W9-BSO-468

THE JOSSEY-BASS HANDBOOK OF NONPROFIT LEADERSHIP AND MANAGEMENT

Third Edition

The Instructor's Guide for the third edition of *The Jossey-Bass Handbook of Nonprofit Leadership & Management* includes chapter-specific teaching materials, including presentations, discussion guides and questions, sample examinations, and related teaching tools. The Instructor's Guide is available free online. If you would like to download and print out a copy of the Guide, please visit: www.wiley.com/college/renz.

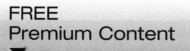

FREE
Premium Content

JOSSEY-BASS ™
An Imprint of
WILEY

This book includes premium content that can be accessed from our Web site when you register at **www.josseybass.com/go/JBHandbook** using the password *professional*.

Essential Texts for Nonprofit and Public Leadership and Management

The Handbook of Nonprofit Governance, by BoardSource

Strategic Planning for Public and Nonprofit Organizations, 3rd Edition, by John M. Bryson

The Effective Public Manager, 4th Edition, by Steven Cohen et al.

Handbook of Human Resources Management in Government, 3rd Edition, by Stephen E. Condrey (Ed.)

The Responsible Administrator, 5th Edition, by Terry L. Cooper

Conducting a Successful Capital Campaign, Revised and Expanded Edition, by Kent E. Dove

The Public Relations Handbook for Nonprofits, by Arthur Feinglass

The Jossey-Bass Handbook of Nonprofit Leadership and Management, 3rd Edition, by David O. Renz, Robert D. Herman, & Associates (Eds.)

Benchmarking in the Public and Nonprofit Sectors, 2nd Edition, by Patricia Keehley et al.

Museum Marketing and Strategy, 2nd Edition, by Neil Kotler et al.

The Ethics Challenge in Public Service, 2nd Edition, by Carol W. Lewis et al.

Leading Across Boundaries, by Russell M. Linden

Designing and Planning Programs for Nonprofit and Government Organizations, by Edward J. Pawlak

Measuring Performance in Public and Nonprofit Organizations, by Theodore H. Poister

Human Resources Management for Public and Nonprofit Organizations: A Strategic Approach, 3rd Edition, by Joan E. Pynes

Understanding and Managing Public Organizations, 4th Edition, by Hal G. Rainey

Designing and Conducting Survey Research, 3rd Edition, by Louis M. Rea et al.

Fundraising Principles and Practice, by Adrian Sargeant, Jen Shang, & Associates

Making Critical Decisions, by Roberta M. Snow et al.

Hank Rosso's Achieving Excellence in Fundraising, 3rd Edition, Eugene R. Tempel, Timothy Seiler, & Eva Aldrich (Eds.)

Handbook of Practical Program Evaluation, 2nd Edition, by Joseph S. Wholey et al. (Eds.)

THE JOSSEY-BASS HANDBOOK OF NONPROFIT LEADERSHIP AND MANAGEMENT

THIRD EDITION

David O. Renz EDITOR

and Associates

Foreword by Robert D. Herman EDITOR EMERITUS

JOSSEY-BASS
A Wiley Imprint
www.josseybass.com

Published by Jossey-Bass
A Wiley Imprint
989 Market Street, San Francisco, CA 94103-1741—www.josseybass.com

Jossey-Bass books and products are available through most bookstores. To contact Jossey-Bass directly call our Customer Care Department within the U.S. at 800-956-7739, outside the U.S. at 317-572-3986, or fax 317-572-4002.

Jossey-Bass also publishes its books in a variety of electronic formats. Some content that appears in print may not be available in electronic books.

Library of Congress Cataloging-in-Publication Data
The Jossey-Bass handbook of nonprofit leadership and management / David O. Renz, editor ; Robert D. Herman, editor emeritus. —3rd ed.
    p. cm. — (Essential texts for nonprofit and public leadership and management ; 18)
  Includes bibliographical references and index.
  ISBN 978-0-470-39250-8 (hardback)
  ISBN 978-0-470-87546-9 (ebk)
  ISBN 978-0-470-87547-6 (ebk)
  ISBN 978-1-118-01349-6 (ebk)
   1. Nonprofit organizations–Management. I. Renz, David O. (David Owen) II. Herman, Robert D., 1946- III. Title: Handbook of nonprofit leadership and management.
  HD62.6.J67 2010
  658′.048—dc22

                                          2010023122

Printed in the United States of America
THIRD EDITION
HB Printing   10 9 8 7 6 5

CONTENTS

PART ONE: THE CONTEXT AND INSTITUTIONAL SETTING OF THE NONPROFIT SECTOR   1

FIGURES, TABLES, AND EXHIBITS

Figures

Tables

Exhibits

THE EDITOR

David O. Renz is the Beth K. Smith/Missouri Chair in Nonprofit Leadership and the director of the Midwest Center for Nonprofit Leadership, the nonprofit leadership research and development center of the Henry W. Bloch School of Business and Public Administration at the University of Missouri–Kansas City. He earned the Master of Arts in Industrial Relations degree in 1978 and a Ph.D. with a concentration in organization theory and administration in 1981, both from the University of Minnesota.

Renz teaches and conducts research on nonprofit and public service governance and leadership and, especially, on strategies for improving nonprofit organization and board effectiveness. He speaks frequently and writes extensively for both the scholarly and practice communities, and has published reports, chapters, and articles in a wide variety of publications, including *Nonprofit Management and Leadership, The Nonprofit Quarterly, Strategic Governance, Public Productivity and Management Review, Public Administration Review,* and *Nonprofit and Voluntary Sector Quarterly.* He currently serves on the editorial boards of *The Nonprofit Quarterly* and *Nonprofit and Voluntary Sector Quarterly.*

Renz has served public service organizations in many leadership capacities, including consulting and service on many councils, task forces, and governing boards. He is past president of the Nonprofit Academic Centers Council, a network of university-based nonprofit research and education centers, and he has served as an officer and governing board member of many nonprofit field-building organizations, including the Association for Nonprofit Research and Voluntary Action (ARNOVA) and the Forum of Regional Associations of Grantmakers. Prior to joining the University of Missouri, he was a Minneapolis-based consultant and taught at the University of St. Thomas. His career includes several senior executive positions in government, including service as executive director of the Metropolitan Council of the Twin Cities and assistant commissioner of administration for the State of Minnesota Department of Labor and Industry.

THE CONTRIBUTORS

Rikki **Abzug** is associate professor of management, Anisfield School of Business, Ramapo College of New Jersey. A researcher of organizational governance, sector theory, social purpose organizations, and neo-institutionalism in organizations, Abzug is coauthor (with Jeffrey Simonoff) of *Nonprofit Trusteeship in Different Contexts* and (with Mary Watson) *Human Resources in Social Purpose Organizations*. Her research has appeared in publications including *The Academy of Management Journal*, *Nonprofit and Voluntary Sector Quarterly* (where she is on the editorial board), *Nonprofit Management & Leadership*, *New York Law School Law Review*, *Organization Science*, and *Voluntas*. Before joining the faculty of the Anisfield School of Business, Abzug was the chair, Nonprofit Management Program, and associate professor at Milano The New School for Management and Urban Policy. In past years, she was the associate director of Yale University's Program on Nonprofit Organizations and a faculty member at New York University's Stern School of Business, Yale, and Wesleyan universities. She has been a management and market research consultant providing consulting services in nonprofit and board development in the United States and Poland. Abzug was on the board of the Association for Researchers in Nonprofit Organizations and Voluntary Action (ARNOVA) and was a founding leadership council member of Governance Matters. She holds a Ph.D. in organizational sociology from Yale University.

Marcia Avner is public policy director with the Minnesota Council of Nonprofits, a statewide association of nonprofits. Her work in Minnesota and nationwide includes writing, training, speaking, advocacy, organizing, and lobbying. Avner is committed to building the field of advocacy, strengthening the will and capacity of nonprofits to engage in mission related advocacy, and increasing grassroots civic engagement. Avner also teaches at the Center on Advocacy and Political Leadership at the University of Minnesota-Duluth and serves as a consultant to nonprofits and foundations on advocacy-related issues. Avner has authored *The Lobbying and Advocacy Handbook for Nonprofit Organizations: Shaping Public Policy at the State and Local Level (*2002), and *The Board Member's Guide to Lobbying and Advocacy* (2004), plus advocacy manuals for national organizations and numerous articles. She serves on the boards of the national Center for Lobbying in the Public Interest, Wellstone Action! and the Wellstone Action Fund, the Nonprofit Information Networking Association (which publishes *The Nonprofit Quarterly)*, and United Family Medicine.

Jeanne Bell is chief executive officer of CompassPoint Nonprofit Services, one of the United States' leading providers of training and consulting services to community-based organizations. She is the coauthor of *Financial Leadership for Nonprofit Executives: Guiding Your Organization to Long Term Success* (2005). In addition to frequent speaking and consulting on nonprofit strategy and finance, Bell has conducted a series of research projects on nonprofit executive leadership, including *Daring to Lead 2006: A National Study of Nonprofit Executive Leadership* and *Securing the Safety Net: A Profile of Community Clinic and Health Center Leadership in California*. Bell is chair of the board of directors of the Alliance for Nonprofit Management and a board member with the Nonprofits' Insurance Alliance of California (NIAC) and with Intersection for the Arts. She serves on the editorial advisory board of *The Nonprofit Quarterly*. Bell holds a Master of Nonprofit Administration (MNA) degree from the University of San Francisco.

Kathy Bonk established the Communications Consortium Media Center (CCMC) in 1988 and is its executive director. Over the past thirty years, she has been at the forefront of media campaigns that marked a sea change in domestic and global policies affecting women, children, and families with the support of major foundations and large donors. Prior to her work in the nonprofit sector, she worked in government as a public information officer in the U.S. Department of State and in the Voting Section of the Civil Rights Division of the Department of Justice. She directed the Media Project for the NOW Legal Defense and Education Fund. Bonk has a degree in communications from the University of Pittsburgh, and in 1988 was awarded a fellowship with the Kellogg Foundation's National Leadership Program.

William A. Brown is an associate professor in the Bush School of Government & Public Service at Texas A&M University and serves as the director of the Nonprofit Management Program. He teaches graduate courses in Nonprofit

Management, Program Evaluation and Volunteer and Human Resources. He received a bachelor of science degree in education from Northeastern University and earned his master's and doctorate from Claremont Graduate University in organizational psychology. Prior to joining Texas A&M University he was an assistant professor at Arizona State University, where he was affiliated with the Center for Nonprofit Leadership & Management. He has worked with numerous organizations in consulting and board governance. His research focuses on nonprofit governance and organizational effectiveness. Specifically he has explored the role of the board in community foundations and incentives for participation by board members. He has authored or coauthored over fifteen research articles, numerous technical reports, and several practice-oriented publications. His work is published in various outlets, including *International Journal of Volunteer Administration, Public Performance and Management Review, Nonprofit and Voluntary Sector Quarterly,* and *Nonprofit Management & Leadership.*

Jeffrey L. Brudney is the Albert A. Levin Chair of Urban Studies and Public Service at Cleveland State University's Maxine Goodman Levin College of Urban Affairs. Brudney has published widely in public administration, the nonprofit sector, and volunteerism. He is the author of *Fostering Volunteer Programs in the Public Sector: Planning, Initiating, and Managing Voluntary Activities* (1990), for which he received the John Grenzebach Award for Outstanding Research in Philanthropy for Education. He has received several other awards from major research associations in business administration, public administration, nonprofit and volunteer administration, and political science for mentoring, service, and scholarship. The Urban Institute calls him "the foremost research expert on volunteer management programs and community volunteer centers in the United States." Brudney is coeditor of the journal, *Nonprofit and Voluntary Sector Quarterly* (NVSQ). NVSQ is the official journal of the Association for Research on Nonprofit Organizations and Voluntary Action (ARNOVA), the largest membership association of academic researchers and practitioners in this field.

John M. Bryson is McKnight Presidential Professor of Planning and Public Affairs at the Hubert H. Humphrey Institute of Public Affairs at the University of Minnesota. He works in the areas of leadership, strategic management, and the design of organizational and community change processes. He wrote the bestselling and award-winning book *Strategic Planning for Public and Nonprofit Organizations* (3rd ed., 2004), and cowrote with Barbara C. Crosby the award-winning *Leadership for the Common Good*, (2nd ed., 2005). Bryson is a Fellow of the National Academy of Public Administration. He has received many awards for his work, including four best book awards, three best article awards, the General Electric Award for Outstanding Research in Strategic Planning from the Academy of Management, and the Distinguished Research Award and Charles H. Levine Memorial Award for Excellence in Public Administration given jointly by the American Society for Public Administration and the National Association of Schools of Public Affairs and Administration. He serves on the editorial boards of the *American Review of Public Administration, International Public Management Journal, Journal of Public Affairs Education,* and *Public Management Review.*

Nancy E. Day is associate professor in human resources and organizational behavior at the Henry W. Bloch School of Business and Public Administration at the University of Missouri–Kansas City (UMKC). Day has taught in undergraduate, graduate, and executive programs. She has a Ph.D. in social psychology from the University of Kansas. Prior to her appointment at UMKC, she was a consultant in compensation, performance management, and human resources issues. Her research focuses primarily on compensation and diversity, including pay communication, sexual orientation, and religious belief in the workplace. She has served on the board of WorldatWork, and is a member of the Society of Industrial and Organizational Psychology and the Academy of Management. Day has published her research in journals such as *Personnel Psychology, Personnel Review,* and *The Journal of Management Education.*

Alnoor Ebrahim is associate professor in the General Management Unit and the Social Enterprise Initiative at the Harvard Business School. His research and teaching focus on the challenges of accountability and performance management facing nonprofit and civil society organizations. He is also affiliated with Harvard University's Hauser Center for Nonprofit Organizations. Among current research projects, Ebrahim leads a global team studying how nonprofits seek to create "systemic change" by influencing national policies on poverty. He also works with nonprofits in the United States on the challenges of organizational learning in urban poverty contexts. His work includes commissioned reports on the World Bank, on NGO accountability at the Inter-American Development Bank, as well as reports for numerous NGOs. Professor Ebrahim is author of the award-winning book *NGOs and Organizational Change: Discourse, Reporting, and Learning* (2005); coeditor with Edward Weisband of *Global Accountabilities: Participation, Pluralism, and Public Ethics* (2007); and the recipient of awards for best article in *Nonprofit Management and Leadership* and *Nonprofit and Voluntary Sector Quarterly.* He holds a B.Sc. degree from the Massachusetts Institute of Technology and a Ph.D. in environmental planning and management from Stanford University.

Robert E. Fogal is an executive coach to professionals in the field of philanthropic fundraising. He has held senior fundraising management positions in higher education, health care, and human services. He is also former director of The Fund Raising School at the Indiana University Center on Philanthropy. Active in the Association of Fundraising Professionals (AFP), he has served on the association's national board of directors, research council, and Advanced

Certified Fund Raising Executive Credentialing Board. He most recently chaired the Research Council Think Tank, "Leadership, Governance, and Giving." He was the founding editor of *New Directions in Philanthropic Fundraising* and for several years was a regular columnist for AFP's *Advancing Philanthropy*. He has led seminars and workshops for more than one-hundred professional, religious, and community organizations in the United States and internationally. He served on the faculty of the Protestant Institute for Advanced Theological Studies in Buenos Aires, Argentina, where he also implemented ethnographic field research. He holds the master of sacred music degree from Union Theological Seminary (New York) and a Ph.D. from Indiana University in folklore and ethnomusicology.

Brenda Gainer is director of the Nonprofit Management and Leadership Program and holds the Royal Bank Professorship in Nonprofit Management at York University in Toronto, Canada. Her main research interests are nonprofit marketing and management; she teaches marketing, resource development and philanthropy, and alternative approaches to social value creation such as social enterprise and cooperatives. Her published work appears in a wide variety of journals and conference proceedings and she is on the editorial board of a number of academic and practitioner journals. Before embarking on an academic career, Brenda worked in the areas of aboriginal rights, women's issues, and culture. She has recently developed capacity-building programs for immigrant and refugee-serving NGOs, social service agencies, and the social housing sector. She currently serves on the board of Canada Helps, a Web-based organization dedicated to increasing philanthropy in Canada. Her professional service includes advisory boards for Statistics Canada and other government agencies and two terms as vice president of the Nonprofit Academic Centers Council. Currently she is president-elect of the International Society for Third Sector Research.

Virginia C. Gross is a shareholder in the Nonprofit Practice Group of Polsinelli Shughart PC. She concentrates her practice in the fields of tax and nonprofit law. She has represented a variety of nonprofit organization clients on tax-exempt matters, including charitable and educational organizations, private foundations, associations, supporting organizations, medical research and other health care organizations, social welfare organizations, and social clubs. Gross is a frequent presenter on nonprofit issues, including federal tax law and governance issues for nonprofit organizations. She has previously coauthored two books on nonprofit law, *Nonprofit Governance: Law Practices & Trends* (2009) and *The New Form 990: Law, Policy & Preparation*. She was listed in *The Best Lawyers of America, Nonprofit Organizations / Charities Law*, for 2008–2010. She has served on numerous boards of directors, and continues to do so. Gross earned her J.D. from the University of Texas in 1986 and her B.S. from Texas A&M University in 1990.

Peter Dobkin Hall is Hauser Lecturer on Nonprofit Organizations at the John F. Kennedy School of Government, Harvard University. Associated with Yale's Program on Non-Profit Organizations from 1978 to 1999, he also held teaching appointments in Yale's Department of History, Divinity School, Ethics, Politics, and Economics Program, and School of Management. Hall's publications include *Sacred Companies: Organizational Aspects of Religion and Religious Aspects of Organizations* (1998), *Inventing the Nonprofit Sector and Other Essays on Philanthropy, Voluntarism, and Nonprofit Organizations* (1992), *Lives in Trust: The Fortunes of Dynastic Families in Late Twentieth Century America* (1992), and *The Organization of American Culture, 1700–1900: Organizations, Elites, and the Origins of American Nationality* (1982).

Scott T. Helm is a senior fellow with the Midwest Center for Nonprofit Leadership and a member of the clinical faculty of the Department of Public Affairs in the Henry W. Bloch School of Business and Public Administration at the University of Missouri–Kansas City, where he teaches program evaluation and policy analysis, social entrepreneurship, and financial management. Helm leads Midwest Center contracted research and evaluation initiatives and facilitates a variety of community planning and development initiatives, including projects in program evaluation, market research, commercialization, business planning, strategic planning, and board training. Helm's academic research and publications are in the area of social entrepreneurship and social enterprise, and his research spans U.S. and European settings. Helm has a B.A. in economics from Washington College in Chestertown, Maryland; an MPA with a concentration in nonprofit management from the University of Missouri–Kansas City, and an interdisciplinary Ph.D. in public administration and economics from University of Missouri-Kansas City.

Robert D. Herman is professor emeritus of the Department of Public Affairs and senior fellow with the Midwest Center for Nonprofit Leadership, both of the Henry W. Bloch School of Business and Public Administration at the University of Missouri–Kansas City (UMKC). He is a founder of UMKC's Master of Public Administration nonprofit management program, one of the first to be created in the United States. Herman's research has concentrated on the effective leadership of nonprofit charitable organizations, including chief executive–board relations, and his most recent research has focused on nonprofit organizational effectiveness. He has published extensively, including in such publications as *Public Administration Review, Nonprofit Management and Leadership,* and *Nonprofit and Voluntary Sector Quarterly,* and he is coauthor of *Executive Leadership in Nonprofit Organizations* (with Richard Heimovics, 1991) and coeditor of *Nonprofit Boards of Directors* (with Jon Van Til, 1989). Herman is the founding editor of the *Jossey-Bass Handbook of Nonprofit Leadership and Management* (1994, 2nd ed. 2005). Herman has served in numerous leadership roles in the field of nonprofit studies, including past president of the Association of Voluntary Action Scholars (now know as the Association for Research on Nonprofit Organizations and Voluntary Action, or ARNOVA). Herman received his B.A. degree in economics from Kansas State University and his M.S. and Ph.D. degrees, both in organizational behavior, from Cornell University.

Melanie Lockwood Herman is the executive director of the Nonprofit Risk Management Center, a resource center serving the nonprofit community in the United States (www.nonprofitrisk.org). The center provides training, technical assistance, and informational resources on a wide range of topics, including risk management, nonprofit governance, employment practices, insurance buying, and protecting vulnerable populations. Melanie has spent her entire career in the nonprofit sector and has authored and coauthored more than fifteen books covering a wide spectrum of nonprofit management issues. Each year she delivers numerous workshops, seminars, and keynote presentations on nonprofit management topics. Her most recent books are *Exposed: A Legal Field Guide for Nonprofit Executives* (2009), *Ready . . . or Not: A Risk Management Guide for Nonprofit Executives* (2009), *Financial Risk Management: A Guide for Nonprofit Executives* (2008), and *Coverage, Claims & Consequences: An Insurance Handbook for Nonprofits* (2nd ed.) (2008). Herman's leadership has brought some of the services provided by the center to nonprofits in Korea, Canada, Australia, and Japan. She is a graduate of American University, where she earned a bachelor of arts in urban affairs. She earned her J.D. from George Mason University School of Law.

Bruce R. Hopkins is a senior partner with the law firm Polsinelli Shughart PC, in its Kansas City, Missouri, office. His practice focuses on tax-exempt organizations. Books he has authored include *The Law of Tax-Exempt Organizations* (9th ed.); *The Tax Law of Charitable Giving* (4th ed.); *Starting and Managing A Nonprofit Organization: A Legal Guide,* (5th ed.); *IRS Audits of Tax-Exempt Organizations: Policies, Practices, and Procedures*; *Private Foundations: Tax Law and Compliance* (3rd ed.) (coauthor); and *Nonprofit Governance: Law, Practices & Trends* (coauthor with Virginia C. Gross). He writes a monthly newsletter, *Bruce R. Hopkins' Nonprofit Counsel* (which won a 2009 Newsletter on Newsletters journalism award for best technical article). He received the Nonprofit Lawyers Award (2007) from the American Bar Association. He has served as an adjunct professor of law in three law schools; he is presently on the faculty of the University of Kansas Law School. He is a graduate of the University of Michigan, and received J.D. and LL.M (taxation) degrees from the George Washington University National Law Center. He is listed in *The Best Lawyers in America* (charity law) (2007–2010).

Thomas H. Jeavons is executive director the Association for Research on Nonprofit Organizations and Voluntary Action (ARNOVA), the leading association of researchers on nonprofit organizations, philanthropy, and voluntarism.

He is also a visiting faculty member of the Indiana University Center on Philanthropy. He served from 1996 until July of 2006 as General Secretary (chief executive) of Philadelphia Yearly Meeting of the Religious Society of Friends (Quakers). Prior to that he was the director of the Center on Philanthropy and Nonprofit Leadership at Grand Valley State University. Jeavons earned a B.A. in philosophy from the University of Colorado (1975), an M.A. in theology from the Earlham School of Religion (1978), and his Ph.D. in management and cultural studies from the Union Institute (1992). He has been a visiting fellow at the Yale University Program on Nonprofit Organizations and at the Yale Divinity School, and a consulting scholar for the SUNY Albany/Pew Roundtable on Religion and Social Welfare Policy. He is the author of *Growing Givers' Hearts: Fundraising as a Ministry* (2000); *When the Bottom Line Is Faithfulness: The Management of Christian Organizations* (1994); and many chapters and articles on nonprofit management, religious organizations, fund raising, ethics, and education.

Vic Murray is adjunct professor in the School of Public Administration at the University of Victoria. From 1983 to 1995, he served as director of the Voluntary Sector Management Program in the Schulich School of Business at York University, Toronto. He is the author of many books, articles, and papers in the fields of organizational behavior and nonprofit management. His most recent publication is *The Management of Nonprofit and Charitable Organizations in Canada,* (2nd ed., 2009). Currently, he is a member of the Advisory Board for the journal *Nonprofit Management and Leadership,* and board member of the Association for Nonprofit and Social Economy Research Canada (ANSER). In 2002 he was awarded ARNOVA's Distinguished Lifetime Achievement Award. He is at present director of the Voluntary Sector Knowledge Network (www.vskn.ca), a Web site of the British Columbia Centre for Nonprofit Management and Sustainability.

Matthew T. A. Nash is managing director of the Center for the Advancement of Social Entrepreneurship (CASE), a research and education center at Duke University's Fuqua School of Business dedicated to promoting the entrepreneurial pursuit of social impact through the thoughtful adaptation of business expertise. Prior to joining the CASE team, he was a senior consultant in strategy and change management with the public sector practice at IBM Business Consulting Services (formerly PricewaterhouseCoopers Consulting). In this position and previous consulting and training capacities, he served a diverse set of clients ranging from community-based organizations to international agencies UNICEF and the U.S. Agency for International Development. Previously, he led the Leadership Institute at Yale's Center for Public Service and volunteered with the U.S. Peace Corps as a nongovernmental organization development consultant in Romania. He is a graduate of the Yale School of Management

(M.B.A.) and Yale College (B.A.), where he received the graduation prize for public service. A recipient of Vice President Al Gore's "Hammer Award" for reinventing government, he was honored with inaugural "Member Achievement Award" by Net Impact, the global network of business professionals seeking to use their skills for social, environmental, and economic impact.

Lester M. Salamon is a professor at the Johns Hopkins University and director of the Johns Hopkins Center for Civil Society Studies and its Comparative Nonprofit Sector and Listening Post projects. Prior to this he served as director of the Center for Governance and Management Research at The Urban Institute and as deputy associate director of the U.S. Office of Management and Budget in the Executive Office of the President. Salamon received his Ph.D. in government from Harvard University and his B.A. in policy studies from Princeton University. He is the author of *Partners in Public Service: Government-Nonprofit Relations in the Modern Welfare State* (1996), *The Tools of Government: A Guide to the New Governance* (2002), *The State of Nonprofit America* (2002), *The Resilient Sector* (2003), and *Global Civil Society: Dimensions of the Nonprofit Sector* (2004). Salamon received the Distinguished Leadership Award from the Association for Research on Nonprofit Organizations and Voluntary Action (ARNOVA) in 2003. He serves on the editorial boards of *Voluntas, Administration and Society, Nonprofit and Voluntary Action Quarterly*, and the Scientific Committee of *Atlantide*.

Steven Rathgeb Smith is the Waldemar A. Nielsen Chair in Philanthropy at the Georgetown Public Policy Institute. He is on leave from the Evans School of Public Affairs at the University of Washington, where he is the Nancy Bell Evans Professor of Public Affairs and director of the Nancy Bell Evans Center on Nonprofits & Philanthropy. Smith was the editor of *Nonprofit and Voluntary Sector Quarterly (NVSQ)*, the journal of the Association for Research on Nonprofit Organizations and Voluntary Action (ARNOVA) from 1998 to 2004. From 2006 to 2008, he served as president of ARNOVA. His publications include *Nonprofits for Hire: The Welfare State in the Age of Contracting* (with Michael Lipsky), *Public Policy for Democracy* (with Helen Ingram), and "The Challenge of Strengthening Nonprofits and Civil Society," *Public Administration Review* (December 2008). His current research focuses on the government-nonprofit relationship in the United States and abroad, the regional variation in American foundations, and the evolving role of nonprofit social services in Europe and the United States.

John Clayton Thomas is professor and former chair in the Department of Public Management and Policy in the Andrew Young School of Policy Studies at Georgia State University in Atlanta, Georgia. He previously taught at and directed the L. P. Cookingham Institute of Public Affairs at the University of Missouri–Kansas City. Thomas has written three books and more than fifty articles in the areas of program evaluation, performance measurement, and other aspects of public management. He has several decades of experience teaching master's- and doctoral-level courses on program evaluation and performance measurement to practitioners from the nonprofit and public sectors. Thomas has also consulted and conducted training for state and local governments and nonprofit agencies in Colorado, Georgia, New York, South Carolina, Pennsylvania, Texas, and Missouri. He holds a Ph.D. in political science from Northwestern University and a B.A. (magna cum laude) and M.A. in journalism and mass communications from the University of Minnesota.

Mary R. Watson is associate professor of management and chair of the Management Programs at Milano The New School for Management and Urban Policy. Her professional work addresses contemporary human capital issues in organizations, with particular emphasis on the social impact of shifting labor market inequalities. Watson has conducted research on global management, executive career paths, recruitment and retention in nonprofit organizations, downsizing and stock prices, the evolution of interorganizational fields, management ethics in multinational operations, and qualitative research methods in management. She has presented her research at more than forty conferences worldwide, and it appears in the *Academy of Management Journal*, previous editions of the *Jossey-Bass Handbook of Nonprofit Leadership and Management*, *Communication Yearbook*, and the *IRRA Research Annals*, among other outlets. Watson has taught undergraduate, graduate and executive education courses in strategy, globalization, organization theory and design, human resources, management and social justice. She is the recipient of The New School's Distinguished University Teaching Award for 2009. Watson earned her Ph.D. in organization studies from the Owen Graduate School of Management at Vanderbilt University.

Carol K. Willen is the inaugural director of the Nonprofit and Public Service Center at Lakeland Community College. As head of the center, she develops educational programming for volunteers and professionals in the nonprofit and public sectors and plays a lead role in the design and delivery of customized consulting services for both individual organizations and groups of organizations. Her academic interest in strategic alliances complements the center's mandate to promote community dialogue and interorganizational collaboration through its capabilities as a catalyst and convener. She is also an adjunct instructor at Case Western Reserve University (CWRU) Mandel School of Applied Social Sciences, where she coteaches a course on nonprofit strategic alliances with coauthor John A. Yankey. Before assuming her position at Lakeland, she was director of academic programs and student services at CWRU's Mandel Center for Nonprofit Organizations. Prior to joining the Mandel Center, she spent fifteen years in philanthropy, including a decade at the Cleveland Foundation, where she served as senior program officer for education. She earned her bachelor's degree at the University of Michigan and her master's and Ph.D. degrees at Harvard University.

John A. Yankey is the Leonard W. Mayo Professor Emeritus at the Mandel School of Applied Social Sciences (MSASS) at Case Western Reserve University (CWRU). A former public administrator, he continues to teach at the Mandel School and Mandel Center for Nonprofit Organizations in the areas of strategic planning and developing strategic nonprofit alliances. During his thirty-seven years at CWRU, he has administered a number of statewide training programs; served in a variety of administrative positions within MSASS including Associate Dean and Acting Dean; served as the Director of Community Services and as Interim Executive Director of the Mandel Center; and, carried out state legislative liaison responsibilities for CWRU as special assistant to the president. During the last twenty years, Yankey has been actively engaged in studying, teaching, and writing about strategic nonprofit alliances development, as well as consulting with nonprofit organizations to create such alliances.

David W. Young is professor of management, emeritus, at Boston University's School of Management, where he was nominated four times for BU's prestigious Metcalf Award for teaching excellence. During each of his last two years at BU, he was voted best professor by Cohort C of the School's MBA students. He has been a core faculty member for the past thirty-two years at Harvard's School of Public Health, where he teaches in the Program for Chiefs of Clinical Service, and the Leadership Development Program in Health Care. In 2006, he received the Special Recognition Award from the Association of Professors of Medicine, an award presented annually to a nonmember who has contributed the most to helping the association meet its mission of providing leadership and direction to academic internal medicine. He is the author of *Management Control in Nonprofit Organization; A Manager's Guide to Creative Cost Cutting; Techniques of Management Accounting;* and *Management Accounting for Health Care Organizations*. He earned a B.A. from Occidental College, an M.A. in economics from the University of California at Los Angeles, and a doctorate from the Harvard Business School. (For more information go to www.DavidYoung.org.)

Dennis R. Young is Bernard B. and Eugenia A. Ramsey Professor of Private Enterprise in the Andrew Young School of Policy Studies at Georgia State University, where he directs the school's Nonprofit Studies Program. From 1988 to 1996 he was director of the Mandel Center for Nonprofit Organizations and Mandel Professor of Nonprofit Management at Case Western Reserve University. He is the founding editor of the journals *Nonprofit Management and Leadership* and *Nonprofit Policy Forum*, and past president of the Association for Research on Nonprofit Organizations and Voluntary Action (ARNOVA). His books include *If Not for Profit for What?*, *A Casebook of Management for Nonprofit*

Organizations, Educating Managers of Nonprofit Organizations (with Michael O'Neill), *Economics for Nonprofit Managers* (with Richard Steinberg), *Corporate Philanthropy at the Crossroads* (with Dwight Burlingame), *The Music of Management*, *Effective Economic Decisionmaking for Nonprofit Organizations*, *Wise Decision-Making in Uncertain Times*, *Financing Nonprofits*, and *Handbook of Research on Nonprofit Economics and Management* (with Bruce A. Seaman). Young received ARNOVA's 2004 Award for Distinguished Achievement and Leadership in Nonprofit and Voluntary Action Research, and the Award for Innovation in Nonprofit Research from the Israeli Center for Third Sector Research at Ben Gurion University in 2005.

FOREWORD

That the *Jossey-Bass Handbook of Nonprofit Leadership and Management* is now in its third edition is, of course, gratifying. That it is now edited by my colleague and friend, Dave Renz, is especially gratifying. I know of no one better qualified and with stronger connections to the scholarly and consultant-practitioner nonprofit management community. Given those connections and the widespread respect Dave has earned for his many contributions to the scholarly and consultant-practitioner communities, it is no wonder that the variety and quality of the contributors and contributions to this third edition is outstanding.

When I began to plan the first edition, I solicited the views of a number of people around the United States and Canada who had developed nonprofit management programs, and the collection of chapters in the first edition represented the topics that nearly all agreed were essential to such a handbook if it were to reflect what was essential in the actual leadership and management of nonprofit charitable organizations. The chapters in this third edition illustrate both continuity and change in the practice of nonprofit management. Many of the topics considered are the "same" as in the first two editions, except of course that research and practice in relation to those topics has advanced and changed, often rapidly. The content of all the chapters addressing the "same" topics thus includes the important recent developments in research and practice. The new chapters address topics and issues that have become more important in the last few years, including increased demands for improved accountability, new sources and more effective management of revenues, and increased innovativeness. This third edition includes several new chapters focused on these concerns: chapters on accountability, strategic communication, strategic management, financial leadership, a generalized framework for nonprofit finance, and chapters on social entrepreneurship and the distinct topic of nonprofit enterprise. As with the first two editions, these chapters are authored by people with strong backgrounds and preparation in these fields.

The previous two editions of the Jossey-Bass handbook were adopted by many faculty for use in nonprofit management programs at universities in the United States and Canada. They were also, I'm glad to write, purchased by actual managers (and an occasional board member). I realize that what nonprofit leaders (whether volunteer board members, other volunteers, or managers) study is seldom the most important factor in how they behave; elements of the immediate situation are. Nonetheless, as I wrote in the preface to the second edition, I believe that those editions did and this third edition continues to present "the best and most practical leadership and management information currently available on a wide range of topics. That the information is the best and most applicable is the result, I believe, of deriving practical implications not solely from current practice but even more from the latest research and the most current theory." I am sure that this edition will be a widely used resource, serving to inform leaders, leaders-to-be, managers, and managers-to-be for years to come.

October, 2010   Robert D. Herman
Kansas City, Missouri

INTRODUCTION TO THE THIRD EDITION

It is a pleasure to have the opportunity, on behalf of founding editor Robert Herman and all of us associated with *The Jossey-Bass Handbook of Nonprofit Leadership and Management*, to present this third edition. With Robert's recent retirement, is has become my privilege to assume the role of editor for the third edition. Needless to say, my aspiration is to sustain the legacy and value of the first two editions while enhancing their relevance and impact with the latest and most substantive of insights into the changing and expanding world of nonprofit leadership and management. All chapters of this third edition of the handbook present the most current of research, theory, and practice in the field of nonprofit leadership and management, written in a manner that is practical and relevant. To ensure that the handbook addresses the changing nature of the field, we have increased emphasis on three important areas. First, we have expanded our attention to the challenges that confront essentially all nonprofit leaders and managers with regard to accountability, transparency, and the increased pressure to demonstrate outcomes and results. To complement the revisions to the second edition chapters, we have added a chapter by Alnoor Ebrahim that expertly examines the complexities and implications of "the many faces of nonprofit accountability."

Second, we have increased our attention to the evolving phenomenon of social entrepreneurship and its implications for nonprofit leadership and management. The foundation for this discussion is a new chapter, "Social Entrepreneurship and Social Enterprise," prepared by Matthew Nash and his colleagues at the Center for the Advancement of Social Entrepreneurship

(CASE) at Duke University, and most chapters of the book have been revised to consider the implications of this phenomenon as relates to their own fields. Integral to this is the increasingly complex and dynamic world of nonprofit financial management. The financial structure and environment of the sector has been changing quite dramatically over the past decade, and the financial section of this edition has been revised significantly to address this. Two new chapters have been added—an excellent framing chapter by Jeanne Bell on financial leadership and an important new chapter that Dennis Young has prepared to explain the increasingly challenging field of nonprofit finance.

This third edition also offers a new type of enhancement: chapter-by-chapter supplemental resources for readers and educators. All who purchase the handbook are invited to visit the Jossey-Bass Premium Content Internet resource site (www.josseybass.com/go/JBHandbook), where they will find an extensive array of supplemental resources designed to help readers make the most of the information presented in each chapter. Among the resource materials on the site are supplemental readings lists, annotated Web site reference lists with hot links to useful chapter-relevant Internet resources, plus application resources such as worksheets and checklists that can be used to begin to apply the knowledge and information relevant to each chapter. In addition, for educators, a special password-protected Web site has been created. Among the resources on this unique access-controlled site are the handbook instructor's manual and chapter-specific teaching materials, including PowerPoint presentations, discussion guides and questions, sample examinations, and related teaching tools. Educators who wish to gain access to these teaching resources should go to www.wiley.com/college/JBHandbook and register to secure access.

This edition of the handbook arrives at a very interesting time in the development of the nonprofit sector (throughout this volume, we use the label "nonprofit sector" to refer to the sector that others sometimes label "the third sector," "civil society," "the independent sector," or "the social sector"). The pace at which the sector and its organizations change continues to accelerate, driven by a complex mix of internal and external dynamics. This edition goes to press as the nonprofit sector finds itself in the midst of one of the most challenging and troubling of economic times. The results and implications of this difficult era are yet to be fully understood, although early signs suggest that the nonprofit world is changing (and being changed) in some fundamental ways. As we make our way through the economic recession that began in 2008, many "lifeline" or "safety net" nonprofits are finding themselves at the mercy of a "triple whammy"—demands for services have increased substantially as more people seek help, philanthropic and governmental financial support has declined significantly with the contraction of the economy, and nonprofits' own internal resources (to the extent they existed) have diminished as investments, endowments, and other assets have declined in value due to the same economic dynamics. As many have observed, the safety nets are fraying, the level of stress throughout the sector is significant and growing, and there is no immediate relief in sight.

Challenges and threats notwithstanding, the dynamics of the current times also offer opportunity and hope. The enthusiasm that many have for the fast-growing interest in social entrepreneurship (no matter how you define it) is bringing new and sometimes different kinds of energy to the field. Many of today's changes are the result of the very innovation and creativity that the nonprofit sector can be so good at fueling—the adoption of new ways of understanding charity and social good and the development of entrepreneurial new ways of meeting the needs of people and communities. In addition, fundamental shifts are under way throughout the United States and many other nations as a direct result of key demographic changes, as new cultures, perspectives, and generations become more fully integrated into the leadership of the sector. The pace and depth of technological change and the increased presence of various social media certainly fuel additional forces for change in the sector. And a new generation of enthusiasm for volunteering and community service seems to be emerging as well. From a leadership and management perspective, the challenges confronting the sector are exceptional. So, too, are the opportunities—for those prepared to step in and make the difference!

The Jossey-Bass Handbook of Nonprofit Leadership and Management emerged in response to the need for a single volume that would offer a comprehensive and thorough treatment of the functions, processes, and strategies integral to effective nonprofit organization leadership and management. Writing in the preface to the second edition of this handbook, editor emeritus Herman observed that all too often advice on financial management, human resource management (for both paid and volunteer personnel), and organizational strategies and leadership has been available only in fragmentary pieces published in far-flung periodicals that are not readily available (p. xvii). In recent years, the volume of literature of the field has grown and developed in impressive ways. And yet the need for a single comprehensive volume on nonprofit leadership and management remains. We are proud that this third edition of the handbook (and its supplemental Internet resources) will extend the legacy as we meet this need with timely, substantive, and readable knowledge and information that is uniquely suited to the challenges of twenty-first-century nonprofit leaders and managers.

Intended Audience

This volume is designed to provide comprehensive and in-depth explanations of effective leadership and management practices, relevant to and applicable throughout any nonprofit organization. We intend the handbook to be of value to all who practice nonprofit leadership or management, as well as those who aspire to do so. It will be especially useful to anyone who has come to a management or leadership position from a program service background, to anyone who has moved from a relatively specialized management niche into a position with wider responsibilities, and to all who seek a solid core of support for the wide range of knowledge and skills that nonprofit leadership and management require. In addition to those in paid staff positions, this volume will benefit board members and other volunteer leaders who are interested in enlarging their understanding of the nature of nonprofit organizations and their management. The handbook also will be useful to those, both in formal education programs and in self-directed learning, who want to develop careers in nonprofit management. Finally, we believe this book will continue to be an important resource to those who work with nonprofit organizations as consultants, technical assistance providers, regulators, and funders.

Overview of the Contents

The volume is organized into five parts, and each part explains a significant part of the puzzle that is nonprofit management and leadership. Part One provides an overall perspective on the context and institutional setting within which nonprofit organizations and the sector as a whole have developed and currently operate, with observations about the ways this context is likely to change for the future. Nonprofit organizations have been shaped and will continue to be shaped by historical times and forces, by social institutions, laws and regulations, and political and economic trends and events. The chapters in Part One examine how these large-scale phenomena have affected and are affecting nonprofit organizations and their leadership and management. In Chapter One, Peter Dobkin Hall deftly describes the complex history of philanthropy and nonprofit organizations in the United States, exploring why and how the nonprofit sector has developed. In Chapter Two, Bruce Hopkins and Virginia Gross offer a timely and current explanation of the legal and regulatory environment in which U.S. nonprofit organizations operate. This chapter provides insight into recent legislative changes and discusses how the U.S. Internal Revenue Service is likely to proceed with implementation and enforcement. In Chapter Three, Lester Salamon updates his analysis of the impact of large-scale economic, political, and demographic forces on various segments of the nonprofit sector. Alnoor Ebrahim, in Chapter Four, discusses the increasingly strong press for accountability in the nonprofit sector, explores multiple ways that accountability can be understood, and offers key insights for ways nonprofit leaders might address them.

Part Two examines the ways that leadership is provided in nonprofit organizations, including the work of governance and management. Boards of directors of nonprofit organizations govern their organizations and, therefore, are central to the process of nonprofit leadership. There is clear evidence that there is an important relationship between board effectiveness and the effectiveness of nonprofit organizations, and nonprofits need effective boards. In Chapter Five, I describe the nature and work of governing boards (including the legal and fiduciary responsibilities of boards and their members), discuss some of the major challenges that confront boards, and offer a board development framework that explains how nonprofit leaders can help build board capacity. In Chapter Six, Robert Herman examines the crucial role of chief executives in leading and managing nonprofit organizations and describes the board-centered, external, and political leadership skills of effective chief executives. Nonprofit executives and other leaders have the challenge of creating and sustaining organizational cultures and practices that uphold the highest of ethical standards. Thomas Jeavons offers important insight into the ethical challenges that leaders must address and provides important advice about how this can be achieved in Chapter Seven.

Leading and managing strategically is essential to the success of nonprofit organizations, and one of the key leadership tasks facing boards and executives is that of strategically designing the organization to most effectively achieve its mission. Recent research indicates that there is an important relationship between strategic planning and organizational effectiveness, and that it is important for boards and executives to be effective strategists. In Chapter Eight William Brown discusses the nature of organizational strategy and the types of strategic choices that are to be made by executives and boards. John Bryson elaborates and applies this perspective in Chapter Nine as he explains the process by which an organization's strategy can be developed and refined using a formal process for strategy development and planning. Nonprofits pursue their missions and strategic goals in many ways, some using very innovative and entrepreneurial approaches. Social entrepreneurship has become a topic of great discussion in the past decade, and Matthew Nash explains in Chapter Ten the various ways that this phenomenon may be understood and implemented.

The contributions in Part Three explain the essentials of nonprofit organizational operations. Nonprofit organizations exist in a balance with their operating environments, and effective nonprofit organizations recognize the need to develop and carefully manage their exchanges with significant constituents and stakeholders. The first four chapters of this section explore various facets of these relationships with the outside world. Brenda Gainer, in Chapter Eleven, provides nonprofit managers and leaders with a thorough explanation of the process of marketing, highlighting important ways that marketing activities are central to mission accomplishment. Chapter Twelve further addresses the process of external relations; Kathy Bonk explains strategic communications and the approaches that nonprofits can use to effectively engage and communicate with their key stakeholders. In Chapter Thirteen, Marcia Avner explains advocacy, lobbying, and the most effective ways for nonprofits to engage government processes to influence and have an impact on legislation and policy. The last of the chapters to address such boundary-spanning activities is Chapter Fourteen. It is increasingly common and necessary for nonprofits to develop substantive ongoing working relationships with other organizations as they work to accomplish their mission, and John Yankey and Carol Willen discuss the most effective ways for nonprofit leaders to develop and sustain effective collaboration and strategic alliances.

The final two chapters of Part Three explore the intersection of management and accountability. Nonprofit organizations implement their missions through programs, and the imperative to ensure program performance and impact is the subject of more and more attention in the field. John Clayton Thomas explains the processes by which program impact and outcomes can be assessed using the techniques of program evaluation in Chapter Fifteen. Questions about effectiveness and performance are not limited to the programs of the organization, however; nonprofit leaders also must ensure organizational effectiveness. Organizational effectiveness is concerned with judgments about the overall performance of a nonprofit organization, typically including considerations of financial performance, community engagement, and more. In Chapter Sixteen, Vic Murray explains the nature and dynamics of assessing nonprofit organizational effectiveness and suggests some useful ways to address this challenge.

Part Four takes up topics crucial to the development and management of financial resources. Jeanne Bell introduces this part of the book in Chapter Seventeen with a thoughtful discussion of the strategic dimensions of financial management—the effective practice of financial leadership. One of the most challenging yet underestimated aspects of nonprofit management is that of securing the financial resources needed to operate the organization. Dennis Young, in Chapter Eighteen, provides insight into a nonprofit organization's financing options and offers guidance to inform crucial revenue choices. Of course, raising money through philanthropic channels is a time-honored approach, and fundraising is a well-developed field of practice; in Chapter Nineteen, Robert Fogal explains how fundraising should be integrated with the mission and culture of the nonprofit organization. A significant number of nonprofits seek to generate financial revenues via social enterprises that produce earned income; in Chapter Twenty, Scott Helm examines the design and development of social enterprises and the opportunities and challenges inherent in this approach to financial development. One of the most common of earned-income strategies for many nonprofits involves contracting with government to provide services. Steven Rathgeb Smith explains the benefits, challenges, and dynamics inherent in nonprofit-government contracting in Chapter Twenty-one. Of course, the process of actually managing and accounting for the flow of money through the nonprofit organization is essential. In Chapter Twenty-two David Young explains the basics of managerial accounting and financial decision making in nonprofits, and discusses how nonprofit managers can use management accounting to enable effective financial and programmatic performance and accountability. One important way that nonprofit organizations can control both costs and exposure to losses is through effective management of risk. Melanie Lockwood Herman provides a thorough guide by which nonprofit leaders can effectively assess and manage their organization's risks in Chapter Twenty-three.

Part Five presents three chapters that address the most significant asset of any nonprofit organization—the people who, whether as employees or volunteers, make the organization what it is. It is essential for every nonprofit to be able to recruit, select, retain, manage, and reward the people who work on its behalf. In Chapter Twenty-four, Mary Watson and Rikki Abzug explain strategic human resource management and the processes and systems that are essential to any well-functioning nonprofit organization, including recruitment, selection, and retention. Nancy Day follows up in Chapter Twenty-five with a comprehensive discussion of the systematic design and operation of a compensation and benefits program that is appropriate to the nonprofit environment. Last but not least in Part Five is Chapter Twenty-six, in which Jeffrey Brudney presents a comprehensive and pragmatic explanation of how a nonprofit can systematically and strategically implement an effective program to attract, organize, lead, and manage volunteers.

Finally, in the Conclusion, I discuss the ways that the sector may be developing and changing and offer a few observations about the future of nonprofit leadership and management. I am optimistic about the future of the sector and the capacity of the talented people who lead and manage it, and I share thoughts about various ways that nonprofit leaders and managers can address the myriad conflicting and complicating forces that buffet the sector and their organizations.

Acknowledgments

It is both a privilege and daunting responsibility to assume the editorship of the third edition of a resource as widely respected and valued as *The Jossey-Bass Handbook of Nonprofit Leadership and Management*, and I want to express my great personal thanks to all who have helped bring this new edition to life. This must of course begin with acknowledgment of editor emeritus, Robert Herman. Bob is an exceptional colleague and friend and, from the start, he has been very supportive of my work on this project. Thank you, Bob, for entrusting the next generation of your legacy to my care; I hope you find it a fitting extension of the work you began more than fifteen years ago when the handbook began!

My acknowledgments also must begin, of course, with a deep thank-you to each and every chapter author. For most, this was their second or third round of service, and I greatly appreciate their willingness to tackle yet another cycle and to do so with such enthusiasm and energy. For some, this was their first opportunity to become a part of the project and they, too, showed great enthusiasm and energy for the work. All confronted tight deadlines and endured regular editorial harassment, yet everyone invested an exceptional amount of effort and delivered their best. This is truly an outstanding group of colleagues and it has been a pleasure to work with them!

I am very appreciative of the excellent support that I have received from Allison Brunner and Justin Frahm, our editors at Jossey-Bass, and their senior editorial assistants, Dani Scoville and Lindsay Morton. They have provided essential encouragement and support throughout the project. New to the editorial role, I required much direction and advice, and they responded with good humor and care as I lurched my way along this path. Thank you for all of your help!

Similarly, a great vote of thanks is due to each of my colleagues at the Midwest Center for Nonprofit Leadership—Mark Culver, Gary Baker, Beth Smith, Scott Helm, Cindy Laufer, Erin Nemenoff, Fredrik Andersson, Iris Gao, and Wendy Herschberger; and to my colleagues in the Department of Public Affairs at the University of Missouri–Kansas City: Arif Ahmed, Joan Gallos, Brent Never, Nick Peroff, and Sam Silveira. All tolerated my cycles of inattention and distraction with grace and encouragement, and they all stepped up to the plate to provide help whenever it was needed. I especially appreciate the assistance that Mark, Iris, Wendy, Scott, and Fredrik provided with specific pieces of this project as we struggled to bring things to closure. To all of you: it is a true pleasure to work with such exceptional professionals!

Finally, and most important, there are no words to adequately express my thanks to Sandy, my wife, and our children, Christian and Sarah. Their care, support, and encouragement throughout this project have meant everything to me, especially since this work has taken so much from our time together! Thanks for everything, guys!!

October, 2010   David O. Renz, Editor
Kansas City, Missouri

THE JOSSEY-BASS HANDBOOK OF NONPROFIT LEADERSHIP AND MANAGEMENT

Third Edition

PART ONE

THE CONTEXT AND INSTITUTIONAL SETTING OF THE NONPROFIT SECTOR

It is important to recognize that the nonprofit sector has developed within a larger institutional and social context, and that nonprofit organizations of today have been and will continue to be shaped by historical forces, social institutions, laws and regulations, and significant political and economic trends and events. All have had an important influence on the modern practice of nonprofit leadership and management, and all have important implications for the future of the sector. The chapters of Part One provide the background and information that are needed to understand this context, and they examine the ways these large-scale phenomena are affecting nonprofit leadership and management.

This part of the book contains four chapters. In Chapter One, Peter Dobkin Hall describes and analyzes the historical evolution of the U.S. nonprofit sector and how nonprofit organizations are affected by and affect many of our society's major institutions. Bruce R. Hopkins and Virginia C. Gross explain in Chapter Two the changing legal and regulatory environment within which U.S. nonprofit organizations, particularly charities, must operate, and discuss the implications for nonprofit practice. In Chapter Three, Lester M. Salamon describes the most significant large-scale changes of the economic, political, and demographic environments of the sector and discusses, in particular, how nonprofit organizations are affected by some of the most recent changes in their evolving relationship with government. Finally, in Chapter Four, a new chapter prepared for this edition, Alnoor Ebrahim examines the increasingly strong push for nonprofit accountability and provides a useful framework by which to consider how nonprofit leaders can understand and respond.

CHAPTER ONE

HISTORICAL PERSPECTIVES ON NONPROFIT ORGANIZATIONS IN THE UNITED STATES

Peter Dobkin Hall

Although charitable, educational, and religious organizations are thousands of years old (for example, the Roman Catholic church) and some in the United States (for example, Harvard College) were founded in colonial times, the concept of "nonprofit organizations" as a unified and coherent "sector" dates back only to the 1970s.

In fact, over 90 percent of nonprofit organizations currently in existence were created since 1950. Worldwide, most nongovernmental organizations (or NGOs, as they are called outside the United States) have come into being in the past thirty years. Nonprofits and NGOs are the most rapidly growing organizational domain in the world.

It is difficult to define what nonprofit organizations are, what they do, and how they do it. They vary enormously in scope and scale, ranging from informal grassroots organizations with no assets and no employees to multi-billion-dollar foundations, universities, religious bodies, and health care complexes with thousands of employees or members. Although some provide traditional charitable, educational, and religious services, the laws in many countries, including the United States, permit them to provide almost any kind of good or service on a not-for-profit basis. Sources of revenue vary: some are supported by donations, others depend on income from sales of goods and services, many receive most or all of their revenues from government. Modes of governance range from the autocracy of sole trustees selected from among the descendants of charitable donors to broadly representative boards composed of *ex officio* elected officials or directors elected by members of organizations.

Because of the complexity and diversity of nonprofit organizations, the term itself has a variety of meanings. It can refer to entities classified by the Internal Revenue Code as 501(c)3 charitable tax-exempts—or to a more inclusive universe of 501(c)4 civic organizations, which are themselves exempt from taxation but do not allow deductibility of donations. Good arguments can be made for including other noncharitable nonprofits such as cemeteries, veterans and fraternal/sororal organizations (such as the Masons and the Elks), political parties, and other organizations covered by Section 501(c). However inclusive, restricting the term to organizations accorded nonprofit status by the tax code remains problematic, since it does not include churches and other religious organizations that enjoy the privileges of 501(c)3s but are not legally required to incorporate or seek exempt status. There is also a vast realm of unincorporated associations (such as Alcoholics Anonymous and other self-help groups) that perform many of the functions of incorporated nonprofits as providers of charitable, educational, and religious services but whose assets do not merit—or ideology does not permit—formal institutionalization.

Because their numbers have grown so rapidly, because they are so diverse, and because their impact is so far-reaching—touching on every aspect of our lives and every level of institutions—nonprofits have been the focus of intense controversy as legislators, the courts, and the public have struggled to come to terms with this organizational revolution. At the same time, because the nonprofit universe has been in a process of emergence, those within it have had to struggle to define and legitimate it.

For all of these reasons—diversity, complexity, and disagreement about how to define them—nonprofits pose particular difficulties for scholars trying to explain their history. Although elements of the "nonprofit sector" date back to Biblical and Classical times (for example, religious bodies), other important aspects of it are entirely new (for example, hospitals and universities). At best, in trying to understand the history of nonprofits, we can identify the various ideas and institutions that constitute today's nonprofit domain and show how they have evolved over time.

Associations in Early America

The basic legal vehicles of today's nonprofits—the corporation and the trust—were known to colonial Americans. Philanthropy and volunteer service—giving money and time—were also features of early American life. But because the colonists understood the role of government and the rights and responsibilities of citizenship so differently, these vehicles and practices little resembled the forms they take in modern America.

To begin with, there was no clear demarcation between public and private realms. All corporations, to the extent that they were permitted to exist, were considered to be public agencies (Davis, 1918; Dodd, 1960; Hurst, 1970; Seavoy, 1982). Most common were municipal corporations: townships (Hartog, 1983). In most colonies, religious congregations were public corporations supported by taxation and enjoying monopoly powers. The early colleges, Harvard (1638), William & Mary (1689), and Yale (1701), were sustained by government grants and governed by clergymen who, as officials of the government-supported ("established") churches, were public actors (Whitehead, 1976). No private corporation as we understand the term today existed in America before the 1780s. Many of these institutions—churches, townships, and colleges—accepted gifts and bequests from donors and held them in trust as endowments, although it would be decades before American courts would have the power to enforce or adjudicate trusts.

Citizens often pitched in to maintain roads, build meeting houses, fight with militias, and assist with other public tasks (McKinney, 1995). Although superficially resembling modern volunteers, these citizens were usually compelled by law to labor on behalf of the public. Service of this kind was a common way of paying taxes in a primitive colonial economy in which barter usually took the place of money. Militia duty and service in public office was often required by law—and those who failed to "volunteer" to serve were often punished by fines.

Despite obvious differences, these colonial institutions resembled modern nonprofits in important ways (Zollmann, 1924). They were self-governing, with decisions made by members who often delegated power to governing boards. More important, they had no owners or stockholders. As public bodies they were exempt from taxation. And, like modern nonprofits, they could accept donations and bequests for charitable purposes, such as supporting education and relief for the poor.

During the eighteenth century, population growth, economic development, and closer contact with England and other European countries changed American institutions. More people and the founding of new towns made it harder to maintain social and political unity. Artisans, merchants, and laborers living in seaports, who depended on trade and were exposed to new ideas from Europe, developed ways of thinking and living that were different from those of subsistence farmers in isolated landlocked villages. Even in the back country, conflict developed between farmers who began to grow crops for sale to urban merchants—thus tying themselves to the emerging market economy—and those who continued to produce largely to satisfy their own needs. To complicate matters, England's efforts to integrate the colonies into its growing commercial empire brought political changes. In many colonies, elected officials were replaced by royal appointees and the Congregationalist religious monopoly was broken by the establishment of Anglican churches.

New ideas accompanied these social, economic, and political changes. Out of a century of religious warfare and political strife in Europe came philosophies that asserted the "natural rights" of citizens, including freedom of speech, assembly, and worship, and questioned the authority of arbitrary and oppressive government (Bailyn, 1992). New ideas also included more sophisticated understandings of law, particularly as it affected economic rights (Katz, 1971; Nelson, 1975; Horowitz, 1977; Katz et al., 1985).

Closer ties to Europe brought not only new ideas, but also new institutions. After an apprenticeship as a printer in London, young Benjamin Franklin returned with firsthand knowledge of the various kinds of voluntary associations being formed by English tradesmen (Morgan, 2003). Freemasonry, a fraternal order whose members were committed to a variety of radical political and religious ideas, spread rapidly through the colonies in the mid-1700s. Masonry provided a model for other forms of private voluntary associations, most notably Franklin's "Junto," a club of young Philadelphia tradesmen who pooled their books, trained one another in debating and writing, and supported one another's political and economic ambitions.

Closer ties with Europe also transformed American religious life as evangelists associated with dissenting sects crossed the ocean to spread their doctrines (Ahlstrom, 1972; Finke and Stark, 1992; Hatch, 1989; Butler, 1990). Soon American cities and towns were filled with competing churches, with Methodists, Baptists, and other religious enthusiasts crowding out the older Congregationalists and Methodists. Although Pennsylvanians and Rhode Islanders had long enjoyed religious toleration, the notion that people could freely choose how to worship and were free to form and support their own congregations, free of government interference, was a novel idea to most Americans. In many places, religious dissenters demanded and succeeded in obtaining many of the same rights as members of established churches, including exemption of their congregations from taxation. This set an important precedent for the secular associations that would proliferate in the nineteenth century.

The American Revolution drew on all these intellectual and organizational developments: religious revivals and political theories that affirmed the importance of individual rights, experience in organizing voluntary associations, and the use of associations in politics. Groups such as the Sons of Liberty and the

Committees of Correspondence helped mobilize citizens to fight for American independence.

Voluntary Associations in the New Republic, 1780–1830

Despite their importance during the Revolution, many Americans distrusted voluntary associations and feared the power of wealthy private institutions. These feelings were fueled by popular uprisings such as Shay's Rebellion, in which Revolutionary veterans led armed resistance to tax collectors, and the establishment of the Society of the Cincinnati, an association of army officers that, critics believed, desired the creation of a titled aristocracy. This distrust fueled resistance to efforts to charter corporations and to enact legal reforms that would make it easier to create and enforce charitable trusts.

Led by Virginia, many states actively discouraged private charity (Wyllie, 1959; Miller, 1961). In 1792, the Commonwealth annulled the British laws that authorized the establishment of charitable trusts and confiscated endowments administered by the Anglican church. Favoring public over private institutions, Virginia established the first state university in 1818 (Dabney, 1981). This would become a common pattern in many southern and western states.

The South was not alone in its suspicion of private charitable enterprise. In 1784, New York established the Regents of the University of the State of New York, a regulatory body that oversaw all charitable, education, religious, and professional organizations. In the 1820s the state enacted laws limiting the size of institutional endowments and the size of bequests that testators could leave to charity.

In contrast, the New England states actively encouraged private initiatives of all sorts. By 1800, Massachusetts and Connecticut had chartered more corporations than all the other states combined. Voluntary associations—formal and informal; religious and secular—flourished. By the 1820s, legal reforms gave further encouragement to private charities by protecting trustees from liability and liberalizing the kinds of investments they could make. As a result, New England states became national centers for education, culture, and science, as the wealth from their industrializing economy poured into the coffers of their colleges, hospitals, libraries, and museums (Hall, 1982).

These growing differences in the treatment of private associations, charity, and philanthropy inevitably had political consequences. With the rise of popular politics and the intensification of efforts to disestablish churches in states where some religious groups still enjoyed monopoly privileges and tax support, conservative elites went on the defensive, using colleges and other private institutions to protect their power. These struggles came to a head in the Dartmouth College Case (Trustees, 1819; Tobias, 1982). In 1819, the U.S. Supreme Court was asked to decide whether the state of New Hampshire had exceeded its powers in taking over a privately endowed educational institution and turning it into a public institution. The court, in ruling that a corporation was a private contract and hence protected by the contracts clause of the United States Constitution, gave assurance to donors that the institutions they founded and supported would be safe from government interference. Later, in the Girard Will Case, the Court would affirm the legal basis for private philanthropy, even in states such as Pennsylvania, which had annulled British charities statutes.

Because the Constitution granted significant power to the states, these federal court decisions had limited impact. Every state had its own laws governing corporations, associations, and charities. Some, like those of New England, encouraged private philanthropy and protected charitable corporations. Most, however, restricted private initiatives and, as a matter of public policy, favored public ones. This preference did not, it should be noted, preclude private giving to public institutions. State colleges and universities, public libraries, and other government-run agencies benefited from this growing practice of public philanthropy.

During the first half of the nineteenth century, voluntary associations played increasingly important roles in the nation's public life. Political parties, which were embryonic in 1800, had become powerful national institutions. As Americans became concerned about slavery, drunkenness, violations of the Sabbath, treatment of the insane, and other causes, voluntary associations, organized on a national basis with state and local chapters, became the preferred vehicles for social movements promoting reform. Churches began organizing themselves into national denominations that supported a wide variety of educational and charitable initiatives, domestic and foreign missions, and substantial publishing enterprises (Foster, 1965; Mathews, 1969). Fraternal organizations, the Masons and Odd Fellows, commanded the loyalties of hundreds of thousands of Americans (Skocpol et al., 1999).

Beginning in the 1830s, emigrants, displaced by war, revolution, and economic distress, began to flock to our shores. Some, like the Germans, brought with them their own rich traditions of voluntary action. Others, like the Irish, brought forms of charitable engagement. The Roman Catholic church, to which many Germans and Irish belonged, began creating a benevolent empire of schools, orphanages, temperance societies, and social welfare organizations to serve its members. Although its hierarchical structure excluded laity from involvement in church governance, the church became an increasingly important factor in the nation's associational life (Dolan, 1992; Oates, 1995).

In addition to these national associations, there were thousands of free-standing local charitable corporations and voluntary associations devoted to practically every imaginable purpose (Ryan,1981). As the French visitor Alexis de Tocqueville noted while visiting America in the 1830s:

> Americans of all ages, all conditions, and all dispositions constantly form associations. They have not only commercial and manufacturing companies, in which all take part, but associations of a thousand other kinds, religious, moral, serious, futile, general or restricted, enormous or diminutive. The Americans make associations to give entertainments, to found seminaries, to build inns, to construct churches, to diffuse books, to send missionaries to the antipodes; in this manner they found hospitals, prisons, and schools. If it is proposed to inculcate some truth or foster some feeling by the encouragement of a great example, they form a society. Wherever at the head of some new undertaking you see the government in France, or a man of rank in England, in the United States you will be sure to find an association (de Tocqueville, [1835] 1945, II, p. 106).

In his enthusiasm, de Tocqueville somewhat exaggerated the universality of voluntary associations. Although they were used for many purposes and by people at all levels of society, including women and African Americans, who were excluded from the political process, there remained significant geographical variations in citizens' willingness to use them, depending on whether state laws restricted their activities and authorities were willing to subsidize them directly, through government grants and contracts, or indirectly through tax-exemption.

In states where private initiative was discouraged, tasks of education, healing, and care for the dependent and disabled were often carried out by public agencies. Public provision did not preclude private support, however. State universities accepted private donations. Fire fighting in most towns and cities was provided by volunteer companies. Along with newer forms of voluntary action, older traditions of public philanthropy and voluntarism continued to flourish.

Nation Building, 1860–1920

Associations, private charities, and giving and volunteering all played prominent roles in the Civil War, which provided opportunities for further advancing the claims of private eleemosynary enterprise. Among the first units to rally to the defense of the Union were private military companies, groups of civilians for whom soldierly training was a form of recreational and social activity. Once the fighting began in earnest, private groups rushed to care for the injured and provide comfort for soldiers still in the field. The United States Sanitary Commission, the United States Christian Commission, and other groups organized fundraising events, made clothing and bandages, and mobilized volunteers in towns and cities throughout the country to meet the medical, public health, and other needs of armed forces (Brockett, 1864; Cross, 1865; Moss, 1968; Frederickson, 1965).

At the war's end, the victorious Union faced the immense task of "reconstructing" states devastated by fierce fighting and preparing millions of free slaves for freedom (Fleming, 1906; McFeely, 1968; Butchart, 1980; Richardson, 1986). To do this, the government turned to voluntary organizations to build and staff schools, teach civic and vocational skills to newly freed men and women, and reform southern industry and agriculture (Swint, 1967). Reconstruction also showed some of the darker possibilities of voluntary associations, as embittered southerners organized groups such as the Ku Klux Klan to terrorize blacks and the northern volunteers who were helping them.

The Civil War transformed America, not only establishing the preeminent authority of the federal government in important areas such as civil rights, but also unifying the country economically and culturally. Military needs had forced standardization of railroad equipment, consolidation of the telegraph industry, and the creation of a national financial market, centered in New York. Government spending and growing demand from an increasingly urbanized population fueled the increases in the scope and scale of manufacturing and commercial enterprises that sought national and international markets. The government-funded Transcontinental Railroad, completed in 1869, opened vast areas of the West for agricultural and industrial development. Growing industries and advancing technology required managers and experts for efficient and profitable operation.

Educational institutions found opportunities in this prospect of unbounded growth. "The American people are fighting the wilderness, physical and moral, on the one hand, and on the other are struggling to work out the awful problem of self-government," declared Harvard's new president, Charles W. Eliot, in 1869. "For this fight they must be trained and armed" (Eliot, 1869). Having spent the war years in Europe studying the relationships between higher education and economic development, Eliot himself was well prepared to lead the transformation of Harvard, a sleepy local college before the war, into a modern research university.

Eliot's clarion call was met with enthusiasm. Gifts and bequests to the university increased from $1.6 million for the period 1841–1865 to $5.9 million for the years 1866–1890 (Sears, 1922). Business leaders largely replaced clergymen and lawyers on its governing boards (Veblen, 1918). Curricular reforms encouraged specialization, while new graduate departments and professional schools provided facilities for advanced training and research (Veysey, 1965; Rudolph, 1968; Hawkins, 1972). Harvard's transformation into a research university set the pace for American higher education—and the generosity and imagination of its donors set a standard for philanthropists throughout the country (Curti and Nash, 1965).

Universities became hubs for a universe of new associational and philanthropic institutions and activities (Bledstein, 1976; Hawkins, 1992; Geiger, 1986, 1993). Hospitals, museums, and other arts organizations became research centers, closely tied to university medical schools, scientific disciplines, and new programs in the fine arts and music (Fox, 1963; Starr, 1982; DiMaggio, 1986). New academic disciplines and professions gave rise to professional and scholarly societies (Buck, 1965; Haskell, 1977). University-trained managers and experts became increasingly important not only to industry, but also to governments, which were beginning to grapple with the social welfare, public health, transportation, and policing problems of growing cities (Wiebe, 1967; Brint, 1994).

Beginning in the 1870s, the American economy was shaken by a series of crises. The collapse of the stock market in 1873 was the beginning of a depression that lasted for years and impoverished hundreds of thousands of workers. Economic distress encouraged the growth of labor unions and radical political organizations whose conflicts with employers and government authorities became increasingly violent. In 1877, a national railroad strike provoked large-scale rioting and looting in major cities. In 1886, labor's campaign for a ten hour workday culminated in the Haymarket bombing in Chicago, which killed a dozen policemen and led to the round-up and execution of radical politicians and journalists.

Among the few calm voices in the period was that of a Pittsburgh steel executive, Andrew Carnegie (Wall, 1970). An immigrant from Scotland, Carnegie had worked his way up from being a child laborer in a textile mill to serving as the right-hand man of the president of the Pennsylvania Railroad. From there, he became a pioneering and fabulously successful steel manufacturer. By the 1880s, he was well on his way to becoming one of America's wealthiest men.

In 1886, Carnegie began writing a series of articles on the labor crisis that argued that shorter hours, better working conditions, and employer recognition of workers' right to organize were in the interests of both capital and labor. At the same time, he suggested that the enlarged scope and scale of modern industry had fundamentally changed not only economic relationships, but also the nature of political life (Carnegie, 1886a, 1886b). He summed up his thinking in an 1889 essay, "Wealth," which urged the "men of affairs" who had most profited from advanced industrial development to use their "genius for affairs" to reinvest their fortunes in society. Inherited wealth, he believed, was bad both for heirs and for society—and he went so far as to recommend confiscatory estate taxation to prevent the passing on of large fortunes (Carnegie, 1889). More important, he argued that intelligent philanthropy could not only eliminate the root causes of social problems, but sustain the competitive processes essential to continuing progress.

Carnegie was harshly critical of traditional charity, which, he believed, only responded to suffering rather than addressing the causes of poverty. "It were better for mankind that the millions of the rich were thrown into the sea," he wrote, "than so spent as to encourage the slothful, the drunken, the unworthy. Of every thousand dollars spent in so-called charity today, it is probable that nine hundred and fifty dollars is unwisely spent—so spent, indeed, as to produce the very evils which it hopes to mitigate or cure" (Carnegie, 1889). "The best means of benefiting the community," Carnegie urged his fellow millionaires, "is to place within its reach the ladders upon which the aspiring can rise"—"institutions of various kinds, which will improve the general condition of the people; in this manner returning their surplus wealth to the mass of their fellows in the forms best calculated to do them lasting good" (Carnegie, 1889). This included libraries, parks, museums, public meeting halls (like New York's famous Carnegie Hall), and educational institutions.

In popularizing the idea that businessmen could use the same "genius for affairs" that had made them rich to reform society, Carnegie set an example for his fellow tycoons. Before Carnegie, most philanthropy had been small-scale and conventional. After Carnegie, philanthropy, organized and focused through foundations, would assume an unprecedented scale and scope, becoming an important source of innovation in addressing problems of education, health, and social welfare.

The consolidation of American political, economic, and social institutions between the Civil War and the First World War was as much the result of the actions of elite institutions such as universities and powerful leaders such as Andrew Carnegie as it was the outcome of associational activity at all levels in society (Sklar, 1988). In the second half of the nineteenth century, America became, in Arthur Schlesinger, Sr.'s phrase, "a nation of joiners" (Schlesinger, 1944, p. 24). Immigrants, who flooded the nation in ever growing numbers, organized mutual benefit associations that gave them solidarity and provided help in times of sickness and distress (Soyer, 1997; Li, 1999). Physicians, lawyers, engineers, and other professionals organized associations to set standards, exchange information, and pressure government (Calhoun, 1965; Calvert, 1967; Auerbach, 1976; Abbott, 1988; Kimball, 1995). Businesses organized trade associations to advocate for legislation favoring their interests (Naylor, 1921). Wage earners organized trade unions to press employers to improve pay and working conditions. War veterans organized the Grand Army of the Republic to promote sociability and advocate for pensions and other benefits. Advocacy groups, which drew members from across the social spectrum, agitated for prohibition, women's suffrage, civil service and charities reform, and other causes (Clemens, 1997). Most important of all were the fraternal and sororal organizations—the Freemasons, Odd Fellows, Knights of Columbus, Rebekahs, and dozens of others—whose chapters became centers of sociability and civic activity, as well as sources of social insurance, for men and women throughout the country (Dumenil, 1984; Beito, 2000; Kaufman, 2002; Skocpol, 2003).

Widespread participation in these broad-based associations was probably the most powerful and effective school of democracy. By participating in associations, citizens learned how to be self-governing, argue and persuade, raise funds and manage finances, and form alliances and coalitions. The fact that most of these associations were national entities whose architecture mirrored that of government itself—with nation, state, and local organizations—helped bind the nation together by accustoming Americans to engaging with one another beyond the locality. If, as de Tocqueville suggested, Americans in the first half of the nineteenth century had learned the principle of association in their schoolyards, in the second half of the century associations became the great school of democracy, teaching adults and children alike the values and skills needed for a vibrant and inclusive public culture.

New Charitable Vehicles, 1890–1930

The kind of large-scale targeted giving Carnegie recommended faced a number of obstacles. The most important of them were legal barriers to private charity in states such as New York. At the time that Carnegie wrote, New York state courts had already invalidated a million dollar bequest to Cornell on grounds that the donation, if accepted, would render the university's endowment larger than the amount that the legislature had authorized it to hold. They had also invalidated former presidential candidate and corporation lawyer Samuel Tilden's multimillion-dollar charitable bequest to establish the New York Public Library (Ames, 1913). Without major legal reform, the wealthy, who were increasingly gravitating to New York—the nation's financial center—could not be philanthropically generous even if they wanted to be.

Another obstacle was the lack of organizational vehicles for large-scale philanthropy. Wealthy men like the devoutly religious John D. Rockefeller, who controlled America's petroleum industry by the 1890s, tried to be conscientious givers, personally considering and carefully weighing the thousands of begging letters that poured into their offices (Harr and Johnson, 1988; Chernow, 1998). Rockefeller's situation was summed up by his chief assistant, John W. Gates, who exclaimed to his employer, "Your fortune is rolling up, rolling up like an avalanche! . . . . You must keep up with it! You must distribute it faster than it grows! If you do not, it will crush you and your children and your children's children" (Harr and Johnson, 1988, p. 82). The solution was the creation of corporate entities, staffed by experts, to scientifically distribute this surplus wealth. The problem was that American charities law had traditionally required that charitable trusts be specific in designating classes of beneficiaries.

The failure of the Tilden Trust, combined with anxieties about the increasing anger of average Americans toward the rich and big business, fueled a coordinated effort to reform charities laws in the leading industrial states ("American Millionaires," 1893). By 1893, New York, Pennsylvania, Ohio, and Illinois had altered their charities statutes, permitting the kind of wholesale philanthropy that Carnegie had advocated. Philanthropists proceeded cautiously onto this new legal ground. The first recognizably modern foundations included Rockefeller's General Education Board (established in 1901) to benefit black schools in the South but later broadened to include higher educational nationally, Andrew Carnegie's Carnegie Endowment for the Advancement of Teaching (established in 1905), and Margaret Olivia Slocum Sage's Russell Sage Foundation (established in 1907) to systematically address social welfare issues on a national basis (Glenn, Brandt, and Andrews, 1947; Fosdick, 1962; Lagemann, 1999; Hammack and Wheeler, 1994). In 1911, Carnegie took the bold step of establishing the largest foundation of all, the Carnegie Corporation of New York, for the general purpose of "the advancement and diffusion of knowledge and understanding" (Lagemann, 1992).

John D. Rockefeller, not to be outdone and smarting from the court-ordered breakup of the Standard Oil monopoly, applied to Congress for a charter for a $100 million foundation dedicated to "the betterment of mankind" (Fosdick, 1952). The request set off a furor among politicians and journalists who worried about the influence foundations of this size could have on public policy and about their economic power. Rockefeller eventually obtained a charter from the New York State legislature in 1913.

Concerns about the power of foundations and the continuing concentration of wealth continued to grow. In 1915, the Congress empanelled a special Commission on Industrial Relations that held well-publicized hearings over a period of two years (U.S. Congress, 1916). The charges aired during these hearings led foundations to be cautious and secretive about their involvement in public affairs—a stance that would fuel public suspicions of philanthropy's motives and methods that would erupt periodically for the rest of the century (Katz, 1981).

Grantmaking foundations were not the only new charitable vehicles created in the decades before the First World War. In 1910, Cleveland, Ohio's Chamber of Commerce convened a committee to consider problems of charitable fraud, abuse, and inefficiency. Appeals for charity were multiplying, but donors had no way of knowing whether they came from reputable organizations. The number of charitable organizations seeking aid was increasing, producing duplicated efforts and wasted resources. The donor base was shrinking, with an increasing proportion of donations coming from a smaller number of donors. The committee eventually brought forth a new kind of charity—the Community Chest (Seeley, 1957; Cutlip, 1965). Led by businessmen, the Chest proposed to conduct a single annual fund drive for all of Cleveland's charities. The Chest's distribution committee would assess the city's charities and allocate funds to the most worthy. The Chest proposed to broaden the donor base by soliciting employees of the city's business firms. Aggressively publicized, the Chest idea spread rapidly. By 1930, hundreds of towns and cities had adopted this form of federated fundraising. The Community Chest is the ancestor of today's United Way.

Cleveland also fostered cooperation among the city's social agencies through its Charities Federation. Establishing lines of communication between agencies allowed them to coordinate their activities, improve their management, and use their resources more efficiently. It also enabled private agencies to work more closely with government to address social problems.

The Community Chest and the Charities Federation addressed problems of current giving and spending. In 1925, Cleveland banker Frederick Goff sought to make the establishment and management of charitable endowments more efficient. He proposed the idea of the community foundation, an institution empowered to receive charitable trusts of various sizes and for various purposes (Hall, 1989a; Hammack, 1989; Magat, 1989). These would be placed under common management under the authority of a board made up of leading bankers. A distribution committee, often made up of public officials and others serving *ex officio*, would allocate undesignated or discretionary funds to worthy organizations. Like the Community Chest, the community foundation was intended to democratize charitable giving while giving civic leaders control of a community's charitable resources.

None of these innovations would have been possible without the enthusiastic backing of business leaders. Not only did their ideas and money sustain charitable, educational, and religious institutions, but their companies became important to the effort to improve society (Heald, 1970; Hall 1989b). Under the banner of "welfare capitalism," corporations not only contributed generously to community institutions, they also established pension plans, initiated educational programs, and supported social and athletic activities for their employees and their families (Brandes, 1976; Brody, 1980). Many firms sold products intended to improve Americans' health and quality of life.

These charitable innovations were only a small part of a far broader associational revolution in the first third of the twentieth century. In the first quarter of the twentieth century, membership in fraternal and sororal organizations peaked in numbers of organizations and membership (Skocpol, 2003). Business-men's service organizations—Rotary, Kiwanis, Lions, and others—appeared in every town and city (Charles, 1993). Businesses organized trade associations to advocate, lobby, and educate the public and government about their interests. Herbert Hoover, writing in 1922, envisioned these trade associations working closely with other kinds of "voluntary organizations for altruistic purposes" to advance public welfare, morals, and charity, to elevate public opinion, to improve public health, and to solve social problems combining the pursuit of self-interested with higher values of cooperation and public service (Hoover, 1922; Galambos, 1966; Hawley, 1974, 1977; Karl, 1969, 1976). A nation based on public interest voluntarism, he believed, would not need the radical remedies of socialism and communism to address problems of inequality and injustice.

Accompanying this associational revolution was a related transformation of fundraising (Cutlip, 1965). As the needs of hospitals, universities, and other organized charities grew, fundraising became professionalized. Firms such as John Price Jones & Company combined sophisticated business methods with aggressive marketing techniques in raising funds for the World War I loan drives and, later, for Harvard and other universities.

Reform-oriented social movements and other kinds of organized advocacy continued to grow during this period (Sealander, 1997). Efforts to eliminate child labor, enfranchise women, restrict immigration, and protect the rights of minori-ties influenced public policy through demonstrations, advertising campaigns, lobbying, and litigation. Particularly notable were the efforts of the NAACP (National Association for the Advancement of Colored People) and other groups in the vanguard of the effort to halt the epidemic of lynchings and race riots in which thousands of black citizens perished between 1890 and 1930. Sadly, perhaps the most influential social movement of the period was the revived Ku Klux Klan, which, during the 1920s, commanded the loyalty of hundreds of thousands of followers throughout the country, directing its energies against African Americans, Jews, Catholics, labor organizers, and others.

Big Government, the Nonprofit Sector, and the Transformation of Public Life, 1930–1980

Between 1930 and 1980, American public life was transformed by huge growth in the scope and scale of government, which in turn stimulated commensurate expansion of private institutions. The two were closely connected, since govern-ment, as it took on increasing responsibilities for managing economic, political, and social domains, was able to use its awesome power to stimulate growth and activity in the private sectors. Just as public sector activities such as construction of the interstate highway system and petroleum industry subsidies stimulated the growth of the privately owned automobile industry, so public sector subsidies of charitable giving (tax breaks for donors, exemptions for charities, voucher programs such as the G.I. Bill, and increasingly generous grants and contracts) stimulated the growth of nonprofit enterprises of every kind.

This was an incremental process. In the 1930s, no one envisioned that the emergency powers assumed by the federal government to deal with the Depression would become permanent and central features of public life. Nor could anyone imagine the extent to which the increasing activism of government would stimulate the growth of the private sector.

The nation was ill-prepared to deal with the catastrophic economic collapse that began with the stock market crash of October 1929. Even if the discipline of economics had been better developed, its retrospective insights could not have offered much understanding of this unprecedented event. In any event, government lacked the necessary tools of economic management to engage problems of mass unemployment and business failure on this scale.

President Hoover, a millionaire mining engineer who had entered politics with an international reputation as a humanitarian, was philosophically opposed to the idea of big government. His attempts to deal with the Depression through the system of voluntary associations whose growth he had fostered as secretary of commerce and later as president, proved ineffective. His successor, Franklin D. Roosevelt, entered office with similarly conservative views. The centerpiece of his recovery program, the National Recovery Administration (NRA)—with its motto, "we do our part"—was similarly based on voluntaristic principles, promoting economic revival through cooperation between business and government (Himmelberg, 1976).

When the NRA was declared unconstitutional in 1935, Roosevelt turned to more activist remedies, with attempts to restore consumer buying power through massive public works projects like the WPA (Works Projects Administration) and the CCC (Civilian Conservation Corps), agricultural subsidies, and through a national system of social insurance (Social Security). He also proposed major tax reforms, which introduced steeply progressive income and estate taxes with the intent of using the tax system to redistribute the wealth owned by the richest Americans. These tax reforms had little impact on average Americans, few of whom earned enough money to owe income tax. But they proved to be a powerful incentive for the wealthy to avoid taxation through large-scale charitable giving.

Roosevelt's New Deal established the paradigm for the later growth of government. Although the federal government increased the scope of its responsibilities and assumed leadership for making policy in important areas, most federal programs were carried out by state and municipal agencies and by nongovernmental organizations funded by government contracts, user fees, and private contributions indirectly subsidized through tax exemptions and deductions.

During the Second World War and afterward, as the United States assumed leadership of the free world, federal government policies played a key role in stimulating growth in the number and importance of nonprofit organizations. The most important of these involved taxation (Witte, 1985; Webber and Wildavsky, 1986). The income tax, which few Americans had had to pay before the 1940s, was universalized: not only were most wage and salary earners subject to it, but also the government began withholding estimated tax liabilities from employees' paychecks. At the same time, tax rates were sharply increased on estates and business corporations. New tax policies were not only intended to gather revenue for government. Through "loopholes"—exemptions, deductions, and tax credits—tax policy was used to encourage charitable giving to private institutions classified as tax exempt by the Internal Revenue Service (IRS) (Howard, 1997). The growth of nonprofit organizations was also stimulated by increased spending in the form of government grants, contracts, and vouchers (like the GI bill, which subsidized higher education for returning soldiers).

These policies had dramatic effects (Weisbrod, 1988). By 1940, there were only 12,500 charitable tax-exempt organizations registered by the IRS—along with 179,742 religious congregations (which did not have to apply for exemption) and 60,000 noncharitable nonprofits (such as labor unions and fraternal associations) that enjoyed various tax privileges.[1] By 1980, there were 320,000 charitable tax exempt nonprofits—as well as 336,000 religious bodies and 526,000 noncharitable nonprofits. By 2006, there would be more than 600,000 charitables, 400,000 religious congregations, and 600,000 noncharitables—a total of more than a million and a half nonprofits of various types (Hall and Burke, 2006). Government policies played a crucial role in fueling the growing scope and number of nonprofit organizations, not only indirectly through creating incentives to individuals and firms for contributing to private organizations serving governmental ends, but also directly, through grants and contracts. By the 1970s, between 12 percent and 55 percent of total nonprofit revenues were direct payments from the federal government (Salamon, 1987).

Although the scope and scale of its responsibilities vastly increased in the second half of the twentieth century, the size of the federal government—at least as measured in the size of its civilian workforce—did not. The number federal civilian employees remained unchanged between 1950 and 2000, while the number of state and local employees doubled and tripled and the number of nonprofit organizations grew from the thousands to over a million. Quite clearly, "big government" as it developed after the second World War took a very different form than conventionally supposed. Doing its work through states and localities and through policies that encouraged flows of resources to private actors, the American welfare state was a remarkable example of what Lester Salamon has called "third-party government." (See Chapter Three for more about the relation between governments and nonprofit organizations.)

Of the proliferating organizations of the nonprofit sector, none attracted more attention in the decades following the war than foundations (Andrews, 1950). As taxes on incomes and estates increased, the founders of the huge fortunes built in the boom years of the twentieth century were increasingly likely to use foundations as mechanisms for avoiding taxation. When Henry Ford died in 1947, stock in his closely held company was divided into two classes (MacDonald, 1956; Greenleaf, 1964; Nielsen, 1971; Sutton, 1987). The voting stock was retained by the family, while the nonvoting securities were given to the Ford Foundation, which sold them at an immense profit. The Ford Motor Company passed to the next generation without paying a penny in taxes—and the largest foundation in the world was created in the process.

Stratagems like this helped fuel an enormous increase in the number and importance of foundations. Numbering only 203 in 1929, the number of foundations with assets exceeding a million dollars grew to 2,058 by 1959—with the vast majority of these established within the decade (*Foundation Directory*, 1960, pp. ix–lv; Andrews, 1956). In 1929, their assets represented only 10.7 percent of the total property controlled by charitable tax-exempt organizations; by 1973, their share was 21.7 percent. Thanks to liberalized laws regarding corporate philanthropy, the growing universe of private and community foundations was further enlarged by corporate foundations and organized corporate contributions programs (Andrews, 1952; Useem, 1987; Hall, 1989b; Himmelstein, 1997).

Although Ford and other foundations established by wealthy families at this time undoubtedly performed valuable services, some politicians and journalists wondered whether average citizens, who were becoming increasingly sensitive to their own tax burdens, either approved of the loopholes that permitted multimillionaires to evade taxes or sympathized with the sometimes controversial uses of foundation grants (Lundberg, 1968; Nielsen, 1971; Andrews, 1969). Between 1952 and 1969, congressional committees' investigations of foundations and "other tax-exempt entities" cast an increasingly skeptical eye on their activities. With the federal government assuming primary responsibility for education, health, and social welfare, many wondered whether private philanthropy, subsidized by tax breaks, had outlived its usefulness.

Despite these periodic outbursts of regulatory enthusiasm, funds from foundations, corporations, and new government programs (such as the National Institutes of Health, National Science Foundation, National Endowment for the

Arts, and National Endowment for the Humanities, among others) continued to fuel the growth and transformation of nonprofit enterprise. On the one hand, industries such as the performing arts and health care, which had been almost entirely for-profit in ownership before 1950, became dominated by nonprofit firms in the course of the next half-century. On the other hand, industries like elder care, which had been largely nonprofit, became for-profit in ownership as government social and medical insurance programs made nursing homes an increasingly profitable enterprise.

The increasing centrality of government also encouraged the growth of special interest advocacy organizations, as stakeholders affected by or benefiting from government programs sought to influence legislators in their favor (Berry, 1977, 1997; Jenkins, 1987; Jenkins and Craig, 1986; Jenkins and Halcli, 1999). Policy research ("think tanks") and policy advocacy groups such as the Business Advisory Council, the Conference Board, the Committee for Economic Development, and the Business Roundtable formed a privatized policy establishment (Critchlow, 1985; Smith, 1991a, 1991b; Rich, 2004).

Increasing government activism and foundation funding also stimulated grassroots social movement activity intended to influence public policy. The Civil Rights movement of the 1950s and 1960s gave rise to a host of movements promoting the rights of women, children, the unborn, and the disabled, the health of the environment, and a variety of international causes (Minkoff, 1995; Proietto, 1999; Berkeley Art Center Association, 2001; Fleischer and Zames, 2001; Minton, 2002; Stroman, 2003). On the whole, these social change organizations differed in significant ways from their nineteenth-century predecessors. Earlier organizations had been broadly based membership organizations in which volunteers and local chapters played central roles. Late twentieth-century social change organizations were increasingly likely to be based in the national capital and to be run by professional managers, policy experts, communications specialists, and lobbyists (Skocpol, 2003).

Changing political culture, combined with a more educated, affluent, and mobile citizenry, helped kill off traditional kinds of voluntary associations. Membership in fraternal and sororal organizations began to drop sharply after the Second World War as Americans moved to the suburbs and substituted television and other privatized forms of entertainment and recreation for more collective forms of social engagement (Skocpol, 1999). Even such venerable organizations as the Parent-Teacher Association (PTA) began to decline, as suburban parents preferred to devote their energies to parent-teacher organizations focusing more narrowly on the schools their own children attended rather than broader educational issues (Crawford and Levitt, 1999). According to political scientist Robert Putnam, all forms of civic engagement—voting, attending public meetings, church attendance, and participation in athletic associations such as bowling leagues—declined sharply after the 1960s (Putnam, 2000).

Taking the place of traditional voluntary and membership-based engagement was a growing domain of narrowly focused, professionally managed nonprofit organizations that drew their revenues from a mix of earned revenues, government and foundation grants and contracts, and corporate contributions (Hall, 2003). These organizations were more likely to provide specific kinds of services (child day care, elder care, education, health services) and to engage in advocacy, lobbying, and public education than to promote generalized sociability and civic engagement. Regarding public culture in the later twentieth century, management guru Peter Drucker would write that "the nonprofit organizations of the so-called third sector . . . create a sphere of effective citizenship . . . , sphere of personal achievement" in which the individual "exercises influence, discharges responsibility, and makes decisions." Drucker concludes,

> In the political culture of mainstream society, individuals, no matter how well-educated, how successful, how achieving, or how wealthy, can only vote and pay taxes. They can only react, can only be passive. In the counterculture of the third sector, they are active citizens. This may be the most important contribution of the third sector (Drucker, 1989, p. 204).

In his enthusiasm for the possibilities of the sector, Drucker overlooked the fact that organizations that did not depend on volunteers or donations, that did not seek to recruit members, and that were narrowly focused on service provision and advocacy were likely to primarily engage the energies and interest of "knowledge workers" empowered by the high-tech economy rather than the mass of citizens.[2] It appeared that the "nation of joiners" celebrated by Schlesinger in 1940 was left without opportunities for joining.

The major exception to this trend was religion. Although rising more slowly than the general population, membership in religious bodies and attendance at worship services increased steadily through the second half of the twentieth century (Finke and Stark, 1992; Fogel, 2000). More impressive were increases in the number of congregations and new religious organizations (Roof, 1999). While the mainstream denominations (Catholic, Protestant, Jewish) declined, their place was being taken by free-standing congregations, often evangelical in persuasion, and by groups that stood outside of Western religious traditions (Wuthnow, 1998; Eck, 2001). In addition, ecumenical and parachurch organizations such as Habitat for Humanity, which drew on members' religious commitment but were nonsectarian, grew steadily (Wuthnow, 1994; Baggett, 2001; Bender, 2003). New religious organizations were more likely to be politically active: the conservative revolution of the 1980s and 1990s owed much to its ability to mobilize voters and bring pressure to bear on legislators (Reed, 1996). More important, the new religious organizations were likely to be broadly based in ways that crossed lines of class, occupation, education, and ethnicity in ways that made them especially potent in imparting civic values and skills (Verba, Schlozman, and Brady, 1995).

As religious organizations have assumed a new visibility in public life generally, they have also gained recognition as centrally important parts of the nonprofit sector (Wuthnow, 1986; Wuthnow, Hodkinson, and Associates, 1990; Cherry and Sherill, 1992; Demerath et al., 1998). This is the case not only because they constitute some 40 percent of the nonprofit universe and command two-thirds of all volunteers and donations, but also because they serve as paths of recruitment into secular activities and as platforms for secular or faith-based service provision in a variety of areas. The debate over charitable choice stemming from the welfare reforms of the mid-1990s was not so much an argument about church-state separation as it was an effort to codify government support for faith-based social services that had been a feature of America's human services regime for decades (Carlson-Theis and Skillen, 1996; Cnaan, 1999, 2002; Chaves, 2001; Hall, 2001).

Originally associated with the conservatives' political agenda, particularly with the programs pushed by the second President Bush, by the end of the first decade of the twenty-first-century charitable choice had been embraced by both parties. The Democrat's abandonment of efforts to maintain a "wall of separation" between church and state was doubtless due to the fact that among the chief beneficiaries of federal funding were the inner city African American congregations crucial to President Obama's 2008 victory.

The Conservative Revolution and the Nonprofit Sector, 1980–2000

For much of the twentieth century, foundations and secular nonprofit organizations had been generally associated with liberal political causes. Conservatives, regarding nonprofits as liberal—if not subversive—organizations had not only sought to curtail their privileges, but also had generally avoided using nonprofits to advance their own purposes. This began to change after the defeat of Barry Goldwater in 1964, when conservative leaders realized that criticizing liberalism was insufficient as a basis for political success: victory required alternative policies and relentless efforts to sway the public in their favor (Hodgson, 1996). To achieve their ends, conservatives would have to overcome their aversion to nonprofits in order to create their own "establishment" of think tanks, advocacy organizations, and foundations (Blumenthal, 1986; Berry, 1997; Rich, 2004).

A number of factors fueled this resolve. One was the emergence of a new cadre of monied conservatives, mostly from fast-developing areas of the South and West, whose wealth was based on defense production and extractive industries (Sale, 1975). They had a vital economic interest in being able to sway government policies in their favor. Another factor was the political mobilization of conservative Christians, particularly in the South, due to civil rights legislation and court decisions—on school prayer, abortion, and tax exemption for segregated private schools—that they believed threatened their way of life. The convergence of big new money and a mass-based religious movement with a social agenda created new opportunities for conservative Republicans to begin organizing around "wedge issues" such as reproductive rights that broke up long-standing liberal political coalitions. The mobilization of conservative voters, in turn, created the conditions for articulating a positive set of conservative policies that could credibly challenge liberal orthodoxies.

Although moderate Republicans regained control of the party after the Goldwater defeat, the conservatives worked doggedly to seize control of the local and state party organizations—helped along by the Watergate scandal, which discredited the moderate leadership of Richard Nixon. By the eve of the 1980 election, conservatives were ready to take power with Ronald Reagan as their standard-bearer.

Reagan assumed office with strong opinions on the role of nonprofit organizations in public life. He believed that big government had stifled private initiative and he intended to undo the damage through a combination of "jawboning" higher levels of corporate giving (through the President's Task Force on Private Initiatives) and by cutting government spending. What he, like most Americans, failed to understand was the extent to which the nonprofit sector had become dependent on government spending. By the time he took office, nearly a third of the annual revenues of private research universities came from government grants and contracts, and direct federal support for nonprofits in industries such as human services ranged as high as 90 percent. All in all, as an influential Urban Institute report pointed out in 1982, the federal government had become the largest single source of revenue for secular nonprofit organizations and, for this reason, massive cuts in government social spending would be likely to devastate the nonprofit sector (Salamon and Abramson, 1982).

Through the 1980s and into the 1990s, the emphasis in conservative social policy was on devolution (shifting responsibilities to states and localities) and privatization (shifting responsibilities for service provision to private sector actors). The rationales for these policies included the belief that more local and private service provision would not only be more flexible and responsive to the needs of beneficiaries, but also that competition for contracts among private providers would produce greater efficiency and effectiveness in service provision (Olasky, 1992).

While it remains to be seen whether privatized social services have fulfilled any of these promises, it is clear that among the most important impacts of these policies was to increase the need for professionally trained nonprofit managers and entrepreneurs—people who could master an increasingly complex and turbulent policy and funding environment. Although Republican leaders like George H. W. Bush might enthuse about the "thousand points of light" comprising America's community-serving nonprofit organizations, the reality was that these organizations were being driven by circumstances into being less and less responsive to client and community needs, while becoming more businesslike in their attitudes and operations. At the same time, as traditional manufacturing and commercial businesses either disappeared or were driven from urban centers to the suburbs, for-profit enterprises were being rapidly replaced by nonprofit service providers, making the nonprofit sector an increasingly important part of the national economy.

Despite the election of centrist Democrat Bill Clinton in 1992, the conservative revolution entered a new and more radical phase in 1994, when Republicans took control of the House of Representatives and increased their plurality in the Senate. Under the banner of a "Contract with America," conservative leaders set out to dismantle the government social programs created during the previous century (Gillespie and Schellhas,1994). This agenda went well beyond the desire to devolve and privatize without altering the basic tasks of social programs. Rather, it was based on a fundamental challenge to a variety of liberal articles of faith: that the tax system should be used to redistribute wealth, that alleviating poverty required changing social conditions, and that church and state should be strictly separated. Asserting that liberal social programs had succeeded in creating a "permanent underclass" by rewarding welfare recipients for deviant behavior, the conservatives proposed to eliminate most entitlement programs and to strictly limit eligibility. The key to dealing with poverty and dependency, conservatives believed, was changing the values and behavior of the poor. The dependent, the disabled, and the unemployed would have to rejoin the workforce and, in doing so, regain their self-respect and self-sufficiency. Not surprising, given their heavily sectarian constituency, conservatives looked to religious bodies and faith-based organizations to play central roles in transforming the values and behavior of the poor. Section 104 of the Personal Responsibility and Work Opportunity Reconciliation Act of 1996 set forth the terms of government's new relationship to religious nonprofits.

Although the conservative revolution in many ways favored nonprofit enterprise, especially with the huge expansion of contracted programs, it also fueled intensified competition between organizations, not only because for-profit businesses were invited to bid against nonprofits for government grants and contracts, but also because of a shift from producer-side subsidies, which went directly to service providers, to consumer-side subsidies, which enabled clients to choose among providers (Salamon, 2005, pp. 84–85). Whereas conservative school reforms encouraged nonprofits through voucher programs and charter schools, they also put nonprofit schools in competition with for-profit enterprises such as the Edison Schools, which, with its access to equity financing, had the capacity to operate entire urban school systems. In such an environment, skilled management, entrepreneurial attitudes, and political acumen became crucial to the survival of nonprofits.

Health care, which until the 1970s had been dominated by nonprofits, underwent major changes as legislators sought to control the rising cost of entitlement programs such as Medicare and Medicaid (Gray, 1983, 1986, 1991). As government became more vigilant about health care costs, hospitals were forced to become more businesslike in their operations. Many converted to for-profit ownership. Others, while remaining nonprofit, turned their operations over to for-profit firms. Seeking economies of scale, hospitals consolidated into national and regional chains, as did formerly nonprofit health insurance plans such as Blue Cross-Blue Shield.

In putting nonprofits in competition with for-profits offering similar services and in demanding higher levels of accountability for decreasing government funding, conservative policies helped erode many of the boundaries between nonprofit and for-profit enterprise (Weisbrod, 1997; Hall, 2003). Nonprofits had to become more commercial and more entrepreneurial to survive. Whether nonprofits' commitments to missions of public service could survive such relentless attention to the bottom line remained in doubt as the twenty-first century dawned (Weisbrod, 1998).

The New Century and the Transformation of Philanthropy

The model of "modern" philanthropy as it had come to be by the middle of the twentieth century was intended to accommodate the essentially undemocratic character of large charitable endowments established by the wealthy with the mores of democratic politics and society. To this end, tax and regulatory regimes strove to reduce donor control, limit opportunities for private benefit, make governance more representative and accountable, and support activities in harmony with established public policies. An important component of this involved promoting the professionalization of management in foundations and their nonprofit beneficiaries on the assumption that trained expertise would be better qualified to discern public priorities than either donors or the general public.

Establishing and maintaining consensus over the way philanthropy should be managed and the purposes it was to serve was fairly easy before the 1980s because most large foundations were concentrated in urban centers in the Northeast and upper Midwest and were run by men who shared similar privileged backgrounds. With a very few exceptions, foundations were pillars of the "Liberal Establishment," which ran the nation's major universities, cultural institutions, and federal government agencies. Henry Ford II alluded to this liberal bias in his 1977 letter of resignation from the board of the Ford Foundation. The fact that "the Foundation is a creature of capitalism," he wrote, is

> a statement that, I'm sure, would be shocking to many professional staff people in the field of philanthropy. It is hard to discern recognition of this fact in anything the Foundation does. It is even more difficult to find an understanding of this in many of the institutions, particularly the universities, that are the beneficiaries of the Foundation's grant programs.[3]

Although the conservative revolution of the 1980s helped broaden the range of viewpoints represented by philanthropic leaders, it did little to change how philanthropy was done, since the new conservative institutional infrastructure followed the pattern of its liberal counterpart, domestically focused, professionally managed, and based on foundation support of conventional nonprofit recipients, such as universities, cultural institutions, and policy think tanks.

What fundamentally changed philanthropy was not political pluralism, but a tidal wave of new wealth accumulation, originating in the revolution in information technology, globalization, and the financialization of the economic system. The new billionaires, largely younger men who were still in their prime as active business leaders, embraced far more activist views of how to manage their surplus wealth. Results-oriented, they expected their philanthropy to express their values and to yield measurable impacts. Because the sources of their wealth were global, they took particular interest in global problems of hunger, disease, environment, and economic development.

The $35 billion Bill and Melinda Gates Foundation, which described itself as "the largest transparently operated private foundation in the world," epitomized many of the features of the contemporary philanthropic revolution. Based in Seattle, Washington, it was established in 1994 by Microsoft founder and chairman Bill Gates to pursue "the interests and passions of the Gates family" (Bill & Melinda Gates Foundation, 2009). The foundation's major foci included a Global Health Program, whose significant grantees have been The Global Alliance for Vaccines and Immunization, The Institute for OneWorld Health, Children's Vaccine Program, University of Washington Department of Global Health, HIV Research, and the Aeras Global TB Vaccine Foundation. Its Global Development Program has funded financial services for the poor (through such social enterprises as the Grameen Bank), agricultural development (focusing on rice research and promoting a green revolution in Africa), Global Libraries, a United States Program (funding schools, libraries, and scholarships). The Gates Foundation's resources were vastly increased in 2006 by financier Warren Buffett's pledge to donate most of his own private fortune—estimated at $30 billion.

Though hardly comparable in size, the philanthropic activities of financier George Soros have been no less globally influential—though in a very different way. A refugee from Nazism, Soros's primary interest has been politics and the development of democratic societies in Central and Eastern Europe. He has also generously funded progressive social movement activity in the United States. Like Gates, he has also given substantial support to poverty eradication efforts in Africa and to social enterprises such as the Grameen Bank.

The philanthropy of Google founders Sergey Brin and Lawrence Page has moved in very different directions from that of Gates, Buffett, and Soros. Founded in 1998 as an online search engine, Google was, as of 2009, valued at more than $23 billion and employed more than 19,000 people worldwide. Although they created a company foundation, their major interest has been the company and its products, which they have viewed—much as Henry Ford viewed the Model T—as primary instruments of social transformation. Their most innovative philanthropic initiative was their establishment in 2006 of Google.org, a for-profit foundation intended to carry out a wide range of activities including product development, political activism, and medical research (Hansell, 2005; Hafner, 2006; Rubin, 2008). Google's philanthropic activities represent an important example of "social enterprise" which, in combining commitments to business and social change, represent a significant departure from traditional conceptions of charity.

Kiva Microfunds, founded in 2005 by California entrepreneurs Matt and Jessica Flannery, offers yet another approach of philanthropy. Drawing its inspiration from the Grameen Bank and other Third World–based microfinance programs, Kiva works globally to match Western microlenders with "field partners" in the developing world (Walker, 2008). Within two years of its establishment Kiva had made nearly $20 million in loans to nearly a quarter million individuals.

Not all big philanthropy has involved the wealthy in the developed world helping the poor in the developing world. A notable feature of economic and cultural globalization has been the growth of diaspora groups who, while living in parts of the world to which they have emigrated, have succeeded in their adopted homelands while retaining significant ties to their countries of origin—and who, although often possessing dual citizenship, make their native lands primary recipients of their philanthropic largesse. These philanthropically active transnational populations now include Indians, Pakistanis, Chinese, Latin Americans, and, of course, Jews, who set the pattern for this kind of transnational philanthropic orientation (see Geithner, Johnson, and Chen, 2004; Merz, 2005; Najam, 2006; Merz, Chen, and Geithner, 2007).

Within a quarter of a century, philanthropy has gone from being centered in North America and Western Europe and focused on aid by advanced industrial nations to developing countries to a genuinely transnational collection of enterprises and initiatives sustaining complex multidirectional flows of aid and influence.

The Nonprofit Sector and the Global Challenge

Nonstate actors—nonprofit organizations, NGOs (nongovernmental organizations), network organizations—are assuming extraordinary importance with the globalization of the world's economy (Salamon and Anheier, 1996, 1997; Anheier and Salamon, 1998).[4] Despite growing global flows of goods, information, and labor, the nation state remains the primary unit of governmental organization, and international governmental bodies remain weak. For this reason, nongovernmental organizations operating transnationally have become the major mechanisms of world governance (Lindenberg, 1999).

These organizations have a variety of forms (Khagram, Riker, and Sikkink, 2002). Some mediate relationships between states (Brown and Fox, 1998; Brown, Khagram, and Moore, 2000; Brown and Moore, 2001). Some, like the U.S. Agency for International Development, are governmental bodies operated to serve the interests of the United States by promoting economic development. Others, like the World Bank, the International Monetary Fund, the World Health Organization, and UNESCO, are international quasigovernmental bodies connected to the United Nations and governed by boards representing the U.N.'s member states.

Many NGOs, such as CARE, the International Red Cross, and a variety of religious charities, are based in the United States or Europe but carry on their operations elsewhere (Biberson and Jean, 1999; Henry, 1999; Offenheiser, Holcombe, and Hopkins, 1999; Gnaerig and MacCormack, 1999; Foreman, 1999). Others are genuinely transnational, based on coalitions of indigenous and transnational NGOs. Often operating in opposition to nation states, these promote human rights, sustainable development, and environmental objectives (Fisher, 1993, 1998; Edwards, 1999). Unlike the quasigovernmental bodies, which deal primarily with governments, these transnational NGOs work directly with indigenous peoples, communities, and organizations. Among the most important of these are groups such as CIVICUS, which promotes the development of nonprofit sectors throughout the world. Some of the largest grantmaking foundations, notably Ford, Rockefeller, and the Bill and Melinda Gates foundations, have global programs that fund health, education, research, and economic development activities in developing countries.

The tragic events of 9/11 called attention to the significance of NGOs and network organizations connected to religious movements. Along with terrorist networks such as Al Qaeda, there are Islamic charities and foundations that operate worldwide to support religious education, provide relief, and support economic and political development in Moslem communities

In some respects, transnational organizations are nothing new. The scientific community has long been transnational and anchored in nongovernmental professional and disciplinary bodies. Transnational human rights advocacy dates back at least as early as the anti-slave trade movement of the late eighteenth century. Most major religious bodies are transnational organizations. International relief organizations have been operating since the nineteenth century. Grantmaking foundations have had international programs since the 1920s (Curti, 1965).

Contemporary global and transnational NGOs differ from their predecessors in important respects. Most important, many are genuinely transnational, located either in many countries or, as in the case of Al Qaeda, not anchored in any nation state. Beyond the reach of national authorities, these entities are difficult to police and control (Brown and Moore, 2001; Goodin, 2003). Of equal importance is the extent to which transnational NGOs are linked to indigenous organizations outside the advanced nations of Europe and North America. Their capacity to give voice to victims of authoritarian regimes, protest economic exploitation, and resist the power of Western corporations and governments has dramatically transformed global public policymaking. Advances in information technology have vastly increased the influence of transnational NGOs by making information available that corporations and governments may attempt to suppress and making it possible for transnational and indigenous groups to form coalitions and alliances. Recent worldwide protests against economic globalization and the U.S. invasion of Iraq may signal the emergence of new kinds of political forces.

The nature of globalization and the role of transnational nonstate actors is far from clear. To some, they represent a kind of neocolonialism, the means by which an integrated global economy, anchored in the advanced nations of the West, is being created. To others, they represent a new empowering force for democracy and social and economic justice. One thing is clear, however: nonprofit organizations, so highly developed in the United States in the course of the twentieth century, offer important possibilities to nations engaged in creating their own civil societies.

Conclusion

This chapter has traced a long and complex strand of institutional development. Beginning in the seventeenth century, when the nation state was still emergent, legal systems primitive, and boundaries between government and private initiative ill-defined, it has traced the ways in which voluntary associations, eleemosynary corporations, and philanthropy became indispensable components of the national state and the industrializing economy in the United States in the nineteenth century. It has suggested that neither business nor government could stand alone: both required broadly based participation by citizens, producers, and consumers in organizations and activities that created the shared values and skills that enabled formal institutions of government and business to function effectively.

In the years between 1830 and 1950, the private, donative, and voluntary character of much of nonprofit enterprise seemed self-evident, as did the boundaries between public and private initiative. In the second half of the twentieth century, these defining characteristics became less well-defined as nonprofits became more dependent on government subsidy and increasingly entrusted with responsibilities formerly borne by government agencies, on the one hand, and more commercial and entrepreneurial, on the other hand.

Globalization, which has enabled nonprofits to operate beyond national borders, has further eroded traditional boundaries between public and private domains and commercial and charitable activities. Because privatization is a global movement, NGOs outside the United States are increasingly taking the place of nation states in service provision, relief, and development assistance. Many development activities, such as microloan programs, more resemble commercial activities than charitable ones. And, overall, important aspects of the emergent global institutional order depend on the governance functions of NGOs rather than governmental entities.

In significant ways, today's centrally important but poorly demarcated roles and responsibilities of nonprofits and NGOs more resemble those of three centuries ago, when the nation state was aborning, than the associations and eleemosynary corporations of a century ago whose character and functions were relatively well defined and clearly bounded.

History shows, if nothing else, that ownerless collectivities of the nonprofit type are remarkably flexible instruments that can be put to a multitude of uses, whether empowering the masses in democracies, shaping public opinion for the benefit of elites, carrying out the tasks of government in authoritarian regimes, promoting peace and prosperity, or spreading terror. What the future holds in store for nonprofits is anybody's guess.

Notes

1. There are few tasks more difficult than accurately counting the number of nonprofit organizations in the United States. The fundamental difficulty involves how to define the nonprofit universe. In corporation law, a nonprofit is any nonstock corporation that does not distribute its surplus, if any, in the form of dividends. Under the federal tax code, a nonprofit is any organization or association classified in Section 501(c) of the IRS Code—a universe that includes not only charitable entities—501(c)3s—but also many other kinds of organizations, including political parties, labor unions, cooperatives, cemetery companies, and black lung trusts. Because some of these noncharitable nonprofits, like those classified as 501(c)4s (social welfare organizations, civic organizations, and associations of employees), engage in many of the same educational and service provision activities as do charitables, though without according to donors' deductibility of donations, excluding them from a definition of the nonprofit sector posits an unreasonably narrow definition. To complicate matters, religious bodies, which enjoy tax exemption and deductibility of donations by right (and hence are not required to apply for these privileges) are not included in IRS statistics of registered nonprofits—despite the fact that they are the largest single category of nonprofit organization in the United States and account for more than half the donated funds received by American nonprofits. To further complicate matters, many groups engaged in charitable, educational, religious, and other activities associated with nonprofits are unincorporated and do not seek exempt status (Smith, 2000).

2. It is impossible to provide exact figures on the number of donative and voluntary non-profits versus those supported by dues, fees, commercial income, and grants and contracts from government, corporations, and foundations. Studies of local organizational populations (Hall, 1999) and national membership associations (Skocpol, 1999, 2003) suggest a vast die-off of traditional donative, voluntary, and membership associations and their replacement by professionally managed nonprofit organizations. Despite these trends, such organizations as religious congregations—one of the most vigorously expansive non-profit domains—remain heavily dependent on volunteers and almost entirely dependent on donations. Counterbalancing this, however, is the huge growth of nonprofit service providers incident to the court-ordered deinstitutionalization of the mentally disabled. These use no volunteers and depend entirely on government subsidies.

3. As quoted in http://www.discoverthenetworks.org/funderProfile.asp?fndid=5176, retrieved December 28, 2009.

4. Walter W. Powell's seminal article on network organizations defines them as "reciprocal patterns of communication and exchange" characterized by "lateral or horizontal patterns of exchange, interdependent flows of resources, and reciprocal lines of communication" (Powell, 1990, pp. 295–296). An example of a network organization is the open source network of computer programmers cooperating to develop the LINUX operating system. These entities lack the hierarchical structures and financial incentives that are typical of conventional firms.

References

Abbott, A. D. *The System of Professions: An Essay on the Division of Expert Labor.* Chicago: University of Chicago Press, 1988.

Ahlstrom, S. E. *A Religious History of the American People.* New Haven, Conn: Yale University Press, 1972.

"American Millionaires and the Public Gifts." *Review of Reviews,* 1893, *37*(7), 48–60.

Ames, J. B. 1913. "The Failure of the Tilden Trust." In J. B. Ames, *Essays in Legal History and Miscellaneous Legal Essays.* Cambridge, Mass.: Harvard University Press, 285–297.

Andrews, F. E. *Philanthropic Giving.* New York: Russell Sage Foundation, 1950.

Andrews, F. E. *Corporation Giving.* New York: Russell Sage Foundation, 1952.

Andrews, F. E. *Philanthropic Foundations.* New York: Russell Sage Foundation, 1956.

Andrews, F. E. *Patman and the Foundations: Review and Assessment.* Occasional Paper Number Three. New York: The Foundation Center, 1969.

Anheier, H. K., and Salamon, L. M. *The Nonprofit Sector in the Developing World: A Comparative Analysis.* New York: St. Martin's Press, 1998.

Auerbach, J. S. *Unequal Justice: Lawyers and Social Change in Modern America.* New York: Oxford University Press, 1976.

Bailyn, B. *The Ideological Origins of the American Revolution.* Cambridge, Mass.: Belknap Press of Harvard University Press, 1992.

Baggett, J. P. *Habitat for Humanity: Building Private Homes, Building Public Religion.* Philadelphia, Penn: Temple University Press, 2001.

Beito, D. T. *From Mutual Aid to the Welfare State: Fraternal Societies and Social Services, 1890–1967.* Chapel Hill, NC: University of North Carolina University Press, 2000.

Bender, C. *Heaven's Kitchen: Living Religion at God's Love We Deliver.* Chicago: University of Chicago Press, 2003.

Berkeley Art Center Association. *The Whole World's Watching: Peace and Social Justice Movements of the 1960s and 1970s.* Berkeley, Calif.: Author, 2001.

Berry, J. M. *Lobbying for the People: The Political Behavior of Public Interest Groups.* Princeton, N.J.: Princeton University Press, 1977.

Berry, J. M. *The Interest Group Society,* 3rd ed. New York: Longman, 1997.

Biberson, P., and Jean, F. "The Challenges of Globalization of International Relief and Development: Medecins Sans Frontieres." *Nonprofit and Voluntary Sector Quarterly,* 1999, *28,* 104–108 (Supplemental).

Bill & Melinda Gates Foundation, "Guiding Principles" at http://www.gatesfoundation.org/about/Pages/guiding-principles.aspx, retrieved December 28, 2009.

Bledstein, B. *The Culture of Professionalism: The Middle Class and the Development of Higher Education in America.* New York: Norton, 1976.

Blumenthal, S. *The Rise of the Counter-Establishment: From Conservative Ideology to Political Power.* New York: Harper & Row, 1986.

Brandes, S. *American Welfare Capitalism.* Chicago: University of Chicago Press, 1976.

Brint, S. *In an Age of Reform: The Changing Role of Professionals in Politics and Public Life.* Princeton, N.J.: Princeton University Press, 1994.

Brockett, L. P. *The Philanthropic Results of the War in America. Collected from official and Other Authentic Sources, by an American Citizen.* Dedicated by permission to the United States Sanitary Commission. New York: Sheldon & Co., 1864.

Brody, D. "The Rise and Decline of American Welfare Capitalism." In D. Brody (ed.), *Workers in Industrial America.* New York: Oxford University Press, 1980, 48–81.

Brown, L. D., and Fox, J. "Transnational Civil Society Coalitions and the World Bank: Lessons from Project and Policy Influence Campaigns." Working Paper #3. Cambridge, Mass.: Hauser Center for Nonprofit Organizations, Harvard University, 1999.

Brown, L. D., and Fox, J. (eds.). *The Struggle for Accountability: The World Bank, NGOs, and Grassroots Movements.* Cambridge, Mass.: MIT Press, 1998.

Brown, L. D., Khagram, S., and Moore, M.H. "Globalization, NGOs and Multi-Sectoral Relations." Working Paper #1. Cambridge, Mass.: Hauser Center for Nonprofit Organizations, Harvard University, 2000.

Brown, L. D., and Moore, M.H. "Accountability, Strategy and International Non-Governmental Organizations." Working Paper #7. Cambridge, Mass.: Hauser Center for Nonprofit Organizations, Harvard University, 2001.

Bryer, D., and Magrath, J. "New Dimensions of Global Advocacy." *Nonprofit and Voluntary Sector Quarterly*, 1999, *28* (Supplemental), 168–177.

Buck, P. H. (ed.). *Social Sciences at Harvard, 1860–1920: From Inculcation to the Open Mind.* Cambridge, Mass.: Harvard University Press, 1965.

Butchart, R. E., *Northern Schools, Southern Blacks, and Reconstruction, 1862–1875.* Westport, Conn.: Greenwood Press, 1980.

Butler, J. *Awash in a Sea of Faith: Christianizing the American People.* Cambridge, Mass.: Harvard University Press, 1990.

Calhoun, D. H. *Professional Lives in America: Structure and Aspiration, 1750–1850.* Cambridge, Mass.: Harvard University Press, 1965.

Calvert, M. A. *The Mechanical Engineer in America: Professional Cultures in Conflict.* Baltimore, Md.: Johns Hopkins University Press, 1967.

Carlson-Thies, S. W., and Skillen, J. W. (eds.). *Welfare in America: Christian Perspectives on a Policy in Crisis.* Grand Rapids, Mich.: Eerdmans, 1996.

Carnegie, A. "An Employer's View of the Labor Question." *Forum*, 1886a, *1*, 114–125.

Carnegie, A. "Results of the Labor Struggle." *Forum*, 1886b, *1*, 538–551.

Carnegie, A. "Wealth." *North American Review*, 1889, *148*, 653–664; *149*, 682–698.

Charles, J. A. *Service Clubs in American Society: Rotary, Kiwanis, and Lions.* Urbana: University of Illinois Press, 1993.

Chaves, M. "Religious Congregations and Welfare Reform: Assessing the Potential." In M. Silk and A. Walsh (eds.), *Can Charitable Choice Work? Covering Religion's Impact on Urban Affairs and Social Services.* Hartford, Conn.: Pew Program on Religion and the News Media, Leonard E. Greenberg Center for the Study of Religion in Public Life, Trinity College, 2001.

Chernow, R. *Titan: The Life of John D. Rockefeller, Sr.* New York: Random House, 1998.

Cherry, C., and Sherrill, R. (eds.). *Religion, the Independent Sector, and American Culture.* Atlanta, Ga.: Scholars Press, 1992.

Clemens, E. S. *The People's Lobby: Organizational Innovation and the Rise of Interest Group Politics in the United States, 1890–1925*. Chicago: University of Chicago Press, 1997.

Cnaan, R. A. *The Newer Deal: Social Work and Religion in Partnership*. New York: Columbia University Press, 1999.

Cnaan, R. A. *The Invisible Caring Hand: American Congregations and the Provision of Welfare*. New York: New York University Press, 2002.

Crawford, S., and Levitt, P. "Social Change and Civic Engagement: The Case of the P.T.A." In T. Skocpol and M. Fiorina (eds.), *Civic Engagement in American Democracy*. Washington, D.C.: Brookings Institution Press, 1999.

Critchlow, D. T. *The Brookings Institution, 1916–1952: Expertise and the Public Interest in a Democratic Society*. DeKalb: Northern Illinois University Press, 1985.

Cross, A. B. *The War and the Christian Commission*. Baltimore, Md.: 1865.

Curti, M. 1965. *American Philanthropy Abroad*. New Brunswick, N.J.: Rutgers University Press.

Curti, M., and Nash, R. *Philanthropy and the Shaping of American Higher Education*. New Brunswick, N.J.: Rutgers University Press, 1965.

Cutlip, S.M. *Fund Raising in the United States: Its Role in America's Philanthropy*. New Brunswick, NJ: Rutgers University Press, 1965.

Dabney, V. *Mr. Jefferson's University: A History*. Charlottesville, Va.: University Press of Virginia, 1981.

Davis, J. S. *Essays on the Earlier History of American Corporations*. Cambridge, Mass.: Harvard University Press, 1918.

Demerath, N. J. III, Hall, P. D., Williams, R. H., and Schmitt, T. (eds.) *Sacred Companies: Organizational Aspects of Religion and Religious Aspects of Organizations*. New York: Oxford University Press, 1998.

DiMaggio, P. J. "Cultural Entrepreneurship in Nineteenth Century Boston." In P. J. DiMaggio (ed.), *Nonprofit Enterprise in the Arts*. New York: Oxford University Press, 1986.

Dodd, E. M. *American Business Corporations until 1860, with Special References to Massachusetts*. Cambridge, Mass.: Harvard University Press, 1960.

Dolan, J. P. *The American Catholic Experience: A History from Colonial Times to the Present*. South Bend, Ind.: University of Notre Dame Press, 1992.

Drucker, P. F. *The New Realities: In Government and Politics, in Economics and Business, in Society and World View*. New York: HarperCollins, 1989.

Dumenil, L. 1984. *Freemasonry and American Culture, 1880–1939*. Princeton, NJ: Princeton University Press.

Eck, D. L. *A New Religious America: How a "Christian Country" Has Become the World's Most Religiously Diverse Nation*. New York: HarperCollins, 2001.

Edwards, M. "International Development NGOs: Agents of Foreign Aid or Vehicles for International Cooperation?" *Nonprofit and Voluntary Sector Quarterly*, 1999, *28* (Supplemental), 25–37.

Eliot, C. W. "The New Education." *Atlantic Monthly*, 1869, *23*, 203–220, 358–367.

Finke, R., and Stark, R. *The Churching of America, 1776–1990: Winners and Losers in Our Religious Economy*. New Brunswick, N.J.: Rutgers University Press, 1992.

Fisher, J. *The Road from Rio: Sustainable Development and the Nongovernmental Movement in the Third World*. Westport, Conn.: Praeger, 1993.

Fisher, J. *Nongovernments: NGOs and the Political Development of the Third World*. West Hartford, Conn.: Kumarian Press, 1998.

Fleischer, D. Z, & Zames, F. *The Disability Rights Movement: From Charity to Confrontation.* Philadelphia: Temple University Press, 2001.

Fleming, W. L. (ed.). *Documentary History of Reconstruction: Political, Military, Social, Religious, Educational & Industrial 1865 to the Present Time.* Cleveland: Arthur H. Clark Company, 1906.

Fogel, R. W. *The Fourth Great Awakening and the Future of Egalitarianism.* Chicago: University of Chicago Press, 2000.

Foreman, K. "Evolving Global Structures and the Challenges Facing International Relief and Developing Organizations." *Nonprofit and Voluntary Sector Quarterly*, 1999, *28* (Supplemental), 178–197.

Fosdick, R. B. *The Story of the Rockefeller Foundation.* New York: Harper & Row, 1952.

Fosdick, R. B. *Adventure in Giving: The Story of the General Education Board, a Foundation Established by John D. Rockefeller.* New York: Harper & Row, 1962.

Foster, C. I. *"An Errand of Mercy": The Evangelical United Front, 1790–1837.* Chapel Hill, N.C.: University of North Carolina Press, 1965.

Foundation Directory — Edition I. New York: Russell Sage Foundation, 1960.

Fox, D. M. *Engines of Culture: Philanthropy and Art Museums.* Madison, Wisc.: State Historical Society of Wisconsin, 1963.

Frederickson, G. M. *The Inner Civil War: Northern Intellectuals and the Crisis of the Union.* New York: HarperCollins, 1965.

Galambos, L. *Competition and Cooperation: The Rise of a National Trade Association.* Baltimore, Md. Johns Hopkins University Press, 1966.

Geiger, R. L. *To Advance Knowledge: The Growth of American Research Universities, 1900–1940.* New York: Oxford University Press, 1986.

Geiger, R. L. *Research and Relevant Knowledge: American Research Universities Since World War II.* New York: Oxford University Press, 1993.

Geithner, P. F., Johnson, P. D., and Chen, L. C. (eds.). *Diaspora Philanthropy and Equitable Development in China and India.* Cambridge, Mass.: Harvard University Press, 2004.

Gillespie, E., and Schellhas, B. (eds.). *Contract with America: The Bold Plan by Rep. Newt Gingrich, Rep. Dick Armey and the House Republicans to Change the Nation.* New York: Times Books, 1994.

Glenn, J. M., Brandt, L., and Andrews, F. E. *The Russell Sage Foundation, 1907–1947.* New York: Russell Sage Foundation, 1947.

Gnaerig, B., and MacCormack, C. F. "The Challenges of Globalizations: Save the Children International." *Nonprofit and Voluntary Sector Quarterly*, 1999, *28* (Supplemental), 140, 146.

Goodin, R. E. "Democratic Accountability: The Third Sector and All." Working Paper #19. Cambridge, Mass.: Hauser Center for Nonprofit Organizations, Harvard University, 2003.

Gray, B. H. (ed.). *The New Health Care For Profit: Doctors and Hospitals in a Competitive Environment.* Washington, D.C.: National Academy Press, 1983.

Gray, B. H. (ed.). *For-Profit Enterprise in Health Care.* Washington, D.C.: National Academy Press, 1986.

Gray, B. H. *The Profit Motive and Patient Care: The Changing Accountability of Doctors and Hospitals.* Cambridge, Mass.: Harvard University Press, 1991.

Greenleaf, W. *From These Beginnings: The Early Philanthropies of Henry and Edsel Ford, 1911–1936.* Detroit, Mich.: Wayne State University Press, 1964.

Hafner, K. "Philanthropy Google's Way: Not the Usual." *New York Times* (September 14, 2006).

Hall, P. D. *The Organization of American Culture, 1700–1900 : Institutions, Elites, and the Origins of American Nationality.* New York: New York University Press, 1982.

Hall, P. D. "The Community Foundation in America." In R. Magat (ed.), *Philanthropic Giving: Studies in Varieties and Goals.* New York: Oxford University Press, 1989a.

Hall, P. D. "Business Giving and Social Investment in the United States." In R. Magat (ed.), *Philanthropic Giving: Studies in Varieties and Goals.* New York: Oxford University Press, 1989b.

Hall, P. D. "Vital Signs: Organizational Population Trends and Civic Engagement in New Haven, Connecticut, 1850–1998." In T. Skocpol and M.P. Fiorina (eds.), *Civic Engagement in American Democracy.* Washington, D.C.: Brookings Institution, 1999.

Hall, P. D. "Historical Perspectives on Religion, Government, and Social Welfare in America." In M. Silk and A. Walsh (eds.), *Can Charitable Choice Work? Covering Religion's Impact on Urban Affairs and Social Services.* Hartford, Conn.: Pew Program on Religion and the News Media, Leonard E. Greenberg Center for the Study of Religion in Public Life, Trinity College, 2001.

Hall, P. D. "The Welfare State and the Careers of Public and Private Institutions since 1945." In L. J. Friedman and M. D. McGarvie (eds.), Charity, Philanthropy, and Civility in American History. New York: Cambridge University Press, 2003.

Hall, P. D., and Burke, C. B. "Voluntary, Nonprofit, and Religious Entities and Activities." In S. Carter, et al. (eds.), *Historical Statistics of the United States — Millennial Edition.* New York: Cambridge University Press, 2006.

Hammack, D. C. 1989. "Community Foundations: The Delicate Question of Purpose." In R. Magat (ed.), *An Agile Servant.* New York: The Foundation Center, 23–50.

Hammack, D. C., and Wheeler, S. 1994. *Social Science in the Making: Essays on the Russell Sage Foundation, 1907–1972.* New York: Russell Sage Foundation, 1994.

Hansell, S. "Google Earmarks $265 Million for Charity and Social Causes." *New York Times* (October 12, 2005).

Harr, J. E., and Johnson, P. J. *The Rockefeller Century.* New York: Scribner, 1988.

Hartog, H. *Public Property and Private Power: The Corporation of the City of New York in American Law, 1730–1870.* Ithaca, N.Y.: Cornell University Press, 1983.

Haskell, T. L. *The Emergence of Professional Social Science: The American Social Science Association and the Nineteenth-Century Crisis of Authority.* Urbana: University of Illinois Press, 1977.

Hatch, N. O. *The Democratization of American Christianity.* New Haven, Conn.: Yale University Press, 1989.

Hawkins, H. *Between Harvard and America: The Educational Leadership of Charles W. Eliot.* New York: Oxford University Press, 1972.

Hawkins, H. *Banding Together: The Rise of National Associations in American Higher Education, 1887–1950.* Baltimore, Md.: Johns Hopkins University Press, 1992.

Hawley, E. W. (ed.). *Herbert Hoover as Secretary of Commerce: Studies in New Era Thought and Practice.* Iowa City: University of Iowa Press, 1974.

Hawley, E. W. "Herbert Hoover, the Commerce Secretariat, and the Vision of an 'Associative State.'" In E. J. Perkins (ed.), *Men and Organizations.* New York: Putnam, 1977.

Heald, M. *The Social Responsibilities of Business: Corporation and Community, 1900–1960.* Cleveland, Oh.: Case Western University Press, 1970.

Henry, K. M. "CARE International: Evolving to Meet the Challenges of the 21st Century." *Nonprofit and Voluntary Sector Quarterly,* 1999, 28 (Supplement), 109–120.

Himmelberg, R. F. *The Origins of the National Recovery Administration: Business, Government, and the Trade Association Issue.* New York: Fordham University Press, 1976.

Himmelstein, J. L. *Looking Good and Doing Good: Corporate Philanthropy and Corporate Power.* Bloomington, Ind: Indiana University Press, 1997.

Hodgson, G. 1996. *The World Turned Right Side Up: A History of the Conservative Ascendancy in America.* Boston, MA: Houghton-Mifflin.

Hoover, H. 1922. *American Individualism.* Garden City, NY: Doubleday.

Horowitz, M. J. *The Transformation of American Law, 1780–1860.* Cambridge, Mass.: Harvard University Press, 1977.

Howard, C. 1997. *The Hidden Welfare State: Tax Expenditures and Social Policy in the United States.* Princeton, NJ: Princeton University Press.

Hurst, J. W. *The Legitimacy of the Business Corporation in the Law of the United States, 1780–1970.* Charlottesville: University Press of Virginia, 1970.

Jenkins, J. C. "Nonprofit Organizations and Policy Advocacy." In W.W. Powell (ed.), *The Nonprofit Sector: A Research Handbook.* New Haven, Conn.: Yale University Press, 1987.

Jenkins, J. C., and Eckert, C. "Channeling Black Insurgency: Elite Patronage and the Development of the Civil Rights Movement." *American Sociological Review 51*, 1986, 812–830.

Jenkins, J. C., and Halcli, A. L. "Grassrooting the System? The Development and Impact of Social Movement Philanthropy, 1953–1990." In E.C. Lagemann (ed.), *Philanthropic Foundations: New Scholarship, New Possibilities.* Bloomington, Ind.: Indiana University Press, 229–256, 1999.

Karl, B. D. "Presidential Planning and Social Science Research: Mr. Hoover's Experts." *Perspectives in American History*, 1969, 347–409.

Karl, B. D. "Philanthropy, Policy Planning, and the Bureaucratization of the Democratic Ideal." *Daedalus* (Fall 1976), 129–149.

Katz, S. N. "The Politics of Law in Colonial America: Controversies over Chancery Courts and Equity Law in the Eighteenth Century." In D. Fleming & B. Bailyn (eds.), *Law in American History.* Boston: Little, Brown, 1971, 257–288.

Katz, S. N. "The American Private Foundation and the Public Sphere, 1890–1930." *Minerva* 1981, *19*, 236–270.

Katz, S. N., Sullivan, B., and Beach, C. P. "Legal Change and Legal Autonomy: Charitable Trusts in New York, 1777–1893," *Law and History Review 3*, 1985, 51–89.

Kaufman, J. *For the Common Good? American Civic Life and the Golden Age of Fraternity.* New York: Oxford University Press, 2002.

Khagram, S., Riker, J. V., and Sikkink, K. (eds.). *Restructuring World Politics: Transnational Social Movements, Networks, and Norms.* Minneapolis, Minn.: University of Minnesota Press, 2002.

Kimball, B. A. *The "True Professional Ideal" in America: A History.* Lanham, Md.: Rowman & Littlefield, 1995.

Lagemann, E. C. 1992. *The Politics of Knowledge: The Carnegie Corporation, Philanthropy, and Public Policy.* Chicago: University of Chicago Press, 1992.

Lagemann, E. C. *Private Power for the Public Good: A History of the Carnegie Foundation for the Advancement of Teaching.* New York: College Entrance Examination Board, 1999.

Li, Ming-huan. *We Need Two Worlds: Chinese Immigrant Associations in a Western Society.* Amsterdam, NL: Amsterdam University Press, 1999.

Lindenberg, M. "Declining State Capacity, Voluntarism, and the Globalization of the Not-For-Profit Sector." *Nonprofit and Voluntary Sector Quarterly*, 1999, *28* (Supplemental), 147–167.

Lundberg, F. *The Rich and the Super-Rich; A Study in the Power of Money Today.* New York: Lyle Stuart, 1968.

MacDonald, D. *The Ford Foundation: The Men and the Millions*. New York: Reynal, 1956.

Magat, R. (ed.). *"An Agile Servant": Community Leadership by Community Foundations*. New York: The Foundation Center, 1989.

Mathews, D. "The Second Great Awakening as an Organizing Process." *American Quarterly* 1969, *21*, 23–43.

McFeely, W. S. *Yankee Stepfather: General O.O. Howard and the Freedmen*. New Haven, Conn.: Yale University Press, 1968.

McKinney, H. J. *The Development of Local Public Services, 1650–1860 : Lessons from Middletown, Connecticut*. Westport, Conn.: Greenwood Press, 1995.

Merz, B. J. (ed.). *New Patterns for Mexico: Observations on Remittances, Philanthropic Giving, and Equitable Development*. Cambridge, Mass.: Harvard University Press, 2005.

Merz, B. J., Chen, L. C., and Geithner, P. F. (eds.). *Diasporas and Development*. Cambridge, Mass.: Harvard University Press, 2007.

Miller, H. S. *The Legal Foundations of American Philanthropy*. Madison: Wisconsin State Historical Society, 1961.

Minkoff, D.C., *Organizing for Equality: The Evolution of Women's and Racial-Ethnic Organizations in America*. New Brunswick, NJ: Rutgers University Press.

Minton, H. L., *Departing from Deviance: A History of Homosexual Rights and Emanicipatory Science in America*. Chicago: University of Chicago Press, 2002.

Morgan, E. S. *Benjamin Franklin*. New Haven, Conn: Yale University Press, 2003.

Moss, L. *Annals of the United States Christian Commission*. Philadelphia: Lippincott, 1968.

Najam, A. *Portrait of a Giving Community: Philanthropy in the Pakistani-American Diaspora*. Cambridge, Mass.: Harvard University Press, 2006.

Naylor, E. H. *Trade Associations: Their Organization and Management*. New York: The Ronald Press Company, 1921.

Nelson, W. E. *Americanization of the Common Law: The Impact of Legal Change on Massachusetts Society, 1760–1830*. Cambridge, Mass.: Harvard University Press, 1975.

Nielsen, W. *The Big Foundations*. New York: Columbia University Press, 1971.

Oates, M. J. *The Catholic Philanthropic Tradition in America*. Bloomington: Indiana University Press, 1995.

Offenheiser, R., Holcombe, S., and Hopkins, N. "Grappling with Globalization, Partnership, and Learning: A Look Inside Oxfam America." *Nonprofit and Voluntary Sector Quarterly*, 1999, *28* (Supplemental), 121–139.

Olasky, M. N. *The Tragedy of American Compassion*. Washington, D.C.: Lanham, Md.: Regnery Gateway; 1992.

Powell, W. W. "Neither Network nor Hierarchy: Network Forms of Organization." *Research in Organizational Behavior 12*. Greenwich, Conn.: JAI Press, 1990.

Proietto, Rosa. "The Ford Foundation and Women's Studies in American Higher Education: Seeds of Change?" In E. C. Lagemann (ed.), *Philanthropic Foundations: New Scholarship, New Possibilities*. Bloomington: Indiana University Press, 229–256, 1999.

Putnam, R. D. *Bowling Alone: The Collapse and Renewal of American Community*. New York: Simon and Schuster, 2000.

Reed, R. *Active Faith: How Christians Are Changing the Soul of American Politics*. New York: Free Press, 1996.

Rich, A. *Think Tanks, Public Policy, and the Politics of Expertise*. New York: Cambridge University Press, 2004.

Richardson, J. M. *Christian Reconstruction: The American Missionary Society and Southern Blacks, 1861–1890.* Athens: University of Georgia Press, 1986.

Roof, W. C. *Spiritual Marketplace: Baby Boomers and the Remaking of American Religion.* Princeton, N.J.: Princeton University Press, 1999.

Rubin, H. "Google Offers a Map for Its Philanthropy." *New York Times* (January 18, 2008).

Rudolph, F. *The American College and University: A History.* New York: Knopf, 1968.

Ryan, M. P. *Cradle of the Middle Class: The Family in Oneida County, New York, 1790–1865.* New York: Cambridge University Press, 1981.

Salamon, L. M. "Partners in Public Service: The Scope and Theory of Government-Nonprofit Relations." In W. W. Powell (ed.), *The Nonprofit Sector: A Research Handbook.* New Haven, Conn.: Yale University Press, 1987.

Salamon, L. M. "The Rise of the Nonprofit Sector." Foreign Affairs, *73*(4), July/August 1994, 110–122.

Salamon, L. M. "The Changing Context of American Nonprofit Management." In R. Herman and Associates (eds.), *The Jossey-Bass Handbook of Nonprofit Leadership and Management* (2nd ed.). San Francisco: Jossey-Bass, 2005.

Salamon, L. M., and Anheier, H. K. *Defining the Nonprofit Sector: A Cross-National Analysis.* New York: St. Martin's Press, 1997.

Salamon, L. M., and Anheier, H.K. *The Emerging Nonprofit Sector: An Overview.* New York: St. Martin's Press, 1996.

Salamon, L. M., & Abramson, A. J. *The Federal Budget and the Nonprofit Sector.* Washington, D.C.: Urban Institute, 1982.

Sale, K. *Power Shift: The Rise of the Southern Rim and Its Challenge to the Eastern Establishment.* New York: Random House, 1975.

Schlesinger, A. M. "Biography of a Nation of Joiners," *American Historical Review,* 1944, *50*(1), 1–25.

Sealander, J. *Private Wealth and Public life: Foundation Philanthropy and* the Reshaping of American Social Policy from the Progressive Era to the New Deal. Baltimore, Md.: Johns Hopkins University Press, 1997.

Sears, J. B. *Philanthropy in the Shaping of American Higher Education.* Washington, DC: Bureau of Education, Department of the Interior, 1922.

Seavoy, R. E. *The Origins of the American Business Corporation, 1784–1855.* Westport, Conn.: Greenwood Press, 1982.

Seeley, J. R., et al. *Community Chest: A Case Study in Philanthropy.* Toronto: University of Toronto Press, 1957.

Sklar, M. J. *The Corporate Reconstruction of American Capitalism, 1890–1916 : The Market, the Law, and Politics.* New York: Cambridge University Press, 1988.

Skocpol, T. "Advocates without Members: The Recent Transformation of American Civic Life." In T. Skocpol and M. Fiorina (eds.), *Civic Engagement in American Democracy.* Washington, D.C.: Brookings Institution Press, 1999, 461–510.

Skocpol, T. *Diminished Democracy: From Membership to Management in American Civic Life.* Norman: University of Oklahoma Press, 2003.

Skocpol, T., et al. "How Americans Became Civic." In T. Skocpol and M. P. Fiorina (eds.), *Civic Engagement in American Democracy.* Washington, D.C.: Brookings Institution, 1999.

Skocpol, T., and Fiorina, M.P. (eds.). *Civic Engagement in American Democracy.* Washington, D.C.: Brookings Institution, 1999.

Smith, D. H. *Grassroots Associations*. Thousand Oaks, Calif.: Sage, 2000.

Smith, J. A. *The Idea Brokers: Think Tanks and the Rise of the New Policy Elite*. New York: Free Press, 1991a.

Smith, J. A. *Brookings at Seventy-five*. Washington, D.C.: Brookings Institution, 1991b.

Soyer, D. *Jewish Immigrant Associations and American Identity in New York, 1880–1939*. Cambridge, Mass.: Harvard University Press, 1997.

Starr, P. *The Social Transformation of American Medicine*. New York: Basic Books, 1982.

Stroman, D. F. *The Disability Rights Movement: From Deinstitutionalization to Self-Determination*. Lanham, Md.: University Press of America, 2003.

Sutton, F. X. "The Ford Foundation: The Early Years." *Daedalus*, 1987, *116*, 42–91.

Swint, H. L. *The Northern Teacher in the South, 1862–1870*. New York: Octagon Books, 1967.

Tobias, M. *Old Dartmouth on Trial*. New York: New York University Press, 1982.

Tocqueville, A. de. *Democracy in America*. (vol. 2) (Henry Reeve, trans.). New York: Random House, 1945 [orig. publ. 1835].

Trustees of Dartmouth College v. *Woodward*, 4 Wheaton 625 (1819).

U.S. Congress. Industrial Relations: Final Report and Testimony Submitted to Congress by the Commission on Industrial Relations. 64th Congress, 1st Session, S. Doc. 154. Washington, D.C. U.S. Government Printing Office, 1916.

Useem, M. "Corporate Philanthropy." In W. W. Powell (ed.), *The Nonprofit Sector: A Research Handbook*. New Haven, CT: Yale University Press, 1987.

Veblen, T. *The Higher Learning in America; A Memorandum on the Conduct of Universities by Business Men*. New York: B. W. Huebsch, 1918.

Verba, S., Schlozman, K. L., & Brady, H. *Voice and Equality: Civic Voluntarism in American Politics*. Cambridge, Mass.: Harvard University Press, 1995.

Veysey, L. R. *The Emergence of the American University*. Chicago: University of Chicago Press, 1965.

Walker, R. "Extra Helping: Kiva.org." *New York Times* (January 27, 2008).

Wall, J. F. *Andrew Carnegie*. New York: Oxford University Press, 1970.

Webber, C., and Wildavsky, A. *A History of Taxation and Expenditure in the Western World*. New York: Simon & Schuster, 1986.

Weisbrod, B. A. *The Nonprofit Economy*. Cambridge, Mass.: Harvard University Press, 1988.

Weisbrod, B. A. "The Future of the Nonprofit Sector." *Journal of Policy Analysis and Management*, 1997, *16*(4), 541–555.

Weisbrod, B. A. (ed.). *To Profit or Not to Profit: The Commercial Transformation of the Nonprofit Sector*. New York: Cambridge University Press, 1998.

Whitehead, J. S. *The Separation of College and State: Columbia, Dartmouth, Harvard, and Yale, 1776–1876*. New Haven, Conn.: Yale University Press, 1976.

Wiebe, R. M. *The Search for Order*. New York: Hill & Wang, 1967.

Witte, J. F. *The Politics and Development of the Federal Income Tax*. Madison: University of Wisconsin Press, 1985.

Wuthnow, R. *After Heaven: Spirituality in America since the 1950s*. Berkeley: University of California Press, 1998.

Wuthnow, R. (ed.). "I come away stronger": *How Small Groups are Shaping American Religion*. Grand Rapids, Mich.: Eerdmans, 1994.

Wuthnow, R., Hodgkinson, V. A., and Associates. *Faith and Philanthropy in America: Exploring the Role of Religion in America's Voluntary Sector*. San Francisco: Jossey-Bass, 1990.

Wuthnow, R. *The Restructuring of American Religion: Society and Faith Since World War II*. Princeton, N.J.: Princeton University Press, 1988.

Wyllie, I. G. "The Search for an American Law of Charity." *Mississippi Valley Historical Review*, 1959, *46*, 203–221.

Zollmann, C. *American Law of Charities*. Milwaukee, Wisc.: Bruce, 1924.

CHAPTER TWO

THE LEGAL FRAMEWORK OF THE NONPROFIT SECTOR IN THE UNITED STATES

Bruce R. Hopkins and Virginia C. Gross

Nonprofit law is derived from many sources, principally the federal tax law, and state corporation and fundraising law. At the federal level, additional bodies of nonprofit law are in the antitrust, consumer protection, health, labor, postal, securities, and other fields. Nonprofit law takes various forms, including statutes enacted by the U.S. Congress and state legislatures, the promulgation by agencies of regulations and rules, and the issuance of federal and state court opinions constitute nonprofit law. Thus, the few pages of this chapter are inherently insufficient to summarize all federal and state law applicable to nonprofit organizations. Nonetheless, the following synopsis of this body of law is provided as an overview to understand the basics of nonprofit law and the governance responsibilities of nonprofit organizations, and to assist the leadership and management of these organizations to be in an informed position to ask questions of legal counsel.

Nonprofit Organizations

A fundamental precept in nonprofit law is the concept of the *nonprofit organization*. This term does not mean an organization that is prohibited by law from earning a profit (that is, an excess of gross earnings over expenses). In fact, it is quite common for nonprofit (and tax-exempt) organizations to generate profits. Rather, the definition of nonprofit organization essentially relates to requirements as to what must be done with the profit earned or otherwise received. This fundamental element of the law is subsumed in the doctrine of private inurement (discussed below).

This concept in law of a nonprofit organization is best understood through a comparison with the concept of a *for-profit* organization. A fundamental distinction between the two types of entities is that the for-profit organization has owners that hold the equity in the enterprise, such as stockholders of a corporation. The for-profit organization is operated for the economic benefit of its owners; the profits of the business undertaking are passed through to them, such as by the payment of dividends on shares of stock. That is what is meant by the term *for-profit organization*: It is an entity that is designed to generate a profit for its owners. The transfer of the profits from the organization to its owners is private inurement—the inurement of net earnings to them in their private (personal) capacity. For-profit organizations are supposed to engage in private inurement.

By contrast, a nonprofit organization is not permitted to distribute its profits (net earnings) to those who control it, such as directors and officers. To do so would be to violate the prohibition against private inurement to which nearly all tax-exempt organizations are subject. That is why the private inurement doctrine is the substantive defining characteristic that distinguishes nonprofit organizations from for-profit organizations for purposes of the law. There are thus two categories of profit: one is at the *entity* level and one is at the *ownership* level. Both nonprofit and for-profit organizations can yield entity-level profit; the distinction in law between the two types of entities pivots on the latter category of profit.

A nonprofit organization can take many forms, most prominently a corporation, an unincorporated association, or a trust. Most states have a statutory regime governing nonprofit corporations and trusts. These regimes address the formation, governance, purposes, operations, and dissolution of the entities.

Tax-Exempt Organizations

A nonprofit organization is not necessarily a tax-exempt organization, although most nonprofit entities qualify for some classification as an exempt entity. Whether a nonprofit organization is entitled to tax exemption, initially or on a continuing basis, is a matter of law. If a nonprofit organization qualifies for a tax exemption, at the federal or state law levels or both, then it is entitled to the exemption. (There is, however, no constitutional law right to a tax exemption, except perhaps for religious organizations.)

The law requires some categories of nonprofit organizations that are eligible for tax-exempt status at the federal law level to apply to the IRS for *recognition* of that exemption. This is generally accomplished by the filing of an application for recognition of exemption (usually Form 1023 or 1024). Most charitable organizations, certain employee benefit organizations, and credit counseling organizations that desire exemption as social welfare organizations are required to apply timely for recognition of exemption. Political organizations must, to be exempt, file a notice with the IRS (Form 8871). For other categories of organizations desiring tax-exempt status, application for recognition of exemption with the IRS is optional but provides some assurance as to the claimed exempt status.

Additional rules apply with respect to *group exemptions*. This is a regime by which organizations that are affiliated with a central tax-exempt organization can be exempt without applying to the IRS for recognition of exemption, provided the central organization successfully files for recognition of tax-exempt status on behalf of the group. This regime can be effective for national or regional organizations with local chapters or affiliates.

The IRS can revoke a recognition of tax exemption for good cause, such as a change in the law, but an organization that has been recognized by the IRS as being exempt generally can rely on that determination as long as there are no substantial changes in its character, purposes, or methods of operation. If material changes occur, the organization should notify the IRS; it may have to undergo a reevaluation of its exempt status.

In a law sense, there really is no such thing as a tax-exempt organization. Nearly all exempt organizations are subject to tax on their unrelated business income. Many types of exempt organizations can have some or all of their investment income taxed if they engage in political activities. Public charities can incur taxes if they undertake legislative or political campaign activities. Private foundations are potentially eligible for a variety of excise taxes, including a tax on their investment income. Social clubs, political organizations, and certain other nonprofit entities are also required to pay tax on their net investment income. Even with complete exemption from federal taxation, a nonprofit organization may have exposure to state or local income, sales, use, or property taxation; each state has its own set of laws regarding qualification for these exemptions.

Categories of Tax-Exempt Organizations

There are over seventy categories of tax-exempt nonprofit organizations in the federal tax law. Not all of them have comparable exemption at the state law level.

Charitable and Like Organizations

Tax exemption is provided for a variety of charitable organizations, which are described in Section 501(c)(3) of the Internal Revenue Code ("Code"). Charitable organizations include those that provide relief for the poor or distressed; promote health; lessen the burdens of government; advance education, science, or religion; promote social welfare; and promote youth sports and protection of the environment. Exemption also is available for cruelty prevention organizations, amateur sports organizations, public safety testing organizations, cooperative hospital service organizations, cooperative educational service organizations, and charitable risk pools. Limitations apply as to private inurement, private benefit, and impermissible advocacy (namely, substantial legislative activities and any political campaign activity).

Religious Organizations

Tax exemption is provided for churches and similar institutions, conventions or associations of churches, integrated auxiliaries of churches, religious orders, apostolic organizations, and other religious organizations, including certain communal groups and retreat facilities. These organizations are also tax-exempt by reason of Code § 501(c)(3).

Educational Organizations

Tax exemption is provided for private schools, including colleges and universities, albeit with a variety of requirements, including the necessity of a disseminated policy as to nondiscrimination on the basis of race. A *school* is an educational institution that has a regular faculty, a regularly enrolled student body, a curriculum, and a place where the educational activities are regularly carried on. Tax exemption is provided as well as for other organizations that instruct individuals or the public, including those that promote sports for the benefit of youth. The term *educational* is not well defined; the federal tax law distinguishes it from *propagandizing*. Nonprofit schools and other educational organizations generally are also tax-exempt by reason of Code § 501(c)(3).

Scientific Organizations

Tax exemption is provided to organizations that engage in scientific research in the public interest. Scientific organizations are typically also tax-exempt by reason of Code § 501(c)(3). There can be controversy as to whether an activity involves *research* as opposed to *commercial testing*.

Social Welfare Organizations

Tax exemption is provided to organizations that operate for the promotion of social welfare (such as civic leagues), in the sense of benefiting those in a community. This category of organizations may include advocacy organizations, that is, those entities that attempt to influence legislation and/or engage in political campaign activity. Generally, these organizations are described in Code § 501(c)(4).

Labor, Agricultural, and Horticultural Organizations

Tax exemption is provided for organizations that engage in collective action to better the working conditions of individuals engaged in a common pursuit. The principal type of this category of tax-exempt organization is the union. Likewise, exemption is provided for organizations that engage in activities to improve the grade of agricultural or horticultural products, and develop a higher degree of efficiency in the activity. Generally, these organizations are described in Code § 501(c)(5).

Business Leagues

Tax exemption is provided for business leagues, namely, associations of person united by common interests, as well as chambers of commerce, boards of trade, real estate boards, and professional football leagues. The principal categories of tax-exempt organizations in this context are trade and business associations, and professional societies. The purpose of these associations is to promote conditions within the line of business they represent. Generally, these organizations are described in Code § 501(c)(6).

Social Clubs

Tax exemption is provided for organizations that provide pleasure and recreation for the benefit of their members. These tax-exempt organizations, which include country clubs and hobby clubs, are required to pay tax on their net investment income. Generally, these organizations are described in Code § 501(c)(7).

Fraternal Societies

Tax exemption is provided for fraternal beneficiary organizations operating under the lodge system and providing certain benefit to their members, and for domestic fraternal societies operating under the lodge system that devote their net earnings to charitable purposes. Generally, these organizations are described in Code § 501(c)(8) or (10).

Veterans' Organizations

Tax exemption is provided for organizations of past or present members of the U.S. armed forces, or related auxiliaries or foundations, when at least 75 percent of the members are past or present members of the U.S. armed forces and substantially all of the other members are spouses or otherwise related to the members. Generally, these organizations are described in Code § 501(c)(19).

Political Organizations

Tax exemption is provided for parties, committees, associations, funds, and other organizations operated primarily for the purpose of accepting contributions or making expenditures, usually for the purpose of assisting one or more individuals in getting elected to public office or preventing a candidate from becoming elected to a public office. Generally, these organizations are described in Code § 527.

Other Tax-Exempt Organizations

Other types of nonprofit organizations that are eligible for tax exemption under the federal tax law are title-holding organizations, credit unions, small insurance companies, various mutual and cooperative organizations, crop financing entities, health maintenance organizations, homeowners' associations, and a variety of employee benefit funds.

Tax-Exempt Organizations Law Basics

Eight principles of law at the federal level compose the basics of the law of tax-exempt organizations, particularly for charitable entities.

Primary Purpose Test

The primary purpose of an organization determines (in part) whether it can qualify as a tax-exempt organization and, if so, which category of exemption is applicable. The focus in this context is on purposes, not activities. These purposes are usually stated in the organizational documents of a tax-exempt entity, such as its articles of incorporation, constitution, or trust document.

Organizational Test

A formal organizational test is applicable to charitable organizations, which focuses on the content of an organization's statement of purposes and the necessity of a dissolution clause in its organizational documents. This statement describes the mission of the entity. A dissolution clause preserves the assets and net income of an organization for charitable purposes, should it dissolve or liquidate. Although there rarely is a formal organizational test for any of the noncharitable tax-exempt organizations, these tests are inherent in each category of exemption.

Operational Test

An operational test is applicable to charitable organizations, which focuses on how an organization functions in relation to the applicable requirements for tax-exempt status. These fundamental requirements are advancement of one or more exempt purposes, and avoidance of private inurement, private benefit, substantial legislative activity, and political campaign activity. Although there rarely is a formal operational test for noncharitable tax-exempt organizations, these tests are inherent in each category of exemption.

Private Inurement Doctrine

The doctrine of private inurement is one of the most important sets of rules constituting the federal law of tax-exempt organizations. This doctrine is a statutory criterion for federal income tax exemption for several categories of exempt organizations, including charitable entities.

The private inurement doctrine requires that a tax-exempt organization be organized and operated so that, in antiquated language, "no part of ... [its] net earnings ... inures to the benefit of any private shareholder or individual." What this doctrine means is that none of the income or assets of a tax-exempt organization subject to the private inurement doctrine may be permitted to directly or indirectly unduly benefit an individual or other person who has a close relationship with the organization, when that person is in a position to exercise a significant degree of control over the entity.

The purpose of the private inurement rule is to ensure that the tax-exempt organization involved is serving exempt rather than private interests. It is thus necessary for an organization subject to the doctrine to be in a position to establish that it is not organized and operated for the benefit of persons in their private capacity, informally referred to as *insiders*, such as the organization's founders, trustees, directors, officers, members of their families, entities controlled by these individuals, or any other persons having a significant personal and private interest in the activities of the organization.

The doctrine of private inurement does not prohibit transactions between a tax-exempt organization subject to the doctrine and those who have a close relationship with it. Rather, the private inurement doctrine requires that these transactions or arrangements be tested against a standard of *reasonableness*. The standard calls for a roughly equal exchange of benefits between the parties; the law is designed to discourage a disproportionate share of the benefits of the exchange flowing to an insider.

The private inurement doctrine does not prohibit the payment of compensation to employees of a charitable organization, provided the compensation is reasonable and not excessive. The reasonableness standard focuses essentially on comparability of data, that is, on how similar organizations, acting prudently, transact their affairs in comparable instances. Thus, the rule addressing the matter of the reasonableness of compensation is that it is generally appropriate to assume that reasonable and true compensation is only such amount as would ordinarily be paid for like services by like enterprises under like circumstances.

The sanction for violation of the private inurement doctrine is revocation (or denial) of the tax-exempt status of the organization involved.

Private Benefit Doctrine

A tax-exempt organization's charitable status can be revoked if there is a finding that the organization is serving a private, rather than a public, benefit. To be exempt, a charitable organization must establish that it is not organized or operated for the benefit of private interests such as designated individuals, the organization's creator or the creator's family members, shareholders of the organization, or persons controlled, directly or indirectly, by such private interests.

The prohibition against private benefit is not limited to situations in which benefits accrue to an organization's insiders. An organization's conferral of benefits on "disinterested persons" (that is, persons who are not insiders) may cause it to serve a private interest. Unlike the private inurement doctrine, the private benefit doctrine permits incidental private benefit. This is an important distinction, inasmuch as, technically, any amount of private inurement may jeopardize a charitable organization's tax-exempt status, whereas an incidental amount of private benefit is allowable. Unlike private inurement, private benefit can exist even when an arrangement is otherwise reasonable. For example, the

IRS has found that a charity was conferring impermissible private benefit on a for-profit management company managing a school, where the management company controlled nearly all the operations of the school.

The sanction for violation of the private benefit doctrine is revocation (or denial) of the tax-exempt status of the organization involved.

Intermediate Sanctions

The intermediate sanctions rules (Code § 4958) provide for the taxation of persons who engaged in impermissible private transactions with certain types of tax-exempt organizations, rather than revocation of the tax-exempt status of these entities. With this approach, tax law sanctions—structured as penalty excise taxes—may be imposed on those persons who improperly benefited from the transaction and on certain managers of the organization who participated in the transaction knowing that it was improper. These taxes are applied to the amount of the excess benefit derived from the transaction. The taxes consist of an *initial* tax and an *additional* tax. The law as to excess benefit transactions applies with respect to tax-exempt public charities and exempt social welfare organizations. These entities are collectively termed, for this purpose, *applicable tax-exempt organizations.*

A person who has a close relationship with an applicable tax-exempt organization is a *disqualified person.* A disqualified person generally is a person who has, or is in a position to have, some type or degree of control over the operations of the applicable tax-exempt organization involved. The term *disqualified person* is defined in this context as (1) any person who was, at any time during the five-year period ending on the date of the transaction involved, in a position to exercise substantial influence over the affairs of the organization (whether by virtue of being an organization manager or otherwise), (2) a member of the family of an individual described in the preceding category, and (3) an entity in which individuals described in the preceding two categories own more than a 35 percent interest.

At the heart of the intermediate sanctions regime is the *excess benefit transaction.* In general, an excess benefit transaction is a transaction in which an economic benefit is provided by an applicable tax-exempt organization, directly or indirectly, to or for the use of a disqualified person, and the value of the economic benefit provided by the organization exceeds the value of the consideration (including the performance of services) received for providing the benefit. Any difference, other than an insubstantial one, between the value provided by the exempt organization and the consideration it received from the disqualified person is an *excess benefit.*

An excess benefit transaction includes a payment of unreasonable (excessive) compensation by an applicable tax-exempt organization to a disqualified person with respect to it. The value of services, in the intermediate sanctions setting, is the amount that ordinarily would be paid for like services by like organizations under like circumstances. Compensation in this context includes all economic benefits (other than certain disregarded benefits) provided by an applicable tax-exempt organization, to or for the use of a person, in exchange for the performance of services, including all forms of cash and noncash compensation.

A key component of the intermediate sanctions rules is the *rebuttable presumption of reasonableness*. When activated, this presumption shifts the burden of proof to the IRS to prove that an element of a transaction or arrangement was unreasonable. (The IRS can rebut this presumption with relevant facts of its own.) This presumption comes into play where the decision to engage in the transaction was made by an independent board or board committee, the board considered appropriate data as to comparability, and the decision was properly and timely documented (including in minutes).

The intermediate sanctions rules entail an initial tax, which is 25 percent of the excess benefit, payable by the disqualified person or persons involved. The transaction must be undone by placing the parties in the same economic position they were in before the transaction was entered into; this is "correction" of the transaction. If the initial tax is not timely paid and the transaction is not timely and properly corrected, an additional tax may have to be paid; this tax is 200 percent of the excess benefit. Board members are subject to a tax of 10 percent of the amount involved if they knowingly participated in the excess benefit transaction, unless the participation was not willful and was due to reasonable cause. The board members subject to the 10 percent excise tax are jointly and severally liable for this tax, which is capped at $20,000 per transaction.

Commensurate Test

Pursuant to an infrequently used standard, termed the *commensurate test*, the IRS may assess whether a charitable organization is maintaining program activities that are commensurate in scope with its financial resources. The IRS has used the commensurate to revoke the tax exemption of charities with high fundraising costs relative to its other expenditures. The IRS has announced that it is going to make greater use of this test.

Public Policy Doctrine

Tax exemption as a charitable organization is available only where the organization is operating in conformance with federal public policy. For example, pursuant to this body of law, a private school cannot be exempt if it has a racially discriminatory policy as to the admission of students, an entity cannot be exempt if it promotes child pornography and exploitation, and an organization cannot qualify for exemption if it impedes IRS inquiries.

Legislative Activities Law

Considerable law restricts the ability of nonprofit organizations to engage in lobbying; these rules are principally directed at charitable organizations. Lobbying involves engaging in activities designed to influence the adoption of legislation, and are distinct from political activities, which involve activities in support of or in opposition to a candidate for political office.

Charitable Organizations. Tax-exempt public charities may engage in legislative activities to the extent that lobbying is not a *substantial* part of their overall functions. This rule is known as the *substantial part test.* Thus, an insubstantial portion of an exempt organization's activities may constitute lobbying; the term *insubstantial* in this context is not well defined. These rules apply with respect to attempts to influence a legislative branch, usually in connection with the development of legislation.

A mechanical test for measuring allowable lobbying, the *expenditure test,* may be elected by a charity. Pursuant to this rule, generally 20 percent of an organization's expenditures may be for lobbying; several exceptions from the concept of lobbying are available under these rules. Excessive lobbying may lead to the imposition of excise taxes, revocation of exemption, or both. More stringent rules are applicable to private foundations.

Social Welfare Organizations. There are no federal tax law limitations on attempts to influence legislation by tax-exempt social welfare organizations, other than the general requirement that the organization primarily engage in efforts to promote social welfare.

Associations (Business Leagues). There are no federal tax law limitations on attempts to influence legislation by tax-exempt business leagues, other than the general requirement that the organization primarily engage in activities appropriate for these organizations. The federal tax law, however, includes rules restricting the tax deductibility of dues paid to these organizations to the extent a portion of the dues is used for lobbying.

Other Exempt Organizations. There are no federal tax law limitations on attempts to influence legislation by any other types of tax-exempt organizations, other than the general requirement that the organization primarily engage in efforts to advance its exempt purpose.

Political Activities Law

The federal tax law generally discourages political campaign activity by nonprofit, tax-exempt organizations. There is an absolute prohibition on political campaign activity by charitable organizations—a rule that is frequently violated.

Charitable Organizations. A charitable organization, to be tax-exempt, may not participate or intervene in a political campaign on behalf of or in opposition to a candidate for public office. This absolute prohibition encompasses political campaign contributions, endorsements, use of facilities, and signage on organization property. Leaders of charitable organizations may, however, engage in political activity in their personal capacity. Political activity may lead to the imposition of excise taxes (Code § 4955), revocation of exemption, or both. More stringent rules are applicable to private foundations.

Social Welfare Organizations. A tax-exempt social welfare organization can engage in political campaign activity without jeopardizing its exemption, but this type of activity cannot be its primary function.

Associations (Business Leagues). There are no federal tax law limitations on political campaign activity by tax-exempt business leagues, other than the general requirement that the organization primarily engage in activities appropriate for these organizations. The federal tax law, however, includes rules restricting the tax deductibility of dues paid to these organizations to the extent a portion of the dues is used for political activity.

Political Organizations. Most political organizations have as their primary exempt function the involvement in political campaign activity, either in support of or in opposition to one or more candidates for public office.

Other Exempt Organizations. The federal tax law is silent as to the extent to which other types of tax-exempt organizations can engage in political campaign activity, in relation to their eligibility for exempt status.

Public Charities and Private Foundations

The realm of charitable organizations is divided into two classes: public charities and private foundations. Every tax-exempt charitable organization is presumed to be a *private foundation* (Code § 508). A showing that the entity is a public charity may rebut this presumption. Because of this presumption, a charitable organization that loses its public charity status becomes, by operation of law, a private foundation.

Definition of Private Foundation

Generically, a private foundation is a charitable entity that is funded from one or just a few sources, has ongoing funding in the form of investment income, and typically makes grants, usually to public charities, for charitable purposes. More technically, a private foundation is a tax-exempt charitable organization that is not a public charity. There are three basic types of charitable organizations that are not private foundations: the institutions, publicly supported charities, and supporting organizations. A fourth form of public charity is the public safety testing organization.

Institutions

Certain tax-exempt *institutions* are classified as public charities regardless of the source of their financial support [Code § 509(a)(1)]. The principal types of institutions are churches, certain other religious organizations, formal educational institutions, hospitals, medical research organizations, and governmental units.

Publicly Supported Organizations

Publicly supported charitable organizations are forms of public charities [Code §§ 170(b)(1)(A)(vi), 509(a)(1)]. The *donative* type of publicly supported charity normally receives a substantial part of its support (other than exempt function revenue) in the forms of contributions or grants from the public or one or more governmental units. The term *substantial* in this context generally means at least one-third, although a charity's public support can be as low as 10 percent if the charity can meet other criteria for public charity status. Generally, support from a member of the public cannot, to be public support, exceed 2 percent of the total amount of support the organization received during the measuring period, which is the entity's most recent five years (including its current year).

The *service provider* type of publicly supported charity [Code § 509(a)(2)] normally receives more than one-third of its support in the form of contributions, grants, membership fees, and fee-for-service revenue from *permitted sources,* and normally does not receive more than one-third of its support in the form of gross investment income and net unrelated business income. Permitted sources do not include disqualified persons with respect to the organization. Public support for these organizations is determined for a measuring period, which is the entity's most recent five years (including its current year).

Supporting Organizations

Supporting organizations are forms of public charities [Code § 509(a)(3)]. Essentially, a *supporting organization* must be organized and operated exclusively for the benefit of, to perform the functions of, or to carry out the purposes of one or more qualified supported organizations. Typical functions of a supporting organization are fundraising, operation of separate programs, and maintenance of an endowment fund. There are four basic types of supporting organizations: Type I, II, III functionally integrated, or Type III nonfunctionally integrated. Stringent law provisions are directed at Type III supporting organizations (both functionally integrated and nonfunctionally integrated), particularly those that are not functionally integrated with a supported organization. These organizations must satisfy a notification requirement, a responsiveness test, and an integral part test. Many Type III supporting organizations must comply with a distribution requirement.

A private foundation may not treat as a qualifying distribution (a permissible grant) an amount paid to a Type III supporting organization that is not a functionally integrated Type III supporting organization or to any other type of supporting organization if a disqualified person with respect to the foundation directly or indirectly controls the supporting organization or a supported organization of the supporting organization. An amount that does not count as a qualifying distribution under this rule is regarded as a taxable expenditure.

A Type III supporting organization must apprise each organization that it supports of information regarding the supporting organization in order to help ensure the responsiveness by the supporting organization to the needs or demands of the supported organization(s). A Type III supporting organization that is organized as a trust must establish, to the satisfaction of the IRS, that it has a sufficiently close and continuous relationship with the supported organization so that the trust is responsive to the needs or demands of the supported organization.

A supporting organization must annually demonstrate that one or more of its disqualified persons [other than its managers and supported organization(s)] do not, directly or indirectly, control it. This is done by means of a certification on its annual information return.

Generally, a supported organization of a supporting organization is a public charity that is classified as one of the institutions or is a publicly supported charity. Under certain circumstances, however, a tax-exempt social welfare organization, labor organization, or business league (association) can qualify as a supported organization.

Private Foundation Rules

Private foundations are subject to a battery of rules prohibiting self-dealing with disqualified persons, excess business holdings, jeopardizing investments, and taxable expenditures. An income payout in the form of qualifying distributions is mandated. (Code §§ 4940–4948.) They must pay an excise tax on their net investment income. The sanctions for violating these rules include a series of excise taxes.

Donor-Advised Funds

A donor-advised fund, although not a separate legal entity, is often seen as an alternative to a private foundation. A *donor-advised fund* is a fund or account (1) that is identified by reference to one or more donors, (2) that is owned and controlled by a sponsoring organization, and (3) as to which a donor or a donor advisor has advisory privileges with respect to the distribution or investment of amounts held in the fund or account. A *sponsoring organization* is a public charity that maintains one or more donor-advised funds. Various impermissible distributions from a donor-advised fund can give rise to a tax (Code §§ 4966, 4967).

Governance

Nonprofit governance is a matter of a great deal of attention in recent years. *Governance* refers to how an organization is governed, meaning how it is controlled and managed. Generally, the body of law applicable to the governance of a tax-exempt organization is state, not federal, law. The nature of the governance of a nonprofit, exempt organization depends mainly on the form of the entity. The state act governing the creation and operation of a nonprofit entity will address matters relating to the organization's governance.

Tax-exempt organizations that are corporations are typically governed by either a board of directors or a board of trustees. If the exempt organization is a trust, it may have a board of trustees or be governed by a single, sometimes corporate, trustee. How the nonprofit organization is organized determines how its directors are selected. Some nonprofit organizations are established with a self-perpetuating board of directors, meaning that the directors elect their successors. In the case of a nonprofit organization formed as a membership entity, the members of the nonprofit organization typically elect the directors. In the rare instance of a nonprofit corporation organized as a stock corporation, which is allowable only in a few states, the stockholders elect the directors. With trusts, the trust document often appoints the trustees. Certain director positions may be ex officio, with the individual serving as a director because of a position held in another entity. However selected, the governing board of a nonprofit organization is responsible for overseeing its affairs. A nonprofit organization's officers are usually elected by the governing body or by the organization's members, with the election process typically governed by the organization's bylaws.

State law usually mandates that at least three individuals serve as the governing body, although some states require only one. Some nonprofit corporations have very large boards of directors; state law does not set a maximum on the number of directors of nonprofit organizations. Some agencies and organizations suggest a minimum of three or five directors in their good governance guidelines, and at least one suggests a fifteen-person maximum. The prevailing view is that nonprofit entities should have enough board members to allow for full deliberation and diversity of thinking on governance and other organization matters.

The composition of a nonprofit organization's governing board is generally a matter of state law, but currently there are four exceptions to this general rule: (1) tax-exempt health care organizations are required to satisfy a community benefit test, which includes having a community board; (2) organizations qualifying as a publicly supported charity by reason of the facts-and-circumstances test may need to have a governing board that is representative of the community, as a community board is one of the factors considered in meeting the test; (3) organizations that qualify as supporting organizations are subject to certain requirements as to their board composition and selection; and (4) entities qualifying as exempt credit counseling organizations are subject to board composition requirements regarding financial independence from the organization.

There is no general requirement that a nonprofit organization have a certain number of independent board members. The inclusion of independent directors on the board of a nonprofit entity is, however, considered a good governance practice. An independent board member is generally one with no financial or family connections with the organization, other than serving as a board member. IRS agents, when reviewing initial applications of exempt organizations, often try to impose their own views on board compositions, such as requiring the addition of independent directors; such views are not correct assertions of the law. One IRS representative stated publicly that "outside of the very smallest organizations, or possibly family foundations," an active, independent, and engaged board of directors is the "gold standard" of board composition.

Duties of Directors

The board of a tax-exempt organization is collectively responsible for developing and advancing the organization's mission; maintaining the organization's tax-exempt status, and (if applicable) its ability to attract charitable contributions; protecting the organization's resources; formulating the organization's budget; hiring and evaluating the chief executive; generally overseeing the organization's management; and supporting and fundraising that the organization undertakes. Embodied in state law are fiduciary duties for members of the governing body of a nonprofit organization. Fiduciary duties arose out of the charitable law of trusts, and impose on directors and trustees standards of conduct and management. One of the principal responsibilities of board members is to maintain financial accountability and effective oversight of the organization they serve. Board members are guardians of the organization's assets, and are expected to exercise due diligence to see that the organization is well managed and has a financial position that is as strong as is reasonable under the circumstances. Fiduciary duty requires board members of nonprofit organizations to be objective, unselfish, responsible, honest, trustworthy, and efficient. Board members, as stewards of the organization, should always act for the organization's good and betterment, rather than for their personal benefit. They should exercise reasonable care in their decision making, and not place the organization under unnecessary risk.

The distinction as to legal liability between the board as a group and the board members as individuals relates to the responsibility of the board for the organization's affairs and the responsibility of individual board members for their actions personally. The board collectively is responsible and may be liable for what transpires within and what happens to the organization. As the ultimate authority, the board should ensure that the organization is operating in compliance with the law and its governing instruments. If legal action ensues, it is often traceable to an inattentive, passive, and/or captive board. Legislators and government regulators are becoming more aggressive in demanding higher levels of involvement by and accountability of board members of tax-exempt organizations; this is causing a dramatic shift in thinking about board functions, away from the concept of mere oversight and toward the precept that board members should be far more involved in policy setting and review, employee supervision, and overall management of the organization. Consequently, many boards of exempt organizations are becoming more vigilant and active in implementing and maintaining sound policies and procedures.

In turn, the board's shared legal responsibilities depend on the actions of individuals. Each board member is liable for his or her acts (commissions and omissions), including those that may be civil law or even criminal law offenses. In practice, this requires board members to hold each other accountable for deeds that prove harmful to the organization.

The duties of the board of directors of a tax-exempt organization essentially are the duty of care, the duty of loyalty, and the duty of obedience. Defined by case law, these are the legal standards against which all actions taken or not taken by directors are measured. They are collective duties adhering to the entire board; the mandate is active participation by all of the board members. Accountability can be demonstrated by showing the effective discharge of these three duties.

The duty of care requires that directors of a tax-exempt organization be reasonably informed about the organization's activities, participate in decision making, and act in good faith and with the care of an ordinarily prudent person in comparable circumstances. In short, the duty of care requires the board—and its members individually—to pay attention to the organization's activities and operations.

The duty of care is satisfied by attendance at meetings of the board and appropriate committees; advance preparation for board meetings, such as reviewing reports and the agenda prior to meetings of the board; obtaining information, before voting, to make appropriate decisions; use of independent judgment; periodic examination of the credentials and performance of those who serve the organization; frequent review of the organization's finances and financial policies; and compliance with filing requirements, particularly annual information returns.

The duty of loyalty requires board members to exercise their power in the interest of the tax-exempt organization and not in their personal interest or the interest of another entity, particularly one with which they have a formal relationship. When acting on behalf of the exempt organization, board members are expected to place the interests of the organization before their personal and professional interests.

The duty of loyalty is satisfied when board members disclose any conflicts of interest; otherwise adhere to the organization's conflict-of-interest policy; avoid the use of corporate opportunities for the individual's personal gain or other benefit; and do not disclose confidential information concerning the information.

The duty of obedience requires that directors of a tax-exempt organization comply with applicable federal, state, and local laws, adhere to the organization's governing documents, and remain guardians of the organization's mission. The duty of obedience is complied with when the board endeavors to be certain that the organization is in compliance with applicable regulatory requirements, complies with and periodically reviews all documents governing the operations of the organization, and makes decisions in advancement of the organization's mission and within the scope of the entity's governing documents.

Developments in Nonprofit Governance

In recent years, Congress, the IRS, and other groups have been attempting to exercise more influence and control over the governance of tax-exempt organizations, especially charities. At this time, however, there is little federal law applicable to the governance of tax-exempt organizations. Although a few provisions of the Sarbanes-Oxley Act passed in 2002 apply to nonprofit organizations, Congress has not yet enacted laws that affect the governance, oversight, and management of nonprofit organizations to any significant degree. The IRS, with its redesign of the Form 990, which is the annual information return filed by most nonprofit organizations, has done more to conform the governance practices of tax-exempt organizations than any other agency. Many in the nonprofit community are questioning the IRS's authority to regulate the manner in which nonprofit organizations are governed. Most believe the IRS is effectively trying to make law by virtue of the questions it asks on the new Form 990 and through the exempt organization application process. The IRS, however, has stated that it has no intentions of backing away from the issue of nonprofit governance and will continue to "educate, engage, and indeed irritate" in the area of nonprofit governance.

Certain states have enacted laws regarding the accountability of nonprofit organizations; the state of California has the most extensive set of rules concerning governance and accountability of nonprofit organizations, mainly due to the state's enactment of the Nonprofit Integrity Act in 2004. Most state provisions, to the extent they exist, require audited financial statements for nonprofit organizations with revenues in excess of a certain threshold.

Corporate Policies

With a few noted exceptions, a nonprofit entity is not legally required to have corporate policies. The prevailing view by the IRS and watchdog organizations in the nonprofit community, however, is that a well-governed nonprofit organization is more effective and more compliant, and that policies and procedures are an indication of a well-governed entity. As a result, tax-exempt organizations should consider implementing policies that are applicable and relevant to their organization both as a matter of good governance, and to demonstrate that they are effectively governed in the event of an audit or investigation. These policies include a conflicts-of-interest policy, whistleblower policy, document retention and destruction policy, code of ethics, investment policy, travel and reimbursement policy, and fundraising policy, just to name a few.

One of the nonprofit buzzwords of the day is "transparency." Most good governance guidelines have, as one of their tenets, a principle that a nonprofit organization should make information regarding the entity widely known and available to the public, including information about its mission, activities, finances, board, and staff. Some of these matters are already part of the law applicable to tax-exempt organizations. Others represent opinions on good governance but are not legal requirements.

As more situations involving apparent lack of governance at the board level over tax-exempt organizations surface, exempt organizations and those that advise them need to pay increasing attention to the entities' governance practices and procedures. Members of the public and nonprofit watchdog organizations are likely to be unsympathetic to an organization bled dry by a wayward executive director or a nonprofit steered away from its original mission by self-interested directors when adherence to good governance principles could have avoided the matter. Exempt organizations should take care to see that its governance affairs are in order, whether or not subject to a legal requirement to do so.

Reporting Rules

Nonprofit, tax-exempt organizations are subject to many reporting rules.

Annual Information Returns. Nearly every organization that is exempt from federal income taxation is required to annually file an information return with the IRS (Code § 6033). For many tax-exempt organizations, this return is Form 990. Small (that is, entities with less than $200,000 in gross receipts or $500,000 in total assets) exempt organizations can file Form 990-EZ. Private foundations (of any size) file Form 990-PF. Political and other exempt organizations may file Form 990, 1120-POL, or both. Homeowners' associations file Form 1120-H. Black lung benefit trusts file Form 990-BL. Very small organizations (that is, those with less than $50,000 in gross receipts) are required to electronically file Form 990-N (the e-postcard). Exceptions to this filing requirement are available.

Unrelated Business Income Tax Returns. A tax-exempt organization with unrelated business income is generally required to file an income tax return, reporting the income, expenses, and any tax due (Form 990-T).

Split-Interest Trust Returns. A split-interest trust is required to annually file a return (generally Form 1041A, perhaps Form 5227) with the IRS.

Nonexempt Charitable Trust Returns. A nonexempt charitable trust is required to annually file a return (Form 1041A, perhaps 5577) with the IRS.

Apostolic Organizations' Returns. Apostolic organizations are required to annually file a partnership return with the IRS (Form 1065).

State Annual Reports. Nonprofit organizations, particularly nonprofit corporations, are generally required to file annual reports with the states in which they are formed, headquartered, and do business.

Charitable Solicitation Act Reports. Charitable and other types of nonprofit organizations that engage in fundraising are generally required to file annual reports with each state in which they solicit funds.

Disposition of Gift Property Rules. A charitable organization that disposes of charitable gift property within three years of the date of the gift is generally required to report the transaction (on Form 8282) to the IRS.

Disclosure Rules

Generally, a tax-exempt organization must make its IRS application for recognition of exemption (including documents submitted in support of the application and any letter or other document issued by the IRS regarding the application) and its three most recent annual information returns available for public inspection. Exempt organizations other than private foundations and political entities are not required to disclose the names and addresses of their donors, and may redact this information prior to providing copies or otherwise making information returns available. Public charities are required to make their Forms 990-T available for public inspection. The IRS has also established a procedure for requesting copies of these documents and returns from the IRS using IRS Form 4506-A, Request for Public Inspection or Copy of Exempt or Political Organization IRS Form.

Documents required to be disclosed must be made available for inspection at the organization's principal office and certain regional or district offices during regular business hours, and organizations are required to provide copies of these documents to those who request them, either in person or in writing. Copies must be provided without charge, other than a reasonable fee for reproduction and mailing costs.

A tax-exempt organization is not required to comply with the requests for copies of its application for recognition of exemption or annual information returns if the organization has made the document widely available. For this purpose, making the documents widely available is satisfied if an organization posts the documents on a Web page that the organization establishes and maintains, or if the documents are posted as part of a database of similar documents by other exempt organizations on a Web page established or maintained by another entity, provided certain other criteria are met. The rules for public inspection of the documents will continue to apply, even if the organization makes the documents widely available to satisfy the requirements regarding copies.

If the IRS determines that a tax-exempt organization is the subject of a harassment campaign and that compliance with the requests would not be in the public interest, the tax-exempt organization does not have to fulfill a request for a copy that it reasonably believes is part of the campaign. The document disclosure rules apply to the notice that must be filed by political organizations to establish their tax-exempt status and to the reports they must file.

Unrelated Business Rules

One of the principal aspects of the law of tax-exempt organizations is the body of law concerning the conduct of unrelated business (Code §§ 511–514).

Requirement of Business

A *business* of a tax-exempt organization is an activity that is carried on for the production of income from the sale of goods or the performance of services. Nearly every undertaking of an exempt organization, including its programs, is a business. Businesses of exempt organizations are, for this purpose, either related or unrelated.

Regularly Carried-on Rule

A business of a tax-exempt organization, to be considered an unrelated business, must be regularly carried on. Generally, this element of regularity is measured annually; if a season is involved, that is the measuring period.

Substantially Related Standard

A business of a tax-exempt organization, to be considered a related business, where the conduct of the business activity has a causal relationship to the achievement of an exempt purpose (other than through the production of income) and the causal relationship is substantial.

Exceptions as to Activities

Various exceptions from treatment as unrelated business are available for activities of tax-exempt organizations, including volunteer-conducted businesses, convenience businesses, sales of gift items, certain entertainment activities, the conduct of trade shows, certain hospital services, the dissemination of low-cost articles, and the exchanging or rental of mailing lists.

Exceptions as to Income

Various exceptions (in the form of *modifications* of the general rule) from treatment as unrelated business income are available for income received by tax-exempt organizations, including dividends, interest, annuities, royalties, rent, capital gains, and research income.

Social Clubs' and Like Organizations' Rules

Special unrelated business rules are applicable to social clubs, veterans' organizations, voluntary employees' beneficiary associations, and supplemental unemployment benefit trusts.

Unrelated Debt-Financed Income Rules

In computing a tax-exempt organization's unrelated business taxable income, there must be included with respect to each debt-financed property that is unrelated to the organization's exempt function—as an item of gross income derived from an unrelated trade or business—an amount of income from the property subject to tax in the proportion to which the property is financed by the debt.

Tax Computation

The unrelated income tax rates payable by most tax-exempt organizations are the corporate rates. In computing unrelated business taxable income, exempt organizations may deduct expenses that are directly connected with the carrying on of the trade or business. A specific deduction of $1,000 is available, as is a charitable deduction. Taxable unrelated business income is reported on Form 990-T.

Subsidiaries

It is common for nonprofit, tax-exempt organizations to have one or more subsidiaries. Generically, this type of arrangement is known as *bifurcation*: a splitting of functions that might otherwise be conducted by one organization so that some of the functions are conducted by one entity and the balance of the functions are conducted by the other entity. Common reasons for formation of a subsidiary by a tax-exempt entity are to insulate the exempt entity from the liability risks of the subsidiary's activity or because the subsidiary's activity is not related to the nonprofit entity's exempt purpose. If one or more subsidiaries exist, the board members should know why; if there are no subsidiaries, the board members should, from time to time, deliberate and seek advice as to whether a subsidiary might be of advantage to the nonprofit organization.

A subsidiary may be a tax-exempt organization or it may be a for-profit organization. Before addressing those distinctions, however, there are six law aspects of the parent-subsidiary relationship that the should be considered, irrespective of the type of subsidiary: the form of the subsidiary, the nature of control of the subsidiary, funding of the subsidiary (initially and on an ongoing basis), day-to-day management of the subsidiary, revenue flow from the subsidiary to the parent, and, perhaps, liquidation of the subsidiary.

- *Form.* If the subsidiary is a nonprofit organization, the legal forms are nonprofit corporation, unincorporated association, trust, or limited liability company. If the subsidiary is a for-profit organization, the typical choices are for-profit corporation or a limited liability company. Matters can become more complicated if the nonprofit parent is not the sole owner of the for-profit subsidiary.
- *Control.* If the subsidiary is a nonprofit organization, the parent can control it by overlapping governing boards, membership (if the parent is the sole member of the subsidiary), appointments, ex officio positions, or some combination of the foregoing. If the subsidiary is a for-profit organization, the control feature will be manifested by ownership, either by stock in the corporation or membership interest in the limited liability company.
- *Funding.* The parent must decide how much money or property, if any, to transfer to the subsidiary and should understand the federal tax consequences of the transfer. If the subsidiary is a for-profit entity, the transfer may be in the nature of a capitalization, such as in exchange for stock or membership interest. The parent may make loans to the subsidiary.
- *Management.* If the parent organization is unduly involved in the day-to-day management of the subsidiary, the activities of the subsidiary may be attributed to the parent. This type of attribution usually causes federal tax problems,

either in the form of endangering tax exemption or unrelated business income taxation.

- *Revenue flow.* Revenue can flow from a subsidiary to a nonprofit parent in two basic ways: payment of net earnings (such a dividends, in the case of a for-profit subsidiary) or payment for services or assistance (such as rent or interest). The second category of these payments may be taxable to the parent as unrelated business income. A special rule (set to expire at the close of 2009) exempts certain types of revenue from a subsidiary from unrelated business income taxation [Code § 512(b)(13)].
- *Liquidation.* If the subsidiary is terminated, and liquidated into the parent, the subsidiary may have to pay income tax on the capital gain resulting from the transfer of assets to the parent that have appreciated in value.

If the subsidiary is a tax-exempt charitable organization, it may be a supporting organization. Typical parents of charitable subsidiaries are social welfare organizations, associations (business leagues), and labor organizations. A charitable organization may be the parent of a charitable subsidiary, such as may be the case with a "foundation" related to a domestic public charity or a fundraising entity affiliated with a foreign charitable organization.

A charitable organization may be the parent entity and have a subsidiary that is a tax-exempt, noncharitable entity. Two common illustrations of this form of bifurcation are lobbying arms (social welfare organizations) of public charities and certification organizations (business leagues) associated with public charities. Other arrangements involving nonprofit, tax-exempt parents and nonprofit, exempt subsidiaries are those using title-holding companies, political action committees and other political organizations (but not by charitable organizations), and various types of employee benefit funds.

Some of these subsidiaries may be for-profit, taxable entities, usually utilized to conduct a business activity that is both substantial and unrelated to the tax-exempt activities of the parent entity. Particular consideration needs to be given to choice of entity in this context; a standard corporation (C corporation) is likely to be the answer, in that flow-through entities (such as S corporations and limited liability companies) can give rise to tax dilemmas for the tax-exempt parent. In some instances, revenue received by an exempt organization parent from its subsidiary is taxable as unrelated business income.

Joint Ventures

Nonprofit, tax-exempt organizations may participate in partnerships and other forms of joint ventures, such as those utilizing limited liability companies. Most of the law in this area concerns public charities as general partners or members in these ventures. Ventures may be whole-entity or ancillary. The IRS is particularly sensitive to the potential for private inurement or private benefit in these circumstances.

The term *partnership* generally has a technical meaning; partnerships are recognized forms of business entities, either as general partnerships or limited partnerships. The term *joint venture*, however, is much broader; a nonprofit organization can be involved in a joint venture with one or more other nonprofit entities or one or more for-profit entities. On occasion, the joint venture form can be imposed on an arrangement between a nonprofit organization and one or more other organizations by operation of law.

A public charity (or perhaps another form of tax-exempt organization) can be a (or the) general partner in a general partnership and not endanger its exempt status where (1) the participation of the exempt organization in the partnership is in furtherance of an exempt purpose, (2) the exempt organization is insulated from the day-to-day responsibilities of being the general partner, and (3) the limited partners are not receiving an unwarranted economic benefit from the partnership.

The federal tax law recognizes the concept of the *whole-entity joint venture*. This type of vehicle was started by tax-exempt health care institutions, which placed the entirety of the institution in a venture (unlike most joint ventures, where only a portion of nonprofit resources are involved). The other venturer(s) may be nonprofit or for-profit. Where it is the latter, the IRS and the courts will look to see whether the exempt venturer has "ceded control" over its operations to the for-profit venturer. If it has, the nonprofit organization will be likely to lose its tax-exempt status, on the basis of violation of the private benefit doctrine.

The federal tax law developed in the context of whole-entity joint ventures is being applied to other ventures involving nonprofit organizations when less than the entire entity is placed in the venture. These are termed *ancillary joint ventures*. It may be that an ancillary joint venture is wholly in furtherance of charitable or other exempt purposes, in which case tax exemption is not at issue. Or the involvement of an exempt organization in an ancillary joint venture may be, from the organization's standpoint, incidental, thus eliminating any private benefit doctrine problems. This open question remains: What happens when a tax-exempt, charitable organization is involved in an ancillary joint venture, to more than an insubstantial extent, and loses control of its resources in the venture to a for-profit co-venturer? The logical, albeit perhaps harsh, answer is that the organization would lose its exempt status.

The joint venture vehicle of choice, when only tax-exempt organizations are involved, is the limited liability company. These companies, which can have one or more members, are generally treated, for federal tax law purposes, as partnerships, which means that they are not themselves taxed, but instead are flow-through entities causing their members to be taxable on the venture's income. Issues may arise, however, with trying to obtain property and sales tax exemptions for these flow-through entities.

Limited liability companies may also be used in situations with for-profit partners. Although the for-profit venturers tend to favor this approach, which avoid double taxation, tax-exempt organizations may want to avoid a flow-through entity, so as not to have taxable unrelated business income and possibly jeopardize their tax-exempt status if the venture does not further exempt purposes. For this reason, some tax-exempt organizations form a for-profit subsidiary to be a member of the joint venture, to serve as a "blocker" entity to escape the unrelated business income tax and perhaps avoid jeopardizing the nonprofit organization's exempt status.

The single-member limited liability company is usually disregarded for tax purposes. This feature allows a tax-exempt organization to place activities in a limited liability company to protect against legal liability, yet still treat them for federal tax purposes as activities directly conducted by the exempt organization.

Other Aspects of Law of Exempt Organizations

Seven other aspects of the law of tax-exempt organizations warrant mention for the benefit of the leadership and management of nonprofit organizations.

Gaming

In general, the conduct of gaming (or gambling) activity by a tax-exempt organization constitutes an unrelated business or a nonexempt function that may jeopardize the organization's exempt status. An exception in the unrelated business context is available for the conduct of bingo games, where they are lawful under state law.

Withholding of Taxes

As is the case with for-profit employers, nonprofit organization employers are required to withhold income and other taxes, and remit them to the appropriate government. Members of the board of nonprofit organizations can be personally liable for these taxes owed (and not paid by the organization).

Unemployment Tax

Tax-exempt organizations generally are required to pay federal and state unemployment taxes with respect to their employees.

Nonexempt Membership Organizations

Special rules apply that can limit the deductibility of expenses in computing taxable income in situations in which a nonprofit organization is a nonexempt membership entity.

Maintenance of Books and Records

Tax-exempt organizations are required to keep records sufficiently showing gross income, expenses, and disbursements and providing substantiation for their annual information returns. The IRS frequently revokes the exempt status of organizations that do not maintain adequate records.

Personal Benefit Contracts

The federal tax law denies a charitable contribution deduction in connection with, and imposes penalties on tax-exempt organizations that engage in transactions involving, certain personal benefit contracts [Code § 170(f)(10)].

Commerciality Doctrine

Tax-exempt organizations, particularly public charities, which operate in a commercial manner (that is, in the same manner as for-profit entities) may have their exemption revoked by the IRS. Commercial activity may alternatively be considered an unrelated business. Factors as to commerciality include the extent of the sale of goods and services to the public, pricing policies, and competition with for-profit businesses.

Charitable Giving

The federal tax law is replete with detailed rules concerning the charitable contribution deduction, for income, gift, and estate tax purposes.

Charitable Deduction. The federal tax law provides for an income tax charitable contribution deduction for gifts to charitable, governmental, and certain other types of tax-exempt organizations (Code § 170). These deductible contributions may be made in the form of money or property. Various percentage limitations may restrict the amount of a charitable contribution deduction in a year. Many special rules apply in this context for particular types of charitable gifts, such as those of inventory, scientific research property, vehicles, and intellectual property. These rules can limit the amount of the charitable deduction, sometimes confining it to the amount of the donor's basis in the property.

Property Valuation. In connection with charitable contributions of property, rather than cash, often the major issue affecting the deductibility of the gift is the matter of the fair market value of the property at the time of its contribution. Various "accuracy related" penalties can apply with respect to an overvaluation of property in this context.

Gift Restrictions. A gift may be made to charity that involves the imposition of conditions or restrictions. In many instances, such a restriction is lawful (such as for scholarships, a form of research, or for an endowment). A restriction or condition may, however, be unlawful, may result in unwarranted private benefit, or reduce or eliminate the amount of the allowable charitable deduction.

Split-Interest Trusts. Contributions may be made to charity by means of a split-interest trust. The resulting charitable contribution deduction (if any) is based on the value of the partial interest contributed to the charity by means of the trust. For a charitable deduction to be available in this context, various requirements must be satisfied, such as those for charitable remainder trusts, pooled income funds, and other types of gifts of remainder interests. These vehicles are used in the realm of the type of charitable fundraising known as *planned giving*. If a charitable organization does not have a planned giving program, the board member may wish to inquire as to why that is the case.

Charitable Remainder Trusts. The *charitable remainder trust* (Code § 664) is the mainstay of a typical planned giving program. This term is nearly self-explanatory: the entity is a trust, in which has been created a remainder interest that is destined for one or more charitable organizations. One or more income interests are also created by means of this type of trust. These trusts, if they qualify under the federal tax law, are tax-exempt entities.

A qualified charitable remainder trust must provide for a specified distribution of income, at least annually, to one or more beneficiaries (at least one of which is not a charitable organization) for life or for a term of no more than twenty years, with an irrevocable remainder interest to be held for the benefit of, or paid over to, the charitable organization. The manner in which the income interests in a charitable remainder trust are ascertained depends on whether the trust is a charitable remainder annuity trust or a charitable remainder unitrust.

In the case of the *charitable remainder annuity trust*, the income payments are a fixed amount (hence the term *annuity*). With a *charitable remainder unitrust*, the income payments are in an amount equal to a fixed percentage of the fair market value of the assets in the trust. Conventionally, once the income interest expires, the assets in a charitable remainder trust are distributed to the charitable organization that is the remainder beneficiary. The assets (or a portion of them) may, however, be retained in the trust; if this type of a retention occurs, the trust will be likely to be classified as a private foundation. With these charitable giving instruments, the person establishing the trust receives a charitable deduction for the value of the charitable remainder interest at the time the trust is established.

Charitable Gift Annuities. A charitable gift annuity is based on an agreement between the donor and the charitable donee. The donor agrees to make a gift and the donee agrees to provide the donor (or someone else or both) with an annuity for a period of time.

Federal Law as to Fundraising

The federal tax law includes five bodies of law that pertain to fundraising.

Special Events. *Special events* are social occasions (such as annual balls, games of chance, and sports events) for the benefit of charities that use ticket sales and underwriting to generate revenue. These events, however, may raise federal tax law issues, such as unrelated business and inappropriate gaming. Special event fundraising is the subject of specific reporting rules as part of the annual information return.

Gift Substantiation Rules. The income tax charitable contribution deduction is not allowed for a contribution of a monetary gift unless the donor maintains a suitable record of the contribution. For a charitable contribution of $250 or more to be deductible, certain substantiation requirements must be met. This principally entails a written communication from the charitable donee to the donor, containing specified information. More detailed substantiation requirements apply in connection with larger noncash contributions. Other charitable gift substantiation rules may arise in other contexts, such as with respect to contributions of vehicles or intellectual property.

Quid Pro Quo Contribution Rules. The federal tax law imposes certain disclosure requirements on charitable organizations that receive *quid pro quo contributions,* which are payments made partially as a contribution and partially in consideration for goods or services provided by the donee organization. Penalties apply for violation of these rules.

Noncharitable Organizations Gifts Disclosure. The federal tax law imposes certain disclosure requirements in connection with contributions to tax-exempt organizations other than charitable entities. These rules, targeted principally at exempt social welfare organizations, are designed to prevent circumstances where donors are led to believe that the gifts are deductible when they are not. Penalties apply for violation of these rules.

Appraisal Requirements. A contribution deduction is not available, in an instance of a gift of property with a value in excess of $5,000, unless certain appraisal requirements are satisfied, including an appraisal obtained by the donor from a qualified appraiser. A *qualified appraisal* is an appraisal document prepared by a qualified appraiser in accordance with generally accepted appraisal standards. A *qualified appraiser* is an individual with verifiable education and experience in valuing the type of property for which the appraisal is performed.

State Law as to Fundraising

Many states have elaborate laws—charitable solicitation acts—that apply to charitable and other nonprofit organizations that engage in fundraising in their jurisdictions. These laws require charitable organizations soliciting gifts to register with and annually report to the state. Fundraising consultants and paid solicitors may also have registration and reporting requirements; bonds may also be necessitated. These laws can impose several other requirements, such as dictation of the contents of a contract between a charity and a professional fundraiser.

Organization of IRS

The leadership of nonprofit organizations, and those who represent these entities, should understand the organization of the IRS. Among the many reasons for this is to gain a perspective on the IRS audit function. Generally, an IRS audit is less traumatic if the overall process is understood.

The IRS is an agency (bureau) of the Department of the Treasury. One of the functions of the Treasury Department is assessment and collection of federal income and other taxes. Congress has authorized the Secretary of the Treasury to, in the language of the Internal Revenue Code, undertake what is necessary for "detecting and bringing to trial and punishment persons guilty of violating the internal revenue laws or conniving at the same." This tax assessment and collection function has largely been assigned to the IRS.

The IRS Web site proclaims that the agency's mission is to "provide America's taxpayers with top quality service by helping them understand and meet their tax responsibilities and by applying the tax law with integrity and fairness to all." The function of the IRS, according to its site, is to "help the large majority of compliant taxpayers with the tax law, while ensuring that the minority who are unwilling to comply pay their fair share."

The IRS is headquartered in Washington, D.C.; its operations there are housed principally in its national office. An Internal Revenue Service Oversight Board is responsible for overseeing the agency in its administration and supervision of the execution of the nation's internal revenue laws. The chief executive of the IRS is the commissioner of internal revenue. The national office is organized into four operating divisions; the pertinent one is the Tax Exempt and Government Entities (TE/GE) Division, headed by the commissioner (TE/GE). Within the TE/GE Division is the Exempt Organizations Division, which develops policy concerning and administers the law of tax-exempt organizations. The components of this division are rulings and agreements, customer education and outreach, exempt organizations electronic initiatives, and examinations.

The examinations office, based in Dallas, Texas, focuses on tax-exempt organizations' examination programs and review projects. This office develops the overall exempt organizations enforcement strategy and goals to enhance compliance consistent with overall TE/GE strategy, and implements and evaluates exempt organizations examination policies and procedures. Two important elements of the examinations function are the Exempt Organizations Compliance Unit and the Data Analysis Unit.

Applications for recognition of exemption are filed with the IRS office in Covington, Kentucky. Tax-exempt organizations file their annual information returns with the IRS office in Ogden, Utah.

IRS Audits

The IRS, of course, has the authority to examine—audit—nonprofit, tax-exempt organizations. Until recently, this has not been a priority for the IRS. With an increase in funding, however, IRS audit activity involving exempt organizations is at an all-time high. Thus, managers of nonprofit organizations are on notice that the chance of their organization getting audited, although inherently slight, is statistically greater than ever.

Reasons for IRS Audits. The reasons for an IRS examination of a nonprofit, tax-exempt organization are manifold. Traditionally, the agency has focused on particular categories of major exempt entities, such as health care institutions, colleges and universities, political organizations, community foundations, and private foundations. Recent years have brought more targeted examinations, such as those involving credit counseling entities and down payment assistance organizations.

An examination of a tax-exempt organization may be initiated on the basis of the size of the organization or the length of time that has elapsed since a prior audit. An examination may be undertaken following the filing of an annual information return or a tax return, inasmuch as one of the functions of the IRS is to ascertain the correctness of returns. An examination may be based on a discrete issue, such as compensation practices or political campaign activity. Other reasons for the development of an examination include media reports, a state attorney general's inquiry, or other third-party reports of alleged wrongdoing.

IRS Audit Issues. The audit of a nonprofit, tax-exempt organization is likely to entail one or more of the following issues:

- The organization's ongoing eligibility for exempt status
- Public charity versus private foundation classification
- Unrelated business activity
- Extensive advocacy undertakings
- One or more excise tax issues
- Whether the organization filed required returns and reports
- Payment of employment taxes
- Involvement in a form of joint venture

Types of IRS Examinations. There are four basic types of IRS examinations of nonprofit, tax-exempt organizations. A compliance check is not technically an audit. Also, there are special procedures for inquiries and examinations of churches.

Common among the types of IRS examinations of tax-exempt organizations are *field examinations,* in which one or more revenue agents (typically, however, only one) review the books, records, and other documents and information of the exempt organization under examination, on the premises of the organization or at the office of its representative. IRS procedures require the examiner to establish the scope of the examination, state the documentation requirements, and summarize the examination techniques (including interviews and tours of facilities).

The IRS's office correspondence examination program entails examinations of tax-exempt organizations by means of office interviews, correspondence, or both. An *office interview* case is one in which the examiner requests an exempt organization's records and reviews them in an IRS office; this may include a conference with a representative of the organization. This type of examination is likely to be of a smaller exempt organization, where the records are not extensive and the issues not particularly complex. A *correspondence examination* involves an IRS request for information from an exempt organization by letter, fax, or e-mail communication.

Office or correspondence examinations generally are limited in scope, usually focusing on no more than three issues, conducted by lower-grade examiners. The import of these examinations should not be minimized, however. A correspondence examination can be converted to an office examination. Worse, an office examination can be upgraded to a field examination.

The newest of the IRS audit approaches is the *team examination program* (TEP). TEP initiatives have a fundamental objective, which is to avoid a fragmenting of the exempt organization examination process by using multiple agents. The essential characteristics of the TEP approach are that the team examinations are being used in connection with a wider array of exempt organizations, the number of revenue agents involved in an examination is somewhat smaller, and the revenue agents are less likely to semipermanently carve out office space in which to live at the exempt organization undergoing the examination. The TEP agents, however, are still likely to want an office for occasional visits and storage of computers and documents.

A TEP case generally is one in which the annual information return of the tax-exempt organization involved reflects either total revenue or assets greater than $100 million (or, in the case of a private foundation, $500 million). Nonetheless, the IRS may initiate a team examination if the case would benefit (from the government's perspective) from the TEP approach or if there is no annual information return filing requirement. IRS examination procedures include a presumption that the team examination approach will be used in all cases satisfying the TEP criteria.

In a TEP case, the examination will proceed under the direction of a case manager. One or more tax-exempt-organizations revenue agents will be accompanied by others, such as employee plans specialists, actuarial examiners, engineers, excise tax agents, international examiners, computer audit specialists, income tax revenue agents, or economists. These examinations may last about two years; a postexamination critique may lead to a cycling of the examination into subsequent years. The IRS examination procedures stipulate the planning that case managers, assisted by team coordinators, should engage in when launching a team examination; these procedures also provide for the exempt organization's involvement in this planning process.

The foregoing types of IRS audits are those normally used to examine nonprofit, tax-exempt organizations. The IRS has within it a Criminal Investigation Division, however, the agents of which occasionally are involved in exempt organizations examinations.

Compliance Checks. An overlay to the IRS program of examinations of tax-exempt organizations is the agency's *compliance check projects,* which focus on specific compliance issues. These projects, orchestrated by the Exempt Organizations Compliance Unit, are a recent invention of the IRS; they are designed to maximize the agency's return (gaining data and assessing compliance) on its investigation efforts. The IRS stated that its exempt organizations examination and compliance-check processes are among the "variety of tools at [the agency's] disposal to make certain that tax-exempt organizations comply with federal tax law designed to ensure they are entitled to any tax exemption they may claim."

Usually, in the commencement of these projects, the IRS contacts exempt organizations only by mail to obtain information pertaining to the particular issue. An exempt organization has a greater chance of being a compliance check target than the subject of a conventional audit. A compliance check, however, can blossom into an examination.

Recent compliance check projects have focused on executive compensation, political campaign activities by public charities, hospitals' compliance with criteria for their exemption, intermediate sanctions reporting, tax-exempt bond financing, community foundations' law compliance, various aspects of the operations of colleges and universities, public charities with large fundraising costs, and exempt organizations with considerable unrelated business income.

CHAPTER THREE

THE CHANGING CONTEXT
OF NONPROFIT LEADERSHIP
AND MANAGEMENT

Lester M. Salamon

The nonprofit sector has long been the hidden subcontinent on the social landscape of American life, regularly revered but rarely seriously scrutinized or understood. In part, this has been due to the role that these organizations play in our national mythologies and in the political ideologies that have been constructed upon them. Indeed, a lively ideological contest has long raged over the extent to which we can rely on nonprofit institutions to handle critical public needs, with conservatives focusing laser-like on the sector's strengths in order to fend off calls for greater reliance on government, and liberals often restricting their attention to its weaknesses instead in order to justify calls for greater government action. Through it all, though largely unheralded and perhaps unrecognized by either side, a classically American compromise has taken shape. This compromise was forged early in the nation's history, but it was broadened and solidified in the 1960s. Under it, nonprofit organizations in an ever-widening range of fields were made the beneficiaries of government support to provide a growing array of services—from health care to scientific research—that Americans wanted but were reluctant to have government directly provide (Salamon and Abramson, 1982, 1996; Salamon, 1987; Smith and Lipsky, 1993). More than any other single factor, this government-nonprofit partnership is

This chapter draws heavily on Lester M. Salamon, *The Resilient Sector: The State of Nonprofit America* (Brookings Institution Press, 2003).

responsible for the emergence of the U.S. nonprofit sector in the shape we see it in today.

During the past thirty years, however, that compromise has come under considerable assault. At the same time, the country's nonprofit institutions have faced an extraordinary range of other challenges as well—significant demographic shifts, fundamental changes in public policy and public attitudes, new commercial impulses, growing competition from for-profit providers, shifts in the basic structure of key industries in which nonprofits are involved, massive technological developments, and changes in lifestyle, to cite just a few. Although nonprofit America has responded with creativity to many of these challenges, the responses have pulled it in directions that are, at best, not well understood, and at worst, corrosive of the sector's special character and role.

This changing context has fundamentally shaped the nature of contemporary nonprofit operations. No serious understanding of nonprofit leadership and management can proceed very far, therefore, without taking this changing context into account.

The purpose of this chapter is to examine some of the salient features of this changing context of nonprofit action. To do so, the discussion falls into three main parts. The first, Challenges and Opportunities: The Changing Context of Nonprofit Action, examines some of the major challenges that American nonprofit organizations have confronted over the recent past and some of the opportunities they have also had available to them. The second, The Nonprofit Response: A Story of Resilience, then assesses the implications these challenges and opportunities have had for nonprofit managers and how the sector's leaders and organizations have responded. Finally, the third part, Implications for Nonprofit Managers, identifies the risks that these responses have brought with them and the steps that may be needed to reduce them.

The fundamental impression that emerges from this analysis is a message of *resilience* of a set of institutions and traditions that has been facing enormous challenges and also important opportunities, but that also has been finding ways to respond to both, often with considerable creativity and resolve. Indeed, nonprofit America appears to be well along in a fundamental process of "reengineering" that calls to mind the similar process that large segments of America's business sector has undergone since the late 1980s (Hammer and Champy, 1993, 1994; Carr and Johnson, 1995). Faced with an increasingly competitive and changing environment, nonprofit organizations and the institutions and traditions that support them have been called on to make fundamental changes in how they operate. And that is just what they have been doing.

Like all processes of change, this one is far from even. Some organizations have thus been swept up in the winds of change while others have hardly felt a breeze, or having felt it, have not been in a position to respond. What is more, it is far from clear which group has made the right decision or left the sector as a whole better off, since the consequences of some of the changes are far from certain and at any rate are mixed.

Challenges and Opportunities: The Changing Context of Nonprofit Action

Nonprofit America has found itself in an extraordinary time of testing in the recent past because of the severe recession that struck towards the end of the century's first decade and continues at this writing. To be sure, it is not alone in this. For-profit corporations and governments have also experienced enormous challenges over the past thirty years. But the challenges facing nonprofit organizations are especially daunting, since they go to the heart of this sector's operations and raise questions about its very existence. Fortunately, however, the sector has also enjoyed a variety of important opportunities. In this section we examine the mixture of challenges and opportunities that has been shaping the context of nonprofit action and that seems likely to continue to do so into the foresee-able future.

Challenges

The challenges recently facing nonprofit organizations in the United States can be grouped for convenience under four main headings.

The Fiscal Challenge. In the first place, these organizations have confronted a significant fiscal squeeze. To be sure, fiscal distress has been a way of life for this sector throughout its history. But this eased significantly during World War II, and even more so in the 1960s, when the federal government expanded its funding, first, of scientific research, and then of a wide range of health and social services. What is not widely recognized is that the government efforts to stimulate science and overcome poverty and ill health during this period relied heavily on nonprofit organizations for their operation, following a pattern that had been established early in our nation's history (Whitehead, 1973; Warner, 1894; for a more complete analysis of this system of government–nonprofit rela-tions see Wilgoren, 2003). By the late 1970s as a consequence, federal support to American nonprofit organizations outdistanced private charitable support by a factor of 2:1, and state and local governments provided additional aid. What is more, this support percolated through a wide swath of the sector, providing needed financial nourishment to colleges, universities, hospitals, health clinics, day care centers, nursing homes, residential treatment facilities, employment and training centers, family service agencies, drug abuse prevention programs, and many more. Indeed, much of the modern nonprofit sector took shape during this period as a direct outgrowth of expanded government support (Salamon and Abramson, 1982; Salamon, 1995).

Federal Retrenchment. This widespread pattern of government support to nonprofit organizations suffered a severe shock, however, in the early 1980s. Committed to a policy of fiscal restraint, and seemingly unaware of the extent to which public resources were underwriting private, nonprofit action, the Reagan administration launched a significant assault on federal spending in precisely the areas where federal support to nonprofit organizations was most extensive—social and human services, education and training, community development, and non-hospital health. Although the budget cuts that occurred during this period were nowhere near as severe as originally proposed, federal support to nonprofit organizations, outside of Medicare and Medicaid, the large federal health finance programs, declined by approximately 25 percent in real dollar terms in the early 1980s and did not return to its 1980 level until the latter 1990s (Abramson, Salamon, and Steurle, 1999). Although some state governments boosted their own spending in many of these fields, the increases were not sufficient to offset the federal reductions. Indeed, outside of pensions, public education, and health, overall government social welfare spending declined by more than $30 billion between 1981 and 1989. Nonprofit organizations in the fields of community development, employment and training, social services, and community health were particularly hard-hit by these reductions.

Although, as we will see, these fiscal pressures eased significantly during the 1990s, the experience of the 1980s and early 1990s left a lingering fiscal scar. That scar has now been reopened, first, in the early years of the new century by a combination of tax reductions, economic recession, and increased military and anti-terror spending that caused new cutbacks in health, education, and social welfare spending, and therefore new pressures on nonprofit finances; and second, by the deep recession that struck the nation late in the century's first decade and generated enormous new strains on nonprofit operations (Wilgoren, 2003; Rosenbaum, 2003; Salamon and Geller, 2009).

From Producer to Consumer Subsidies: The Changing Forms of Public Support. Not just the amount, but also the form of government support to the nonprofit sector changed during this period, moreover. For one thing, during the 1980s and 1990s government program managers were encouraged to promote for-profit involvement in government contract work, including that for human services (Kettl, 1993). More significantly, instead of relying on producer-side subsidies such as grants and contracts to finance services, the federal government shifted to forms of assistance such as vouchers and tax expenditures that channel aid to the consumers of services instead, thus requiring nonprofits to compete for clients in the market, where for-profits have traditionally had the edge (Salamon, 2002c). Already by 1980, the majority (53 percent) of federal assistance to nonprofit organizations took the form of such consumer subsidies, much of it through the Medicare and Medicaid programs. By 1986 this stood at 70 percent, and it continued to rise into the 1990s (Salamon, 1995, p. 208).

In part, this shift toward consumer subsidies resulted from the concentration of the budget cuts of the 1980s on the so-called discretionary spending programs, which tended to be producer-side grant and contract programs, while Medicare and Medicaid—both of them consumer-side subsidies—continued to grow. In part also, however, the shift toward consumer-side subsidies reflected the ascendance of conservative political forces that favored forms of assistance that maximized consumer choice in the marketplace. The price of securing conservative support for new or expanded programs of relevance to nonprofit organizations in the late 1980s and early 1990s, therefore, was to make them vouchers or tax expenditures. The new Child Care and Development Block Grant enacted in 1990 and then reauthorized and expanded as part of the welfare reform legislation in 1996, for example, specifically gave states the option to use the $5 billion in federal funds provided for day care to finance voucher payments to eligible families rather than grants or contracts to day-care providers, and most states exercised this option. As of 1998, therefore, well over 80 percent of the children receiving day-care assistance under this program were receiving it through such voucher certificates and an additional $2 billion in federal day-care subsidies was delivered through a special child-care tax credit (U.S. House, Committee on Ways and Means, 2000, pp. 912, 923). Nearly $7 billion was thus provided in new consumer-side day-care subsidies, much more than the $2.8 billion allocated for producer-side subsidies to social service providers for day care and all other forms of social services under the federal government's Social Services Block Grant. What is more, by 2009, a decade later, the value of the tax subsidies had doubled to $4.3 billion (U.S. Office of Management and Budget, 2010, p. 217). Nonprofit day-care providers, like their counterparts in other fields, have thus been thrown increasingly into the private market to secure even public funding for their activities. In the process, they were obliged to master complex billing and reimbursement systems and to learn how to "market" their services to potential "customers." Worse yet, the reimbursement rates in many of these programs have often failed to keep pace with rising costs, putting a further squeeze on nonprofit budgets and making it harder to sustain mission-critical functions such as advocacy and charity care (Gray and Schlesinger, 2002).

Not only did government support to nonprofit organizations change its form during this period, but so did important elements of private support. The most notable development here was the emergence of "managed care" in the health field, displacing the traditional pattern of fee-for-service medicine. By 1997, close to 75 percent of the employees in medium and large establishments, and 62 percent of the employees in small establishments, were covered by some type of managed care plan (U.S. Census Bureau, 2000, p. 119). More recently, managed care has expanded into the social services field, subjecting nonprofit drug treatment, rehabilitation service, and mental health treatment facilities to the same competitive pressures and reimbursement limits as hospitals have been confronting.

Tepid Growth of Private Giving. Adding to the fiscal pressure nonprofits have been facing has been the continued inability of private philanthropy to offset cutbacks in government support and finance expanded nonprofit responses to community needs. To be sure, private giving has grown considerably over the recent past. Between 1998 and 2004, for example, nonprofit revenue from private philanthropy grew by nearly 25 percent after adjusting for inflation.[1] But overall nonprofit revenue increased by nearly 30 percent, so that the giving share of the total actually declined. Indeed, as a share of personal income, private giving has been declining steadily in the United States: from an average of 1.89 percent in the early 1970s, down to 1.75 percent in the early 1980s, and to 1.64 percent in the early to mid-1990s (Salamon, 2003, p. 20). Although this trend was reversed in the boom times of the late 1990s, moreover, it resumed its downward course in the early part of the first decade of the new century (AAFRC Trust for Philanthropy, 2002, p. 170). As a consequence, private philanthropy actually lost ground as a share of total nonprofit income, falling from 18 percent of the total outside of religion in 1977 to 12 percent in 1997, and slipping to below 12 percent by 2004 (Salamon, forthcoming). Given the emasculation of assets caused by the recession that began in 2008, moreover, these downward pressures have only intensified. Indeed, overall private giving declined in absolute, and not just relative, terms in 2008 (Giving USA, 2009, p. 1).

The Competition Challenge. In addition to a fiscal challenge, nonprofit America has also faced a serious competition challenge. This, too, is not a wholly new development. But the changing forms of public sector support coupled with the difficulties nonprofit organizations have confronted in securing capital for new technologies seem to have enticed for-profit competitors into an ever-widening

TABLE 3.1. GROWING FOR-PROFIT COMPETITION IN SELECTED FIELDS, 1982–1997

Dimension Field	Percentage nonprofit		Percentage change in relative nonprofit share
	1982	1997	
Employment			
Child day care	52	38	−27
Job training	93	89	−4
Individual and family services	94	91	−3
Home health	60	28	−53
Kidney dialysis centers	22	15	−32
Facilities, Participation			
Dialysis centers	58[a]	32	−45
Rehabilitation hospitals	70[a]	36	−50
Home health agencies	64[a]	33	−48
Health maintenance organizations	65[a]	26	−60
Residential treatment facilities for children	87[b]	68	−22
Psychiatric hospitals	19[a]	16	−16
Hospices	89[c]	76	−15
Mental health clinics	64[b]	57	−11
Higher education enrollments	96	89	−7
Nursing homes	20[b]	28	+40
Acute care hospitals	58[a]	59	+2

Source: U.S. Census Bureau 1999; Gray and Schlesinger 2002, pp. 68–69; National Center for Education Statistics, 2000, pp. 202–203, 209.

[a]Initial year for data is 1985, not 1982.

[b]Initial year for data is 1986, not 1982.

[c]Initial year for data is 1992.

range of fields and to have given them a competitive edge. Thus, as shown in Table 3.1, the nonprofit share of day-care jobs dropped from 52 percent to 38 percent between 1982 and 1997, a decline of some 27 percent. Similarly sharp declines in the relative nonprofit share occurred among rehabilitation hospitals, home health agencies, health maintenance organizations, kidney dialysis centers, mental health clinics, and hospices. In many of these fields the absolute number of nonprofit facilities continued to grow, but the for-profit growth outpaced it. And in at least one crucial field—acute care hospitals—whereas the nonprofit *share* increased slightly, a significant reduction occurred in the *absolute number* of nonprofit (as well as public) facilities, so that the for-profit share of the total increased even more.

TABLE 3.2. CHANGE IN NONPROFIT SHARE OF EMPLOYMENT, SELECTED FIELDS, 1997–2007

Field	Change in Nonprofit Share
Outpatient care facilities	−8%
Home health care facilities	−19%
Specialty hospitals (other than psychiatric)	−13%
Nursing care facilities	−3%
Community care facilities for the elderly	−20%
Other residential care facilities	−3%
Individual and family services	−23%
Child day care	−2%

Source: U.S. Census Bureau, 2000, 2009.

This trend has continued in more recent years, however. Thus, as Table 3.2 reveals, between 1997 and 2007 the nonprofit sector continued to lose ground to for-profit providers in terms of its share of employment in the fields of individual and family services (−23 percent), home health care (−19 percent), day care (−2 percent); and these fields were joined by outpatient care centers (−8 percent), specialty hospitals (−13 percent), nursing care facilities (−3 percent), and community care facilities for the elderly (−20 percent) (U.S. Census Bureau, 2000, and 2009).

The range of for-profit firms competing with nonprofits has grown increasingly broad, moreover. For example, the recent welfare reform legislation, which seeks to move large numbers of welfare recipients from welfare dependence to employment, attracted defense contractors like Lockheed-Martin into the social welfare field. What these firms offer is less knowledge of human services than information-processing technology and contract management skills gained from serving as master contractors on huge military system projects, precisely the skills now needed to manage the subcontracting systems required to prepare welfare recipients for work. Similarly, for-profits have made substantial in-roads in the field of higher education. Between 1980 and 2005, while enrollment in public and nonprofit higher education institutions each grew by roughly 37 percent, enrollment in for-profit institutions expanded by 800 percent—from just over 110,000 to more than 1 million students (U.S. Department of Education, 2007). Even the sacrosanct field of charitable fundraising has recently experienced a significant for-profit incursion in the form of financial service firms such as Fidelity and Merrill Lynch. By 2000, the Fidelity Charitable Gift Fund had attracted more assets than the nation's largest community foundation, and distributed three times as much in grants (AAFRC Trust for Philanthropy, 2001, p. 53).

The Effectiveness Challenge. One consequence of the increased competition nonprofits are facing has been to intensify the pressure on them to perform, and to demonstrate that performance. This runs counter to long-standing theories in the nonprofit field that have emphasized this sector's distinctive advantage precisely in fields where "information asymmetry" makes it difficult to demonstrate performance, and where "trust" is consequently needed instead (Hansmann, 1981).

In the current climate, however, such theories have few remaining adherents, at least among those who control the sector's purse strings. Government managers, themselves under pressure to demonstrate results because of the recent Government Performance and Results Act, are increasingly pressing their nonprofit contractors to deliver measurable results, too. Not to be outdone, prominent philanthropic institutions have jumped onto the performance bandwagon. United Way of America, for example, thus launched a bold performance measurement system in the mid-1990s complete with Web site, performance measurement manual, and video in order to induce member agencies to require performance measurement as a condition of local funding. Numerous foundations have moved in a similar direction, increasing the emphasis on evaluation both of their grantees and of their own programming (Porter and Kramer, 1999). In addition, a new "venture philanthropy" model stressing focused attention on performance measures has been attracting increased attention and numerous adherents (Letts, Ryan, and Grossman, 1997).

The Technology Challenge. Pressures from for-profit competitors have also accelerated the demands on nonprofits to incorporate new technology into their operations. Indeed, technology has become one of the great wildcards in the evolution of the contemporary nonprofit sector, as it has of the contemporary for-profit and government sectors. Like the other challenges identified here, technology's impact is by no means wholly negative. For example, new information technology is increasing the capacity of nonprofits to advocate, reducing the costs of mobilizing constituents, and connecting to policymakers and allies. Technology is also opening new ways to tap charitable contributions. The September 11 tragedy may well have marked a turning point in this regard, since some 10 percent of the funds raised came via the Internet (Wallace, 2001, p. 22), and the response to the Haiti earthquake in 2010 saw Internet giving come fully into its own.

But enticing as the opportunities opened by technological change may be to the nation's nonprofit institutions, they pose equally enormous challenges. This is due in important measure to the capital requirements that technology poses, requirements that are especially difficult for nonprofits to meet because of their inability to enter the equity markets and raise funds. But new technologies are also raising a variety of philosophical issues involving such matters as creative control and intellectual property rights in the arts (Wyszomirski, 2002, pp. 198–202).

The Opportunities

But challenges are not all that nonprofit America has confronted in the recent past. It has also had available a number of opportunities, four of which deserve special attention.

Social and Demographic Shifts. In the first place, nonprofit America has been the beneficiary of a significant range of social and demographic shifts that have increased not only the need, but also the demand, for its services. Included here are the following:

- The doubling of the country's population of seniors seventy-five years and older between 1980 and 2008 on top of a doubling of the sixty-five and older population between 1960 and 2000 and the prospect that there will be two times as many seventy-five-year-old and over Americans in 2030 as in 2010, which will increase the need for nursing home and other elderly services.
- The jump in the labor force participation rate for women, particularly married women, from less than 20 percent in 1960 to 64 percent in 1998, and its holding at that level since, which translates into increased demand for child-care services (U.S. Census Bureau 2000, pp. 408–409; U.S. Census Bureau, 2010, Table 576).
- The doubling of the country's divorce rate from one in every four marriages in the 1960s to one in every two marriages in the 1980s and thereafter; and a resulting sharp jump in the number of children involved in divorces from less than 500,000 in 1960 to over 1 million per year in the 1980s and 1990s (U.S. Census Bureau 2000, p. 101).
- A five-fold increase in the number of out-of-wedlock births, from roughly 225,000 in 1960 to more than 1.25 million per year by the mid-1990s, and a further increase beyond, to the point where the share of births to unmarried mothers reached 40 percent in 2007, which has increased the need for a variety of work-readiness, health, and child-care services (U.S. Census Bureau 2000, p. 71; U.S. Census Bureau 2010, Table 89).
- The nearly tripling that occurred in the number of people obtaining legal permanent resident status from 3.3 million in the decade of the 1960s to 8.3 million in just the first eight years of the decade of the 2000s (U.S. Census Bureau, 2010, Table 68).

Taken together, these and other sociodemographic changes have expanded the demand for many of the services that nonprofit organizations have traditionally provided, such as child day care, home health and nursing home care for the elderly, family counseling, foster care, relocation assistance, and substance abuse treatment and prevention. The pressure on the foster care system alone, for example, has ballooned as the number of children in foster care doubled between the early 1980s and the early 1990s. At the same time, the welfare reform legislation enacted in 1996, with its stress on job readiness, created additional demand for the services that nonprofits typically offer. The demand for these services has spread well beyond the poor and now encompasses middle class households with resources to pay for them, a phenomenon that one analyst has called "the transformation of social services" (Gilbert, 1977).

The New Philanthropy. Also working to the benefit of the nonprofit sector are a series of developments potentially affecting private philanthropy. These include the *intergenerational transfer of wealth* between the Depression-era generation and the postwar baby boomers that has been anticipated over the next forty years (Avery and Rendell, 1990; Havens and Schervish, 1999), though the short drop in home prices beginning in 2008 and the rising cost of health care for the baby boom generation seems likely to take a large bite out of this; the greater corporate willingness to engage in partnerships and collaborations with nonprofit organizations that has resulted from globalization (Smith, 1994; Nelson, 1996; Salamon, 2010); the dot-com phenomenon, which accumulated substantial fortunes in the hands of a small group of high-tech entrepreneurs, some of whom have turned their newfound wealth into charitable ventures (Bishop and Green, 2008); and the emergence of a host of new actors and new tools for channeling private investment capital into support of social and environmental objectives (Godeke and Bauer, 2008; Salamon, 2011 [forthcoming]; Wood and Hoff, n.d. [2007]). Together, these developments are injecting a substantial amount of new blood and new energy into the philanthropic field.

Greater Visibility and Policy Salience. Another factor working to the advantage of nonprofit organizations has been a recent spate of political and policy developments that has substantially increased the visibility of these organizations. This has included the neoliberal ideology popularized by the Thatcher and Reagan regimes in the United Kingdom and the United States, with their anti-government rhetoric and emphasis on the private sector; the significant role that "civil society" organizations played in the collapse of communism in Central Europe in the latter 1980s; the recent emphasis on the importance of "social capital" to the development of democracy and the market system; and the Obama administration's support for "social innovation" and the "social entrepreneurs" that promote it.

Resumption of Government Social Welfare Spending Growth. Finally, and perhaps most important, government social welfare spending, which had stalled and in some cases reversed course in the early 1980s, resumed its growth in the late 1980s and into the 1990s. The principal reason for this was a steady broadening of eligibility and coverage under the basic federal entitlement programs—Medicare, Medicaid, and the Supplemental Security Income Program (SSI). For example, the number of children covered by SSI, a program originally created to provide income support to the elderly poor, increased from 71,000 in 1974 to over 1 million in 1996, largely as a result of aggressive efforts to enroll disabled children following a 1990 Supreme Court decision that liberalized SSI eligibility requirements. Medicaid coverage was extended to fifty distinct subgroups during the latter 1980s and early 1990s, including various groups of women and children, the homeless, newly legalized aliens, AIDS sufferers, recipients of adoption assistance and foster care, and broader categories of the disabled and the elderly. At the same time, states found new veins of federal funding to tap as old ones ran dry. The most striking example here is what became known as the "Medicaid maximization strategy," under which programs formerly funded entirely by the states, or by federal discretionary programs subjected to Reagan-era budget cuts, were reconfigured to make them eligible for funding under the more lucrative and still-growing Medicaid or SSI programs (Coughlin, Ku, and Holahan, 1994; U.S. House, Committee on Ways and Means, 2000, p. 901). Between 1980 and 1998, as a consequence, Medicaid coverage doubled and the program was transformed from a relatively narrow health and nursing home program into a veritable social service entitlement program (U.S. House, Committee on Ways and Means, 2000, p. 892–893).

What is more, federal policymakers also created a variety of new programs during this period to improve the life chances of children, and provide assistance for homeless people, AIDS sufferers, children and youth, people with disabilities, voluntarism promotion, drug and alcohol treatment, and home health care (Smith, 2002). Renewed federal activism was mirrored, and in some cases anticipated, moreover, by activism at the state and local level.

Thanks to these and other changes, spending on the major federal entitlement programs jumped more than 175 percent in real terms between 1980 and 1994, more than three times the 52 percent real growth in the U.S. gross domestic product (See Table 3.3). Although reimbursement rates under these programs were still often insufficient to cover the full costs of the services, the expansion in the pool of resources available was substantial. What is more, Medicaid spending

TABLE 3.3. GROWTH IN FEDERAL ENTITLEMENT PROGRAM SPENDING, 1980–2008 (IN CONSTANT 2005 $)

Program	Amount			Change (%)	
	1980	1994	2008	1980–1994	1994–1908
Medicare	93.4	239.6	423.0	219%	45%
Medicaid	62.7	200.5	291.8	220%	75%
Supplemental Security Income	15.2	32.8	35.1	115%	7%
Total	171.3	472.9	749.9	176%	59%
Gross Domestic Product (GDP)	5,839.0	8,870.7	13,312.2	52%	50%

Source: U.S Department of Commerce, Bureau of Economic Analysis, National Income and Product Accounts, http://www.bea.gov/national/nipaweb/Index.asp, Table 3.12. Accessed January 23, 2010.

continued to grow at a rate that was 50 percent greater than the overall growth rate of GDP during the subsequent fourteen-year period, although the growth rate of some of the other entitlement programs slowed in this more recent period.

Fortunately for nonprofits even during at least a portion of this latter period, however, the federal welfare reform legislation enacted in 1996 produced a fiscal windfall for the states when welfare rolls surprisingly began to fall while federal payments to the states remained fixed at their 1996 level. Under the welfare reform legislation, states were permitted to use these funds to finance a variety of work-readiness, child-care, and related human service programs considered necessary to help welfare recipients find work, and many of these are run by nonprofit organizations.

The Nonprofit Response: A Story of Resilience

How has nonprofit America responded to this combination of challenges and opportunities? Conventional wisdom would lead us not to expect much. Nonprofits are not to be trusted, Professor Regina Herzlinger (1996, p. 98) thus explained to readers of the *Harvard Business Review* in 1996, because they lack the three basic accountability measures that ensure effective and efficient operations in the business world: the self-interest of owners, competition, and the ultimate bottom-line measure of profitability.

In fact, however, nonprofit America has responded with amazing resilience. To be sure, the resulting changes are hardly universal. What is more, there are serious questions about whether they are in a wholly desirable direction. Yet there is no denying the dominant picture of resilience, adaptation, and change. More specifically, four broad threads of change are apparent.

Overall Growth

Perhaps the most vivid evidence of the nonprofit sector's resilience is the striking record of recent sector growth. Between 1977 and 1997, the revenues of America's nonprofit organizations increased 144 percent after adjusting for inflation, nearly twice the 81 percent growth rate of the nation's economy. Nonprofit revenue growth was particularly robust among arts and culture organizations, social service organizations, and health organizations, for each of which the rate of growth was at least twice that of the U.S. economy. However, even the most laggard components of the nonprofit sector (education and civic organizations) grew at a rate that equaled or exceeded overall U.S. economic growth (Salamon, 2003, p. 51).

Growth occurred, moreover, not only in the revenues of the sector, which can be affected by the performance of just the larger organizations, but also in the number of organizations. Between 1977 and 1997 the number of 501(c)(3) and 501(c)(4) organizations registered with the Internal Revenue Service increased by 115 percent, or about 23,000 organizations a year, and growth was faster in the more recent part of the period than in the earlier part (Weitzman et al., 2002, p. 4–5).

This growth rate moderated a bit in the subsequent eight years, between 1997 and 2005 (the latest year for which data are available). During this period as well, however, nonprofit revenues, adjusted for inflation, grew at a rate twice the rate of growth of U.S. GDP (54 percent vs. 26 percent). Nonprofit health organizations reported the most robust growth during this period, led by hospitals, which boosted their revenues by 66 percent. But education and human service organizations also exceeded the rate of growth of GDP (46 percent and 43 percent, respectively, vs. 26 percent). Revenue growth was least robust among nonprofit arts and culture organizations, but even these kept pace with overall GDP growth (27 percent vs. 26 percent).[2]

Commercialization

What accounts for this record of robust growth? Although many factors are responsible the dominant one appears to be the vigor with which nonprofit America embraced the spirit and the techniques of the market. The clearest reflection of this is the substantial rise in nonprofit income from fees and

TABLE 3.4. CHANGING STRUCTURE OF NONPROFIT REVENUE, 1977–1997

Revenue Source	Change (%), 1977–1997	All		Without Religion		Share of Revenue Growth, 1977–1997	
		1977	1997	1977	1997	All	Without religion
Fees, charges	145	46	47	51	51	47	51
Government	195	27	33	31	37	37	42
Philanthropy	90	27	20	18	12	16	8
Total	144	100	100	100	100	100	100

Source: Weitzman et al., 2002; Council of Economic Advisors, 2002.

charges, indicative of the success with which nonprofit organizations succeeded in marketing their services to a clientele increasingly able to afford them. In fact, even with religious congregations included, fees and charges accounted for nearly half (47 percent) of the growth in nonprofit revenue between 1977 and 1997—more than any other source (see Table 3.4).

Fee income not only grew in scale, but also spread to ever broader components of the sector. Thus, after adjusting for inflation, the fee income of arts and culture organizations jumped 272 percent, of civic organizations 220 percent, and of social service organizations over 500 percent between 1977 and 1997 (Salamon, 2003, p. 52). Even religious organizations boosted their commercial income during this period, largely from the sale or rental of church property (Chaves, 2002, p. 284).

What is more, this trend seems to have intensified in more recent years. Nonprofit revenue grew between 1998 and 2004 to the degree that fee income became 51 percent of total nonprofit revenue with religious congregations included.[3]

Another reflection of the commercialization of the nonprofit sector has been its success in adapting to the new terrain of public funding, which has also grown more commercial as a consequence of the shift to "consumer-side" subsidies. Despite this shift, nonprofits managed to boost their government support 195 percent in real terms between 1977 and 1997, proportionally more than any other source, and these figures do not include the windfall from welfare reform. Government accounted for 37 percent of the sector's substantial growth during this period as a consequence, increasing its share of the total from 27 percent in 1977 to 33 percent in 1997. And with religious congregations excluded (since they do not receive much government support), government's share of the sector's revenue increased from 31 percent to 37 percent (Salamon, 2003, p. 54).

And this process, too, continued in more recent years, so that by 2004, nonprofit revenue from government, even with religious congregations included, stood at 38 percent.[4]

Also indicative of the commercialization of the nonprofit sector has been the significant growth of commercial ventures within the sector and the expanding pattern of partnerships with business. Commercial ventures such as museum gift shops and online stores, the rental of social halls by churches, and licensing agreements between research universities and commercial firms, have long been a feature of nonprofit operations, but they have recently undergone substantial growth (Lipman and Schwinn, 2001, p. 25). Especially interesting has been the emergence of "social ventures," that is, business ventures that serve not primarily to generate income but to carry out the basic charitable missions of nonprofit organizations (such as training ex-convicts for productive jobs by establishing a catering business in which they work and are trained) (Young and Salamon, 2002, pp. 431–434).

These developments point, in turn, to a broader and deeper penetration of the market culture into the fabric of nonprofit operations. Nonprofit organizations are increasingly "marketing" their "products," viewing their clients as "customers," segmenting their markets, differentiating their output, identifying their "market niche," formulating "business plans," and generally incorporating the language, and the style, of business management into the operation of their agencies. Indeed, management expert Kevin Kearns (2000, p. 25) argues that nonprofit executives are now "among the most entrepreneurial managers to be found anywhere, including the private for-profit sector."

As the culture of the market has spread into the fabric of nonprofit operations, old suspicions between the nonprofit and business sectors have significantly softened, opening the way for nonprofit acceptance of the business community not simply as a source of charitable support but as a legitimate partner for a wide range of nonprofit endeavors. This perspective has been championed by charismatic sector leaders such as Billy Shore, who urge nonprofits to stop thinking about how to get donations and start thinking about how to "market" the considerable "assets" they control, including particularly the asset represented by their reputations (Shore, 1995). This has meshed nicely with the growing readiness of businesses to forge strategic alliances with nonprofits in order to generate "reputational capital." The upshot has been a notable upsurge in strategic partnerships between nonprofit organizations and businesses manifested, for example, in a variety of "cause-related marketing" arrangements and increasingly in broader partnerships that mobilize corporate personnel, finances, and know-how in support of nonprofit activities (Austin, 2000).

Professionalization

If commercialization has been the chief vehicle for the nonprofit sector's response to the challenges and opportunities it has recently faced, professionalization has been a close second. Nonprofit America has undergone a massive professionalization over the past two decades. This process began in the fundraising sphere, where a veritable revolution has occurred as reflected in the emergence and growth of specialized fundraising organizations, such as the National Society of Fund-Raising Executives (1960) now the Association of Fund-Raising Professionals (AFP); the Council for the Advancement and Support of Education (1974); the Association for Healthcare Philanthropy (1967); and the National Committee for Planned Giving (1988). Equally impressive has been the transformation in the technology of charitable giving through the development of such devices as workplace solicitation, telethons, direct mail campaigns, telephone solicitation, e-philanthropy, and a host of complex "planning giving" vehicles such as "charitable remainder trusts." Entire organizations have surfaced to manage this process of extracting funds, and for-profit businesses, such as Fidelity Investments, have also gotten into the act.

Other evidence of the growing professionalization of the nonprofit field has included the construction of a set of sectorwide infrastructure institutions, such as Independent Sector, the Council on Foundations, the Association of Small Foundations, the Forum of Regional Associations of Grantmakers, and state nonprofit organizations (Abramson and McCarthy, 2002); the development of a sizable research and educational apparatus focused on this sector, including nonprofit degree or certificate programs in close to 100 colleges and universities; and the creation of a nonprofit press (*The Chronicle of Philanthropy*, *Nonprofit Times*, *The Nonprofit Quarterly*). What was once a scatteration of largely overlooked institutions has thus become a booming cottage industry attracting organizations, personnel, publications, services, conferences, Web sites, head-hunting firms, consultants, rituals, and fads—all premised on the proposition that nonprofit organizations are distinctive institutions with enough commonalities despite their many differences to be studied, represented, serviced, and trained as a group.

Implications for Nonprofit Managers

Nonprofit America has thus responded with extraordinary creativity and resilience to the challenges and opportunities it has confronted over the past twenty years. The sector has grown enormously as a consequence—in numbers, in revenues, and in the range of purposes it serves. In addition, it seems to have expanded its competencies and improved its management, though these are more difficult to gauge with precision. To be sure, not all components of the sector have experienced these changes to the same degree or even in the same direction. Yet what is striking is how widespread the adaptations seem to have been.

On balance, these changes seem to have worked to the advantage of the nonprofit sector, strengthening its fiscal base, upgrading its operations, enlisting new partners and new resources in its activities, and generally improving its reputation for effectiveness. But they have also brought significant risks, and the risks may well overwhelm the gains.

The Risks

More specifically, the nonprofit sector's response to the challenges of the past twenty years, creative as it has been, has exposed the sector to at least five important risks.

Growing Identity Crisis. In the first place, nonprofit America is increasingly confronting an identity crisis as a result of a growing tension between the market character of the services it is providing and the continued nonprofit character of the institutions providing them. This tension has become especially stark in the health field, where third-party payers, such as Medicare and private HMOs, increasingly downplay values other than actual service cost in setting reimbursement rates; where bond rating agencies discount community service in determining the economic worth of bond issues and hence the price that nonprofit hospitals have to pay for capital; and where fierce for-profit competition leaves little room for conscious pursuit of social goals (Gray and Schlesinger, 2002, pp. 72, 74–75). Left to their own devices, nonprofit institutions have had little choice but to adjust to these pressures, but at some cost to the features that make them distinctive. Under these circumstances, it is no wonder that scholars have been finding it so difficult to detect real differences between the performance of for-profit and nonprofit hospitals and why many nonprofit HMOs and hospitals have willingly surrendered the nonprofit form or sold out to for-profit firms (Rosner, 1982; Herzlinger and Krasker, 1987; Salkever and Frank, 1992; James, 1998).

Increased Demands on Nonprofit Managers. These tensions have naturally complicated the job of the nonprofit executive, requiring these officials to master not only the substantive dimensions of their fields, but also the broader private markets within which they operate, the numerous public policies that increasingly affect them, and the massive new developments in technology and management with which they must contend. They must do all this, moreover, while balancing an increasingly complex array of stakeholders that includes not only clients, staff, board members, and private donors, but also regulators, government program officials, for-profit competitors, and business partners; and while also demonstrating performance and competing with other nonprofits and with for-profit firms for fees, board members, customers, contracts, grants, donations, gifts, bequests, visibility, prestige, political influence, and volunteers. No wonder that burn-out has become such a serious problem in the field despite the excitement and fulfillment the role entails.

Increased Threat to Nonprofit Missions. Inevitably, these pressures pose threats to the continued pursuit of nonprofit missions. Nonprofit organizations forced to rely on fees and charges naturally begin to skew their service offerings to clientele who are able to pay. What start out as sliding fee scales designed to cross-subsidize services for the needy become core revenue sources essential for agency survival. Organizations needing to raise capital to expand are naturally tempted to locate new facilities in places with a client base able to finance the borrowing costs. When charity care, advocacy, and research are not covered in government or private reimbursement rates, institutions have little choice but to curtail these activities.

How far these pressures have proceeded is difficult to say with any precision. As William Diaz has observed, support for the poor has never been the exclusive, or the primary, focus of nonprofit action (Diaz, 2002). Nor need it be. What is more, many of the developments identified above have usefully mobilized market resources to support genuinely charitable purposes. Yet the nonprofit sector's movement toward the market is creating significant pressures to move away from those in greatest need, to focus on amenities that appeal to those who can pay, and to apply the market test to all facets of their operations (James, 1998; Joassart-Marcelli, 2011).

Disadvantaging Small Agencies. A fourth risk resulting from the nonprofit sector's recent move to the market is to put smaller agencies at an increasing disadvantage. Successful adaptation to the prevailing market pressures increasingly requires access to advanced technology, professional marketing, corporate partners, sophisticated fundraising, and complex government reimbursement systems, all of which are problematic for smaller agencies. Market pressures are therefore creating not just a digital divide, but a much broader "sustainability chasm" that smaller organizations are finding it increasingly difficult to bridge. Although such agencies can cope with these pressures in part through

collaborations and partnerships, these devices themselves often require sophisticated management and absorb precious managerial energies. As the barriers to
entry, and particularly to sustainability, rise, the nonprofit sector is thus at risk of
losing one of its most precious qualities—its ease of entry and its availability as a
testing ground for new ideas.

Potential Loss of Public Trust. All of this, finally, poses a further threat to the public trust on which the nonprofit sector ultimately depends. Thanks to the pressures
they are under, and the agility they have shown in response to them, American
nonprofit organizations have moved well beyond the quaint Norman Rockwell
stereotype of selfless volunteers ministering to the needy and supported largely
by charitable gifts. Yet popular and press images remain wedded to this older
image and far too little attention has been given to bringing popular perceptions
into better alignment with the realities that now exist, and to justifying these
realities to a skeptical citizenry and press. As a consequence, nonprofits find
themselves vulnerable when highly visible events, such as the September 11
tragedy, let alone instances of mismanagement or scandal, reveal them to be far
more complex and commercially engaged institutions than the public suspects.
Reflecting this, the proportion of respondents in recent polls registering "a great
deal of confidence" in nonprofit organizations stood at only 18 percent as of
May 2002, and by March 2008 was down to 16 percent (Light, 2008). The more
successfully nonprofit organizations respond to the dominant market pressures
they are facing, therefore, the greater the risk they face of sacrificing the public
trust on which they ultimately depend.

Resetting the Balance: The Task Ahead

What all of this suggests is that a better balance may need to be struck
between what Bradford Gray and Mark Schlesinger term the nonprofit sector's
"distinctiveness imperative," that is, the things that make nonprofits special; and
the sector's "survival imperative," that is, the things nonprofits need to do in
order to survive (Gray and Schlesinger, 2002). To be sure, these two imperatives
are not wholly in conflict. Nevertheless, the tensions between them are real and
there is increasing reason to worry that the survival imperative may be gaining
the upper hand. To correct this, steps will be needed in both domains, and the
steps will require support from many different quarters.

Steps to address the nonprofit sector's distinctiveness imperative could
include revisiting the sector's fundamental rationale through organizational
strategic retreats and broader sectorwide positioning exercises, more sustained
public information campaigns designed to clarify the actual operations of

contemporary nonprofit institutions, and possible shifts in public policy to increase the salience of the sector's public benefit activities. Actions on the survival side of the equation could include passage of tax incentives to help even the playing field for nonprofit generation of capital, reconfiguring government and private reimbursement systems to make provision for mission-critical nonprofit functions, and shifting from a tax deduction to a tax credit system for charitable contributions in order to provide additional stimulus to private charitable giving.

Conclusion

The context of nonprofit management has changed massively in recent years. Up to now, nonprofit managers have had to fend for themselves in deciding what risks it was acceptable to take in order to respond to this changing context. Given the stake that American society has in the preservation of these institutions and in the protection of their ability to perform their distinctive roles, this may now need to change. Americans need to rethink in a more explicit way whether the balance between survival and distinctiveness that nonprofit institutions have had to strike in recent years is the right one for the future, and, if not, what steps might now be needed to allow nonprofit managers to shift this balance for the years ahead.

Notes

1. Author's estimates based on Internal Revenue Service Form 990 tabulations available from IRS Statistics of Income Web site.
2. Author's estimates are based on data in Wing, Pollak, and Blackwood (2008, pp. 134–136).
3. Author's estimates based on data in Internal Revenue Service IRS Return tabulations. Accessed at: http://www.irs.gov/taxstats/charitablestats/article/0,,id=97176,00.html#2 on January 23, 2010.
4. Author's estimates based on IRS 990 return tabulations and Census Bureau Services Annual Survey.

References

Abramson, A. J., Salamon, L. M., and Steurle, C. E., "The Nonprofit Sector and the Federal Budget: Recent History and Future Directions." In E. T. Boris and C. E. Steurle, *Nonprofits and Government: Collaboration and Conflict.* Washington, D.C.: The Urban Institute Press, 1999.

Abramson, A. J., and McCarthy, R., "Infrastructure Organizations." In L. M. Salamon (ed.), *The State of Nonprofit America.* Washington, D.C.: Brookings Institution Press, 2002, 331–354.

AAFRC Trust for Philanthropy. *Giving USA 2000.* Indianapolis: AAFRC Trust for Philanthropy, 2002.

Avery, R., and Rendell, M., 1990. "Estimating the Size and Distribution of the Baby Boomers' Prospective, Inheritances." Ithaca, N.Y.: Cornell University, Department of Consumer Economics.

Austin, J. *The Collaboration Challenge: How Nonprofits and Businesses Succeed Through Strategic Alliances.* San Francisco: Jossey-Bass, 2000.

Bishop, M., and Green, M., *Philanthrocapitalism: How the Rich Can Save the World.* New York: Bloomsbury Press, 2008.

Carr, D. K., and Johnson, H. J., 1995. *Best Practices in Reengineering: What Works and What Doesn't in the Reengineering Process.* New York: McGraw-Hill.

Chaves, M. "Religious Congregations." In L.M. Salamon (ed.), *The State of Nonprofit America.* Washington, D.C.: Brookings Institution Press, 2002.

Coughlin, T. A., Ku, L., and Holahan, J., *Medicaid Since 1980: Costs, Coverage and the Shifting Alliance between the Federal Government and the States.* Washington, D.C.: Urban Institute Press, 1994.

Diaz, W. "For Whom and for What: The Contributions of the Nonprofit Sector." In L. M. Salamon (ed.), *The State of Nonprofit America.* Washington, D.C.: Brookings Institution Press, 2002.

Gilbert, N. "The Transformation of Social Services." *Social Services Review*, *51*(4) (Dec. 1977), 624–641.

Giving USA. Indianapolis: Giving USA Foundation, 2009.

Godeke, S., and Bauer, D., *Mission-Related Investing: Philanthropy's New Passing Gear. A Policy and Implementation Guide for Foundation Trustees.* New York: Rockefeller Philanthropy Advisors, 2008.

Gray, B., and Schlesinger, M., "Health." In L. M. Salamon (ed.), *The State of Nonprofit America.* Washington, D.C.: Brookings Institution Press, 2002, 65–106.

Hammer, M., and Champy, J., *Reengineering the Corporation: A Manifesto for Business Revolution.* London: Nicholas Brealy, 1993.

Hammer, M., and Champy, J., *Reengineering the Corporation: A Manifesto for Business Revolution.* Revised Paperback Edition. London: Nicholas Brealey, 1994.

Hansmann, H. 1981. "The Role of Nonprofit Enterprise." *Yale Law Journal*, *89*(5), 835–901.

Havens, J. J., and Schervish, P. G., "Millionaires and the Millennium: New Estimates of the Forthcoming Wealth Transfer and the Prospects for a Golden Age of Philanthropy." Boston College, Social Welfare Research Institute, 1999.

Herzlinger, R. "Can Public Trust in Nonprofits and Governments be Restored?" *Harvard Business Review* (March-April), 1996.

Herzlinger, R., and Krasker, W. S., "Who Profits from Nonprofits?" *Harvard Business Review* (January/February), 1987, 93–106.

James, E. "Commercialism Among Nonprofits: Objectives, Opportunities, and Constraints." In B. Weisbrod (ed.), *To Profit or Not to Profit: The Commercial Transformation of the Nonprofit Sector.* New York: Cambridge University Press, 1998.

Joassart-Marcelli, P. "For Whom and For What? Who Really Benefits from Nonprofits?" in Lester M. Salamon, ed., *The State of Nonprofit America.* Second Edition. Washington, D.C.: Brookings Institution Press, 2011.

Kearns, K. P. *Private Sector Strategies for Social Sector Success: The Guide to Strategy and Planning for Pubic and Nonprofit Organizations.* San Francisco: Jossey-Bass, 2000.

Kettl, D. *Shared Power: Public Governance and Private Markets.* Washington, D.C.: Brookings Institution Press, 1993.

Letts, C. W., Ryan, W., and Grossman, A. "Virtuous Capital: What Foundations Can Learn from Venture Capitalists." *Harvard Business Review,* 1997 (March/April), 2–7.

Light, P. "How Americans View Charities: A Report on Charitable Confidence, 2008." *Issues in Governance Studies,* 2008 (Apr.), No. 13.

Lipman, H., and Schwinn, E., "The Business of Charity: Nonprofit Groups Reap Billions in Tax-Free Income Annually." *The Chronicle of Philanthropy,* 2001 (Oct. 18), 25.

National Center for Education Statistics. *Digest of Education Statistics 2000.* Washington, D.C.: Department of Education, National Center for Education Statistics, 2000, pp. 202–203, 209.

Nelson, J. *Business as Partners in Development: Creating Wealth for Countries, Companies, and Communities.* London: Prince of Wales Business Leaders Forum, 1996.

Porter, M., and Kramer, M. R., "Philanthropy's New Agenda: Creating Value," *Harvard Business Review,* 1999 (November-December), 121–130.

Rosenbaum, D. "Bush Plans Little More Money for Bulk of Federal Programs," *The New York Times,* January 22, 2003, p. A19.

Rosner, D. *A Once Charitable Enterprise: Hospitals and Health Care in Brooklyn and New York, 1885–1915.* Princeton, N. J.: Princeton University Press, 1982.

Salamon, L. M. "Partners in Public Service." In W. W. Powell (ed.), *The Nonprofit Sector: A Research Handbook.* New Haven, Conn.: Yale University Press, 1987, 99–117.

Salamon, L. M. *Partners in Public Service: Government-Nonprofit Relations in the Modern Welfare State.* Baltimore, Md.: Johns Hopkins University Press, 1995.

Salamon, L. M. *The State of Nonprofit America.* Washington, D.C.: Brookings Institution Press, 2002a.

Salamon, L. M. 2002. "The New Governance and the Tools of Public Action: An Introduction," in Lester M. Salamon, editor, *The Tools of Government: A Guide to the New Governance* New York: Oxford University Press, 2002b, pp. 1–47.

Salamon, L. M. (ed.). *The Tools of Government: A Guide to the New Governance.* New York: Oxford University Press, 2002c.

Salamon, L. M. *Rethinking Corporate Social Engagement: Lessons from Latin America.* Sterling, Va.: Kumarian Press, 2010.

Salamon, L. M., editor. *The State of Nonprofit America.* Second Edition. Washington, D.C.: Brookings Institution Press, 2011.

Salamon, L. M. (ed.) *New Frontiers of Philanthropy: A Guide to the New Tools and New Actors That Are Reshaping Global Philanthropy and Social Investing.* San Francisco: Jossey-Bass, 2011.

Salamon, L. M., and Abramson, A.J. *The Federal Budget and the Nonprofit Sector.* Washington, D.C.: Urban Institute Press, 1982.

Salamon, L. M., and Abramson, A. J., "The Federal Budget and the Nonprofit Sector: Implications of the *Contract with America.*" in D. F. Burlingame, W. A. Diaz, W. F. Ilchman and Associates (eds.), *Capacity for Change? The Nonprofit World in the Age of Devolution.* Indianapolis: Indiana University Center on Philanthropy, 1996.

Salamon, L. M., and Geller, S. L., *Impact of the 2007–09 Recession on Nonprofit Organizations.* Communique No. 14. Baltimore, MD: Johns Hopkins Center for Civil Society Studies, 2009. (Available at www.ccss.jhu.edu).

Salkever, D. S., and Frank, R. G., "Health Services." In C. T. Clotfelter (ed.), *Who Benefits from the Nonprofit Sector.* Chicago: University of Chicago Press, 1992, 24–54.

Shore, B. *Revolution of the Heart: A New Strategy for Creating Wealth and Meaningful Change.* New York: Riverhead Books, 1995.

Smith, C. "The New Corporate Philanthropy," *Harvard Business Review,* May/June 1994.

Smith, S. R. "Social Services." In Lester M. Salamon (ed.), *The State of Nonprofit America.* Washington, D.C.: Brookings Institution Press, 2002, 149–186.

Smith, S. R., and Lipsky, M. *Nonprofits for Hire: The Welfare State in the Age of Contracting.* Cambridge, Mass: Harvard University Press, 1993.

U.S. Census Bureau, *U.S. Economic Census.* Washington, D.C.: U.S. Government Printing Office, 1999.

U.S. Census Bureau, *Economic Census 1997.* Washington, D.C.: U.S. Government Printing Office, 2000a.

U.S. Census Bureau, *Statistical Abstract of the United States: 2000.* 120th ed. Washington, D.C.: U.S. Government Printing Office, 2000b.

U.S. Census Bureau, *Economic Census 2007.* Washington, D.C.: U.S. Government Printing Office, 2009.

U.S. Census Bureau. *Statistical Abstract of the United States: 2010.* Washington, D.C.: U.S. Government Printing Office, 2010. http://www.census.gov/compendia/statab/, accessed June 15, 2010.

U.S. Department of Education. *Digest of Education Statistics 2007.* Washington, D.C.: Government Printing Office, 2007.

U.S. House, Committee on Ways and Means. *2000 Green Book: Background Material and Data on Programs within the Jurisdiction of the Committee on Ways and Means,* 106th Congress, 2nd Session (Oct. 6), 2000.

U.S. Internal Revenue Service. *SOI Tax Stats: Charities & Other Tax-Exempt Organizations Statistics.* http://www.irs.gov/taxstats/charitablestats/article/0,,id=97176,00.html#2, accessed January 23, 2010.

U.S. Office of Management and Budget. *Special Analysis, Budget of the United States Government, Fiscal Year 2011.* Washington, D.C.: Government Printing Office, 2010.

Wallace, N. "Online Giving Soars as Donors Turn to the Internet Following Attacks." *The Chronicle of Philanthropy,* 2001, (Oct. 4), p. 22.

Warner, A. *American Charities: A Study in Philanthropy and Economics.* New York: Thomas Y. Crowell, 1894.

Weitzman, M. S., Tai Jalandoni, N., Lampkin, L. M., and Pollack, T. H., *The New Nonprofit Almanac and Desk Reference.* San Francisco: Jossey Bass, 2002.

Whitehead, J. S. *The Separation of College and State: Columbia, Dartmouth, Harvard, and Yale.* New Haven, Conn.: Yale University Press, 1973.

Wilgoren, J. "New Governors Discover the Ink Is Turning Redder." *The New York Times,* 2003, (Jan. 14), p. A 20.

Wing, K. T., Pollak, T. H., and Blackwood, A., *The Nonprofit Almanac 2008.* Washington, D.C.: Urban Institute, 2008.

Wood, D., and Hoff, B., *Handbook on Responsible Investment Across Asset Classes.* Boston: Institute for Responsible Investment, n.d. [2007].

Wyzsomirski, M. "Arts and Culture." In L. M. Salamon (ed.), *The State of Nonprofit America.* Washington, D.C.: Brookings Institution Press, 2002, 187–218.

Young, D., and Salamon, L. M., "Commercialization and Social Ventures." In L. M. Salamon (ed.), *The State of Nonprofit America,* Washington, D.C.: Brookings Institution Press, 2002, 423–443.

CHAPTER FOUR

THE MANY FACES OF NONPROFIT ACCOUNTABILITY

Alnoor Ebrahim

Calls for greater accountability are not new. Leaders of organizations, be they nonprofit, business, or government, face a constant stream of demands from various constituents for accountable behavior. But what does it mean to be accountable?

At its core, accountability is about trust. By and large, nonprofit leaders tend to pay attention to accountability once a problem of trust arises—a scandal in the sector or in their own organization, questions from citizens or donors who want to know whether their money is being well spent, or pressure from regulators to demonstrate that they are serving a public purpose and thus merit tax-exempt status. Amid this clamor for accountability, it is tempting to accept the popular normative view that more accountability is better. But is it feasible, or even desirable, for nonprofit organizations to be accountable to everyone for everything? The challenge for leadership and management is to prioritize among competing accountability demands. This involves deciding both *to whom* and *for what* they owe accountability. The purpose of this chapter is to provide an overview of the current debates on nonprofit accountability while also examining the trade-offs inherent in a range of accountability mechanisms.

This chapter is a much expanded and revised version of an entry that was first published in the *International Encyclopedia of Civil Society* (Ebrahim, 2009); adapted with permission.

Numerous definitions of accountability have been offered by scholars and practitioners in the nonprofit and nongovernmental sector. Many describe accountability in terms of a "process of holding actors responsible for actions" (Fox and Brown, 1998, p. 12) or as "the means by which individuals and organizations report to a recognized authority (or authorities) and are held responsible for their actions" (Edwards and Hulme, 1996b, p. 967). The literature further identifies four core components of accountability (Ebrahim and Weisband, 2007):

1. *Transparency*, which involves collecting information and making it available and accessible for public scrutiny
2. *Answerability or justification*, which requires providing clear reasoning for actions and decisions, including those not adopted, so that they may reasonably be questioned
3. *Compliance*, through the monitoring and evaluation of procedures and outcomes, combined with transparency in reporting those findings
4. *Enforcement or sanctions* for shortfalls in compliance, justification, or transparency

For many observers, it is enforceability that ultimately gives any accountability mechanism power or "teeth." Other observers, however, find such an approach to be too narrow in its dependence on punitive forms of compliance. They broaden this perspective by suggesting that accountability is not just about responding to others but also about "taking responsibility" for oneself (Cornwall, Lucas, and Pasteur, 2000, p. 3). As such, accountability has both an *external* dimension in terms of "an obligation to meet prescribed standards of behavior" (Chisolm, 1995, p. 141) and an *internal* one motivated by "felt responsibility" as expressed through individual action and organizational mission (Fry, 1995). For example, the One World Trust in the United Kingdom, which assesses the accountability of large global organizations—multinational corporations, international NGOs, and intergovernmental agencies—defines accountability as "the processes through which an organization makes a commitment to respond to and balance the needs of stakeholders in its decision making processes and activities, and delivers against this commitment" (Lloyd, Oatham, and Hammer, 2007, p. 11).

At the very least, what the preceding definitions share is an understanding that accountability centers on the relationships among various actors, with some giving accounts of their behavior and others receiving and judging those accounts. Most discussions about the concept thus also pose two further questions: Accountability to whom? And accountability for what?

Accountability to Whom?

Accountability relationships are complicated by the fact that nonprofits are expected to be accountable to multiple actors: upward to their funders or patrons, downward to clients, and internally to themselves and their missions (Edwards and Hulme, 1996a; Kearns, 1996; Lindenberg and Bryant, 2001; Najam, 1996). "Upward" accountability usually refers to relationships with donors, foundations, and governments and is often focused on the use of funds. Accountability to clients refers primarily to "downward" relationships with groups receiving services, although it may also include communities or regions indirectly impacted by nonprofit programs. The third category of accountability concerns nonprofits themselves. This internal (or horizontal) accountability centers on an organization's responsibility to its mission and staff, which includes decision makers as well as field-level implementers. Some scholars have even suggested that there are as many types of accountability as there are distinct relationships among people and organizations; some characterize this condition as "multiple accountabilities disorder" (Koppell, 2005; Lerner and Tetlock, 1999).

At a minimum, to whom one is accountable varies with organization type, be it a membership organization, a service-delivery nonprofit, or a network engaged in policy advocacy. Although these three "types" of nonprofits do not capture the diversity in the sector, they illustrate critical differences:

• *Membership organizations* are largely oriented toward serving the interests of their members, and are often run by and for their members (for example, the American Association of Retired Persons, cooperatives and unions, and clubs and societies). The mechanisms of accountability available to members include the exercise of "voice" by voting for the organization's leaders, "exit" by revoking membership and dues or joining another organization, and "loyalty" by attempting to reform the organization either by influencing leaders or by running for a leadership position.[1] Because the members or clients are internal to the organization, membership organizations combine internal accountability (to members of the organizations) with downward accountability (to clients, who are members). In short, there is a structural equality between principals and agents, and thus a significant potential for the use of exit, voice, and loyalty options.

• *Service* organizations typically provide a range of services to their clients or beneficiaries, ranging from health and education to housing and rural development. Their clients are usually not involved in creating the nonprofit in the way that members are; they are external actors to the organization and therefore have less voice in shaping its activities and direction. For many, the demands of funders or patrons (such as upward accountability) tend to be the most formalized; for example, through grant contracts, reporting requirements, and formal evaluations. This imbalance is reproduced in their relations with clients, who are often in a "take it or leave it" relationship with respect to services offered (Uphoff, 1996, p. 25), except in highly competitive contexts in which clients have multiple service providers from which to choose. A key accountability challenge lies in increasing "downward" accountability from funders to the nonprofit, and from the nonprofit to clients.

• *Policy advocacy networks* display characteristics that are common to membership as well as service organizations, and also characteristics that are unique. For example, organizations such as the Sierra Club and Amnesty International both have individual members who pay dues and thus have the option of taking their dues elsewhere should the organization fail to satisfy their interests. But they are not self-help organizations in the way that cooperatives are, and most members do not have direct access to organizational decision making or even to other members (nor do they necessarily desire such access), despite the fact that they elect board members. They are more like clients of service organizations. In other words, although their options for exit (revoking membership dues) are potentially powerful, their actions are likely to be remote and isolated. On the other hand, some network organizations attract members by virtue of their policy advocacy work—thereby seeking to hold policymakers and public officials accountable to the views and values of their members. The mechanisms of accountability available to them are advocacy-oriented (voice), including lobbying, litigation, protest, negotiation, fact-finding, and demanding transparency in the reporting of information and events. Networks in which the members are organizations, rather than individuals, involve an additional layer of accountability that depends on negotiation and coordination among member organizations. Accountability is collective in the sense that it depends on reliable coordination and pooling of resources among key players.[2]

In short, the demands of accountability "to whom" are multifold and can seldom be reduced to simple terms. Accountability is a relational concept; it varies according to the relationships among actors, and it also varies across different types of organizations (for example, membership, service, and advocacy networks). Furthermore, asymmetric relationships among stakeholders are likely to result in a skewing toward accountability mechanisms that satisfy the interests of the most powerful actors. In other words, accountability is also about power, in that asymmetries in resources become important in influencing who is able to hold whom to account.

Accountability for What?

Given that nonprofit organizations face demands for accountability from multiple actors, it follows that they are expected to be accountable for different things by different people. These expectations may be broken down into four broad, but far from comprehensive, categories: accountability for finances, governance, performance, and mission (Behn, 2001; Ebrahim, 2009a).

Questions about *finances* have received considerable attention in the wake of various accounting scandals and crises not only in the nonprofit world but also in the private sector (for example, the fall of firms such as Enron and WorldCom in 2001 and 2002, as well as industry-wide failures in mortgage-backed securities and financial derivatives markets in 2008). Public policy responses, particularly to firm-level failures, typically call for greater disclosure of financial transactions, transparency in the use and oversight of funds by executives and trustees, and protections for whistleblowers who reveal information about mismanagement. Accountability in this context is constituted as coercive or punitive, with an emphasis on disclosure and a reliance on legislative or regulatory oversight, backed up by threats of sanctions for noncompliance, such as fines, imprisonment, or loss of tax-exempt status.

The second type of expectation focuses on organizational *governance*, which, especially in the United States and United Kingdom, has often centered on the role of the board of directors. The board is the nexus of standards of care, loyalty, and obedience: board members are responsible for seeking and considering adequate information on which to base decisions (care), for disclosing conflicts of interest and placing the organization's interests over personal ones (loyalty), and for acting within the organization's mission while also adhering to internal organizational protocols for decision making (obedience). The board's fiduciary responsibilities typically focus on its financial oversight role, about how the organization raises and spends money, follows donor intent, and whether it is in compliance with the law. The basic premise is that boards are responsible for oversight of internal controls and legal compliance, such that failures within an organization are reflective of failures of guidance and oversight at the board level. But boards are increasingly also expected to be accountable for the broader purposes of the organization: for its performance in achieving results, for identifying an effective strategy, and for focusing on a mission that creates the greatest social value.[3] These functions require much more than fiduciary oversight, demanding that boards play a more "generative" role (Chait et al., 2005), particularly in the development and maintenance of mission (McFarlan and Epstein, 2009). Chapter Five of this volume focuses more broadly on the design and work of nonprofit organization governing boards, and Chapter Two includes important information about their legal characteristics.

Thus, the third broad stream of accountability demands centers on *performance*, built on the premise that organizations should be held to account for what they deliver. The purpose of such accountability is to demonstrate "results." Performance-based accountability often uses tools such as logic models (called logical framework analysis in the international development world), in which a project's objectives and expected results are identified in a matrix with a list of indicators used in measuring and verifying progress. This kind of accountability relies on a range of technical and professional skills related to performance measurement, indicator development, evaluation and impact assessment, all of which converge toward metrics that link goals to outcomes. This type of accountability is encouraged by funder reporting requirements that reward clear outputs and outcomes. Some critical observers have cautioned, however, that an overemphasis on measurable outcomes can lead to a push for quick fixes, potentially conflicting with or even undermining the work of nonprofits engaged in relationship building and empowerment-related work, and whose efforts may take time to bear fruit (Benjamin, 2008; Lindenberg and Bryant, 2001, p. 214). They stress a need to examine long-term effectiveness and less easily measurable goals related to political and social change.

This leads to a fourth and more emergent type of accountability that focuses on the very core of nonprofit activity: organizational *mission*. If nonprofits exist for purposes of public good, why not ask them to demonstrate progress toward achieving that mission? One might describe this as a mission-centered variant of performance-based accountability, which it extends in two respects. First, it embraces a long-term view of performance measurement by emphasizing iteration and learning—on the basis that nonprofit managers are unlikely to know how best to achieve their goals and what to measure along the way, but repeated trials and critical scrutiny can lead to new insights and convergence. This suggests there are no panaceas to social problems, but instead that social problem solving requires an ability to cope with uncertainty and changing circumstances. It also indicates a critical role for nonprofit boards in internalizing the mission, regularly monitoring performance against it, and periodically reviewing it in light of changing external conditions (McFarlan and Epstein, 2009). And second, organizational goals and strategies are themselves subject to adaptation, as managers learn more about the social problems that they are trying to understand and solve. A central managerial challenge becomes putting in place processes that can engender systematic critical reflection and adaptation while remaining focused on solving social problems (Ebrahim, 2005).

These four "whats" of accountability—for finances, governance, performance, and mission—are not mutually exclusive but are instead integrative. For example, boards have not only fiduciary responsibility but also serve the mission and oversee performance. Donors consider mission in selecting which organizations to fund, and many provide considerable flexibility with respect to performance assessment. And chief executives are expected to work with boards and staff to align mission, strategy, and performance.

Accountability How?

If nonprofits are expected to be accountable to multiple actors (accountability to whom) and for multiple purposes (accountability for what), what then are the mechanisms of accountability actually available to them (accountability how)? And how can we compare these mechanisms?

The following discussion explores five broad (but far from comprehensive) types of accountability mechanisms used by nonprofits in practice: reports and disclosure statements, evaluations and performance assessments, industry self-regulation, participation, and adaptive learning (Ebrahim, 2003). The comparative strengths and weaknesses of each of these mechanisms are also further analyzed. This discussion does not examine challenges of democratic accountability, in which nonprofits may claim to represent the views of a specific community; this would require a separate discussion on representation.

To begin, it may be helpful to differentiate between those mechanisms that are "tools" and those that are "processes." In basic terms, accountability tools refer to discrete devices or techniques used to achieve accountability. They are often applied over a limited period of time, can be tangibly documented, and can be repeated. For example, financial reports and disclosures are tools that are applied and repeated quarterly or annually and are documented as financial statements, ledgers, or reports. Performance evaluations are also often carried out at specific points in time, usually at the end of a specific project, and result in an evaluation report. However, process mechanisms such as participation and adaptive learning are generally more broad and multifaceted than tools, while also being less tangible and time-bound, although each may use a set of tools for achieving accountability. Process mechanisms thus emphasize a course of action rather than a distinct end product, in which the means are important in and of themselves. These distinctions are discussed in greater detail below.

Disclosure Statements and Reports

Disclosure statements and reports are among the most widely used tools of accountability and are frequently required by federal or state laws in many countries. These include, for example, application requirements for tax exemption under section 501(c)(3) of the Internal Revenue Code, and annual filings of the Form 990 which requests disclosures on finances, organizational structure, and programs. Furthermore, state law provisions also often include registration and reporting statutes that involve annual financial reporting (Fremont-Smith, 2004).

On the one hand, such legal disclosures enable some degree of accountability to donors, clients, and members who wish to access these reports, and also serve as means for nonprofit boards to fulfill their fiduciary responsibilities. On the other hand, donors and clients of a nonprofit organization in the United States generally have very limited legal standing to challenge an organization for falling short of legal requirements, with primary responsibility falling on the attorney general as the representative of society at large or on the Internal Revenue Service for matters of tax exemption. At the same time, legal requirements can also be abused by governments to keep tabs on organizations that challenge them, as has been documented in many parts of the world (International Center for Not-for-Profit Law (ICNL), 2006). These problems have become more pronounced in a post 9/11 context, where nonprofit activities are subject to greater scrutiny by their governments, funders are being asked to prove that their moneys are not being channeled to activities of concern to state security, and some subsectors, such as Muslim charities, suffer "from a loss of the presumption of innocence" (Jordan and Van Tuijl, 2006, p. 8). Apart from legally mandated reports, donors require regular reports from organizations that they fund. The nature of these reports varies considerably among funders and projects, and it is not uncommon for nonprofit staff to complain about multiple reporting requirements.

Such reports and legal disclosures are significant tools of accountability in that they make available (either to the public or to oversight bodies) basic data on nonprofit operations. Their distinct and tangible nature makes them easily accessible. Yet the bulk of this reporting emphasizes upward reporting of financial data, with only limited indication of the quality of nonprofit work and almost no attention to downward accountability to stakeholders. These are external approaches to accountability, enforced through punitive threats such as the loss of nonprofit status or revocation of funds. Although no doubt important as deterrents, these external approaches have limited potential for encouraging organizations and individuals to take internal responsibility for shaping their organizational mission, values, and performance or for promoting ethical behavior.

Evaluation and Performance Assessment

Another widely used set of tools for facilitating accountability includes various kinds of evaluation, including performance and impact assessments. Funders commonly conduct external evaluations of nonprofit work near the end of a grant or program phase, and are increasingly employing midterm assessments as well. Such evaluations typically aim to assess whether and to what extent program goals and objectives have been achieved, and they can be pivotal to future funding. These appraisals may focus on short-term results (that is, activities or outputs, such as training programs offered or jobs secured) or medium- and long-term results (that is, outcomes and impacts, such as sustained improvements in client income, health, natural resource base, and so on). Internal evaluations are also common, in which nonprofit staff gauge their own progress, either toward the objectives of externally funded programs or toward internal goals and missions.

As a means of accountability, evaluations often run into conflicts among nonprofits and funders over whether they should be assessing activities, processes, outputs, or outcomes and impacts (accountability for what). As donors increasingly demand information about long-term outcomes and impacts, many nonprofit leaders have expressed concern about the difficulty, reliability, and expense of such measurement, particularly in accounting for causal factors well beyond their control. Randomized control trials, regarded by some as a gold standard for evaluation, are costly to conduct and are feasible only when cause-effect relationships are sufficiently linear and testable (Center for Global Development, 2006; Jones et al., 2009; Rogers, 2009; White, 2009). Moreover, the question of what should be evaluated may vary according to different stakeholders (accountability to whom). When an organization's work is fairly straightforward to measure (such as a nonprofit that aims to serve meals to the poor), and performance criteria are likely to be shared across different stakeholder groups, a simple logic model can be helpful in clarifying results. However, when performance criteria vary among stakeholders, such as in empowerment and rights-based work or policy advocacy, nonprofit leaders face the challenge of prioritizing and coordinating among multiple interests and constituents.

Control over evaluations thus remains a central tension between nonprofits and their stakeholders, and particularly with funders who must make decisions on allocating or cutting funding. Some scholars have shown that funders can come to somewhat different conclusions about the same set of nonprofits as a result of how they frame their evaluations (Tassie, Murray, and Cutt, 1998, p. 63). A related concern raised by small nonprofits is that their limited staff and resources are stretched too thin by evaluation and reporting requests of funders, and that nonprofit size and capacity should be key factors in determining the scale of an appraisal. These concerns notwithstanding, the strength of evaluation as a mechanism of accountability lies in its explicit attention to results (whether those be outputs or outcomes) and the impetus it provides to nonprofits for collecting some form of performance data.

Self-Regulation

Nonprofits have also increasingly turned to industry-wide accountability standards. The term *self-regulation*, as used here, refers specifically to efforts by nonprofit networks to develop standards or codes of behavior and performance. These standards have emerged partly as an effort to redeem the image of the sector (as a result of public scandals or exaggerated claims of performance) while establishing norms around quality, and in some instances to forestall potentially restrictive government regulation.

Standards and their certification are most ubiquitous and long-standing in the education and health care sectors, where there is a mix of government oversight and industry self-regulation, and a combination of public, private, and nonprofit players. In education, for example, certification of teachers and educational facilities is common but not always required. Moreover, the entire higher education industry is organized around programs that must be accredited in order to grant degrees (for example, in business, law, medicine, education, public administration, public health, accounting, city planning, and social work, to name just a handful). Similarly, the health care field relies on certification and licensing of its professionals (doctors, nurses, administrators, technicians, and so on) and also offers certification of facilities and services.

More broadly, the past two decades have seen the emergence of an array of voluntary codes of conduct and third-party certification standards across nonprofit industries—intended to send signals of good housekeeping to the outside world. Hundreds of national and international codes have been documented globally. For example, the Independent Sector in the United States, and Bond in the United Kingdom (formerly British Overseas NGOs for Development), together list over a hundred standards and codes promoted by charity watchdogs, nonprofit and NGO associations, foundations, individual organizations, and governments.[4] Some standards systems are inclusive in nature, seeking to improve governance across a spectrum of nonprofits, and are typically sponsored by umbrella associations. Others are exclusive in nature, seeking to screen organizations and professions through a certification process (Gugerty and Prakash, 2010).

In the United States, a widely cited set of standards was developed in 1993 by InterAction, a membership association of U.S. private voluntary organizations active in international development. The 1990s also saw the rise of state-level nonprofit associations adopting and promoting codes and certification standards; the most heavily promoted was the "Standards of Excellence" developed by the Maryland Association of Nonprofit Organizations (MANO). Most of these standards lay out, in considerable detail, requirements concerning governance, organizational integrity, finances, public communication and disclosure, management and hiring practices, and public policy involvement. For instance, governance standards typically require organizations to have an independent board of directors and even specify some of the tasks of the board and minimum frequency of meetings. Integrity standards emphasize truthfulness in conduct and require that each organization develop a written standard of conduct (including conflict of interest) for its directors, employees, and volunteers. InterAction's code further provides guidelines and requirements for promoting gender equity, diversity, and people with disabilities. These standards have had impacts beyond the United States. For example, a code of ethics used by the Canadian Council for International Co-operation contains content very similar to InterAction's code. Although implementation of these standards is often based on self-certification (such as InterAction), some organizations require external or third-party certification (such as MANO).

Whether and how the adoption of such self-regulation actually improves nonprofit accountability remains to be empirically tested. At the very least, their value is symbolic, sending signals about sector identity and values to an increasingly skeptical public. Even then, self-regulatory efforts face at least two challenges. First, as the number of such standards has grown, it has become difficult for donors and citizens to compare them. Their power as seals of good housekeeping may thus rely on two distinct pathways—either more clear differentiation among codes or a consolidation among them. Second, although most self-regulatory efforts have focused internally on the governance and operations of their members (accountability for what), few have been explicit about accountability to key constituents (accountability to whom). A notable exception is the Humanitarian Accountability Partnership, established in 2003, which specifically prioritizes accountability to its intended beneficiaries (disaster survivors), and which requires all participating organizations to articulate an explicit "accountability framework."[5]

Participation

As an accountability mechanism, participation is quite distinct from disclosure reports and evaluations because it is a process rather than a tool, and it is thus part of ongoing routines in an organization. In examining participation, it is helpful to distinguish between four levels or kinds of participation common to nonprofit and public activities (Arnstein, 1969; Gardner and Lewis, 1996). At one level, participation refers to information about a planned intervention being made available to the public, and can include public meetings or hearings, surveys, or a formal dialogue on project options. In this form, participation involves consultation with community leaders and members, but decision-making power remains with the project planners. A second level of participation includes public involvement in actual project-related activities, and it may be in the form of community contribution toward labor and funds for project implementation, and possibly in the maintenance of services or facilities. At a third level, citizens are able to negotiate and bargain over decisions with nonprofits or state agencies, or even hold veto power over decisions. At this level, citizens are able to exercise greater control over local resources and development activities. And finally, at a fourth tier of participation, are people's own initiatives that occur independently of nonprofit- and state-sponsored projects. Examples of this kind of participation include social movements such as the environmental and women's movements.

The first two forms of participation are commonly espoused by state agencies, donors, and nonprofits, and are based on an assumption that social problems such as poverty can be eliminated by increasing local access to resources and services. At both of these levels, little decision-making authority is vested in communities or clients, and actual project objectives are determined by nonprofits and funders long before any participation occurs. This sort of participation has been criticized by some observers as being a feel-good exercise in which "the sham of participation translates into the sham of accountability" because "[u]nlike donors, [communities] cannot withdraw their funding; unlike governments, they cannot impose conditionalities" (Najam, 1996, pp. 346–347). The act of participation or the exercise of "voice" and "exit" is largely symbolic in such settings. The primary argument is that without some mechanism for addressing unequal power relations, participation appears unlikely to lead to downward accountability (Cooke and Kothari, 2001).

There have been a number of innovations in this area since the year 2000, especially in combining participation with evaluation to involve communities in evaluating nonprofits, or nonprofits in evaluating funders. For example, the Grantee Perception Reports, developed by the Center for Effective Philanthropy in the United States, seek anonymous feedback from nonprofit grantees about their relationships with funders (Center for Effective Philanthropy, 2004). Similarly, a Comparative Constituency Feedback tool developed by Keystone Accountability in the United Kingdom aims to give nonprofits or funders data on how their constituents view and evaluate their relationships and interventions

(Bonbright, Campbell, and Nguyen, 2009). There have also been innovations in participatory budgeting, pioneered by citizens in municipalities in Brazil, and social audits and public hearings in which citizens assess the work of NGOs and governments (Malena, Forster, and Singh, 2004). Each of these approaches combine tools of evaluation and performance assessment with processes of participation to enhance downward accountability.

Adaptive Learning

Another process mechanism is adaptive learning, in which nonprofits create regular opportunities for critical reflection and analysis in order to make progress toward achieving their missions. Building such learning into an organization requires at least three sets of building blocks: *a supportive learning environment*, where staff are given time for reflection and the psychological safety to discuss mistakes or express disagreement; *concrete learning processes* and practices that enable experimentation, analysis, capacity building, and forums for sharing information; and, *supportive leadership* that reinforces learning by encouraging dialogue and debate and by providing resources for reflection (Garvin, Edmondson, and Gino, 2008). Learning, as such, seeks to "improv[e] actions through better knowledge and understanding" (Fiol and Lyles, 1985, p. 803) or, in more technical terms, to "encod[e] inferences from history into routines that guide behavior" (Levitt and March, 1988, p. 320).

As an accountability mechanism, adaptive learning focuses internally on organizational mission rather than externally on accountability to funders, although it may also enhance the latter. It also offers a way for nonprofit leaders to address a common myopia—the focus on immediate short-term demands at the expense of longer-term and more sustained results. The central managerial challenge becomes to put in place processes that can engender systematic critical reflection and remain focused on achieving the mission.

This is easier said than done. Evaluations or performance assessments that reward success while punishing failure (for example, through revocation of funds or additional conditions on funding) seem unlikely to engender learning since they encourage nonprofits to exaggerate successes while discouraging them from revealing and closely scrutinizing their mistakes. At the same time, onerous data requirements can lead nonprofits to develop monitoring and evaluation systems that, although satisfying donor needs for information, are of limited value for internal learning and decision making.

Despite these impediments, a number of global nonprofit organizations have been experimenting over the past decade with building learning into their work. This has been especially true of multisite organizations seeking to share knowledge across teams in dozens of countries. For example, ActionAid International revamped its entire planning and reporting processes in 2000, launching a new Accountability, Learning, and Planning System (ALPS). Its aim was to reduce unnecessary internal bureaucracy, while reshaping the expert-driven task of measurement and reporting into a more critical and reflective process (ActionAid International, 2006, p. 4; David and Mancini, 2004). Many other international nonprofits, such as CARE and Oxfam, have undertaken their own experiments to find practical and useful approaches to measurement, reporting, and learning. At the same time, there has been a burst in the development of participatory tools for evaluation and learning such as outcome mapping, constituency feedback, and most significant changes techniques (Bonbright et al., 2009; Davies and Dart, 2005; Earl, Carden, and Smutylo, 2001; Khagram et al., forthcoming).

Discussion and Implications

Key characteristics of the accountability mechanisms discussed in this chapter are summarized in Table 4.1. The first column lists each of the five mechanisms and distinguishes among those that are tools and those that are processes. The second and third columns respond to the questions of "accountability to whom" and "accountability for what"? For example, disclosure statements and reports are currently used primarily for upward accountability from nonprofits to donors, and tend to focus on reporting about annual or quarterly performance and finances. Similarly, tools of evaluation and performance assessment are also mostly targeted toward satisfying funder demands for assessing performance, although they have a tremendous, underutilized potential for downward accountability—by making nonprofits more accountable to communities and by making funders more accountable to nonprofits. Although funders frequently require nonprofits to seek community input in evaluating projects, they rarely seek nonprofit input in evaluating themselves. Similarly, participation, which is primarily conceived by nonprofits as a tool of downward accountability to communities, has received only scant attention as a tool for increasing the responsiveness of funders to nonprofits. Self-regulation, often driven by a crisis of confidence in the sector, is seen as enabling accountability within the sector and also to donors who seek a seal of good housekeeping. And it is only adaptive learning processes that tend to focus on accountability to organizational mission, although related mechanisms such as performance assessment also have the potential to do so.

There are several broad implications to these observations. First, although traditional approaches to improving accountability, such as increased oversight through reporting and disclosure requirements, enable a degree of upward

TABLE 4.1. CHARACTERISTICS OF ACCOUNTABILITY MECHANISMS

Accountability How? (tool or process)	Accountability to Whom? (upward, downward, internal)	Accountability for What? (finances, governance, performance, mission)	Inducement (internal or external)	Organizational Response (compliance or strategic)
Disclosures / reports (tool)	Upward to funders and oversight agencies Downward (to a lesser degree) to clients or members who read the reports	Finances and performance, depending on what is being reported	Legal requirement Tax status Funding requirement (external threat of loss of funding or tax status)	Primarily compliance, with a focus on letter of law and short-term results
Evaluation and performance assessment (tool)	Upward to funders Significant potential for downward from nonprofits to communities and from funders to nonprofits	Performance, often short-term outputs but with increasing emphasis on impacts	Funding requirement (external) Potential to become a learning tool (internal)	Primarily compliance at present, with possibilities for longer-term strategic assessments
Self-regulation (tool and process)	To nonprofits themselves, as a sector To donors as a seal of good housekeeping	Finances and governance, depending on what the codes or standards emphasize	Erosion of public confidence due to scandals and exaggeration of accomplishments (external loss of funds; internal loss of reputation)	Strategic if it raises industry standards and enables policy voice Compliance if standards are weak and adopted pro forma
Participation (process)	Downward from nonprofits to clients and communities Internally to nonprofits themselves Significant potential downward from funders to nonprofits	Depends on the purpose of participation, e.g., whether it is to seek input on implementation (performance) or to influence agendas (governance)	Organizational values (internal) Funding requirement (external)	Primarily compliance if participation is limited to consultation and implementation Strategic if it increases power of clients in influencing nonprofit agendas or increases power of nonprofits in influencing funders
Adaptive learning (process)	To nonprofits themselves Downward and upward to stakeholders	Mission and performance	Improve performance in order to achieve mission (internal)	Strategic if it focuses attention and resources on how to solve social problems

accountability, they are of limited use for enhancing downward accountability. A more balanced approach thus requires a greater role for nonprofits in evaluating funders and for clients in evaluating nonprofits. The emergence of feedback tools such as grantee perception reports and constituency voice suggest that it is possible to find low-risk ways for nonprofits to express their views on funders. These efforts notwithstanding, the key point is that downward accountability mechanisms remain comparatively underdeveloped.

A second implication is that improving accountability within nonprofits themselves also needs attention to a range of mechanisms. The fourth column in Table 4.1 focuses on the inducements or drivers behind each accountability mechanism. In many cases the inducements are external, such as legal requirements for annual reports (for example, for retaining nonprofit tax status) or requests by donors for quarterly progress data, backed up by sanctions for noncompliance (such as loss of funding). External inducements can also be more subtle, such as the erosion of public confidence in nonprofits as a result of scandals or exaggerated claims of achievement.

The key point here is that although externally driven mechanisms matter, the legitimacy and reputation of the social sector needs to be buttressed by internally driven mechanisms. To be sure, internal inducements exist and are often driven by core values, such as those regarding participation and democratic practice. But for a sector that views itself as largely mission-driven, there is an urgent need for nonprofit leaders to take performance assessment seriously in order to justify activities with substantiated evidence rather than with anecdote or rhetoric. Funders and regulators also bear responsibility in this regard. Funders that want nonprofits to measure impacts, but at the same time are unwilling to fund management capacity building and overhead costs for performance measurement, end up undermining both the nonprofits and themselves.

The third implication concerns the primary type of organizational response that a mechanism generates—whether it is *compliance-driven* or *strategy-driven* (see last column in Table 4.1). Compliance-driven accountability is a reactive response to concerns about public trust. It is about doing what one has to do, such as complying with the law, disclosing whatever information is necessary in order to account for resource use, and taking fiduciary responsibility seriously in order to prevent fraud or malfeasance. Under this approach, nonprofit leaders share information about their performance or operations largely because funders or regulators demand it. Strategy-driven accountability, on the other hand, is a proactive approach to addressing concerns about public trust (Brown, Moore, and Honan, 2004; Jordan, 2007). It is focused on improving performance and achieving mission. Under this approach, nonprofit leaders seek and share information that can help them achieve their long-term goals.

The most common mechanisms of accountability, such as disclosure statements, reports, and project evaluations, mainly serve a compliance purpose because they tend to focus on accounting for funds and reporting their short-term results (often within specified budget cycles). The complex nature of nonprofit work suggests, however, that attention to more strategic processes of accountability are necessary for lasting social and political change. While reporting requirements that are biased in favor of easily measurable assessments of progress might be sufficient for funding and regulatory purposes, they undervalue adaptive assessments that are essential for understanding how a nonprofit might improve its work. A strategy-driven accountability requires building internal capacity in nonprofits for adaptive learning.

Self-regulation may also be seen as a strategic response in the sense that it is targeted toward change at a sectorwide level, not only by raising the standards for an industry, but also by forming umbrella organizations that can engage in national-level policy debates. But self-regulation also runs the risk of becoming a compliance response if the adopted standards are weak, pro forma, and do not actually improve behavior.

Conclusions

In the end, accountability is both about being held to account by external actors and standards and about taking internal responsibility for actions. An integrated perspective suggests that nonprofit leaders face multiple, and sometimes competing, accountability demands: from numerous actors (upward, downward, internal), for varying purposes (finances, governance, performance, mission), and requiring various levels of organizational response (compliance and strategic).

The current emphasis among nonprofits and funders on the upward and compliance dimensions of accountability is problematic, as it skews organizational attention toward the interests of those who control critical resources. In such cases, patrons hold powers of punishment and can revoke funds, impose conditionalities, or even tarnish nonprofit reputations. The predominant emphasis on compliance-driven accountability tends to reward nonprofits for short-term responses with quick and tangible impacts, while neglecting longer-term strategic responses or riskier innovations that can address more systemic issues of social and political change.

Yet it is inescapable that nonprofits will continue to face multiple and competing accountability demands. After all, funders have a right to demand accountability for their resources, and many are increasingly attentive to the concerns and interests of nonprofits they support. The critical challenge for nonprofit leaders lies in finding a balance between upward accountability to their patrons while remaining true to their missions. At the same time, few nonprofits have paid serious attention to how they might be more accountable to the communities they seek to serve. The above review of accountability offers four key insights for practice:

- Nonprofit leaders must be deliberate in prioritizing among accountabilities. They cannot be accountable to everyone for everything. But it is a fact of life in the social sector that they will continue to be pulled in all directions. Rather than aiming simply to comply with the demands of the most powerful actors, nonprofit leaders need to focus their attention on accountabilities that really matter.
- Nonprofits are expected to be accountable for multiple purposes: finances, governance, performance, and mission. These expectations cannot be handled separately, but require integration and alignment throughout the organization.
- There are many mechanisms of accountability available to nonprofits— including, for example, better information disclosure, evaluation and performance assessment, industry codes and standards, participation, and adaptive learning (to name just a few). Nonprofit leaders must adapt any such mechanisms to suit their organization—whether it is a membership-based organization, a service-delivery nonprofit, or an advocacy network (among others).

The broader conclusion is that accountability is not simply about compliance with laws or industry standards but is, more deeply, connected to organizational purpose and public trust. Nonprofit leaders might thus pay greater attention to strategy-driven forms of accountability that can help them achieve their missions. New innovations are unlikely to lie in oversight and punishment, but in creative forms of adaptation and learning in order to solve pressing societal problems.

Notes

1. These options of exit, voice, or loyalty draw from Hirschman (1970).
2. Nonprofit organizations engaged in policy advocacy face an additional accountability challenge increasingly leveled by their critics: "Whom do you represent? Who elected you?" This challenge is less of a problem for organizations that are membership based, and who can thus claim to be accountable to their members for their lobbying and advocacy activities. Nonmembership organizations, however, tend to claim authorization on the grounds of what, rather than whom, they represent—such as a set of values, a social purpose or mission, expertise and experience in an issue area such as health or education, or

a particular set of interests such as those of marginalized or unorganized groups (Peruzzotti, 2006, pp. 52–53).

3. The author is grateful to Herman "Dutch" Leonard for this insight, which underpins a "Governing for Nonprofit Excellence" executive education program at Harvard Business School chaired by Professor Leonard.

4. See www.independentsector.org/issues/accountability/standards2.html and www.bond. org.uk/pages/quality-standards-codes-and-inititatives-2.html (both accessed November 11, 2009).

5. For examples of codes, see InterAction (www.gdrc.org/ngo/pvo-stand.html), Maryland Association for Nonprofits (www.marylandnonprofits.org/html/standards/index.asp), the Philippine Council for NGO Certification (www.pcnc.com.ph), the International NGO Accountability Charter (www.ingoaccountabilitycharter.org), and the Humanitarian Accountability Partnership (www.hapinternational.org/standards.aspx); accessed November 24, 2009.

References

ActionAid International. "ALPS: Accountability, Learning and Planning System." Johannesburg: ActionAid International. 2006.

Arnstein, S. R. "A Ladder of Citizen Participation." *American Institute of Planning Journal*, 1969, *35*(4), 216–224.

Behn, R. D. *Rethinking Democratic Accountability* . Washington, D.C.: Brookings Institution Press, 2001.

Benjamin, L. M. "Account Space: How Accountability Requirements Shape Nonprofit Practice." *Nonprofit and Voluntary Sector Quarterly*, 2008, *37*(2), 201–223.

Bonbright, D., Campbell, D., and Nguyen, L. "The 21st Century Potential of Constituency Voice: Opportunities for Reform in the United States Human Services Sector." Alliance for Children & Families, United Neighborhood Centers of America, and Keystone Accountability, 2009.

Brown, L. D., Moore, M. H., and Honan, J. "Building Strategic Accountability Systems for International NGOs." *Accountability Forum*, 2004, 31–43.

Center for Effective Philanthropy. "Listening to Grantees: What Nonprofits Value in Their Foundation Funders." Cambridge, Mass.: The Center for Effective Philanthropy (CEP), 2004.

Center for Global Development. "When Will We Ever Learn? Improving Lives through Impact Evaluation." Washington, D.C.: Evaluation Gap Working Group, Center for Global Development, 2006.

Chait, R. P., Ryan, W. P., and Taylor, B. E. *Governance as Leadership: Reframing the Work of Nonprofit Boards*. Hoboken, N.J.: Wiley, 2005.

Chisolm, L. B. "Accountability of Nonprofit Organizations and Those Who Control Them: The Legal Framework." *Nonprofit Management and Leadership*, 1995, *6*(2), 141–156.

Cooke, B., and Kothari, U. (eds.). *Participation: The New Tyranny?* London and New York: Zed Books. 2001.

Cornwall, A., Lucas, H., and Pasteur, K. "Introduction: Accountability through Participation: Developing Workable Partnership Models in the Health Sector." *IDS Bulletin*. 2001, *31*(1), 1–13.

David, R., and Mancini, A. "Going Against the Flow: Making Organisational Systems Part of the Solution Rather than Part of the Problem." *Lessons for Change in Policy & Organisations* (No. 8), 2004.

Davies, R., and Dart, J. "The 'Most Significant Change' (MSC) Technique: A Guide to Its Use." 2005. Available at http://www.mande.co.uk/docs/MSCGuide.htm.

Earl, S., Carden, F., and Smutylo, T. *Outcome Mapping: Building Learning and Reflection into Development*. Ottawa: International Development Research Centre, 2001.

Ebrahim, A. "Accountability in Practice: Mechanisms for NGOs." *World Development* 2003, *31*(5), 813–829.

Ebrahim, A. "Accountability Myopia: Losing Sight of Organizational Learning." *Nonprofit and Voluntary Sector Quarterly*, 2005, *34*(1), 56–87.

Ebrahim, A. "Placing the Normative Logics of Accountability in 'Thick' Perspective." *American Behavioral Scientist* 2009a, *52*(6), 885–904.

Ebrahim, A. "Accountability." In H. Anheier and S. Toepler (eds.), *International Encyclopedia of Civil Society*. New York: Springer. 2009b.

Ebrahim, A., and E. Weisband (eds.). *Global Accountabilities: Participation, Pluralism, and Public Ethics*. Cambridge, U.K.: Cambridge University Press. 2007.

Edwards, M., and Hulme, D. (eds.). *Beyond the Magic Bullet: NGO Performance and Accountability in the Post-Cold War World*. West Hartford, Conn.: Kumarian Press, 1996a.

Edwards, M., and Hulme, D. "Too Close for Comfort? The Impact of Official Aid on Nongovernmental Organizations." *World Development*, 1996b, *24*(6), 961–973.

Fiol, C. M., and Lyles, M. A. "Organizational Learning." *Academy of Management Review*, 1985, *10*(4), 803–813.

Fox, J. A., and Brown, L. D. (eds.). *The Struggle for Accountability: The World Bank, NGOs, and Grassroots Movements*. Cambridge, Mass.: The MIT Press, 1998.

Fremont-Smith, M. R. *Governing Nonprofit Organizations: Federal and State Law and Regulation*. Cambridge, Mass.: Belknap Press of Harvard University Press, 2004.

Fry, R. E. "Accountability in Organizational Life: Problem or Opportunity for Nonprofits?" *Nonprofit Management and Leadership*, 1995, *6*(2), 181–195.

Gardner, K., and Lewis, D. *Anthropology, Development and the Post-Modern Challenge*, London: Pluto Press, 1996.

Garvin, D. A., Edmondson, A. C., and Gino, F. "Is Yours a Learning Organization?" *Harvard Business Review*, 2008, 109–116.

Gugerty, M. K., and Prakash, A. (eds.). *Voluntary Regulation of NGOs and Nonprofits: An Accountability Club Framework*. Cambridge, Mass.: Cambridge University Press, 2010.

Hirschman, A. O. *Exit, Voice, and Loyalty: Responses to Decline in Firms, Organizations, and States*. Cambridge, Mass.: Harvard University Press, 1970.

International Center for Not-for-Profit Law (ICNL). "Recent Laws and Legislative Proposals to Restrict Civil Society and Civil Society Organizations." *International Journal of Not-for-Profit Law*, 2006, *8*(4), 76–85.

Jones, N., Jones, H., Steer, L., and Datta, A. *Improving Impact Evaluation Production and Use*. London: Overseas Development Institute, 2009.

Jordan, L. "A Rights-Based Approach to Accountability." In A. Ebrahim and E. Weisband (eds.), *Global Accountabilities: Participation, Pluralism, and Public Ethics*. Cambridge, U.K.: Cambridge University Press, 2007, 151–167.

Jordan, L., and P. Van Tuijl (eds.). *NGO Accountability: Politics, Principles, and Innovations*. London and Sterling, Va.: Earthscan, 2006.

Kearns, K. P. *Managing for Accountability: Preserving the Public Trust in Nonprofit Organizations.* San Francisco: Jossey-Bass, 1996.

Khagram, S., Thomas, C., Lucero, C., and Mathes, S. "Evidence for Development Effectiveness." *Journal of Development Effectiveness.* 2009, *1*(3), 247–270.

Koppell, J. G. S. "Pathologies of Accountability: ICANN and the Challenge of Multiple Accountabilities Disorder." *Public Administration Review*, 2005, *65*(1), 94–108.

Lerner, J. S., and Tetlock, P. E. "Accounting for the Effects of Accountability." *Psychological Bulletin*, 1999, *125*(2), 255–275.

Levitt, B., and March, J. G. "Organizational Learning." *Annual Review of Sociology*, 1988, *14*, 319–40.

Lindenberg, M., and Bryant, C. *Going Global: Transforming Relief and Development NGOs.* Bloomfield, Conn.: Kumarian Press, 2001.

Lloyd, R., Oatham, J., and Hammer, M. "2007 Global Accountability Report." London: One World Trust, 2007.

Malena, C., Forster, R., and Singh, J. "Social Accountability: An Introduction to the Concept and Emerging Practice." Washington, D.C.: The World Bank, 2004.

McFarlan, F. W., and Epstein, M. W. "Non-Profit Boards: It's Different: A Businessman's Perspective." Draft book manuscript (cited with permission), 2009.

Najam, A. "NGO Accountability: A Conceptual Framework." *Development Policy Review*, 1996, *14*, 339–353.

Peruzzotti, E. "Civil Society, Representation and Accountability." In L. Jordan and P. Van Tuijl (eds.), *NGO Accountability: Politics, Principles and Innovations.* London and Sterling, Va.: Earthscan, 2006, 43–58.

Rogers, P. "Matching Impact Evaluation Design to the Nature of the Intervention and the Purpose of the Evaluation." In R. Chambers, D. Karlan, M. Ravallion, and P. Rogers (eds.), *Designing Impact Evaluations: Different Perspectives*, Working Paper 4. New Delhi: International Initiative for Impact Evaluation, 2009. Available at 3ieimpact.org.

Tassie, B., Murray, V., and Cutt, J. "Evaluating Social Service Agencies: Fuzzy Pictures of Organizational Effectiveness." *Voluntas: International Journal of Voluntary and Nonprofit Organizations*, 1998, *9*(1), 59–79.

Uphoff, N. "Why NGOs Are Not a Third Sector: A Sectoral Analysis with Some Thoughts on Accountability, Sustainability, and Evaluation." In M. Edwards and D. Hulme (eds.), *Beyond the Magic Bullet: NGO Performance and Accountability in the Post-Cold War.* West Hartford, Conn.: Kumarian, 1996, 23–39.

White, H. "We All Agree We Need Better Evidence. But What Is It and Will It Be Used?" In M. W. Lipsey and E. Noonan (eds.), *Better Evidence for a Better World.* Working Paper 2. New Delhi: International Initiative for Impact Evaluation (3ie), 2009. Available at 3ieimpact.org.

PART TWO

LEADING AND GOVERNING NONPROFIT ORGANIZATIONS

Governance and leadership are important areas in which nonprofit organizations differ significantly from businesses and government agencies, and this part of the handbook examines the various ways that leadership and strategic direction are provided to nonprofit organizations. Governing boards (that is, boards of directors or boards of trustees) of nonprofit organizations are legally accountable for leadership, governance, and management of the affairs of the nonprofit organization, and they are expected to provide effective leadership in establishing and developing their organizations' missions, visions, values, and strategic directions. No less central in providing organizational leadership are those who serve as chief executives of nonprofit organizations. They work with their governing boards to provide leadership, develop strategic direction, and manage the operations of their organizations.

The six chapters in Part Two of this volume collectively examine the leadership roles that boards and chief executives are expected to serve in nonprofit organizations, explore the difficulties that sometimes prevent boards or executives from carrying out their prescribed roles, and discuss various strategies and techniques that have proved useful in enhancing the leadership effectiveness of both boards and executives. The first chapter in this part, Chapter Five, explains the work of governing boards and draws on the increasing body of research to discuss ways for boards and their members to implement their roles more effectively. In Chapter Six, Robert D. Herman examines the many roles of chief executives, including their pivotal role in helping boards perform effectively. In Chapter Seven, Thomas H. Jeavons discusses the work of executives in creating and sustaining organizational cultures and practices that uphold the highest of ethical standards.

Leading and managing strategically is essential to nonprofit success, and one of the key leadership tasks facing boards and executives is that of strategically designing the organization to most effectively achieve its mission. In Chapters Eight and Nine, William A. Brown and John M. Bryson discuss the work of developing organizational strategy and the processes by which this might best be accomplished. In the final chapter of this part, Chapter Ten, Matthew T. A. Nash explains and discusses the implications of a broad strategic direction that more and more nonprofit leaders are embracing: social entrepreneurship. Each of these chapters provides important information about the practices and issues that influence the effectiveness by which nonprofit organizations are governed and led.

CHAPTER FIVE

LEADERSHIP, GOVERNANCE, AND THE WORK OF THE BOARD

David O. Renz

Governing boards have become the focus of substantial attention and interest in the past decade as more and more people have become aware of the ways that boards can affect nonprofit performance and success. Boards are charged with leading nonprofits in an increasingly dynamic and complex environment, and the challenges of doing so well have intensified interest in nonprofit boards, the work they do, how they are organized, and how they can and should contribute to the success and effectiveness of the organizations they govern.

When we review most of what is known about the field of nonprofit governance, we find our knowledge relies to a surprising degree on conventional wisdom, anecdotes, horror stories, and the impressions and prescriptions of various board consultants and authors. Ostrower and Stone, in their recent survey of the formal research literature on nonprofit governance, observe that progress is being made yet "major gaps in our theoretical and empirical knowledge about boards continue to exist" (2006, p. 612). They explain this is partly because "boards are complex entities that defy sweeping generalizations," and partly because there is an incredible degree of heterogeneity in the range of settings in which boards work. It can be very difficult to know just what guidance should apply to any one particular board, given this exceptional diversity. Nonetheless,

---

The beginning of this chapter is adapted from the author's chapter on "Governance of Nonprofits" (Renz, 2004b), and has been adapted with permission.

a core body of knowledge and information informs the design and practice of nonprofit governance and the work of boards, and that is the focus of this chapter.

I discuss nonprofit boards and governance from two perspectives. First, and as a foundation, I discuss governance and the work that typically is the province of a nonprofit board. This section includes basic information about the duties and responsibilities of governing boards and those who serve as members of boards, and describes some of the changes in expectations for their service. Second, I explore some of the key concerns that have been voiced regarding board performance and present a general framework for building board capacity. In presenting this framework, I highlight some of the important findings of recent research on board performance and discuss strategies for enhancing board effectiveness.

Governance, Strategy, and the Board

Every incorporated nonprofit organization in the United States and in most other nations of the world is legally required to have a formally established governing body. Typically labeled a "board of directors" or "board of trustees," this governing board is the group of people entrusted with and accountable for the leadership and governance of the nonprofit corporation. It is the board that has the ultimate authority and responsibility for the performance of a nonprofit organization and, even when the organization employs people in executive and staff roles, it is the board that ultimately is accountable to the community, to the state, and to clients and beneficiaries.

As common as nonprofit boards are, they and their work tend to be quite misunderstood—even by those who work with and serve on them! Central to the confusion is the blurring of two key concepts: governance and board. The two are fundamentally different: *governance* is an organizational function, whereas a *board* is a structure of the organization that exists (at least theoretically) to govern—to perform the work of governance. When we treat them as the same thing, we plant the seeds of much of the confusion that bedevils our understanding of boards and board effectiveness.

Governing boards, by definition, exist to govern. They often do more, as discussed in the next section, but at the least they are supposed to govern. For a nonprofit organization, what does this mean? Governance is the process of providing strategic leadership to the organization. It comprises the functions of setting direction, making decisions about policy and strategy, overseeing and monitoring organizational performance, and ensuring overall accountability. Nonprofit governance is a political and organizational process involving multiple functions and engaging multiple stakeholders. There is significant evidence that effective governance is closely related to the success of the nonprofit organization (summarized in Herman and Renz, 2008). Governance is primarily the province of an organization's governing board, yet often it will not be theirs alone. This is especially true in larger organizations that employ staff, where it is not unusual for the chief executive officer (such as executive director) and sometimes others to play a part in the governance process, as well.

Governance constitutes the most strategic decision process to be implemented by an organization, and its practice is grounded in the assumption that organizations can cause desired results to occur by choosing appropriate courses of action. Therefore, governance involves strategy, that is, the process of selecting among alternative courses of action—using the organization's mission, outcomes, and goals as the basis for the selection—and implementing these strategies to achieve the desired results and outcomes. In other words, governance is the process of providing direction that begins with making informed organizational choices: choices about why we're here, what we want to accomplish, how best to achieve those results, the resources we'll need to do these things and how we will secure them, and how we will know whether we are making a difference.

Effective governance and strategy are integral to the sustainability and long-term effectiveness of a nonprofit operating in today's complex and competitive world. To succeed, nonprofits (like all organizations) must continuously renew the link between what they do and the needs and interests of the community they serve. The strategy part of governance involves gathering information and using it to inform the key decisions, with the expectation that good strategic choices will result in organizational success. Unlike the for-profit world, where these choices are largely grounded in options for making money for someone, nonprofits essentially always begin with a focus on mission accomplishment—and their choices are about how best to have an impact. They must ensure they are providing the services needed and valued by their clients and constituents, and in ways that are consistent with the organization's core values and principles. As the organization serves its clients and the community, governance involves making assessments about how well or poorly the organization is doing and then making choices about how to refine its work to be more effective. (The strategy development process is explained in depth in Chapter Nine.)

The Work of the Board of Directors

The board of directors of the typical nonprofit organization has multiple roles and responsibilities. In this section, I describe the most common and fundamental of these, beginning with the legal and fiduciary duties that apply to essentially all governing boards and concluding with a discussion of the core functions of the nonprofit governing board. In the following section, I discuss the roles and responsibilities of the people who serve as individual members of a board.

The Legal Duties of the Board[1]

The board of directors is the primary group of people entrusted with and accountable for the leadership and governance of the nonprofit corporation. Nonprofit corporations are entities authorized by a state to be formed for the purpose of engaging in some form of public service, and state laws generally require that each such corporation has a governing body that oversees the work and ultimately is legally accountable. Acting as a collective, this governing body has both the authority and the accountability for the work of the organization. It is common for many boards to hire staff to do the actual work of the organization, often with support from volunteers. Nonetheless, it is the governing board that ultimately is accountable for all acts undertaken in the name of the organization (including by staff and volunteers), whether or not those acts are formally approved or implemented by the board itself. This accountability exists regardless of the size or nature of the nonprofit organization and regardless of whether the organization employs staff.

From a legal perspective, a nonprofit board and its members have three fundamental duties:

- *Duty of care*, which is taking the care and exercising the judgment that any reasonable and prudent person would exhibit in the process of making informed decisions, including acting in good faith consistent with what you as a member of the board truly believe is in the best interest of the organization. The law recognizes and accepts that board members may not always be correct in their choices or decisions, but it holds them accountable for being attentive, diligent, and thoughtful in considering and acting on a policy, course of action, or other decision. Active preparation for and participation in board meetings where important decisions are to be made is an integral element of the duty of care.
- *Duty of loyalty*, which calls upon the board and its members to consider and act in good faith to advance the interests of the organization. In other words, board members will not authorize or engage in transactions except those by which the best possible outcomes or terms for the organization can be achieved. This standard constrains a board member from participating in board discussions and decisions when they as an individual have a conflict of

interest (that is, their personal interests conflict with organizational interests, or they serve multiple organizations whose interests conflict).

- *Duty of obedience*, which requires obedience to the organization's mission, bylaws, and policies, as well as honoring the terms and conditions of other standards of appropriate behavior such as laws, rules, and regulations.

Board members are obligated to honor these standards with regard to all decisions and actions of the board, and those who do not may be subject to civil and even criminal sanctions (including, in the United States, sanctions imposed by the federal Internal Revenue Service in cases of inappropriate personal benefit).

During the past decade, there has been a significant increase in the attention paid to the legal responsibilities of nonprofit boards and their members. National, state, and provincial authorities all have placed increased emphasis on the need for nonprofit boards to be accountable for the quality of their governance and oversight of their organizations, and a number of governments have adopted legislation to require improved nonprofit performance and accountability. Many also have provided formal policy "guidance" and direction intended to spur increased self-regulation (see, for example, the U.S. Internal Revenue Service, 2010; The Panel on the Nonprofit Sector, 2005). The increasingly competitive and demanding environment of nonprofits, including increased competition between nonprofits and for-profit businesses, is likely to lead to calls for even more legal accountability in the future.

It is worth noting that there are many others who want boards to improve their practice as well, and some of them are more troubled by many boards' lack of connectedness and accountability to their constituent communities. Nonprofits exist to serve these communities, these advocates assert, so it is time for boards to develop new and more effective ways to engage more fully and effectively with their clients and beneficiaries (see, for example, Freiwirth and Letona, 2006). While there is less direct legal accountability for this aspect of board work, some communities are beginning to explore ways to enhance this type of accountability as well.

The Fiduciary Responsibility of Boards

Boards and board members often are reminded that they have a "fiduciary responsibility" to the organization and, ultimately, to the larger community within which they serve. At its core, "fiduciary responsibility" is the responsibility to treat the resources of the organization as a trust, and the responsible board will ensure that these resources are utilized in a reasonable, appropriate, and legally accountable manner. Although the phrase often is used to refer specifically to financial resources, it actually applies to the stewardship of all of the assets and resources of the organization.

In general, the appropriate exercise of fiduciary responsibility includes

- Adoption of a set of policies to govern the acquisition and use of financial and other resources
- Establishment, on a regular basis (usually annual), of a budget that allocates financial resources to the programs and activities that will accomplish the organization's mission, vision, and goals and outcomes (preferably, in alignment with a strategic plan)
- Development and implementation of an ongoing system for monitoring and holding staff and volunteers accountable for their performance with regard to these policies and budgets
- Development and implementation of an ongoing system to monitor, assess, and report on the overall fiscal condition and financial performance of the organization
- Implementation of an independent external review process (such as an independent audit) on a regular basis (usually annual), to assess the organization's fiscal condition and health, including the effectiveness of its systems and policies for the protection and appropriate use of financial resources

The Core Functions of the Typical Nonprofit Board

As already explained, most nonprofit boards do much more than govern. Thus, numerous nonprofit board consultants and authors have created lists of core functions and responsibilities to help boards understand their work. There is some variation among lists, and no one list is applicable to all organizations and boards, yet there are key themes that appear in one form or another on almost all lists.

It is typically the governing board's responsibility to

1. *Lead the organization:* provide overall leadership and strategic direction (including mission, vision and key goals) for the organization.
2. *Establish policy:* be proactive in establishing policies that will guide the organization.
3. *Secure essential resources:* make sure that the organization secures the resources that it needs to accomplish its mission, vision, and goals.
4. *Ensure effective resource use:* ensure that the organization makes effective use of its resources to accomplish its mission, vision, and goals.

5. *Lead and manage chief executive performance:* provide strategic direction, support and advice, and performance feedback to the organization's chief executive (such as the executive director). (*Note:* Even in organizations that do not employ staff, the board still is responsible for providing direction and oversight to the person or persons who manage and implement the work of the organization.)

6. *Engage with constituents:* actively help the organization develop and sustain an effective ongoing relationship with its key constituents.

7. *Ensure and enable accountability:* make certain that the organization has established standards and implemented systems by which to ensure that it is accountable and effective in serving the community it exists to serve.

8. *Ensure board effectiveness:* see that the board itself operates at a high level of performance and effectiveness.

Exhibit 5.1 identifies the key activities that are associated with each core function.

EXHIBIT 5.1. THE CORE FUNCTIONS OF THE PUBLIC SERVICE GOVERNING BOARD

A. Lead

Lead the Organization

1. Articulate the mission and an inspiring vision for the organization
2. Determine the organization's strategic direction and focus, and how the organization fits into the "bigger picture" for the future
3. Instill and maintain a strategic perspective and focus for the work of the organization (this is governance versus management)
4. Specify the organization's long-term (multiyear) goals and outcomes
5. Determine the core programs and services of the organization
6. Provide advice and counsel to executive leadership
7. Seek and nurture opportunities for service and innovation

B. Establish Policy

Establish Proactive Policy to Guide Organizational Action

1. Establish policies to guide executive decision making and action and the implementation of organizational programs and operations
2. Establish key intermediate-term organizational goals (1–3 years)
3. Approve overall organizational design (structure and core processes)
4. Ensure that strategic plans and policies guide resource allocation

C. Secure Essential Resources

Ensure That the Organization Secures the Resources Needed to Accomplish Its Mission, Vision, and Goals

1. Enable the organization to secure the resources necessary to implement the programs and services that are central to the achievement of the mission, vision, and goals
2. Make sure that the resource mix is appropriate to the mission, vision, and long-term goals

D. Ensure Effective Resource Use

Ensure That the Organization Makes Effective Use of Resources to Accomplish Its Mission, Vision, and Goals

1. Allocate resources to implement the organization's strategic plans (i.e., budget)
2. Ensure that effective systems are in place to enable the board and executive leadership to monitor and document that financial and other resources are managed and used effectively to accomplish the organization's purposes and plans
3. Make sure that the organization's systems and policies are adequate to safeguard and guide the use of resources and assets (including appropriate management of risk)

E. Lead and Manage Chief Executive Performance

Ensure Effective CEO Performance

1. Recruit, select, hire, and set appropriate compensation for the chief executive
2. Provide regular performance direction and feedback to the chief executive
3. Serve as a confidential sounding board and resource advisor
4. Articulate board and executive roles and role distinctions (avoid micromanagement)
5. Ensure that there is a clear performance management structure in place that enables appropriate levels of accountability throughout the organization

F. Engage with Constituents

Ensure an Effective Ongoing Relationship Between Organization and Key Constituents

1. Maintain strong relationships with key stakeholders
2. Facilitate and enhance effective two-way, ongoing communication with key stakeholders

3. Enhance the external image and credibility of the organization
4. Make sure that organizational accountability information is regularly and accurately reported to relevant stakeholders
5. Encourage and support the processes for enhancing inter-organizational and inter-agency communication and coordination
6. Discern and evaluate external trends and dynamics to assess their implications for the organization, and share this information with the organization
7. Help constituents link with appropriate parts of the organization (as they have needs and problems to address)
8. Keep private the information that legally or ethically must remain private

G. Ensure and Enable Accountability

Ensure Organizational Accountability and Stewardship

1. Ensure that appropriate systems exist and function well to monitor, assess, and document organizational performance and outcomes
2. Ensure that appropriate systems exist and function well to assess, document, and report on organizational compliance with policies, regulations, bylaws, and other mandates and guides for organizational action (including "sunshine laws," etc.)
3. Ensure that organizational performance and outcomes information are reported in a timely, accurate, and useful manner to all relevant stakeholders
4. Monitor use of financial and other resources to ensure that they are managed and used efficiently and effectively to accomplish the organization's purposes and plans
5. Determine the performance information to be reported to the board, in what forms and manner, and how often (per above, items 1, 2, and 4)
6. Ensure that the organization is responsive to constituent requests for information
7. Clarify to whom the organization is to be accountable and ensure that systematic accountability is maintained with them.

H. Ensure Board Effectiveness

Ensure a High Level of Board Performance and Effectiveness

1. Attract and retain well-qualified, committed members to serve on the board
2. Establish and monitor compliance with policies to guide board operations
3. Clarify board roles and responsibilities in helping the organization accomplish its mission, vision, and long-term goals (including maintenance of distinctions between governance and management roles in the organization)

4. Prepare and educate members to work and serve effectively (including orientation, member education, ongoing information, and education sessions)
5. Establish and regularly refine a functional, effective board design (structure and process for board and all subsidiary entities)
6. Engage in regular self-assessment and development planning (including individual member performance feedback)

The Work of Board Members

Interest in nonprofit boards and how they work has grown substantially in recent years, and more and more people are embracing the opportunity to serve on a board. This is good news. But the trend has a challenging side to it, as well. The average person working with a governing board, executive and board member alike, has limited understanding of the work to be done by a board or what is expected of him or her as they work with that board. In spite of all the talk about the importance of effective boards and good governance, we find that the majority of people in the nonprofit sector (including even a significant share of those who have prior board experience) actually have only vague and general notions about the fundamental roles and responsibilities of the board and the work of governance.

The uncertainty and confusion are understandable. We have not done a good job of preparing people for their work on and with boards. This may be partly because every board seems to be a little (or a lot) different from any standard model, and partly because we are so busy that we don't feel that we can afford to take the time to be sure that we're all on the same page. We become so busy doing the work that we don't take the time to make sure that we understand the work! The lack of shared understanding is amplified by our discomfort with our uncertainty. A good share of the time, an executive or board member with questions assumes he or she is the only one who is uncertain—and yet that person is rarely alone in his or her uncertainty.

The Legal Responsibilities of the Individual Board Member

The legal responsibilities of a board member flow directly from the responsibilities of the board as a whole. Each board member, individually, is accountable for honoring the same three fiduciary duties as is the entire board: to exhibit due care, loyalty, and obedience on behalf of the organization on whose board the member serves. This standard of personal conduct requires active and informed preparation and participation in the conduct of board business, including raising questions and issues that would reasonably be raised by any prudent person. Of course, a board member who does not attend meetings or who attends but does not participate or know what is under consideration does not meet these standards. At best, such members are not helping the organization; at worst they are endangering the organization and the interests of the people it serves. Such members also are at risk of personal liability and "intermediate sanctions" should certain kinds of inappropriate organizational or board behavior occur. (See Chapter Twenty-three for more information on risk management and the liability of board members and other volunteers, and see Chapter Two for general information about nonprofit law.)

All board members are responsible for doing their best to help ensure that the board as a whole is performing its legal responsibilities, and individual board members can be held liable as individuals for inappropriate organizational acts. Among the circumstances under which board members have been held personally liable (for more information, see Herman, 2006) are the following:

- When the organization has not paid certain taxes, especially payroll taxes
- The board enters into inappropriate arrangements or contracts with a board member, particularly including conflicts of interest
- The board has violated employment laws or contracts (a common example: the handling of the termination of an executive director)
- The board has failed to take reasonable steps to protect others from harm in a situation they knew or should have known was potentially dangerous (for example, in addressing dangerous facilities conditions, or in failing to address inappropriate individual behaviors of staff such as harassment or sexual misconduct)

Beyond the Legal Obligations

Obviously, it is important for every board member to honor his or her legal responsibilities, but the roles and responsibilities of the individual board member of a typical nonprofit board are more extensive than mere legal compliance. Every board should develop its own set of member expectations that addresses the needs and interests of that specific organization and what it needs from its board. However, the following are among the most common of responsibilities or expectations that a typical nonprofit is likely to have of its board members:

- Participate actively (for example, attend all meetings of the board, serve on committees or task forces, prepare in advance for meetings and other key board activities, engage in independent and critical thought in all areas of board work, and attend special events and other key organizational activities as requested).

- Be knowledgeable and ensure that they understand and act consistently with the mission, vision, and overall work and strategic direction of the organization; the bylaws and policies that guide the work of the board; and the board's expectations of them as a member of the board.
- Do their homework to ensure that they are appropriately informed about issues and matters that will be the subjects of board deliberation, decision making, or monitoring, and important issues that are likely to have an impact on the success of the board and organization.
- Provide active support for the fundraising and other resource development activities of the organization, including making a regular personal financial contribution to the organization (at a significant level, according to the member's capacity) and assisting the organization in connecting with those people and organizations that may be able to assist in funding and supporting the organization.
- Serve as an ambassador and advocate on behalf of the organization, helping support networking and the development of connections with community and other leaders.
- Provide encouragement and active support for the work of the staff and volunteers, taking care that board activities do not interfere with staff roles or functions.
- Serve with honor and integrity, including to
  - Help enhance the image and credibility of the organization through their work, taking care that their personal behavior reflects well on the work and reputation of the organization.
  - Address sensitive matters in confidence and with discretion, exhibiting the best of ethical performance.
  - Honor and actively support all board decisions, once they have been made, and treat the content of board deliberations with confidence and discretion.
  - Avoid actual and perceived conflicts of interest, to the greatest degree possible, and exhibit the highest of ethical standards in all personal conduct.
- Support and actively contribute to the board's efforts to work effectively as a team, including taking an active and constructive role in helping the board do its work, embracing the challenges and opportunities of board work with a positive attitude and energy, bringing a sense of perspective and humor to the work of the board, and providing encouragement and support to fellow board members (including taking time to celebrate the successes and accomplishments of the organization, the board and its members).

Characteristics of Typical Nonprofit Boards

As noted earlier in this chapter, nonprofit boards are an exceptionally diverse and heterogeneous lot, so a discussion of "typical" characteristics must be broad and general. Nonprofit boards typically have specific positions (offices) and work units (committees and task forces) that help the board organize and accomplish its work. The typical nonprofit board has twelve to twenty-four members; according to a recent survey of U.S. nonprofits (Ostrower, 2007, p. 25), the average for nonprofit board size in America is thirteen members (median size is eleven). Most board members also serve for specified terms of office (three-year terms are most common), and about two-thirds of all U.S. nonprofits limit consecutive reelection to a maximum of three terms (most common is a limit of two consecutive terms).

Officers

Most nonprofit organizations have multiple officers, and the laws of most states of the United States require certain offices—most commonly, chair (sometimes called president), secretary, and treasurer (sometimes the roles of secretary and treasurer are combined).

Chair. The board chair is the chief voluntary officer of the organization and is responsible for organizing and conducting the meetings of the board. Further, it is the chair's responsibility to facilitate the board's work as a team and to ensure that meetings and other board activities are conducted in an effective manner. It is common for the board chair to oversee the performance of the organization's chief executive on behalf of the board, although some organizations elaborate the process by assigning the chair to lead a process in conjunction with a committee of the board (often the executive committee) or even the full board. Although there is little research to date, recent research (Harrison and Murray, 2007) affirms what many would expect: the effectiveness of the board chair has significant impact on the effectiveness of the board and the satisfaction of its members.

Secretary. The work of a corporate secretary involves ensuring that accurate records are retained for the nonprofit, including copies of all official documents, communications, and correspondence of the organization (including articles of incorporation, bylaws, and legal notices and filings), as well as notices and minutes of all official meetings of the board. The secretary might or might not personally prepare the minutes but is accountable for ensuring that accurate and complete minutes of all official meetings are kept.

Treasurer. The treasurer oversees the processes of financial management and accountability for the organization, helping make sure that all resources are used appropriately and their use is documented. This includes ensuring the preparation and retention of complete and accurate financial reports and records. In small organizations, the treasurer often is involved in the actual financial operations of the organization; in larger organizations he or she maintains general oversight of financial affairs and sees that regular reports are provided to the board, regulators, and other key stakeholders. The treasurer might or might not personally keep financial records and maintain accounts, but he or she is accountable for ensuring that these records are maintained and available to authorities.

Committees and Task Forces

Boards engage in much of their work as a full group and, ideally, all members work as a team to accomplish the work of the board. Nonetheless, more than 90 percent of U.S. nonprofit boards also have created committees and task forces to help the board do its work (Ostrower, 2007), and these entities are part of the governance system of the organization. For most boards, some of these units are permanent or "standing" structures whereas others accomplish a specific task and then disappear. It is increasingly common for boards to refer to the permanent structures as "committees" and the limited term entities as "task forces" or "ad hoc committees," although some organizations do use the labels interchangeably. It is common for board committees to be composed entirely of board members, yet an increasingly large number of nonprofits also invite non–board members with unique expertise, knowledge, or interests to serve. Typically, the key standing committees are specified in the organization's bylaws, which also should explain their purpose and role(s).

The following are among the most common types of standing committees:

1. *Executive committee.* This committee is typically composed of the officers, and sometimes also will include committee chairs or selected other board members. It usually has the authority to act on behalf of the board between meetings and to address organizational emergencies. Some executive committees have the authority to act independently, but many are required to have their actions subsequently ratified by the full board.
2. *Nominating committee.* This committee has the responsibility for recruiting candidates for board and committee membership and preparing a "slate" of candidates or nominees for consideration and action by the full board; many also nominate officers. It is increasingly common to define this committee's responsibilities to include a year-round cycle of board development activities, including new member orientation, member self-assessment, board

self-assessment and development, and the development of board training programs and retreats. When operating with this enlarged portfolio, such committees often are called board development or governance committees.

3. *Fundraising or development committee.* This committee usually is responsible for working with staff and board to organize and implement the organization's fundraising events and activities, including the solicitation of major gifts and grants.

4. *Finance committee.* This committee is responsible for planning, monitoring, and overseeing the organization's use of its financial resources, including developing a budget to allocate the organization's funds. This committee will develop for board action the financial policies the organization requires. Unless the organization has a separate audit committee, the finance committee also will oversee and review the organization's independent audit or financial review.

5. *Personnel committee.* This committee usually is responsible for planning, monitoring, and overseeing the organization's use of its human resources (paid and volunteer). This committee will develop needed personnel policies, including policies guiding performance management and supervision, employee compensation and benefits, and handling of grievances.

6. *Program committee.* It is not unusual for nonprofits to have one or more committees to oversee the organization's system(s) for delivering quality services to clients, and to engage in some form of monitoring and oversight to ensure that these services are provided in a timely and responsible manner. Such committees may handle certain relations with community leaders and interest groups that have key interests in the programs of the organization, as well as planning for program development or refinement to meet future needs.

It is important that committees and task forces only do work that legitimately is the responsibility of the board, and care must be taken to ensure that these structures do not interfere with either the staff operations of the organization or with the oversight that should be provided by the full board. Many boards in older organizations have concluded that they have too many committees, and it has become something of a trend among U.S. nonprofit boards to decrease the number of standing committees and use task forces more frequently to address specific issues of strategic importance as they arise (Taylor, Chait, and Holland, 1996).

Building Board Capacity to Serve

Nonprofit boards are today feeling more pressure than ever to perform well, and these demands to perform more effectively are coming from nearly all quarters. Although each group is demanding something a little different, the federal and state regulatory officials, various taxation authorities (such as the Internal Revenue Service and state departments of revenue), the foundation community, donors, and even clients and other key beneficiaries are calling for boards to be better, stronger, and more effective. Even board members themselves, for the most part, say their boards could be more effective.

The Characteristics of the Strong Nonprofit Board

What are the characteristics of the well-developed board—the board that is able to recruit, retain, and mobilize its members to do the essential work of a board of directors? A review of the literature suggests the following key characteristics:

- The effective board organizes its work in ways that make judicious (and often creative) use of the limited amount of time that members can commit to the organization.
- The effective board is good at matching the work it needs to do with the skills, abilities, and interests of its members, and it invests in preparing these members to do this work.
- The effective board understands that, at core, success is grounded in building effective relationships—relationships among the members of the board, relationships between each member and the board as a whole, and relationships between the member and the overall organization. These boards take care to help these relationships develop and grow from the very beginning.
- The effective board recognizes that one of the most valuable assets it brings to the nonprofit is its members—their time, talent, and service. It understands that the highest and best use of member time is to provide leadership, strategic direction, and oversight to the agency, and it recognizes the opportunity cost inherent in dribbling away member time by involving them in irrelevant activities that divert their attention from the most important work they could do.
- The effective board creates an infrastructure of support that helps members accomplish their work efficiently. Member time and talent are successfully leveraged because the support, systems, and technology exist to enable their work. Two kinds of infrastructure are provided:
  - Infrastructure that supports members' work together, such as communications technologies and information systems
  - Systems to provide the information that the board needs to accomplish its work
- The effective board is thoughtful about and takes the time to reflect on what its does well and what could be improved—and it uses this information to

improve both board performance and the quality of each member's experience as a board member. The successful board understands that board effectiveness is a journey and a process, not a specific state of being. It is thoughtful about growing its capacity to perform, and focuses on the high-leverage targets of opportunity for growing board capacity.

Competencies of Effective Boards

What are the key elements of nonprofit board effectiveness? Why do some boards perform well when many others do not? One of the foundational research initiatives to examine these questions was implemented by Richard Chait and colleagues in the mid-1990s. They examined the differences between boards that were reported to be more versus less effective and identified six core competencies that were associated with the best-performing of these boards (Taylor, Chait, and Holland, 1996). Even the most effective of these boards varied in the degree to which they had mastered each of the six, but there were clear relationships between the degree to which each board exhibited each of the competencies and their overall performance as a board. The six key dimensions of board competence are the following (Holland and Jackson, 1998, pp. 122–123):

- *Contextual competence:* the board understands and takes into account the culture, values, mission, and norms of the organization it governs.
- *Educational competence:* the board takes the necessary steps to ensure that members are well informed about the organization, the professions working there, and the board's own roles, responsibilities, and performance.
- *Interpersonal competence:* the board nurtures the development of its members *as a group*, attends to the board's collective welfare, and fosters a sense of cohesiveness and teamwork.
- *Analytical competence*: the board recognizes complexities and subtleties in the issues its faces, and it draws upon multiple perspectives to dissect complex problems and to synthesize appropriate responses.
- *Political competence:* the board accepts that one of its primary responsibilities is to develop and maintain healthy two-way communications and positive relationships with key constituencies.
- *Strategic competence:* the board helps envision and shape institutional direction and ensures a strategic approach to the organization's future.

Helping Boards Meet the Challenge

It is time to recognize that we're really not doing enough to help governing boards and their members to be successful as they serve in these special roles of public trust. Relatively few boards engage in a regular program of board development (Ostrower, 2007), yet there are many reasons to believe that nonprofit boards that engage in a regular ongoing systematic approach to board development are more effective and their members are happier and more productive on behalf of the organization. A number of recent studies have documented that board development activities can have an impact on board member performance and overall board effectiveness. For example, one study (Brown, 2007) reports that effective member recruitment, selection, and orientation practices enhance board member performance; another study suggests that a well-designed program of board development can make a difference in the performance of a nonprofit board and, ultimately, in the financial performance of the organization (Holland and Jackson, 1998). Similarly, Cornforth (2001) reports a direct relationship between the effectiveness of nonprofit boards and (a) the knowledge and skills of board members, (b) the clarity of their board member roles and responsibilities, and (c) board members and executives coming together on a periodic basis to assess how well they are working together. It is reasonable to conclude that activities that improve board members' knowledge and skills and clarify their roles and responsibilities will therefore enhance board effectiveness as well.

One of the major impediments that keeps the typical board from engaging in ongoing board development is the sense (or worry) that it will involve too much effort and time, and that it will be a distraction from "our real work." An effective board development approach will not divert attention from important matters. To the contrary, it will focus attention in a more efficient way on one of the core responsibilities of every nonprofit board—the responsibility to be a good steward of its members' time and talent and to ensure its own effectiveness. In other words, effective boards engage in a systematic ongoing process of development because they understand that this will make a difference in the value they deliver for the organization, and because it makes a difference to those who serve on the board. It's no fun to serve on a dysfunctional board!

Being systematic does not require a board to be exceptionally elaborate about its approach, nor to consume hundreds of hours of member time each year. Indeed, one of the greatest challenges confronting most boards today is that they barely can find the time to get enough members together to handle the regular required business, much less the time for what some might consider "add on" activities. Thus, efficiency in the development process is important. However, the irony is that those boards that take a minimalist approach to development generally undercut their capacity to bring members together for the minimal agenda of regular business, because service on their board is so boring and unrewarding that their members attend meetings (if they do at all) because of a sense of obligation rather than because they feel their time and talents are being used well. Efforts to minimize development time actually can backfire when it comes to member commitment as well as performance!

Eight Core Principles for Growing a Board

Board leaders should recognize eight fundamental principles as they explore the ways they might wish to build their boards' capacity.

> *Principle 1.* Nonprofit organizations cannot be successful for the long term unless they have governing boards that are effective. There is a high correlation between nonprofit organizational effectiveness and board effectiveness (Herman and Renz, 2008; Brown, 2007). Therefore, a board's effectiveness is important to the organization's performance and service to the community.

> *Principle 2.* Board design is about the future, and all board development needs to be done with the future in mind—both the conditions that the organization will face in the future and the organization's needs for the future to address those conditions. Hockey star Wayne Gretzky is reputed to have said that his success as a hockey player was due to the fact that he always made it a point to "skate to *where the puck was going to be!*" Boards should take this point to heart! We are preparing to serve in the future—do we know "where it will be?"

> *Principle 3.* There is no one single design or model for board development that automatically will be best for all organizations. The board is part of two larger systems—the organization and the larger community environment—and so its design and development need to be aligned with the needs and characteristics of these environs. Boards serve different functions and roles at different points in the life and development of their organizations, and these differences must be taken into account when determining the most useful board development process. Further, the research to date on board development initiatives suggests no one model seems to be better than another. In fact, there is evidence that what makes a difference in board development is the organized use of any thoughtful and well-developed systematic approach to development (Nobbie and Brudney, 2003; Brudney and Murray, 1998).

> *Principle 4.* Focus on principles, not "best practices." The notion that there are practices that are universally best is flawed—at best, there are "promising practices" that are worthy of consideration, but one can never claim that a given practice will be "best" until the organization's issues, needs, and circumstances are taken into account (Herman and Renz, 2008; 2004).

There are many good resources that offer examples of useful practices (for example, checklists, training programs, board development tools—consult the Internet resource site of this handbook for further information), but until the organization knows what it needs, these are merely resources.

Principle 5. Leadership is critical and pivotal to board success and, therefore, to board development. Every change process, including every development process, needs to have at least one champion who will make it their goal to help advance the development process (Kotter, 1996). However, serving as "champion" is not the only leadership role in any board; responsibility for leadership must be shared among all members of a team, as they provide both mutual support and encourage mutual accountability for the board's work.

Principle 6. Structures never guarantee performance in organizations (or communities), although they can get in the way and screw things up. Performance derives from the behavior of people, and it is not possible to guarantee performance through the creation of structures, so retain only as many board structures (for example, offices, committees, terms, reporting relationships) as are essential. Likewise, take care to nurture the "soft" or process aspects of the board's work, because the processes are the dynamic vehicles for bringing structures to life (see the next principle).

Principle 7. Effective boards, by definition, are teams. Teams are groups of people who are working together to accomplish a shared goal or outcome (Katzenbach and Smith, 2003). If this definition does not describe a governing board, then that board is not living up to its legal and ethical obligations as a board! The shared outcome always is defined as the success of the organization. Thus, team building is always an important dimension of any legitimate approach to board development.

Principle 8. Every effective development process must "meet" the organization or team "where they are," and each organization and board must build from the level of development and capacity that exists at the time they begin the development process. Regardless of what you wish, the board is currently at some level of development that must be recognized for what it is—the starting point for growing the board. So the process starts at this point—start here, start now, and initiate a process that will be manageable in scale and scope. Further, it must be recognized that there are going to be limits to how much can be done or what a board can accomplish in a given time period. It makes no sense to assume or wish that a board is better positioned than it is (nor worse than its situation is); it is essential to build from whatever stage of development exists. Nowhere is this going to be more true than in working with an all-volunteer group of people from the community, people who always will need to balance their board work with the other demands of life, family, and work. Finally, do not wait until the "perfect time" to start a development process—conditions never will be close to perfect for any typical board, so start now and begin with whatever is feasible to begin to help your board develop

The Board Builder's Challenge: Taking the Long-Term, Developmental Perspective

Strong and effective boards do not happen by accident, and they do not develop overnight. They also do not remain effective indefinitely. Successful nonprofits invest time, energy, and even money in building and sustaining strong boards. This section introduces a board development framework, discusses the process by which boards develop and grow, and explores the ways that the concepts of the framework might be used to guide board development activity. Effective boards capitalize on all facets of a board's development process, taking a long-term developmental or continuous-improvement approach to growing their boards. Effective boards grow and develop (intentionally or not) through an ongoing cycle of eight relatively sequential overlapping elements. Each element adds unique value to the capacity and impact of the board, each poses its own design and development challenges, and each has a set of developmental activities that enhance its contribution to board success. We discuss how the cycle begins for new organizations with new boards, but our emphasis is on the ways that existing boards can use this development cycle approach to build their capacity and impact.

It is most useful for nonprofit leaders who are interested in building their boards' capacity to approach their capacity-building work from the perspective of a larger and longer-term integrated board development process—a process that reflects a complete board development cycle. Even though many board leaders cannot afford to address all facets of the board development process at one time, their ability to make a substantive long-term difference will be considerably enhanced if they recognize that each of the various facets exists and that, collectively, they affect a board's capacity to succeed. Strong and effective boards grow to be effective because their leaders have chosen to invest in their capacity.

Understanding and Implementing a Developmental Cycle Approach to Build Your Board

Effective boards engage in a thoughtful ongoing process of board development because they understand that this makes a difference in the value and impact that their board delivers for the organization, and because they understand that it makes a difference to those who serve on the board. And a truly useful approach recognizes that all of the elements of board development interact in a systematic way. It may make sense for a board to tackle only one or two of these elements at any given time, yet it is essential to be systematic about the process by which it does so. To fail to take the larger perspective will be both inefficient and, ultimately, without impact.

When we observe nonprofit boards and think about how they emerge and develop, we see a relatively predictable process that includes specific phases and key elements of development. Although these elements of development do not occur in a distinct linear sequence, we do observe that there is a general flow that is common to most boards, and this flow of development becomes a recurring cycle that effective boards recognize and use to their advantage. This process is often implemented rather intuitively, since few boards give much systematic thought to their growth and development. However, when understood and used in a systematic manner, it becomes possible for boards to grow and develop in more efficient and effective ways.

There are eight elements that every board addresses in its development. The effective board will develop its capacity to serve by making sure that it

- *Organizes* itself to efficiently and effectively accomplish the work it must do for the organization
- *Attracts* to the board table a group of people who will enable it to do this work well
- *Prepares* these people to effectively serve in their roles as members
- *Helps* these members work together as a team to accomplish their work
- *Focuses* members' attention on the right issues and questions
- *Engages and motivates* its members to retain their involvement and service
- *Employs* members' time well, in meetings and other activities
- *Evaluates and develops* its own performance, as a group, and uses this information to refine its design and practices to improve its effectiveness for the future

When a board first organizes to govern and lead an organization, these tend to be the stages that it will go through as it creates itself. Of course, in real organizational life, the elements tend to overlap and interact in ways that cause them to influence each other. Further, in young and relatively undeveloped boards, many of these elements tend to be executed informally and even unknowingly— yet each of these elements is in fact implemented in some way by every board that actually grows to operate as a board. Figure 5.1 illustrates the general sequence and flow of these eight elements.

FIGURE 5.1. THE BOARD DEVELOPMENT CYCLE.

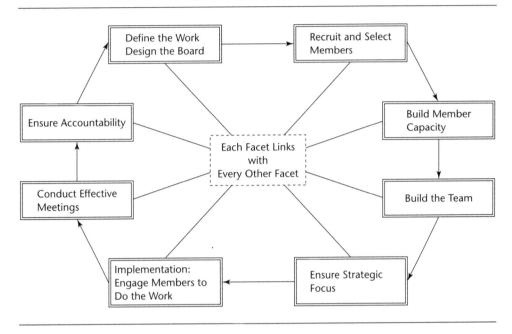

The Key Elements of the Board Development Cycle

Each of the eight elements of the board development cycle contributes uniquely to the capacity of a board. Each alone offers specific utility for building board capacity, and the activities associated with each may be implemented alone. However, the extended value of the board development cycle framework lies in the recognition that the value that each element offers is substantially enhanced by linking it to and growing it from other elements in the cycle. Some of these elements are most usefully implemented in a sequence (for example, recruiting and selecting members usefully precedes building member capacity). However, it also is likely that many of these elements should overlap in their implementation (for example, "ensuring strategic focus" relates to each of the other elements). Therefore, it is essential to recognize that the eight elements of board development are neither mutually exclusive nor do they occur in a purely sequential, lockstep way.

Working from the perspective of a new start-up organization, I now provide a brief overview of the eight elements of the board development cycle. Additional information about each of the eight is available at the Internet resource site for this book. Included on the site are ideas and suggestions for various development options and activities that might be considered useful by a board working to address each element.

Element A: Define the Work, Design the Board. The effective board is designed to effectively accomplish the work that it will need to do. Board organization comprises multiple elements, including structures (such as committees, task forces, offices) and processes (such as leading, meeting, making decisions, monitoring, communicating). It will include clear delineation of the roles that the board will play in the leadership, governance, and management of the organization, and, for the organization with staff (paid or volunteer), this definition will include explicit distinctions regarding the roles to be served by the board and by the executive or other staff. The complex and sensitive topic of the board–executive relationship is very important but, since it is addressed extensively in Chapter Six, I will not discuss this in any depth here.

The wise board organizes from the perspective of the work that it is to accomplish and, in particular, the work that it needs to do during the organization's next stage of development. Until the board knows what is needed from it, it cannot determine what it should do or how to organize to do it. The contributions that must be made by the board of a small start-up organization are going to be relatively different from the contributions of the board of a mature organization. The work is going to be different. And some board designs match some stages of organization development better than do others.

Thus the focus of Element A is this: the board of directors of a nonprofit organization should design itself based on the needs of the organization and the work that the board will need to do.

Element B: Recruit and Select Members. Recruiting and selecting members is one of the most commonly practiced elements of board development. Every board must find people to serve, and every board somehow engages in activities that will make this happen. But the key issue is whether the board is thoughtful and systematic about its member recruitment. To echo the findings that business author Jim Collins (2005) has described in his recent work, an essential element of organizational success is to ensure that you have "the right people on the bus." Far too many boards haphazardly pursue the wrong candidates for the wrong reasons, place them on the board, and then become terribly frustrated when things go poorly. A large proportion of board performance problems can be traced directly back to an ineffective or counterproductive member recruitment and selection process. Ignore this element at your peril!

The effective nonprofit board will engage in a thoughtful process that builds on the insights it gained during its work on Element A (Define the Work, Design the Board). From its understanding of the work it needs to do for the organization, it will then determine its next-generation needs (such as knowledge, skills, abilities, and other characteristics), evaluate its current membership from the perspective of these needs, and then engage in a systematic process of seeking, locating, and recruiting the people who will meet next-generation of the board. It will take care to find the right matches among its needs and the needs and interests of prospective members, including taking care to ensure that its membership is appropriately diverse and reflective of the community the organization exists to serve. Recent research has documented that effective recruitment and selection practice is very significant to board effectiveness (see, for example, Brown, 2007; Cornforth, 2001). None of this is to suggest that this element must be implemented in a drawn-out and bureaucratic way: it is possible to be proactive and systematic without getting bogged down in an excessive process.

Element C: Prepare Members to Serve. Effective boards recruit people to serve as members because they bring knowledge, skill, and an array of talents and assets that the board envisions to be important to its future success. But it is not enough to simply bring the right people to the board; the effective board will help its members put these talents to work in ways that are most useful for both the organization and the member. This type of preparation often begins with helping the new member understand the nature and scope of his or her role as he or she becomes an active member of the board, and an increasing number of boards are beginning to offer some kind of useful member-orientation process for their new members. In fact, this member preparation usually begins at the recruitment and selection stage with an explicit description of the roles and expectations that the board has for its members (for example, requirements for meeting attendance or whether members work on fundraising).

This is a good start, but the effective board will provide much more in the way of preparation and support for its members. Here, too, recent research confirms that new member orientation and ongoing education activities for all members are positively related to effective board performance (see Brown, 2007; Holland and Jackson, 1998). Such development helps members better understand their work, the work of the organization, the challenges that the organization and board believe will be most important to address as they proceed with their work, and what they envision will be the board's role in helping to address these issues. Further, a strong board will provide regular ongoing support to all of its members to help them serve effectively, not only those who are new. Unless nothing is changing in either the organization or its operating environment, member knowledge and understanding will need to grow and develop as the organization's circumstances evolve. This dimension of support for members is not only important from a board perspective; many board members value their time on a board because they gained new knowledge or skills or perspectives through their board service. This preparation can even be a motivator as well as a support for the content of the board's work.

Element D: Build the Board as a Team.   Preparing the individual board members to play their roles is important but not enough when it comes to nonprofit board service. Much of the power of the effective board comes from the synergy of the individuals coming together to do things that they could not do as well by themselves. When individual board members come together, they are a group. Yet board work is inherently *teamwork*. As explained earlier, the board's authority and responsibility, legally and ethically, derives from its work as a *collective* body. The thoughts and decisions of specific individuals, no matter how bright or relevant, cannot be represented as the work of the board unless and until the board *collectively* adopts them as its own.

In other words, a board must develop to the level of working as a team in order to serve effectively. Taylor et al. (1996) report that leading-edge boards are focusing directly on building their capacity for teamwork—in their words, these boards are "focusing on the constellation, not the stars!" Some debate whether a board is or needs to be a team—yet it is entirely clear (as a matter of definition) that a board cannot truly serve as a board unless its members come together to serve as a team. If there is no shared purpose the board members are working together to accomplish, they cannot possibly be serving effectively as a board. If nothing else, the duty of loyalty compels it! But of course the typical board member usually joins a board for just this purpose—they join to work with others to help see that the organization progresses in its efforts to accomplish its mission and vision.

Of course, it is one thing to assert that a board is or should be working as a team, it is another to actually achieve this. Thus, a critical yet often overlooked element of board effectiveness is the explicit attention to building the capacity of the board's members to work *together* effectively, to work as a team. This is the core of the work of this element of board development. Ironically, many board members and leaders know much about teams, how effective teams sustain their success, and how to help teams enhance their performance—they've had formal team development training provided by their employers! And yet it is quite unusual to find a board that is overtly working to tap the power of the wide-ranging literature on team development and performance to enhance board effectiveness.

Element E: Create and Sustain a Strategic Focus.   Boards are "all over the map" when it comes to their work. Some operate exclusively at the policy governance and leadership level of work, some serve in both governing and management roles, and still others serve all roles in the organization—as governor, manager, and as operations staff. But the one level at which all boards must work is the strategic level, the work of governance and leadership. And one of the greatest challenges many boards face is that of sustaining their focus at the strategic level. For understandable but problematic reasons, boards much too often become so involved in the details that they lose all sense of their unique responsibility to make strategic choices. Indeed, in organizations with staff, this often becomes a critical source of tension between the board and the organization's top levels of executive management; board members become heavily involved in management or operations and become resented for their duplication of or interference with the work of the rest of the organization.

This is one board development element that intertwines with all other elements of the board development cycle. There are aspects of creating and sustaining a strategic focus that must be integrated with each of the other phases. For example, the issue of strategic focus and the board's role obviously is central to the question of board design. But the challenge of strategic focus is equally relevant when we implement that design through recruiting members to serve on the board. If a board does not ensure that the members it recruits are able to work with an appropriately strategic focus, then it is doomed to fighting an uphill battle for its entire tenure.

There are multiple ways that boards and their leaders can help ensure that the board works with and provides the strategic focus that the organization needs. Many of these ideas are discussed on the *Handbook* Internet resource site.

Element F: Implementation: Accomplish the Board's Work. There are certain aspects of board development that are likely to be most effectively accomplished as the board and its members actually engage in the process of implementation; that is, doing the work planned and organized during the earlier stages of board development. Key among them is the set of issues around engaging and motivating members to play their roles—the entire process of handling board members as a special type of volunteer. We know quite a lot about volunteer management and what it takes to engage and motivate volunteers yet, similar to our lack of utilization of the team development literature, we find that most boards are not adequately attentive to matters of engaging the board member as volunteer. (The guidance on volunteer management provided in Chapter Twenty-six is especially relevant to this point.)

Element G: Conduct Effective Meetings. The crucible within which boards do much of their most critical and essential work is the meeting—the time during which board members come together to organize and begin to implement their work on behalf of the organization. Too long, too short, too disorganized, too narrow, too unfocused—the complaints and concerns are multiple and frequent. Meetings are among the most disliked elements of board service for many members, yet the typical board leader spends surprisingly little time organizing and conducting meetings to ensure that they are efficient and effective venues for board work. There are boards that have developed strategies to use meetings to full advantage to conduct business and to do so in ways that are motivating and energizing for all who participate. These meetings capitalize on the diverse and unique talents at the table, and they create a productive environment that results in board accomplishment. These meetings are used as tools to advance board performance, and they are effectively organized and conducted by chairs who have mastered the art of the effective meeting.

As with the topics of team development and volunteer management, there is a practical body of literature that exists to help board leaders understand how to organize and conduct meetings effectively. And as with the topic of team development, board leaders as a group have tended to ignore the practical advice that this literature offers for using the board meeting effectively.

Element H: Assess and Enhance Board and Member Accountability. Accountability is an increasingly critical issue in all corners of the nonprofit world, and it is an issue that boards must address at multiple levels. New guidelines and expectations are being proposed and sometimes even mandated by a myriad of actors, including state and federal regulators, watchdog agencies, funders, and even constituent advocacy groups. Growing pressures are developing across the sector for enhanced "self-regulation." But the effective board is not reacting to these external calls for accountability; it is taking the lead. Relatively few nonprofit boards today engage in any regular systematic process by which to assess their performance and impact, yet a growing number are beginning to recognize both the imperative and potential benefits of doing so.

Effective boards set goals for their own performance, both long and short term, and they implement processes by which to assess their accomplishment and evaluate how they could be more successful. Some boards have initiated self-assessment processes to gather information to ascertain whether board members meet the expectations that they set (such as attendance, personal giving). Some board members are uncomfortable with such activities, but a growing number support board self-assessment and consider such efforts appropriate and beneficial. These boards are proactively developing their own systems and practices for gathering performance information at multiple levels—about organization performance, board performance, and even about the performance of individual board members. It is essential to point out, however, that the focus of these systems is not merely on gathering performance information with a "report card" mentality, it is about using this information as the basis for refining and redesigning operations to continuously improve nonprofit and board effectiveness. Several useful tools exist to help boards engage in self-assessment initiatives (for example, see the Holland and Jackson [1998] Board Self-Assessment Questionnaire that is based on the six competencies discussed earlier in this chapter, or the BoardSource self-assessment tool based on Ingram's ten core responsibilities of nonprofit boards [Ingram, 1996]).

Regardless of approach, effective boards take time on a regular basis to reflect on what is working well and what might be improved, and they use this information to help inform how they might refine their design and practices to be of most value to the organization and to the board's own members. And this discussion is not couched in terms of "what's bad?" or (even worse) "who's to blame?" It is couched as a learning discussion that focuses on two key themes: (1) What does our organization need of us, in our next generation of work as a board, to uniquely add value to the accomplishment of the organization's mission? and (2) How might we refine the way we are organized and do our work to make the most effective use of the resources that we, as a board, have at our disposal? As the board considers its findings from the assessment process, the next step is to use these findings to refine the board's design for its next generation of work—which is the focus of Element A (Define the Work, Design the Board).

Where to Start?

A nonprofit organization might begin the development cycle with any of the elements, although there are two most likely phases at which a board will enter the cycle. For the board of a new organization that is just beginning to organize its governing board, the organization usually will begin (knowingly or not) with Element A: "Define the Work, Design the Board." Those engaged in creating the board are going to engage in some form of design, and their design will be based on some sense of what the board's work needs to be. They may be analytical and thoughtful about the work to be done and the design that best advances it, or they may simply imitate some other board design (too many boards simply copy their bylaws from those of another organization without giving any thought to whether those bylaws will be suited to the work their board needs to do). But the fact is that some kind of design is adopted when an organization officially starts its existence.

For the board of the nonprofit that has been in operation for some time, it would be typical for the organization to enter the cycle at Element H: the "Assess and Enhance Board and Member Accountability" phase. This is the phase during which the organization takes stock of its situation, assesses how well its design and actual performance meet the needs and expectations of the organization, and considers what this means for its next generation of service. It is during this phase that the organization determines whether changes are likely to be needed and, if so, generates information that will inform the next phase of work.

Effective nonprofit agencies invest time, energy, and money in building and sustaining their effectiveness. This section of the chapter has explained how boards may be developed and sustained through the use of a board development cycle comprising eight relatively sequential overlapping elements. Each element adds unique value to the success of the board, each poses its own design and development challenges, and each contributes in its own way to board success.

Conclusion

Governance is a central and essential dimension in the leadership of nonprofit organizations, and the boards of directors that engage in the work of governance are central to the success of the organizations they serve. This chapter provides a basic overview of the nature and scope of a typical nonprofit organization's governance processes, including the basic ways that boards of directors typically provide leadership and direction to their organizations, and explains how these practices affect the success of the organization. There is no question that when knowledgeable and motivated volunteers take the time to serve on community and other nonprofit boards, we all benefit. Likewise, serving as a member of a nonprofit organization's board of directors can be one of the most influential and enjoyable roles that any volunteer can play, and the rewards of effective service accrue to both the volunteer and their community. Such service is essential to the future of our civil society.

Note

1. As with any general discussion of legal matters, we must present an important warning and disclaimer. This chapter is intended only to offer general information and its contents do not constitute legal advice. Boards and members with specific legal questions and concerns should consult legal counsel and the relevant regulatory authorities for definitive information and answers. Please also recognize that this chapter focuses largely on nonprofit organizations in the United States. Laws and legal expectations vary from state to state, even though a large number of states in the United States have adopted nonprofit corporation laws that are based on the same model statute, and nonprofit laws vary even more

substantially from nation to nation. It makes a significant difference where the organization was founded and incorporated, and where it operates its programs and services. To assist readers, reference and resource materials and Internet links are provided at the end of this chapter.

References

Brown, W. "Board Development Practices and Competent Board Members: Implications for Performance." *Nonprofit Management and Leadership.* 2007, *17*(3), 301–317.

Brudney, J. L., and Murray, V. "Do Intentional Efforts to Improve Boards Really Work? The Views of Nonprofit CEOs." *Nonprofit Management and Leadership,* 1998, *8*(4), 333–348.

Collins, J. *Good to Great and the Social Sector.* San Francisco: HarperCollins, 2005.

Cornforth, C. (ed.) *What Do Boards Do? The Governance of Public and Nonprofit Organizations.* London: Routledge, 2001.

Freiwirth, J., and Letona, M. E. "System-Wide Governance for Community Empowerment." *Nonprofit Quarterly,* 2006, *13*(4), 24–27.

Harrison, Y., and Murray, V. "The Role and Impact of Chairs of Nonprofit Organization Boards of Directors: An Exploratory Study." Paper presented at Networks, Stakeholders, and Nonprofit Organization Governance conference, Midwest Center for Nonprofit Leadership, University of Missouri–Kansas City, Mo. Apr. 26–27, 2007.

Herman, M. L. *Pillars of Accountability: A Risk Management Guide for Nonprofit Boards.* (2nd ed.). Washington, D.C.: Nonprofit Risk Management Center. 2006.

Herman, R. D., and Renz, D. O. "Doing Things Right and Effectiveness in Local Nonprofit Organizations: A Panel Study." *Public Administration Review,* 2004, *64*, 694–704.

Herman, R. D., and Renz, D. O. "Advancing Nonprofit Organizational Effectiveness Research and Theory: Nine Theses." *Nonprofit Management and Leadership,* 2008, *18*, 399–415.

Holland, T., and Jackson, D. "Strengthening Board Performance: Findings and Lessons from Demonstration Projects." *Nonprofit Management and Leadership.* 1998, *9*(2), 121–134.

Ingram, R. T. *Ten Basic Responsibilities of Nonprofit Boards* (2nd ed.). Washington, D.C.: BoardSource, 1996.

Katzenbach, J., and Smith, D. K. *The Wisdom of Teams: Creating the High-Performance Organization.* New York: HarperBusiness Essentials, 2003.

Kotter, J. P. *Leading Change.* Boston: Harvard Business School Press, 1996.

Nobbie, P. D., and Brudney, J. L., "Testing the Testing the Implementation, Board Performance, and Organizational Effectiveness of the Policy Governance Model in Nonprofit Boards of Directors." *Nonprofit and Voluntary Sector Quarterly,* 2003, *32* (4), 571–595.

Ostrower, F. *National Survey of Nonprofit Governance.* Washington, D.C.: Urban Institute, 2007.

Ostrower, F., and Stone, M. "Boards of Nonprofit Organizations: Research Trends, Findings, and Prospects for the Future." In W. W. Powell and R. Steinberg (eds.), *The Nonprofit Sector: A Research Handbook* (2nd ed.). New Haven, Conn.: Yale University Press, 2006.

The Panel on the Nonprofit Sector. *Strengthening Transparency, Governance, Accountability of Charitable Organizations: A Final Report to Congress and the Nonprofit Sector.* Washington, D.C.: Independent Sector, June 2005.

Renz, D. O. "Governance of Nonprofits." In D. Burlingame (ed.), *Philanthropy in the U.S: An Encyclopedia.* Santa Barbara, Calif.: ABC-CLIO, 2004b, 191–199.

Taylor, B. E., Chait, R. P., and Holland, T. P. "The New Work of Nonprofit Boards." *Harvard Business Review,* 1996.

U.S. Internal Revenue Service. "Governance and Related Topics. 501(c)(3) Organizations." http://www.irs.gov/pub/irs-tege/governance_practices.pdf (retrieved January 31, 2010).

CHAPTER SIX

EXECUTIVE LEADERSHIP

Robert D. Herman

Nonprofit organizations are distinctive forms of organization, differing in fundamental ways from business and government. Like businesses, nonprofit organizations engage in voluntary exchanges to obtain revenues and other resources, and like governments, they often provide service with public goods characteristics. Unlike businesses, nonprofit charitable organizations have no conceptually clear maximization criterion. Unlike governments, they cannot levy taxes. Robert Payton (1988) described philanthropy as voluntary (private) action for the public purposes. Nonprofit organizations—particularly those classed as 501(c)(3) publicly supported charities under the U.S. Internal Revenue Code—are the chief instruments for actualizing philanthropy.

The distinctive character of nonprofit organizations presents special challenges for the executive (top staff) leadership of such organizations. A chief executive, in conjunction with the board, must integrate the realms of mission, resource acquisition, and strategy. To oversimplify but phrase the issue more memorably, *mission, money, and management* are interdependent. Making progress on mission achievement depends, in part, on the potential for resource acquisition. Any mission, no matter how worthy, is likely to fail if the organization lacks necessary and sufficient resources to pursue it. Conversely, the acquisition of some kinds of resources can influence the mission. Moreover, decisions about strategies for acquiring resources must be consistent with the mission and ethical values of the organizations. Actions in one realm affect the other realms. The leadership

157

challenge is to see that decisions and actions in one realm are not only consistent with those in other realms but also mutually reinforcing.

Obviously leadership does not and cannot occur only at the top of an organization; however, leadership is fundamentally the responsibility of the chief executive and the board. In fact, the chief executive–board relationship is crucial to effective organizational leadership. The chief executive position in nonprofit organizations is usually demanding and difficult. Those demands and difficulties can be more effectively met if CEOs both understand and develop the skills to focus on the essential relationships and tasks it entails. In these pages, I first describe the psychological centrality of CEOs. In spite of the formal hierarchical structure that makes the CEO subordinate to the board, the day-to-day reality as it is experienced by most CEOs, board members, and staff is that CEOs are expected to accept the central leadership role in nonprofit organizations. This often requires that CEOs take responsibility for enabling their boards to carry out the boards' duties.

Leadership issues are among the most studied and written about in management and the social sciences generally. This chapter will not review the general leadership literature, though it will rely on some findings that are especially germane to the position of nonprofit CEOs. By and large I will rely on research that has specifically focused on CEOs of nonprofit organizations. I begin with a description of the central role that CEOs perform in nonprofit organizations and then consider the skills that differentiate effective chief executives from those who are not as effective; those skills focus on the executives' relation with their boards. Next, I address the importance of executive leadership in the external environment—specifying strategies for leadership across boundaries. I continue by describing research on the "political" skills of effective CEOs and provide guidelines for thinking and acting in politically effective ways. The importance of this criterion of leadership is also examined in light of the hesitancy of chief executives to espouse or advocate political action as an important aspect of their leadership. The closing summary emphasizes that the essence of effective executive leadership is a responsive external orientation in which the strategies pursued are directed at the tasks of mission accomplishment and resource acquisition.

Executive Centrality

Similar to other formal organizations, a nonprofit organization is typically understood as necessarily hierarchical, with the board of directors in the superior position. The board is expected to define mission, establish policies, oversee programs, and use performance standards to assess financial and program achievements. The chief executive is hired to assist the board and works at the board's pleasure. This conception is the application of what organizational theorists have labeled the "purposive-rational" model (Pfeffer, 1982) or the "managed systems" model (Elmore, 1978) to nonprofit organizations. This model, generally derived from Max Weber's description of bureaucracy (1946), as well as the nature of many organizations over the last century or two, conceives of organizations as goal-directed instruments under the control of rational decision makers where responsibility and authority are hierarchically arranged. This rational, managed systems model is also the commonplace or conventional "theory" of many organizational participants. It is how, many people believe, organizations do and should work.

Much of the substantial normative literature on nonprofit boards accepts this conventional model (for example, Houle, 1997, and Carver, 1997), putting the board at the top of the hierarchy and at the center of leadership responsibility. Based on a legal requirement and a moral assumption, the normative literature has advanced a heroic ideal (Herman, 1989) for nonprofit boards. United States law holds that a nonprofit board is ultimately responsible for the affairs and conduct of the organization. The moral assumption is that the board conducts the organization's affairs as a steward of the public interest, in a manner consistent with the wishes and needs of the larger community. Notwithstanding the wide dissemination of this normative model, a substantial body of research over the past three decades shows the actual performance of boards often falls short of the ideal. Ostrower and Stone (2006) review much of that literature. Bell, Moyers, and Wolfred (2006), in a survey of nearly 2,000 U.S. nonprofit chief executives, report that 75 percent plan to leave their jobs in the coming five years and that dissatisfaction with board performance is strongly correlated with chief executive turnover. Clearly the relationship between chief executives and boards is often a difficult one.

The notion that chief executives are simply agents of the board cannot be supported. Recognizing that the relationship between boards and chief executives is more complex than the normative model envisions, many people have invoked a "partnership" or "team" metaphor to describe (and prescribe) the executive-board relationship. Such terms are more appropriate than the conventional model's depiction of the relation as superior-subordinate. However, the partnership and team conceptions remain misleading.

Middleton (1987, p. 149) used the phrase "strange loops and tangled hierarchies" to describe more accurately the complex executive-board relationship. Boards retain their legal and hierarchical superiority (and sometimes must exercise it), whereas executives typically have greater information, more expertise, and a greater stake in and identification with the organization. Thus both parties are dependent on the other, but they are not exactly equals. This complex, interdependent relation is not fundamentally changed even when nonprofit organizations adopt the corporate model of designating the chief executive "president" and letting the executive vote on board decisions. Ostrower's study (2007) of U.S. nonprofit organizations based on a stratified sample drawn from the IRS form 990 database found that having CEOs as voting board members is negatively associated with the accountability practices of having an audit, a conflict of interest policy, and a whistle-blower policy, indicating some shortcomings of that practice.

The complex executive-board relationship can be better understood, and more effective standards and practices relating to the executive-board working relationship can be developed, if other organizational models are used. Herman and Renz (2004, 2008) have found that a "social constructionist model" of organizations provides important insights into the chief executive's organizational role and the dynamics of effective executive-board relations. In contrast to the managed systems model, the social constructionist perspective abandons assumptions of hierarchically imposed order and rationality, emphasizing that what an organization is and does emerges from the interaction of participants as they attempt to arrange organizational practices and routines to fit their perceptions, needs, and interests. The social constructionist model recognizes that official or intended goals, structures, and procedures may exist only on paper. Actual goals, structures, and procedures emerge and change as participants interact and socially construct the meaning of ongoing events.

In research on critical events in nonprofit organizations Heimovics and Herman (1990) studied the "self-serving" hypothesis, which holds that individuals see themselves as causes of successful outcomes and others or luck as responsible for failure. In studying local nonprofit charitable organizations they found that in successful events board presidents, chief executives, and senior staff credited chief executives with contributing the most to that outcome, though presidents and staff also attributed high responsibility to themselves. In unsuccessful events, board presidents and staff, consistent with this hypothesis, saw the chief executive as most responsible, assigning less responsibility to themselves or to luck. However, in the unsuccessful events, chief executives assigned more blame to themselves than to others. Accepting responsibility for things not going well is very unusual (and may contribute to burnout and turnover). In short, all (including chief executives themselves) see the executive as centrally responsible for what happens in nonprofit organizations. What does the reality of executive centrality imply for more effective action?

I believe that two possibilities are indicated. One, since chief executives are going to be held responsible, they should take full control, running things as they think best. The board then becomes either the proverbial rubber stamp or a combination rubber stamp and cash cow. Obviously, there are many instances of this manipulative pattern. Alternatively, since chief executives are going to be held responsible and since they accept responsibility for mission accomplishment and public stewardship, they should work to see that boards fulfill their legal, organizational, and public roles. I believe that this second implication is the much wiser choice. Not only is it consistent with legal and ethical duties, but it is also more likely to enhance organizational effectiveness. I am not advocating that chief executives dominate or "demote" their boards. Boards, in addition to their legal and moral duties, can contribute a great deal to achieving their organizations' missions. What the research results and experience demonstrate is that chief executives can seldom expect boards to do their best unless chief executives, recognizing their centrality, accept the responsibility to develop, promote, and enable their boards' effective functioning.

Board-Centered Leadership Skills of Chief Executives

The view that chief executives must often enable and develop their boards' abilities to carry out their duties and responsibilities is based on research on the leadership skills of effective nonprofit chief executives. Herman and Heimovics (1990) wanted to determine what behaviors or skills distinguished especially effective nonprofit chief executives from others. A sample of especially effective chief executives was created by asking several knowledgeable participants in a metropolitan nonprofit sector to identify executives they judged to be highly effective. The nominators held positions—such as heads of foundations, federated funding agencies, technical assistance providers, and coalitional organizations—that required them to make and act on judgments of executive effectiveness. Chief executives who received at least two independent nominations as highly effective were included in the effective sample.

A comparison sample was selected from among executives who received no nominations and who had held their position for at least eighteen months. Executives from both the effective and comparison samples were interviewed, via the critical event approach. The transcribed interviews were coded by trained raters to note the presence of various leadership behaviors by using an inventory developed by Quinn (1983). Recognizing that a CEO's relationships with the board and staff would probably differ, the raters coded executive leadership in relation to each.

The results confirmed the importance of distinguishing between executive leadership in relation to the board and the staff. Analysis showed that executive leadership in relation to staff and in relation to the board are independent and distinct factors. Effective and comparison executives differed little in leadership with their staffs. The most important finding was that the effective executives provided significantly more leadership to their boards. This does not mean that the effective executives ordered their boards around. Rather, as the descriptions of their behavior in the critical events showed, the effective executives accepted responsibility for supporting and facilitating their board's work. The effective executives valued and respected their boards. As a result, they see their boards as at the center of their work. Their leadership is board-centered.

The comparison executives' relations to their boards often fit the pattern described by Murray et al. (1992) as that of CEO dominance. In an Israeli study of nonprofit chief executives, Iecovich and Bar-Mor (2007) find CEO dominance to be the most common pattern and that although a number of variables are related to CEO dominance in bivariate analyses, in a regression analysis only the number of hours spent by the board chair in his or her duties predicts (negatively) CEO dominance. In a few cases the boards seemed to dominate the CEO.

The following six behaviors specifically characterize the board-centered leadership of the especially effective executives:

- *Facilitating interaction in board relationships.*
  The effective chief executive is aware of, and works to see that board members engage in, satisfying and productive interaction with each other and with the executive. The executive is skilled at listening (that is, at hearing the concerns behind the words) and at helping the board resolve differences.
- *Showing consideration and respect toward board members.*
  The effective executive knows that board service is an exchange and seeks to be aware of the needs of individual board members. The executive also works with the board president to find assignments that meet those needs.
- *Envisioning change and innovation for the organization with the board.*
  Given their psychological centrality and their centrality in information flows, chief executives are in the best position to monitor and understand the organization's position in a changing environment. However, appropriate response to this external flux requires that board members be apprised of the trends, forces, and unexpected occurrences that could call for adaptation or innovation. The executive encourages the board to examine new opportunities and to look for better ways of doing things and better things to do. In short, the executive challenges the board consistently to think and rethink the connections among mission, money (and other resources), and management strategy.

- *Providing useful and helpful information to the board.*
  In addition to the usual routine information, such as financial statements, budget reports, and program service data, boards need relevant and timely information that can aid in decision making. Since the executive will have access to a great deal of information of all kinds and quality, he or she must find ways of separating the important from the trivial and of communicating the important to the board. One key rule followed by effective executives is "no surprises." The temptation to hide or delay bad news is understandable, but it must be resisted. Effective executives realize that problems are inevitable and know that by sharing the bad news, solutions are more likely to be found.
- *Initiating and maintaining structure for the board.*
  Like other work groups, boards require the materials, schedules, and work plans necessary to achieve their tasks. Effective executives take responsibility to work with the board president and other members to develop and maintain consistent procedures. In many effective organizations, the board has annual objectives. It is important that the chief executive support the work of the board in reaching those objectives.
- *Promoting board accomplishments and productivity.*
  The effective executive helps set and maintain high standards (about attendance, effort, and giving). Through the board president and committee chairpersons, the executive encourages board members to complete tasks and meet deadlines.

These findings, based on research on nonprofit charitable CEOs, are reinforced by the results of research in general leadership. Based on his review and integration of the literature Yukl (2010) has concluded that several skills are the most important leadership functions of effective managerial leaders. Among those are (1) creating alignment on objectives and strategies, (2) building task commitment and optimism, (3) building mutual trust and cooperation, (4) strengthening collective identity, (5) organizing and coordinating activities, (6) encouraging and facilitating collective learning, and (7) developing and empowering people. The similarities of these behaviors to those discussed above are obvious.

Executives who have (somehow) learned how to use these leadership skills in relation to their boards, as well as their staffs (including volunteers), have hard-working, effective boards. It is not clear how some chief executives learned these board-centered leadership skills. Perhaps they had coaching in such skills by a mentor who has those skills. Perhaps they are people who have always been attentive and responsive to others. Perhaps they have developed such skills based on tacit knowledge (or intuition). Ritchie et al. (2007) found that nonprofit chief executive intuition was positively related to three of four organizational effectiveness measures. Clearly, work on understanding how board-centered leadership skills are developed is needed.

Leadership Across the Boundaries: Impact in the External World

As noted above, the board-centered executive is likely to be effective, in large part, because he or she has grasped that the work of the board is critical in adapting to and affecting the constraints and opportunities in the environment. In short, the effective executive knows that leadership is not solely an internal activity. Research specifically on nonprofit charitable CEOs (see Herman and Heimovics, 1990, 1991), as well as other research, suggests a number of specific strategies for enhancing external impact.

Spend Time on External Relations

Spending time on external relations may seem too obvious to deserve mention. However, both systematic evidence and experience show that routine activities and the inevitable day-to-day office problems can easily absorb nearly all an executive's time. Executives must learn to delegate much of the management of internal affairs and focus on the external. Dollinger (1984) found that small business owners and managers who spent more time on boundary-spanning or external activities were more successful.

Develop an Informal Information Network

Information about what happened in the past (such as is found in financial statements and program evaluations) is important, but information about what might happen in the future (whether that future is next week or next year) is even more important. Information on possible futures is much more likely to be widely scattered, partial, and ambiguous. To acquire, evaluate, and integrate this "soft" information, executives (and others) need to communicate with government agencies, foundations, accrediting bodies, professional associations, similar nonprofit organizations, and so forth. They must attend meetings and lunches, breakfasts and legislative sessions.

Important, useful information is more likely to flow when the parties are more than acquaintances. Face-to-face communication helps build reciprocal credibility and trust.

A successful network is built and sustained when people are willing and able to understand and accept the interests of others, and it requires exchanging reliable information without violating confidentiality. It means not only investing time but also helping others with their concerns in exchange for help with your own. As Huff (1985) observes, a network is important for more than sharing information. Networks are also deeply involved in making sense of an often rapidly changing field. Different kinds of information are available from different parts of an organization's environment. Information gleaned from a professional associate will be different from that available from a corporate giving officer. Both are likely to be important to a particular policy or program delivery issue. The whole network has an important role in defining emerging issues and in pointing the way to new program practices.

Know Your Agenda

Strategic planning provides organizations with a rational process for deriving specific goals and objectives from their missions. Thus the strategic plan structures the executive's work. Both Kotter (1982) and Huff (1985) found that executives supplement the strategic plan with agendas that are both more immediate and more long-range. The executive's agenda, whether taken directly from the plan or consistently supplemental to it, provides a short list of goals or outcomes that the executive sees as crucial. Knowing and using the agenda to focus work offers a basis for effectively allocating time and effort. A limited, focused agenda also helps bring order and direction in a complex and rapidly changing environment. Concentrating on the agenda also allows the executive to use external interactions to advance those goals. Huff (1985) has described three strategies effective executives often employ in advancing their agenda as dramatizing events, "laying a bread crumb trail," and simplifying.

Dramatizing events entails calling attention to the relationship between networking events and the executive's agenda. For example, an executive who wants to add staff fluent in Spanish to expand services to Spanish-speaking communities might send information about growth in the city's Latino population and its service needs to board members. The executive might also feature a digest of such stories in the organization's newsletter and see that the newsletter goes to regular funders. The key is to dramatically or memorably connect public issues to the organization's agenda.

Another good example of how to dramatize events comes from the chief executive of an agency serving the developmentally disabled. She encouraged a friend who taught creative writing at a local university to engage a class in developing a story about a day in the life of her agency. The story was included in the materials made available to those attending an annual banquet and awards dinner for the organization. The story was presented to many stakeholders and others to give them a "real feel for the work of the agency." Clearly, the executive director had additional uses for the story. The description skillfully catalogued the creative work of a staff constrained by limited resources. Copies of the story became part of the publicity program of the agency and were included in reports to funders and in grant applications.

Just as dramatizing external events is a way of focusing attention, so is the "laying of a bread crumb trail." Over time, through various communications, a chief executive points the way to an important decision. As Huff (1985, p. 175) puts it, organizational action requires that an executive edit his or her concerns "into a smaller number of items that can be comprehended by others. Repetition of these concerns is almost always necessary to gain the attention of others and convince them of serious intent." Such a strategy is probably widely applicable, but we find it especially germane in executive-board relations. Consider, for instance, the strategy of the chief executive of an organization that operates group homes for the mentally ill. The organization's original facility, called Tracy House, was an old building in great need of repair. Operations at the house did not quite break even. Surpluses from the operation of other facilities covered the shortfall. The executive, based on what he was hearing from the network of licensing, funding, and accrediting bodies, believed that new standards would require modifications that, combined with no growth in state daily rates, would mean operating the facility at a larger deficit. So he began laying a bread crumb trail for board members, both formally in board meetings and informally in conversations in other settings. Part of his problem was that a few board members had a strong emotional attachment to Tracy House; they had personally painted it and made repairs to meet licensing standards. Instead of pointing out again that Tracy House was decrepit, he provided an update on the state funding prospects, noting the financial implications for each facility, which made the burden of carrying the home's deficit obvious. Some time later, he mentioned the possibility of federal housing funds' becoming available for group home construction, observing that this would permit the organization to "get out from under" Tracy House. In this way, when the decision was finally made to sell Tracy House, it was a foregone conclusion. The trail of markers not only defined and focused the issue but also brought everyone to the same conclusion, making what could have been a painful decision easy.

The last strategy identified by Huff is to keep things as simple as possible. A complex and interdependent world enhances the tendency for inaction and drift. Before we can make a decision about X, we have to see what happens with Y, and Y depends on what A and B do. To make decisions and take action, individuals must risk simplifying the situation. As Huff (1985) observes, behaving as though the situation is simpler than you know it to be can help bring about more simplicity. Acting in relation to the agenda is an important way of simplifying, or creating order in a disorderly world.

Improvise and Accept Multiple Partial Solutions

The point of leadership across the boundary is to position the organization in the larger environment and match its capabilities with the demands for its services and the resources available. Of course, the inevitable fact is that neither organizational capabilities nor environmental demands and resources are static. A short, clear agenda and the strategies to carry it out provide a compass pointing the way to where the executive, who has integrated to the greatest extent possible the preferences of the stakeholders, wants to go.

The metaphor of the compass, however, is not complete because the executive (reflecting the stakeholders' varying preferences) wants to go to several places. For example, the agenda might include increasing total revenues, diversifying revenue sources, acquiring a new facility, and expanding a particular program. Not only are these different goals, but there are likely to be different paths to each. Furthermore, the most direct path to one may make paths to the others longer or more difficult to find. Finding the combination of paths that most efficiently leads to goals may often be beyond calculation, particularly when the environment keeps changing. The upshot is that executives must sometimes be willing and able to improvise, to take an unexpected path when it presents itself. Sometimes chief executives find they cannot, at least within a crucial period, reach a goal in exactly the form imagined. As Huff (1985, p. 167) observes, an "administrator's ability to perceive issues is almost always bigger than the ability to act on issues. As a result, the administrator often must be content to work on a small part of the larger whole." That is, sometimes the organization may have to go someplace a little different from what was at one time imagined because that is where the only available path leads. Huff suggests that a "specific action should rarely be taken unless it is compatible with several different issues" (p. 168). Or in the terms of our metaphor, an action that leads to movement on paths to two or three places at once is particularly useful.

For an especially compelling illustration of this sort of creative leadership, consider the case of a nonprofit organization that required a facility with large spaces. For several years, the organization used an old warehouse that a business corporation provided for free. However, the corporation made it clear that it was interested in selling the warehouse and that the organization might have to relocate. As a few years passed and the corporation lacked success in selling the warehouse and had little apparent necessity for doing so, the issue of obtaining a suitable, more permanent facility was increasingly put on the back burner.

One day, the chief executive received a call from a corporate officer saying that a tentative agreement to sell the warehouse had been reached and that the organization would have to vacate in six months. The first thing the chief executive did was to call the board. Staff members were also quickly informed to avoid the spread of rumors. The chief executive found that many board members and staff assumed that the organization should try to find another old warehouse. However, the executive knew that old warehouses had disadvantages: high energy costs, lack of parking, inaccessibility, and so forth. The executive thought this was an excellent opportunity to rethink what sort of facility would be most appropriate.

After conferring with the board chairman and other key board members, a facility planning committee was formed. The executive was interested in connecting the facility issue to other agenda issues, especially those of enhancing collaboration with other community organizations and adding a demonstration day-care program for children. As the facility planning committee identified alternative ways of securing a replacement facility and the costs associated with each, a board member suggested that the executive meet with an official from a local community college. Although the college was not in the same service field as the organization, the college had enough money available through a bond issue to construct a new building but not enough money to finish and equip the building. Following quick negotiations, the organization agreed to provide funds to finish and equip the facility in exchange for a ten-year lease of two floors at a very low rental rate. This solution, though not perfect, moved the organization along on several agenda issues simultaneously. This progress was achieved because the executive worked with and through the board and linked action on one issue with progress on others.

Promote Responsiveness to Stakeholders

In studying the effectiveness of nonprofit charitable organizations, Herman and Renz (2004) adapted an instrument developed by Tsui (1984). In an important study of managerial effectiveness Tsui et al. (1995) used her instrument to measure how those who work with a ("focal") manager assess the effectiveness of that manager. The items Tsui et al. used asked respondents (in their study, respondents were subordinates, peers, and superiors of the focal managers) to assess the extent to which the manager was performing the way the respondent would like, was meeting the respondent's expectations, and extent to which the respondent would change how the manager behaved. Tsui et al. identify several strategies managers might use when facing discrepant or conflicting expectations from stakeholders, including making an extra effort to meet expectations, trying to influence expectations, explaining actions, distorting feedback from stakeholders, revising their own expectations downward, and avoiding dissatisfied stakeholders. They collected data from and about mid-level managers in both business (94 managers, 713 respondents) and government (316 focal managers, 1,906 respondents). Their results showed that extra effort was very strongly related and explaining action strongly related to effectiveness ratings, whereas avoidance and trying to influence stakeholder expectations were negatively related to effectiveness (because distorting feedback and revising expectations are not observable by stakeholders these strategies were not studied). Their results also showed that managers who were rated as frequently using extra effort and explanation seldom used avoidance or attempted influence, and vice versa. Managers were also found to behave consistently with all types of stakeholders. These results, demonstrating that individuals judge managerial effectiveness of the basis of the responsiveness to their expectations, seemed to Herman and Renz (2004) likely to apply throughout an organization. Nonprofit leaders, chief executives and boards, who practice responsiveness are likely to encourage and promote such practices throughout the organization.

Herman and Renz (2004) found that an adapted instrument measuring stakeholder judgments of *organizational responsiveness* was highly correlated to a different measure of organizational effectiveness, including for institutional funders as well as board members and senior staff. Though they collected no direct evidence on whether organizational members exhibited extra effort, explained actions, or engaged in other ways of being responsive to stakeholders, this set of results (from Tsui et al. and Herman and Renz) seems strong enough to warrant including promoting responsiveness to stakeholders, as well as external stakeholders, as a skill for chief executives (and others) to develop and practice.

These five admonitions are also reinforced by Yukl's integration of the general leadership literature (2010). Among the skills he concludes as most important for effective managerial leadership are helping interpret the meaning of events and obtaining necessary resources and support. These skills seem, in the case of nonprofit CEOs, especially relevant in relation to the external stakeholders, though they could also be included in the list presented pages 162–163, as some of the skills listed there could be listed here as well.

In emphasizing the importance of externally oriented leadership, I do not wish to suggest that internal operations can be ignored by chief executives. However, I believe that nearly all executives and boards are well aware of the importance of managing internal operations well. What seems to be less well comprehended is the importance of understanding and influencing, when possible, people and systems beyond the organization's boundaries. Effective executive leadership beyond the boundaries is based, in part, on a "political" orientation and on political skills. In the next section, I define what I mean by a political orientation, describe research that finds effective executives are more politically skillful than others, and suggest how executives can enhance their political acumen.

Using the Political Frame

Research has shown that not only do successful executives provide significantly more leadership for their boards than those not deemed especially effective, but they also work with and through their boards to position their organization in its environment. Special effort is extended externally across the boundaries of the organization to manage the organization's dependence on the factors that determine the availability of the resources to carry out the mission and to establish the legitimacy of the organization. In short, effective executives cross boundaries to seek and act on opportunities in the environment to help shape the future health and direction of the organization.

Effective executives have been found to be more likely than other executives to "frame" their orientations toward external events in political ways. This political orientation helps explain how effective executives work "entrepreneurially" to find resources and revitalize missions for their organizations.

Effective chief executives use a political frame to understand and deal with the challenges of resource dependency their organizations face (Heimovics, Herman, and Coughlin, 1993; Heimovics, Herman, and Jurkiewicz, 1995). A multiple-frame analysis for understanding organizations and leadership developed by Bolman and Deal (2008) forms the basis for understanding the political orientation of the effective executive. Bolman and Deal identify four distinct organizational perspectives, or "frames," that leaders may adopt to think about the many realities of organizational life: (1) structural, (2) human resource, (3) political, and (4) symbolic. Knowledge of these frames, their various strengths, and their appropriate use can help leaders understand and intervene in their organizations more effectively. The following brief discussion summarizes these frames.

In the structural frame, clarity in goal setting and role expectations provides order and continuity in organizations. Clear procedures and policies and the view of the organization as a rational and hierarchical system are characteristic of this frame. Adherence to accepted standards, conformity to rules, and the creation of administrative systems confer on the organization its form and logic. Following procedures (for example, personnel systems and board performance standards) to define individual and organizational effectiveness is also characteristic of this frame, as is the emphasis on certainty in mission and clarity of direction.

Leaders who rely strongly on the structural frame regard effectiveness as largely determined by clear procedures and clear goals.

According to the human resource frame, people are the most valuable resource of any organization. The effective leader, as defined by this frame, searches for an important balance between the goals of the organization and the hopes and aspirations of its members by attending to individual hopes, feelings, and preferences, valuing relationships and feelings, and advocating effective delegation. Nonprofit leaders who use this frame believe in delegation because it not only "empowers" others to take initiative but also provides opportunities for personal growth and development. This frame defines problems and issues in interpersonal terms and encourages open communication, team building, and collaboration.

The political frame assumes ongoing conflict or tension over the allocation of scarce resources or the resolution of differences—most often triggered by the need to bargain or negotiate to acquire or allocate resources. As viewed within the political frame, conflict resolution skills are necessary to build alliances and networks with prominent actors or stakeholders to influence decisions about the allocation of resources. The informal realities of organizational life include the influence of coalitions and interest groups. Politically oriented leaders not only understand how interest groups and coalitions evolve but can also influence the impact these groups have on the organization. Those who use the political frame exercise their personal and organizational power and are sensitive to external factors that may influence internal decisions and policies.

According to the symbolic frame, realities of organizational life are socially constructed. Organizations are cultural and historical systems of shared meaning wherein group membership determines individual interpretations of organizational phenomena. Organizational structure, politics, and human relations are inventions of the cultural and historical system. Leaders evoke ceremonies, rituals, or artifacts to create a unifying system of beliefs. This frame calls for charismatic leaders to arouse "visions of a preferred organizational future" and evoke emotional responses to enhance an organization's identity, transforming it to a higher plane of performance and value (Bass, 1985).

Heimovics, Herman, and Coughlin (1993) began research on the use of frames by revisiting the critical-incident interviews that served as the source of data for Herman and Heimovics's (1990) work on board-centered behaviors and the psychological centrality of the chief executive. Analysis revealed that the structural frame was the dominant frame for both the effective and comparison executives. The substantial reliance on the structural frame may be a reflection of the attention paid by both groups of executives to aspects of events that may be relatively close at hand, immediately demanding, and perhaps amenable to action.

The use of the political frame differed significantly, however, between effective and comparison executives. The comparison executives were almost twice as likely to employ the structural frame and 70 percent more likely to use the human resource frame than the political frame. By contrast, the political frame was the second most common frame for the effective executives, who were almost as likely to use it as the structural frame. Most significant, effective executives were twice as likely as the comparison executives to engage in actions defined by the political frame.

The findings on the substantial use of the political frame by effective executives are reinforced by additional data. Most of the critical events described by both groups of executives occurred in the environment external to their organizations. Both effective and comparison executives were more likely to choose an external event than an internal event to describe as critical. Examples of environmental events were usually incidents that dealt with the challenges of resource dependency, such as mergers, alliances, fundraising strategies, legislative lobbying, collaboration with other agencies, relations with government officials, new program developments, or program decline. These kinds of events were distinguished from internal critical events, such as a personnel action or problems with implementing an administrative system or procedure. Analysis of the data by location of events (internal or external) was undertaken to determine whether this variable explained differences in frame use. Again significant differences between in the use of the political frame were found in the two groups of executives. Comparison executives were substantially less likely to rely on the political frame than the effective executives were when dealing with events in the external environment of the organization, where the political frame is often likely to be most important.

Effective executives not only relied more on the political frame but also dealt with events in more cognitively complex ways than those not deemed to be especially effective. That is, effective executives integrate and employ multiple frames and do not rely on single perspectives, as the comparison executives do. It seems very likely that the use of multiple frames by effective executives contributes to a deeper understanding of the complexities and volatility of the leadership challenges faced in the fast-changing and complicated environment of nonprofit organizations. The ability of nonprofit executives to understand and act politically, as well as through other frames, in relation to complex sets of interrelated actors helps explain why some executives are more effective than others.

Heimovics, Herman, and Jurkiewicz (1995) provide an interesting extension to the findings about the political orientation of effective chief executives. They conducted a second, independent four-frame analysis of the interviews using

Argyris's distinctions between espoused theories and theories-in-use. For Argyris (1982), espoused theories are values and actions about which individuals are conscious and aware and which they often use to describe (their) effective leadership as distinct from what they might actually do, their theory-in-use. An espoused theory could be considered a personal philosophy or a statement of a leadership belief, but it is not necessarily a description of a particular action taken. Argyris has shown that commonly there are incongruities between what people espouse as their leadership action and how they actually behave. This was the case in this research.

Recall that effective executives were twice as likely as the comparison executives to engage in actions defined in the political frame. However, both sets of executives were much more inclined to present (espouse) their leadership from the structural and human resource frame than the political. Furthermore, both the effective executives and those not deemed especially effective enacted more political behavior than they espoused. In summary, whereas the use of the political frame was the most strongly distinguishing criterion of executive effectiveness, executives without respect to effectiveness acted in political ways and advocated a less politicized philosophy. Why might this be the case?

The espoused structural frame argues for the importance of rationality and the values of structures that best fit organizational purposes and environmental demands. Apparently, nonprofit executives prefer to present themselves as structured and orderly and embracing of the human resource frame. Perhaps it is important to appear as if one is ordered and rational and concerned about others regardless of whether one predominantly behaves that way. Pfeffer (1981) argues that power is most effectively exercised unobtrusively and that overt political pronouncements are divisive and likely to be met with challenges. Wrong (1988) distinguished between political operatives who say and those who do. He concludes that the doers are more effective. In short, it may be important and effective to act in accordance with the political frame; it may not be acceptable to espouse this frame as part of a leadership philosophy. Nonetheless the research clearly suggests that nonprofit executive leadership effectiveness must encompass the ability to operate within a political framework, regardless of the proclivity to espouse a political agenda.

Summary

Nonprofit leaders continually face the challenge of integrating mission, money, and management strategy. Both boards and chief executives play crucial and interdependent roles in meeting this continuing challenge. Both must ask,

"How well are we collectively meeting our responsibilities—to define and refine the organization's mission, to secure the resources necessary to achieve our mission, and to select and implement strategies appropriate to and effective in mission accomplishment and resource acquisition?" Chief executives must ask this question not only of themselves but also in relation to their boards. Are their boards meeting these responsibilities? If the answer is yes, a chief executive will surely want to understand how this happy state of affairs has been achieved and take pains to see that it is maintained. If the answer is no, a chief executive will want to consider the following four fundamental executive leadership strategies. The research described here suggests that executives who use these strategies are more likely to lead organizations that effectively meet their responsibilities.

- *Effective executives accept and act on their psychological centrality.*
  The research shows that chief executives, board members, and others often regard the chief executive as primarily responsible for the conduct of organizational affairs. This is, I'm sure, a frequent fact of life in nonprofit organizations, no matter how strongly any of us might want it to be otherwise. This fact suggests that chief executives must often accept the responsibility for enabling their boards to carry out their leadership roles.
- *Effective executives provide facilitative leadership for their boards.*
  Boards can make a difference in how nonprofit organizations meet the challenge of integrating mission, money, and management. Boards are much more likely to be active, effective bodies when they are supported by a chief executive who, recognizing his or her psychological centrality, is willing and able to serve the board as enabler and facilitator.
- *Effective executives emphasize leadership beyond their organizations' boundaries.*
  Given the extensive dependence of nonprofit organizations on their external environment, executives generally recognize the importance of "networking" and other external activities for understanding the changes in that environment. Beyond the information-gathering value of external relations, some executives recognize the importance and value of affecting events in the environment. Exercising external leadership is difficult and demanding, since executives often can bring little, if any, financial or political power to bear. The leadership resources they are likely to have in greater abundance are expertise, trustworthiness, the moral stature of their organizations, skills in coalition building and conflict resolution, and their organizations' responsiveness to external stakeholders.

- *Effective executives think and act in political ways.*
  Effective executives are realists. They recognize and accept that their organizations and the larger world are composed of groups with differing interests. Thus an important part of the leadership role consists of building coalitions, bargaining, and resolving conflicts. Politically astute executives are not immoral or manipulative. However, they are comfortable with the fact that interests differ and sometimes conflict. They are also comfortable with and skilled at negotiating, compromising, and forming alliances, although they are unlikely to proclaim these political skills as an aspect of their leadership strategies.

These four executive leadership strategies are highly interrelated. An executive who enhances his or her board-centered leadership skills is also likely to become more attentive to externally oriented leadership. An executive who becomes more active in and skilled at leadership in the external environment will be likely to develop more politically-oriented ways of thinking and behaving. Obviously, these skills are increments to a solid base of other knowledge and skills, such as those of program services, financial management, human resource management, fundraising, planning, evaluation, and the like. These board-centered, external, and political leadership skills are what distinguish especially effective nonprofit chief executives.

References

Argyris, C. *Reasoning, Learning, and Action: Individual and Organizational*. San Francisco: Jossey-Bass, 1982.

Bass, B. M. *Leadership and Performance Beyond Expectations*. New York: Free Press, 1985.

Bell, J., Moyers, R., and Wolfred, T. *Daring to Lead 2006: A National Study of Nonprofit Executive Leadership*. San Francisco: CompassPoint Nonprofit Services and Meyer Foundation, 2006.

Bolman, L. G., and Deal, T. E. *Reframing Organizations: Artistry, Choice, and Organizations*. (4th ed.) San Francisco: Jossey-Bass, 2008.

Carver, J. *Boards That Make a Difference*. (2nd ed.) San Francisco: Jossey-Bass, 1997.

Dollinger, M. J. "Environmental Boundary Spanning and Information Processing Effects on Organizational Performance." *Academy of Management Journal*, 1984, *27*, 351–368.

Elmore, R. F. "Organizational Models of Social Program Implementation." *Public Policy*, 1978, *26*, 185–228.

Heimovics, R. D., and Herman, R. D. "Responsibility for Critical Events in Nonprofit Organizations." *Nonprofit and Voluntary Sector Quarterly*, 1990, *19*, 59–72.

Heimovics, R. D., Herman, R. D., and Coughlin, C.L.J. "Executive Leadership and Resource Dependence in Nonprofit Organizations: A Frame Analysis." *Public Administration Review*, 1993, *53*, 419–427.

Heimovics, R. D., Herman, R. D., and Jurkiewicz, C. L. "The Political Dimension of Effective Nonprofit Executive Leadership." *Nonprofit Management and Leadership*, 1995, *5*, 233–248.

Herman, R. D. "Concluding Thoughts on Closing the Board Gap." In R. D. Herman and J. Van Til (eds.), *Nonprofit Boards of Directors: Analyses and Applications*. New Brunswick, N.J.: Transaction, 1989.

Herman, R. D., and Heimovics, R. D. "An Investigation of Leadership Skill Differences in Chief Executives of Nonprofit Organizations." *American Review of Public Administration*, 1990, *20*, 107–124.

Herman, R. D., and Heimovics, R. D. *Executive Leadership in Nonprofit Organizations: New Strategies for Shaping Executive-Board Dynamics*. San Francisco: Jossey-Bass, 1991.

Herman, R. D., and Renz, D. O. "Multiple Constituencies and the Social Construction of Nonprofit Organization Effectiveness." *Nonprofit and Voluntary Sector Quarterly*, 1997, *26*, 185–206.

Herman, R. D., and Renz, D. O. "Doing Things Right and Effectiveness in Local Nonprofit Organizations: A Panel Study." *Public Administration Review*, 2004, *64*, 694–704.

Herman, R. D., and Renz, D. O. "Advancing Nonprofit Organizational Effectiveness Research and Theory: Nine Theses." *Nonprofit Management and Leadership*, 2008, *18*, 399–415.

Houle, C. O. *Governing Boards*. San Francisco: Jossey-Bass, 1997.

Huff, A. S. "Managerial Implications of the Emerging Paradigm." In Y. S. Lincoln (ed.), *Organizational Theory and Inquiry: The Paradigm Revolution*. Thousand Oaks, Calif.: Sage, 1985.

Iecovich, E., and Bar-Mor, H. "Relationships between Chairpersons and CEOs in Nonprofit Organizations." *Administration in Social Work*, 2007, *31*, 21–40.

Kotter, J. P. *The General Managers*. New York: Free Press, 1982.

Middleton, M. "Nonprofit Boards of Directors: Beyond the Governance Function." In W. W. Powell (ed.), *The Nonprofit Sector: A Research Handbook*. New Haven, Conn.: Yale University Press, 1987.

Murray, V. V., Bradshaw, P., and Wolpin, J. "Power in and Around Nonprofit Boards: A Neglected Dimension of Governance." *Nonprofit Management and Leadership*, 1992, *3*, 165–182.

Ostrower, F. "Nonprofit Governance in the United States: Findings on Performance and Accountability from the First Representative National Study." Urban Institute Center on Nonprofits and Philanthropy [http://www.urban.org/publications/411479.html], 2007.

Ostrower, F., and Stone, M. "Boards of Nonprofit Organizations: Research Trends, Findings, and Prospects for the Future." In W. W. Powell and R. Steinberg (eds.), *The Nonprofit Sector: A Research Handbook* (2nd ed.) New Haven, Conn.: Yale University Press, 2006.

Payton, R. *Philanthropy: Voluntary Action for the Public Good*. Old Tappan, N.J.: Macmillan, 1988.

Pfeffer, J. *Power in Organizations*. New York: Ballinger, 1981.

Pfeffer, J. *Organizations and Organization Theory*. Boston: Pitman, 1982.

Quinn, R. E. "Applying the Competing Values Approach to Leadership: Toward an Integrative Framework." In J. G. Hunt and others (eds.), *Managerial Work and Leadership: International Perspectives*. New York: Pergamon, 1983.

Ritchie, W. J., Kolodinsky, R. W., and Eastwood, K. "Does Executive Intuition Matter? An Empirical Analysis of Its Relationship with Nonprofit Organization Financial Performance." *Nonprofit and Voluntary Sector Quarterly*, 2007, *36*, 140–155.

Tsui, A. S. "A Role Set Analysis of Managerial Reputation." *Organizational Behavior and Human Performance*, 1984, *34*, 64–96.

Tsui, A. S., Ashford, S., St. Clair, L., and Xin, K. "Dealing with Discrepant Expectations: Response Strategies and Managerial Effectiveness." *Academy of Management Journal*, 1995, *38*, 1515–1543.

Weber, M. *From Max Weber: Essays in Sociology* (H. H. Gerth and C. W. Mills, trans. and eds.). New York: Oxford University Press, 1946.

Wrong, D. *Power: Its Forms, Bases, and Uses*. Chicago: University of Chicago Press, 1988.

Yukl, G. A. Leadership in Organizations. (7th ed.) Upper Saddle River, N.J.: Prentice Hall, 2010.

CHAPTER SEVEN

ETHICAL NONPROFIT MANAGEMENT

Core Values and Key Practices

Thomas H. Jeavons

Over the last two decades scandals in the nonprofit sector and the corporate world have given rise to heightened concerns about ethics, accountability, and public trust for all types of organizations. Charitable organizations and those who run them have sometimes behaved badly on occasion before, but they have probably never received such intense public scrutiny. In a new era of twenty-four-hour news networks and the Internet even small missteps can become major public relations nightmares. Moreover, the public's readiness to believe the worst about all institutions has been strongly reinforced most recently by the growing evidence of the moral myopia of major corporations and the widespread economic chaos and human suffering to which it has contributed.

The results of similar problems have been seen before. During the 1990s, following the United Way of America scandal, the public's faith in nonprofit institutions generally fell. Then, in the aftermath of efforts to make nonprofits more accountable, there was some rebound in public trust (Independent Sector, 2002). But more recently the frauds, abuses of power, failures of governance, and evasions of accountability that have been so evident in cases like those of the American Red Cross, the Smithsonian, and the Catholic Church (to name just a few prominent examples) have generated reasons for public faith in nonprofits to erode again.

Since 1973 a significant decline in public confidence in many major institutions has been widespread (O'Neill, 2009, pp. 251–52). This represents a real problem for government and business, but even more so for nonprofits. Why more so for nonprofits? Because nonprofit organizations—at least public charities (the 501(c)(3)s)—are especially dependent on the public's trust and goodwill to gain the support they need for the work they do. These organizations are sometimes described as "values-expressive," as being instrumental and critical to building "social capital" (a concept that centers on trust), and as being instruments of collective action for serving the public good (Lohmann, 1992; Putnam, 2000; Payton and Moody, 2008). If they are not organizations of integrity, organizations that are trustworthy, then they generally will not be able to function effectively. Why would people want to give their money or time to an organization if they have reason to doubt that organization is representing itself and the work it does honestly and is using the contributions it receives well for the purpose of fulfilling its stated mission?

The responsibility for assuring the ethical behavior of a nonprofit organization resides with both managers and trustees or board members of nonprofits. The roles and responsibilities of governing boards are spoken to elsewhere in this volume, so this chapter focuses primarily on the responsibilities of professional staff, the managers. The discussion here is about "professional ethics."

Attention to professional ethics has followed an interesting trajectory over the last four decades. There was a notable surge of interest in these matters following the Watergate scandal in the mid-1970s after it was observed that the majority of those involved were educated at some of the nation's most prestigious law schools. A similar surge of interest in ethics has risen in the aftermath of high-profile, corporate scandals in the first decade of this century. Yet the responses of commentators and institutional leaders, and the changes in professional school curricula over the last thirty years, have been inadequate to abate the cycle of recurring scandals, and they often reflect two troubling assumptions about ethics and the professions.

The first assumption is that careful, skilled thinking about ethical matters is more the business of philosophers and academics than of practitioners. Although persons "training for the professions" may be required to take courses in or complete assignments relating to ethical issues of their profession, many involved—especially the students—assume that these courses and assignments are of secondary importance. Why would they assume that? Because both practitioners and students can see (from observing their fields) that the skills one must master to build a "successful career" are the technical and practical skills of their profession; and that an inability to think clearly about and act appropriately on the ethical issues has not often created a major stumbling block to professional advancement. (If they were, persons of questionable character would rise to leadership far less often.)

The second problematic assumption is found among many who, even while they admit the importance of ethical questions and issues, believe these questions and issues may be dealt with as discrete concerns in professional practice, isolated from others. This perspective is evident in the tendency to have one course on ethics in a professional program, or to have one or two sessions in courses on other subjects take up ethical issues, rather than trying to have the ethical implications of every aspect of professional practice dealt with wherever they might arise in a professional education.

I lift up these assumptions here because they are both, I believe, patently false. Both undermine the maintenance of appropriate ethical standards and behavior in the management and operation of nonprofit organizations. (Indeed, this is true for organizations of any kind.)

The analysis that follows builds, in fact, on two contrary assumptions. The first is that reflecting critically and actively on ethical issues is an obligation of every professional, including nonprofit managers. The capacity for and inclination to socially responsive, historically grounded, critical, ethical judgment should be one outcome of any sound professional education program, and one of the capacities of a "professional" as "reflective practitioner" (Schon, 1983, 1987). The second is that a concern for the ethical implications of one's decisions and actions is salient in every aspect of professional practice and—for the considerations of this volume—in relation to every facet of the life of nonprofit organizations.

Indeed, I argue here, as the chapter title implies, that we are most likely to see consistently ethical behavior among nonprofit managers and organizations only where an emphasis on ethical values and behavior is deeply embedded in the cultures of these organizations. So, building and reinforcing that kind of organizational culture becomes a primary responsibility for those desiring that ethical practice be a hallmark of all the functions, including the management, of their organization.

An Overview of the Chapter

The argument I make here is that ethical behavior in and by nonprofit organizations cannot be effectively assured by employing encouraging rhetoric about ethics, nor just by establishing specific rules for ethical behavior. This point can be readily demonstrated by examining the historical record and the common experience of most managers and organizational analysts. Anyone with significant experience in organizational life knows there is often a marked disparity between rhetoric and practice, between "espoused values" and "operative values," in organizational behavior (Argyris and Schon, 1978). He or she also knows that rules about ethics (and other matters) can be, and frequently are, followed "in the letter" while being totally ignored or violated "in the spirit."

Thus, the claim argued here is that truly ethical behavior will be assured only by creating an organizational culture in which key ethical ideals and expectations are incorporated in the "core values" (Schein, 1985) of an organization and thus permeate its operations. This process will almost certainly involve the use of appropriate rhetoric about values, and may involve promulgating codes of ethics within the organization. More important, though, it must involve modeling of the core values in the behavior of key individuals in an organization, and reinforcement of those values through the organization's structures and reward systems.

In addition, I argue that because of the unique historical, societal dimensions of their character and function, the expectations about what constitutes ethical behavior in and by nonprofit, public benefit charities differ from those placed on other organizations. Specifically, questions of trust and integrity go to the essence of the reason for the existence of these organizations and their ability to satisfy public expectations. The existence of most charitable nonprofit organizations, their capacity to garner resources—and so to survive and carry out their missions—depends on their moral standing and consistency (see Hansmann, 1987; Douglas, 1987; Ostrander and Schervish, 1990; Jeavons, 1992; Payton and Moody, 2008).

There is an implicit social contract supporting the presence and function of private, public benefit nonprofits in our society. Simply summarized, these organizations are given special standing and specific legal advantages over other private organizations with the understanding they will serve the public good. The public expects these organizations to be motivated by and adhere to such a commitment in their performance. The public also expects these organizations will honor a set of widely accepted moral and humanitarian values—deriving from the organizations' historical and philosophical roots—and that they will not act in a self-serving manner.

Accordingly, if the managers of public benefit nonprofits wish to ensure the ethical behavior of their organizations, staffs, and themselves, then they need to create and maintain organizational cultures that honor in practice (as fundamental) a set of "core values" that are in keeping with the historic, philosophical, moral, and religious roots of the voluntary sector, and that meet current public expectations. In this context, trust is the essential lifeblood of the nonprofit sector—trust that nonprofits will fulfill this implicit social contract. To ensure that this trust is sustained, I argue, five core values must permeate these organizations, shaping their ethics. These values are integrity, openness, accountability, service, and charity (in the original sense of that term).

To frame this argument we must begin by considering what ethics are and are not. We will look at a number of definitions of ethics, with a particular eye toward the origins, character, and purposes of ethical norms or standards. Then we need to examine more closely the kinds of ethical norms that are usually applied to nonprofit, public benefit organizations in American culture, the factors that have shaped these norms, and the purposes they serve.

Having formed a well-grounded perspective on the norms or standards for ethical behavior in and by nonprofit organizations, we next need to ask how such behavior can be assured. What is the relationship between values and behavior? Assuming an organization does ascribe to or articulate the "right" values, how can one help ensure that those values are captured and reflected in all aspects of its operations, by all its members?

In essence, this is to ask about the integrity of an organization, about how to make certain that it is—and will continue to be—what it claims to be. Specifically, how can one make certain that there will be continuity between the values an organization claims to represent and the purposes it says it intends to serve, on the one hand, and its actual operations, on the other? Finally, this chapter concludes with some specific suggestions about how a "culture of integrity" can be created and sustained in nonprofit organizations, for assuming nonprofit organizations wish to act ethically, it is only by creating and sustaining such an organizational culture that this intention is likely to be fulfilled consistently. Let us begin, then, by examining the nature of "ethics" and "ethical behavior."

What Are "Ethics"?

As a field of study, *ethics* refers to "the study of moral topics, including moral issues, moral responsibilities, and moral ideals of character."[1] In a normative sense, "ethics" may be seen as referring to "justified moral standards"—which is to say, not just what people do believe about how they should act, but also what they should believe. As this chapter is directed more to practitioners of management and other "lay people" than to scholars, however, we need to think more about more common uses of the term *ethics*.

Webster's New World Dictionary of the American Language (2nd College Edition, 1970) defines *ethics* as a "system or code of morals of a particular person, religion, group, profession; etc." The Oxford English Dictionary (Compact Edition, 1971) notes that the word *ethics* comes from the Greek term *ethos*, meaning "custom, usage, manner or habit," and goes on to offer the following definitions (for *ethics*): "the moral principles by which a person is guided" and "the rules of conduct recognized in certain associations or departments of human life." The derivations of the term, as well as the differences we see in these common definitions, highlight two facets of the origins and purposes of ethics it is useful to examine.

One set of issues involves the derivations of and justifications for specific ethical systems and values. Exploring various types of ethical theories—duty ethics, utilitarianism, virtue ethics—can be a valuable exercise. However, given limitations of space, it would not be helpful here as it would divert us from our intended focus on questions about applied ethics in nonprofit management.

Yet the definitions of ethics just examined also remind us that much of what we typically think about as ethical principles or judgments, especially when our concern is application and practice, do not derive from philosophical absolutes, but rather from reference points of social or community standards. To play with the words, one's *ethics* (as we typically use the term) may be as much a matter of *ethos*—what is expected or socially acceptable, what is customary—as they are a matter of indisputable moral vision. Of course, these two aspects of ethics are often intertwined. What a particular community views as ethically acceptable will often be determined by what its members believe some source of absolute moral authority (God, perhaps) requires.

Understanding these things about the origins and meaning of ethics makes it clear that when we raise and examine questions about ethics—ethics generally, professional ethics, the ethics of nonprofit managers, or the ethics of the behavior of nonprofit organizations—there are two reference points we need always to bear in mind in our considerations. One is a point of moral absolutes, and the other of community standards and expectations. For our purposes, when we think about the ethics of nonprofit organizations and their management, I believe we must then be asking two kinds of questions: First, what are we morally obligated to do and not do? Second, what does society require or expect of us? Moreover, ethical questions should be considered in that order, giving preference to moral obligations over customary ones.

Professional Ethics

One book claims that ethics are "a set of rules that apply to human beings over the totality of their interrelationships with one another, and that take precedence over all other rules" (Gellerman, Frankel, and Ladenson, 1990, p. 41). If we accept this, then we need to ask, How are such rules more specifically defined by and applied to particular spheres of professional activity, in contrast to the broader reach of our lives? (For a wonderfully insightful exploration of the interplay between professional and personal ethics, see Martin, 2000.)

Some scholars claim that one of the elements that define a *profession* (as opposed to other kinds of work) is that every specific profession involves a commitment to publicly articulated goals and social and societal purposes for that profession's practice, and to standards for and approaches to that practice which should be shared by all its practitioners. It is because they meet societal needs with special expertise, it is argued, that professions are given certain privileges, such as self-regulation, control over standards for training and entry into practice, and (thus) control over their own markets and competition. These prerogatives are provided in exchange for the profession's commitment (implicit, at least) to meet public needs and serve the public good (see Bellah and others, 1985; Flores, 1988; Larson, 1977; Martin, 2000). Here we have another implicit social contract. A classic paradigm for this is the medical profession and doctors with their Hippocratic Oath and the other specific expectations about their obligations to society in the provision of medical care.

Following this line of reasoning, one commentator on "professional values" argues that in our culture "professionals are viewed as morally committed to pursuing the dominant value that defines the goals of their professional practice.... They are expected to pursue such goals on a social as well as individual level.... And they are expected to do so even when self-interest may have to be sacrificed in that pursuit" (Alan Goldman, cited in Gellerman, Frankel, Ladenson, 1990, p. 5).

It may not be immediately clear what "the dominant value" that defines the goals of the practice of management generally is or should be. Still, it can be argued that the dominant value that should define the practice of management of public benefit nonprofits is "a commitment to serve the greater good." Such organizations are (or were) often created specifically to advance the common good, usually by providing services, and (as I will show) often in situations in which the establishment of trust in the integrity and commitment to service of the agency is a paramount concern.

In sum, the claim here is that the ethical operation of nonprofit agencies and ethical nonprofit management require the articulation and internalization of standards for behavior and ways of being for those agencies and their managers that adequately reflect the sector's origins in the moral spheres of our culture, and that meet the current, morally justifiable expectations of our society. Before moving on to look closely at those origins and expectations and the standards for behavior they necessitate, however, I want to comment briefly on how this perspective contrasts with some current views of the purposes of professional ethics, because those views are especially dangerous if they are adopted in the nonprofit world.

Misunderstanding Professional Ethics

One commonly articulated rationale for ethical behavior in professional practice is that it is simply "good for business." This may be the case. It may well be possible to demonstrate that it is (generally) true that "honesty [and other ethical behavior] is the best policy." Looking at some of the business practices that led to the economic crisis of 2008–2009, it is certainly clear that unethical behavior can have disastrous consequences for the common good. What is also clear, however, is that this utilitarian perspective does not provide an adequate underpinning for behaving ethically. Still, this is often the only, or at least the most prominent, rationale or motivation given for the development and practice of "sound business ethics."

Consider, for example, a long-running advertisement for a prestigious business school's seminars on ethics that said the reasons for learning and, presumably, practicing "good business ethics" is to "build stable, profitable relationships, strengthen employee loyalty . . . and avoid litigation." One would hope that all these results would ensue for the ethical organization. Still, we need to ask, How well does a focus on these goals hold up as the rationale or motivation for behaving ethically? What if lying about something that has recently occurred is likely to help a firm avoid litigation more than telling the truth? Is lying acceptable then? What if misusing funds to provide extra perquisites for employees is more effective in gaining their loyalty than using funds properly? What if there are cases in which "more stable, profitable relationships" can be better secured through bribery or deceit than through honest competition? The point here is that when commitments to or judgments about ethical behavior are based primarily on utilitarian cost-benefit calculations, they may be weak indeed.

It is easy to argue for the practical benefits of ethical behavior as the primary justification for adhering to ethical standards. But as the examples just cited highlight, such a justification is easily undermined. Ironically it is most easily undermined in just those situations in which sound ethical choices may be most difficult to discern and most important to make.

One potential advantage of nonprofit, public benefit organizations in this sphere is that they can—and should—root their judgments about commitments to ethical behavior in the moral traditions from which the nonprofit sector sprang. As one scholar reminds us, "Institutions that enunciate, transmit, and defend ethical values fall within the boundaries of nonprofit sector. Educational, religious, and advocacy organizations constitute a majority of [the] membership and have shaped the sector itself" (Mason, 1992a). Put more plainly, as a monograph entitled *Ethics and the Nation's Voluntary and Philanthropic Community* noted, "Those who presume to serve the public good assume a public trust" (Independent Sector, 1991, p. 1).

Understanding that ethical judgments must be based on firmer moral and social considerations, let us look more closely at the particular ethical values—and the character of the public trust—that can and should shape the ethical perspectives of nonprofit managers, whatever the practical advantages (or disadvantages) of ethical behavior may be.

Core Values for the Voluntary Sector

Many explanations have been offered for the origins and use of the nonprofit organizational form. Scholars differ as to which explanations are most valid. (For useful discussions of this question, see Columbo and Hall, 1995; Douglas, 1987; Hansmann, 1987; Hopkins, 1998; O'Neill, 2003; Salamon, 1999; Van Til, 1988.) One explanation that holds substantial explanatory power revolves around two issues or dynamics that economists and organizational theorists call "market failure" and "contract failure" (or an "agency problem").

Too simply put, the market failure theory suggests that private nonprofits tend to arise to provide services when agencies of governments cannot or will not provide the service for some reason, and the nature of the service needed is such that for-profit businesses cannot make a sufficient return on their investment to be induced to offer it. Contract failure and agency theory suggest nonprofits are needed to provide services when those who want a service offered are not in a position to provide it themselves, and it is also the case that those paying for the service are unable to judge the quality of that service because of the nature, location, or setting of the service to be provided. In such circumstances, it is argued, people create or use private nonprofit (rather than for-profit) organizations because they feel nonprofits will have less incentive to cheat either consumers or supporters. That is, they think this type of organization—acting as their agent—is less likely to skimp on the amounts or quality of services offered because its board and managers have less opportunity to enrich themselves by that behavior in this organizational structure.

Note it is assumed that in these cases the people paying for the services are often not the consumers of the services. Often they are donors. This being so, they prefer to work through an organization that, as an agent, can be expected to provide that service in the manner that they (the donors) would provide it themselves if they could. Consequently, they seek an agent they believe to be highly committed for moral reasons to providing that service for others. Crassly put, they want an agent that is involved "for the cause," not "for the money."

A quick analysis of both these situations tells us what is likely to be one of the most important and desirable ethical qualities of nonprofit organizations in the public's eyes. In these circumstances trust is a key consideration. That being so, we can project what operational and ethical values will need to be evident in organizations to earn and retain the public's trust. Among the most significant, as already noted, are integrity, openness, accountability, and service.

Also on that earlier list, though, is *charity*, in the original sense of the term, from the Latin *caritas*. Obviously, there are some nonprofit organizations that would not be expected to be charitable as that word is often used—that is "generous" or "eleemosynary." Most people do not expect these to be characteristics of trade associations, for example. Still, the majority of the organizations that populate the nonprofit or voluntary sector are service providers dependent in some way on the philanthropic traditions and practices of our society. Indeed, the majority are religious, or have religious roots (Jeavons, 2003). And all these are expected in that context to be basically "caring" organizations, willing to put the public good and the welfare of others above their own private interests.

It is important to understand how this last expectation presumes a moral quality ascribed to such organizations deriving from their historical and sociological functions in our society. The fact is nonprofit philanthropic and service organizations occupy a distinctive place in American society because of their origins—largely in religious or other idealistic voluntary associations—and because they have traditionally been vehicles for preserving, transmitting, or promoting social values. Because of their historical development and their contemporary roles, these institutions carry much of the burden of mediating civic, moral, and spiritual values in the public realm and from one generation to the next (Curti, 1958; Parsons, 1960). Thus, they are objects of special public expectations that they will behave in morally honorable ways.

So there are ethical qualities that are essential in the character and behavior of public benefit nonprofits. These organizations are expected to—and should—demonstrate integrity, openness, accountability, service, and a caring demeanor. And what is required of managers in this context is that they give continuing attention to assure that these ethical values are reflected in every aspect of these organizations. This requires that the managers model ethical qualities in their own behavior as well as articulate and foster them as ideals for others. Considering carefully the meaning of these values in organizational behavior should allow us to see better how managers can undertake these responsibilities and work toward creating a culture of integrity.

Ethical Management in Ethical Organizations

It will be useful now to consider the key ethical attributes of nonprofit managers and their organizations more fully. In this process we should undertake an analysis at two levels—the individual and the organizational—asking, for example, What does it mean for a manager to do his or her work with integrity, and for an organization to operate with integrity?

It is important to say that I cannot, in this one section, make an exhaustive analysis or offer numerous illustrations of how these ethical qualities would be evident in each of the many aspects of the operations and management of nonprofit organizations. Authors of other chapters in this volume that address other aspects of nonprofit management discuss questions and offer considerations of ethical issues specifically relevant to different facets of the work of nonprofit organizations. At this point, my intention is to offer a broader context within which to think further in ethical terms about the material presented in the other chapters (and in real life). Ideally, the relationship between this chapter, focused specifically on ethics, and those other chapters, addressing various facets of nonprofit management, should set the ground for a dialogue about a wide range of ethical issues nonprofit managers face.

Integrity

It may be most useful to describe integrity as "honesty writ large." That is to say, integrity has to do with continuity between appearance and reality, between intention and action, between promise and performance, in every aspect of a person's or organization's existence. If trust is essential to support the operation of charitable nonprofit organizations, and if being trustworthy is one of the most basic qualities the public looks for in them, then integrity in this sense becomes a fundamental ethical characteristic they must possess.

At the organizational level, integrity is most obviously demonstrated to be present or absent by comparing an organization's own literature—fundraising materials, reports, mission statements, and such—with its actual program priorities and performance. For instance, an organization that claims to exist to serve the poor but regularly spends extensive resources on enlarging itself, enhancing its own image before the public, or attending to the comfort of its staff must be suspect. So, too, one wonders about educational institutions that say they are devoted to providing the best education possible to students but spend more of their resources on things intended to improve their own status—image enhancing athletics, high-profile research projects, or "star" faculty members—than on facilities and activities for teaching and learning.

This is not to say that staff in such organizations should not have reasonable salaries and benefits; that being in the public eye for fundraising purposes is not important to support the work to be done; or that an organization might not be able to improve its service delivery by growing or its teaching by employing active researchers. However, it is to say that a careful examination of budgets, allocations of staff time, and the application of other resources sometimes show that nonprofit organizations that were created to serve the public good are giving more attention to caring for and improving themselves than others. Moreover, the public is highly sensitive to these issues. If we need proof of this, we would do well to recall the huge controversies involving United Way of America or some television ministries in the early 1990s; or more recent controversies that have centered on compensation levels for CEOs of large universities and foundations.

It is instructive, in fact, to review in more detail the story of the United Way of America, because its scandal caused long-term and profound damage to almost all local United Ways and injured the credibility of charities more generally. In the spring of 1992 it was revealed that the head of the United Way of America was receiving a salary of almost $500,000, traveling about the world first-class, and setting up subsidiary organizations run by his friends and relatives. When millions of small donors to local United Ways found out that a portion of their gifts were going to support a lavish lifestyle for an executive of a charitable organization, many were outraged. Despite the massive efforts of local United Ways to explain that only a tiny portion of income went to the national organization, which was a legally separate entity, the giving to local United Ways (and so to many community service agencies) fell significantly the next year and in many cases took years to recover. Some would argue the declining influence of United Ways in many places, while having multiple causes, began its downward trend here.

This case illustrates how clear disparities between the ethical promise (implicit or explicit) and the real performance of one charitable organization may precipitate dramatic difficulties for the entire nonprofit sector. As one of the first economists to study the nonprofit sector carefully observed, "Whenever any nonprofit is found to have abused its trusted position, the reputation of trustworthy nonprofits also suffers" (Weisbrod, 1988, p. 13). This observation of twenty years ago seems only to grow more true as media scrutiny of nonprofits intensifies.

Indeed, we have seen this anew in the last decade. From 2002 to 2008 the charitable sector and the public were treated to a long-running spectacle staged by the Senate Finance Committee chaired by Senator Charles Grassley. Under Grassley's leadership the committee launched one investigation after another—and broadcasted one charge after another—about the alleged misuse and waste of funds by nonprofits. Seizing on a relatively small number of cases, some of which were admittedly egregious, the Senator and Finance Committee staff were able to generate an extraordinary amount of bad publicity for charitable institutions as a whole. These investigations raised significant questions about nonprofits' operations that in many cases need attention. But in a broader context all the noise made by the Senate Finance Committee simply served to make all nonprofits ethically suspect because of the bad behavior of a very small minority.

A specific example of the kind of behavior that raises such issues about integrity can be drawn from a smaller study of relief and development agencies (Jeavons, 1994). One of the agencies studied engaged in practices that were not illegal but would certainly have caused questions in the minds of donors (and others), if they had become aware of them. At least two practices were ethically questionable.

First, this agency sometimes used what are called "representational" images in their fundraising materials. That is to say, brochures told stories about a family or person in need, often desperate need, and included pictures of their plight that were quite striking. However, sometimes these stories were actually composites of stories of a number of people in the impoverished area, put together for maximum effect; or the pictures were not of the particular persons or family mentioned at all, but rather were pictures that the agency calculated were most likely to "pull on donors' heart strings." The needs were real, and the stories and pictures conveyed the needs quite effectively; but this approach lacked integrity because the stories and pictures were not, finally, factually true.

Some persons would argue that this is morally wrong because, simply enough, it is a form of dishonesty, regardless of the fact that it raises money for a good purpose. Others argued the ends justified the means, because the stories were essentially true. Yet even persons within this organization admitted that if donors had become aware of this practice they might have been upset. The donors' expectations of high moral standards—in this case, higher standards of truthfulness—for such an organization would have been violated.

Second, this same agency often made general appeals with brochures featuring projects for which it could most easily raise money, and the brochures gave a strong impression (though not a specific promise) that the money raised would go to those particular projects. But in fact, those projects were fully funded from other sources, and the donations were used for other purposes. Again, this was done in a way that ensured there was no illegality, but neither was there clear integrity.

One is left to wonder, in such an organizational climate, what other ethical standards were allowed to slide and how well the funds that were raised were being used. If one is inclined to think that these kinds of decisions can be seen purely as matters of strategic choice, one needs to see the contrast between this organization and other relief and development agencies that were studied.

Many other agencies had specific rules against using "representational images" and policies that require donors to be consulted before their gifts are used for projects other than the ones for which they were solicited. The managers in those agencies described their standards and policies as points of pride, as conscious choices made to uphold the ethical character of their organizations and their work. And those managers pointed out that it was vital to maintain the highest moral standards in all facets of their operations, lest the willingness to compromise at one point become the beginning of a lowering of standards more generally—the first step on the proverbial "slippery slope."

This small example from long ago presaged similar, more recent problems for a much more visible charity. Charges like these, but on a far larger scale, were raised about the Red Cross's fundraising in the aftermath of the terrorist attacks on the United States on September 11, 2001. Although there may have been good, even compelling reasons that some of the millions of dollars of funds not needed in New York City should have been set aside for emergencies elsewhere, doing so without prior permission from (or explanations to) donors was not acceptable to the public. The fallout caused that organization great embarrassment.

So all this asks us to examine again the meaning of integrity at the individual level for managers and management. *Integrity* may have different meanings for different individuals, but in the context of professional ethics it must mean doing one's job as honestly and as fully in adherence to one's professed principles as possible. Careful observers of organizational behavior have noted that managers and leaders in organizations, or particular parts of organizations, can have a significant effect in setting behavioral standards, either as a matter of personal influence or because of their control of reward systems, or for both reasons.

The manager who wants her or his employees to deal honestly with others had better deal honestly with them and, further, had better reward honesty and discourage any dishonesty. If the manager is willing to cut corners, tell "little" lies, or act in self-serving ways, it becomes more likely that employees, too, will see this as acceptable, at least in the work setting. A manager who wants the organization she or he oversees to be known for its integrity and to be trustworthy must begin by being completely trustworthy in her or his dealings with all those who are part of the organization, and make it clear that similar behavior is expected of all those people.

Put more simply, integrity must be one of the hallmarks of nonprofit management. It is an ethical obligation, both as a matter of morality, because it is right, and as a matter of societal necessity, because the public expects nonprofit organizations to do these things. Recent history shows that failing to uphold the highest standards for personal and organizational integrity can have enormous consequences for nonprofit managers and their agencies or institutions.

Openness

It would not be accurate to call the quality of openness a "moral" value, at least within the context of the most common value systems of American culture. So the claim to be made here about openness as an ethical value is not based so much on moral absolutes—as may be the case for integrity—as on social values and expectations. In this context, we might think of openness as a "derivative virtue." We might also note, however, that in businesses, as well as nonprofits, efforts to make organizations more transparent to stakeholders are gaining ground as leaders recognize that being trustworthy is often critical to success in both spheres.

In any case, in the history of philanthropy in America, whenever organizations or individuals try to hide their philanthropic endeavors from public view, the result—if they are discovered—has almost always been to raise profound skepticism about the motivation for and character of those endeavors. The public's attitude here has been, "If they are really doing good, why would they be reluctant (or embarrassed) to have us see what they are doing?"

This is especially true for organizations. It is possible to put forth a reasonable argument, even one based on religious grounds (see Matthew 6:2–4 or the Mishnah Torah), for individuals "doing good works" anonymously or in secret. However, organizations operating in the public sphere, especially in areas of service or advocacy that can have an impact on public policy or community life, find it hard to argue convincingly that there is any value to secrecy about how they make their choices and do their work. Indeed, it may be crucial for these organizations to conduct their business in a way that is open to public scrutiny.

One compelling reason for this is that openness undergirds other ethical behavior. The organization that operates openly cannot afford to cut other ethical corners. Being "transparent" —something of a buzzword in governance discussions now—makes integrity mandatory, unless one wants to suffer serious criticism. For example, in the case of the relief and development agencies (above), it seems clear that the one that engaged in questionable tactics would not have been able to operate transparently and retain its donor base.

Another reason for openness is historical. There have long been critical questions raised about the roles philanthropic and service organizations play in shaping people's and communities' lives. (See, for instance, Griffin, 1957, or Nielsen, 1985.) One cause for this concern is that some organizations appear to have had ulterior motives—for example, intentions of "social control" or protection of the interests of the privileged—embedded in their work. It is clear that some of the impetus for legislation regulating the operation of foundations (in 1969) came from supposedly philanthropic entities being formed and using their tax-exempt status as a way to protect family fortunes from taxation while still controlling family businesses (Bremner, 1988). Here again, recent scandals in the conduct of nonprofit some organizations reinforce the case to be made for their being subject to public scrutiny.

In addition, those who are concerned about the continuing vitality of nonprofit organizations, and recognize that maintaining a climate of trust is essential to that vitality, argue that operating openly is one of the best ways to build trust. Organizations that wish to engage people's support and good faith can find no better way to do so than to do good works well, and then welcome the inquiries and inspection by anyone interested in their methods.

A similar logic applies to those who lead these organizations, in terms of their leadership and management. In the effort to build the support and commitment of staff, volunteers, and donors, a manager's willingness to talk openly and honestly about rationales for programs, the reasons for and ways in which decisions are made, and approaches to problem solving can be invaluable. Also, many nonprofits (as voluntary associations) come out of a populist democratic tradition in American culture. It can be argued that they really ought to be operated in such a democratic manner to represent and further that tradition, so this may be another significant part of their role and social obligation in this society. (For a very helpful discussion of these issues, see Lohmann, 1992; O'Neill, 2003; & Van Til, 1988.)

Finally, this means that openness should be seen as a core ethical value for nonprofit organizations and their managers in the business of decision making, in matters of raising and allocating resources, and generally in the manner of their operation. Moreover, openness is a necessary prerequisite to accountability, which is the next core value we should examine.

Accountability

Not only is it important for nonprofit, public benefit organizations to be open about the things they do and how and why they do them, it is also important that they be ready to explain and generally be accountable for their choices. This is an extension of the implicit social contract of privilege and trust these organizations enjoy in our society. By accepting the privilege of tax-exemption and the right to solicit tax-deductible contributions, public benefit nonprofits also accept an obligation to be ready to answer for their behavior and performance—and not only to their membership, but also to the communities they serve, and to the broader public as well. For they are using financial resources that would otherwise have gone into the public treasury.

Looked at in contractual terms, we see these organizations are granted the right to solicit tax-deductible contributions, or at least are granted tax-exempt status, on the assumption that they are serving the public good and will put their resources to work as directly and efficiently as possible on behalf of the causes or people they claim to serve. Indeed, the character and language of the legal discourse about these issues—employing terms such as "public benefit" or "mutual benefit" organizations—confirms these assumptions (see, for example, Simon, 1987). From this implicit social contract derives a clear ethical obligation to perform according to promise, to be subject to evaluation, and be answerable for a failure to perform.

In fact, issues of nonprofits' accountability are very complicated, much more so than public discussions of these issues typically suggest. To really understand these issues for different nonprofits, one must ask multiple questions. "To whom is a nonprofit accountable?" is only the first; and the answer is likely to be, "to multiple constituencies." In addition, one should also ask, "For what aspects of their operations should they be accountable, and by whom will they be held accountable, and in what manner?" Some would argue that although all nonprofits should have some public accountability, these specifics of "to whom and how" are matters that should be thought about strategically and that need to be determined according to the stakeholders involved (Kearns, 1996). Chapter Four offers an extensive discussion of many different ways that nonprofit accountability can be understood and addressed.

All of this is to say that in social and contractual terms, all nonprofit organizations have an ethical responsibility to be accountable to their supporters, their members, and their donors; and most of all, the public benefit organizations, have a larger responsibility to be accountable to the broader public for how they undertake to fulfill their philanthropic purposes. Evidence of increasing public expectations in this regard can be found in the growth in recent years of "watch-dog" groups like the Better Business Bureau's Wise Giving Alliance and Guidestar. Nonprofits themselves have manifested their willingness to be more accountable by forming mutual accountability networks in particular fields, such as the Evangelical Council for Financial Accountability. Most recently Independent Sector issued a report on *Principles of Good Governance and Ethical*

Practice (2007), which they encouraged all their members (and others) to see as an outline of the ideals and behaviors all nonprofits should pursue, and for which they should be prepared to be accountable. In addition, more states have enacted laws to mandate financial disclosure and regulate fundraising practices of nonprofits.

How does this obligation of accountability extend to nonprofit managers? In much the same way as the obligations of integrity and openness do. First, if this is a quality managers and leaders want to see others demonstrate in their organization, then it is one the managers better model in their own behavior. Then it becomes an expectation that they can articulate credibly to other staff, trustees, and volunteers.

Second, managers can establish this commitment most firmly by holding themselves accountable to their organization's board, and working to build a board that will hold them properly accountable for their performance. Executives that view themselves as free agents, trying to isolate their boards from full information about and active involvement in the work of the organization, and boards that hire an executive, and then fall into passive, "rubber stamp" role in evaluation and governance have been two key contributing factors to poor performance and ethical problems in a number of nonprofits. The most useful literature on the board and executive relationships has pointed out that a full and vital partnership between executives and managers is essential to the most effective leadership in nonprofit organizations (Drucker, 1990; Herman and Heimovics, 1991; Middleton, 1987).

Ironically, one of the things this may require of an executive is that he or she encourage (or even educate) a board to play a more active role in evaluating the executive's—and the organization's—performance. In this way, if the board is representative of, or at least in touch with, the needs and feelings of the larger community, then the executive is soliciting oversight, and potentially helpful feedback from those the organization should serve. In this the executive is also modeling a quality she or he should hope to encourage in all staff—general accountability for performance and receptivity to constructive criticism.

Service

The grounds for the ethical obligation here are virtually identical with those for accountability. Nonprofit organizations, especially public benefit organizations, exist and are granted specific privileges (as noted above) with the explicit understanding that they are committed in some way to serve the public good. Those that are classified as "mutual benefit" organizations—which include trade associations, fraternal organizations, and such—are not beholden in the same way to serve "the public" in the broadest sense, but they are still certainly expected to serve their membership. The point is that service, service to people or service to a cause, is at the heart of the reason for being of all these organizations. (Note: Sometimes that service includes advocacy, speaking out about community needs and assets to others, as well as the organizations trying to meet those needs themselves.)

The social contract extended to these organizations assumes that they will devote themselves primarily to service. In accepting the privileges they have been granted, these organizations incur the ethical obligation to be service oriented. Moreover, in accepting the support—membership dues, donations, volunteers' time—of people who sustain them, these organizations reinforce their ethical obligations in this regard.

The ethical obligation to service should be manifest in the conduct of managers in a number of ways. A commitment to service should be manifest in those managers making practical and strategic choices that give precedence to fulfilling the mission of their organization over possibilities for advancing their own status and careers. Often, and we hope most often, these two goals can go hand-in-hand. But there are situations in which executives can make a choice that yields a short-term gain for the organization and makes the executive look good—improving his or her chances for a better next job—even though that choice harms the organization in the long run.

Many people now make a career of work in the nonprofit sector, especially in the field of fundraising. We could not have a meaningful discussion, as we do in this book, of nonprofit management as a "profession" if people did not commit themselves to and build careers in this area. This creates the ground for our discussion of professional ethics. However, it also creates a context in which managers can easily work with more concern for their own advancement than for the people or cause their organization is supposed to serve—and that can be problematic.

Now this is not to say that managers are required to sacrifice themselves—their health, their basic financial security, or their personal well-being—for the benefit of their organization. Nonprofit organizations, especially cause-oriented ones, are notorious for exploiting their staff in the name of noble ideals (see Greene, 1991). But this is to say that the undergirding values of the nonprofit sector are altruistic, or at least service-centered; and although it is fine to be concerned for one's own career, it is never acceptable for managers to advance themselves at the expense of the people and causes they have promised to serve.

In addition, observation suggests that the willingness of managers and leaders to see themselves as servants of others may be crucial to focusing others in an organization on that organization's commitment to service. Here the notion of "servant leadership" (Greenleaf, 1977) takes on both profound significance and immediate salience.

Charity

Finally, the last, but certainly not least important ethical obligation of nonprofit, public benefit organizations is to charity, in the original sense of the term. The word *charity* comes from the Latin *caritas*. This means more than giving to those in need. It originally was translated as "love"—not romantic love, but the love of neighbor and committed concern for the welfare of others as illustrated in the parable of the Good Samaritan. It meant caring, putting the welfare of others on a par with one's own. It meant being generous with one's own resources, not out of a sense of pity, but out of a sense of relationship with and concern for others.

It can surely be argued that for nonprofit organizations an ethical obligation to "charity" in this sense derives from reciprocity. That is, many of these organizations depend on the generosity of their supporters for their existence, and ought to display such generosity themselves. Furthermore, at least in the case of many public benefit nonprofits, the motivation of most of their supporters rests in no small way on a belief that these organizations are committed to caring for others. As noted in earlier discussion of origins of nonprofit organizations and the voluntary sector, the basis of many of these organizations' support is the expectation that they will be vehicles for building a better world or a more caring and just society.

This expectation is manifest in an interesting range of phenomena. For instance, the preference of many clients and supporters of social service agencies for private nonprofit groups appears to be based on an assumption that they will provide services in a more personal, more caring way than a government agency. In industries where potential employees—for example, teachers, nurses, or social workers—might work for either government or private organizations, the preference of some for private nonprofits is often explained in terms of their expectation (or experience) of these organizations as more caring work environments. And this expectation is certainly confirmed by the public indignation that is often evident when an organization that is itself the beneficiary of charity turns around and acts in uncaring ways.

Once more, the way in which this expectation applies to the ethics of management seems obvious. An uncaring or mean-spirited manager can undermine the caring quality of an organization as fast as any negative influence imaginable. If one wants the participants in an organization to treat its clients (and one another) with love and respect, it is hardly likely that treating the participants coldly or unfairly will help that occur. Managers and leaders help set the tone of an organization's life—whether they intend to or not—and that tone is almost certainly going to be reflected in the way that organization and all of its staff interact at every level with its various constituencies.

Finally, we should see again that the organizations of the nonprofit sector have been seen as having a special role in transmitting civic, social, and ethical values in our society from one generation to the next. If that is true, then we have yet another reason to be concerned that these organizations reflect the highest ideals for a caring society. And it is clear that some managers do see their responsibilities in this light. Discussing the kind of "witness" his organization wants to make to all those which deal with it, the president of a Christian relief and development agency said, "We have a major challenge in living up to our commitment [to care for people]; not just for children eight thousand miles away, but also for the people at our elbow" (Jeavons, 1994, p. 265).

From Ideals to Operative Values

If we can agree, then, that these five concepts or ideals—integrity, openness, accountability, service, and charity—describe key ethical qualities and obligations of nonprofit organizations and their managers, we are still left to ask how these ideals get translated into behavior.

At the individual level, this may be easy. If one assumes that people can choose what to value and choose to embody those values in their actions, then for individuals ethical behavior is primarily a matter of choice and will. If this is the case, then the managers of nonprofit organizations simply need to choose to act with integrity, to be open and accountable in their work, and to make commitment to service and charity a cornerstone for their decision making and interaction with others. They need to do these things because they are the right things to do. They need to do these things because that is what the public that supports (and can withdraw its support from) these organizations expects (and even demands) of them; and because the failure to uphold these obligations can have very significant negative consequences for their organizations and others. However, this still leaves open the question of how these ethical ideals become the operational values of an organization as a whole.

At this point, we need to turn to the work that has been done on "organizational culture." This offers valuable insights to our discussion. In particular, I want to draw heavily on the careful research and analysis reported by Edgar Schein in *Organizational Culture and Leadership* (1985).

Some early thinking about organizational culture tended to focus, sometimes shallowly, on "rites and rituals" of organizational life (see Deal and

Kennedy, 1982; Peters and Waterman, 1982). Schein takes a different tack, arguing that an excessive focus on what he calls "the manifestations of culture" will obscure the fact that very similar rituals, conventions, or regular practices in various companies are undertaken for very different reasons. Thus, he claims, to understand organizational culture one must focus on the essential values these visible practices are meant to express. These values are "the substance of culture," in Schein's view.

Indeed, Schein argues that some values represent the basic assumptions of a group of people, like the membership of an organization, about the way the world is and how they, as a group, can function most successfully in it. These "core values" will shape the organization's behavior, not only by dictating what are right or acceptable responses to different kinds of situations, but even more fundamentally by shaping the way those situations are perceived, by influencing what people see as important or unimportant information.

Schein's views are reinforced by other scholars of organizations who contend that the most effective (and "unobtrusive") controls on the behavior of individuals in organizations may be achieved by either selecting people who will come to the organization with certain (shared) basic understandings about organizational or professional goals and practices, or by orienting them toward those understandings, goals, and practices once they arrive (Perrow, 1986).

In this vein, Schein argues that leaders or managers can shape the direction, character, and operations of an organization most fundamentally and effectively by shaping the core values of the participants within it, or by selecting new participants who share those values. Indeed, he claims "there is a possibility— underemphasized in leadership research—that the only things of real importance that leaders do is to create and manage culture" (1985, p. 2). The implications of this for people who are concerned about creating and maintaining organizations that behave ethically are obvious.

Managers' capacities to create a culture of integrity take root in the connection between the ethical behavior of those managers and the maintenance of the highest ethical standards of behavior of their nonprofit organizations. This is a culture in which the ethical ideals we have been discussing come to be accepted as "givens," and in which the expectation that these ideals will be honored in the life and work of the organization permeates every participant's thinking. This can only occur when these ethical values are both articulated and modeled by those in positions of responsibility and leadership. In this way, leaders and managers can shape the core values of an organization as a whole—and the individuals within it—around these ethical ideals.

One place where such a dynamic can most readily be observed is in some religious service organizations that maintain a strong commitment to honor very clear and sometimes constricting ethical ideals in their operations, while still competing successfully for donor support in a highly competitive market. (For a detailed description of such groups, see Jeavons, 1994.)

Creating and Maintaining a Culture of Integrity

Finally we must see that clear, strong commitments to ethical ideals and behavior on the part of managers is a prerequisite to creating organizational cultures of integrity in nonprofits that will enable the organizations themselves to behave ethically. The importance of the example of leadership in this process cannot be overemphasized. As one commentator has observed, "CEOs . . . are ultimately accountable for [their] organization's ethical posture. . . . No organization can rise above the ethical level of its manager" (Mason, 1992b, p. 30).

Clearly, a manager who tells others about the importance of behaving ethically while behaving otherwise himself or herself is likely to have little positive influence on the organization. In fact, such a manager is likely to have a destructive influence, generating cynicism about and indifference to ethical concerns throughout the organization. And ultimately a manager whose own behavior models all the best of these values but who does not talk about their significance for the organization's life may still have a less positive influence than is needed.

Still, even where the management of an organization is consistent in both preaching and practicing the desired values, more will probably be needed to create and sustain a culture of integrity. Organizational structures and reward systems must also support and encourage ethical behavior among all employees and volunteers. People's best intentions can be undermined or confused by organizational structures and processes that lead them to make choices that have negative ethical consequences.

One wonders, for instance, how often in nonprofit service agencies (of various types) reports of problems with programs or relationships to their clients are stifled, or mistakes that could reveal ways to improve their service are never mentioned, because their staffs (and volunteers) are rewarded only for successes. As in many organizations that are hierarchically ordered, some nonprofits have a tendency to punish the bearers of bad news—and even reward the bearers of false news, when it is good. Encouraging employees to be less than honest about policies and programs that are failing leaves an organization less able to perform its mission. The leadership and management of a nonprofit organization must put in place systems that reward participants for honesty in every form, even forms that lead to the revelation of difficulties and deficiencies of the organization.

Similarly, one has to wonder about organizations that constantly emphasize short-term goals and focus solely on raw numbers (of dollars raised) in evaluating development efforts, rather than asking questions about the quality of relationships with donors and other potentially positive effects of fundraising—such as its educational impact on constituencies they are trying to reach. Where narrower emphases and reward systems dominate, what is the impact on fundraisers' approaches to donors? Are they as honest and caring as they should be? What is the effect on individual and organizational reporting? Is the information about fundraising costs and results as complete and fully revealing as it should be? (For a fuller examination of these issues, see Jeavons and Basinger, 2000.)

These kinds of questions about the relationship between reward systems and structures and ethical behavior become even more complex, but no less important, when the behaviors at issue are not so simple, or when more subtle matters are involved. For instance, what about a situation in which questions are being asked about whether a "progressive nonprofit organization" is exploiting its employees, or whether it is being true to the values it claims to represent in the ways it treat them?

By way of example, I once worked with an organization that claimed that one of the principles to which it was committed was that it "values people . . . [and] does not permit the accomplishment of goals at the expense of people." However, the organization had a structure for and approach to fundraising that emphasized continually increasing the number of dollars raised and reducing administrative costs without consideration for the effects of such goals and policies on the relationships among staff or between donors and staff. Furthermore, rewards in the organization—both raises and promotions—were distributed in a highly competitive system according to an assessment of performance based almost solely on quantitative measures. The outcome was that managers tended to push staff to achieve "more impressive" results—that is, raise more money—without regard to the impact that pressure might have on either the donors they worked with or the staff themselves. These practices seemed a direct contradiction to articulated values, and led to high staff turnover.

One could look also at the famous United Way of America scandal mentioned earlier. How did an organization that was formed specifically to serve and support local United Ways and to promote a philosophy of service, volunteering, and giving come to be an example of self-serving, empire-building management practices? In part, at least, this seems to have been a result of organizational structures that insulated the top management from the constituencies they were supposed to be serving, making them less aware of and accountable to the people the organization most needed to hear—that is, local United Ways' donors and clients.

In addition, the staff leadership seemed to spend most of its time with, and came to pattern itself after, business leaders in the effort to gain support and resources from them. However, in the process, the United Way of America's executive leadership came to think like for-profit corporate executives and apparently to believe that organizational growth was an end worth pursuing in itself for United Way of America. That particular strategies for attaining this end were undermining United Way's stated mission was overlooked. The result was a misuse of donated funds, a clear abuse of public trust, and some erosion of the very spirit of giving and volunteering the organization was suppose to promote.

The point is that organizational structures and processes and systems of rewards and disincentives must be put in place and consciously maintained to reinforce whatever rhetoric about ethical values an organization puts forth. Moreover, all this must be supported by the managers and leaders of the organization who demonstrate personal commitment to those ethical values in their own behavior. The creation and maintenance of an organizational culture of integrity—one where integrity, openness, accountability, service, and charity consistently predominate; one that will lead to consistently ethical behavior on the part of nonprofit organizations—cannot be achieved absent these elements in an organization's life.

Summary

This chapter has demonstrated that ethical questions and issues must be primary concerns of all nonprofit managers, and that these issues and questions are salient in all aspects of the operation of nonprofit organizations. It has been argued that the ethical values most important for nonprofit managers and organizations to honor center on the qualities of integrity, openness, accountability, service, and charity. We have seen how these particular ethical ideals are prescribed for nonprofit organizations by virtue of the distinctive history of the voluntary and nonprofit sector and the roles that these organizations play in American society. It is crucial that nonprofit organizations embody these ethical ideals in practice, both because ethical conduct and character are what moral duty requires—it is right—and because the public expects this of nonprofit organizations that say they are serving the public good. Only in this way can nonprofits fulfill the implicit social contract that supports their existence in our society.

It is important to note the educational implications of this. The last two decades have seen the emergence of a number of programs around the country to educate people specifically for the work of managing nonprofit organizations. How much attention do these programs give to helping those people understand the special history and unique roles and expectations that should shape the way these organizations function and are managed? (Some would say not enough.) Those being educated to take on the responsibilities of management and leadership in nonprofit organizations must be taught sound approaches to, and the profound importance of, careful, responsible reflection on the ethical issues embedded in the various facets of the life of these organizations.

Managing an organization so that core ethical values will be consistently embodied in the organization's life requires more than rhetoric. It requires that managers demonstrate these values in their own conduct in their professional lives and service. It also requires that they create and maintain organizational structures and dynamics by which ethical conduct is rewarded and unethical conduct, in any manifestation, is discouraged. This has to involve an examination of all organizational systems and structures, from fundraising strategies to human resources policies to accounting systems, to ensure that those structures and systems do not generate pressures on personnel to ignore or violate the standards and assumptions for ethical behavior espoused in broader contexts. Other chapters offer more illustrations of how ethical questions might arise in specific facets of the work of nonprofit organizations and their managers.

The significance of these matters cannot be overemphasized. The lifeblood of the nonprofit sector is trust. Without trust on the part of donors, clients, and the larger public, nonprofit organizations will not be able to do the important work and fulfill the crucial roles that are theirs in our society. And nothing will erode this foundation of trust, for the good nonprofits as well as the bad, as quickly as new (or continuing) scandals involving unethical behavior by nonprofit organizations and their managers.

When faced with the temptation to cut an ethical corner, tell a little lie, not bother with full disclosure, or let the ends justify the means, it is essential that the leadership and management of nonprofit organizations understand the implications of such actions and refuse to compromise on upholding rigorous ethical standards. We have to remember that ultimately noble ends are never served by ignoble means. We have to understand that inevitably our "ethical chickens will come home to roost."

Nonprofit, public benefit organizations have special responsibilities to serve the public good in our society, to do the right thing—for those in need, and for important causes and those who care about them—because it is right. This represents the ethical and essential foundation of the nonprofit sector. Without this foundation intact, it is quite likely the whole structure of the sector, including its moral and social capital and the special privileges that support its operations, could slowly dissolve. Attention to sustaining the highest levels of ethical conduct must be a primary concern of every nonprofit manager.

Note

1. I am indebted for this definition, and for much of the formulation of the material that follows on ethical theory, to Mike W. Martin, professor of philosophy at Chapman University.

References

Argyris, C., and Schon, D. A. *Organizational Learning*. Reading, Mass.; Addison-Wesley, 1978.

Bellah, R. N., et al. *Habits of the Heart: Individualism and Commitment in American Life*. Berkeley: University of California Press, 1985.

Bremner, R. H. *American Philanthropy*. (2nd ed.) Chicago: University of Chicago Press, 1988.

Columbo, J. D., and Hall, M. H. *The Charitable Tax Exemption*. Boulder, Colo.; Westview Press, 1995.

Curti, M. "American Philanthropy and the National Character." *American Quarterly*, 1958, *10*, 420–437.

Deal, T. E., and Kennedy, A. A. *Corporate Cultures: The Rites and Rituals of Corporate Life*. Reading, Mass.: Addison-Wesley, 1982.

Douglas, J. "Political Theories of Nonprofit Organization." In W. Powell (ed.), *The Nonprofit Sector: A Research Handbook*. New Haven, Conn.: Yale University Press, 1987.

Drucker, P. F. *Managing the Nonprofit Organization*. New York: HarperCollins, 1990.

Flores, A. (Ed.) *Professional Ideals*. Belmont, Calif.: Wadsworth Publishing, 1988.

Gellerman, W., Frankel, M. S., and Ladenson, R. (eds.). *Values and Ethics in Organization and Human Systems Development*. San Francisco: Jossey-Bass, 1990.

Goldman, A. H. "Professional Values and the Problem of Regulation." *Business and Professional Ethics Journal*, n.d., *5*(2), 47–59.

Greene, S. G. "Poor Pay Threatens Leadership." *Chronicle of Philanthropy*, March 26, 1991, 28–31.

Greenleaf, R. K. *Servant Leadership*. Ramsey, N.J.: Paulist Press, 1977.

Griffin, C. S. "Religious Benevolence as Social Control, 1815–1860." *Mississippi Historical Review*, 1957, *44*(3), 423–444.

Hansmann, H. "Economic Theories of the Nonprofit Sector." In W. Powell (ed.), *The Nonprofit Sector: A Research Handbook*. New Haven, Conn.: Yale University Press, 1987.

Herman, R. D., and Heimovics, R. D. *Executive Leadership in Nonprofit Organizations: New Strategies for Shaping Executive-Board Dynamics*. San Francisco: Jossey-Bass, 1991.

Hopkins, B. R. *The Law of Tax-Exempt Organizations*. (7th ed.) Somerset, N.J.: Wiley, 1998.

Independent Sector. *Ethics and the Nation's Voluntary and Philanthropic Community*. Washington, D.C.: Independent Sector, 1991.

Independent Sector. "Keeping the Trust: Confidence in Charitable Organizations in an Age of Scrutiny." Washington, D.C.: Independent Sector, 2002.

Independent Sector. *Principles for Good Governance and Ethical Practice: A Guide for Charities and Foundations*. Washington, DC: Independent Sector, 2007.

Jeavons, T. H. "When Management Is the Message: Relating Values to Management Practice in Nonprofit Organizations." *Nonprofit Management & Leadership*, 1992, *2*(4), 403–421.

Jeavons, T. H. *When the Bottom Line Is Faithfulness: The Management of Christian Service Organizations*. Bloomington: Indiana University Press, 1994.

Jeavons, T. H. "The Vitality and Independence of Religious Organizations." *Society*, 2003, *40*(4), 27–36.

Jeavons, T. H., and Basinger, R. B. *Growing Givers Hearts: Treating Fundraising as Ministry.* San Francisco: Jossey-Bass, 2000.

Kearns, K. P. *Managing for Accountability.* San Francisco: Jossey-Bass, 1996.

Larson, M. S. *The Rise of Professionalism: A Sociological Analysis.* Berkeley: University of California Press, 1977.

Lohmann, R. *The Commons: New Perspectives on Nonprofit Organizations and Voluntary Action.* San Francisco: Jossey-Bass, 1992.

Martin, M. W. *Meaningful Work: Rethinking Professional Ethics.* New York: Oxford University Press, 2000.

Mason, D. E. "Keepers of the Springs: Why Ethics Make Good Sense for Nonprofit Leaders." *Nonprofit World*, 1992a, *10*(2), 25–27.

Mason, D. E. "Ethics and the Nonprofit Leader." *Nonprofit World*, 1992b, *10*(4), 30–32.

Middleton, M. "Nonprofit Boards of Directors: Beyond the Governance Function." In W. Powell (ed.), *The Nonprofit Sector: A Research Handbook.* New Haven, Conn.: Yale University Press, 1987.

Nielsen, W. *The Golden Donors: A New Anatomy of the Great Foundations.* New York: Dutton, 1985.

O'Neill, M. *Nonprofit Nation: A New Look at the Third America.* San Francisco: Jossey-Bass, 2003.

O'Neill, M. "Public Confidence in Nonprofit Organizations." *Nonprofit and Voluntary Sector Quarterly*, 2009, *38*(2), 237–269.

Ostrander, S. A., and Schervish, P. G. "Giving and Getting: Philanthropy as a Social Relation." In Van Til and Associates, *Critical Issues in American Philanthropy: Strengthening Theory and Practice.* San Francisco: Jossey-Bass, 1990.

Parsons, T. *Structures and Process in Modern Societies.* Glencoe, Ill: Free Press, 1960.

Payton, R. L., and Michael M. *Understanding Philanthropy.* Bloomington: Indiana University Press, 2008.

Perrow, C. *Complex Organizations: A Critical Essay.* (3rd ed.) New York: Random House, 1986.

Peters, T. J., and Waterman, R. *In Search of Excellence.* New York: HarperCollins. 1982.

Putnam, R. *Bowling Alone: The Collapse and Revival of American Community.* New York: Simon & Schuster, 2000.

Salamon, L.M., *America's Nonprofit Sector: A Primer.* New York: Foundation Center, 1999.

Schein, E. *Organizational Culture and Leadership.* (2nd ed.) San Francisco: Jossey-Bass, 1985.

Schon, D. A. *The Reflective Practitioner.* San Francisco: Jossey-Bass, 1983.

Schon, D. A. *Educating the Reflective Practitioner: Toward a New Design for Teaching and Learning in the Professions.* San Francisco: Jossey-Bass, 1987.

Simon, J. G. "The Tax Treatment of Nonprofit Organizations: A Review of Federal and State Policies." In W. Powell (ed.), *The Nonprofit Sector: A Research Handbook.* New Haven, Conn.: Yale University Press, 1987.

Van Til, J. *Mapping the Third Sector.* New Brunswick, N.J.: Transaction Press, 1988.

Weisbrod, B. *The Nonprofit Economy.* Cambridge, Mass.: Harvard University Press, 1988.

CHAPTER EIGHT

STRATEGIC MANAGEMENT

William A. Brown

This chapter explores the decisions that nonprofit managers need to consider as they think and act strategically, as they make specific choices in order to accomplish particular outcomes or goals. The strategy process is focused on the desire to achieve some sense of alignment and coherence among management practices and to ensure that there is a framework to guide decision making and that the framework is discussed, evaluated, and modified according to operational conditions. As Bryson explains in his chapter on the Strategy Change Cycle (Chapter Nine of this handbook), *strategy* is "a pattern of purposes, policies, programs, actions, decisions, or resource allocations that define what an organization is, what it does, and why it does it." Strategic management involves the ability to achieve some sense of alignment and coherence and to understand external market opportunities and challenges and weave together service delivery systems to address the needs of the multiple stakeholders that are affected by the actions of the organization.

For many nonprofit professionals strategic management is the same as strategic planning. It is not. Strategic management is a larger process that comprises two phases—strategy formation (what are we going to do?) and strategy implementation (how are we going to do it?) (Hitt, Ireland, and Hoskisson, 2007). Strategic planning is a process that guides conversations about an organization's purpose, helps integrate perspectives from multiple stakeholders, and provides the steps to develop goals and objectives that will move the organization forward. Even as he explains strategic planning, (Chapter Nine) Bryson emphasizes that that effective planning must be linked to "strategic thinking and acting." A disconnected planning process is not helpful and is a waste of time and resources.

Miles and Snow (1978) explain that strategy encompasses interpreting environmental conditions and designing the organization's systems to foster success: "the effectiveness of organizational adaptation hinges on the dominant coalition's perceptions of environmental conditions and the decisions it makes concerning how well the organization will cope with these conditions" (p. 21).

Successful strategy is contingent on appropriate interpretation of environmental conditions and formulating an organizational response to address those conditions (Mintzberg, 1979). The dominant coalition is the set of key decision makers who guide priorities and control resources. Strategic management encompasses most of the topics discussed in this handbook (such as managing operations, developing financial resources, and managing people); effective strategic managers develop coherent approaches that integrate the work of these different areas. No organization can drive out all of the paradoxes and contradictions, but strategic management is the process by which to facilitate alignment among the various functions and activities in the organization.

Before discussing nonprofit strategic management in detail it is necessary to note some key concepts from the strategic management literature. First, strategy is often within the mind of the executive or leadership team (that is, the dominant coalition). The founder or executive has an idea of how to get things done and that philosophy guides operations. Leaders cocreate the philosophical perspective and activities that guide how the organization operates, who it serves, and which funders to work with. Second, changes to strategic orientations are typically *incremental* and happen through modest adjustments to practices (Quinn, 1989). Third, managers need to ensure that their strategic perspective is articulated and shared. Rarely is it fully captured in a plan binder on a shelf, but key decision makers should understand and agree on the general perspective that will guide the organization's operations. Fourth is the idea of agreement and consistency among organizational participants and structures, which is called *alignment*. The empirical literature documents that greater alignment among organizational elements is better (Schiemann, 2009).

To understand alignment, Miles and Snow (1978) developed a typology to guide strategic thinking. Drawing from their own and others' research, they identified four basic strategic orientations of organizations: Prospectors,

Defenders, Analyzers, and Reactors. *Prospectors* are innovators seeking to expand and create new products and services, while *Defenders* seek efficiency and consistency in a select number of services. *Analyzers* are not the first to develop services but are quick to integrate service innovations once identified. *Reactors* lack a coherent method and are inconsistent and unable to implement tactics reliably. Research across organizational forms (nonprofit, for-profit, international, small, and large firms) suggests that these organizational "types" are identifiable and, depending on the operational context, prospector, defender, or analyzer may be a reasonable strategic model by which to frame management decisions (see, for example, Andrews, Boyne, Law and Walker, 2009; Ketchen et al., 1997; Miles, Snow, Mathews, Miles, and Coleman, 1997). Reactors, however, are non-optimal performers. These "types" are not necessarily pure throughout an organization (Andrews, Boyne, Law, and Walker, 2009). Some departments and divisions might be more entrepreneurial (that is, prospector-like) whereas other departments or divisions might be working to improve efficiencies (that is, defender-like). These typological boundaries are not concrete, yet they provide a useful tool to consider how organizational systems work together to improve performance.

Fundamental to strategic management is the idea of *differentiation*. In order to be successful an organization should consider how it is distinctive from others. In a for-profit context, the other entities are typically competitors trying to attract *customers*. For nonprofits that might be less true, but the concept of *competitive advantage* is useful because, even in cooperative relationships, organizational entities look for distinctive or unique capabilities in a potential partner. Furthermore in a competitive funding environment (I discuss this more in the next section), nonprofits need to consider how they are unique in the services they provide and the values they embody. As nonprofit managers address the various contingencies of their organization they should consider how they are *positioned* to differentiate their own organization from other entities.

One more contingency element that informs this chapter is the recognition that many nonprofits are small- to moderate-sized organizations, and this limits choices. Nonprofit managers confront needs far bigger than their organization can address and experience resource constraints that frustrate even the best and brightest. So I'll try to keep the ideas simple and identify priorities for nonprofit managers. This chapter is designed to relate to, yet not duplicate, the guidance offered by other chapters throughout this handbook. For example, I acknowledge and note the importance of collaboration and alliances and effective human resource practices with the expectation that the reader will then review the content of each related chapter for additional information on each of these topics.

Nonprofit Strategic Management Cycle

Nonprofit strategy is becoming more sophisticated to better reflect the unique character of nonprofits (see, for example, Backman, Grossman and Rangan, 2000; Chew and Osborn, 2009; Courtney, 2002; Kong, 2007), including the need to consider multiple stakeholders, the potential for collaborations, and the mixed influences of market forces. This chapter draws on a modified version of the "adaptive cycle" model proposed by Miles and Snow (1978) in their cutting-edge study exploring *Organizational Strategy, Structures, and Processes*, to offer guidance on decision making that is relevant to the unique conditions nonprofit managers confront. The model identifies the three main topics in strategic management (see Figure 8.1). Nonprofit managers make strategic decisions that address

1. The need for *services and resource opportunities* (that is, market opportunities)
2. The mechanisms that will be used to offer services and secure resources (that is, *delivery systems and capabilities*)
3. The practices used to monitor *performance and control* operations

   In this chapter I address each of these decision areas or "problems." First, I consider the market opportunities available to a nonprofit organization.

FIGURE 8.1. NONPROFIT STRATEGIC MANAGEMENT CYCLE.

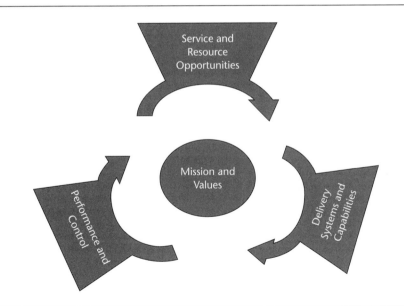

For nonprofits, the market entails not only a demand or need for services but also the resource environment. Second, I review the challenges of developing a service delivery system that relies on paid and unpaid organizational participants. Further, I examine how nonprofits often form alliances and work cooperatively in ways that are not common in a for-profit context. Finally, I identify the processes a nonprofit can put in place to monitor and address performance. This is particularly important for nonprofit strategy because of the difficulty of determining success. All of these "problems" are interconnected and, although I address them one by one, a key principle in strategic management is to recognize that organizational practices are interrelated and that decisions about one area are associated with the other two. All parts of the nonprofit strategic management cycle work together to constrain choices and facilitate performance.

Service and Resource Opportunities

Nonprofits must consider the need or demand for their products and services and their resource opportunities. For-profit entities typically have an easier time identifying their customer because there is, in most cases, an integral connection between the product or service, the customer and resource generation. The for-profit organization has significantly improved its chances for success if there is a "market" opportunity. For-profit managers still need to decide how to deliver that product or service in an efficient and effective manner, but meeting the need is synonymous with revenue generation. This is not necessarily the case for nonprofits. It is unusual for nonprofits to operate in an exchange relationship comparable to selling a product (Moore, 2000). So although it might seem a bit crass to suggest that nonprofits must not only look at "needs" in the community but also the potential resource market, it is vitally important to balance the purpose with resources.

Without a doubt the first "problem" a nonprofit manager considers is the purpose of the nonprofit—why it exists. As a tax-exempt entity, a nonprofit is typically organized for one of three reasons: religious purposes (that is, churches and houses of worship), public benefit purposes to meet needs in the community (that is, all 501(c)(3) charitable nonprofits exist to provide a public benefit), or mutual or member benefit purposes (for example, professional and trade associations that exist to provide services to their members) (State of California, 2009). Clarifying and establishing the purpose and reason for being is preeminent in strategic decision making for a nonprofit. This is captured in the organization's mission, vision, and values statements. That is why the mission, vision, and values are at the center of the strategic management cycle (Figure 8.1). The mission helps frame how an organization approaches everything it does. It is the core or heart of a nonprofit. In addition to creating the mission nonprofit managers need to consider the resource market. Who might fund and support our work? Although a "pure" nonprofit operates to fulfill its tax-exempt purposes, a realistic nonprofit meets those needs by considering the resource environment. Nonprofits must consider resources as part of their market because funders have a significant impact on the types of services provided and, some say, nonprofits also serve to facilitate philanthropic needs (Jeavons, 1994). This idea is not without controversy (Eikenberry, 2009). Some contend that resources are the "means" to achieve the "ends" articulated in the mission statement and hence are not comparable to the "real" market nonprofits exist to serve. However, the resource dependent nature of nonprofits and the lack of exchange with beneficiaries (that is, customers) imply that "the reason for being" is also driven by the practicalities of resources. This is a fundamental, if uncomfortable, reality for many nonprofits.

Multiple "Markets"

A nonprofit can benefit by considering primary markets (the tax-exempt purposes) and secondary markets (resource opportunities). The nonprofit "market" includes the need for services, the potential funding opportunities, workforce potential (that is, a labor pool of volunteers and paid employees), and the nature of other service providers (see Figure 8.2). The market is at a minimum "two-headed," and the existence of multiple target audiences makes it much harder to satisfy everyone (Andreasen and Kotler, 2007). Extensive literature is dedicated to analyzing market opportunities and evaluating the strengths and weaknesses of other providers (Chew and Osborne, 2009; Porter, 1998), and several chapters in this handbook discuss alternative ways that nonprofits can examine their options.

"Where does my organization fit in relation to other providers?" This is a basic question in strategic management. There is some concern that the nonprofit sector is cluttered—there are too many nonprofits doing more or less the same thing. Nonprofit managers should be cognizant of other organizations and stakeholders operating in a similar service arena. It is vital to consider how one nonprofit differentiates itself from another. Nonprofits may appear similar but there should be several ways that each is unique (including the values that explain how a nonprofit fits or works with other players in the field [Weisbrod, 1998; Frumkin and Andre-Clark, 2000]). This differentiation is important for meeting community needs but also to attract resources.

An example is a recent start-up of a volunteer center that is trying to determine where and how to move forward with the idea of "promoting volunteerism"

FIGURE 8.2. MULTIPLE NONPROFIT MARKETS AND STRATEGIC INPUTS.

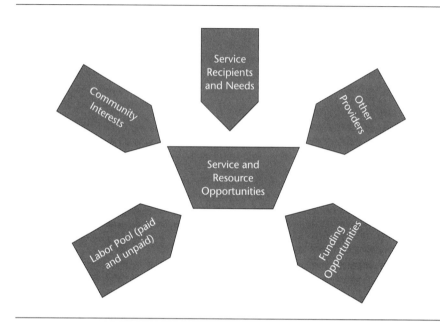

in a particular regional area. The very existence of the volunteer center was instigated by a funder. The community has recognized for quite some time that there is a need for more coordinated services and infrastructure organizations to serve the nonprofit community. It wasn't until a key funder helped get the center established that the "need" was addressed. Based on the interests of the key funder certain market choices are already determined, such as the geographic service area. The funder becomes part of the "dominant coalition" of decision makers helping to articulate and define the strategic purposes (as illustrated in Lake, Reis, and Spann, 2000). There are of course numerous choices to be made. For example, there are various pools of volunteers (that is, corporate, students, faith-based, individual community member, and required community service) and the center needs to decide which to prioritize. The center will also consider who else is providing similar services. For instance, this center is in a university town and needs to understand how the university does or does not meet the needs of student volunteers. The center needs to consider the interests of placement entities. How much help do nonprofits need to locate and manage volunteers? Inevitably, resources will also influence the focus of activities. Who else will help pay for the services? So, resource questions will also guide how the center develops in addition to the needs and demands of the beneficiaries.

A related concept is the existence of multiple "bottom lines" (Jeavons, 1994). Take for example, Teach for America that seeks to "eliminate educational inequity." Their strategy provides teachers to some of the most disadvantaged student populations in America. Concurrently, Teach for America seeks to recruit and influence some of the best and brightest college educated students (that is, future leaders) in America. They hope to influence and change the volunteers, while meeting needs. They are educating not only school-age students, they are educating their volunteers about the American education system. Only some "corps members" will remain as teachers, but the corps members will forever understand challenges in American education. Part of Teach for America's success is related to understanding the multiple markets. There was indeed a need for teachers in the communities they serve, but there was also a desire among well-educated socially conscious individuals to make a difference, and Teach for America was able to serve both of these objectives simultaneously. This recognition of multiple markets (resources and needs) is fundamental to nonprofit strategy. These examples illustrate the complex and multifaceted "markets" that nonprofits understand when deciding on their service and resource niches. (Chapter Eleven of this handbook offers an extensive discussion of the practice of nonprofit marketing.)

Strategic Orientations

Beyond considering the purpose and market, strategic managers consider how they approach that market. Revisiting the four strategic orientations proposed by Miles and Snow (Prospectors, Defenders, Analyzers, and Reactors), we can see how organizations might respond differently to market opportunities and strategic inputs. Prospectors are more entrepreneurial, seeking innovation and new methods to meet opportunities within their market areas. They also tend to conceptualize their market opportunities more broadly. Alternatively, Defenders are more concerned with perfecting the system of service delivery while expecting the market to remain fairly static. Prospectors are better suited to a turbulent and highly competitive environment, where new products and services are constantly in demand and must be created regularly. Those organizations first to provide a service (or approach a new funder) gain significant benefit. Defenders are better suited to a more stable market where we don't need new services but we need efficiency; we need to extract more from what we are currently doing. Analyzers believe this is true but we also need to innovate in selected areas, expanding our market reach while striving to be efficient. Figure 8.2 depicts the nature of the external environment (that is, stable versus turbulent) across key areas such as funding, and illustrates how needs influence management decisions. These strategic orientations can provide coherence to the strategic managers' complex set of market decisions. I'll briefly review some of the challenges managers confront in trying to understand the "need for services" and resource opportunities.

Service Recipients and Needs: Understanding the Need for Services

There are many factors to consider regarding market stability and the appropriate strategic orientation to adopt. One reality is that needs and demands for services can shift and change and thereby make the current level of services unnecessary. The best case of this: a nonprofit was instrumental in overcoming the issue and as a result its services are no longer needed. In other instances, communities and needs may change and nonprofits must adjust. Nonprofits do not necessarily respond to such market changes in a "typical" or business fashion (Lynk, 1995; Zaleski and Esposto, 2007). When a for-profit hospital is the "only game in town" we expect to see some price inflation, because competition tends to drive prices down. This doesn't happen in every instance, and there also are plenty of examples of nonprofit hospitals that seem to abandon their charitable purposes (Starkweather, 1993) as they act like for-profits, but some studies document that nonprofits don't take advantage of the market dominance in a "typical" way. Under such conditions, it appears they may expand services or take on more difficult cases. In other words, they used the surplus market power to extend their charitable purposes. Confusion with market forces is not all that surprising because nonprofits do not operate exclusively on the exchange basis (services = revenue). Other factors drive those decisions, including resources, governance models, and executive leadership.

This lack of market sensitivity might indeed be a good thing because it means nonprofits remain focused on their charitable purposes. However, given the potential for power differentials between service recipients and the nonprofit hospital, there is some recognition that nonprofits may not attend to the needs of beneficiaries in the way they should (Bruce, 1995; Pavicic, Alfirevic, and Mihanovic, 2009). Some explanations include the recognition that in many instances the nonprofit is the only service provider. Beneficiaries often don't have a choice of providers and have to accept what is given. Even if there are other providers, the need or demand for services often outstrips the capabilities of all providers, so providers do what they can but are cognizant of the excessive demand. There is also the potential for providers to assume a professional or even moral justification to control services because they "know what is best." In an effort to get something done nonprofits might inadvertently overlook beneficiary preferences. Nonprofits are morally accountable to beneficiaries but not financially accountable, and the ambiguity and power differential can be difficult to negotiate. (Chapter Four of this volume discusses in depth the multiple dynamics of nonprofit accountabilities.)

Funding Opportunities

Even more pressing for some nonprofits than demand for service is the nature of the resource environment. There is tremendous complexity in the funding environment given the range of revenue sources, such as government, corporations, individuals, foundations and the various mechanisms through which donors can participate (such as grants, major gifts, annual contributions) (Delfin and Tang, 2008; Grønbjerg, 1993). Nonprofits must ensure consistent and reliable funding.

Funders can lose interest and shift priorities. An example is an organization dedicated to prevention services, primarily by providing programming on public school campuses. They were quite good at providing clinical and educational services related to drug abuse prevention and addiction within the school system. Most if not all of their services were offered on campus. Funding came through contracts with the local school district. As the educational priorities changed, demand increased for time on academics, and resources were limited, so the program was losing contracts with the school. This captured the board's attention when contracts were either not renewed or significantly curtailed. The organization needed to consider how to respond—"our primary market is going away." Some on the board thought, "This is it, we were good at what we did and now the sponsor no longer wants our services. Our program is over." Others on the board and, in particular, the new executive director felt the organization was about *prevention* and, although they had operated in one way in the past, they needed to consider other ways to provide services to the community at large. The need for prevention services and drug abuse treatment wasn't going away—if anything, drug use and abuse was going up. The sponsor, however, was not interested in paying for those services in the same way they had.

The executive pushed forward and developed a new program model that allowed them to expand their "market" (community-based prevention services) while staying true to their mission. They might never have become involved in what became an award-winning community program without this push from the funder. The organization continued to expand their funding base to limit the influence of just one sponsor. For most nonprofits it is inevitable that a major funder is going to have a significant impact on their services. Funding can be a "push" as, in this instance, a lack of resources pushed the organization out of a service niche. Funding can also be a "pull" whereby organizations are drawn toward particular funding opportunities. If not careful, this can become a source of "mission creep"—the condition in which a nonprofit loses track of its purpose and spends too much energy following the resource market, slowly and modestly shifting to accommodate resource opportunities at the expense of attention to mission. It is important to remember that funding considerations need to be addressed in alignment with mission and service priorities (Jennings, 2004). One without the other is not optimal.

Leadership in Strategic Management

The story of prevention services also illustrates other factors that determine market strategies—specifically, the role of the executive and board (Goodstein and Boeker, 1991; Ritchie, Kolodinsky, and Eastwood, 2007). Changes at the top allow an opportunity to implement new models and new thinking. Strategic perspectives are often held in the mind of key decision makers, sometimes articulated but rarely captured in their entirety, or in a plan sitting on a shelf. As an example, when discussing the role of the mission statement in decision making in one organization, one executive explained that the mission was used to contain ideas for services and could be used to block new ideas. "We could do that if you want to change the mission statement," he would say to board members who suggested ideas he felt were outside the organization's purview. His strategic orientation was that of a defender.

Other executives might frame the mission more like a planter from which program ideas "grow." For them, the mission statement is used to build new ideas and strategies. This is how the new executive at prevention services described what was happening to their organization. Neither one of these frames is necessarily "right" or "wrong" in a generic sense. Strategic orientations should be grounded in the context, but these examples illustrate that executives have a strong influence over how the nonprofit operates. Therefore, changes at the top can, by design or at times inadvertently, shift the way a nonprofit does business.

The influence of executives is often quite pronounced when long-time founders leave the organization. Founders typically have a specific strategic orientation, one that likely worked well during a particular life stage of their organization. Successful founders often have excellent intuition about strategic direction and how to operate the organization (Ritchie, Kolodinsky, and Eastwood, 2007). However, if that strategy was not shared with board members, or board members deferred to the executive in ways that were not healthy, then it is possible that there might be significant differences of strategic opinion between them and a new executive about how the organization operates. A new executive may well bring a different program model, one that may be needed given the developmental state of the organization, yet this can lead to conflict because "that's not the way we do things around here." If those perspectives are not well articulated then there might be trouble. This is what happened in the earlier example of the organization providing prevention services. The shift to expand the market did not come without conflict on the board. Many board members were dedicated to the older model, and it took time to educate them about the new opportunity and the shifting resource environment.

Riding Against the Wind

One more illustration about recognizing the power of external market opportunities might be helpful. I ride road bikes with a group of friends and every Saturday we go for forty- to fifty-mile bike rides. Imagine our group is a nonprofit organization. We have several purposes: mostly we want to get some exercise and we want to have fun. One of things we consider when we head out is which way the wind is blowing. Imagine if you will that the resource environment is like the wind. When the wind is at our back we go faster, feel stronger, and generally have more fun, and all the while we don't have to work as hard. We travel more miles with less effort. If the wind is blowing at us, we have to work a lot harder to go the same distance. We also have to coordinate our effort a lot more. By working together and taking turns at the front we can get through the wind. We don't mind doing that sometimes because it does make us stronger. The wind isn't always at our back but, at the same time, we are not always "riding against the wind."

The dynamics of the resource and service market are similar to the degree that nonprofits should position themselves to take advantage of the prevailing winds. If we fight the wind in every ride we will be exhausted and potentially give up in frustration. Of course, following every breeze isn't viable either because we would never get home. So we consider how much we can benefit from the prevailing wind to make the best use of our energy while making sure we can get home. Nonprofits that ignore the resource and market opportunities are like bike riders always heading into the wind or, worse, riders who don't even know which way the wind is blowing. Some days they sail along without any effort—getting further and further from home, having a grand time. Other days the wind works against them. They are not ready and may be even somewhat clueless about why it is so hard. External forces are quite powerful and to ignore them or to operate as if they don't matter is to operate in peril.

Delivery Systems and Capabilities

The high level "strategic" conversations related to markets and opportunities often engage board members and other constituencies. There is, however, a whole other level of management activity that might be conceptualized as "operational" in nature. In the strategic management literature, it has to do with implementation. Considering how the "system" is created and works is critical for senior managers to guide. Once questions about market opportunities are resolved, the next strategic issue is how we are going to get this done. Structure and purpose are indeed commingled. According to the planning literature, we consider opportunities and capabilities while crafting our implementation. Opportunities are only viable if we have the ability to capitalize on them. Part of the grief experienced in strategic planning results from the disconnect that can happen when ideas and opportunities are discussed apart from the practicalities of organizational systems. Miles and Snow called this the "engineering" program, based on the idea that for manufacturing firms the challenges were often technological. For nonprofits this is rarely the case. Nonprofit managers need to address issues such as: ensuring that beneficiaries have access to services, building diversified revenue streams, engaging the political system, collaborating with key service partners, and building values into organizational decision making (see Figure 8.3). One of the most fundamental aspects of the "engineering problem" is the nature of human resources. Who can carry out the services we have chosen? Strategic human resource management is an extensive field, encompassing a large number of elements, including job design, recruitment, selection, evaluation, and performance (Pynes, 2004).

Committed Human Resources

With upward of 70–80 percent of expenditures allocated to staffing costs in the typical nonprofit, human resource capabilities are the most significant lever to achieve organizational objectives. Furthermore, for many nonprofits, volunteer labor exponentially expands the work force. Kong (2007) makes the case that it is the "intellectual capital" that makes nonprofits unique and that strategic objectives should be framed to consider how a nonprofit can better utilize their people and relationships. The human resource school of strategic management also recognizes that working with people makes everything possible (Courtney, 2002). Traditional human resource dimensions include motivation factors, person-organizational fit, job design, and the like. Given the strategic management focus of this chapter, I only introduce these topics

FIGURE 8.3. FACTORS THAT INFLUENCE SERVICE DELIVERY.

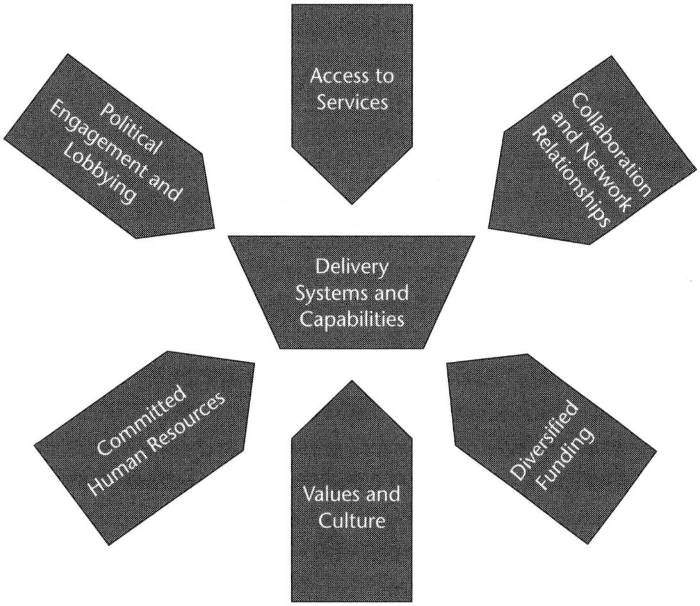

Access to Services

Political Engagement and Lobbying

Collaboration and Network Relationships

Delivery Systems and Capabilities

Committed Human Resources

Values and Culture

Diversified Funding

here—Part Four of the handbook is devoted entirely to managing the human resource domain.

The strategic human resource management field recognizes that human resource practices make a difference in organizational performance. However, nonprofits often have some unique constraints in how such practices are utilized (Akingbola, 2006; Rodwell and Teo, 2008). Part of this is explained by the small size of most nonprofits, yet some argue that nonprofits' challenges are due to a lack of discipline to implement more rigorous practices. The implementation of effective practice is further complicated by the engagement of unpaid staff members—that is, volunteers. Leading and managing volunteers poses its own unique challenges, as Jeffrey Brudney discusses in Chapter Twenty-six. Volunteers can be difficult to control, and the ease with which they enter and exit from various roles in the organization (leadership, fund raising, program delivery) further complicates how volunteers are managed (Pearce, 1993).

Further, as is discussed in depth in Chapter Twenty-four, organizational commitment is an important issue that has significant strategic implications across the entire nonprofit "workforce." A committed workforce, whether paid or unpaid, is motivated to work harder and achieve better results for the organization. Several studies suggest that commitment to the organization and the mission are fundamentally important and a unique advantage for nonprofits (see, for example, Brown and Yoshioka, 2003; Preston and Brown, 2005). As values-based organizations, nonprofits attract and retain workers partly because they tap into the expressive needs of employees (Mason, 1995). People join and stay with nonprofits because they want to make a difference; they believe in the values and purposes. The extent to which nonprofits emphasize the expressive benefits of and help workers "see" a connection between their work and the purposes of the organization affects the degree to which people are going to be satisfied with their role in the organization, and this increases the likelihood they will put forth the effort necessary to achieve organizational priorities.

How do we encourage commitment? It is not simple but, from a strategic perspective, nonprofit executives need to ensure a high level of alignment and consistency in values and ethical practices. The chapter on ethical management (Chapter Seven) clearly makes the case that nonprofits need to be able to rely on trust and cooperation because of the inherent difficulty in determining performance measures; stakeholders inside (paid and unpaid employees) and outside the organization need to be able to trust nonprofit leaders to operate ethically. Nonprofits are held to that higher standard because of the very nature of who they are. Employee commitment is partially driven by the ethical practices of leadership and supervisors. Since in most instances nonprofits are not going to be able to pay as much as the for-profit counterpart, nor are nonprofits able to offer the employment stability of the public sector, organizational participants expect a positive work environment that reflects the principles and values espoused by the organization. Their values propositions are potentially the most distinctive aspect of a nonprofit organization and can make them very appealing to donors, volunteers, and paid employees (Frumkin and Andre-Clark, 2000).

Collaboration and Network Relationships

Another important consideration in the development of service delivery is the potential of collaborative relationships. If an organization doesn't have adequate internal capacity, a good option may be to work with other organizations to achieve organizational objectives. This is particularly true for nonprofits in complex operating environments with multifaceted social issues and the challenges of resource limitations (Sowa, 2009). Collaborative strategies can be difficult, yet they often are necessary and sometimes may even be the only approach to achieve broader objectives. John Yankey and Carol Willen provide an excellent discussion of the value, benefits, and challenges of various forms of collaborations and strategic alliances in Chapter Fourteen.

Less common but also reasonable to consider is the option to acquire or merge with another organization. This is less common in nonprofits, yet there are many examples of how nonprofits have been successfully acquired or merged. The merger of the Points of Light Foundation and Hands On Network is an interesting example. The Points of Light Foundation was by all indications the historical infrastructure organization in volunteer management; it represented the national network of volunteer centers. Points of Light employed a fairly traditional model to facilitate volunteer placements with partner nonprofits. In contrast, Hands On Network was a younger organization that framed volunteer engagement slightly differently; they were more about organizing projects and developed "make-a-difference" day. Each of these partner organizations brought a slightly different orientation toward supporting volunteers and together they have integrated multiple approaches in an effort to enhance their sustainability and impact. This illustrates how two different types of organizations interested in the same cause (supporting volunteerism) strategically joined forces to address real challenges in the field.

Political Engagement and Lobbying

In addition to direct service collaborations to achieve program goals, nonprofits can seek to influence broader political forces. The classic parable of babies floating down the river helps illustrate this concept.

There is a fisherman that lives in a town along a river and one day he discovers a baby floating down the river. Through heroic effort he pulls the baby from the river. The town decides they need to watch the river on a regular basis. As more and more babies come floating down the river the town develops an elaborate system to pull the babies from the water and get them placed in good homes. They have developed a sophisticated service delivery system that saves the babies, cleans them up, and places them with adoptive parents. At some point the town realizes they can't keep raising these babies. So someone goes upstream to see if they can stop the flow of babies. They find an ogre stealing babies and tossing them into the river. The downstream town joins forces with the upstream town and they kill the ogre, thereby ending the need for saving babies from the river.

The downstream town changed the system so that now it is unnecessary to save babies from the river. Nonprofits need to provide services, but they should also work to change the system so their services are no longer needed. It is not just about finding a need, securing resources, and developing an amazing service delivery system, it is also about changing the system to limit the need for services altogether. In many instances this means changing the laws and rules to help eliminate the problem. MADD is an example of a nonprofit that set out to change the rules about drunk driving. By organizing and campaigning they helped changed the way Americans thought about drinking and driving. MADD wasn't just about victim services and supporting mothers who had lost children. They were about changing the system so that there were fewer grieving mothers (MADD, 2005).

Performance and Control

The third component of the strategic cycle is related to control and performance (see Figure 8.4). This section considers how organizations monitor and control the various aspects of the organizational system to obtain value for key participants.

FIGURE 8.4. ISSUES TO CONSIDER IN PERFORMANCE AND CONTROL.

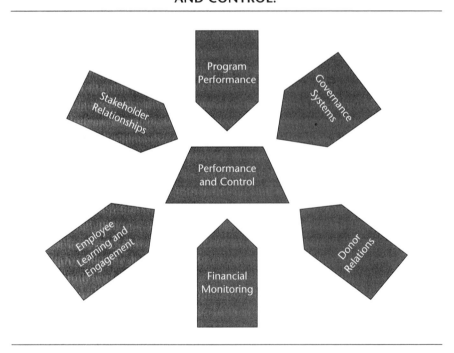

It is about learning and knowledge to guide organizational participants. How do we improve our practices? It is also about performance and impact. Performance is a critical concern for nonprofits because it is often difficult to know the effectiveness of service initiatives. It is also why the adaptive cycle developed by Miles and Snow (1978) is particularly relevant; it identifies the instrumental function that control and performance issues play in nonprofit organizations (Moore, 2000).

There are, of course, many organizational effectiveness assessment systems available to nonprofits (for example, balanced scorecard and total quality management), and there is an excellent chapter in this handbook (Chapter Sixteen) that discusses these practices in more detail. Related are program evaluation systems that determine impact of program initiatives (Chapter Fifteen focuses on program evaluation). The strategic management balance is to determine how much of an administrative bureaucracy is necessary for monitoring organizational activities. As executives make decisions about staffing or about which programs to expand or discontinue, there need to be logic and objective criteria behind the decision. Unfortunately, it doesn't always work that way. That is not always because of "weak" management; many other factors (that is, resources and capabilities) influence service delivery. It is complicated because there are multiple constituents who seek information about performance and operations, so developing and using effective performance assessment systems is a major concern. Donors, volunteers, and even service methodologies can be resistant to organizational control strategies; executives, too, may resist utilizing control processes. Consequently, this important part of the strategic management system might not get enough attention. As already discussed, decision making is often owned by the executive and senior leadership (paid and unpaid), and often it is the intuitions of the executive that drive the design of performance management practices. Performance and control are not just about counting numbers and objective indicators, it also is about relationships and monitoring the status of key stakeholders.

Centralized Versus Decentralized Structures

An additional organizational consideration is that of how centralized or decentralized to structure the organization (Miles and Snow, 1978). A centralized system tends to have tighter and more thorough control systems and authorization structures. In a human service context highly regulated environments tend to enact tighter control mechanism to ensure compliance. Centralized systems are intended to limit unauthorized behavior by organizational participants but also to capitalize on systems and processes that streamline choices to facilitate efficiency. A Defender orientation, for example, is to limit operational choices via adoption of "best practices" that seek to achieve optimal efficiency, and replicate these practices throughout the organizational system. Use of a decentralized organizational system is intended to allow a bit more discretionary decision making by organizational participants. Brown and Iverson (2004) report that Prospectors are more likely to adopt a decentralized structure because it allows for more eyes scanning the external environment to identify opportunities and suggest responses. Those using a decentralized structure are willing to bear the cost of some inefficiency either because independence might foster innovation or because the cost of control is too high. For example, different divisions and branches may be duplicating control systems or even creating less-sophisticated approaches, but the argument to allow this is that those approaches are appropriately adapted to their context and the effort to control and monitor is not worth the cost.

However, even in a decentralized system there has to be some mechanism to monitor organizational activities and describe performance achievements. Let's consider an example from Big Brothers Big Sisters. I worked with a Big Brothers Big Sisters affiliate that was predominantly defender oriented. One of their initiatives was to increase the efficiency of how they placed prospective mentors. They found that limiting the time between inquiry and placement was very important and that if they could get prospective mentors placed more quickly they could increase the number of matches. In an effort to develop best practices and to improve efficiencies of paid staff, they spent a fair amount of time modifying and perfecting the system to place volunteers quickly (Brown and Yoshioka, 2005). They implemented a new service delivery model to minimize the loss of prospective volunteers. They changed job descriptions and created new positions. They implemented controls to monitor and track success on these rates of conversion. This is an example of a fairly tight and centralized system. Every volunteer was supposed to be treated according to this protocol because it would increase placements. Conversely, they have features of a decentralized system for the volunteer mentors. After receiving training, the mentors are expected to create and develop a "relationship" with their "little." It is very difficult if not impossible to control exactly how that happens. Each mentor and "little" need to negotiate a relationship that works for them. Part of the frustration volunteers sometimes experience is that there are lots of uncontrollable variables that make it difficult to benchmark clear consistent techniques. This reflects the nature of many nonprofit initiatives. They can monitor some aspects (such as placement rates), while others are inherently difficult to control (such as relationship development between a mentor and a mentee).

Issues in Control and Performance

The nonprofit context suggests several performance and control issues that warrant priority consideration, and Figure 8.4 depicts the key areas nonprofits should monitor. Other chapters in this handbook address each of these topics in detail, so this section merely highlights some of the key strategic management issues for each area.

Financial Stewardship. Monitoring financial indicators through effective budgeting and reporting consumes a significant amount of time for nonprofit managers. With just concern, nonprofits often operate with limited reserve capabilities and stewardship expectations that require high quality practices in this area. Donors and granting entities expect resources to be used judiciously. Frivolous expenditures, excessive compensation, or, heaven forbid, fraudulent practices can have a detrimental impact on an organization and the entire sector. Like so many of the management challenges confronted by nonprofit executives, financial management is a paradox. Take, for example, discussion about how much money should be kept in reserves: too much and some contend the money is not being put to "good use"; not enough and the nonprofit runs the risk of falling short and being unable to met obligations. Financial performance often becomes a proxy for organizational health, and executives need to consider how "the numbers" are reflective of other key operational issues such as program performance and donor relationships.

Governance. Board oversight is critical for nonprofit organizations in a number of ways. The board sets the tone and, more important, seeks to ensure consistency in organizational practices so as to achieve success across the organization. Boards help guide the organization and keep it on track. Alignment among organizational practices and participants is an important aspect of effective strategic management. The board should help identify priorities related to strategic inputs and operational practices. The board should not meddle in the details of how services are delivered; it should approve major initiatives and have a general understanding of how management is moving forward to achieve priorities across the key inputs. Furthermore, the board should monitor information that enables it to assess progress on these priorities. The board helps keep management accountable but is also a partner in helping management overcome challenges and alter course as necessary. Executives look to the board to provide guidance and direction about operational gray areas. By staying attuned to the priorities of the organization and progress reports in these areas, boards can become active partners while fulfilling the most important function they have—oversight. The board is often the intermediary to the market and key stakeholders. It exists to verify that the organization is operating honestly and according to its purposes. The role is not as an outsider, critical and confrontational, but as a partner to help achieve the priorities and objectives. The board is essential to strategic management because, with so many activities, opportunities, and challenges confronting nonprofits, managers need regular guidance on strategic priorities and decisions. This can only be accomplished with regular feedback and conversation. As Chapter Six on executive leadership makes clear, it is part of the executive's responsibility to help structure the board's activities so they can fulfill this function. It is apparent that without a coordinated effort and a shared sense of importance that most boards are incapable of holding the executive accountable without his or her consent. It is indeed an interesting paradox that the oversight body within the organization is dependent on the goodwill of executives, but given the complexities confronted and ambiguous performance standards, boards need to be partners that ask tough questions about performance.

Program Evaluation and Performance. Managers confront many challenges when trying to implement evaluation systems. In many cases it is difficult, if not impossible, to know exactly the benefit that programs obtain for service beneficiaries. Furthermore, using rigorous evaluation methodologies is often beyond the scope of many nonprofits. The principle is to encourage learning among providers while being realistic about the quality of evaluation of activities. The value of evaluation is when it is part of the culture of the organization. It should be natural for program providers to boast about program successes that emphasize the beneficiaries, but they also should discuss and identify program weaknesses. It is not easy, but nonprofits need to stay attuned to the needs and perceptions of program beneficiaries, and good evaluation practices are critical.

Managing Relationships. Finally, it is essential that a strategic manager maintain a regular process by which to monitor the tone and quality of relationships with each of three key stakeholder groups: donors, paid and unpaid employees, and key decision makers in the external operating environment (such as regulators, political officials, and other service providers). Each of these constituencies plays a significant role in the strategic management choices of the organization, and the processes by which to maintain and assess these relationships are discussed in some depth in subsequent chapters of this handbook.

Conclusion

This chapter examines the decisions and processes that nonprofit managers employ as they work to think and act strategically to accomplish their organization's goals and outcomes. Strategic management in nonprofit organizations is the ability to understand external market opportunities and challenges while weaving together service delivery systems to address the needs and interests of the multiple stakeholders of the organization. Effective strategic managers guide, strengthen, and modify their programs and operations according to learning that is based on objective quantifiable information and the best guidance and intuition of the organization's leadership. Using the adaptive cycle developed by Miles and Snow (1978), the chapter discussed three key strategic "problems" for nonprofit managers: (1) understanding service and resource opportunities, (2) creating service delivery systems that utilize organizational capabilities, and (3) building control and performance management systems that foster learning.

Strategic management is informed by the desire to achieve alignment and coherence among organizational processes and practices. A fundamental element of strategic management is to ensure there is a framework to guide decision making and that the framework is discussed, evaluated, and modified according to operational conditions. Even organizations that have been successful run the risk of losing their relevance and impact as circumstances change if they fail to practice strategic management.

References

Akingbola, K. "Strategy and HRM in nonprofit organizations: Evidence from Canada." *International Journal of Human Resource Management*, 2006, *17*(10), 1707–1725.

Andreasen, A. R., and Kotler, P. *Strategic Marketing for Nonprofit Organizations*. (7th ed.) Upper Saddle River, N.J.: Prentice Hall. 2007.

Andrews, R., Boyne, G. A., Law, J., and Walker, R. M. "Strategy, Structure and Process in the Public Sector: A Test of the Miles and Snow Model." *Public Administration*, 2009, *87*(4), 732–749.

Backman, E. V., Grossman, A., and Rangan, V. K. "Introduction: New Directions in Nonprofit Strategy." *Nonprofit and Voluntary Sector Quarterly*, 2000, *29*(1), 2–8.

Brown W. A., and Iverson, J. O. "Exploring Strategy and Board Structure in Nonprofit Organizations." *Nonprofit and Voluntary Sector Quarterly*, 2004, *33*(3), 377–400.

Brown, W. A., and Yoshioka, C. "A New Service Delivery Model to Support Volunteer Mentoring Relationships." *Journal of Volunteer Administration*, 2005, *23*(3), 44–46.

Brown, W. A., and Yoshioka, C. "Mission Attachment and Satisfaction as Factors in Employee Retention." *Nonprofit Leadership and Management*, 2003, *14*(1), 5–18.

Bruce, I. "Do Not-for-Profits Value Their Customers and Their Needs?" *International Marketing Review*, 1995, *12*(4), 77–84.

Chew, C., and Osborne, S. P. "Identifying Factors that Influence Positioning Strategy in U.K. Charitable Organizations that Provide Public Services." *Nonprofit and Voluntary Sector Quarterly*, 2009, *38*(1), 29–50.

Courtney, R. *Strategic Management for Voluntary Nonprofit Organizations*. New York: Routledge, 2002.

Delfin, F. G., and Tang, S. Y. "Foundation Impact on Environmental Nongovernmental Organizations." *Nonprofit and Voluntary Sector Quarterly*, 2008, *37*(4), 603–625.

Eikenberry, A. "Refusing the Market: A Democratic Discourse for Voluntary and Nonprofit Organizations." *Nonprofit and Voluntary Sector*, 2009, *38*(4), 582–596.

Frumkin, P., and Andre-Clark, A. "When Missions, Markets and Politics Collide: Values and Strategy in Nonprofit Human Services." *Nonprofit and Voluntary Sector Quarterly*, 2000, *29*(1), 141–163.

Goodstein, J., Boeker, W. "Turbulence at the Top: A New Perspective on Governance Structure Changes and Strategic Change." *Academy of Management Journal*, 1991, *34*(2), 306–330.

Grønbjerg, K. A. *Understanding Nonprofit Funding: Managing Revenues in Social Service and Community Development Organizations*. San Francisco: Jossey-Bass, 1993.

Hitt, M. A., Ireland, R. D, and Hoskisson, R. E. *Strategic Management*. (7th ed.) Mason, Ohio: Thomson Southwest, 2007.

Jeavons, T. *When the Bottom Line Is Faithfulness*. Bloomington: Indiana University Press, 1994.

Jennings, K. N. "Which Came First, the Project or the Fundraising?" *The Bottom Line*, 2004, *17*(3), 108.

Ketchen, D. J., Combs, J. G., Russell, C. J., Shook, C., Dean, M. A., and Runge, J. "Organizational Configurations and Performance: A Meta-Analysis." *Academy of Management Journal*, 1997, *40*, 223–240.

Kong, E. "A Review of the Strategic Management Literature: The Importance of Intellectual Capital in the Nonprofit Sector." 28th McMaster World Congress on Intellectual Capital and Innovation, McMaster University, Hamilton, Ontario, Canada, 24–26 January 2007.

Lake, K. E., Reis, T. K., and Spann, J. "From Grant Making to Change Making: How the W. K. Kellogg Foundation's Impact Services Model Evolved to Enhance the Management and Social Effects of Large Initiatives." *Nonprofit and Voluntary Sector Quarterly*, 2000, *29*(1), 41–68.

Lynk, W. J. "Non-Profit Hospital Mergers and the Exercise of Market Power." *Journal of Law and Economics*, 1995, *38*(2), 437–461.

MADD. "Secrets to Success." *Driven*, 2005, 22–25. Available at www.madd.org/About-us/About-us/History.aspx. Accessed Jan. 11, 2010.

Mason, D. E. *Leading and Managing the Expressive Dimension*. San Francisco: Wiley, 1995.

Miles, R. E., and Snow, C. C. *Organizational Strategy, Structure and Process*. New York: McGraw-Hill, 1978.

Miles, R. E., Snow, C. C., Mathews, J. A., Miles, G., and Coleman, H. J., Jr. "Organizing in the Knowledge Age: Anticipating the Cellular Form." *Academy of Management Review*, 1997, *11*, 7–24.

Mintzberg, H. T. *The Structuring of Organizations*. Englewood Cliffs, N. J.: Prentice-Hall, 1979.

Moore, M. H. "Managing for Value: Organizational Strategy in For-Profit, Nonprofit and Governmental Organizations." *Nonprofit and Voluntary Sector Quarterly*, 2000, *29*(1), 183–204.

Pavicic, J., Alfirevic, N., and Mihanovic, Z. "Market Orientation in Managing Relationships with Multiple Constituencies of Croatian Higher Education." *Higher Education*, 2009, *57*, 191–207.

Pearce, J. L. *Volunteers: The Organizational Behavior of Unpaid Workers*. New York: Routledge, 1993.

Porter, M. E. *Competitive Strategy*. New York: The Free Press, 1998.

Preston, B. J., and Brown, W. A. "Commitment and Performance of Nonprofit Board Members." *Nonprofit Management and Leadership*, 2005, *15*(2), 221–238.

Pynes, J. E. *Human Resources Management for Public and Nonprofit Organizations*. San Francisco: Jossey-Bass, 2004.

Quinn J. B. "Strategic Change: 'Logical Incrementalism.'" *Sloan Management Review*, 1989, *30*(4), 45–60.

Ritchie, W. J., Kolodinsky, R. W., and Eastwood, K. "Does Executive Intuition Matter? An Empirical Analysis of Its Relationship With Nonprofit Organization Financial Performance." *Nonprofit and Voluntary Sector Quarterly*, 2007, *36*(1), 140–155.

Rodwell, J. J., and Teo, S. T. T. "The Influence of Strategic HRM and Sector on Perceived Performance in Health Service Organizations." *International Journal of Human Resource Management*, 2008, *19*(10), 1825–1841.

Schiemann, W. A. "Aligning Performance with Organizational Strategy, Values and Goals." In J. W. Smither and M. London (eds.), *Performance Management*, pp. 45–87. San Francisco: Jossey-Bass, 2009.

Sowa, J. E. "The Collaboration Decision in Nonprofit Organizations." *Nonprofit and Voluntary Sector Quarterly*, 2009, *38*(6), 1003–1025.

Starkweather, D. B. "Profit Making by Nonprofit Hospitals." In D. Hammack and D. Young (eds.), *Nonprofit Organizations in a Market Economy*, pp. 105–137. San Francisco: Jossey-Bass, 1994.

State of California Organization of California Nonprofit, Nonstock Corporation. Sacramento: Secretary of State, Business and Program Division, 2009.

Weisbrod, B. A. "The Nonprofit Mission and Its Financing: Growing Links Between Nonprofits and the Rest of the Economy." In B. A. Weisbrod (ed.), *To Profit or Not To Profit*, pp. 1–22. New York: Cambridge University Press, 1998.

Zaleski, P. A., and Esposto, A. G. "The Response to Market Power: Non-Profit Hospitals Versus For-Profit Hospitals." *Atlantic Economic Journal*, 2007, *35*, 315–325.

CHAPTER NINE

STRATEGIC PLANNING AND THE STRATEGY CHANGE CYCLE

John M. Bryson

This chapter presents an approach to strategic planning for nonprofit organizations and collaborations. The process, called the Strategy Change Cycle, does what Poister and Streib (1999, pp. 309–310) assert strategic planning should do. Specifically, they believe strategic planning should

- Be concerned with identifying and responding to the most fundamental issues facing an organization
- Address the subjective question of purpose and the often competing values that influence mission and strategies
- Emphasize the importance of external trends and forces as they are likely to affect the organization and its mission
- Attempt to be politically realistic by taking into account the concerns and preferences of internal, and especially external, stakeholders
- Rely heavily on the active involvement of senior level managers, and in the case of nonprofits, board members, assisted by staff support where needed
- Require the candid confrontation of critical issues by key participants in order to build commitment to plans
- Be action oriented and stress the importance of developing plans for implementing strategies
- Focus on implementing decisions now in order to position the organization favorably for the future

The Strategy Change Cycle becomes a *strategic management* process—and not just a *strategic planning* process—to the extent that it is used to link planning and implementation and to manage an organization in a strategic way on an ongoing basis (Poister and Streib, 1999, pp. 311–314). The Strategy Change Cycle draws on a considerable body of research and practical experience, applying it specifically to nonprofit organizations.

Two quotations help make the point that strategic thinking, acting, and learning are more important than any particular approach to strategic planning. Consider first the humorous statement of Daniel Boone, the famous eighteenth and nineteenth century American frontiersman: "No, I can't say as I ever was lost, but once I was bewildered pretty bad for three days" (Faragher, 1992, p. 65). When you are lost in the wilderness—*bewildered*—no fixed plan will do. You must think, act, and learn your way to safety. Boone had a destination of at least a general sort in mind, but not a route. He had to wander around reconnoitering, gathering information, assessing directions, trying out options, and in general thinking, acting, and learning his way into where he wanted to be. In Weick and Sutcliffe's words (2007), he had to "act thinkingly," which often meant acting first and then thinking about it (Weick, 1995). Ultimately—but not initially, or even much before he got to there—Boone was able to establish a clear destination and a route that worked to get him there. Boone thus had a strategy of purposeful wandering, and it is true that he was not exactly lost; rather, he was working at finding himself where he wanted to be. So wandering with a purpose is an important aspect of strategic planning, in which thinking, acting, and learning clearly matter most.

Next, consider this from poet and essayist Diane Ackerman: "Make-believe is at the heart of play, and also at the heart of so much that passes for work. Let's make-believe we can shoot a rocket to the moon" (Ackerman, 1999, p. 7). She makes the point that almost anything is possible with enough imagination, ambition, direction, intelligence, education and training, organization, resources, will, and staying power. We have been to the moon, Mars, Venus, and a host of other places. We as citizens of the world have won world wars and cold wars, ended or avoided depressions, virtually eliminated small pox, unraveled the human genome, watched a reasonably united and integrated Europe emerge, and seen democracy spread where it was thought unimaginable. But there obviously is much more to do, and previous triumphs are never permanent. So let's think about joining others already focused on thinking, doing, and learning about how to have a good job for everyone, adequate food and housing for everyone everywhere, universal health care coverage, drastically reduced crime, effective educational systems, secure pensions and retirements, a dramatic reduction in greenhouse emissions, the elimination of terrorism and weapons of mass destruction, the elimination of HIV/AIDS, the realization in practice of the Universal Declaration on Human Rights, and so on. We can create institutions, policies, projects, products, and services of lasting public value by drawing on our diverse talents—and have done so again and again throughout history (Boyte, 2005), and clearly nonprofit organizations have an important role to play (Light, 2002; Powell and Steinberg, 2006). We can use strategic planning to help us think, act, and learn strategically—to figure out what we should want, why, and how to get it. Think of strategic planning as organizing hope, as what makes hope reasonable.

A Ten-Step Strategic Planning Process

Now, with the caution that strategic thinking, acting, and learning matter most, let us proceed to a more detailed exploration of the ten-step Strategy Change Cycle. The process, presented in Figure 9.1, is more orderly, deliberative, and participative than the process followed by an essayist such as Ackerman, or a wanderer like Boone. The process is designed to "create public value" (Moore, 2000) through fashioning an effective mission, meeting applicable mandates, organizing participation, creating ideas for strategic interventions, building a winning coalition, and implementing strategies. The Strategy Change Cycle may be thought of as a *processual model of decision making* (Barzelay, 2001, p. 56), or a *process strategy* (Mintzberg, Ahlstrand, and Lampel, 2005), where a leadership group manages the process, but leaves much of the content of what the strategies will be to others. The ten steps (or designed set of occasions for dialogue and decision) are as follows:

1. Initiate and agree on a strategic planning process.
2. Identify organizational mandates.
3. Clarify organizational mission and values.
4. Assess the external and internal environments to identify strengths, weaknesses, opportunities, and threats.
5. Identify the strategic issue facing the organization.
6. Formulate strategies to manage the issues.
7. Review and adopt the strategic plan or plans.
8. Establish an effective organizational vision.
9. Develop an effective implementation process.
10. Reassess strategies and the strategic planning process.

These ten steps should lead to actions, results, evaluation, and learning. It must be emphasized that actions, results, evaluative judgments, and learning

FIGURE 9.1. THE STRATEGY CHANGE CYCLE.

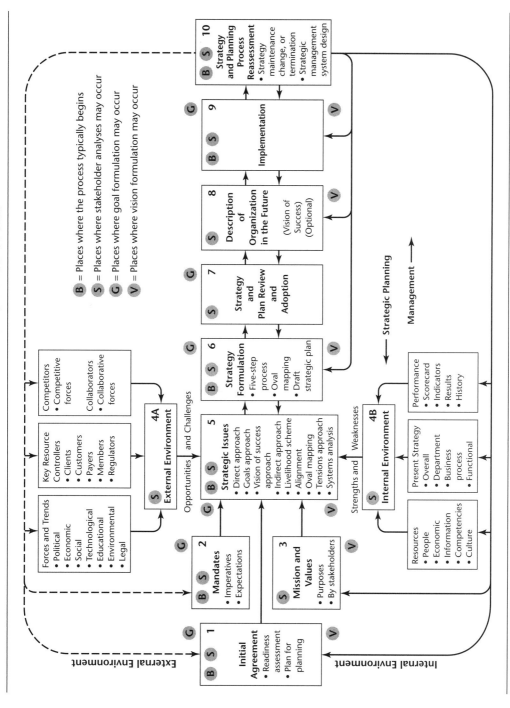

B = Places where the process typically begins
S = Places where stakeholder analyses may occur
G = Places where goal formulation may occur
V = Places where vision formulation may occur

Source: Copyright © 1995, 2003 by John M. Bryson; revised for this volume.

should emerge at each step in the process. In other words, implementation and evaluation should not wait until the "end" of the process, but should be an integral and ongoing part of it.

The process is applicable to nonprofit organizations and collaborations. The only general requirements are a "dominant coalition" (Thompson, 2003), or at least a "coalition of the willing" (Cleveland, 2002), able to sponsor and follow the process, and a process champion willing to push it. For small nonprofit organizations, many well-informed strategic planning teams that are familiar with, and believe in, the process should be able to complete most of the steps in a two- or perhaps three-day retreat, with an additional one-day meeting scheduled three to four weeks later to review the resulting strategic plan. Responsibility for preparing the plan can be delegated to a planner assigned to work with the team, or the organization's chief executive may choose to draft the plan personally. Additional reviews and signoffs by key decision makers might take more time. Additional time also might be necessary to secure information or advice for specific parts of the plan, especially its recommended strategies. For large organizations, however, more time and effort are likely to be needed for the process. And when applied to a collaboration, the effort is likely to be considerably more time consuming in order to promote the involvement of substantial numbers of leaders, organizations, and perhaps members or citizens (Huxham and Vangen, 2005; Bryson, Crosby, and Stone, 2006).

Note that in practice the Strategy Change Cycle bears little resemblance to the caricature of strategic planning occasionally found in the literature as a rigid, formal, detached process (see, for example, Mintzberg, Ahlstrand, and Lampel, 2005; Bryson, Crosby, and Bryson, 2009). Instead, the Strategy Change Cycle is intended to enhance strategic thinking, acting, and learning; to engage key actors with what is, as well as with what can be; to engage with the important details while abstracting the strategic message in them; and to link strategy formulation with implementation in wise, technically workable, and politically intelligent ways. You might think of the Strategy Change Cycle as identifying and helping organize a *deliberative pathway* to promote mutual persuasion and learning among stakeholders about what to do, how, and why in order to fulfill an organization's mission and meet its mandates (Garston, 2006; Moynihan and Landuyt, 2009).

Step 1: Initiating and Agreeing on a Strategic Planning Process

The purpose of the first step is to negotiate agreement among key internal (and perhaps external) decision makers or opinion leaders about the overall strategic planning effort and the key planning steps. The support and commitment of key decision makers are vital if strategic planning in an organization is to succeed.

Further, the involvement of key decision makers outside the organization usually is crucial to the success of nonprofit programs if implementation will involve multiple parties and organizations (Light, 1998, 2002; Bryson, 2004a).

Obviously, some person or group must initiate the process. One of the initiators' first tasks is to identify exactly who the key decision makers are. The next task is to identify which persons, groups, units, or organizations should be involved in the effort. These two steps will require some preliminary stakeholder analysis, which is discussed in more detail below. The initial agreement will be negotiated with at least some of these decision makers, groups, units, or organizations. In practice, a *series* of agreements typically must be struck among various parties as support for the process builds and key stakeholders and decision makers sign on. Strategic planning for a nonprofit organization or collaboration is especially likely to work well if an effective policymaking body is in place to oversee the effort.

The agreement itself should cover

- The purpose of the effort
- Preferred steps in the process
- The form and timing of reports
- The role, functions, and membership of any group or committee empowered to oversee the effort, such as a strategic planning coordinating committee (SPCC)
- The role, functions, and membership of the strategic planning team
- The commitment of necessary resources to proceed with the effort
- Any important limitations or boundaries on the effort

As noted, at least some stakeholder analysis work will be needed in order to figure out whom to include in the series of initial agreements. A *stakeholder* is defined as any person, group, or organization that can place a claim on an organization's (or other entity's) attention, resources, or output or that is affected by that output. Examples of a nonprofit organization's stakeholders include clients or customers, third-party payers or funders, employees, the board of directors, members, volunteers, other nonprofit organizations providing complementary services or involved as co-venturers in projects, banks holding mortgages or notes, and suppliers.

Attention to stakeholder concerns is crucial: *the key to success in nonprofit organizations and collaborations is the satisfaction of key stakeholders* (Light, 1998, 2002; Bryson, 2004a). A stakeholder analysis is a way for the organization's decision makers and planning team to immerse themselves in the networks and politics surrounding the organization. An understanding of the relationships—actual or potential—that help define the organization's context can provide invaluable clues to identifying strategic issues and developing effective strategies (Bryson, 2004a; Patton, 2008). In this regard, note that the definition of stakeholder is deliberately quite broad for both practical and ethical reasons. Thinking broadly, at least initially, about who the stakeholders are is a way of opening people's eyes to the various webs of relationships within which the organization exists (Feldman and Khademian, 2002) and of assuring that the organization is alerted to its ethical and democratic accountability responsibilities, since they always involve clarifying *who* and *what* count (Mitchell, Agle, and Wood, 1997; Lynn and Hill, 2008).

For many nonprofit organizations, the label "customer" will be given to their key stakeholder. The customer label can be useful, particularly for organizations that need to improve their "customer service." In other situations, the customer language actually can be problematic. One danger is that focusing on a single "customer" may lead these organizations inadvertently to ignore other important stakeholder groups. Another danger is that the customer label can undermine the values and virtues of active citizenship that many nonprofit organizations are trying to promote (deLeon and Denhardt, 2000; Boyte, 2005). In addition, many community-based nonprofit organizations and those relying on government funding also face very complex stakeholder environments (Stone and Sandfort, 2009).

The organizers of the planning effort should count on using several different techniques, including as a starting point what I call the Basic Stakeholder Analysis Technique (Bryson, 2004a, 2004b). This technique requires the strategic planning team to brainstorm a list of the organization's stakeholders, their criteria for judging the performance of the organization (that is, their "stake" in the organization or its output), and how well the organization performs against those criteria *from the stakeholders' points of view*. If there is time, additional steps (perhaps involving additional analysis techniques) should be considered, including understanding how the stakeholders influence the organization, identifying what the organization needs from its various stakeholders (money, staff, political support), and determining in general how important the various stakeholders are. Looking ahead, a stakeholder analysis will help clarify whether the organization needs to have different missions and perhaps different strategies for different stakeholders, whether it should seek to have its mandates changed, and in general what its strategic issues are. (A variety of other useful techniques will be found in Bryson [2004a, 2004b].)

Step 2: Identifying Organizational Mandates

The formal and informal mandates placed on the organization consist of the various "musts" it confronts, meaning the requirements, restrictions, and expectations it faces. Actually, it is surprising how few organizations know precisely what they are (and are not) formally mandated to do. Typically, few members of any organization have ever read, for example, the relevant legislation, policies, ordinances, charters, regulations, articles, and contracts that outline the organization's formal mandates. Many organizational members also do not understand the informal mandates—which are typically political in the broadest sense—that the organization faces. It may not be surprising, then, that most organizations make one or more of three fundamental mistakes. First, by not articulating or knowing what they must do, they are unlikely to do it. Second, they may believe they are more tightly constrained in their actions than they actually are. And third, they may assume that if they are not explicitly told to do something, they are not allowed to do it.

Step 3: Clarifying Organizational Mission and Values

An organization's mission, or purpose, in tandem with its mandates, provides the organization's *raison d'être*, the social justification for its existence. An organization's mission and mandates also point the way toward the ultimate organizational end of creating public value. For a nonprofit organization, this means there must be identifiable social or political demands or needs that the organization seeks to fill in a way that accords with its nonprofit status (Bryce, 2000). Viewed in this light, nonprofit organizations must always be seen as a means to an end, not as an end in and of themselves. For a collaboration, it means identifying the "collaborative advantage" to be gained by working together, that is, what can be gained together that creates public value that cannot be achieved alone (Huxham and Vangen, 2005).

Identifying the mission, however, does more than merely justify the organization's existence. Clarifying purpose can eliminate a great deal of unnecessary conflict in an organization and can help channel discussion and activity productively (Thompson, 2001; Nutt, 2002). Agreement on purpose also defines the arenas within which the organization will collaborate or compete and, at least in broad outline, charts the future course of the organization. Agreement on purpose thus serves as a kind of taken-for-granted framework that bounds the plausibility and acceptability of arguments (Bolman and Deal, 2008). Agreement on purpose can go even further and provide a kind of premise control that constrains thinking, learning, and acting (Perrow, 1986; Weick, 1995) and even legitimacy (Suchman, 1995). Moreover, an important and socially-justifiable mission is a source of inspiration and guidance to key stakeholders, particularly employees (Kouzes and Posner, 2008). Indeed, it is doubtful whether any organization ever achieved greatness or excellence without a basic consensus among its key stakeholders on an inspiring mission (Collins and Porras, 1997; Light, 2002).

Some careful stakeholder analysis work should precede development or modification of an existing mission statement, so that attention to purpose can be informed by thinking about purpose *for whom*. If the purposes of key stakeholders are not served, then the organization may be engaging in what historian Barbara Tuchman (1984) aptly calls folly. The mission statement itself might be very short, perhaps not more than a paragraph or a slogan. But development of the mission statement should grow out of lengthy dialogue about the organization's identity, its abiding purpose, desired responses to key stakeholders, its philosophy and core values, and its ethical standards. These discussions may also provide a basic outline for a description of the organization in the future, or its "vision of success," described in Step 8. Considerable intermediate work is necessary, however, before a complete vision of success can be articulated.

Step 4: Assessing the Organization's External and Internal Environments

The planning team should explore the environment outside the organization to identify the opportunities and threats the organization faces (Step 4a). It should explore the environment inside the organization to identify strengths and weaknesses, and particularly existing or needed organizational competencies (Step 4b). Basically, "outside" factors are those not under the organization's control, while "inside" factors are those that are. Opportunities and threats usually (though not necessarily) are more about the future than the present, whereas strengths and weakness are about the present and not the future (Nutt and Backoff, 1992).

Monitoring a variety of forces and trends, including political, economic, social, educational, technological, and physical environmental ones, can help planners and decision makers discern opportunities and threats. Unfortunately, organizations all too often focus only on the negative or threatening aspects of these changes, and not on the opportunities they present, so care must be taken to assure a balanced view. In other words, attending to threats and weaknesses should be seen as an opportunity to build strengths and improve performance (Ackermann, Eden, and Brown, 2004; Weick and Sutcliffe, 2007).

Besides monitoring trends and events, the strategic planning team also should monitor various important external stakeholder groups, including especially those that affect resource flows (directly or indirectly). These groups would include customers, clients, payers or funders, dues-paying members, regulators, and relevant policy bodies. The team also should attend to competitors, competitive forces, and possible sources of competitive advantage, as well as to collaborators, collaborative forces, and potential sources of collaborative advantage.

The organization might construct various scenarios to explore alternative futures in the external environment, a practice typical of much strategic planning in large private-sector organizations. Scenarios are particularly good at demonstrating how various forces and trends are likely to interact, which are amenable to organizational influence, and which are not. Scenarios also offer an effective way of challenging the organization's "official future" when necessary. The "official future" is the presumed or taken-for-granted future that makes current strategies sensible (Schwartz, 1991). Organizations unwilling to challenge this future are the ones most likely to be blindsided by changes (Marcus, 2009).

Members of an organization's governing body (particularly if they are elected) may be better at identifying and assessing external threats and opportunities (particularly present ones) than are the organization's employees. This is partly due to a governing board's responsibility for relating an organization to its external environment and vice versa (Bryce, 2000; Carver, 2006). Unfortunately, neither governing boards nor employees usually do a systematic or effective job of external scanning. As a result, most organizations are like ships trying to navigate troubled or treacherous waters without benefit of human lookouts, global positioning systems, radar, or sonar. All too often the result is a very unwelcome surprise (Weick and Sutcliffe, 2007).

Because of this, both employees and governing board members should consider relying on a somewhat formal external assessment process to supplement their informal efforts. The technology of external assessment is fairly simple, and allows organizations to cheaply, pragmatically, and effectively keep tabs on what is happening in the larger world that is likely to have an effect on the organization and the pursuit of its mission. Clip services, Internet alerts, discussion groups and listservs, regular participation in professional conferences, and periodic retreats, for example, might be used in part to explore forces and trends and their potential impact. The key, however, is to avoid being captured by existing categories of classification and search, since they tend to formalize and routinize the past, rather than open one to the surprises of the future (Mintzberg, Alstrand, and Lampel, 2005; Weick and Sutcliffe, 2007).

Attention to opportunities and threats, along with a stakeholder analysis, can be used to identify the organization's "critical success factors" (Johnson, Scholes, and Whittington, 2008). These may overlap with mandates, in the sense that they are the things the organization must do, or criteria it must meet, in order for it to be successful in the eyes of its key stakeholders, especially those in the external environment. Ideally, the organization will excel in these areas, and must do so in order to outperform or stave off competitors.

To identify internal strengths and weaknesses, the organization might monitor resources (inputs), present strategy (process), and performance (outputs). Most nonprofit organizations, in my experience, have information on many of their inputs, such as salaries, supplies, physical plant, and full time equivalent (FTE) personnel. Unfortunately, too few organizations have a very clear idea of their philosophy, core values, distinctive competencies, and culture, a crucial set of inputs both for ensuring stability and managing change.

Organizations also tend to have an unclear idea of their present strategy, either overall, by subunit, or by function. And typically they cannot say enough about their outputs, let alone the effects, or outcomes, those outputs create for clients, customers, or payers, although this, too, is changing. However, some nonprofit organizations have been able to pull their input, process, and outcome measures together in the form of a Balanced Scorecard (BSC) that shows, in effect, the organization's "theory of action" and allows it to monitor how it is doing in terms of the theory's predictions (Niven, 2008). BSCs attempt to show the linkages and achieve a "balance" among measures of customer or stakeholder satisfaction, financial performance, internal management or production process performance, and accomplishments in the areas of employee and organizational learning and growth. BSCs are likely to become far more widely used in the future by nonprofit organizations.

A lack of performance information presents problems both for the organization and its stakeholders. Stakeholders judge an organization according to the criteria *they* choose, which are not necessarily the same criteria the organization would choose. For external stakeholders in particular, these criteria typically relate to performance. If an organization cannot effectively meet its stakeholders' performance criteria at a reasonable cost, then regardless of its "inherent" worth, the stakeholders are likely to withdraw their support.

An absence of performance information may also create—or harden— major organizational conflicts. Without performance criteria and information, there is no way to reasonably and objectively evaluate the relative effectiveness of alternative strategies, resource allocations, organizational designs, and distributions of power. As a result, organizational conflicts are likely to occur more often than they should, serve narrow partisan interests, and be resolved in ways that don't further the organization's mission (Flyvbjerg, 1998; Gerzon, 2006). The difficulties of measuring performance are well known (Radin, 2006; Moynihan, 2008). But regardless of the difficulties, organizations are continually challenged to demonstrate effective performance to their stakeholders.

A consideration of the organization's strengths and weaknesses can also lead to an identification of its "distinctive competencies" (Selznick, 1957), or what have been referred to more generally as "core competencies" (Prahalad and Hamel, 1990; Johnson, Scholes, and Whittington, 2008) or "capabilities" (Stalk, Evans, and Shulman, 1992). These are the organization's most important abilities or practices on which it can draw routinely to perform well. What makes these abilities "distinctive" is the inability of others to replicate them easily, if at all, because of the way they are interlinked with one another (Eden and Ackermann, forthcoming). Nonprofit organizations should seriously consider taking the time to identify the existing and/or needed competencies and distinctive competencies necessary to achieve their aspirations (Bryson, Ackermann, and Eden, 2007). A clear statement that focuses solely on identifying and linking the existing or needed competencies and distinctive competencies to the nonprofit organization's mission and goals is sometimes referred to as its "livelihood scheme" and can provide the core logic of a strategic plan (Ackermann, Eden and Brown, 2004). A livelihood scheme can also facilitate the identification of strategic issues (see next section).

Step 5: Identifying the Strategic Issues Facing an Organization

Together the first four elements of the process lead to the fifth, the identification of strategic issues. *Strategic issues* are fundamental policy questions or critical challenges affecting the organization's mandates, mission, and values; product or service level and mix; clients, users or payers; cost, financing, organization, or management. Finding the best way to frame these issues typically requires considerable wisdom, dialogue, and deep understanding of organizational purposes, operations, stakeholder interests, and external demands and possibilities. The first four steps of the process are designed deliberately to slow things down so that there is enough information and interaction for the needed wisdom to emerge. The process is designed, in other words, to "unfreeze" people's thinking (Lewin, 1951; Dalton, 1970) so that knowledge exploration, development, and learning might occur (March,1991; Crossan, Lane, and White, 1999). This knowledge will be exploited in this and later phases.

Strategic planning focuses on achieving the best "fit" between an organization and its environment. Attention to mandates and the external environment, therefore, can be thought of as planning from the outside in. Attention to mission and organizational values and the internal environment can be considered planning from the inside out. Usually, it is vital that pressing strategic issues be dealt with expeditiously and effectively if the organization is to survive and prosper. An organization that does not respond to a strategic issue can expect undesirable results from a threat, a missed opportunity, or both.

The iterative nature of the strategic planning process often becomes apparent in this step when participants find that information created or discussed in earlier steps presents itself again as part of a strategic issue. For example, many strategic planning teams begin strategic planning with the belief that they know what their organization's mission is. They often find out in this step, however, that one of the key issues their organizations faces is the need to clarify exactly what its mission ought to be. In other words, the organization's present mission is found to be inappropriate, given the team members' new understanding of the situation the organization faces, and a new mission must be created.

Strategic issues, virtually by definition, involve conflicts of one sort or another. The conflicts may involve ends (what); means (how or how much); philosophy (why); location (where); timing (when); and who might be advantaged or disadvantaged by different ways of resolving the issue (who). In order for the issues to be raised and resolved effectively, the organization must be prepared to deal with the almost inevitable conflicts that will occur. Conflict, shifts in understanding, and shifts in preferences will all evoke participants' emotions (Weick, 1995; Gerzon, 2006; Heifetz, Grashow, and Linsky, 2009). It is therefore in this stage that the importance of emotion will become dramatically apparent, along with the concomitant need for emotional intelligence on the part of participants if the emotions are to be dealt with effectively (Goleman, 1995; Goleman, Boyatzis, and McKee, 2002; Heifitz, Grashow, and Linsky, 2009).

A statement of a strategic issue should contain three elements. First, the issue should be described succinctly, preferably in a single paragraph. The issue should be framed as a question that the organization can do something about. If the organization cannot do anything about it, it is best not to think of it as an issue for the organization; it is simply a condition. An organization's attention is limited enough without wasting it on issues it cannot address effectively. The question also should have more than one answer, as a way of broadening the search for viable strategies. Too often organizations "jump to solutions" without fully understanding what else might be possible, and without learning more about the issue by understanding more about the range of possible answers (Nutt, 2002; Ackermann, Eden, and Brown, 2004; Burton, 2008).

Second, the factors that make the issue a fundamental challenge should be listed. In particular, what is it about the organization's mandates, mission, values, or internal strengths and weaknesses, and external opportunities and threats that make this a strategic issue for the organization? Listing these factors will become useful in the next step, strategy development. Every effective strategy builds on strengths (and especially competencies and distinctive competencies) and takes advantage of opportunities, while minimizing or overcoming weaknesses and threats. The framing of strategic issues is therefore very important because it will provide much of the basis for the issues' resolution (Eden and Ackermann, 1998; Nutt, 2002; Crosby and Bryson, 2005).

Finally, the planning team should prepare a statement of the consequences of failure to address the issue. This will help organizational leaders decide just how strategic, or important, various issues are. If no consequences will ensue from failure to address a particular issue, then it is not a strategic issue. At the other extreme, if the organization will be destroyed or will miss a valuable opportunity by failing to address a particular issue, then the issue is clearly *very* strategic and is worth attending to immediately. Thus, the step of identifying strategic issues is aimed at focusing organizational attention on what is truly important for the survival, prosperity, and effectiveness of the organization.

Once statements of the issues are prepared, the organization will know what kinds of issues it faces and just how strategic they are. There are several kinds of strategic issues:

- Those that alter the organization and especially its "core business" and for which there is no real organizational precedent (or what might be called *developmental* issues), and those that do not (or what might be called *nondevelopmental* issues) (Nutt, 2001). Developmental issues involve a fundamental change in products or services, customers or clients, service or distribution channels, sources of revenue, identity or image, or some other aspect of the organization for which there is no real organizational precedent. Nondevelopmental issues involve less ambiguity because most of the aspects of the organization's overall strategy will not change. Nondevelopmental issues therefore may still be very important, but are more operational than strategic.
- Those that require an immediate response and therefore cannot be handled in a more routine way.
- Those that are coming up on the horizon and are likely to require some action in the future, and perhaps some action now. For the most part, these issues can be handled as part of the organization's regular strategic planning cycle.
- Those where no organizational action is required at present, but which must be continuously monitored.

Nine basic approaches to the identification of strategic issues will be discussed. The *direct* approach goes straight from a discussion of mandates, mission, and SWOTs (strengths, weaknesses, opportunities, and threats) to the identification of strategic issues.

The *goals* approach starts with goals (or performance indicators) and then identifies issues that must be addressed before the goals (or indicators) can be achieved. Sometimes a careful goals clarification exercise is necessary in order to be clear just what the goals-in-practice are (Patton, 2008, pp. 97–149). The *vision of success* approach starts with at least a sketch of a vision of success in order to identify issues that must be dealt with before the vision can be realized. This approach is probably necessary in situations involving developmental decisions, where fundamental change is needed but the organization lacks a precedent (Nutt, 2001).

The *indirect* approach begins with brainstorming about several different kinds of options before identifying issues. Each option is put on a separate card or self-adhesive label. The sets of options include actions the organization could take to meet stakeholders' performance expectations, build on strengths, take advantage of opportunities, and minimize or overcome weaknesses and threats, as well as incorporate any other important aspect of background studies or reports or present circumstances. These options are then merged into a single set of potential actions that are then clustered according to potential themes or issue categories.

The *oval mapping* approach involves using oval-shaped cards (but they can be other shapes as well) to create word-and-arrow diagrams in which statements about potential actions the organization might take, how they might be taken, and why, are linked by arrows indicating the cause-effect or influence relationships between them. In other words, the arrows indicate that action A may cause or influence B, which in turn may cause or influence C, and so on; if the organization does A, it can expect to produce outcome B, which in turn may be expected to produce outcome C. These maps can consist of dozens, and sometimes hundreds, of interconnected relationships, showing differing areas of interest and their relationships to one another. Important clusters of potential actions may comprise strategic issues. A strategy in response to the issue would consist of the specific choices regarding actions to undertake in the issue area, how to undertake them, and why (see following; also see Eden and Ackermann, 1998; Bryson, Ackermann, Eden, and Finn, 2004).

The approach is particularly useful when participants are having trouble making sense of complex issue areas, time is short, the emphasis must be on action, and commitment on the part of those involved is particularly important. Participants simply brainstorm possible actions, cluster them according to similar themes, and then figure out what causes what and which statements count as actions, issues, strategies, and goals or mission. Beyond that, the idea of causal mapping—that is, of placing statements on a page, flipchart sheet, or wall and linking them with arrows to indicate cause-effect relationships—can be used in tandem with the other approaches to indicate whatever logic is being followed.

The *livelihood scheme* approach makes use of a causal map that focuses specifically on aspirations (for example mission, goals, critical success factors, important performance indicators) and links these to competencies and distinctive competencies (Bryson, Ackermann, and Eden, 2007). The issues then relate to what might be necessary to take advantage of existing or needed links between aspirations and competencies. In other words, if a livelihood scheme outlines the core logic of a strategic plan, it thereby helps clarify what issues might need to be addressed in order to bring that logic to life in practice. The approach can be paired with the goals approach.

The *alignment* approach focuses on clarifying the issues involved in aligning mission, goals, resource deployments, strategies, and operations. In its simplest form, it involves just asking the planning team and/or key stakeholders what issues of organizational or stakeholder alignment, or both, need to be addressed for the mission and goals to be better achieved and for existing strategies and operations to be more effective. The approach may also make use of a balanced scorecard strategy map to help outline possible areas of misalignment among stakeholder desires or expectations, financial measures, production processes, and organizational competencies and learning needs (Kaplan and Norton, 2006; Niven, 2008).

The *tensions* approach was developed by Nutt and Backoff (1992) and elaborated in Nutt, Backoff, and Hogan (2000). These authors argue that there are always four basic tensions around any strategic issue. These tensions involve human resources and, especially, *equity* concerns; *innovation and change*; maintenance of *tradition*; and *productivity improvement*; and their various combinations. The authors suggest critiquing how issues are framed by using these tensions separately and in combination in order to find the best way to frame the issue. The critiques may be used in tandem with any of the other approaches and may need to run through several cycles before the wisest way to frame the issue is found. Finally, *systems analysis* can be used to help discern the best way to frame issues when the system contains complex feedback effects and must be formally modeled in order to understand it (Senge, 1990; Sterman, 2000).

By stating that there are nine different approaches to the identification of strategic issues, I may raise the hackles of some planning theorists and practitioners who believe you should *always* start with either issues, goals, vision, or analysis. I argue that what will work best depends on the situation and that the wise planner should choose an approach accordingly.

Step 6: Formulating Strategies and Plans to Manage the Issues

A *strategy* is defined as a pattern of purposes, policies, programs, actions, decisions, or resource allocations that define what an organization is, what it does, and why it does it. Strategies can vary by level, function, and time frame. Strategies are developed to deal with the issues identified in the previous step.

This definition is purposely broad, in order to focus attention on the creation of consistency across *rhetoric* (what people say), *choices* (what people decide and are willing to pay for), *actions* (what people do), and the *consequences* of those actions. Effective strategy formulation and implementation processes link rhetoric, choices, actions, and consequences into reasonably coherent and consistent patterns across levels, functions, and time (Eden and Ackermann, 1998). The reasoning behind and argumentation for the links should be clear and practical

(Garsten, 2006; Heinrichs, 2007). They also will be tailored to fit an organization's culture, even if the purpose of the strategy or strategies is to reconfigure that culture in some way (Johnson, Scholes, and Whittington, 2008). Draft strategies, and perhaps drafts of formal strategic plans, will be formulated in this step to articulate desired patterns. They may also be reviewed and adopted at the end of this step if the strategic planning processes is relatively simple, small-scale, and involves a single organization. (Such a process would merge this step and Step 7.)

A Five-Part Strategy Development Process. There are numerous approaches to strategy development (Bryson and Anderson, 2000; Holman, Devane, and Cady, 2007). I generally favor either of two approaches. The first is a five-part, fairly speedy process based on the work of the Institute of Cultural Affairs (Spencer, 1996). The second can be used if there is a need or desire to articulate more clearly the relationships among multiple options to show how they fit together as part of a pattern.

The first part of the five-part process begins with identification of practical alternatives and dreams or visions for resolving the strategic issues. Each option should be phrased in action terms; that is, it should begin with an imperative, such as "do," "get," "buy," "achieve," and so forth. Phrasing options in action terms helps make the options seem more "real" to participants.

Next, the planning team should enumerate the barriers to achieving those alternatives, dreams, or visions, and not directly on their achievement. Focusing on barriers at this point is not typical of most strategic planning processes. But doing so is one way of assuring that any strategies developed deal with implementation difficulties directly rather than haphazardly.

Once alternatives, dreams, and visions, along with barriers to their realization, are listed, the team develops major proposals for achieving the alternatives, dreams, or visions directly, or else indirectly through overcoming the barriers. (Alternatively, the team might solicit proposals from key organizational units, various stakeholder groups, task forces, or selected individuals.)

After major proposals are submitted, two final tasks remain in order to develop effective strategies. Actions that must be taken over the next two to three years to implement the major proposals must be identified. And finally, a detailed work program for the next six months to a year must be spelled out to implement the actions. These last two tasks shade over into the work of Step 9, but that is good, because strategies always should be developed with implementation in mind. As Mintzberg explains (1994, p. 25), "Every failure of implementation is, by definition, also a failure of formulation." In some circumstances, Steps 6 and 9 may be merged—for example, when a single organization is planning for itself. In addition, in collaborative settings, implementation details must often be worked out first by the various parties before they are willing to commit to shared strategic plans (Innes, 1996; Bardach, 1998; Huxham and Vangen, 2005). In situations such as these, implementation planning may have to precede strategy or plan adoption.

Structuring Relationships Among Strategic Options to Develop Strategies.

The second method is based on the Strategic Options Development and Analysis (SODA) method developed by Colin Eden, Fran Ackermann, and their associates (Eden and Ackermann, 1998, 2001; Bryson, Ackermann, Eden, and Finn, 2004). The SODA method builds on the oval mapping method discussed above and involves listing multiple options to address each strategic issue, where each option again is phrased in imperative, action terms. The options are then linked by arrows indicating which options cause or influence the achievement of other options. An option can be a part of more than one chain. The result is a "map" of action-to-outcome (cause-effect, means-to-an-end) relationships; those options toward the end of a chain of arrows are possible goals or perhaps even mission statements. Presumably, these goals can be achieved by accomplishing at least some of the actions leading up to them, although additional analysis and work on the arrow chains may be necessary to determine and clearly articulate action-to-outcome relationships. The option maps can be reviewed and revised and particular action-to-outcome chains selected as strategies. (Additional detail and numerous examples will be found in Bryson, Ackermann, Eden, and Finn, 2004.)

An effective strategy must meet several criteria. It must be technically workable and politically acceptable to key stakeholders, and must fit the organization's philosophy and core values. Further, it should be ethical, moral, and legal, and should further the creation of public value. It must also deal with the strategic issue it was supposed to address. All too often I have seen otherwise desirable strategies that were technically, politically, morally, ethically, and legally workable but did not deal with the issues they were presumed to address. Effective strategies thus meet a rather severe set of tests. Careful, thoughtful dialogue—and often bargaining and negotiation—among key decision makers who have adequate information and are politically astute are usually necessary before strategies can be developed that meet these tests. Some of this work typically must occur in this step; some is likely to occur in the next step.

Step 7: Reviewing and Adopting the Strategies and Plan

Once strategies have been formulated, the planning team may need to obtain an official decision to adopt them and proceed with their implementation. The same is true if a formal strategic plan has been prepared. This decision will help affirm the desired changes and move the organization toward "refreezing" in the new pattern (Lewin, 1951; Dalton, 1970), where the knowledge exploration of previous steps can be exploited (March, 1991). When strategies and plans are developed for a single organization, particularly a small one, this step actually may merge with Step 6. But a separate step will likely be necessary when strategic planning is undertaken for a large organization, network of organizations, or community. The SPCC will need to approve the resulting strategies or plan, relevant policymaking bodies; and other implementing groups and organizations are also likely to have to approve the strategies or plan, or at least parts of it, in order for implementation to proceed effectively.

In order to secure passage of any strategy or plan, it will be necessary to continue to pay attention to the goals, concerns, and interests of all key internal and external stakeholders (Borins, 2000). Finding or creating inducements that can be traded for support can also be useful. But there are numerous ways to defeat any proposal in formal decision-making arenas. So it is important for the plan to be sponsored and championed by actors whose knowledge of how to negotiate the intricacies of the relevant arenas can help assure passage (Crosby and Bryson, 2005).

Step 8: Establishing an Effective Organizational Vision

In this step, the organization develops a description of what it should look like once it has successfully implemented its strategies and achieved its full potential. This description is the organization's "vision of success." Few organizations have such a description or vision, yet the importance of such descriptions has long been recognized by well-managed companies, organizational psychologists, and management theorists (Collins and Porras, 1997; Kouzes and Posner, 2008). Such descriptions can include the organization's mission, its values and philosophy, basic strategies, its performance criteria, some important decision rules, and the ethical standards expected of all employees.

The description, to the extent that it is widely circulated and discussed within the organization, allows organization members to know what is expected of them, without constant managerial oversight. Members are freed to act on their own initiative on the organization's behalf to an extent not otherwise possible. The result should be a mobilization of members' energy toward pursuing the organization's purposes, and a reduced need for direct supervision (Nutt, 2001; Moynihan and Landuyt, 2009).

Some might question why developing a vision of success comes at this point in the process rather than much earlier. There are two basic answers to this question. First, it does not have to come here for all organizations. Some organizations are able to develop a clearly articulated, agreed-upon vision of success much earlier in the process. And some organizations start with "visioning" exercises in order to develop enough of a consensus on purposes and values to guide issue identification and strategy formulation efforts. Figure 9.1 therefore indicates the many different points at which participants may find it useful to develop some sort of guiding vision. Some processes may start with a visionary statement. Others may use visions to help them figure out what the strategic issues are or to help them develop strategies. And still others may use visions to convince key decision makers to adopt strategies or plans, or to guide implementation efforts. The further along in the process a vision is found, the more likely it is to be more fully articulated.

Second, most organizations typically will not be able to develop a detailed vision of success until they have gone through several iterations of strategic planning—if they are able to develop a vision at all. A challenging yet achievable vision embodies the tension between what an organization wants and what it can have (Senge, 1990; Rughase, 2007). Often, several cycles of strategic planning are necessary before organizational members know what they want, what they can have, and what the difference is between the two. A vision that motivates people will be challenging enough to spur action, yet not so impossible to achieve that it demotivates and demoralizes people. Most organizations, in other words, will find that their visions of success are likely to serve more as a guide for strategy implementation than strategy formulation.

Further, for most organizations, development of a vision of success is not necessary in order to produce marked improvements in performance. In my experience, most organizations can demonstrate a substantial improvement in effectiveness if they simply identify and satisfactorily resolve a few strategic issues. Most organizations simply do not address often enough what is truly important; just gathering key decision makers to deal with a few important matters in a timely way can enhance organizational performance substantially. For these reasons the step is labeled optional in Figure 9.1.

Step 9: Developing an Effective Implementation Process

Just creating a strategic plan is not enough. The changes indicated by the adopted strategies must be incorporated throughout the system for them to be brought to life and for real value to be created for the organization and its stakeholders. Thinking strategically about implementation and developing an effective implementation plan are important tasks on the road to realizing the strategies developed in Step 6. For example, in some circumstances direct implementation at all sites will be the wisest strategic choice, whereas in other situations some form of staged implementation may be best (Crosby and Bryson, 2005, pp. 312–339).

Again, if strategies and an implementation plan have been developed for a single organization, particularly a small one, or if the planning is for a collaboration, this step may need to be incorporated into Step 7, Strategy Formulation. However, in many multi-organizational situations, a separate step will be required to assure that relevant groups and organizations do the action planning necessary for implementation success.

Action plans should detail the following:

- Implementation roles and responsibilities of oversight bodies, organizational teams or task forces, and individuals
- Expected results and specific objectives and milestones
- Specific action steps and relevant details
- Schedules
- Resource requirements and sources
- A communication process
- Review, monitoring, and midcourse correction procedures
- Accountability procedures

It is important to build into action plans enough sponsors, champions, and other personnel—along with enough time, money, attention, administrative and support services, and other resources—to assure successful implementation. You must "budget the plan" wisely to assure implementation goes well. In interorganizational situations, it is almost impossible to underestimate the requirements for communications, the nurturance of relationships, and attention to operational detail (Huxham and Vangen, 2005).

It is also important to work quickly to avoid unnecessary or undesirable competition with new priorities. Whenever important opportunities to implement strategies and achieve objectives arise, they should be taken. In other words, it is important to be opportunistic as well as deliberate. And it is important to remember that what actually happens in practice will always be some blend of what is intended with what emerges along the way (Mintzberg, Ahlstrand, and Lampel, 2005).

Successfully implemented and institutionalized strategies result in the establishment of a new "regime," a "set of implicit or explicit principles, norms, rules, and decision-making procedures around which actors' expectations converge in a given area" (Krasner, 1983, p. 2; see also Crossan, Lane, and White, 1999; Crosby and Bryson, 2005). Regime building is necessary to preserve gains in the face of competing demands. Unfortunately, regimes can outlive their usefulness and must be changed, which involves the next step in the process.

Step 10: Reassessing Strategies and the Strategic Planning Process

Once the implementation process has been under way for some time, it is important to review the strategies and the strategic planning process as a prelude to a new round of strategic planning. Much of the work of this phase may occur as part of the ongoing implementation process. However, if the organization has not engaged in strategic planning for a while, this will be a separate phase. Attention should be focused on successful strategies and whether they should be maintained, replaced by other strategies, or terminated for one reason or another. Unsuccessful strategies should be replaced or terminated. The strategic planning process also should be examined, its strengths and weaknesses noted, and modifications suggested to improve the next round of strategic planning. Effectiveness in this step really does depend on effective organizational learning, which means taking a hard look at what is really happening and being open to new information, and designing forums within which knowledge can be developed and shared (Moynihan and Landuyt, 2009). As Weick and Sutcliffe (2007, p. 18) say, "The whole point of a learning organization is that it needs to get a better handle on the fact that it doesn't know what it doesn't know." Viewing strategic planning as a kind of action research can help embed learning into the entire process and make sure the kind of information, feedback, and dialogue necessary for learning occur (Eden and Huxham, 1996).

Tailoring the Process to Specific Circumstances

The Strategy Change Cycle is a general approach to strategic planning and management. Like any planning and management process, it therefore must be tailored carefully to specific situations if it is to be useful (Wenger, 1998; Johnson, Langley, Melin, and Whittington, 2007). A number of adaptations, or variations on the general theme, are discussed in this section.

Sequencing the Steps

Although the steps (or occasions for dialogue and decision) are laid out in a linear sequence, it must be emphasized that the Strategy Change Cycle, as its name suggests, is iterative in practice. Participants typically rethink what they have done several times before they reach final decisions. Moreover, the process does not always begin at the beginning. Organizations typically find themselves confronted with a new mandate (Step 2), a pressing strategic issue (Step 5), a failing strategy (Step 6 or 9), or the need to reassess what they have been doing

(Step 10) and that leads them to engage in strategic planning. Once engaged, the organization is likely to go back and begin at the beginning, particularly with a reexamination of its mission. Indeed, it usually does not matter where you start, you always end up back at mission.

In addition, implementation usually begins before all of the planning is complete. As soon as useful actions are identified, they are taken, as long as they do not jeopardize future actions that might prove valuable. In other words, in a linear, sequential process, the first eight steps of the process would be followed by implementing the planned actions and evaluating the results. However, implementation typically does not, and should not, wait until the eight steps have been completed. For example, if the organization's mission needs to be redrafted, then it should be. If the SWOT analysis turns up weaknesses or threats that need to be addressed immediately, they should be. If aspects of a desirable strategy can be implemented without awaiting further developments, they should be. And so on. As noted earlier, strategic thinking *and* acting *and* learning are important, and all of the thinking does not have to occur before any actions are taken. Or as Mintzberg, Ahlstrand, and Lampel (2005, p. 71) note, "Effective strategy making connects acting to thinking which in turn connects implementation to formulation. We think in order to act, to be sure, but we also act in order to think." And learn, they might add. Strategic planning's iterative, flexible, action-oriented nature is precisely what often makes it so attractive to public and nonprofit leaders and managers.

Making Use of Vision, Goals, and Issues

In the discussion of Step 8, it was noted that different organizations or collaborations may wish to start their process with a vision statement. Such a statement may foster a consensus and provide important inspiration and guidance for the rest of the process, even though it is unlikely to be as detailed as a statement developed later in the process. As indicated in Figure 9.1, there are other points at which it might be possible to develop a vision statement (or statements). Vision thus may be used to prompt the identification of strategic issues, guide the search for and development of strategies, inspire the adoption of strategic plans, or guide implementation efforts. The Amherst H. Wilder Foundation of St. Paul, Minnesota, for example, has been guided for years by the following vision (with only minor word changes from time to time) (Wilder Foundation, 2008):

> The Foundation's vision for the greater Saint Paul area is that it will be a vibrant community where all individuals, families and neighborhoods can prosper, with opportunities to work, to be engaged in their communities, to live in decent housing, to attend good schools and to receive support during times of need.

It uses the vision to help identify issues to be addressed and to develop strategies to be used to realize the vision. The decision to develop a vision statement should hinge on whether one is needed to provide direction to subsequent efforts; whether people will be able to develop a vision that is meaningful enough, detailed enough, *and* broadly supported; and whether there will be enough energy left after the visioning effort to push ahead.

Similarly, as indicated in Figure 9.1, it is possible to develop goals in many different places in the process. Some strategic planning processes will begin with the goals of new boards of directors, executive directors, or other top-level decision makers. These goals embody a reform agenda for the organization or collaboration. Other strategic planning processes may start with goals that are part of mandates. For example, government agencies often require nonprofit organizations on which they rely for legislated policy implementation to develop plans that include results and outcome measures that will show how the intent of the legislation is to be achieved. A *starting* goal for these nonprofits, therefore, is to identify results and outcomes they want to be measured against that also are in accord with legislative intent. The goal thus helps these organizations identify an important *strategic issue*—namely, what the results and outcomes should be. Subsequent strategic planning efforts are then likely to start with the desired outcomes the organization thinks are important.

Still other strategic planning processes will articulate goals to guide strategy formulation in response to specific issues or to guide implementation of specific strategies. Goals developed at these later stages of the process are likely to be more detailed and specific than those developed earlier in the process. Goals may be developed any time they would be useful to guide subsequent efforts in the process *and* when they will have sufficient support among key parties to produce desired action.

In my experience, however, strategic planning processes generally start neither with vision nor with goals. In part, this is because in my experience strategic planning rarely starts with Step 1. Instead, people sense something is not right about the current situation—they face strategic issues of one sort or another, or they are pursuing a strategy that is failing, or about to fail—and they want to know what to do (Borins, 1998; Nutt, 2001; Ackermann, Eden, and Brown, 2004). One of the crucial features of issue-driven planning (and political decision making in general) is that you do not have to agree on goals to agree on next steps (Huxham and Vangen, 2005; Crosby and Bryson, 2005). You simply need to agree on a strategy that will address the issue and further the interests of the organization or collaboration and its key stakeholders. Goals are likely to be developed once viable strategies have been developed to address the issues. The goals typically will be strategy-specific.

Articulating goals or describing a vision in this way may help provide a better feeling for where an agreed strategy or interconnected set of strategies should lead (Nutt, 2001; Ackermann, Eden, and Brown, 2004). Goals and vision are thus more likely to come toward the end of the process than the beginning. But there are clear exceptions and process designers should think carefully about why, when, and how—if at all—to bring goals and vision into the process.

Applying the Process Across Organizational Subunits, Levels, and Functions on an Ongoing Basis

Strategic thinking, acting and learning depend upon getting key people together, getting them to focus wisely and creatively on what is really important, and getting them to do something about it. At its most basic, the technology of strategic planning thus involves deliberations, decisions, and actions. The steps in the Strategy Change Cycle help make the process reasonably orderly to increase the likelihood that what is important is actually recognized and addressed, and to allow more people to participate in the process. When the process is applied to an organization as a whole on an ongoing basis (rather than as a one-shot deal), or at least to significant parts of it, usually it is usually necessary to construct a *strategic planning system*. The system allows the various parts of the process to be integrated in appropriate ways, and engages the organization in strategic *management*, not just strategic planning (Poister and Streib, 1999). In the best circumstances, the system will include the actors and knowledge necessary to act wisely, foster systems thinking, and prompt quick and effective action, since inclusion, systems thinking, and speed are increasingly required of nonprofit organizations (Bryson, 2003; Moynihan, 2008).

The process might be applied across subunits, levels, and functions in an organization as outlined in Figure 9.2. The application is based on the "layered" or "stacked units of management" system used by many corporations. The system's first cycle consists of "bottom up" development of strategic plans within a framework established at the top, followed by reviews and reconciliations at each succeeding level. In the second cycle, operating plans are developed to implement the strategic plans. Depending on the situation, decisions at the top of the organizational hierarchy may or may not require policy board approval (which is why the line depicting the process flow diverges at the top). The system may be supported by a set of performance indicators and strategies embodied in a Balanced Score Card (BSC) (Niven, 2008).

Strategic planning systems for nonprofit organizations usually are not as formalized and integrated as the one outlined in Figure 9.2. More typical is a "strategic issues management" system, which attempts to manage specific strategic issues without seeking integration of the resultant strategies across all

FIGURE 9.2. STRATEGIC PLANNING SYSTEMS FOR INTEGRATED UNITS OF MANAGEMENT.

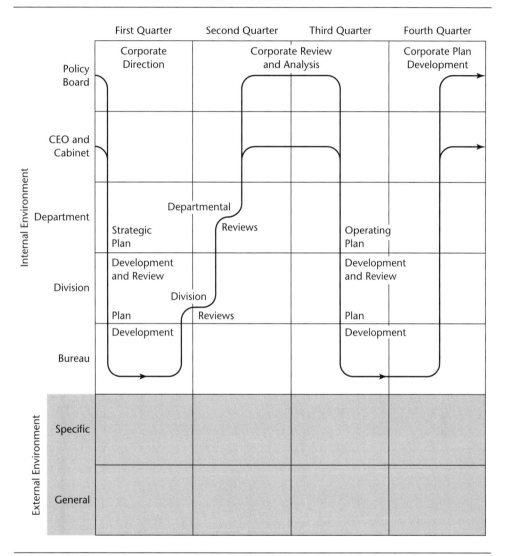

Source: Adapted from Bryson and Roering (1987), p. 16.

subunits, levels, and functions. Tight integration is not necessary because most issues do not affect all parts of the organization, are subject to different politics, and are on their own time frame. Other common public and nonprofit strategic planning systems include the "contract model," in which there is a contract or agreement between a "center" and related units, such as between a headquarters organization and local affiliates; "goal model," in which there are goals, but little else to assure implementation; and "portfolio model," in which organizational subunits or programs are managed as part of an overall organizational portfolio.

If the organization is fairly large, then specific linkages will be necessary in order to join the strategic planning and implementation process to different functions and levels in the organization so that it can proceed in a reasonably orderly and integrated manner. One effective way to achieve such a linkage is to appoint the heads of all major units to the strategic planning team. All unit heads can then be sure that their units' information and interests are represented in strategy formulation, and can oversee strategy implementation in their unit.

Indeed, key decision makers might wish to form themselves into a permanent strategic planning committee or cabinet. I certainly would recommend this approach, if it appears workable for the organization, as it emphasizes the role of line managers as strategic planners and the role of strategic planners as facilitators of decision making by the line managers. Pragmatic and effective strategies and plans are likely to result. Temporary task forces, strategic planning committees, or a cabinet can work; but whatever the arrangement, there is no substitute for the direct involvement of key decision makers in the process.

Applying the Process to Collaborations

When applied to a collaboration, the process probably will need to be sponsored by a committee or task force of key decision makers, opinion leaders, "influentials," or "notables" representing important stakeholder groups. Additional working groups or task forces probably will need to be organized at various times to deal with specific strategic issues or to oversee the implementation of specific strategies. Because so many more people and groups will need to be involved, and because implementation will have to rely more on consent than authority, the process is likely to be much more time consuming and iterative than strategic planning applied to an organization (Bardach, 1998; Huxham and Vangen, 2005; Agranoff, 2007).

Roles for Planners, Decision Makers, Implementers, and Citizens

Planners can play many different roles in a strategic planning process. In many cases, the "planners" are not people with the job title planner, but are in fact policymakers or line managers (Mintzberg, Ahlstrand, and Lampel, 2005). The people with the title planner often act primarily as facilitators of decision making by policymakers or line managers, as technical experts in substantive areas, or both. In other cases, planners operate in a variety of different roles. Sometimes the planner is an expert regarding different kinds of expertise who can ease different experts in and out of the process for different purposes at different times. At still other times, they are "finders" of strategy, who do their job by interpreting existing actions and recognizing important patterns in the organization and its environment; "analysts" of existing or potential strategies; "catalysts" for promoting strategic thought and action; or, finally, "strategists" themselves (Mintzberg, 1994, pp. 361–396).

Since the most important thing about strategic planning is the development of strategic thought, action and learning, it may not matter much which person does what. However, it does seem that strategic planning done by boards, executive directors, or line managers is most likely to be implemented. Exactly how people formally designated as planners contribute to that formulation is unclear. In any particular situation they should be involved in such a way that strategic thinking, acting, and learning are enhanced, along with commitment to agreed-upon strategies.

When a nonprofit organization is the principal focus of attention, for good or ill, there often is little participation by "outsiders" in the planning process other than that of board members. One reason may be that the organization may already possess the necessary knowledge and expertise in-house and therefore involvement by others may be redundant and excessively time-consuming. In addition, insiders typically are the chief implementers of strategies, so their ownership of the process and resultant decisions may be what is most crucial. Further, participation by outsiders may not be necessary to legitimize the process because the board is directly involved and its members are seen as legitimate representatives of a larger public. The absence of participation by ordinary outsiders would parallel much private-sector corporate planning practice. On the other hand, it is easy to be wrong about how much one "knows," or needs to know, and how much perceived legitimacy the process needs (Suchman, 1995; Nutt, 2002). Interviews, focus groups and surveys of outsiders, and external sounding boards of various sorts, such as advisory boards or councils, often are worth their weight in gold when they open insiders' eyes to information they have missed, add legitimacy to the effort, and keep insiders from reaching the wrong conclusions or making the wrong decisions (Thomas, 1997; Nutt, 2002). So a word of caution is in order, and that is to remember, as the Greeks believed, that nemesis always walks in the footsteps of hubris!

Program-focused strategic planning appears to be much more likely to involve outsiders, particularly in their capacity as clients or customers. Outsiders' involvement in program planning thus is roughly analogous to extensive consumer involvement in private-sector marketing research and development projects. Finally, planning on behalf of a collaboration almost always involves substantial participation, but who is inside and who is outside can be difficult to determine (Huxham and Vangen, 2005).

Summary

This chapter has outlined a process called the Strategy Change Cycle for promoting strategic thinking, acting and learning in nonprofit organizations and collaborations. Although the process is presented in a linear, sequential fashion for pedagogical reasons, it proceeds iteratively as groups continuously rethink connections among the various elements of the process, take action, and learn on their way to formulating effective strategies. In addition, the process often does not start with Step 1 but instead starts somewhere else and then cycles back to Step 1. The steps also are not steps precisely, but instead occasions for deliberation, decisions, and actions in part of a continuous flow of strategic thinking, acting and learning; knowledge exploration and exploitation; and strategy formulation and implementation. Mintzberg, Ahlstrand, and Lampel (2005, p. 195) assert that "All real strategic behavior has to combine deliberate control with emergent learning." The Strategy Change Cycle is designed to promote just this kind of strategic behavior.

References

Ackerman, D. *Deep Play*. New York: Vintage, 1999.

Ackermann, F., Eden, C., and Brown, I. *The Practice of Making Strategy: A Step-by-Step Guide*. London: Sage, 2005.

Agranoff, R. *Managing Within Networks: Adding Value to Public Organizations*. Washington, D.C.: Georgetown University Press, 2007.

Bardach, E. *Getting Agencies to Work Together*. Washington, D.C.: Brookings, 1998.

Barzelay, M. *The New Public Management: Improving Research and Policy Dialogue*. Berkeley and New York: University of California Press and Russell Sage Foundation, 2001.

Bolman, L., and Deal, T. *Reframing Organizations*. San Francisco: Jossey-Bass, 2008.

Borins, S. *Innovating with Integrity: How Local Heroes Are Transforming American Government*. Washington, D.C.: Georgetown University Press, 1998.

Borins, S. "Loose Cannons and Rule Breakers, or Enterprising Leaders? Some Evidence About Innovative Public Managers." *Public Administration Review*, 2000, *60*(6), 498–507.

Boyte, H. C. *Everyday Politics: Reconnecting Citizens and Public Life*. Philadelphia: University of Pennsylvania Press, 2005.

Bryce, H. J. *Financial and Strategic Management for Nonprofit Organizations*. San Francisco: Jossey-Bass, 2000.

Bryson, J. M. *Strategic Planning for Public and Nonprofit Organizations* (3rd ed.). San Francisco: Jossey-Bass, 2004a.

Bryson, J. M. "What to Do When Stakeholders Matter: Stakeholder Identification and Analysis Techniques." *Public Management Review*, 2004b, *6*(1), 21–53.

Bryson, J. M. "Strategic Planning and Management." In G. Peters and J. Pierre (Eds.), *Handbook of Public Administration*. Thousand Oaks, Calif.: Sage, 2003.

Bryson, J. M., Ackermann, F., Eden, C., and Finn, C. *Visible Thinking: Unlocking Causal Mapping for Practical Business Results*. Chichester, U.K.: Wiley, 2004.

Bryson, J. M., and Anderson, S. R. "Applying Large-Group Interaction Methods in the Planning and Implementation of Major Change Efforts." *Public Administration Review*, 2000, *60*(2), 143–162.

Bryson, J. M., Crosby, B. C., and Bryson, J. K. "Understanding Strategic Planning and the Formulation and Implementation of Strategic Plans as a Way of Knowing: The Contributions of Actor-Network Theory." *International Public Management Journal*, 2009, *12*(2), 172–207.

Bryson, J. M., Crosby, B. C., and Stone, M. M. "The Design and Implementation of Cross-Sector Collaborations: Propositions From the Literature." *Public Administration Review*, 2006, *66*(s1), 44–55.

Burton, R. A. *On Being Certain: Believing You Are Right Even When You're Not*. New York: St. Martin's Griffin, 2008.

Carver, J. *Boards That Make a Difference: A New Design for Leadership in Nonprofit and Public Organizations*. San Francisco: Jossey-Bass, 2006.

Cleveland, H. *Nobody in Charge: Essays on the Future of Leadership*. New York: Wiley, 2002.

Collins, J. C., and Porras, J. I. *Built to Last: Successful Habits of Visionary Companies*. New York: HarperBusiness, 1997.

Crosby, B. C., and Bryson, J. M. *Leadership for the Common Good: Tackling Public Problems in a Shared-Power World*. San Francisco: Jossey-Bass, 2005.

Crossan, M. M., Lane, H. W., and White, R. E. (1999). "An Organizational Learning Framework: From Intuition to Institution." *Academy of Management Review*, *24*(3), 522–537.

Dalton, G. W. "Influence and Organization Change." In G. Dalton, P. Lawrence, and L. Greiner (eds.), *Organization Change and Development*. Homewood, Il.: Irwin, 1970.

deLeon, L., and Denhardt, R. B. (2000). "The Political Theory of Reinvention." *Public Administration Review*, *60*(2), 89–97.

Eden, C., and Ackermann, F. *Making Strategy: The Journey of Strategic Management*. London: Sage, 1998.

Eden, C., and Ackermann, F. "A Mapping Framework for Strategy Making." In A. S. Huff and M. Jenkins (eds.), *Mapping Strategic Knowledge*. London: Wiley, 2001, 173–195.

Eden, C., and Ackermann, F. *Making Strategy: The Journey of Strategic Management*. (2nd ed.) London: Sage, forthcoming.

Eden, C., and Huxham, C. "Action Research for Management Research." *British Journal of Management*, 1996, *7*, 75–86.

Faragher, J. M. *Daniel Boone: The Life and Legacy of an American Pioneer*. New York: Henry Holt, 1992.

Feldman, M. S., and Khademian, A. M. "To Manage Is to Govern." *Public Administration Review*, 2002, *62*(5), 541–554.

Flyvbjerg, B. *Rationality and Power: Democracy in Practice* (new ed.). Chicago: University of Chicago Press, 1998.

Garsten, B. *Saving Persuasion: A Defense of Rhetoric and Judgment*. Cambridge, Mass.: Harvard University Press, 2006.

Gerzon, M. *Leading Through Conflict*. Cambridge, Mass.: Harvard Business School Press, 2006.

Goleman, D., Boyatzis, R., and McKee, A. *Primal Leadership: Realizing the Power of Emotional Intelligence*. Boston: Harvard Business School Press, 2002.

Goleman, D. *Emotional Intelligence*. New York: Bantam, 1995.

Heifetz, R. A., Grashow, A., and Linsky, M. *The Practice of Adaptive Leadership*. Boston: Cambridge Leadership Associates, 2009.

Heinrichs, J. *Thank You for Arguing*. New York: Three Rivers Press, 2007.

Holman, P., Devane, T., and Cady, S. *The Change Handbook: Group Methods for Shaping the Future*. San Francisco: Berrett-Koehler, 2007.

Huxham, C., and Vangen, S. *Managing to Collaborate: The Theory and Practice of Collaborative Advantage*. New York: Routledge, 2005.

Innes, J. E. "Planning Through Consensus Building: A New View of the Comprehensive Planning Ideal." *Journal of the American Planning Association*, Autumn 1996, 460–472.

Johnson, G., Langley, A., Melin, L., and Whittington, R. *Strategy as Practice: Research Directions and Resources*. New York: Cambridge University Press, 2007.

Johnson, G., Scholes, K., and Whittington, R. (eds.). (2008). *Exploring Corporate Strategy* (8th ed.). London: Prentice Hall.

Kaplan, R. S., and Norton, D. P. "How to Implement a New Strategy Without Disrupting Your Organization." *Harvard Business Review*, 2006, *84*.

Kouzes, J. M., and Posner, B. Z. *The Leadership Challenge* (4th ed.). San Francisco: Jossey-Bass, 2008.

Krasner, S. D. "Structural Causes and Regime Consequences: Regimes as Intervening Variables." In S. D. Krasner (ed.), *International Regimes*. Ithaca, N.Y.: Cornell University Press, 1983.

Lewin, C. W. *Field Theory in Social Science*. New York: Harper, 1951.

Light, P. C. *Sustaining Innovation: Creating Nonprofit and Government Organizations That Innovate Naturally*. San Francisco: Jossey-Bass, 1998.

Light, P. C. *Pathways to Nonprofit Excellence*. Washington, D.C.: Brookings Institutions Press, 2002.

Lynn, L. E., Jr., and Hill, C. J., *Public Management: A Three-Dimensional Approach*. Washington, D.C.: CQ Press, 2008.

March, J. G. "Exploration and Exploitation in Organizational Learning." *Organization Science*, 1991, *2*, 71–87.

Marcus, A. *Strategic Foresight: A New Look at Scenarios*. New York: Palgrave Macmillan, 2009.

Mintzberg, H. *The Rise and Fall of Strategic Planning: Reconceiving Roles for Planning, Plans, Planners*. New York: Free Press, 1994.

Mintzberg, H., Ahlstrand, B., and Lampel, J. *Strategy Safari: A Guided Tour Through the Wilds of Strategic Management*. New York: Free Press, 1998.

Mitchell, R. K., Agle, B. R., and Wood, D. J. "Toward a Theory of Stakeholder Identification and Salience: Defining the Principle of Who and What Really Counts." *Academy of Management Review*, 1997, *22*(4), 853–886.

Moore, M. H. "Managing for Value: Organizational Strategy in For-Profit, Nonprofit, and Governmental Organizations." *Nonprofit and Voluntary Sector Quarterly*, 2000, *29*(1), 183–204.

Moynihan, D. P. *The Dynamics of Performance Management*. Washington, D.C.: Georgetown University Press, 2008.

Moynihan, D. P., and Landuyt, N. "How Do Public Organizations Learn? Bridging Structural and Cultural Divides." *Public Administration Review*, 2009, *69*(6), 1097–1105.

Niven, P. R. *Balanced Scorecard Step-By-Step for Government and Nonprofit Agencies* (2nd ed.). New York: Wiley, 2008.

Nutt, P. C. Strategic Decision-Making. In M. A. Hitt, R. E. Freeman, and J. S. Harrison (eds.), *Blackwell Handbook of Strategic Management*. Malden, Mass.: Blackwell Business, 2001.

Nutt, P. C. *Why Decisions Fail: Avoiding the Blunders and Traps That Lead to Debacles*. San Francisco: Berrett-Koehler, 2002.

Nutt, P. C., and Backoff, R. W. *Strategic Management of Public and Third Sector Organizations: A Handbook for Leaders*. San Francisco: Jossey-Bass, 1992.

Nutt, P. C., Backoff, R. W., and Hogan, M. F. "Managing the Paradoxes of Strategic Change." *Journal of Applied Management Studies*, 2000, *9*, 5–31.

Patton, M. Q. *Utilization-Focused Evaluation* (4th ed.). Thousand Oaks, Calif.: Sage, 2008.

Perrow, C. *Complex Organizations: A Critical Essay*. New York: Random House, 1986.

Poister, T. H., and Streib, G. "Strategic Management in the Public Sector: Concepts, Models, and Processes." *Public Productivity and Management Review*, 1999, *22*, 308–325.

Powell, W. W., and Steinberg, R. (Eds.). *The Nonprofit Sector: A Research Handbook*. (2nd ed.). New Haven, Conn.: Yale University Press. 2006.

Prahalad, C. K., and Hamel, G. "The Core Competence of the Corporation." *Harvard Business Review*, 1990 (May-June), 79–91.

Radin, B. A. *Challenging the Performance Movement: Accountability, Complexity and Democratic Values*. Washington, D.C.: Georgetown University Press, 2006.

Rughase, O. *Identity and Strategy*. Northampton, Mass.: Edward Elgar, 2007.

Schwartz, P. *The Art of the Long View: Planning for the Future in an Uncertain World*. New York: Doubleday Currency, 1991.

Selznick, P. *Leadership in Administration: A Sociological Interpretation*. Berkeley: University of California Press, 1957.

Senge, P. M. "The Leader's New Work: Building Learning Organizations." *Sloan Management Review*, 1990, (Fall), 7–23.

Spencer, L. *Winning Through Participation*. Dubuque, Iowa: Kendall/Hunt, 1996.

Stalk, G., Evans, P., and Shulman, L. E. "Competing on Capabilities: The New Rules of Corporate Strategy." *Harvard Business Review*, 1992, *70* (Mar.–Apr.), 57–69.

Sterman, J. *Business Dynamics: Systems Thinking and Modeling for a Complex World*. New York: Irwin/McGraw-Hill, 2000.

Stone, M. M., and Sandfort, J. R. "Building a Policy Fields Framework to Inform Research on Nonprofit Organizations." *Nonprofit and Voluntary Sector Quarterly*. 2009, *38*, 1054–1075.

Suchman, M. C. "Managing Legitimacy: Strategic and Institutional Approaches." *Academy of Management Review*, 1995, *20*(3), 571–610.

Thompson, J. D. *Organizations in Action*. Edison, N. J.: Transaction, 2003.

Thompson, L. *The Mind and Heart of the Negotiator*. Upper Saddle River, N. J.: Prentice-Hall, 2001.

Tuchman, B. *The March of Folly: From Troy to Vietnam*. New York: Knopf, 1984.

Weick, K. E. *Sensemaking in Organizations*. Thousand Oaks, Calif.: Sage, 1995.

Weick, K. E., and Sutcliffe, K. M. *Managing the Unexpected: Resilient Performance in an Age of Uncertainty*. San Francisco: Jossey-Bass.

Wenger, E. *Communities of Practice: Learning, Meaning, and Identity*. Cambridge, U.K.: Cambridge University Press, 1998.

CHAPTER TEN

SOCIAL ENTREPRENEURSHIP AND SOCIAL ENTERPRISE

Matthew T. A. Nash

What business entrepreneurs are to the economy, social entrepreneurs are to social change. They are the driven, creative individuals who question the status quo, exploit new opportunities, refuse to give up, and remake the world for the better.

DAVID BORNSTEIN, *HOW TO CHANGE THE WORLD: SOCIAL ENTREPRENEURS*
AND THE POWER OF NEW IDEAS

Few concepts in the social sector have caught on as quickly and have captured the imagination of so many, or have been the subject of such intense debate, as has social entrepreneurship. For the first time in human history, within just a few keystrokes on a computer and from the embarrassing comfort of our homes, we have the ability to witness the horrors of widespread hunger, intractable and epidemic disease, gripping poverty, entrenched conflicts, global climate change, unimaginable natural disasters, and inevitable economic turbulence and dislocation. Against this sobering backdrop has emerged a new generation of "social entrepreneurs"—those some have called "new heroes" (Byker et al., 2005) or "unreasonable people," possessed of a relentless drive to pioneer breakthrough approaches to some of the world's most pressing problems

I am indebted for the definition of social entrepreneurship and for the formulation of much of the material on social entrepreneurship theory to my colleague, J. Gregory Dees, professor of the practice of social entrepreneurship and founding faculty director of the Center for the Advancement of Social Entrepreneurship (CASE) at Duke University's Fuqua School of Business. This chapter draws heavily on his work and that of our current and former colleagues at CASE, especially Paul N. Bloom, Beth Battle Anderson, and Catherine Clark and is adapted and reprinted with their permission.

(Elkington and Hartigan, 2008). Many of these social entrepreneurs draw upon and adapt principles, practices, and models from the business world, blurring the traditional boundaries between the public, private, and social sectors.

Although the concept of social entrepreneurship started to gain serious attention in the mid-1990s, the field has gained the momentum of a social movement over the past ten years. Social entrepreneurs have garnered public attention as recipients of prestigious prizes such as the MacArthur "genius awards," the Presidential Medal of Freedom, and even the Nobel Peace Prize; and stories about social entrepreneurs now appear regularly in newspapers and magazines such as the *New York Times*, *The Economist*, and the *Financial Times*. By many accounts, David Bornstein's 2004 book, *How to Change the World: Social Entrepreneurs and the Power of New Ideas*, may deserve the greatest credit for inspiring the public's admiration of these social innovators.

Since the first known course on social entrepreneurship was offered by Prof. J. Gregory Dees at Harvard Business School in the early 1990s, scores of other universities have offered courses or started research initiatives on social entrepreneurship. New academic journals such as the *Stanford Social Innovation Review*, *Innovations* (MIT), and the newly announced *Journal of Social Entrepreneurship* (Oxford) have emerged to provide a much-needed forum for academic discourse. And new kinds of student organizations such as Net Impact and Starting Bloc inspire their young members to pursue careers that achieve a social and environmental impact in addition to financial returns.

As some social entrepreneurs experiment with business models that aim to achieve a "blended value" of social, environmental, and economic impact, entirely new forms of corporate structure are being advanced, such as the "community interest company" in the United Kingdom, the "social business" proposed by Muhammad Yunus, and the low-profit limited liability company (L3C) and for-benefit "B corporation" in the United States.

The embrace of social entrepreneurship has crossed boundaries into the business sector, where a growing number of companies engage in partnerships with social entrepreneurs—some as a more fundamental approach to philanthropy and "corporate citizenship" that is strategically aligned with their corporate missions and values, some as a strategy to develop new business models and access new markets at the base of the economic pyramid (Chesbrough et al., 2006), and some to pursue other opportunities that may generate social and economic value (Austin et al., 2006).[1]

Perhaps the most influential vote of confidence in the promise of social entrepreneurship has come from President Barack Obama, who established in 2009 the White House Office of Social Innovation in fulfillment of a campaign pledge to identify the most promising, innovative, results-oriented social innovations and support their replication across the country. Committed to investing in "what works," the Office, in partnership with the Corporation for National and Community Service, launched in 2010 the Social Innovation Fund to deliver growth capital needed to enable programs with demonstrated results to scale their impact. With $50 million in seed capital from the federal government, the fund will leverage private donations, requiring all grantees to secure a dollar-for-dollar match.

Social Entrepreneurship Is Responding to the "New Realities"

For those who believe that social entrepreneurship represents an important new lens through which to view social change, these developments are encouraging, perhaps even exhilarating. However, the concept of social entrepreneurship did not arise in a vacuum.

One important historical shift that may be contributing to the ascent of social entrepreneurship, at least within the United States, is a widespread recognition of the limits of top-down government solutions to social problems. In the social sector, philanthropy and development aid continue to move away from simple charity and toward more pragmatic, results-oriented strategies, perhaps driven in turn by an engaged citizenry that increasingly demands lasting solutions.

Over the past two decades, as nonprofits competed for limited dollars from government and philanthropic funders, a growing number of organizations began to adopt market-driven approaches and experiment with practices drawn from the business sector, including the launch of earned-revenue ventures, both mission-related social enterprises and unrelated businesses.[2]

As societies seek to harness private initiative, ingenuity, and investment to find new and better ways to solve social problems, the concept of social entrepreneurship captures the spirit of that search. It reflects broader and deeper social trends that are driving change in how we approach social problems. The rapid growth in popularity of social entrepreneurship can be seen, at least in part, as one response to these trends. Whether it will grow into a significant expression of a new mindset remains to be seen. It depends, in part, on the ability of proponents of social entrepreneurship to capitalize on these propitious circumstances (CASE at Duke, 2008).

What Is Social Entrepreneurship?

The concept of "social entrepreneurship" is relatively new, even if the practice arguably has been around for a very long time. As with many new concepts, its definition is open to debate. Different people and organizations use the term differently, and the number of academic definitions escalates each year as scholars endeavor to refine and clarify the concept. This discourse is healthy as definitional disputes are common in many fields. Indeed, the term "entrepreneurship" has been around for more than two hundred years, but dozens of definitions circulate in scholarly literature, perhaps contributing to the debate within the field of social entrepreneurship.

Reviewing the development of the field of social entrepreneurship, Dees and Anderson trace the evolution of two major schools of thought and practice — *social enterprise*, which tends to focus on the application of business practices in the social sector, including the generation of earned revenue to serve a social mission; and *social innovation*, which is focused on establishing new and more effective ways to address social problems or meet social needs. "While these schools are often conflated in popular discourse, they reflect different perspectives, priorities, and, to some extent, values. At times, their proponents have been at odds. But both schools have been critical to the growth of the field of social entrepreneurship" (Dees and Anderson, 2006, p. 41).

The Social Enterprise School of Thought

Typifying the "social enterprise school" of thought are those who subscribe to the conventional definition of entrepreneurship as the act of starting a business. Indeed, the Merriam-Webster dictionary online defines "entrepreneur" as "one who organizes, manages, and assumes the risks of a business or enterprise" (www.merriam-webster.com). Columbia Business School Professor Amar Bhide concurs, "Following common usage, I call individuals who start their own businesses entrepreneurs. Theorists attribute a variety of functions to entrepreneurs, such as coordination, risk-taking, innovation, and arbitrage.... I refrain from debating which of these roles are truly 'entrepreneurial'" (2000, pp. 25–26).

The rise of social enterprise in the 1980s and 1990s came about as a result of an increasing interest among nonprofit organizations in finding new sources of revenue to supplement donor and government funding, as well as by a desire among some business executives to promote the provision of human social services by for-profit companies (Dees and Anderson, 2006). An important emphasis among adherents of the social enterprise school is the blurring of the lines between the business and social sectors, often through experimentation with market-based solutions to social problems that seek to align economic and social value creation. One example is the launch of earned-revenue ventures, both mission-related enterprises that aim to create social and economic value and unrelated enterprises whose main purpose is to make money to subsidize more direct social purpose activities.

The Social Innovation School of Thought

Although it may be commonplace to think of an entrepreneur as someone who starts and runs a business, many scholars contend that the definition of social entrepreneurship should be grounded in a more robust interpretation drawing upon the rich tradition of scholarly research and writing on the concept of entrepreneurship.

The Nature of Entrepreneurship. The term "entrepreneur" was first introduced in the eighteenth century by French economists, who drew upon the word *entreprendre* from Old French, meaning "to undertake." According to Jean-Baptiste Say (1803), "entrepreneurs" are value creators who shift resources from areas of lower and into areas of higher productivity and yield. Although the precise definitions of the terms "entrepreneur" and "entrepreneurship" have been debated ever since, these terms have almost always been reserved for the business context. Writing in the first half of the twentieth century, Austrian economist Joseph Schumpeter (1934), suggested that entrepreneurs perform their value creating function through innovations, the carrying out of "new combinations" (pp. 65–66), including the creation of a new good or service as well as producing and delivering an existing good or service in a new way or to a new market. Schumpeter declared, "the function of entrepreneurs is to reform or revolutionize the pattern of production" (p. 132).

More recently, leading management scholar Peter Drucker pointed out that entrepreneurs constantly search for and exploit the opportunities created by change (in technology, consumer preferences, social norms, and so on) (Drucker, 1985). Put another way, entrepreneurs have a mindset that sees the possibilities rather than the problems created by change. Howard Stevenson carried this idea further, observing that entrepreneurs pursue these opportunities without being limited by the resources they have in hand; instead, entrepreneurs mobilize resources from others to achieve their objectives (Stevenson and Gumpert, 1985).

Although these scholars were writing about business entrepreneurs, their theories—and the skills, practices, and mindset of an entrepreneur—apply equally as well in the social sector. In this way, a social entrepreneur can be thought of as one type of entrepreneur. Simply put, social entrepreneurs are entrepreneurs whose "business" (or mission) is to achieve social impact. A business entrepreneur may seek to create economic value for private benefit, whereas the social entrepreneur seeks above all to create social value for the benefit of society; they measure their productivity in terms of social impact and seek a social return on investment.

Social Innovation. Proponents of the "social innovation school" assert that social entrepreneurs combine the opportunity orientation identified by Drucker, the innovation as revolutionary change agents as described by Schumpeter, and create value through new and better ways of doing things, as described by Say, though the value that the social entrepreneur seeks to create and sustain is social value. According to this view, social entrepreneurs are individuals who reform or revolutionize the patterns of producing social value, shifting resources into areas of higher yield for society. Adherents to the social innovation school do not restrict their definition of social entrepreneurship to the nonprofit sector. Instead, the selection of legal form of incorporation—nonprofit, for-profit, cooperative, or hybrid—is seen as an important decision that the social entrepreneur must make when crafting the strategy for attracting resources and when considering various restrictions associated with each form of incorporation.

In a similar spirit, and building on the scholarly literature on entrepreneurship, in the widely cited "The Meaning of Social Entrepreneurship" (1998b, rev. 2001), Dees elaborates on the proposition that social entrepreneurs play the role of change agents in the social sector by

- Adopting a mission to create and sustain social value (not just private value)
- Recognizing and relentlessly pursuing new opportunities to serve that mission
- Engaging in a process of continuous innovation, adaptation, and learning
- Acting boldly without being limited by resources currently in hand
- Exhibiting a heightened sense of accountability to the constituencies served and for the outcomes created

---

Social Entrepreneurship Is About Innovation and Impact, Not Income

Having worked in this field for a while, I am always delighted to find that people are increasingly familiar with the term "social entrepreneur." Too often, however, they identify social entrepreneurship with nonprofits generating earned income. When the Schwab Foundation for Social Entrepreneurship named Linda and Millard Fuller of Habitat for Humanity and Wendy Kopp of Teach for America, among others, as outstanding social entrepreneurs, it must have confused many people. Both organizations are well known, but neither of them is known for its earned income strategies. They rely heavily on grants and donations. In fact, these social entrepreneurs are masterful at attracting philanthropic donations. What makes them entrepreneurial is that each of them has pioneered creative ways of addressing social problems and marshaled the resources to support their work. Habitat mobilizes volunteers to build affordable houses for the poor. Teach for America recruits talented college graduates to teach in economically distressed schools. Schwab was following a view long endorsed by Bill Drayton at Ashoka that social entrepreneurship is about innovation and impact, not income. This view is well grounded in entrepreneurship theory (see my paper on "The Meaning of Social Entrepreneurship," [Dees, 2001]) but not sufficiently.

Despite efforts to spread an innovation-based definition, far too many people still think of social entrepreneurship in terms of nonprofits generating earned income. This is a dangerously narrow view. It shifts attention away from the ultimate goal of any self-respecting social entrepreneur, namely social impact, and focuses it on one particular method of generating resources. Earned income is only a means to a social end, and it is not always the best means. It can even be detrimental-taking valuable talent and energy away from activities more central to delivering on the organization's social mission. Though it is very popular right now, it is just one funding strategy among many and must be assessed on a case-by-case basis. The key is finding a resource strategy that works.

Focusing on earned income leads people to embrace the problematic idea of a "double bottom line." Profits should not be treated with equal importance to social results. No amount of profit makes up for failure on the social impact side of the equation. Any social entrepreneur who generates profits, but then fails to convert them into meaningful social impact in a cost effective way has wasted valuable resources. From a management point of view, the financial "bottom line" is certainly important, but it is not on the same level as social impact. Social entrepreneurs have only one ultimate bottom line by which to measure their success. It is their intended social impact, whether that is housing for the homeless, a cleaner environment, improved access to health care, more effective education, reduced poverty, protection of abused children, deeper appreciation of the arts, or some other social improvement.

Many activities that generate earned income are not entrepreneurial at all. Earned income has become commonplace. In fact, if religious congregations are excluded, earned income has exceeded donations as a source of funds for public charities in the U. S. for many years now. Hospitals charge fees for medical services; private schools charge tuition; performing arts groups sell tickets; many museums charge admission and often have gift shops in their lobbies. No one thinks of these practices as examples of "social entrepreneurship" even though they all involve generating earned income. It would be absurd to give a social entrepreneurship award, for instance, to a major hospital simply because of its extremely high percentage of earned income from patient fees and the record profits at its gift shop and parking garage. Yet, this would be a logical implication of taking earned income as the yardstick of social entrepreneurship. High levels of earned income are often not innovative and may not be correlated with high levels of social impact.

Any form of social entrepreneurship that is worth promoting broadly must be about establishing new and better ways to improve the world. Social entrepreneurs implement innovative programs, organizational structures, or resource strategies that increase their chances of achieving deep, broad, lasting, and cost-effective social impact. To borrow from J.B. Say, the eighteenth century French economist who first popularized the term "entrepreneur," they shift resources into areas of higher productivity and yield. Habitat persuades volunteers to shift their time from recreational activities to building a house. Teach for America persuades bright college graduates who did not major in education to devote two years of their careers to teaching in schools that have a difficult time finding teachers. This resource-shifting function is essential to progress. As Peter Drucker (1985) has said, "What we need is an entrepreneurial society in which innovation and entrepreneurship are normal, steady, and continuous."

Of course, some exciting forms of social entrepreneurship use earned income strategies to achieve social impact. We should encourage social sector leaders to explore innovative financial strategies that make their organizations more effective in serving social needs while leveraging social assets. Creative efforts to harness business methods to serve social objectives are often entrepreneurial in the best sense of that term. Consider Grameen Bank that was built around an innovative approach of using peer-groups to improve the economics and effectiveness of micro-enterprise lending as a tool to fight poverty in Bangladesh. Or consider Delancey Street Foundation, a residential community of hardcore substance abusers in San Francisco that runs several businesses to provide productive employment to community members and generate funds for the organization. These are powerful examples of how social sector leaders can blend business methods with social objectives. What makes them entrepreneurial is not the source of income, but their innovations and their impact.

Earned income ventures are socially entrepreneurial only when they have a social purpose beyond simply making money. If social entrepreneurship is to be distinctive in any way, it must be because social objectives matter in how the venture is organized and managed. If the only way a venture serves your mission is by generating funds, it may be business entrepreneurship, but it is not social entrepreneurship. If I start a bakery to make money that will be used to support my sailing hobby, we do not call the bakery a "sailing venture." Likewise using the proceeds of the bakery for a social purpose does not make it into a "social" venture. It is a social venture only if social considerations are integrated into its objectives and management. A purely moneymaking venture can be managed using straight business principles. It makes no difference if the owner intends to use the cash generated by the venture to buy a bigger sailboat or to serve the homeless. True social ventures often require a more complex skill set than straight business ventures.

Only if we can embrace a definition of social entrepreneurship that focuses on innovation and impact can we put funding strategies in their proper perspective. It is not surprising that people are drawn to the earned income definition of social entrepreneurship. Resources are scarce and social needs are great. Everyone wants to explore new avenues for generating resources and earned income seems promising. Unfortunately, some social sector leaders appear to be more concerned about attracting resources and sustaining their organizations than they are about assessing, sustaining, and improving their social impact. They assume they are doing a great job on the social side and that they deserve the additional funding, often without much systematic evidence. These are risky assumptions. Finding ways to sustain organizations that are not cost-effectively delivering social value is a terrible waste of energy and resources. Social sector leaders should look for creative resource strategies that enhance their impact, rather than simply sustain their organizations. By embracing a definition of social entrepreneurship that focuses on innovation and impact, we can assure that social objectives are taken seriously in the entrepreneurial process. In the end, social entrepreneurship must be about creating social value, not simply about making money.

J. Gregory Dees, Adjunct Professor and Faculty Director, Fuqua School of Business Center for the Advancement of Social Entrepreneurship (CASE), Duke University. This article originally appeared on The Skoll Foundation's Social Edge in September 2003. It is reprinted here by permission.

The Imperative of Systemic Change.   One important tenet of the social innovation school is that social entrepreneurship aims to effect large scale, sustainable, and systemic change. Writing in the *Stanford Social Innovation Review* in 2007, Martin and Osberg argued that social entrepreneurship is characterized by three fundamental components:

- Identifying a stable but inherently unjust equilibrium that causes the exclusion, marginalization, or suffering of a segment of humanity that lacks the financial means or political clout to achieve any transformative benefit on its own
- Identifying an opportunity in this unjust equilibrium, developing a social value proposition, and bringing to bear inspiration, creativity, direct action, courage, and fortitude, thereby challenging the stable state's hegemony
- Forging a new, stable equilibrium that releases trapped potential or alleviates the suffering of the targeted group, and through imitation and the creation of a stable ecosystem around the new equilibrium ensuring a better future for the targeted group and even society at large (p. 35)

Martin and Osberg draw a strong distinction between social entrepreneurship and two other forms of social engagement—social activism and social service provision—noting that the former is an indirect form of social engagement and arguing that the latter does not set out to achieve and sustain a new equilibrium (see Figure 10.1). Acknowledging the distinctive value that each form of social engagement brings to society, Martin and Osberg note that social activists, social service providers, and social entrepreneurs may borrow and adapt one another's strategies and develop hybrid models.

The emphasis on transformational systems change, at the core of this definition of social entrepreneurship, has long been championed by Bill Drayton,

FIGURE 10.1. PURE FORMS OF SOCIAL ENGAGEMENT.

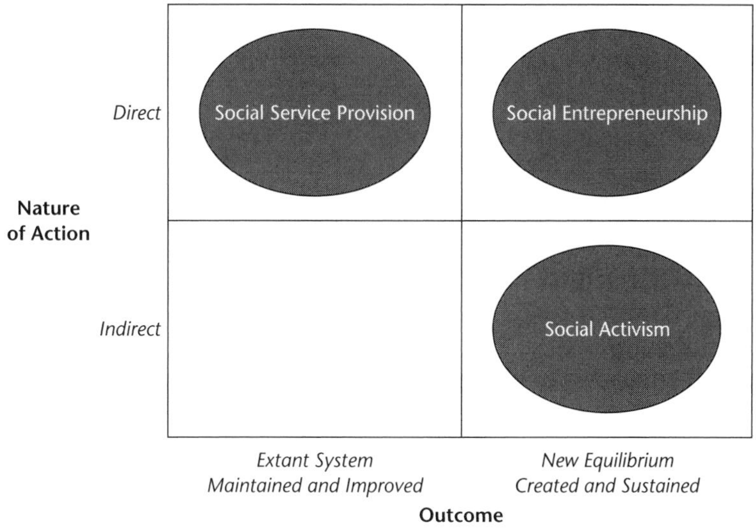

Source: Martin and Osberg, 2007, reprinted with permission.

who is arguably the primary driving force advancing the social innovation school of thought. In 1980, Drayton founded Ashoka, the global network of leading social entrepreneurs and framed its mission to find and support "outstanding individuals with pattern setting ideas for social change" (Drayton and MacDonald, 1993, p. i). Setting a high standard for those who would consider themselves social entrepreneurs, Drayton asserts, "The job of a social entrepreneur is to recognize when a part of society is stuck and to provide new ways to get it unstuck. He or she finds what is not working and solves the problem by changing the system, spreading the solution and persuading entire societies to take new leaps. Social entrepreneurs are not content just to give a fish or teach how to fish. They will not rest until they have revolutionized the fishing industry" (Leviner, Crutchfield, and Wells, 2006).

Toward a Shared Theory of Social Entrepreneurship

It is easy to see how these points of difference can lead to significant confusion over what "counts" as social entrepreneurship and what does not. Shared definitions will likely emerge from a give-and-take process among participants and the media outlets that popularize the term. In order to propel this field forward, we must find definitional solutions that increase precision and clarity while allowing healthy disagreements, respecting different perspectives. Too broad a definition will dilute the focus of the community, but too narrow a definition could exclude too many and result in a field that is "too special" for mainstream attention.

We have observed that a vibrant and diverse community of practice is emerging, including those who embrace all the different definitions mentioned above. In order to maintain the interest, commitment, and participation of key players, while also allowing for academic discourse to advance the state of knowledge within the field, CASE at Duke suggests a path forward that balances increased clarity with openness and respect for differences and that frames this emerging field of inquiry in a way that builds upon the rich work of reflective practitioners and scholars who have led the way thus far.

For those in the field with a vested interest in resolving the confusions about definitions, CASE has suggested the following guidelines (CASE at Duke, 2008):

- Clearly distinguish "social entrepreneurship," focused on innovation, from "social enterprise," focused on the use of business methods to generate income.
- For the foreseeable future, define the community of practice and knowledge to include both social entrepreneurship and social enterprise.
- Find a vocabulary to distinguish the different forms of socially entrepreneurial behavior (that is, to distinguish independent start-ups led by one or two people from organizations engaged in finding innovative solutions to social problems; and to distinguish the revolutionaries, aiming for major systemic change, from the reformers, aiming for more incremental improvements).
- Recognize the importance and legitimacy of all these forms of entrepreneurial behavior, and acknowledge that they have enough problems, concerns, and passions in common to be part of a shared community of practice and knowledge.
- Respect that it is healthy for key community participants to focus their work on forms of socially entrepreneurial behavior that they deem most important, interesting, and a good fit for them.

These guidelines should allow for the development of a diverse and vibrant community with some critical mass but without all the confusion that currently exists in the field. Participants need to respect honest differences while working together to help find new and better solutions to social problems.

As in many fields, consensus on a basic definition of the field may not emerge for some time. However, the critical need for rigorous research and high-quality teaching requires the field to make advances in the absence of full consensus. Observing encouraging signs of convergence between the two main schools of thought, CASE proposes a way of framing this new field of inquiry that raises a distinctive set of intellectual questions that cut across disciplinary boundaries. Dees and Anderson contend that the most promising arena for academic inquiry lies at the intersection of social enterprise and social innovation, which they identify as "enterprising social innovation," defined as "carrying out innovations that blend methods from the worlds of business and philanthropy to create social value that is sustainable and has the potential for large-scale impact" (Dees and Anderson, 2006, p. 50). This framing forces scholars and practitioners to acknowledge the intimate connection between social and economic realities and the role of markets in the social sector. "In order to be considered 'enterprising,' the innovation must involve some business-inspired elements, whether through the adaptation of business methods to create or enhance social value, the operation of a social-purpose business, or the formation of cross-sector partnerships" (p. 51).

This framing on ventures that blend business and philanthropic methods has the potential to raise theoretically interesting questions and engage a broad range of scholars working in diverse disciplines and domains. Selected areas of academic inquiry could include

- Aligning market dynamics with social outcomes
- Strengths and limits of different economic strategies (philanthropic and commercial)
- Role of different legal forms of organization
- Bias toward commercial market solutions
- Competitive advantage of social orientation
- Market discipline and accountability
- Efficiency in the social sector capital markets

Observing the accelerating trend of blurring of the boundaries between the public, private, and social sectors, Dees and Anderson call upon academics and thoughtful practitioners to seek to understand better what may lie ahead for the field of social entrepreneurship. "If we do not deepen our knowledge of these kinds of approaches, we are likely to fumble around in the dark, making more mistakes than necessary. Success will depend on a better understanding of how to effectively combine elements from the business world and the social sector, and how to recognize the limits and risks. This arena is where we should focus most of our limited time and resources. Doing so will not only serve both schools of thought and academia well; more importantly, it will be of great value to society" (p. 61).

The Process of Social Entrepreneurship: Creating Worthy Opportunities

All acts of entrepreneurship start with a vision of an attractive opportunity (Stevenson and Gumpert, 1985). All entrepreneurs, whether business or social entrepreneurs, must uncover or create new opportunities through a dynamic process of exploration, innovation, experimentation, and resource mobilization (Dees, 2007). The difference for the social entrepreneur is that opportunities worthy of serious pursuit must have sufficient potential for positive social impact in order to justify the investment of time, money, and energy required to pursue it seriously. Social entrepreneurs must have the same commitment and determination as a business entrepreneur, plus a deep passion for the social cause, minus an expectation of significant financial gains.

Drawing extensively upon the work of Guclu, Dees, and Anderson (2002), in the following pages we will discuss a useful process framework that social entrepreneurs may use to guide the discovery or creation of such an opportunity. This process is illustrated in Figure 10.2.

Step 1: Generate Promising Ideas

For entrepreneurs, whether business entrepreneurs or social entrepreneurs, the entrepreneurial journey begins with a promising idea. Though ideas commonly have their roots in personal experience, in identifying, exploring, and

FIGURE 10.2. THE OPPORTUNITY CREATION PROCESS.

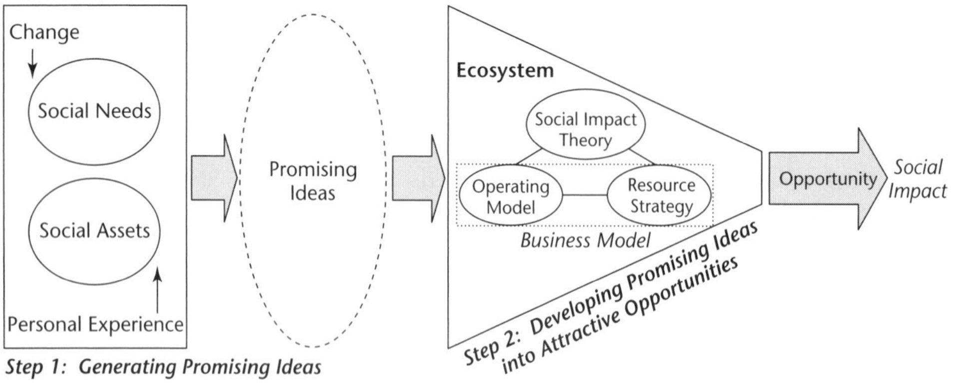

Source: Guclu, Dees, and Anderson, 2002. Reprinted with permission.

developing promising ideas, the social entrepreneur may also draw upon his or her understanding of social needs, social assets, and relevant changes in society.

Personal Experience. Personal experience often motivates, inspires, or informs the idea generation process. Not surprising, many successful new venture ideas arise from the entrepreneur's education, work experience, and hobbies (Vesper, 1979). Dissatisfaction with the status quo often spurs entrepreneurial creativity, prompting social entrepreneurs to look for new approaches to problems and frustrations they have encountered personally, witnessed among family or friends, or seen on the job. Note that relevant experience does not have to be in the same field in which the new venture would operate. Sometimes experience and knowledge of practices in other fields can help the social entrepreneur see new ways of doing things.

Social Needs. Sound entrepreneurial ideas respond to genuine needs. For business ventures, these are unmet or poorly met consumer needs. Likewise, social entrepreneurs would be wise to look beyond their personal preferences in the search for promising ideas, basing them on an understanding of social needs, gaps between socially desirable conditions and the existing reality. They rest on some vision of a better world and are grounded in personal values. These values can provide a sense of moral imperative that may serve as a powerful motivator for social entrepreneurs and their ideas. Calling to mind the famous quote from Robert Kennedy, social entrepreneurs are unwilling to settle for the status quo; instead, they "dream of things that never were, and ask why not?"

Social Assets. Understanding the tangible and intangible assets in a community can lead to the development of promising ideas. Although it is important to ground ideas for new ventures in a plausible diagnosis of social needs, there is a danger of over emphasizing the negative. Some argue that the social sector concentrates too much on needs and that better ideas emerge out of an appreciative focus on assets. The latter presents the community in a new light and may inspire creative new ideas that would not be visible if social entrepreneurs looked only at needs or "problems."

Change. It is common to think of entrepreneurs as creating change, but entrepreneurs are often inspired by the changes all around them. As discussed earlier, Peter Drucker has argued that entrepreneurs "always search for change, respond to it and exploit it as an opportunity" (Drucker, 1985). In framing their ideas, social entrepreneurs may be stimulated by changing demographics, values, cultures, technologies, industry structures, knowledge, public policies, and preferences. These changes can create new needs, new assets, or both, opening up new possibilities and prompting social entrepreneurs to generate promising new ideas.

Step 1 Summary. Personal experience, social needs, social assets, and change can stimulate promising ideas, but only if the social entrepreneur also adopts an opportunity-oriented mindset, actively looking for new possibilities to have significant positive social impact. Successful social entrepreneurs embody this "how can" attitude, particularly in the idea generation phase, as they ask themselves

- How can I draw upon my personal experience in seeking to achieve broad social impact?
- How can I address a particular social need or make the most of existing social assets to improve society?
- How can I capitalize on recent changes to create new opportunities for social impact?

Effective social entrepreneurs carry this orientation into the opportunity-development process, engaging in continuous innovation, adaptation, analysis, and learning along the way.

Step 2: Develop Promising Ideas into Attractive Opportunities

The second step for the aspiring social entrepreneur is to convert an initially appealing idea into a worthwhile opportunity, combining rigorous analysis with creative adjustment as the social entrepreneur tests and refines the ideas through a mixture of research, innovation, and action. The chances of success are significantly increased if the envisioned social venture idea is grounded in a set of plausible hypotheses about the underlying *social impact theory* (also known as a "theory of change") and a plausible *business model*, consisting of an effective operating model describing the activities, structures, and systems required by the social impact theory, and a viable strategy for attracting the necessary human and financial resources required by the operating model. The most attractive opportunities have strong social impact theories and business models that fit with the working environment and the personal characteristics of the social entrepreneur.

Social Impact Theory. As we have seen, social entrepreneurs are driven by a desire to achieve results—to create social value for their primary constituents or beneficiaries, society, and the world. Underlying any promising new social venture is a carefully conceived and testable hypothesis about how the venture will achieve its intended social impact. Expressing the cause-and-effect logic by which the venture's operating model connects inputs, activities, and outputs to generate desired outcomes, this "social impact theory," also known as a "theory of change," is central to the venture's strategy and generally embodies the organization's mission and values (Guclu, Dees, and Anderson, 2002). The articulation of this theory linking action to results should include a "convincing statement of how program inputs will produce a sequence first of intermediate and then ultimate outcomes, . . . and some indication of the bases, in experience, for expecting a cascade of results" (Szanton as quoted in Grossman and Curran, 1990). By clearly defining the venture's intended outcomes and means for achieving them, the theory also provides a precise description of the ultimate social impacts for which the organization will hold itself accountable (Campbell and Haley, 2006).

A well-articulated social impact theory should also identify the critical assumptions underlying the hypothesis. We can think of these assumptions as the necessary preconditions that should hold in order for the social impact theory to lead to achieving the intended impact. Considered alongside the intermediate outcomes that will jointly cause the intended impact, these assumptions complete the "if/then" logic inherent in the social impact theory. Whenever possible, critical assumptions should be identified and tested prior to launching a venture by comparing the social impact theory to existing relevant knowledge in the field or by doing new research and analysis. Despite their need and bias for action, social entrepreneurs should structure their actions carefully in such a way that they can test as many critical assumptions as feasible before making major, irreversible investments (McGrath and MacMillan, 1995).

To aid in developing and refining their social impact theory, the social entrepreneur may wish to create a simple logic model that clearly identifies the specific resources or "inputs" required, the major activities of the venture, the "outputs" produced by those activities, and the "outcomes" resulting from the activities. Another useful tool is the "outcomes framework"—an inductive logic tree that illustrates the hypothesis implicit in the social impact theory, the causal logic among the intermediate outcomes and ultimate intended impact, and any critical assumptions that should hold in order for the social impact theory to lead to achieving the intended impact. Logic models and outcome frameworks can become valuable tools for planning, communications, and management and should be reviewed and updated regularly.

Defining and refining a social impact theory is a dynamic process that blends creativity and out-of-the-box thinking with concrete analysis and assessment of results. Social entrepreneurs should regularly test and, if necessary, revise their social impact theory to assure they are pursuing a worthwhile opportunity and are on track to achieving their ultimate intended impact. Since social impact is so hard to measure and many social entrepreneurs aim for long-term, sustainable lasting impact, the testing process can take significant amounts of time. Having a clearly articulated social impact theory helps make the testing process more systematic and timely.

Business Model. In addition to a compelling social impact theory, every worthwhile opportunity needs to be supported by a plausible business model that includes an effective operating model coupled with a viable resource strategy. In many cases, social entrepreneurs are most creative and add the greatest value in the design of their business model—they employ a wide range of options for structuring their ventures, acquiring capital, pricing their services, paying their workers, and coming to terms with suppliers.

For the socially entrepreneurial venture, the business model includes two key elements:

1. An *operating model* that includes internal organizational structure and external partnerships that are crucial for creating the organization's intended impact
2. A *resource strategy* that defines where and on what terms the organization will acquire needed resources (financial and human capital)

These two elements of the business model work closely together to bring the social impact theory to life. In this sense, the business model is essentially the conduit through which a social entrepreneur converts inputs into outcomes. It determines the organization's financial and talent needs, the extent and nature of dependence on different resource providers, and the efficiency with which resources are converted into impact, which factors into the social return on investment.

Regardless of how effective an innovation is at achieving impact, the business model must be "sustainable" over the period of time required to achieve widespread, lasting impact. If the business model is not capable of being scaled or replicated, widespread impact will be impossible to achieve. If the business model is not aligned with the mission and intended impact of an organization, the organization may be sustained and it may scale, but its ultimate impact will be undermined. This can even be a problem for for-profit social ventures that discover their mission impact would be better served through activities and costs that cannot be adequately covered by their revenues.

Operating Model. A fundamental component of the business model, the operating model describes how the social impact theory will be implemented in practice. It is a combination of specific activities, structures, and support systems that are designed to work together to bring about the intended impact.

In developing an operating model, the first step is to trace a chain of activity from inputs to outcomes, identifying every step that is necessary in between. These direct productive activities will usually need to be supported by administrative functions, such as accounting, human resources, fundraising, and so on. When all of these elements are put together (see Figure 10.3), the result looks similar to the "value chain" in a business, a concept introduced by strategist Michael Porter (1985) as a tool for analyzing potential sources of competitive advantage for a firm.

This framework can be used to identify the major activities through which a social entrepreneurial venture can create or enhance social value. Social entrepreneurs may create social value at any of the steps in this process. For example, microfinance institutions such Grameen Bank create social value by making loans to people who otherwise would not have access to the capital they need. Perhaps Muhammad Yunus's most important innovation was to eliminate the requirement of assets as collateral for loans, an insurmountable barrier to the poor; instead Yunus created peer-lending groups, small groups of women borrowers from the same village who meet regularly, support each other, and share responsibility for repayment of loans made to anyone in the group, thus pooling risk and increasing return.

Fair trade organizations such as Forests of the World create social value in how and from whom they purchase the goods they sell. Other social ventures, such as Rubicon Bakery, create value through employing disadvantaged populations. Some, such as Triangle Residential Opportunities for Substance Abusers (TROSA) engage their beneficiaries in earned revenue ventures as a form of rehabilitative therapy and to foster job skills needed for reintegration in the community, thus increasing likely social impact. With hospice care, the social value is inherent in the design of the value or service. Through their distribution chains, both KickStart and VisionSpring harness the powerful incentives of small business ownership to sell foot-operated water pumps and deliver eye care services and products in rural villages in developing countries.

Once the social entrepreneur has identified all key activities in the value chain, she must make structural decisions, such as choosing a form of incorporation and

FIGURE 10.3. THE SIMPLIFIED SOCIAL VALUE CHAIN.

Source: Guclu, Dees, and Anderson, 2002. Reprinted with permission.

defining the division of labor and coordination of activities. Social entrepreneurs may choose to incorporate their venture as a nonprofit organization, a for-profit social venture, or a hybrid; this decision may be based on a number of factors including the desired sources of capital. A for-profit form of incorporation (proprietorships, partnerships, corporations, limited liability companies, and cooperatives) will be necessary if the social entrepreneur seeks to tap into private capital markets for investment funds, whether at or below market rate of return (Dees and Anderson, 2003).

The major labor division question concerns what the new venture should do and control versus what could be left to affiliates, partners, suppliers, contractors, or providers of complementary services. This decision should be driven largely by the importance of the activity, the presence or lack of competencies and efficiencies within the organization, and the value of maintaining control over it.

Finally, social entrepreneurs should consider the support systems that may need to be in place to assure effective and efficient social value creation, including systems for monitoring organizational performance and assessing outcomes, as well as intangible support systems such as the organization's culture.

With these pieces in place, the operating model should allow social entrepreneurs to trace a plausible and specific causal path through a chain of activities, structures, and support systems to the intended social impact. As with the social impact theory, any proposed operating model will rest on assumptions that may be tested before anyone can say that the operating model is likely to be effective.

Resource Strategy. Whether in business or in the social sector, an operating model cannot begin to create value unless it is aligned with and supported by a viable resource strategy. At the most fundamental resource level, the social entrepreneur needs *people* (including their skills, knowledge, contacts, credentials, passions, and reputations) and *things* (including everything from office space to patents). Unlike the business entrepreneurs, in the social sector, entrepreneurs may acquire both people and things with or without using money.

In developing a resource strategy, social entrepreneurs must first identify resource requirements; these may be deduced from the proposed operating model, along with performance and growth objectives. Resource needs cannot be determined without a specific operating model in mind that converts the resources into the capabilities necessary to create the intended social impact efficiently and effectively. Of course, as the idea is refined, the original operating model may need to be adjusted to fit the realities of resource mobilization.

Next, social entrepreneurs must determine how best to mobilize the resources required through one or more of the following options:

- Building partnerships or alliances
- Attracting donations
- Paying for the resources

Although some partnerships may be desirable as part of the operating model, others are driven more by resource considerations. When resources are scarce or hard to mobilize, as is often the case during a start-up stage, it may be wise to build resource-based partnerships with others that have (perhaps underutilized) resources of the kind required. However, social entrepreneurs should carefully consider benefits, costs, and risks of any partnership, particularly if it is not ideal from the operations point of view.

Social entrepreneurs may also attempt to acquire resources through volunteers and in-kind donations, which can reduce the cash needed to achieve social impact. Some organizations, such as Habitat for Humanity, rely heavily on volunteers and in-kind donations for core activities. Other social entrepreneurs have decided that operational effectiveness requires paying for key resources. For example, whereas most youth mentoring organizations typically rely on volunteers, Friends of the Children, winner of the Purpose Prize for 2009, has challenged that model, arguing that the use of paid mentors for at-risk kids leads to better social outcomes.

Even for those things that are purchased, social entrepreneurs can sometimes offer below-market compensation or seek discounts. For example, many organizations have been able to attract and retain high-quality workers with below-business-market wages, perhaps due to the personal satisfaction that people get from working for a cause that is deeply meaningful to them. Also, social ventures may qualify for discounted prices on equipment, supplies, services, professional fees, and so on, though the pool of available resources may be limited and the quality of services provided at reduced cost may be lower than desirable.

Finally, when considering the acquisition of costly equipment and facilities, social entrepreneurs must also decide if they will purchase outright or whether they will simply rent or lease. When risk is high, renting or leasing is typically the optimal option.

Based on these decisions, social entrepreneurs should estimate the cash needs for their ventures and begin to identify plausible sources of funding. Though many social entrepreneurs would love for their ventures to be "self-sufficient," charging customers enough to cover all the operating costs (as occurs in the private sector) is often not optimal from the point of view of creating social impact.

Although third-party payers (such as government agencies or corporations) may be found to cover costs, in many domains in which social entrepreneurs operate, revenues gained from service fees and contracts will fall short of what is needed to have the desired impact. In these cases, the resource strategy must include a plausible fundraising plan. However, social entrepreneurs must be vigilant about selecting cash income streams that do not pull the venture away from its core mission.

In summary, the social entrepreneur should craft the resource strategy based upon assumptions about resource requirements and methods of meeting them, asking questions such as

- How many staff and volunteers will be necessary for successful service delivery?
- Can the venture attract and retain staff with the requisite skills at the proposed levels of compensation? Can it recruit, train, and effectively manage the required volunteers?
- Will projected in-kind donations come with too many strings attached or have serious operating costs?
- Who may pay for the venture's activities? Who may be willing to donate to subsidize it? Will revenue sources be aligned with the mission?

Although some of the assumptions embedded in the model may be highly plausible based on past experience, social entrepreneurs should carefully identify those uncertain assumptions to which the resource strategy is most sensitive and make sure they are tested and adjusted as the venture rolls out. The topic of nonprofit finance is discussed in depth by Dennis Young in Chapter Eighteen of this handbook, and all of the chapters in Part Five address the challenges of recruiting, retaining, and motivating both staff and volunteers.

As with the rest of the process of social entrepreneurship, developing an attractive resource strategy requires creativity, especially given the intense competition for funding in the social sector. In some instances, an innovative resource strategy might even drive, or significantly impact, the social venture's operating model. However, a resourceful approach does not undermine the effectiveness of the business model and ultimate social impact of the venture. In fact, the most attractive resource strategies actually enhance social impact.

Business Model Summary. There are numerous ways by which a social entrepreneur may create social value. In designing a social venture, the social entrepreneur has a wide range of options for structuring their ventures, acquiring capital, pricing their services, paying their workers, and coming to terms with

FIGURE 10.4. THE SOCIAL ENTERPRISE SPECTRUM.

	Purely Charitable	← Mixed →	Purely Commercial
Motives, Methods and Goals	Appeal to goodwill Mission-driven Social value creation	Mixed motives Balance of mission and market Social and economic value	Appeal to self-interest Market-driven Economic value creation
Key Stakeholders			
Targeted Customers	Pay nothing	Subsidized rates, and/or mix of full payers and those who pay nothing	Pay full market rates
Capital Providers	Donations and Grants	Below-market capital and/or mix of donations and market rate capital	Market rate capital
Work Force	Volunteers	Below-market wages and/or mix of volunteers and fully paid staff	Market rate compensation
Suppliers	Make in-kind donations	Special discounts and/or mix of in-kind and full price	Charge full market prices

Source: Dees and Anderson (2006).

suppliers. In exploring these various options, it may be helpful to consider the "Social Enterprise Spectrum" illustrated in Figure 10.4 (Dees 1996, 1998a).

This spectrum describes the full range of business models available to social entrepreneurs, from purely philanthropic to purely commercial, with many variations in between. Philanthropic methods are involved any time an organization falls short of the far right side on at least one dimension of the spectrum, indicating some form of subsidy or sacrifice. Excluding purely philanthropic or purely commercial ventures is not a major sacrifice in scope because very few social-purpose organizations exist at either extreme (Dees and Anderson, 2006).

Ultimately, the selection of a business model should be made upon careful reflection on the following questions:

- Does the business model use resources efficiently and effectively?
- Will it attract sufficient resources to achieve the intended social impact?
- How well does it fit with the ecosystems in which you want to operate?
- Is it sufficiently robust and scalable?
- Are the incentives in the business model aligned with your social impact theory?

It is important to note that no single business model is best for all social entrepreneurs in all settings. Potential trade-offs and risks have to be assessed on a case-by-case basis, and the operating model may need to be adjusted accordingly. However, designing an effective business model is an essential part of the creative learning process of crafting, testing, and refining the hypotheses and assumptions inherent in the social entrepreneur's social impact theory. This process of learning and refinement should continue well after the launch of the venture as the social entrepreneur gains experience and as the venture is affected by changes in the ecosystem in which it operates.

Ecosystem (or Operating Environment)

Drawing upon the science of biology, scholars of strategy and management have begun to study and apply ecosystems theory to reveal lessons for business and entrepreneurship. So, too, social entrepreneurs hoping to create significant and sustainable social impact should also develop an understanding of, and may endeavor to alter, the broad environment in which they operate. This is true especially if they seek to leverage complex systems of interacting players in rapidly evolving political, economic, physical, and cultural environments. Indeed, changes in these conditions may determine whether and when a window of opportunity is open or closed to the social entrepreneur.

Ecosystem Players[3]. Just as biological ecosystems are made up of complex webs of interrelated organisms, social ecosystems operate in much the same way. Social entrepreneurs get help from some individuals and organizations, give help to others, fend off threats from others, and compete with still others. To assist social entrepreneurs in identifying and mapping all of the relevant ecosystem players and the roles that they play, Bloom and Dees (2008) recommend dividing the players into six roles:

- *Resource providers*, including providers of financial, human, knowledge, networking, and technological resources, and any brokers or intermediaries that channel these resources to those who want them. Resource provides may include third-party payers, donors, volunteers, and workers, anyone who must voluntarily participate in the venture in order for it to be successful. Social entrepreneurs must have a plausible value proposition for each group of resource provider.
- *Competitors*, including organizations that compete with the social entrepreneur's organization for resources as well as those that compete to serve the same beneficiaries.

- *Complementary organizations and allies*, including organizations or individuals that facilitate a social entrepreneur's ability to create impact, such as partners who perform critical steps in the social entrepreneur's theory of change, individuals and organizations supporting the same cause, and those providing important complementary services.
- *Beneficiaries and customers*, including clients, patients, customers, and others who benefit from social entrepreneurs' activities, whether or not the ultimate beneficiaries interact directly with the organization.
- *Opponents and problem makers*, including organizations and individuals that contribute to the problems social entrepreneurs are addressing, undermine the ability of the organizations to achieve and sustain their intended impact, or oppose their efforts politically.
- *Affected or influential bystanders*, including players who have no direct impact now, but who are affected by the social entrepreneur's efforts—especially those that could be harmed if the social entrepreneur succeeds and those that can be turned into allies or resource providers if convinced of the benefits of the social entrepreneur's efforts—or those who could influence her success, either positively or negatively, such as members of the media.

Bloom and Dees note that the categories of ecosystem players listed above are dynamic and not mutually exclusive (2008). Organizations may play more than one role or may switch over time; paradoxically, the same organization can be both an ally (for example, when it comes to advocating for legislation to serve the same cause) yet also a competitor (for example, when vying for limited funding). As in for-profit industries, new players may enter the ecosystem at any time, posing new threats or presenting opportunities for the social entrepreneur and her venture to benefit.

Environmental Conditions. Biological ecosystems are made up not only of other organisms, but also of environmental conditions (for example, soil, weather, sunlight, and water) that have a significant impact on the type of organisms that can exist, as well as on their relationships with one another. So, too, with social ecosystems, although organizations and people can, in turn, influence the environmental conditions and bring about change within the social ecosystems of which they are a part. To aid social entrepreneurs in identifying relevant changes or trends that can influence their ability to create and sustain the intended social impact, Bloom and Dees (2008) identify four sets of environmental conditions that should be considered by the social entrepreneur:

- *Politics and administrative structures*, including rules and regulations—and the processes and procedures for adopting, enforcing, and reforming these rules—along with the political dynamics of the jurisdictions in which social entrepreneurs operate, including potential sources of public support or resistance.

- *Economics and markets*, including the overall economic health of the regions in which social entrepreneurs operate and seek resources, as well as the region's distribution of wealth and income, economic prospects, levels of entrepreneurial activity, and relevant markets.
- *Geography and infrastructure*, including not only the physical terrain and location, but also the infrastructure that social entrepreneurs count on for transportation, communication, and other operating needs.
- *Culture and social fabric*, including the norms and values, important subgroups, social networks, and demographic trends of the people living in the area. For example, many microfinance institutions and global health initiatives target women in hopes of achieving greater social and economic impact for the women and their families. However, local cultural norms about the role of women in the economy may pose significant challenges and present promising opportunities for the social entrepreneur.

Mapping the Ecosystem. Although the relevant features of the ecosystem will vary from venture to venture and will depend on the specifics of the venture idea, including the social impact theory and the business model, most social entrepreneurs will make crucial assumptions about their markets, the industry structure, the political environment, and the culture. In studying and making assumptions about the ecosystem in which operate, social entrepreneurs may choose to construct a simplified ecosystem map illustrating the key ecosystem players and environmental conditions, noting key relationships and trends, and anticipating potential changes that may positively or negatively affect their ability to achieve the desired social impact. Mapping the ecosystem in this way is a dynamic process that may yield significant strategic insights (Bloom and Dees, 2008).

In summary, an ecosystems framework can help social entrepreneurs in many ways, including

- Imparting a deeper understanding of an organization's social impact theory by making the environmental conditions and relationships on which the organization depends more visible, possibly leading to a revision of that theory.
- Mapping the resource flows into and within the ecosystem, revealing constraints, bottlenecks, and underused sources, perhaps suggesting alternative resource strategies for the organization.
- Identifying new operating partnerships, perhaps with complementary organizations, that fall short of systemic change but that promise to enhance the

social entrepreneurs' impact by increasing the coordination of otherwise independent players.

- Determining the minimum critical environmental conditions required for an organization's operating model to be a success and using that information to guide the social entrepreneurs' efforts to take the model into new areas.
- Developing different operating models for different ecosystems, or a more robust operating model that works in a variety of different ecosystems. (Bloom and Dees, 2008, p. 53)

As social entrepreneurs flesh out the three core elements of their opportunities, they will inevitably make assumptions about their ecosystem or operating environment. The potential success of the venture depends largely on whether the assumptions accurately represent the context. Thus, a promising opportunity must fit with the characteristics of its environment. However, in the social sector as in the business world, windows of opportunity may close as quickly as they open.

Windows of Opportunity. Since ecosystems are dynamic, it is also helpful for social entrepreneurs to be sensitive to the window of opportunity, the time frame in which conditions are expected to be favorable for pursuing a given opportunity. In studying the conditions necessary for social entrepreneurship, respected nonprofit scholar Paul Light has asserted that such windows of opportunity are rare, cannot be predicted, tend to occur in great punctuations when the demand for change reaches a tipping point, emerge when entry costs are low, open, and close quickly, favor competition over collaboration, and appear to the special few (Light, 2008, p. 203).

Social entrepreneurs may have better chances of success if they can take advantage of windows that are opening and that will stay open long enough for the venture to have its intended impact. Changes in the ecosystem or other external conditions may increase or decrease receptivity to new ideas, or may affect the viability of a proposed business model, thus opening or closing the window of opportunity. Such changes include the growth or decline of the social need being addressed, the number of people affected by the need, the visibility of the need and expected media coverage, perceptions of urgency or relative importance by key resource providers, levels of satisfaction with existing approaches, technological changes, changes in public policy, and popular trends or fashions in relevant fields (Guclu, Dees, and Anderson, 2002).

Personal Fit. As social entrepreneurs develop their ideas into worthwhile opportunities, they also have to be sensitive to personal fit. Even if they have identified an attractive opportunity, it may not be a good opportunity for them when assessed in relation to other options. Before seeking to launch a social venture, aspiring social entrepreneurs should conduct an honest self-assessment, asking themselves

- Do I have the time, energy, fortitude, commitment, and determination required to coordinate ambitious social impact goals with scarce income sources, and to satisfy excess need for services with an overstretched staff and limited time?
- Do I have healthy support systems and strong personal and professional networks that can help me forestall and/or handle the burnout that not infrequently accompanies launching and managing an entrepreneurial venture?[4]
- Do I have the skills, expertise, credibility, credentials, contacts, and assets needed to launch this venture? Can I attract a strong team to help compensate for any critical shortcomings?
- Is this right time in my life to pursue this kind of opportunity? Are there career and family or other personal considerations that must be taken into account?

New ventures of any sort are tremendously demanding. Social ventures are even more so. Ultimately, aspiring social entrepreneurs would be wise to pursue only opportunities that fit their personal commitment, qualifications, income requirements, and stage in life, embarking on their entrepreneurial journey with full awareness of the risks involved.

Ecosystem Summary. In order to determine whether a promising idea can be transformed into an opportunity worthy of serious pursuit, it is essential for the social entrepreneur to articulate a compelling social impact theory and a plausible business model. Developing a plausible business model requires designing an effective operating model and crafting a viable resource strategy. These pieces must fit together, and the assumptions embedded in them must be credible given the environment in which the social entrepreneur intends to operate. Finally, the requirements of the venture must fit the commitment, qualifications, and life stage of the entrepreneur considering it. When all these elements are feasible and aligned, the chances for success are relatively high and those involved can make a more informed estimate of the potential for social impact.

Strengthening the "Ecosystem" of Social Entrepreneurship

In the fall of 2006, the Center for the Advancement of Social Entrepreneurship (CASE) at Duke University, with the support of the Skoll Foundation, launched a groundbreaking project to identify opportunities for further building the field of social entrepreneurship, both as a field of practice and as a field of inquiry, knowledge, and learning related to that practice. The CASE team conducted in-depth interviews with eighty-five social entrepreneurs, funders, academics, consultants, journalists and authors, and others knowledgeable about the field. As a result of this study, CASE recommended a set of critical initiatives for strengthening the ecosystem in which the practice of social entrepreneurship takes place (CASE at Duke, 2008). By the term *ecosystem,* we refer to the environmental factors that affect the ability of social entrepreneurs to achieve their intended social impacts.

To inform its research, CASE developed a simplified framework to describe the key elements of this ecosystem. Figure 10.5 presents this framework, illustrating the richness and complexity of the environment in which social entrepreneurs operate and the various determinants of their effectiveness.

The elements of the ecosystem are presented in two broad categories. The first category consists of the resources, or types of "capital," social entrepreneurs depend on to do their work, including financial capital, human capital, intellectual capital, and social/political capital. Though social entrepreneurs can, to some extent, develop these forms of capital through their operations, most social entrepreneurs rely on outside organizations to help them get or build the capital they need. Note that these subcategories are broadly defined, including capital creators, providers, and related intermediaries. The second broad category includes the context-setting factors, or external conditions, that could support or undermine the practice of social entrepreneurship. These conditions are divided into four subcategories: policy and politics, media, economic and social conditions, and related fields. These factors tend to have their influence indirectly, and they are highly diverse. Each of these factors has the potential to affect social entrepreneurs, various players in the capital infrastructure, and the other context-setting factors.

Finding Key Leverage Points in the Ecosystem

During the CASE field-building study, nearly all interviewees identified inefficiencies and obstacles in the ecosystem and discussed how these might be remedied so that the potential of social entrepreneurship may be more fully realized. While all agreed that serious challenges exist for those who want to improve the ecosystem, most interviewees felt optimistic that these challenges could be met with creative solutions, dedicated attention, and increased collaboration. Based largely on suggestions made by participants in the field research, the CASE team identified five potential leverage points that are particularly crucial to address in order for the field to advance, and offered suggestions for moving forward on each of them.

FIGURE 10.5. ECOSYSTEM OF SOCIAL ENTREPRENEURSHIP.

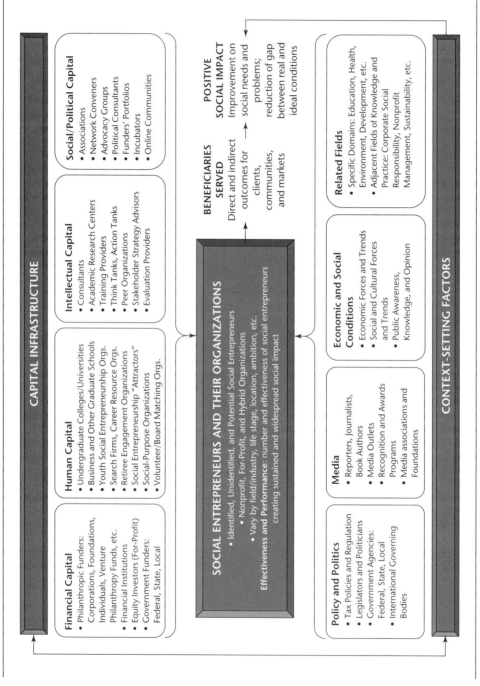

Source: Center for the Advancement of Social Entrepreneurship, Duke University, 2008. Reprinted with permission.

Making Financial Markets More Efficient and Responsive

In almost every interview for the CASE field-building study, participants identified the financial markets as a critical challenge for the field, agreeing that social sector capital markets are deficient in many ways. Funding is insufficient, especially to achieve scale, and the funding that is available often does not flow to its best uses (that is, the highest social return relative to the risk). Funders often do not know which use will produce the greatest benefits, and they seem to make their decisions based on factors that are not clearly related to performance. The financial markets for social ventures are full of inefficiencies. The search costs—the time and energy it takes to make the right match between social entrepreneurs and financiers—are high. The financial products, services, and terms of engagement often do not fit the needs of social entrepreneurs at different stages of development, or they impose burdensome conditions on the social entrepreneurs. Overall, social financial markets tend to be fragmented (often around different causes or interests), disjointed (different funders with different standards and requirements), and relatively small (compared to mainstream capital markets).

Those who want to strengthen the ecosystem for social entrepreneurs should consider doing or supporting the following:

- Develop specialized financial intermediaries who have the expertise to make sound funding decisions and the marketing skill to attract funding
- Create new financial "instruments" or "deal structures" designed to address the different kinds of business models and different stages of development
- Support high-quality, independent "analysts" to assess social ventures and provide platforms to distribute their reports to funders who would find them useful
- Experiment with more collaborative funding models in which major funders invest in each other's "deals," sharing the risks and the lessons
- Work toward common grant applications, requests for proposals, and reporting requirements for foundation funding
- Establish standardized tools for social entrepreneurs to track the information that would be relevant to funders
- Organize online information marketplaces to make it easier for social entrepreneurs and suitable funders to find each other more easily

Refining and Standardizing Performance Measurement Tools

Reliable, timely, and cost-effective measures of social value are crucial for demonstrating success, providing better information to the financial markets, and informing the strategic decisions of social entrepreneurs. Yet, social value is notoriously difficult to measure and to attribute to a specific intervention and many of the most important ways in which social entrepreneurs can make the world a better place are long-term, intangible, qualitative, not easily reduced to any single common metric. Funders, who have a crucial role in developing suitable systems and standards, and others seeking to drive progress in this area, may consider the following suggestions:

- Make social entrepreneurs aware of the different tools currently available, as well as the pros and cons of each
- Encourage use of and continued experimentation with impact-oriented performance measures by social entrepreneurs, making sure to include qualitative elements as well as signs, symptoms, and indicators of intangible and long-term impact
- Favor measurement systems that produce information that is valued by and useful to social entrepreneurs (usually including process measures as well as outcome measures for learning purposes)
- Distinguish what is publicly reported from what is available for internal, managerial use
- Reward candor, learning, and informed strategic adjustments, not just raw outcome performance
- Avoid the situation in which different funders impose significantly different and demanding measurement methodologies on a single organization
- Use intermediaries to design and implement external reporting standards in a way that provides the information that capital providers want in forms that are meaningful and engaging
- Make the values and assumptions behind any measurement scheme transparent and open to challenge
- Recognize that judgment is required and make sure performance data are accompanied by information that helps users make sensible judgments and comparisons

Helping Social Entrepreneurs Find Effective Pathways to Scale

In the CASE field research, nearly all interviewees seemed to agree that success for this field requires that social entrepreneurs ultimately achieve significant "scale" relative to the magnitude of the problems they tackling. The successful spread of innovations and the growth of social ventures in the past indicates that it is possible to achieve considerable impact even in this flawed ecosystem. Proponents need to help social entrepreneurs find viable paths to achieve scale and widespread impact.

Those who wish to improve the ability of social entrepreneurs to scale may want to

- Identify and document successful paths to achieving scale in an imperfect world, analyzing success stories and drawing on the best strategic thinking
- Encourage innovation in the scaling process and capture the lessons from the experiments
- Recognize that no one path fits all social ventures—each strategy needs to be designed for the circumstances at hand
- Provide social entrepreneurs and their teams with knowledge about different scaling strategies, frameworks for designing their own, and opportunities for learning with and from others struggling with the same issues
- Capture and share lessons learned along the way
- Refrain from overemphasizing the need to scale quickly, which may result in premature efforts to scale
- Acknowledge that not every "successful" local innovation or venture is scalable or worthy of scaling
- Acknowledge that the role of the founding social entrepreneur may change through the scaling process and that other talented individuals may be needed to play a leading role

Building New Talent Pipelines

In the business world, it is widely recognized that talent is the key to success. Venture capitalists know the importance of investing in high performing management teams. Business leaders see themselves in a "battle for talent." Human capital is no less important for the success of social entrepreneurs. The ecosystem needs new talent pipelines and development programs to prepare social entrepreneurs and their teams for the challenges of sustainability, scale, and the creation of new equilibria. Those who want to strengthen this part of the ecosystem should consider the following:

- Invest in programs that increase "hybrid" management and leadership skills, particularly those that address the needs of social entrepreneurs to scale their impact and sustain their ventures
- Support team-building efforts and educational programs that work with teams, rather than just individuals
- Facilitate peer learning, not only among social entrepreneurs, but also among members of the senior teams working with the social entrepreneurs
- Explore emerging talent pools such as those embarking on second careers

- Experiment with new approaches to draw on motivated talent from the business sector, adapt it to the needs of social entrepreneurs, and use it to develop internal capabilities
- Find ways to reward talented people who work in this field, through reasonable compensation and attractive (but rarely offered) benefits, such as pensions, health care, insurance, training, and paid sabbaticals
- Encourage suitable undergraduate and graduate programs (in business, public policy, education, social work, public health, environment, and engineering schools, and so on) to offer tracks that make it possible for students to develop hybrid skills

Providing Better Guidance on Effective Business Models

Social entrepreneurs will be successful only if their innovations are supported by sufficiently sustainable, scalable, and aligned business models. Greater attention to business model design could also force social entrepreneurs to think about how to mobilize the talent and knowledge they need on favorable and sustainable terms, perhaps through partnerships. Proponents of social entrepreneurship who want to strengthen the field should consider taking the following steps to strengthen social entrepreneurs' ability to develop robust and effective business models:

- Recognize that no single business model will work for all social entrepreneurs and that models drawn from the world of business may not be appropriate
- Support research efforts to develop better knowledge of alternative business models for social entrepreneurs and to frame some design principles
- Encourage experimentation with different business models, capturing the lessons from the experiments
- Provide strategic assistance to social entrepreneurs who have attractive innovations but business models that limit their potential in serious ways
- Develop funding schemes for foundations and social investors that encourage resource-smart business model redesign and help recipients make the transition to the new business models

These five issues—financial markets, performance measurement, scaling strategies, talent development, and business models—emerged as priorities as the CASE team analyzed the data from interviews and conversations. Addressing these issues could go a long way toward strengthening the ecosystem, assuring greater success of social entrepreneurs, and building the field.

Ecosystem Summary: Providing Support with Discipline

It is essential to create a supportive ecosystem for social entrepreneurs if the field is to thrive. By contrast, business entrepreneurs benefit from a very supportive ecosystem, particularly in the United States. Yet there is an important difference between business entrepreneurship and social entrepreneurship that should not be neglected—business entrepreneurs face significant market discipline from both customer markets and financial markets. Customers determine whether the good or service provided creates more value for them than it costs to produce. Investors determine if the venture is likely to provide sufficient returns to justify their investments. For social entrepreneurs, the ultimate test is social impact, and that value is not guaranteed by market discipline. We need other mechanisms.

If the ecosystem is to do its job of enhancing chances of success for the field as a whole, we must mimic this kind of market discipline, using the best measures and judgments available at the time. We need to create a healthy, vibrant ecosystem that supports innovative social entrepreneurs, but with appropriate discipline to assure that capital is directed to its best uses. Without some devices to filter out the under-performers, scarce forms of capital and other support will be spread among those who put it to good use and those who do not. Fortunately, a number of innovative and exciting efforts are under way to address these issues. Many in this field cautiously hope that the next five to ten years will bring about significant advances in the development of the field of social entrepreneurship. These advances could have a beneficial impact on the social sector as a whole.

Conclusion

"New concepts are introduced all the time. Some never catch on. Others experience great popularity for a period, but then decline and are viewed as passing fads. A few concepts have staying power and sustained impact. In rare cases, a new concept serves as a foundation for a whole new field of practice and knowledge. Social entrepreneurship has the potential to be one of those rare field-creating concepts" (CASE at Duke, 2008, p. v).

As elaborated in this chapter, social entrepreneurship is about crafting innovative and sustainable solutions to social problems. Fundamentally, effective social entrepreneurship is a learning process that combines a valid social impact theory with a supportive business model. Social entrepreneurs are innovative, resourceful, and results oriented. They draw upon the best thinking in both the business and nonprofit worlds to develop strategies that maximize their social impact. These entrepreneurial leaders operate across a broad spectrum of organizations: large and small; new and old; nonprofit, for-profit, and hybrid.

We are at an undeniably exciting time for the field of social entrepreneurship. Having experienced dramatic growth in recent years, social entrepreneurship has attracted strong interest from policymakers, philanthropists, aid agencies, and academics, despite the fact that it is still being developed and researched. However, many thoughtful observers, including advocates, are concerned that the recent momentum could fade or be undermined before a solid foundation is laid for the future of this emerging field. Success for the field will require a healthy institutional and social environment to support the practice. We refer to this as the "ecosystem of social entrepreneurship."

It is essential to create a supportive ecosystem for social entrepreneurs if the field is to thrive. By contrast, business entrepreneurs benefit from a very supportive ecosystem, particularly in the U.S. Yet, there is an important difference between business entrepreneurship and social entrepreneurship that should not be neglected—business entrepreneurs face significant "market discipline" that makes businesses efficient and helps assure they are creating something of value to their customers while also providing sufficient returns to investors. If the ecosystem of social entrepreneurship is to do its job of enhancing chances of success for the field as a whole, it must mimic this kind of market discipline, using the best measures and judgments available to assure that social entrepreneurs are using resources well to create impacts that are valuable to society.

We need to create a healthy, vibrant ecosystem that supports innovative social entrepreneurs, but with appropriate discipline to ensure that capital is directed to its best uses. Without some devices to filter out the under-performers, scarce resources will be spread among those who put it to good use and those who do not. Fortunately, a number of innovative and exciting efforts are underway to address these issues. Many in this field express cautious hope that the next decade will bring significant advances in the development of the field of social entrepreneurship. These advances could have a beneficial impact on the social sector as a whole.

Notes

1. We accept as the definition of corporate social entrepreneurship as "the process of extending the firm's domain of competence and corresponding opportunity set through innovative leveraging of resources, both within and outside its direct control, aimed at the simultaneous creation of economic and social value" (Austin, Leonard, Reficco, and Wei-Skillern, 2006).
2. For the purpose of this chapter, we have adopted the definition of *social enterprise* advanced by Kim Alter: "a socially oriented venture (nonprofit/for-profit or hybrid) created to solve a social problem or market failure through entrepreneurial private sector approaches that increase effectiveness and sustainability while ultimately creating social benefit or change" (Alter, 2005).

3. The content of this section is drawn from Bloom and Dees, 2008, and is reprinted with permission.

4. For an insightful discussion on building strong support networks, see Gergen and Vanourek, *Life Entrepreneurs: Ordinary People Leading Extraordinary Lives* (San Francisco: Jossey-Bass), 2008, pp. 111–128. The authors draw upon extensive interviews of successful business entrepreneurs and social entrepreneurs.

References

Alter, K. "Social Enterprise Definition." Virtue Ventures, 2005. Available at http://virtueventures.com.

Austin, J., Leonard, H., Reficco E., and Wei-Skillern, J. "Social Entrepreneurship: It Is for Corporations, Too." In *Social Entrepreneurship: New Models of Sustainable Social Change*, Alex Nicholls, (ed.). New York: Oxford University Press, 2006.

Bhide, A. V. *The Origin and Evolution of New Business Ventures*. New York: Oxford University Press, 2000.

Bloom, P. N., and Dees, J. G. "Cultivate Your Ecosystem." *Stanford Social Innovation Review*, Winter 2008, *6*(1), 46–53.

Bornstein, D. *How to Change the World: Social Entrepreneurs and the Power of New Ideas*. New York: Oxford University Press, 2004.

Byker, C., Stuart, C., Cohen, B., et al. (producers). *The New Heroes*. Video series. Oregon Public Broadcasting, 2005.

Campbell, K., and Haley, B. "Business Planning for Nonprofits: What It Is and Why It Matters." The Bridgespan Group, 2006.

CASE at Duke, "Developing the Field of Social Entrepreneurship," Center for the Advancement of Social Entrepreneurship, Duke University, the Fuqua School of Business, 2008.

Chesbrough, H. M., Ahern, S., Finn, M., and Guerraz, S. "Business Models for Technology in the Developing World: The Role of Non-Governmental Organizations." *California Management Review*, 2006, *48*(3).

Dees, J. G. *The Social Enterprise Spectrum: Philanthropy to Commerce*. Boston: Harvard Business School Publishing, Case # 9–396–343, 1996.

Dees, J. G. *The Meaning of Social Entrepreneurship*. Self-published essay. 1998b. Revised May 2001. Available at www.caseatduke.org/documents/dees_sedef.pdf.

Dees, J. G. "Taking Social Entrepreneurship Seriously." *Society*, 2007, *44*(3), 24–31.

Dees, J. G., and Anderson, B. B. "Framing a Theory of Social Entrepreneurship: Building on Two Schools of Practice and Thought." in *Research on Social Entrepreneurship: Understanding and Contributing to an Emerging Field*, Mosher-Williams, R. (ed.). Association for Research on Nonprofit Organizations and Voluntary Action, ARNOVA Occasional Paper Series, 2006, *1*(3), 41.

Dees, J. G., and Anderson, B. B. "For-Profit Social Ventures." In M. L. Kourilsky and W. B. Walstad (Eds.), *Social Entrepreneurship*. Dublin, Ireland: Senate Hall Academic Publishing. A special issue of the *International Journal of Entrepreneurship Education*, 2, 1–26, 2003.

Drayton, W., and MacDonald, S. *Leading Public Entrepreneurs*. Arlington, Va.: Ashoka: Innovators for the Public, 1993.

Drucker, P. *Innovation and Entrepreneurship*. New York: Harper & Row, 1985.

Elkington, J., and Hartigan, P. *The Power of Unreasonable People: How Social Entrepreneurs Create Markets That Change the World*. Boston: Harvard Business Press, 2008.

Gergen, C., and Vanourek, G. *Life Entrepreneurs: Ordinary People Leading Extraordinary Lives*. San Francisco: Jossey-Bass, 2008.

Guclu, A., Dees, J. G., and Anderson, B. B. "The Process of Social Entrepreneurship: Creating Opportunities Worthy of Serious Pursuit." Center for the Advancement of Social Entrepreneurship, Duke University, The Fuqua School of Business, 2002.

Grossman, A., and Curran, D. F. quoting Peter Szanton in, *EMCF: A New Approach at an Old Foundation*. Boston: Harvard Business School Publishing, Case # 9–302–090, 1990, p. 4.

Leviner, N., Crutchfield, L., and Wells, D. "Understanding the Impact of Social Entrepreneurs: Ashoka's Answer to the Challenge of Measuring Effectiveness." In *Research on Social Entrepreneurship: Understanding and Contributing to an Emerging Field*, Mosher-Williams, R. (ed.). Association for Research on Nonprofit Organizations and Voluntary Action, ARNOVA Occasional Paper Series, 2006, *1*(3), 93.

Light, P. *The Search for Social Entrepreneurship*. Washington, D.C.: Brookings Institution Press, 2008.

Martin, R., and Osberg, S. "Social Entrepreneurship: The Case for Definition." *Stanford Social Innovation Review*, Spring 2007, p. 29–39.

McGrath, R., and MacMillan, I. "Discovery-Driven Planning," *Harvard Business Review*, July-August 1995.

Porter, M. E. *Competitive Advantage: Creating and Sustaining Superior Performance*. New York: The Free Press, 1985.

Say, J. B. (1803). Traité d'économie politique, ou simple exposition de la manière dont se forment, se distribuent et se consomment les richesses (1st ed.). Paris: Deterville.

Schumpeter, J. A. *The Theory of Economic Development: An Inquiry into Profits, Capital, Credit, Interest, and the Business Cycle* (trans. Redvers Opie). Cambridge, Mass.: Harvard University Press, 1934.

Stevenson, H. H., and Gumpert, D. E. "The Heart of Entrepreneurship." *Harvard Business Review*, 1985, *63*(2), 85–95.

Vesper, K. "New Venture Ideas: Do Not Overlook the Experience Factor." *Harvard Business Review*, 1979.

PART THREE

MANAGING NONPROFIT OPERATIONS

Nonprofit organizations exist in a careful balance with their operating environments, and effective nonprofit organizations recognize the need to organize and carefully manage their exchanges with significant constituents and stakeholders. The first four chapters of this part of the handbook explore various facets of these relationships with the outside world. In the first chapter, Chapter Eleven, Brenda Gainer describes the process of nonprofit marketing and explains the most important ways in which nonprofits can use marketing concepts and skills to advance their impact. In Chapter Twelve Kathy Bonk provides information on a key way to operationalize this process and explains in depth the process by which strategic communications can be employed to effectively engage and communicate with key stakeholders. One of the most important and underutilized of exchange relationships is that of advocacy and lobbying. In Chapter Thirteen, Marcia Avner explains the advocacy process and discusses the most effective ways by which nonprofits can engage in formal governmental processes to influence to have an impact on legislation and policy. In the fourth of the chapters in this part, Chapter Fourteen, John A. Yankey and Carol K. Willen examine the increasingly common practice of developing intensive working relationships with other organizations and explain the most effective ways to advance mission accomplishment through collaboration and strategic alliances.

As various parties that engage in exchanges with nonprofit organizations have become increasingly concerned with accountability and evidence of performance, nonprofit organizations have been challenged to develop better ways to analyze program and organizational effectiveness. The final two chapters of Part Three explore the intersection of management and accountability. In Chapter Fifteen, John Clayton Thomas explains the processes by which program impact and outcomes can be assessed and describes tools to assess outcomes and evaluate programs. Questions about effectiveness and performance are not limited to the programs of the organization, however; nonprofit leaders must be concerned with questions of organization effectiveness as well. Organizational effectiveness is concerned with judgments about the overall performance of a nonprofit organization, typically including considerations of financial performance, community involvement, and other factors. In the final chapter of this part, Chapter Sixteen, Vic Murray explains the nature and dynamics of assessing nonprofit organizational effectiveness and suggests some useful ways of addressing the challenges.

CHAPTER ELEVEN

MARKETING FOR NONPROFIT ORGANIZATIONS

Brenda Gainer

Marketing has long been defined as the science of exchange (Bagozzi, 1975). In the for-profit sector, marketing is the management discipline that is focused on developing and maintaining exchange relationships with customers. In the nonprofit sector, marketing pertains not only to customers or clients but also to exchange relationships with a wide range of donors, funders, supporters, users, suppliers, partners, and adherents—as well as taxpayers and public opinion. Although the facilitation of exchanges with many of these groups is called by names other than "marketing" in nonprofit organizations (for example, fundraising, grant writing, volunteer and employee recruitment, program development, communications, or public relations), the marketing paradigm articulates an approach to value creation and exchange as being at the heart of an organization's interaction with and responsiveness to the individuals and institutions in its environment.

The conceptual framework upon which strategic marketing is based asserts that satisfying the needs and wants of key target groups through exchange results in organizational "success" (the achievement of the organization's goals). Research in the private sector has demonstrated that higher levels of organizational orientation toward the market are associated with performance outcomes such as return on investment (Narver and Slater, 1990). Of course in the nonprofit sector organizational goals comprise many complex ambitions beyond the simple goal of profitability that is paramount in the for-profit sector. Research on nonprofit organizations has shown that market orientation not only predicts success in attracting financial resources but is also associated with other important mission-based outcomes such as higher degrees of client satisfaction (Gainer and Padanyi, 2002). This supports the notion that a focus on value creation with respect to all the different stakeholder groups with which the organization interacts is at the heart of realizing its ambitions.

Because marketing theory was developed in the private sector and focuses directly on profitability derived from customers, controversy has existed for years among marketing scholars about the "boundaries" of marketing and whether its concepts and tools can be applied to the nonprofit sector (Parson et al., 2008). Hutton (2001) has argued that the customer metaphor is fundamentally incompatible with an organization charged with the mission of social value creation. Nevertheless, prominent marketing scholars have argued that the marketing paradigm is extremely relevant to conceptualizing the relationship of the nonprofit organization to its environment (Andreasen and Kotler, 2008; Sargeant and Wymer, 2007).

However, in the field there often remains a very limited view of what marketing entails. Marketing is often implemented primarily in terms of a few key marketing subfields such as communications or public relations and associated with information, education, and persuasion processes. As a result of this narrow conceptualization of marketing, the value that a strategic marketing "mindset" can contribute at the leadership level to overall organization performance and success is often less than it could be.

In the for-profit sector, marketing is associated with both resource attraction and resource allocation—marketing is used to influence customers to buy products and services (resource attraction) and it is also the functional area that ultimately decides which products and services will be developed in order to attract those sales (resource allocations). Perhaps because of this reciprocal relationship between the resource attraction and resource allocation functions of marketing in the private sector, acceptance of marketing as a component of high-level strategic management and leadership in the nonprofit sector has been controversial. There has been an assumption that organizations that respond to "market forces" will drift away from a focus on their mission because they will begin to allocate funds to the development of "market-driven" programs associated with resource attraction in preference to "mission-driven" programs associated with resource allocation.

However, although occasionally conflict may arise in nonprofits over decisions with respect to the "market" for resources and the "mission" associated with expenditures, these constructs are not dichotomous opposites nor mutually exclusive. The adoption of a strategic marketing mindset in a nonprofit organization does not mean that financial considerations will take precedence over operations or that devoting resources to marketing will erode spending on programs. Instead the implementation of the marketing concept and the development in the nonprofit sector of what has been called a "market orientation" in the private sector will mean that the nonprofit organization becomes more responsive to the wants and needs of the multiplicity of stakeholder groups with which it interacts—as well as to society more generally (Sargeant, Foreman, and Liao, 2002).

In the for-profit sector, marketing is the means through which firms engage in transactions with customers that are based on an exchange of value. Successful firms are those that are able to understand the needs and wants of their customers better than their competitors. In the nonprofit sector, marketing is based on a similar notion, although vastly more complicated in execution.

First, those who provide revenues to the firm are not often "customers" buying goods or services. Therefore the "value exchange" is often nonmonetary— though nonetheless valuable. For example, in exchange for financial contributions, labor (paid and unpaid), political support, or behavioral change, a nonprofit organization may provide achievement, inclusion, sociability, status, skills, social networks, advocacy, enactment of public policy, and—extremely difficult to measure but nonetheless very "real" in terms of value—better communities and a better world.

And second, in nonprofit marketing, the idea of multiparty as opposed to dyadic, or two-party, exchange is critical. There are many more constituencies with which a nonprofit organization engages in exchange transactions than "customers." Those for whom programs are designed are not always those who support the organization and even if earned revenue is substantial, resources are almost always attracted from a variety of sources (Young, 2006). The key concept here is that in each of the "markets" in which a nonprofit organization transacts, the notion of value exchange applies—government funders are looking for a means of implementing public policies and volunteers are looking for skill development, social engagement, or a way to contribute meaningful activity to their community. If a nonprofit organization wants to be successful in attracting resources, it will have to deliver sufficient value to the providers of those resources while providing value to the different constituencies that "consume" those resources.

Of course in practice, as an organization attempts to devote limited financial and human resources to the creation of value for all of the various constituencies that form the context in which it is embedded, conflict may emerge. A strategic marketing approach will not dictate that resources go to the "market" as opposed to the "mission" but it will provide a logical and defensible framework for analysis and planning that can lead to the most efficient *and* effective use of resources to build long-term organizational success, defined as the organization's ability to achieve its mission over the long-term. A marketing approach is based on the recognition that nonprofit organizations must be responsive to many different constituencies, understand the unique needs and wants of each, and take steps to create the tangible and intangible value that will form the basis of stable, sustainable, long-term exchange relationships.

The long-term quality of the relationship between an organization and its exchange partners is coming to be recognized as more important than using marketing techniques and tools to trigger isolated transactions (Conway, 1997). It is becoming increasingly important to consider the "lifetime" value of a client in the nonprofit sector because long-term relationships are associated with lower costs over time (Brennan and Brady, 1999). It is particularly difficult to continue investing in long-term relationships in organizations whose revenues are unpredictable from year to year and, moreover, are under substantial pressure to spend as much money as possible on programs and services and not on fundraising or recruitment or other kinds of "administrative" expenses. A marketing analysis based on value exchange would suggest, however, that investments in long-term relationships pay off not only in terms of cutting costs that come from "losing" clients and then having to pay more later to attract new ones, but also from the ability to move long-term relationships to higher levels of value exchange.

It is through marketing research that nonprofit leaders come to understand the needs of the people and institutions on which the organization depends and it is through marketing analysis that they develop appropriate responses to those needs that lead to engagement in meaningful relationships through which both parties—the organization and its stakeholders—achieve greater value. I begin this chapter with an exposition of this basic framework and the concepts and theories that underpin a strategic approach to nonprofit markets and marketing. In the second part of the chapter I examine the four primary subfields of marketing (programs and products, communications, pricing, and distribution) and the key models, tools, and techniques that have been developed to apply marketing thinking to nonprofit operations.

The Strategic Marketing Framework

In order to understand the markets with which a nonprofit organization interacts, research is required. Research will allow an organization to identify the potential groups of people or institutions it wishes to engage and also to clarify what other choices or alternatives exist that may also serve their needs. With this information about the market, decisions can be made about which groups it makes the most sense to serve or to target, based on analysis of the possible clienteles, the competitive situation, the human and financial resources that are available, and the organization's mission. Once these strategic choices have been made, an organization can develop a marketing mix of appropriate programs and services, communications, pricing, and delivery systems that will maximize the exchange potential with its target markets.

This strategic marketing approach—a step-by-step process which is based on both research and analysis—is mapped in Figure 11.1. The boxes in the diagram represent decisions an organization needs to make about what target markets to serve, how to position the organization and its value against alternatives, and what kind of marketing mix will serve those markets best. All of the inputs to the decision processes mapped in this chart are based on an understanding of an organization's constituencies developed through market research. It should be noted that the analytical process used to develop marketing strategies will be applied to each "market" that a nonprofit organization interacts with—for example, segmentation, the first decision point at the top of the chart, will be done differently depending on whether marketing to donors, clients, volunteers, or the general public is under consideration.

FIGURE 11.1. THE STRATEGIC MARKETING PROCESS.

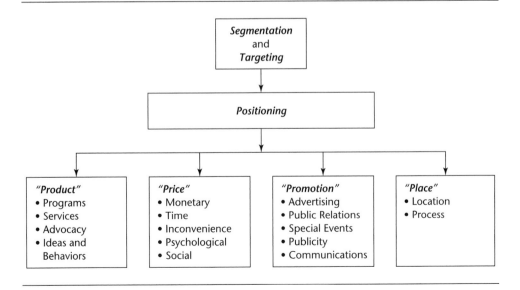

The Role of Research in the Marketing Process

Formal market research in nonprofit enterprises is quite rare and usually limited to the larger fundraising organizations (universities, colleges, hospitals, and some of the large medical research and service organizations). The cost of research is often prohibitive, but there are other reasons that nonprofits are reluctant to undertake research. One is that many nonprofit organizations are convinced that they already understand their markets and what they need, a notion that results from the fact that many nonprofits offer services provided by highly trained and specialized professionals such as social workers, psychologists, educators, artists, scientists, or medical personnel. Market studies may appear unwarranted because the service deliverer seems to be in a better position than the user to specify the appropriate service or program. The service deliverer may see it as a duty to prescribe what services the other party should receive. Other reasons that many nonprofit organizations fail to see value in research is that they often operate on a small scale and know the individuals with whom they interact personally, they deal with end users directly as opposed to through intermediaries, and many of the transactions in which they engage with clients provide substantial personal information already. For example, organizations that sell tickets or accept donations or hold raffles or lotteries may collect personal information as part of that exchange, which can then be "mined" to yield information on market segmentation.

Although formal market research may be expensive and therefore conducted infrequently, there is a wealth of information that already exists in many nonprofits that can provide highly useful insights. For example, many organizations could easily collect and organize in a more systematic way information that they are already receiving through frontline staff such as receptionists, counselors, nurses, box office attendants, or community workers. Nonprofits can also rely on publicly available secondary data sources such as the United Way or municipal governments or national statistical agencies (Moyer, 1994). Nonprofits occasionally undertake joint projects with organizations with a common interest—these research consortia may include government, university, foundation, and nonprofit sector partners with a common interest in large-scale issues such as immigrant and refugee settlement, capacity building and leadership succession, housing, or poverty.

It is important that nonprofit organizations undertake some form of research if only to combat organizational myopia that stems from being too close to an issue and, more important, to a particular organizational culture that has defined the external environment in a particular way. Research is a way to engage in critical thinking about an issue and the people involved with it; it allows managers and leaders to look at questions from different perspectives and to reframe issues. For example, despite the fact that there is a widely held belief that corporate donations are motivated by a "bottom line" perspective, research on corporations suggests that their primary motive for supporting or partnering with charities is philanthropic (Gan, 2006; Sargeant and Stephenson, 1997; Young, 2003). This enduring finding suggests that advertising benefits may not be as important to corporations as we have thought and that opening opportunities for corporations and their employees to engage in service delivery may actually result in larger and more sustained support. With regard to clients, it has been suggested that because clients and funders are separate constituencies in nonprofit organizations, there is no direct feedback loop as in the private sector—a gap that can lead to poor-quality service over long periods (Connor, 1999). Moreover, when clients are ill-served, their remedies may be few and frail. Clients of many social or community service organizations are more likely to be disadvantaged and vulnerable, to have fewer opportunities to switch to other providers, and to be more afraid of complaining. Anonymous and confidential research may give these important stakeholders opportunities to provide information that should be part of nonprofit organizations' decision processes.

Segmentation and Target Marketing

Target marketing is the process whereby decisions are made about which groups an organization will choose to serve within specific markets. For example, in the market for donations, an organization may divide individual donors into several groups, such as board members, former clients (for example, students, audience members, patients, and so on), prominent philanthropists, and people who may be affected by the cause at some time in the future. Organizational resources will not usually allow a nonprofit to target all of these segments, so decisions need to be made about which market segments best fit the organization's objectives and abilities and then how to tailor marketing programs to create the most value for each of the chosen segments.

Choosing to "target" certain groups while ignoring others may seem a questionable, if not unacceptable, approach in the nonprofit sector. Choosing some segments means not choosing others—which is to say that focusing on some people means not serving or communicating with others. In a field in which turning no one away or achieving mass social change is often a cherished norm, neglecting some possible clients as a matter of policy can seem to degrade fundamental organizational values.

However, the case for target marketing is both strong and responsible. In an environment in which human needs are escalating while resources are constrained and shrinking, no organization can reach all possible constituencies. The question then is not whether the enterprise will constrain its domain, but how. Market segmentation allows nonprofit organizations to control whom they serve by choosing where they will be most effective, based on their competencies, or where it is most important for them to act, according to organizational mandate or mission, and to spend limited resources efficiently, as opposed to letting the limits of their funding arbitrarily decide which markets they cannot serve when they run out of funds. Segmentation helps an organization focus its resources on the clienteles that best fit its mission, capabilities, and aspirations.

The first step in segmentation is to divide the market into meaningful groups. Segments are considered meaningful when they are "homogeneous within, heterogeneous without." This means that the people or organizations within a segment are considered to behave the same way in response to particular marketing programs, and differently from people in other segments. There are a number of variables that may be used to define segments. The most conventional are demographic, geographic, and socioeconomic. These variables are convenient because available data are most often arrayed along these lines, and they serve as useful surrogates for deeper psychological and behavioral motivations that marketers cannot always access.

Other data, although more difficult to collect and interpret, can often provide a more nuanced approach to segmentation. Psychographics, based on information about lifestyles, values, attitudes, and opinions, can be particularly important in segmenting for social marketing efforts designed to change attitudes and behaviors. Personality variables such as empathy and self-esteem have been suggested as useful segmentation variables for recruiting volunteers (Wymer, 1997). Benefit segmentation is efficacious because, being rooted in the fundamental notion of market exchange, it not only identifies homogeneous client clusters but also is suggestive of the most relevant offer for each. Benefit segmentation is useful in volunteer marketing and is also used to good effect in fundraising. Usage segmentation (heavy versus light users) is relevant to many causes; heavy users are especially propitious targets.

Finally, because marketing aims ultimately to consummate exchanges, the marketer may find it logical and advantageous to cluster people or organizations by how they respond to marketing variables. For example, if some potential donors are moved by sympathy for people who have a given disease while others react to a warning that they may contract it, a segmentation scheme that identifies these as two separate groups may be warranted. In a case such as this, the decision will be made on the basis of whether the expected reward from appeals tailored more specifically to the needs of individual groups will outweigh the costs associated with developing multiple campaigns.

In choosing which segments to target, several criteria come into play. The first, of course, is whether a particular segment fits the mission of the enterprise. A second test is whether the segment aligns with the organization's capabilities. In appraising the goodness of fit of a potential target market with an organization's capabilities, organizations must be careful not to overvalue their own capabilities and underestimate the strengths and competencies of competitors.

A third criterion is whether the segment is sufficiently large to justify a special marketing treatment. Arriving at an answer to this question can be complicated in the nonprofit sector. In a commercial firm, the projected value of a superior return from an investment in a unique marketing program is usually the only arbiter of acceptable segment size. In a charitable enterprise, financial considerations may be overridden. This may be acceptable if the organization is able to cross-subsidize special programs through revenues from more "profitable" segments but not if the loss associated with serving small segments endangers the survival of the organization.

A final consideration in target selection is whether particular segments can be accessed by special marketing programs. Often targets are difficult to estimate and the members are hard to reach through specialized marketing programs. Ideally, the idea of targeting specific markets is to use a "rifle" approach in which only the specified clients are reached by specialized media, messages, pricing, and so forth, but it is often necessary, and more economical, to use a "shotgun" campaign, which targets a mass market and leaves it to members of the target population to "come into the market" through a process of self-selection.

Competition, Positioning, and Branding

Competition is an idea that is often troubling in the nonprofit sector. Adherents of economic theories of the nonprofit sector that consider these organizations to have developed out of market failure argue that nonprofit organizations respond to need and do not compete. Often there is a philosophical aversion to the idea of competition on the part of those who work in the nonprofit sector, who would prefer to think of the nonprofit sector as being engaged in cooperative, as opposed to competitive, behavior.

Nevertheless, competition is a reality in the nonprofit sector (Oster, 1995). In many countries the number of nonprofit organizations has exploded, and many of them have been founded specifically because they intend to provide alternative programs or philosophies to the offerings of existing organizations.

Moreover, many nonprofit organizations are trying to influence attitudes and behavior and their target markets always have choices about how they think and behave—even if it means continuing with their old habits and patterns.

Positioning refers to the place that an agency occupies in the minds of the individuals in its target market (Trout and Rivkin, 1997). It is always related to how an organization and its offerings are evaluated in terms of the set of alternatives (or competition) known to those in the target market. The first step in developing a positioning strategy involves understanding the dimensions that the target market used to compare organizations and alternatives, and the second seeks to place the alternatives, relative to each other, in the space defined by those dimensions. For example, if potential clients evaluate immigrant-serving organizations along the dimensions of "multiple service offerings" and "effectiveness in service outcomes," different settlement organizations would be placed in different positions on a grid formed with the two dimensions as axes (see Figure 11.2).

One of the troubling realities of positioning in the nonprofit sector is that the multiple constituencies with which organizations interact often evaluate

FIGURE 11.2. POSITIONING MAP FOR HYPOTHETICAL IMMIGRANT-SERVING AGENCIES.

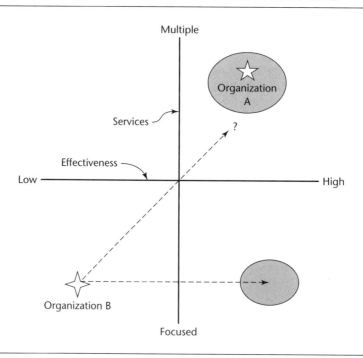

both the dimensions that they use to compare agencies and the position of individual agencies along those dimensions differently. For example, wealthy potential donors may compare arts organizations in terms of the service and opportunities for recognition that they provide to their major patrons, while government granting agencies that support artistic work may compare the same organizations on different dimensions such as originality or creativity. It may also happen that different market constituencies use the same dimensions but evaluate competitors differently. Both clients and foundations officials may evaluate and compare social service agencies in terms of their effectiveness, but clients may evaluate a particular agency as highly effective while a funder may rate the same agency low on effectiveness. The key point is that positioning refers to the dimensions and the relative positions along those dimensions that are in the minds of *each* clientele with which the marketing organization interacts. A nonprofit organization that serves several clienteles (donors, clients, foundation funders) will develop a unique map for each market constituency that will dictate a unique strategy for each separate clientele.

Of course the grids cannot be mapped unless the perceptions of the target markets are known, and the best way to collect this information is through some form of market research. However, even a dispassionate and objective "back of the envelope" grid can be mapped without expensive data if managers are willing to talk to their potential audiences and listen to what they say about the evaluative dimensions that matter to them and how they see the alternatives before them in terms of these dimensions.

Once an organization has determined its positioning, the next step is to develop a positioning strategy. Positioning is based on the key marketing idea of *differentiation*—in other words, an organization is positioned on the grid on the basis of how it differs from its competitors on the dimensions of interest. The important thing to notice about Figure 11.2 is that even if an organization has given no thought to positioning and is not interested in the process, it is still positioned on the grid in the minds of its target market.

An organization may choose to maintain its current position by continuing to emphasize those factors that differentiate it in positive ways or it may choose to emphasize characteristics that would differentiate it in more positive ways by using elements of the marketing mix to move to a more advantageous position on the grid. In either case, it is important to keep in mind that not all competitors should plan to locate themselves in the same position on the grid (different segments will be located in different places in accordance to their particular preferences). The trick is to find a group of sufficient size who wants a particular combination of attributes and evaluate whether a particular organization has the capacity to serve them better than the alternatives.

In Figure 11.2 the shaded circles represent the size of market segments and their preferences. We can see that Organization A is well positioned and Organization B is not. What should Organization A's strategy be? It should continue to emphasize the fact that it offers "one stop shopping" (multiple services) and that it is effective in delivering desired outcomes. What should Organization B's strategy be? This organization has two choices: it must definitely improve the public perception of its effectiveness, but instead of adding more programs and services in order to move up and serve the segment located in the upper right quadrant, where it would have to compete directly with Organization A, it would be better off to target the segment in the lower right quadrant interested in, say, effective language training but not particularly looking for job training, child counseling, or computer training. It should also be noted that there may be several ways that it could "move" to the right on the grid and target the segment we see there. It may be that this organization is, in fact, highly effective but that is not well known. In that case a communications or advertising strategy would be effective in "moving" the organization to the right. If, on the other hand, the organization has not had a record of high achievement in language training, it will need to change or improve its programs in order to increase the perception of its effectiveness in this area.

An important marketing idea related to positioning is branding. A brand is a shortcut means of identifying an organization, program, or cause in a way that differentiates it from alternatives. It embodies a set of characteristics that external communities believe will be delivered consistently. It can convey the organization's position in the market, build trust between the organization and its clienteles, raise an organization's profile, and provide insulation from competition (Ritchie, Swami and Weinberg,1999).

Branding has recently become a popular concept among nonprofit organizations. There are particular challenges to branding in the third sector. First, branding can absorb considerable financial resources because of the advertising required to develop and sustain the brand. Second, to create a successful brand is not primarily an advertising task—every element of the organization must support the ideas that the brand is trying to communicate. This means that "buy-in" across all functional areas and at all organizational levels must occur and that it must involve more than inventing a logo or a tagline and rest upon concrete results in changing service delivery modes and program elements to be consistent with the brand image. Third, in global or large national organizations with multiple branches with a high degree of local autonomy, it can be very difficult to standardize not only advertising materials but also organizational cultures and decision making around the values inherent in the brand (Quelch and Laidler-Kylander, 2006).

Managing the Marketing Mix

Having chosen target markets through a thoughtful approach to segmentation and determined a positioning strategy on the basis of competitive analysis, the marketing organization is in a position to use the tactical elements of the marketing mix to facilitate exchange relationships with its chosen targets by offering them better value than alternatives. Value is the ratio of benefits to costs and this, of course, includes not only material benefits and financial costs but also intangible benefits (for example, experience, status, social networks) and costs (time, inconvenience, hard work). In other words, value is often a perceptual construct.

Marketers, in an excessive devotion to alliteration, sometimes define the elements of the marketing mix as the 4 P's, namely product, place, price, and promotion. None of these is a very exact term. In the nonprofit sector, *product* is the element of the marketing mix that refers to services, programs, advocacy, or ideas for which the organization wants to find users or supporters. *Place* refers to choices about distribution channels; *price* refers to all of the costs, tangible and intangible, that are considered by potential exchange partners; and *promotion* extends well beyond a technical definition of promotion to include all marketing communications.

Product Marketing in the Nonprofit Sector

The marketing of physical products, although it occurs in the nonprofit sector, is relatively uncommon. Instead most nonprofit organizations are engaged in service marketing, social marketing (behaviors and ideas), or both. Physical products such as items in a thrift store, baked goods in a sheltered kitchen, or merchandise offered to those who buy membership is relatively easy for potential clients to evaluate. The same is not true of services such as literacy programs or home care for senior citizens, and it is even more difficult for potential supporters to evaluate such intangibles as anti-racism, a political candidate, or recycling.

Programs, Services, Behaviors, and Ideas

Some of the key differences between marketing products and marketing services are well documented in the marketing literature. Services are generally considered to be harder for users to evaluate, harder to control in terms of standardization of quality, and impossible to inventory, all of which poses greater challenges for organizations in the nonprofit sector who are service producers. Recently scholars have also defined some of the key features that distinguish social marketing from product and service marketing: it is often controversial (for example, safe sex, gay and lesbian rights, the banning of "obscene" art), it is often deeply embedded in individuals' lives, cultures, and psyches (for example, racial prejudice, overeating, corporal punishment of children), and it often involves target markets that are entire populations (for example, changing to the metric system) or subsets of populations that are pitted against each other (for example, ownership of handguns, support of political parties) (Kotler and Lee, 2007; Andreasen, 2006).

All of this suggests that the "product" markets in which most nonprofit organizations typically engage are the most complex and challenging in which to succeed. Further challenges to making effective decisions about "product marketing" are posed by the internal circumstances of most nonprofit organizations. First, because competition is often considered to be weak or nonexistent, it is difficult to make a case for spending resources on research about market preferences or about new programs or services. In addition, where a case can be made for upgrading, downgrading, or eliminating a program, internal deliberations can be complicated by the attachment of founders, directors, funders, staff, or volunteers to preserving or protecting certain programs at the expense of other priorities. Underlying all of these obstacles to timely and rational planning of the "product line" is the absence of a market mechanism to arbitrate disagreements as to the proper adding, dropping, or changing of nonprofit programs. This can lead to extreme waste of resources as sentiment about heritage programs can outweigh a focus on overall organizational effectiveness in terms of goal attainment. Most nonprofit organizations, especially larger ones but even small ones to some extent, are an assemblage of enterprises. Such organizations confront decisions not unlike those of a corporation that must determine which product lines to promote, maintain, or drop.

Portfolio analysis is a formal analytical process that is useful in allocating limited resources for maximum effectiveness in a nonprofit organization. Essentially portfolio analysis identifies the main programs of an organization, establishes a set of criteria for judging the relative importance of these units, and evaluates each program against those criteria. Matrix models are often used to conceptualize and manage the decision processes inherent in portfolio analysis. Individual criteria can be clustered to produce a summary evaluation of the contribution of each program to the organization's goals on two or three key dimensions. Often one of the dimensions used to evaluate a particular program is "contribution to (or centrality of) mission" and others may be such factors as the size and growth of the market it serves, its quality and reputation, community need, contribution to revenue, or the likelihood of breaking even. The summary appraisals are often mapped visually in a grid that yields a convenient visual representation (MacMillan, 1983) or fitted into a table in which "scores" are assigned to each program on each dimension and then summed.

The Product Life Cycle

Programs, services, and policies need to be constantly reappraised over the course of their lives as the environment in which they are developed changes. Important changes that affect nonprofit sector "products" are the entry of new services or service providers, the emergence of new community needs, and the loss of a major source of funding. A tool that has been useful in terms of understanding and managing the lifecycles of nonprofit causes, organizations, and specific programs and services is the product life cycle, based on the similarity of a marketplace to an ecological environment. The product life cycle (PLC) is visually represented as an S-shaped curve mapped against two axes: in a nonprofit context the curving line represents the number of "exchanges" that take place as a program or service or organization engaged in market relationships over time. Verbal models divide this evolution into stages of introduction, growth, maturity, and decline and the curve rises rapidly in the introductory and growth stages but flattens dramatically in the mature stage of the life cycle.

Each phase of the PLC not only describes changes in both clients and competitors at different stages of evolution but also prescribes useful changes in marketing strategies to maximize the number of marketing exchanges at each phase. As shifts in the awareness, demand, and behavior of clients and the pressures of competitors emerge over time, nonprofit organizations need to change the elements of their marketing mix in order to achieve maximum effectiveness in terms of mission achievement. One of the most important insights from the PLC for nonprofits is that an organization that is offering a relatively new program may grow quickly in the early stage with little investment in communications or strategic positioning. However, as its success attracts more clients and competitors and the market reaches maturity, nonprofits will have to devote more resources to competing for clients and funding and can expect the ratio of revenues to costs to decline substantially. Although in the for-profit sector this would lead to a "shake out" in which firms leave the market, in the nonprofit sector this may suggest that mergers or partnerships are indicated (Gainer, 1989).

Adoption and Diffusion

In guiding products through their life cycles, particularly the "behavioral" products characteristic of social marketing, nonprofit organizations can also take advantage of what is known about how innovations are adopted and diffused throughout populations. Sociologists have discovered that new ways of thinking and behaving are accepted by certain groups of people within a population first and that subsequent groups join in only after others have gone ahead. This diffusion process is represented visually by a "bell curve" diagram with "time" on the horizontal axis. Innovators or opinion leaders are represented by the small tail on the left, followed, as time passes, by a larger group of people known as early adopters. As the curve rises toward its peak more and more people, eventually constituting the majority of the population, adopt the behavior or ideas. As the curve slopes downward again, the late adopters and finally the laggards are converted.

The implications of a model like this for nonprofit organizations are clear. One of the aspects of diffusion is that special interest should be directed toward finding and persuading those who are likely to be active and influential at the outset of the life cycle of a new idea or behavior. Rogers (1995) has generalized that compared to those who "get on board" later, early adopters in a social system tend to be younger, of higher social status, financially better off, more plugged into impersonal and cosmopolitan information sources, and in closer contact with the origins of new ideas. The model not only suggests that it is important to reach these people early in the process of developing new programs or behavior but also that it is a waste of organizational resources to target people who are more likely to be in the majority or late adopter categories—even if these are the people who are particularly important to reach. Even if the target market most closely aligned with organizational mission is older, more conservative, and of lower socioeconomic status, it is unlikely that a new idea of behavior will be adopted by this group until it has become more widely diffused in the general population.

Pricing in the Nonprofit Sector

Too often in nonprofit organizations, prices (including a decision to deliver goods or services at no fee, as in, say, a food bank or a crisis center) are set in arbitrary and casual ways. Moreover, prices are often set on the basis of attitudes or beliefs such as that services of a nonprofit organization should always be delivered free or that the target market cannot afford to pay anything when this is not necessarily the case. Many nonprofit organizations need to revisit their pricing policies on the basis of objective research into the needs and means of the target markets and decide whether they are accepting an unnecessary loss of revenue—and, as a result, perhaps accepting a diminution of available benefits to their clients. Moreover, as more and more nonprofits address the revenue crises they face through activities associated with social enterprise, they are going to be setting prices in a competitive marketplace. For these reasons, pricing decisions in the nonprofit sector need to be made in a logical and analytical manner.

Reducing Nonfinancial Costs: A "Value" Approach to Pricing. Before describing useful approaches to setting monetary prices, it is worthwhile considering that the "price" of using a service or accepting an idea or adopting a behavior will include nonfinancial costs. Such nonfinancial costs might include awkwardness or embarrassment, time costs such as missing work or having to travel to remote and difficult locations, ancillary financial costs such as having to pay for parking or child care, or psychological costs associated with giving up familiar or pleasurable habits.

A marketing perspective would put forward the idea that before putting resources into promoting a service or a behavior, one should search out opportunities to reduce each of these costs. A "value" approach to pricing would suggest that customers compare the benefits they receive for the costs they incur. Lowering the costs to the clientele, including nonfinancial costs, can thus increase the value of the offering substantially. Increasing the value of a product by cutting social, psychological, and time costs may be particularly important in a situation where the organization is about to start charging for a service that has previously been free.

Pricing Objectives. If an organization has made the decision to set a financial price for the first time or to revisit existing pricing policies, one of the first considerations is to get a clear sense of the organization's pricing objectives. There are a number of pricing objectives; for enterprises that are designed to raise money to cross-subsidize mission-based programs (such as museum shops), profit maximization may be the dominant goal. In other cases the goal may be cost recovery—in other words, instead of aiming for profits that can be used to subsidize other programs or services, the goal is to be able to offer services or programs so that their costs are covered by the people who use them. Cost recovery is used in situations where an organization does not have the capacity or the desire to raise funds for certain programs from grants or donations. Setting prices according to "ability to pay" is also a scheme used by many nonprofits that use sliding scales based on income; objectives here are cost recovery but also social justice. Other social aims that may modify pricing schemes developed solely on the basis of profit maximization or cost recovery are such considerations as not wanting to discourage use, be considered elitist or exclusive, be thought insensitive, or incur charges of unfair competition from private sector suppliers of similar services.

Pricing Strategies

Cost-Based Pricing. One of the easiest pricing strategies to understand and implement is cost-based pricing. The only complication in calculating the costs of services or programs is when an organization has a portfolio of multiple programs and decisions need to be made about the allocation of costs that are incurred jointly to individual programs (such as the rent paid for common facilities, or the executive director's salary). As when diverse products come out of a single factory, an organization needs to arrive at a basis for allocating charges that seems rational under the circumstances (see Chapter Twenty-two for details about cost allocation methods). Once a method of cost allocation has been developed, it is a simple matter to calculate the total cost of providing a particular program within an organization.

However, setting the price to charge each client who accesses that program is a more complicated matter. One of the most crucial pieces of information needed for this decision is a break-even analysis. This analysis takes into account how many "units" would have to be "sold" at a given price in order to cover all costs to produce it. One begins by separating expenses that vary with the number of clients (variable costs) from costs that are fixed regardless of how many people access the service or program (fixed costs).

For example, if we think of a language class for new immigrants, it is clear that printing costs for handout materials vary according to how many people sign up for the class (variable costs), whereas the cost for the instructor's salary and the cost for the classroom space and heat and light (allocated as above) are the same regardless of how many people are in the class (fixed costs).

A second important pricing concept is that of "contribution per unit." To develop a concrete example, consider that the class described above has variable printing costs of $200 per person for handouts and fixed costs of $1750 for the teacher and $750 allocated for the room, light, and heat. The contribution per unit will be calculated by comparing the expected revenue per student (say we are considering a price of $250) and the variable cost per student (which is $200 for printing). The difference between these two amounts is how much we get from each student that will go to covering the fixed costs. Here our contribution per student is $50.

With this figure, we can calculate how many students we need to attract to this course to "break even" or, in other words, cover all of the fixed and variable costs. The break-even calculation would be done as follows:

$$
\begin{aligned}
\text{Break-even volume} &= \frac{\text{Fixed costs}}{\text{Contribution per unit}} \\
&= \frac{\text{Fixed costs}}{\text{Price} - \text{variable cost per unit}} \\
&= \frac{\text{Instructor fee} + \text{rent}}{\text{Student fee} - \text{cost of printing per person}} \\
&= \frac{\$2500}{\$250 - \$200} \\
&= 50 \text{ students}
\end{aligned}
$$

In other words to break even, we need to attract 50 students to this course.

What if it appears that this is very unlikely? What if the organization's experience or knowledge of its target market suggests that fewer students might attend? A series of calculations can be performed that indicate to organizers what fee they would have to charge to break even at different levels of participation. For example, the calculation below would indicate what fee would have to be charged to break even if they only expect 25 participants.

$$\text{Break-even fee} = \frac{\text{Total cost}}{\text{Number of participants}}$$
$$= \frac{\text{Fixed costs} + \text{variable costs}}{\text{Number of participants}}$$
$$= \frac{\$2500 + (25 \times \$200)}{25}$$
$$= \$300$$

The question then would be whether $300 is a price that the intended participants would pay. If it is, then $300 is the price that they need to charge to recover their full costs. If it that seems unlikely that 25 people in the target market would be able to attend (that is, that a fee of $300 would depress attendance), then the organizers know that they will have to charge less than this amount to get the attendance they think is important. This calculation tells them exactly how much extra money they would have to find to subsidize this program or how much they would have to reduce from their variable costs.

Demand-Based Pricing. Note that whereas the organization began with costs to calculate the break-even price, it was soon led to consider how prospective clients would respond to that price. This example demonstrates that it is critically important to understand the concept of *break even* in order to plan fundraising or grant-writing efforts, but that it is equally important to understand that cost analysis is linked to demand analysis when actually setting prices. A useful concept in analyzing demand is that of elasticity. Price elasticity is the responsiveness of demand to changes in price. When a large change in price causes little change in demand, demand is said to be "price inelastic." When a small change in price causes big changes in demand, the demand curve is said to be elastic at that point. In general, inelastic demand means that an organization can increase revenues by raising prices, whereas elastic demand means that it is best to avoid price increases and, if the goal is to expand the number of users of a product or service, to lower prices. Clearly knowledge of the elasticity of demand can be helpful in deciding whether to initiate user fees and at what level to set them.

Elasticity of demand may vary dramatically across market segments. That variability invites different prices for different segments. The differential pricing of seats in a theater, the offering of lower-priced services for students or seniors, and the subsidization of some children in a camp all represent pricing schemes that recognize and respond to differing demand elasticities. Of course differential pricing involves ethical as well as economic decision making, which nonprofit leaders must recognize, resolve, and defend.

Demand-based pricing requires that the price-setting organization knows or is able to estimate accurately the value of the offer as perceived by the "buyer." This has important implications for nonprofit leaders. Those who are insulated from their markets may substitute their own beliefs about their clients for facts and thereby invent inaccurate pricing data. This can lead nonprofit organizations to price their services too low based on beliefs about clients considering nonprofit programs to be "second rate" or on beliefs about what clients will want to or be able to pay.

Competitive Pricing. Pressed to keep up with the demand for services, nonprofit organizations often react as though they have no competition and dismiss competitive analysis as irrelevant. Yet the intended clienteles of most nonprofit enterprises do have alternatives for their patronage. End users often define relevant competitors as those that offer similar benefits, rather than just similar-looking products or services delivered by similar-looking nonprofit agencies. Appraising competition can be useful in several ways. First, it will help identify the ceiling—the highest price that can be charged. Studying competitors' prices, both monetary and nonmonetary, can also reveal ways in which service deliverers can offer better products at lower prices. However, nonprofit managers must also consider the ethical implications of competitive pricing. Sometimes competitors, particularly in the private sector, are able to offer low prices through extremely low wage policies or by hiring less-qualified service deliverers than nonprofit agencies are comfortable with. Moreover, private sector firms in high-demand markets may choose to serve only those segments with high-profit potential whereas nonprofit agencies may feel ethically bound to make their services available to those market segments with more limited means. However, private sector companies may feel that nonprofits are unfairly undercutting their prices because they are not subject to the same tax demands as for-profit companies. Thus, although competitive analysis is a useful and essential input to the pricing process, it must be examined in conjunction with costs, market demand, and social and ethical considerations.

Designing Marketing Channels

Decisions about how best to distribute an offering to a market can have a major effect on the fortunes of the offering itself. In some respects, the choice of channels can be more critical in the third sector than in the private sector. When the product is a service, it is often consumed at the same time and place that it is produced, thereby putting the nonprofit employee in direct contact with end users. Religious, psychological, health, and educational services tend to be of that sort. The buyer-seller contact may be inherently sensitive and intrusive, making the quality of the channel offering unusually critical to a satisfactory outcome and requiring that the nonprofit marketer is a client-oriented channel manager. It follows from this that the first step in channel design should be to analyze the requirements of the end user, and a basic building block in building a market channel is the user's specification of acceptable performance.

In designing service facilities, management may find it useful to invoke a categorization common in retailing: that of convenience, shopping, and specialty goods. Convenience products are those that the shopper will not exert much effort to investigate; at the other extreme, specialty goods are those that call forth considerable effort. Shopping goods lie somewhere in between. These definitions, derived from clients, have implications for logistics: convenience products must be readily accessible while specialty products can be successfully distributed through few and more remote channels. Thus social marketing messages that advocate changes in behavior will not be sought out by the target market and must be readily accessible and ubiquitous in order to reach the target because people will not seek out this information or put effort into finding it. Yet an organization that provides specialized home care for a unique market segment can probably expect that their services will be sought out.

Where alternative suppliers are absent, as they often are in the nonprofit sector, suppliers are inclined to design distribution systems that suit their convenience more than the end user's in order to save costs. Nevertheless, the organization has to balance the client's desire for convenience with the service deliverer's need for operating efficiency. There are several ways to manage this trade-off (Lovelock and Weinberg, 1989). One is to decentralize the client contact function while centralizing the technical operations—this is the Red Cross model of blood collection in which blood is collected where it is convenient to the donors but processed centrally. This model is also used by international and national charities that centralize direct mail fundraising, for example, but have many local and regional offices that provide "high touch" engagement of volunteers who raise funds through special events and social networks. A third variation of this solution is to offer more limited services at branches than at the main site, and a fourth is to join with other providers of compatible products to offer a larger meaningful assortment at a local site—information agencies or entertainment ticket agencies are examples of this channel strategy.

Related to a channel's accessibility is the question of the kind and quality of the experience it will deliver. In the past, museums and hospitals have attracted critical comment for their forbidding atmosphere. In contrast, a settlement agency may record its answering message in many different languages in order to communicate a multilingual and multicultural atmosphere for callers contacting the agency for the first time.

Finally, although there are often advantages for the short, controlled distribution channels that are characteristic of most nonprofit organizations, it is sometimes necessary or advisable to use channel intermediaries. These channels may be cheaper, more quickly activated, more expert, or more accessible to end users. Nonprofit organizations also use channel collaborators in order to achieve their goals. To illustrate, advocacy alone may persuade some smokers that they should quit, but their behavior is more likely to change if it is validated by medical judgments, mandated by laws, and supported by workplace regulations. No organization acting alone can deliver all of these components, but out of such imperatives come marketing partnerships among hospitals, cancer societies, medical associations, school boards, industry associations, and government departments.

Where there are interinstitutional relationships, however, there will also be conflict. Even institutions that want to collaborate will bring to the table, in addition to complementary knowledge and skills, potentially competing values, goals, and priorities. Because charitable enterprises are highly value-driven, imprinted with founders' visions, protective of their turf, and in competition for scarce funds, they are just as likely as business firms to experience conflict in the distribution chain. Third-sector organizations need to be assiduous about forming partnerships that work to the advantage of the distribution system as a whole, including the end user, and about recognizing the need for continuous attention to the power relationships and their management that a complex channel requires. In the field of early intervention services for children with disabilities, for example, it has been suggested that neutral brokers may help parents or caregivers access the best services by resolving some of the channel conflict that clients may lack the power to resolve on their own (Fugate, 2000).

Marketing Communications

It was observed earlier that third-sector managers often tend to equate marketing with advertising or other forms of communications such as public relations. Regrettably, those managers are then inclined to define all marketing challenges as "communication" problems; to rush to judgment about mounting promotional efforts; to overlook opportunities for improved products, pricing strategies, and channels; and, as a consequence, to burden communications with an unrealistically heavy part of the total marketing task—and unattainable goals.

The marketing communications program must flow logically from, and fit consistently with, the other parts of the overall strategic approach to an organization's multiple markets. Moreover, all the different parts of the marketing communications must be carefully integrated with each other. The environment in which current marketing communication takes place is one of major fragmentation. Target groups are splintering as both a multiplicity of needs develops and demands for having those needs specifically served proliferate. Distribution channels are fragmenting as organizations distribute their services through new emerging channels or in nontraditional mixes with the offerings of other organizations. Media fragmentation is resulting from more specific media usage and from a huge growth in hard-to-measure online usage. And finally the organization of marketing communications is fragmenting as new suppliers emerge such as special events planners, sponsorship specialists, or Internet experts (Middleton, 2009). All of these changes mean that more than ever it is important to integrate marketing communications across all the different media and contact points through which the various clienteles of interest interact with a nonprofit organization.

Marketing communications in contemporary organizations consist of three types of messages. Planned messages are the most obvious—the traditional form of controlled communications comprising advertising, public relations, direct response marketing, licensing, Web sites, and Internet marketing. However, communication does not only consist of messages that organizations send out to their audiences, but also what messages are actually received by target markets of interest. Recently it has come to be understood that unplanned (and uncontrolled) messages play an equally important part in terms of organizational communications. Employee behavior, media stories and investigations, chat groups and social network sites, government investigations, blogs, and Twitter all convey information about an organization, its programs and services, its policies and advocacy, and its brand. And there is a third, "unconsidered" aspect of communications as well—factors such as service, facilities, and the other elements of the marketing mix such as pricing, distribution channels, and programs and services communicate volumes about an organization and its brand. These unconsidered elements of marketing communications are, in fact, controllable and serve to underline the point that not only do the formal elements of the communications mix (such as advertising and direct mail and public relations) need to be integrated but all of the messages through which an organization communicates to its target markets need to be considered, planned, and controlled insofar as possible.

For many years and in many nonprofit organizations, a communications department was charged with writing press releases to obtain publicity while a separate fundraising department engaged in direct mail, telemarketing, or both to raise funds. If the organization also engaged in sales activity as, for example, in an arts organization, separate advertising and other marketing communications would be created there. Those who managed volunteers often created a newsletter and different communications reached clients. Increasingly we have seen a movement towards an "integrated look" in many nonprofit organizations as communications departments have emerged that take on the role of "policing" the colors, fonts, taglines, and logos that may be used to represent the organization and its programs and services.

Simply coordinating the look of marketing communications does nothing to integrate the fragmented messages that contemporary clients receive, however. To truly "brand" an organization so that it represents a clear, differentiated and trusted place in clients' minds, the messages that they receive must be integrated and consistently delivered—and not only across the different media an organization uses to get its messages out but also across all the different aspects of the organization with which clients interact.

The traditional elements of the marketing communications mix used by for-profit organizations are advertising, publicity, public relations, direct response, sales promotions, and personal selling. Increasingly new media, especially the Internet, and sponsorships and events are coming to be seen as important channels of communication as well. More and more marketing communications take place in the street or online as opposed to in the home through advertising, mail, telephone, and news media. This shift represents not only the emergence of new communications technology but also the emergence of a new trend in marketing communications, namely participation. As people become less and less inclined to simply "receive" marketing communications and more engaged in participating in the creation of communications through events and social media, nonprofit organizations need to recognize that while marketing communication still occurs through commercial channels, it is also delivered through cultural and community contexts (Hanna and Middleton, 2008).

This is both good news and bad news for the third sector. On the one hand, it means that unplanned and uncontrolled communication abounds about organizations that have traditionally already been subject to a very high degree of public scrutiny and misinformation. On the other hand, it means that in a sector deprived of the resources necessary to undertake expensive advertising campaigns and media buys an organization can, through strategic communications planning, capitalize on one of its greatest assets—the engagement and participation of citizens embedded in the social networks that constitute communities. (Chapter Twelve complements the information provided in this section of this chapter with additional information on the topic of strategic communications for nonprofits.)

Summary

Marketing is the management discipline charged with facilitating exchanges with key constituencies. The marketing concept posits that organizational success is achieved through satisfying the needs and wants of exchange partners better than competitors. In large nonprofits and particularly in those which deliver services in return for payment or create programs that attract large donations, we have seen the adoption of sophisticated marketing systems and thinking across organizational departments and levels, sometimes characterized as a "market orientation." In many other organizations and particularly those which are most reliant on grant income (transfer payments), the importance of external constituencies is much less evident to leaders, and marketing is still considered to be limited to the fields of communications and public relations. A value-based approach to clients (both providers and users of resources), a strategic approach to competitors, and an analytical approach to organizational programs, services, and competencies is lacking in many nonprofits. Moreover in some nonprofit organizations, a fear persists that a "marketing approach" to decision making will derail an organization from its mission.

In part this is because marketing theory as applied to the for-profit sector dictates that the marketing department has control over all of the "four Ps" whereas this notion is rejected almost universally in the nonprofit sector. In fact, in many organizations there is a "dual leadership" function that is designed precisely to separate decision making that pertains to operations and programs from that which pertains to income development. In some arts organizations this is formalized by having two "equal" leaders at the top of an organizational hierarchy (Reid and Karambaya, 2009), whereas in other nonprofit settings the duality may reside in one senior leader who takes advice on programs from different experts than those who offer marketing advice. For example, in a live performing arts company, the repertoire is largely chosen by the artistic director; in a family service agency, the programs to be mounted are primarily determined by professional social workers or psychologists; in a university, the curriculum is mostly shaped by the faculty; in a public arts gallery, decisions about acquisitions lie primarily with curators; and in a hospital, the type and quality of care are governed largely by physicians, nurses, and other health care workers.

These customary organizational arrangements are highly significant for nonprofit marketing. They testify to the fact that in many parts of the nonprofit sector, key decisions about the most pivotal parts of the "marketing mix" are made by experts who, in their training and their experience, have little exposure to or regard for marketing. Whereas the primary purpose of for-profit organizations is to make money for their owners or shareholders and thus it is appropriate for marketing managers to have control over much of the production of these organizations, the primary purpose of nonprofit organizations is to serve the public good through the production of goods, services, and ideas that are generated on the basis of expert knowledge and not necessarily on the basis of demand.

However, while marketing experts in the nonprofit sector must understand and accept that "subject matter" expertise is critical to achieving the mission of nonprofit organizations, it is equally important to recognize that facilitating mutually advantageous exchanges between the organization and its environments is critical. Nonprofit organizations achieve their mission not merely through producing services and advocacy but also by ensuring that this production is adequately funded and that their services and ideas reach those for whom they are produced.

Marketing is the aspect of management in nonprofit organizations that is most often to be found advocating for responsiveness to external clienteles and environments. For-profit organizations have unambiguous feedback from a conventional market mechanism, but nonprofit organizations must find other ways to ensure that they respond effectively to clients' wants and needs. Marketing facilitates this responsiveness not by developing programs and ideas that are within the domain of subject-matter experts, but by monitoring the environment, undertaking market research, communicating changing wants and needs of key client groups, participating in portfolio analysis, suggesting suitable segmentation schemes and target markets, creating and maintaining a consistent brand internally and externally, establishing differentiation, and, most important, by fostering the relationships that are crucial to the long-term survival of the organization. It is particularly important to recognize that although many of these relationships may provide financial resources that contribute to sustainability, many others provide equally important "nonfinancial" support—attitudinal and behavioral change, public trust, political pressure, or volunteer commitment and engagement.

Progressive nonprofit organizations realize that in an era of increasing emphasis on notions of transparency, accountability, participation, engagement, equity, and democracy, a more systematic and strategic approach to both understanding and responding to the needs of the multiple constituencies with an interest in the organization is necessary. Organizations need to pay more than lip service to the notion of including the needs of key constituencies, both internal and external, in their decision making and activities and to the need for increasing participation in and engagement with civil society organizations. Marketing is the discipline of management that is charged with "boundary-spanning" activities and bringing the perspectives and ideas of external constituencies inside the nonprofit organization. Incorporating the insights and analysis of marketing into decision making at all levels of the nonprofit organization is thus a critical aspect of a new third-sector leadership that is focused not only on increasing the resource base and visibility of the third sector but also on enhancing its role in building connected communities and an active and engaged citizenry.

References

Andreasen, A. *Social Marketing for the 21st Century*. Thousand Oaks, Calif.: Sage, 2006.

Andreasen, A. R., and Kotler, P. *Strategic Marketing for Nonprofit Organizations* (7th ed.). Upper Saddle River, N. J.: Prentice Hall, 2008.

Bagozzi, R. P. "Marketing as Exchange." *Journal of Marketing*, 1975, *39*, 32–39.

Brennan, L., and Brady, E. "Relating to Marketing? Why Relationship Marketing Works for Not-for-Profit Organisations." *International Journal of Nonprofit and Voluntary Sector Marketing*, 1999, *4*, 327–337.

Connor, R. "How Responsive Are Charities to Market Needs?" *International Journal of Nonprofit and Voluntary Sector Marketing*, 1999, *4*, 338–348.

Conway, T. "Strategy vs. Tactics in the Not-for-Profit Sector: A Role for Relationship Marketing?" *International Journal of Nonprofit and Voluntary Sector Marketing*, 1997, *2*, 42–51.

Fugate, D. L. "Channel Design for Early Intervention Services: Is There a Role for Brokers?" *Journal of Nonprofit and Public Sector Marketing*, 2000, *7*(4), 3–15.

Gainer, B. "The Business of High Art: Marketing the Performing Arts in Canada." *Service Industries Journal*, 1989, *9*, 143–161.

Gainer, B., and Padanyi, P. "Applying the Marketing Concept to Cultural Organizations: An Empirical Study." *International Journal of Nonprofit and Voluntary Sector Marketing*, 2002, *7*, 182–193.

Gan, A. "The Impact of Public Scrutiny on Corporate Philanthropy." *Journal of Business Ethics*, 2006, *69*(3), 217–236.

Hanna, J., and Middleton, A. *Ikonica— A Fieldguide to Canada's Brandscape*. Vancouver, B.C.: Douglas and McIntyre, 2008.

Hutton, J. G. "Narrowing the Concept of Marketing." *Journal of Nonprofit and Public Sector Marketing*, 2001, *9*(4), 5–24.

Kotler, P., and Lee, N. *Social Marketing: Influencing Behaviors for Good* (3rd ed.). Thousand Oaks, Calif.: Sage, 2007.

Lovelock, C., and Weinberg, C. B. *Marketing for Public and Nonprofit Managers*. (2nd ed.) Redwood City, Calif.: Scientific Press, 1989.

MacMillan, I. C. "Competitive Strategies for Not-for-Profit Agencies." Advances in Strategic Management, 1983, *1*, 61–68, reprinted in Oster, S. M. *Strategic Management for Nonprofit Organizations: Theory and Cases*. New York: Oxford University Press, 1995.

Middleton, A. "Marketing Communications at Work and the Importance of Integration." Speech to Masters Certificate in Marketing Communications Leadership, Association of Canadian Advertisers and the Schulich School of Business, 2009.

Moyer, M. S. "Marketing for Nonprofit Managers." In R. D. Herman and Associates (eds.), *The Jossey-Bass Handbook of Nonprofit Leadership and Management*. San Francisco: Jossey-Bass, 1994.

Narver, J. C., and Slater, S. F. "The Effect of a Marketing Orientation on Business Profitability." *Journal of Marketing*, 1990, *54*, 20–35.

Oster, S. M. *Strategic Management for Nonprofit Organizations: Theory and Cases*. New York: Oxford University Press, 1995.

Parson, L., Maclaran, P., and Tadajewski, M. (eds.) *Nonprofit Marketing* (3 vols.). Thousand Oaks, Calif.: Sage, 2008.

Quelch, J. A., and Laidler-Kylander, N. *The New Global Brands: Managing Non-government Organizations in the 21st Century*. Mason, Ohio.: Southwestern Publishing Company, 2006.

Reid, W., and Karambayya, R. "Impact of Dual Executive Leadership in Creative Organizations." *Human Relations*, 2009, *62*(7), 1073–1112.

Ritchie, R., Swami, S., and Weinberg, C. B. "A Brand New World for Nonprofits." *Journal of Nonprofit and Voluntary Sector Marketing*, 1999, *4*(1), 26–42.

Rogers, E. *The Diffusion of Innovations*. (4th ed.) New York: Free Press, 1995.

Sargeant, A., Foreman, S., and Liao, M. "Operationalizing the Marketing Concept in the Nonprofit Sector." *Journal of Nonprofit and Public Sector Marketing*, 2002, *10*(2), 41–45.

Sargeant, A., and Stephenson, H. "Corporate Giving: Targeting the Likely Donor." *Journal of Nonprofit and Voluntary Sector Marketing*, 1997, *2*(1), 64–79.

Sargeant, A., and Wymer, W. *The Routledge Companion to Nonprofit Marketing*. Oxford: Routledge, 2007.

Trout, J., and Rivkin, S. *The New Positioning: The Latest on the World's #1 Business Strategy*. New York: McGraw-Hill, 1997.

Wymer, W. W., Jr. "Segmenting Volunteers Using Values, Self-Esteem, Empathy, and Facilitation as Determinant Variables." *Journal of Nonprofit and Public Sector Marketing*, 1997, *5*(2), 3–28.

Young, D. R. (ed.) *Financing Nonprofits: Putting Theory into Practice*. Lanham, Md.: AltaMira Press, 2006.

Young, S. *Moral Capitalism: Reconciling Private Interest with the Public Good*. San Francisco, Berrett-Koehler, 2003.

CHAPTER TWELVE

STRATEGIC COMMUNICATIONS

Kathy Bonk

Strategic communications is a way for nonprofits to approach public outreach and media relations not as stand-alone activities but rather as an integration of critical organizational functions, similar to fundraising or membership development. Being strategic is not simply reacting to events, it is anticipating and creating them in a systematic and planned manner. When successfully integrated into other management functions, strategic communication activities are important tools for nonprofit leaders to use both in day-to-day operations and long-range planning for the growth and success of the entire organization. Even today, too many nonprofit organizations operate as though e-mailing press releases and reaction statements and holding press conferences now and then are, sufficient ways to rally support. By themselves, these are not enough.

Good media coverage is a prized commodity, and it is built on a foundation of strong working relationships with key journalists and media gatekeepers and pursued through a well-thought-out plan of action. Such a plan typically includes carefully defining target audiences, crafting messages, targeting reporters on a story-by-story basis, and receiving strategic guidance from polls and

This chapter is adapted from *Strategic Communications for Nonprofits, A Step-by-Step Guide to Working with the Media*, a Jossey-Bass Guidebook by Kathy Bonk, Emily Tynes, Henry Griggs, and Phil Sparks (2008).

market research (which can be surprisingly affordable). Other important action elements include building internal teams, framing messages, telling stories that will resonate with target audiences, training spokespeople, developing and marketing appropriate written materials, identifying opportunities to make news, and creating a system by which to evaluate progress.

Perhaps the first strategic insight for nonprofit communications is that there is a built-in advantage in simply being a nonprofit—what we are "pitching" to reporters is meant to make a better world, not a bigger profit or enhanced bottom line; that often means a better story for journalists to cover. Nonprofits may also be in a better position to provide personal stories and appeals to conscience and emotion than for-profit businesses. Finding good real-life stories in the ranks of an organization's members, volunteers, or partners is important for a strategic communications plan (regardless of whether the work is strictly charitable, directed to policy change, or somewhere in between). For many target audiences within the general public (and as a general trend in an age of information overload) personal stories are the ones that really matter. Reporters are always looking to "put a face" on their stories. Fortunately, many of the same stories and appeals that make for good media outreach have equal value in fundraising, membership recruitment, and social networking.

When developing strategies around communications, it is important to understand the simple fact that news or entertainment coverage of organizations and issues rarely just happens. It usually appears as a function of the conscious efforts of interested parties to cultivate reporters and educate target audiences. This is true whether we are talking about the public, donors, or policymakers.

The elements of strategic communications are basically the same for a small advocacy group, a large not-for-profit hospital, a museum, a university, a service provider, or a foundation. Strategic communications plans affirm and should be driven by (1) an organization's goals and outcomes; (2) its vision, as expressed in the mission statement; and (3) its values and beliefs.

Strategic communication planning starts by setting overall communications goals.

Setting Overall Communications Goals

Goals are important, but they must also be measurable in order to gauge progress along the way and know what has been achieved. If, for example, the goal is to recruit more members, the nonprofit leader needs to state how many are to be added and by when. If a plan is about raising awareness about an issue, they must decide how best to measure success. Will it be by responses to a Web site? Through an increase in the number of services provided? By the number of media contacts and resulting coverage? In short, final communications outcomes should answer for the organization the question: So what?

If an organization has only been reactive in its dealings with media, it may be time for a proactive effort that includes a minimum number of press events, meetings with and regular outreach to journalists and bloggers, an enhanced Web site, and other activities that support an organization's overall communications goals.

Building on a Vision and Mission Statement

A nonprofit's mission statement should be the cornerstone of its strategic communications plan, driving the overall direction of media activities. Include this mission statement at the very beginning of a communications plan to remind staff, board members, and other internal decision makers that all of the media-related activities should flow from the core mission and vision of the organization (not just from its communications department). Media outreach activities should not overshadow the bigger picture of "what and organization stands for." Rather, strategic communications should be a building block to help with fundraising, advocacy, membership recruitment, social networking, and supporting the overall purpose of the nonprofit.

Integrating Organizational Values and Beliefs

Every nonprofit organization, foundation, public agency, and institution has at its heart a system of values and beliefs. Unlike opinions, which can shift in a short period, values are long lasting. They emerge in the context of conflicts over government versus individual rights, individual freedoms versus group responsibility, and diversity versus tradition. Everything stems from those core values; they are the organization's reason for being and should be reflected in any new plans and goals the organization creates, including communications goals. For example, the Annie E. Casey Foundation of Baltimore firmly believes that "children do best in families"; its grantmaking and communications plans support this. The Sierra Club's slogan, "Explore, enjoy and protect our planet" clearly states its values and aligns the organization unequivocally with the primary environmental connections of most Americans.

If a nonprofit is planning to initiate a strategic communications effort (whether for the first time or to reinvigorate an earlier effort), it should address these fundamental questions:

- Who does a group want to reach? Is the purpose of the strategic communications activities to inform key audiences about an issue, direct services, and raise awareness? Or is it to enhance the importance or saliency of the organizations? Are people being asked to take some kind of action?
- What is the name recognition of the organization and knowledge of their mission and goals? Is there a general lack of awareness of the nonprofit?
- Does the public already support the goals of the organization? If so, then the challenge is to marshal the resources needed to mobilize people.
- Is there opposition to the group's mission or a scandal that must first be addressed with an effort to reframe or change public opinion?
- What is the appropriate communications strategy, given the level of public understanding? What are the available funds and resources that can be devoted to a strategic communications plan? Who are the most effective messengers and what are the messages that will resonate the most with the target audiences?

Seven elements are critical to building a communications strategy:

1. Definition and understanding of target audiences and how to reach them
2. Research into past media coverage and public opinion about a particular nonprofit and its issues or services
3. Messages to be delivered and relevant messengers
4. Materials to be produced, on paper and online
5. Resources and a budget from which staff, consultants, travel, expenses, and equipment will be drawn
6. A written work plan
7. A feedback system that enables a nonprofit to evaluate the impact of its efforts

The importance of identifying these elements and putting them in place before implementing day-to-day activities cannot be overstated. Outcomes are likely to be determined by the success in pulling these basic elements together.

Identifying Key Target Audiences

One of the first steps in devising a communications plan is to identify target audiences and determine how best to reach them. If, for example, the main objective is to use media to support fundraising efforts, then target audiences may include large donors, appropriate committees of state legislatures, budget committees of a city council, foundation leaders, or select residents of a specific neighborhood or town. Individual large business donors with higher incomes and a history of making contributions are likely to be reading college alumni magazines or the *Wall Street Journal*. If, by contrast, a nonprofit is building a program for younger adults, social networking sites such as MySpace or Facebook are important platforms.

Nonprofit leadership strategists should start by listing the categories of people who are important to the success of a communications effort and by identifying the media they consume and whose word they will respect. For example, if the audience a nonprofit is trying to reach is more progressive or independent minded with a college education, local affiliates of National Public Radio, the *New York Times* and its Web site, stories by the Associated Press and cable's MSNBC, or select CNN programs along with other mainstream media outlets will top the list of media to cultivate. On the other side of the political spectrum, conservatives more likely are found as followers of Fox News cable stations and AM radio conservative talk-show hosts, along with magazines such as the *National Review* and its Web site.

With so many segmented and specialized media now in operation, the concept of a "general public" hardly exists anymore. Nonprofits do not need to communicate to the entire public all at once. Rather, they can focus on carefully chosen segments or, in the case of policymakers and other influential people, a very narrow slice of the population. Fortunately, media outlets can often supply data on the size and demographics of their readership or viewing audiences, typically packaged as marketing information for advertisers, at no cost. This can be especially helpful as a nonprofit begins media placement efforts with reporters and editors.

Conducting Research into Media Coverage, Public Opinion, and Supporting Facts

How are nonprofit organizations and their services or issues perceived by those they seeking to influence? Positioning an organization, framing issues, soliciting funds, and describing services are all elements of strategic communications. A review of past coverage, of lack of it, can help build for the future. Through Internet searches and with the help of Web-based resources, nonprofits can develop an instructive profile of how issues are covered in the media, how often an organization is quoted, how others describe it, and what public opinion polls have been conducted on relevant topics.

Two relatively simple projects can enhance the implementation of a communications plan. The first is a media trend analysis that looks at the quantity, quality, and character of press coverage, news reporting, editorial commentary, and popular culture. The second involves taking stock of public opinion to determine whether the goal is to mobilize people already supportive of a group or issue, to win the support of those sitting on a fence, or to raise overall awareness of an issue or nonprofit.

Media Trend Analysis

Effective communications with prime audiences in the future requires a thorough understanding of coverage from the past. It also demands detailed attention to aspects of reporting that are crucial to knowing how organizations or issues are perceived by the media, including the following:

- *Story placement.* Is past coverage hard news, on page one or the Web site home page of newspapers, or the lead piece of a video newscast? Or is coverage mainly by feature writers or in the lifestyle or "softer" sections in media outlets? Or positioned as "News You Can Use" info-bites? Or featured in more popular culture such as films, documentaries, daytime talk shows, and so forth?
- *Tone.* Are stories dry renderings of events or exposes of scandals?
- *Bylines.* Does the same reporter cover an issue or group or is it done by journalists in shifting beats who rotate from issue to issue?
- *Spokespeople.* Who is quoted or interviewed on a specific topic? Government officials? Business leaders? Nonprofit officials and advocates?
- *Messages.* How has the media portrayed an organization in the past? How do the spokespeople frame the issue? Does the coverage suggest action that can be taken by readers or viewers such as volunteering, joining, or participating with the group in some way? Do stories show both the problem and the solution to important social issues?
- *Timing and new hooks.* Are there seasonal or other patterns to coverage that an organization can take better advantage of for future communications?

Once a good sample of media coverage is assembled, one person should review stories to analyze them by date, placement, tone, length, reporter or blogger interest, words and phrases used to describe the group and its issues, spokespeople, and so on. After reviewing even several dozen stories, patterns and trends will emerge that can help guide future communications strategies and be important for evaluation purposes on the impact of a strategic communications effort.

Quantitative and Qualitative Research

If a communications strategy will be used to recruit new members, for example, informal or formal focus group discussions or surveys of existing members can be invaluable research tools for targeting media and helping to develop messages. Public opinion research falls into these two main categories. The most familiar is quantitative, such as public opinion polls or surveys conducted among scientifically drawn samples of several hundred to several thousand people. A well-designed public opinion poll can (1) gather information needed for message development; (2) measure public awareness of an organization, its mission, and issue agenda; (3) quantify people's level of support and reaction to test messages; and (4) identify target audiences. Costs can vary from several thousand to several hundred thousands of dollars. Fortunately for smaller nonprofits, there are ways to access existing polling data at a fraction of that price through the University of Connecticut's Roper Center's iPoll Databank (www.ropercenter.uconn.edu).

Qualitative research is the second and equally important strategy for targeting audiences and developing messages. This can include facilitating focus groups, conducting dozens of one-on-one interviews, and utilizing work of cognitive linguists who bring knowledge of how the brain processes information via a values-based approach.

Typically, a *focus group* is a collection of twelve to twenty people selected according to certain characteristics for a two-hour, moderated discussion. Focus groups can be used to uncover new themes that persuade people, test reactions to specific language and messages, and provide valuable feedback on visual presentations. Unlike polls, focus groups explore the values, beliefs, and motivations underlying participants' opinions.

As the name implies, *in-depth interviews,* also called IDIs, focus on one or two people at time. They are best for probing sensitive or confidential information that is hard to discuss in a small-group setting, or for learning the opinions of people who are unlikely to attend a focus group.

Considering that about 75 percent of adults in the United States regularly use the Internet, virtual qualitative research has increasingly more advantages. *Online research* can provide a representative sample of hard-to-reach populations and allow for greater geographic dispersal of participants and high response rates, as respondents can participate at their convenience. Formats include chatrooms, bulletin boards, and online survey forms.

Dial sessions allow participants, using instant-response dial technology, to register their reactions to information presented to them. These "people meters" are regularly being used by broadcast and cable outlets around political debates or mega-events such as presidential speeches. Participants are given wireless devices and they "dial" from 1 (negative) to 100 (positive). Reactions are captured instantaneously and displayed in a line superimposed over a video. Each time the line rises or falls, something significant usually has occurred and is evaluated by the researchers.

Packaging Supporting Facts and Figures

Part of a strategic communications plan should be to collect data on the issues or services in formats that reporters and editors can easily use to answer the "who, what, when, where, why, and how" in every story. A side benefit to that approach is that it transforms the data needed to help shape communications into a virtual gold mine in outreach to reporters. This process starts by categorizing all available internal data according to its usefulness to journalists, and when the time comes to answer their questions, a group will be well prepared.

But facts and figures about a specific nonprofit or its issues are not enough. The facts need to be put into a context and help tell a story. More and more reporters say, "Help me find a personal story" to tell my readers or viewers. They need to tell stories, based on facts, and this is where messaging and framing become important parts of a strategic communications plan.

Developing and Framing Messages versus Branding Nonprofits

Logos, taglines, elevator speeches, sound bites, quotes, brochures, speeches, digital videos, B-roll, press kits, Web site design and content, blogs, twitters, direct mail solicitations, e-mail alerts, business cards, and more are all part of your strategic communications efforts.

By targeting audiences, a nonprofit is deciding what segments of the public should be reached and sometimes what segments should be ignored. By properly framing messages, a nonprofit builds a communications strategy on widely held values that shape opinions. Within those frames, a group can target messages and assemble the specific concepts and language that will resonate with those who are persuadable and ready to move to action. Nearly all nonprofits have a mission statement based on core values and principles, as discussed above. For some groups, these may be values of care for one's family, personal liberty, integrity, equality, or fairness. Others may base their mission on values of improving education or promoting democracy, equal opportunity, or global health. For several decades, pollsters and academics have been doing research and writing about the connections among values, framing, and communications (for example, Yankelovich, Kemton, Kidder).

In the 1990s, the nonprofit Frameworks Institute developed a multidisciplinary approach to communications called Strategic Frame Analysis. This approach uses techniques from cognitive and social sciences to document the public's deeply held worldviews and widely held assumptions. Among the core tenets of this approach are the following observations:

- People are not blank slates.
- Communications are interactive and frame-based.
- Communications resonate with people's deeply held values and worldviews.
- People routinely default to the "pictures in their heads."
- People can be redirected to a different way of thinking if the composition and order of communications is changed.

To help people further understand how this approach can be used to communicate to audiences, the Frameworks Institute explored framing elements at three "levels of thinking" based on research related to how human brains process information: Level One is about big ideas and values such as responsibility, opportunity, safety, family, and other bigger concepts; Level Two focuses on issues, movements, networks, and the drivers for change; Level Three is about specific policies, actions, and services. Experts and advocates usually operate at Level Three, with a specialized vocabulary and language; the larger public generally operates at Level One, with a more universal language.

Nonprofits need to ask: Can the conversation be opened at Level One? How best can messages be framed to as to increase awareness, concern, and saliency and move people to action?

In contrast, if the target audience is with leading experts and academics, then communications need to be at their level of thinking. Messages need to be crafted at the level and language where the audience resides with a focus on one or two, but no more than three, key ideas of message points.

Nonprofits should ask: What is the main message of our communications? If a story is written about the group, what three to six words should go between the two commas to describe it?

If asked in an elevator about their work, what does the nonprofit person do? How would a staff member or volunteer answer with just a few floors during which to have the conversation? What is the headline or feature story about the group? If the group is clear about its messages to reporters, donors, potential members, consumers, and others, target audiences will also be clear and more likely to support it.

Work back from this headline to fill in the missing elements: Who made the story happen? What obstacles did they encounter? Why is this important to others in the community and throughout the country? What role did the organization play? These are the things reporters want to know to write or produce a story. And think visually. What possible photographs or creative video can be supplied with the story?

A useful exercise for staying on message is to develop a "message box" with "talking points" for spokespeople to use whenever they talk to reporters. The box contains key or central points, and around it are supporting facts, a call to action, and other secondary messages. Thinking in terms of a box, rather than a list, can help people remember to jump back to the central argument throughout the interview.

In recent years, many foundations and nonprofit organizations have focused on branding as part of their overall communications plans. Branding is an attempt to define a single organization or its activities as a unique brand. Commonly used to individualize commercial products ranging from soap to automobiles, it can also be used by nonprofits. Organizations may adopt a slogan to distinguish themselves from others, or try to make the point more powerfully with paid advertising (see discussion under Producing High-Quality Materials). The key here is the availability of resources to provide the drumbeat for a branding repetition. There is another challenge to branding (apart from the high cost). The most successful advocacy efforts in the nonprofit world tend to involve the collaboration of many different groups working toward the same objective. The use of branding to uniquely characterize a particular organization within the coalition may foster competition or promote the hoarding of proprietary information, defeating the purpose of the joint effort in which the groups downplay their individual identities. Thus, branding is generally not effective in collaborative situations and usually requires a sizable budget for paid advertising for individual nonprofits.

Producing High-Quality Materials

Traditional public relations materials are important tools for reaching reporters, donors, policymakers, influentials, and others in your target group. The nonprofit toolbox should include the following:

- A good logo and stationery design that will last awhile; the logo should be easy to read on paper and in an electronic format
- An easy-to-understand, one-page fact sheet about the work of the nonprofit
- At least one press kit on highlighted services, issues, and activities for media, with a one-page fact sheet on each

- Brochures that can be printed on paper and adapted for a Web site
- Photos, videos, slides, overheads, and computer presentations that tell your story
- Reports and studies for public release as news items
- Short bios and a top-quality photo of leaders and spokespeople
- Current newsletter, if there is one
- Copies of published news or feature articles from mainstream media and Web sites as validators of the group's work and importance

All of these should be produced in formats that can be posted on Web sites with a clearly marked media or "press room" button on a home page with "press room" hyperlinks on all pages.

Assessing Resources

Spell out how you will allocate staff time, budgets, computers, databases, in-house and contract services, and volunteer or intern help to implement the plan. A communications, public affairs, or media director is a must for midsize to large organizations. In agencies with fewer than ten employees or volunteers, everyone from the executive director to the person who answers the phone should be a part of the communications team. A resource review should be completed to do the following:

- Assess staff time, in-house services, and consultant support.
- Evaluate existing media technologies with follow-up staff training and upgrades as needed.
- Designate or hire staff that will be responsible for communications.
- Develop a budget that includes provisions for such outside services as freelance writing, video production, database management, graphic design, and Web site management.
- Build or expand access to executive loan programs, internships, pro bono media support, donations, and grants.

Writing a Work Plan for Ongoing Media Outreach and Related Activities

Specific strategies for winning positive media coverage, editorial endorsements, or media partnerships are as varied as the media landscape and the communities a nonprofit may serve, but the elements of a basic strategic plan, discussed in this chapter, are fairly constant. What follows are eight fairly typical communications goals and functions, along with suggested ongoing activities for achieving or maintaining them. This list is a menu from which to adopt or modify activities for specific situations.

Ensure Positive Media Coverage

Positive stories in the media are earned through an investment of funds and resources over time. The term *earned media* is now used widely to describe what used to be called public relations or free media (as opposed to paid media or advertising). If a nonprofit is already newsworthy or can make news, it should develop a strategy for regular positive coverage. If not, take these basic steps:

- Cultivate personal relationships with reporters, editors, and media gatekeepers.
- Develop a calendar of events around key issues or activities, such as the release of a report, reoccurring special dates, such as back-to-school or holiday seasons.
- Plan and initiate additional news events to expand media coverage opportunities.
- Coordinate written materials for print media, develop visuals for photographers and broadcasters, and make tapes for audio news feeds.
- Schedule press conferences sparingly when a group has real news and media briefings when warranted.
- Distribute press releases on significant developments by e-mail, fax, hand delivery and snail mail—which very few groups use these days and are often opened more regularly than other forms of communications.
- Update Web sites with new information and materials on a regular basis with special alerts to media when warranted.

Feature stories or "softer" news items about people, places, and issues attract diverse audiences and tend to be "evergreen." In other words, they do not have the urgency or timeliness of "hard" breaking news. To pitch a feature piece to a reporter, outline your desired approach to the story before you call. It may take several tries and different story ideas before a reporter responds positively. Don't get discouraged. Also, the increasing use of voice mail means you may have to try several times to reach reporters with your pitch.

Writing articles for publication and scheduling broadcast or cable appearances on public affairs programming featuring your spokespeople are good ways to get your messages across in their purest form, without a reporter's interpretation. Try the following:

- Write and place bylined opinion articles or op-eds in newspapers and move ideas up the media food chain to radio, cable, television, and popular culture.

- Coordinate timely, sharp, and relevant letters to the editor and one-liner responses to specific stories and features.
- Join Internet media Web sites for chats and instant responses to news stories and features.
- Schedule regular appearances on talk radio and television public affairs shows.
- Offer comments on news developments to producers of news and news-magazine shows. They may be interested in having your spokesperson discuss them on the air.

Secure Editorial Endorsements and Columnist, Opinion Writer, and Blogger Support

Newspapers and many local news programs take positions on issues and endorse or participate in nonprofit activities such as walkathons. The *New York Times*, for example, runs a yearly winter holiday series about "The Neediest Cases," with specific examples chosen by the seven agencies supporting a Times-administered fund by the same name. Local media outlets do the same with those with whom they have relationships. To attain editorial support, nonprofits need to

- Set up face-to-face editorial board meetings at daily, weekly, or neighborhood papers. Be prepared with "an ask" of the editorial board—a request for them to take a position on the editorial page. That is their job, and the arguments and data you provide can help them decide.
- Generate mailings, e-mails, and faxes with clips and fact sheets about issues or activities, along with requests for support.
- Send columnists story ideas and opinions about issues that they may want to address.
- Get to know key bloggers who are trend spotters and trendsetters who will carry messages forward to new and younger audiences.

Identify Spokespeople and Train Them in Media-Readiness Skills

Successful strategies require articulate, respected messengers for public presentations and interviews with print and electronic journalists. Before any interview, nonprofit communications staff should do their homework to find out as much as possible about the reporters and their publication or broadcast outlet—and their Web sites. Staff should read the reporter's stories and call colleagues who may have experience working with the reporter. Ask: Is the story a profile, hard news, or an investigative piece? If a newspaper reporter is doing the interview, find out whether photographs or videos will be taken or whether the organization may supply background video or photographs.

Being interviewed successfully, especially in front of a camera, is a learned skill. No one should just "wing it" with on-air interviews, especially in an Internet world where today's performance is tomorrow's Facebook and YouTube postings. Larger nonprofits should use the services of a professional media trainer, such as former television or cable correspondents with extensive on-air experience. Quick tips for effective interviews:

- Use the interview to state the key messages the organization wants to get across. One way to stay on message is to prepare a message box or a short, one-page list of key talking points.
- Speak in complete sentences, especially in reply to a question. Monosyllabic answers, like yes or no, are not likely to be quoted or broadcast.
- Don't fake it. If you do not know the answer to a question, volunteer to get back with the information later.
- Say the organization's full name. There is a tendency in an interview to use a full name just in the beginning and use abbreviated references later (such as "the Center" or "the Council"). The first reference may be edited out and later ones may not make sense.
- Watch or listen in advance to the show or appearances or interviews. Clothing choices should be solid colors that will contrast slightly but not blend into the set.
- Be animated with passion. Do not play "rock in a seat," or bounce or nod at each remark; rather, look at the camera and talk to the thousands in the audience, not just the one person doing an interview.
- Regularly tape radio, television, and cable appearances. Ask several trusted advisers for feedback, which includes strong positive comments and gentle but firm criticisms. Often very smart people who may not be prone to coaching or receiving honest feedback from staff will see themselves on video and do an immediate course correction to improve on dress, hairstyle, jewelry, and other distractions that can easily be improved.

Research indicates that audiences most respond to and remember a visual presentation (55 percent); they are next most impressed by vocal (38 percent); only 7 percent remember the verbal part of a presentation. Yes, words do matter, but form, style, looks, appearance, tone, eye contact, style, and nonverbal communications play an important role—especially on television, cable, and video online networks.

Build Media Partnerships

Always remember that the news media are businesses first. They are major corporations that keep stockholders' interests firmly in mind, and they want to build audiences and sell advertising. Nonprofits may be in a position to help them do both.

The less controversial a nonprofit is, the more willing a media outlet will be to forge a partnership with it. Across the country, media have provided institutional support for worthy causes, with events ranging from lengthy broadcast telethons to fifteen-second public service announcements. Some mount impressive multipart or episodic campaigns that give viewers and readers information about major current issues such as health care or child welfare. Others promote community activities or other free services on their news programs or pages. Media personalities volunteer time and money. The *Washington Post,* for example, joined efforts to help reform District of Columbia schools by offering summer training programs for teachers. The *Post*'s local foundation also makes grants to community groups and organizations in the arts and to organizations that help minorities advance in the fields of journalism and communications.

Public service advertising can also be an important way to reach target audiences, along with local calendar of events sections in newspapers and on radio and television (including Web sites) to provide information to audiences about events and to enhance an organization's name recognition.

Media partnerships might include

- Public service announcements (PSAs) that advertise events, recruit members, explain service delivery, and build the organization's image.
- National and local documentaries or feature films.
- Billboard and transit campaigns on buses and subways.
- Agreements by corporate advertisers to "barter" space in the media for a nonprofit that is supported by the company in order to help its cause. An agency may be able to negotiate a free thirty-second spot for a nonprofit for every ten to fifty spots purchased by a corporate client.

Be Mindful of Internal Communications

Staff members, boards of directors, and volunteers can be a nonprofit's best asset. But they need regularly updated information about what an organization is doing. Otherwise, they cannot accurately represent causes to friends, family, neighbors, and others in their circles of influence. When it comes to working with the media, staff also needs to be trained and ready to deal with press calls and inquiries. This applies as much to the receptionist who answers the phone as to top spokespeople.

Consider Paid Advertising

Advertising takes thousands of forms, from skywriting and blimps to special showcases in bookstores and magazine racks. Buying media time or space guarantees that your messages will be delivered in the exact words you choose and to your target audiences. In 2008, U.S. businesses invested $136 billion in paid advertising. Politicians running for office typically spend 50 to 75 percent of their campaign funds on paid advertising.

Nonprofits sometimes ignore or even disdain paid advertising in favor of public service announcements and earned media coverage. That sentiment is misguided for two reasons. First, the tools and techniques of advertising are generally adaptable to any communications strategy. Survey research, media content analysis, focus groups, and other components of a communications strategy all started in the world of commercial marketing and advertising. Before launching a multimillion-dollar national ad campaign of any kind, themes and language are tested on scientifically selected groups that represent potential audiences of consumers. Thus, potential flaws can be caught and refinements made before committing serious resources of tens of millions of dollars. Second, paid advertising can jump-start a media outreach effort or complement it over the long term. Combining earned and paid media usually will guarantee that target audiences are reached with key messages.

Investing in advertising is an art, not a science. Most nonprofits simply do not have the resources to make significant expenditures on paid media. An investment in finding a creative ad agency that knows how to make nonprofits vibrant and relevant is well worth the time and energy.

Develop a Crisis Control and Backlash Plan

Regardless of how noncontroversial a nonprofit's services or issues may be, management should prepare for a crisis or backlash in the media. Unfortunately, people make mistakes, systems break down, and organizations do not always perform according to expectations. A crisis turned public with extensive media exposure can occur at any time, causing long-term damage to individual reputations and organizations. For nonprofits responsible for people's safety and well-being, even a slight error can have devastating consequences. Examples of situations that have caused damage to nonprofits because crisis management has not been properly handled include

- People die or are seriously injured while in the care of a nonprofit hospital, college or university, child welfare contractor, or nursing home.
- A nonprofit is sued for violations of civil rights, fair labor standards, sexual harassment, discrimination, or other employment-related charges.
- Sexual exploitation is revealed by employees or affiliates.

- Interpersonal tensions explode between members of boards of directors, or among local chapters and staff, with one side using media as a weapon to build public sympathy.
- Serious mismanagement of funds, exposing a nonprofit to pubic scrutiny and a challenge to its tax status. Numerous nonprofits appeal for and dispense large sums of money when emergency situations or natural disasters occur, which is usually followed by clamors for accountability. If funds go awry or are not getting to those most in need, a public scandal can erupt.

Think of a crisis management plan as a fire drill. It is preparation for an emergency that can erupt at any time, even though it may never happen at all. There are three basic rules of a crisis communications plan: (1) prepare for the worst, (2) remain calm and in control if a crisis happens, and (3) be proactive after it occurs. Very few media frenzies based on a crisis die off and fade. Three critical elements of a plan include (1) identify a crisis coordination team that monitors media coverage and possible negative exposure, (2) develop a special communications plan to ensure timely and appropriate responses, and (3) conduct internal briefings about how fast and when to begin implementing damage control procedures.

If a nonprofit puts efficient systems in place, things generally will not fall apart when something goes wrong. At those times, it is more important than ever to stay in control. Keep target audiences in mind, have clearly developed messages and clearly defined roles, decide who will speak to the media, monitor coverage especially online, maintain internal communications, be truthful and honest, and provide a quick analysis of the situation and its impact.

The key to managing a crisis is prevention. But if a crisis does occur, nonprofit managers should be accountable, take action, and make a commitment to change and improve as needed. It is important to recognize the difference between a crisis and a controversy. Media regularly cover controversy and see controversy as news. It is important to differentiate work on controversial issues such as immigration or abortion from being caught in a serious crisis. A single event or series of events can negatively change the tone and focus of media coverage on social issues. Even in the absence of unfavorable events, critics may attack an organization to get attention or hurt a cause. This is when framing an issue becomes an important skill. Often, whoever frames the debate wins the debate. Once a backlash based on controversy starts, it can be hard to turn around. There is an old saying that "journalists are like crows on a wire; when one flies off, the rest will follow."

Conduct Evaluations and Establish Accountability

Impartial assessment is a prerequisite for continued improvements. It ensures accountability, facilitates coordination, points the way to next steps, and creates a record against which future activities can be judged. Every strategic communications plan should have an integral evaluation component to establish accountability and make improvements over time. Major activities might include analyzing media content and monitoring certain developments, such as shifts in public opinion, policy changes, increased memberships and organizational participation, and improved institutional capacity.

Nonprofits need to assess process as well as outcomes. Among the process questions to ask: (a) What information and what services are being delivered and by whom? and (b) How many communications activities were tried and executed, and at what cost? Among the outcome questions to ask: (a) Did the nonprofit make a discernible difference? and (b) Why does that matter? In other words, so what?

Summary

An effective communications and outreach program and the effective use of new communications technologies will advance the goals of the nonprofit organization and provide new and exciting opportunities for development. In this era, when the Internet turns into high-speed digital, journalism turns into 24/7 news cycles, Web sites turn into radio and television stations, and the industrialized world operates on information overload, nonprofits need to be strategic about communications and media.

CHAPTER THIRTEEN

ADVOCACY, LOBBYING, AND SOCIAL CHANGE

Marcia Avner

Nonprofit advocates and lobbyists have been involved in nearly every major public policy accomplishment in the country—from civil rights to environmental protection to health care. These are not abstract issues. Tens of thousands of lives have been saved by passing laws that improve car safety and reduce drunk driving. Hunger and disease for millions of children have been reduced by passing laws that advance public health as well as food and nutrition programs. . . . In other words, nonprofit advocacy is an honorable tradition, a paean to our American heritage, the First Amendment, and free speech.

GARY BASS, OMB WATCH, "ADVOCACY IN THE PUBLIC INTEREST," 2009

Charities make an enormous contribution to our national life, and a good share of that is accomplished through direct services. Unfortunately, as the founder of the Center for Lobbying in the Public Interest, Bob Smucker, laments, charities seldom organize or mobilize their volunteers to address one of the most valuable of services they could provide—speaking out to policymakers about the needs and interests of the people they serve and the results that their organizations seek. Observes Smucker, "This is a huge loss, not only for the people and causes that charities serve but also for the nation as a whole; the right of citizens to petition their government is basic to our democracy, and charities are one of the most effective vehicles for allowing citizen participation to shape public policy. Our democratic system can only be strengthened by charities and their volunteers telling public officials about the needs as they see them—firsthand" (2005, p. 231).

This chapter introduces the topic of nonprofit advocacy and lobbying and provides readers an understanding of what constitutes public policy advocacy, why nonprofits are uniquely positioned to be effective advocates, the potential benefits, and how to make this an integral part of a nonprofit's strategy for meeting mission.

Why Should Nonprofits Advocate and Lobby?

Nonprofits have the potential to create public policy changes that have a profound impact on peoples' lives. Imagine the power and the reach of the nonprofit sector, given the experience, expertise, intellect, and commitment of boards, staff, volunteers, participants, and donors! Nonprofits connect to essentially all members of our society. More and more nonprofits recognize that the combination of knowledge, community involvement, and a broad base of support position this sector to lead the way in shaping policy strategies that address our local, state, and national problems in sound and responsible ways.

How Do We Know That Nonprofits Make a Difference?

There is a long history of nonprofit achievement in shaping policy. In a short period of time, starting at the local level, nonprofits dedicated to preventing cancer, lung disease, heart disease, and unhealthy workplaces have built a "smoke free" movement that has achieved nationwide changes in indoor environments. These organizations' advocacy efforts have led to changes in the laws and, most important, changes in personal behavior and cultural norms. And through a diverse group of nonprofits, working consistently over many decades, nonprofit advocacy has led to creative solutions to family violence, such as crisis nurseries and anti-bullying programs. Advocacy works.

What Do We Mean by Advocacy, Lobbying, Organizing?

Advocacy is general support for an idea or issue, and *direct lobbying* is a specific form of advocacy. Nonprofit lobbying involves asking an elected official to take a particular position on a specific legislative proposal. For instance, asserting that "We have 7,000 homeless people a night in our city and we need more affordable housing" is an advocacy position. Moving to the specific opportunity and asking a state legislator, "Will you vote yes on Senate Bill 6643, which ensures that all publicly subsidized housing requires eligible tenants to pay less than 30 percent of their income in rent?" is direct lobbying. Lobbying is asking for a particular action on a discrete proposal. *Organizing* is the ability to understand who is likely to support the issues and positions that you champion and to engage people and institutions in working with you, in becoming part of your base of support. Grassroots organizing, which engages people who are likely to be directly affected by the decisions that are under consideration, builds the power and resources of your organization. Constituents in their community have unique access to elected officials, and when they are involved in your advocacy and lobbying, they expand your impact through their relationships and numbers. A nonprofit that advocates through organizing and lobbying can achieve change.

So Why Don't More Nonprofits Advocate and Lobby?

The call to advocacy is clear. Yet recent research on nonprofit participation in advocacy and lobbying (see, for example, Arons, 2002) makes clear that many 501(c)(3) public charities, especially those dedicated to providing social and human services, are not engaging in or maximizing their potential to fulfill their mission because they are meeting needs but not addressing the reason that so many basic needs exist.

Bob Smucker sheds light on the reluctance of some nonprofits to advocate and lobby, noting that

> The importance of government decisions on nonprofit programs and the government funding of those programs argues strongly for the development by nonprofits of lobbying skills and knowledge of the laws governing nonprofit lobbying. However, managers of nonprofits and their boards of directors have been slow to recognize and act on this point. Many still doubt that lobbying is a proper and legal nonprofit activity. . . . The law is absolutely clear about the legality of lobbying. . . . In 1976 legislation was passed that clarified and vastly expanded the amount of lobbying nonprofits can conduct. Equally important, on August 31, 1990, the Internal Revenue Service promulgated regulations that support both the spirit and the intent of the 1976 law. Together the law and the regulations provide more lobbying leeway than 99 percent of all nonprofits will ever need or want. (2005, pp. 231–232)

Even when a nonprofit organization's leaders understand that lobbying is legal and that it is, in fact, a responsible activity for nonprofits to undertake, many are still uncertain about how to build an advocacy and lobbying effort. Put doubts to rest. The following pages offer a practical understanding of how to plan and act to have an impact on public policy debates.

The Role of Nonprofits in the Public Dialogue

Nonprofit public policy advocacy strategies are essential to mission accomplishment. Nonprofits in a diverse array of activity areas share a common commitment to meeting the interests and needs of people and communities. Their work on programs, services, and excellence in management are directed to the changes they want to make in society. The work of nonprofits is different from the work of political and business institutions, and nonprofits advance goals, ideas, movements, and programs separate from governmental and market priorities. Nonprofits bring values, information, and the voices of the community to their work with government. Often nonprofits are a countervailing force to the influence of the marketplace on governmental decisions at all jurisdictional levels. Because of their unique and essential role in ensuring a fully informed public dialogue, nonprofits need to fulfill their key role in decisions about government programs, policies, and priorities.

Nonprofits often work with people at the individual and community level. Public charities often have the most far-reaching, trusted, and comfortable of relationships with people in their communities. Based on those ongoing and respected relationships, nonprofits have the potential to encourage individuals and groups to step up to their place in a healthy democracy. And nonprofits provide public leaders with insights about community interests. These organizations hold government accountable to a broad public, present the diverse values reflected in society, and advance issues that are not otherwise addressed. And they are a vehicle through which many members of the society have a voice in the policy and political process.

Public policy need not be mysterious. Nonprofits need to recognize that, at the core, *public policy embodies the decisions we make about how we will care for one another, our communities, and the land.* Regardless of whether a particular organization's issues are addressed at the federal, state, or local level, nonprofits have the opportunity and the responsibility to shape policies. Without policy work, nonprofits might never have seen an Americans with Disabilities Act provide access to countless spaces and resources for people whom they may serve. Without public policy work, nonprofits could not have shaped some responses to welfare reform that enable people to get out of poverty, not just off of welfare. Without public policy, nonprofit arts organizations would not have resources to play their role in building quality of life and serving as economic engines in communities. Without public policy, nonprofits would have lost their sector's rights to lobby, engage in voter registration, benefit from tax exemptions, and secure what funding exists for the programs and services they offer.

Their public policy work is essential to nonprofit mission, but it is also essential to policymakers. Elected officials must be generalists. Nonprofits bring to them expertise and experience that is needed for a fully informed public debate. Charities have information: research, data, stories, measures of support. Since policy decisions will be made with or without nonprofit input, the choice to enrich the policy dialogue with our knowledge and point of view becomes an imperative.

It long has been the role of the sector to engage people in the decisions that affect their lives; this is yet another dimension of a nonprofit's role in a democratic society. Through nonprofit information and organizing efforts, individuals who would otherwise be silent add their ideas, interests, and insights to the policy debate. Through nonprofit, nonpartisan political activity, people who are not engaged in the public life of the community may become voters, participate in community and public sector decision making, and exercise their potential to work for their communities' interests.

Nonprofit advocacy work is not abstract. It is a concrete component of an organization's work to identify and meet needs, protect community resources, and ensure that individuals are using the power they have to be a voice on issues. Collectively, nonprofits promote, protect, and support policies and reforms that have an impact on quality of life, community vitality, economic security, and justice.

> Americans have a long-standing tradition of association and expression on political issues . . . they largely organize their voices through a variety of nonprofit organizations. In fact, nonprofit organizations are a familiar institutional force in American politics on almost every side of every issue. They promote the interests, values, and preferences of a diverse civic culture that includes the mainstream and minority, social service providers and their clients. . . . Along with elected officials and formal institutions of government, nonprofits are part of the system of representation in American democracy. (Reid, 2006, pp. 343–344)

What Activities Constitute Advocacy?

Advocacy is general support for an idea or issue. We are all advocates. As individuals and as organizational leaders, managers, and staff, we embrace causes and work to persuade others to support our issues and our point of view.

Lobbying is a very specific form of advocacy. Lobbying is explicitly defined by the IRS in its regulation of nonprofit organizations. Details about what constitutes lobbying and how nonprofits report such activity are included later in this chapter and in extensive online resources. Basically, lobbying involves you, or those whom you organize and mobilize, asking elected officials or others who can make policy decisions to act in a particular way on a specific policy proposal. Although advocacy includes broad promotion, education, persuasion, and lobbying, lobbying is that limited component of advocacy that includes a request for a particular action on a specific policy.

Organizing involves building, engaging, preparing, and mobilizing a base of supporters. Included in organizing is the ability to understand who is likely to support the issues and positions that you champion and to engage those people and institutions in working with you on behalf of an issue. Grassroots organizing, which engages people who are likely to be affected by the decisions that are on the table, builds the power and resources of your organization. Constituents in their community have unique access to elected officials and, when constituents are involved in your advocacy and lobbying, they expand your impact through their relationships and numbers. A nonprofit that advocates through organizing and lobbying can achieve change.

Building and Contributing to Social Change Movements

While it is great to "win" on single specific issues, nonprofits have the knowledge, leaders, power base, and regional and national networks to inspire, implement, build, and sustain *social change movements*. In so doing, nonprofits shape the broad political will to remedy societal problems. Social change movements have revolutionized the way Americans understand and respond in values and policies to an exceptional array of issues, including domestic violence, food safety, substance abuse, abuses of corporate power, human rights, poverty alleviation, public art, medical care, early childhood education, and so much more. Individually and collectively, movements work to change systems, rules, and regulations in ways that improve conditions for programs and services that people count on in their community.

An Example

Imagine a nonprofit that provides shelter and programs for the homeless. They are also advocates for more shelters to meet existing and future needs and for increased units of affordable permanent housing. This nonprofit, "Coalition for the Homeless," engages in a wide range of activities. Staff works with local university faculty to research the numbers of people experiencing homelessness, the diverse reasons for individuals and families to be homeless, the numbers and effectiveness of services for the homeless, and the unmet needs in the community. In sharing that information and their concern that more be done to alleviate homelessness, the coalition's nonprofit advocates communicate with all those connected with their organization, with allied organizations and coalitions, with the media, with Facebook friends, and probably include what they know and are passionate about in most conversations. They may have general discussions with elected officials about the problem as they understand it.

In preparing to be effective advocates, the organization carries out a well-planned organizing campaign. It identifies those who are already on board with their work, those who have an interest in the success of the work, and those who will be most directly affected by the proposed changes. In reaching out, often on a one-to-one basis, they learn about the individual or organization's specific interests and capacity to support an advocacy campaign. As they target, recruit, educate, prepare, and mobilize the supporters whom they can win over, the nonprofit builds a powerful community base that can leverage change.

As they work for particular reforms or laws as part of the solution to the problem of homelessness, their advocacy effort has a lobbying component. Lobbying is the work that the organization does to prepare for the "ask"—the request, for instance, to the head of the State House of Representative's Housing Committee to support a particular proposal. The lobbying component builds on all of the advocacy that the coalition has done and is the step that focuses on the effort to get decision makers to "Vote to stop the bill that cuts funding for the homeless," or "Vote 'yes' for House File 220 to fund 300 units of affordable housing at scattered sites in Santa Fe."

Because affordable housing is a nationwide need, nonprofit networks and coalitions combine their efforts to do public education, organizing, and advocacy. They work to build a movement to raise public awareness and inspire broad public support for making housing a priority in communities across the nation. Countless groups working at the local level change attitudes and reach deeply into the community. The work at the local level connects to similar efforts in other places, often through nonprofit networks and national associations. As values change, as the issue becomes a national priority, as increasing numbers of political leaders and officials take up the issue to satisfy the needs of their constituents and communities, an affordable housing movement expands and elevates the issue in public and political life.

Civic engagement is one of many terms used to describe efforts to sustain and expand participation in all forms of activities that relate to democratic society. Some nonprofits increase civic engagement by convening groups to understand an issue. For example, they hold "Eggs and Issues" breakfasts or community town hall meetings to encourage people to understand and get involved in issues of concern, from the placement of a stoplight at a dangerous intersection to the elements of national health care reform. Many nonprofits encourage the people with whom they work to be active with advocacy groups that are working to address an issue or to volunteer to serve on the citizen task forces and committees that inform governmental activities.

For increasingly large numbers of nonprofits, nonpartisan voter mobilization builds on the organization's trusted role in the community to encourage those eligible to vote to learn the election process, register to vote, know about issues and candidates, and vote. These activities have drawn many people into exercising their proper role in democracy in the interests of themselves and their community. In Minneapolis, for example, a neighborhood association that included forty buildings in two precincts decided that their needs were getting little if any attention from city or state officials. Therefore, the leaders of this "High Rise Council" sought training in nonpartisan voter engagement work and implemented voter registration drives, candidate forums, and voter turnout reminders that enabled them to meet their goal: 90 percent of eligible voters in the forty buildings voted. They are now on the radar of those who decide where precious resources go and whose phone calls to return.

Nonprofits that are involved in advocacy and civic engagement build ongoing efforts to advance issues in multiple ways. They also create opportunities for supporters to stay engaged in advancing issues on many fronts.

FIGURE 13.1. ADVOCACY CYCLE.

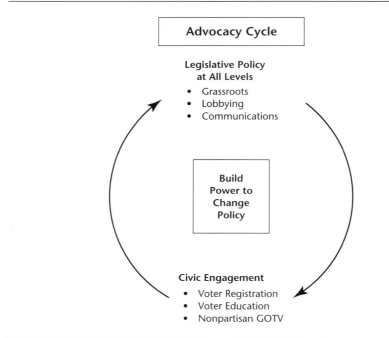

Source: Grassroots Solutions (www.grassrootssolutions.org). © 2009 Grassroots Solutions, Minneapolis, MN. Reprinted by permission.

Nonprofit Activism and the Law[1]

Nonprofits have the opportunity and responsibility to engage in democracy-supporting activities as discussed here; nonprofit executives and board members need to recognize that lobbying is legal and encouraged.

In the United States, the federal Internal Revenue Service (IRS) regulates lobbying activities. At the federal level, the oldest standard for lobbying limits has been the 1934 "insubstantial part test," which states that "no substantial part of a charity's activities...may be carrying on propaganda or otherwise attempting to influence legislation." This dangerously vague standard frustrated and intimidated proponents of nonprofit lobbying and led to successful pressure for the passage of the 1976 Lobby Law, which established a "bright line test" for the limits of permissible lobbying. (See Chapter Two for more on all facets of U.S. nonprofit law.)

The IRS developed rules under the 1976 law that establish a clear expenditure test for 501(c)3 lobbying. This bright line test requires nonprofits to file IRS Form 5768, known as the "h election" because it refers to Section 501(h) in the Internal Revenue Code. The h election provides a generous allowance for lobbying activity, capped at $1 million in lobbying expenditures:

- 20 percent of the first $500,000 of exempt purpose expenditures, plus
- 15 percent of the next $500,000 of exempt purpose expenditures, plus
- 10 percent of the next $500,000 of exempt purpose expenditures, plus
- 5 percent of the remaining exempt purpose expenditures up to $1 million

More of the expenditures allowed under the h election may be used for direct lobbying than for grassroots lobbying. Direct lobbying, in which the nonprofit and its members ask legislators to vote or act in a particular way on a specific issue, may be used for the full amount of the allowed expenditure. If the nonprofit reaches out to the broader public, which constitutes grassroots lobbying, only 25 percent of the allowable expenditure may be dedicated to that work.

Many activities are not counted as lobbying, thus making the lobby limits even more generous. Activities *not* counted as lobbying include

- Contact with elected officials or executive branch officials on proposed regulation (as opposed to legislation)
- Lobbying by volunteers (because no money is expended; only reimbursement for travel or meals for volunteers is counted)
- Response to written requests to testify before legislative bodies

Lobbying activity is reported as a component of a nonprofit's Form 990 filing with the IRS. Nonprofits that have taken the h election have a much simpler expenditure report than those that choose not to use the h election. Those not choosing the h election need to provide detailed descriptions of all lobbying activity. It is recommended that nonprofits that are comfortable with the $1 million cap on the lobby limits file for the h election.

In spite of the clarity of the bright line expenditure test option, studies of 2000 organizations were conducted by Jeff Berry and David Arons in 2003; they concluded that most view the rules as overly complex. For this reason, the rules and reporting requirements have had a chilling effect on nonprofit lobbying.

The perception that lobbying is not permissible and that nonprofits will be overly burdened by reporting requirements needs to be tackled in two ways. First, national organizations that lobby on behalf of the nonprofit sector need to continue to educate nonprofits and work for lobby reform. The Alliance for Justice, the Center for Lobbying in the Public Interest, and OMB Watch are good resources. As Elizabeth Reid notes (2006, p. 355), "These nonprofit-sector trade organizations and coalitions represent a formidable lobby on behalf of the nonprofit sector, defending the advocacy of nonprofits as critical public input to developing policies responsive to communities and opposing regulation that might further dampen nonprofit advocacy activity."

Second, individual nonprofit board and staff leaders need to take advantage of the resources available to help them understand the rules that govern lobbying and assure that their organizations choose to elect as appropriate and then have in place the simple systems required for tracking time and expenditures that need to be reported.

More detailed information about the lobby law itself and action steps for nonprofits that choose the h election are available on the Internet resource site for this handbook. There readers will find samples of IRS form 5768, sample forms to enable a nonprofit to track time and expenditures for lobbying activity, and samples of 990 reporting. Organizations that provide information, training, and work for lobby law reform are easy to access from this resource site, as well.

Nonprofit Nonpartisan Election Activities and the Law

Nonprofits are prohibited from participating in partisan political activity, and they may not take any steps to influence the outcome of an election by supporting individual candidates or parties. Nonetheless, nonprofits (while taking care to be rigorously nonpartisan) have an important role to play in elections. In

2004, nonprofits in over sixteen states participated in National Voice, a broad alliance of nonprofits that used the strength of their relationships with their constituencies to engage them in the election. Many reached out to educate potential voters about the issues at stake. Others called on new and infrequent voters to learn about the issues and candidates and to vote, so that they and their community had a voice in the election and a powerful presence that elected officials would remember. Some nonprofits worked to ensure that those they serve registered, if eligible. Nonprofits as diverse as the League of Women Voters, NAACP, YWCA, Community Action Agency, and Arts Alliances combined efforts at the local level to host candidate forums. Working together, they had the strength of numbers to draw the candidates and the voters together to discuss issues and learn about candidates' positions. In all instances, they trusted the voters to decide how to vote. The nonprofits' work was to educate, inform, and mobilize often hard-to-reach voters.

National Voice was one organized C3 effort at engaging voters in dynamic dialogue and high turnout efforts, and nonprofit work in this arena has been growing rapidly since 2004. In the 2008 election cycle nonprofits across the country and from diverse perspectives engaged in education on major issues and inspired increased voting.

The national Nonprofit Voter Engagement Network serves as a resource to 501(c)(3) organizations nationwide by providing them with basics of the law, toolkits, and materials for reaching voters and conducting nonpartisan voter registration efforts, candidate and voter education, and Get-Out-the-Vote. The Alliance for Justice has excellent training and materials for nonprofits and delves into the differences among charities and the permissible activity for them as compared to other organizations—for example, public welfare organizations, unions, and political action committees.

These efforts to strengthen democracy go hand in hand with issue advocacy, as nonprofits inspire and activate higher levels of informed engagement in elections and policy formation. Nonprofits and their supporters can work for change by staying engaged in permissible lobbying and civic engagement activities.

Checklist: Preparing Your Organization for Nonprofit Advocacy Engagement

Nonprofit advocacy and nonpartisan voter engagement are legal. But what steps do nonprofits need to take to do this work well? Here is a checklist of preparatory steps:

- Formalize the organization's commitment to advocacy
- Know the laws governing nonprofit lobbying and election activity
- Develop a strategic plan for advocacy work

- Identify capacity needs and plan to build the capacity needed
- Be issue experts: conduct and prepare research and communications
- Learn about policy arenas where you will be working
- Target and recruit allies and partners
- Study and prepare to respond to opponents
- Build advocacy and organizing skills

Build Advocacy Capacity

Although it is easy to identify many nonprofits that have an ongoing commitment to public policy advocacy and to celebrate their accomplishments, most small and midsize nonprofits have engaged in little intentional planning for advocacy as a key strategy. Nonprofit leaders, good stewards for their organizations, step forward when there is an immediate threat of cuts in government funding, but they don't build the commitment, capacity, or skills to sustain their advocacy efforts. To advance their ability to use advocacy as a tool for shaping change, nonprofits would benefit from the following specific steps:

Make a commitment. The board and staff of a nonprofit need to agree that advocacy is a key component of their work. Organizations that do so often design board-level policy committees or policy councils that include program participants, sister organizations, and community leaders to ensure there is good counsel and focused attention to policy work.

Plan. Advocacy should be included in an overall strategic plan, or an advocacy plan can be developed and integrated into the organization's overall strategic plan. Sample planning guides are available on this chapter's section of the handbook's Internet resource site. Among the core planning questions: Is our organization making a short-term or long-term commitment to advocacy? What are our near and long-term policy goals? What systems do we need to develop to support issue selection, timely decision making, and securing the resources and skills needed for the work? Who will shape and implement the advocacy plan and serve in the role of policy coordinator?

Build capacity. The organization needs to identify needs and current capacity. There are guides available to support nonprofits in assessing their capacity needs (see the Internet resource site). In addition to a strong strategic plan for advocacy, nonprofits can rely on a growing field of publications to determine

- The organization's decision-making processes
- Criteria for issue selection

- Processes and protocols in targeted executive and legislative arenas of influence at the local, state, or national level
- Commitments of staff time and resources to advocacy at levels that are carefully matched to advocacy goals
- Communication systems for internal and external information dissemination

Strengthen the knowledge base. Conduct research. Collect information. Format the data and stories that your organization has built over time. Understand where there are additional informational resources. Nonprofits add value to the policy dialogue because of the experience and information that they bring to the table. Be sure that you make a strong case for your position by having user-friendly data and well-developed and presented stories.

Know the arenas for change. At all levels of government, Internet-based information is available about how policies and budgets progress through a policy process, timelines for action, and the roles and background of key decision makers. Often the elected officials who champion the issues that you are working on and those elected in the areas that you serve can be your guides. Staff for individual elected officials and for committees that work with your issues can provide essential information about the process and the history of the issues.

Identify partners. Many issues are important to multiple nonprofits and the people they serve. A nonprofit new to advocacy rarely has to discover and do this work alone. It is often most productive to work with existing or emerging alliances and coalitions with which your organization has a common agenda. It is useful to find partners and mentors, and state or national organizations can be helpful matchmakers. The National Council of Nonprofits can identify state-level associations of nonprofits; these associations can facilitate connections to like-minded organizations. National organizations that focus on your issues can be especially helpful with materials, model advocacy efforts, and identification of allies.

Understand the opposition. Knowing who opposes your position and why enables your nonprofit to prepare responses to other points of view. Elected officials appreciate knowing what you know about all "sides" on an issue. In addition, knowing the opposition's case allows you to preempt their key messages by addressing them in your own case statements.

Build skills. Much nonprofit advocacy depends on relational skills, and nonprofits can gain training in the key components of advocacy, lobbying, and civic engagement from state or national infrastructure organizations.

State associations of nonprofits usually provide training and materials to their members and others, and entities such as the Center for Lobbying in the Public Interest, United Way of America, the Building Movement Project, Wellstone Action, and universities with leadership programs do skill-building training.

Framework for Advocacy: A Pragmatic Approach to Advocacy and Lobbying

Checklist: Steps in Developing and Implementing a Lobbying Plan

The following are essential to do as you develop and prepare to implement your lobbying plan:

- Understand the framework for an advocacy action plan (presented following) and apply it to your issue and our planning process
- Set your policy issue goals
- Prepare your key messages and materials
- Include messages about your organization as well as your issues
- Identify and prepare your key messengers: lobbyists and organizational spokespersons

Once nonprofits understand that advocacy is part of their work and have made a commitment to implement advocacy strategies, it is important to understand how to act on policy issues. Whether the objective is to propose a new policy, join efforts to pass legislation, or stop a proposal deemed harmful, nonprofits can be rapid responders to immediate needs and can build effective advocacy and lobbying strategies with a pragmatic and systematic approach.

The Advocacy Triangle of Figure 13.2 poses four key questions that a nonprofit should address with a high level of specificity. Once the nonprofit decides on what it wants to happen, and how to talk about it, there are three core tactics to be considered: direct lobbying, grassroots organizing, and media advocacy.

Core Questions

1. What is the problem or opportunity?
2. What do you want to have happen?
3. Who decides?
4. How do you influence them?

FIGURE 13.2. THE ADVOCACY TRIANGLE.

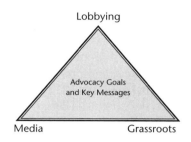

Set Goals: What Do You Want to Have Happen?

Advocacy and lobbying are heavily influenced by external factors that the nonprofit cannot control. Although nonprofits do this work to create sound policies by passing laws and ensuring that they are implemented, there are many objectives to be met along the way to achieving a "win." It is important to set goals and specific objectives related to the policy result to be achieved, but also aim to

- Establish your organization as a trusted resource to elected officials and staff
- Insert your experience, expertise, and point of view into the policy dialogue
- Build support from likely and unexpected sources
- Establish ongoing connections to the base of supporters to build power for the long term
- Build positive working relationships with decision makers, staff, and media
- Position your work to be covered favorably in traditional and social media
- Strengthen internal capacity, including board capacity for engagement in advocacy (including an active policy committee)

Focus on Position and Power

Remember, nonprofit advocacy is most effective if it is based on a long-term, sustained effort to work for change relating to your organization's values, vision, and mission. In setting goals, place a premium on *positioning your organization* to be a resource and a valuable leader in the public dialogue and *building power* to work for the changes that are needed.

Prepare Key Messages and Messengers

Nonprofits need to be able to provide clear and compelling case statements. What is the problem or opportunity? What is the proposed solution and why? What is your organization and what is your expertise and position?

Once these questions are addressed in thoughtful message development, they become the background for consistent messaging throughout an advocacy campaign. The core message should be used internally in building and expanding the base, in conversations with elected officials and other leaders, and in media messages. The challenge is to present the core message in a way that is effective with the intended audience. (Chapter Twelve, Strategic Communications, includes additional ideas for this process.) Once the case statement is prepared, short versions of the key themes work well in introductory meetings with all target audiences.

Match the depth of detail in the message, the tone of the message, and the medium for moving the message to the intended audience. What do they care about? How do you connect your cause to their interests? What do they need to know about the issue and your position even if they have only a brief amount of time with you?

It is useful to assess each audience by asking: What do they need to know? Who do they need to hear from? The messenger is as important as the message. The organization should determine who manages the message as it adapts to the evolution of the dialogue, who prepares messengers, and ways to have a consistent and disciplined message while reaching out to many audiences.

In most organizations, members of the board and executive staff are strong candidates for the position of organizational spokesperson. These are the people whom the press and public expect to hear from on your key issues. Lobbyists can be these same people, but it is usually wise to have those who are doing direct lobbying include issue experts and grassroots advocates who are constituents of the elected official whom you are approaching. Develop a strategy of matching the messenger to the audience.

Primary Advocacy Actions: Direct Lobbying, Grassroots Organizing, and Media Advocacy

Effective nonprofit advocacy comprises a number of specific processes and activities, including direct lobbying, grassroots organizing, and media advocacy. Each offers its own unique leverage and value in the advocacy process, and the choice to employ one or more is an important strategic decision.

Direct Lobbying

Lobbying, and the relationship building, education, and advocacy that lead to lobbying, are most effective when organizations begin to work with policy decision makers well prior to the "ask" for a "yes" or "no" vote on specific legislation.

Checklist: Steps in Direct Lobbying

The following are essential to do as you prepare to engage in direct lobbying:

- Identify and learn about the decision makers whom you need to influence and whose support you need to win
- Establish strong working relationships with key elected officials as early as possible
- Identify the elected officials who are your champions and work closely with them
- Present your information to targeted elected officials and their staff
- Ask decision makers to support your position
- Respond to decision makers based on their level of agreement with you

Targeting. Early in an advocacy effort, determine which elected officials you need to work with most closely. This can be ascertained by where you have the most power because your organizations and the people you serve are constituents. It is prudent to build the best possible relationships with those who are designated representatives for your area and where the official is held accountable at election time by those in the district. Other priority targets should be based on the power, position, and passion of the elected official. Identify

- Who has cared about this or similar issues and is likely to share our values and position? Who serves on the committees that will hear our policy issue?
- Who is a champion for our cause who is in the political majority and has a power advantage?
- Who will demonstrate broad support if added to our list of allies based on geography, ethnicity, gender, political party, leadership within the city council, legislature, or Congress?
- Who will work well across party lines and between legislative bodies—House and Senate, for example.

Build Strategic Relationships. If your organization is to be a trusted resource for elected officials and in a position to influence them, it is important that they know your organization and that you articulate common interests. Research helps. Check Web sites, blogs, and press coverage to learn about officials you wish to influence. Examine what they have supported in the past. Understand the issues that are key in the official's district and to her political party. And then begin to meet.

Some meeting options:

- Meet at your organization's site. This is especially appropriate for the officials who represent the district, but anyone interested in your issues should be invited to a "kitchen table" meeting with a few people (for example, board, staff, program participants) who can explain who you are, what you care about, and why. These site meetings are often the best venue for listening to the elected official. Ask her to share her goals, expectations, and hopes for the work ahead. Understand where there is shared experience—perhaps with illness in the family or an experience with an injustice, or a shared frustration with a system that isn't meeting its public purpose.
- Convince the elected official that you can be or are a resource in your issue areas, and provide information and "real people" who can tell their stories as part of the policy debate.
- Invite elected officials to tell you how they prefer to receive communications with you (for example, which e-mail address? Which phone number? In their office or at home in the community?).
- Stay in touch. Consider your advocacy to be an ongoing conversation with those whose support you have and want. Information updates, a presence at their community meetings, all strengthen relationships.
- Maintain the trust. Always tell the truth, get information that is requested, and deliver what you promise.

Identify Elected Officials Who Are Your Champions. Early in your lobbying effort, identify the elected officials who are likely to be your strongest supporters and who are also in a position to advance your cause. It is useful to have champions who are passionate about your issue, respected by their peers and able to garner bipartisan support, and in positions of power on the committees that will carry primary responsibility for your issue area. Your champions may turn out to be authors of the bills that you propose or support. The policy leaders with whom you work in partnership have the ability to guide you through the intricacies of legislative processes as they advance the issue. And they will count on you to be a good partner. The nonprofit organization's role is to ensure that the legislative champions for the issue have accurate and compelling information, visible and broad support in the community, and people who will work in support of the issue.

And Let the Lobbying Begin. Present your ideas to elected officials whom you have identified as the decision makers whom you need to influence. The messages, messengers, and materials that you prepared early in your planning and preparation swing into action mode now.

Prepare elected officials by communicating with them about your issue and position. Nonprofits often take advantage of the time before elected officials are in decision-making mode to meet with them at the nonprofit site, in the district, or at their offices to introduce the organization and the issue. Preliminary meetings establish your presence on an issue and can encourage the elected official to recognize you as a resource on the issue as well as an organization that wants to be at the table as the issue is addressed. The more time spent educating and persuading elected officials with meetings, letters, e-mails, and calls before they have to make a decision the better. Nonprofits sometimes create events, including legislative forums or a "Day on the Hill." Such events may attract media attention and become a forum for both explaining your position and demonstrating how many people support your position.

As the time nears for decision making, be sure to build on early contacts and work hard to persuade elected officials to commit to supporting you or to letting you know how you might win their support. Grassroots advocacy, discussed under that heading below, is one component of persuasion. In direct lobbying, however, nonprofits are best served by having a small group meet with the targeted elected officials. These are most often leaders on the issue, members of the committee who will hear the bill, and legislative leaders.

The nonprofit should have a small group participate in the meeting, including a person with expertise on the issue, a constituent when possible, someone with a story to tell to illustrate the importance of the position that you are advocating. People learn from stories, and elected officials like to have facts and illustrative examples to use in their thinking and in their own discussions about the issue.

Set up meetings by contacting the staff person who schedules the elected official's appointments. Be sure to identify the nonprofit, the issue, and indicate whenever possible that a constituent will be part of the small group at the meeting.

Keep a few tips in mind for your meeting with an elected official:

- Be on time and be prepared. It is a good idea to "rehearse" legislative meetings when you are new to this effort.
- Identify yourself to the staff and tell staff a little about your issue. Offer thanks for setting up the meeting and provide contact information to the staff in case he or she or the elected official need to reach you at a future time.
- Greet the official warmly and introduce the members of your team by identifying their role in your organization and on the issue. It is effective to have one person on the team serve as the key facilitator for your team.

- Verify the amount of time that the official has for the meeting so that you can get to your key points in a timely way.
- Remind the official of your previous discussions or contacts.
- Be direct and clear: explain why you are there and what you want.
- Provide brief, clear, materials.
- Provide an opportunity for the official to ask questions.
- Make a direct ask: Do you support us and will you vote for our position?
- Next steps depend upon the elected official's answer.

Be clear when you ask an elected official for support for your position. What do you want? Why? What is your counter to opposing arguments? And who cares? If constituents, other elected officials, your base and allies care, then share that information.

> *The answer is yes.* When an elected official supports your position, thanks are in order. Push to understand how much the elected official is willing to do in addition to voting in the way that you have requested. Will she talk to other legislators? Author an ordinance or bill? Ask for a hearing? Talk to the press? And be sure to provide elected officials who are your advocates with the information and insights that will help them.
>
> *The answer is "I don't know yet."* This is the time to ask: What do you need to know? Who do you need to hear from? And then follow through to the extent possible with information and contacts.
>
> *And "absolutely not!"* It isn't worth spending too much time with those who clearly oppose your position and tell you that they are immovable. It is worth asking whether anything would change their position. But a strong tactic is to avoid an unnecessarily negative exchange. The opponent on one issue can surface as the supporter on another. "Thank you for meeting with us. We hope we can work together on issues in the future," is an exit line that prevents you from making an enemy.

In all exchanges with elected officials, it is helpful to have brief and compelling materials, back-up documents for those who want to delve into the issue, and a list of contact people whom the official can reach with questions and requests.

A word about staff: When elected officials have staff who work for them, those staff should be included in your relationship-building approach. Often the staff person maintains the information files, contact lists, and requests that you make. More important is the reality that staff facilitates everything from your access to an individual elected official to who is on the agenda when a policy proposal is being heard. Respect the time pressures and responsibilities of staff, but recognize their important to the process. Distinguish your organization by thanking them for their help!

Lobbying includes meetings, calls, letters, e-mails, testimony, press events, and other communication formats that request support. Be strategic in matching your approach to the interests and styles of the officials and staff as you get to know them and as you demonstrate that you add value to the public policy debate. Purely public charities are often trusted because of the information and people they bring to the table. Nonprofits can position themselves to be seen as the ethical voice of the community in contrast with the self-interest of private sector lobbyists. Maintain the trust.

Grassroots Organizing

Grassroots organizing is the most essential of the strategies central to effective nonprofit advocacy to achieve short-term and long-term policy reforms. Grassroots community-based organizing is the process through which people plan and build shared efforts to work for the changes that they want on their issues. Organizing enables people to build the power they need to advance issues, challenge failed systems, and become respected participants in decisions that affect their lives.

After he graduated from college and before he entered Harvard Law School, Barack Obama worked for three years as a community organizer on Chicago's south side. According to Obama (1990):

> Organizing begins with the premise that (1) the problems facing inner-city communities do not result from a lack of effective solutions, but from a lack of power to implement these solutions; (2) that the only way for communities to build viable long-term power is by organizing people and money around a common vision; and (3) that a viable organization can only be achieved if a broadly based indigenous leadership—and not one or two charismatic leaders—can knit together the diverse interests of their local institutions.

Nonprofits are often quite effective at mobilizing those who support them for a short-term effort. But mobilizing is only one component of organizing. Organizing builds a sustainable base, builds power, and builds leadership. Mobilizing is one tool that organizers use to activate their base at strategic points. Nonprofits are well served if they focus on organizing and building an ever growing and regularly engaged base.

Marshall Ganz, now at Harvard's Kennedy School, has developed theories of leadership and organizing that provide helpful background to nonprofits moving into this arena of advocacy. He underscores that "Organizers identify, recruit, and develop leadership; build community around leadership, and build power out of community" (Ganz, 2009, pp. 16–17).

Short-term and long-term advocacy initiatives benefit from effective organizing, base building, and advocacy. Nonprofits working on issue campaigns are most likely to achieve desired policies if they build, sustain, and activate a base of support that is able to use its collective power to influence public awareness, political will, and decision makers.

Organizing is especially important in the highly polarized political landscape that dominates policy dialogues at the federal, state, and local level. Elected officials are demonstrating high levels of loyalty to partisan agendas. To override the demands for disciplined support for political party agendas, nonprofits have to rely on the individual values of a particular legislator or build enough pressure in the elected official's district to persuade her or him that the official's community has placed a high priority on your issue and position. Good organizing includes holding decision makers accountable, and community voices have a keen influence in many instances.

Organizing support for public policy issues will require each organization to determine its particular approach to this work. For organizations already working with an activated constituency, the ongoing engagement and expansion of the base is important. For organizations new to this work, starting within the organization and reaching out to potential allies, both organizations and individuals, will be a starting point. The common components of nonprofit grassroots organizing are targeting supporters, recruiting supporters, engaging supporters, mobilizing the base, evaluation of activities, and reengagement.

Checklist: Key Organizing Actions

- Identify existing supporters.
- Develop a list of potential supporters. These are your "targets."
- Recruit. Reach out to have conversations with potential supporters. Understand their interests and allow those interests to influence your organizing and advocacy strategies.
- Engage supporters and make them an integral part of your team. Provide information, gather their knowledge and stories, include them in planning and strategy sessions, and be responsive in dialogue with them.
- Prepare your base so that people have training in the skills that you are asking them to use and know what they will be asked to do and when.
- Mobilize the base when the time is ripe for their advocacy in activities ranging from e-mails to meetings to events.

- Debrief and evaluate your collective efforts. Celebrate accomplishments and the rewards of working collectively.
- Reengage for the next tier of action on your issues.

Analysis of Potential Supporters. A nonprofit has rarely reached all those who care about the success of its policy efforts. Mapping stakeholder potential allows a nonprofit to be strategic in targeting outreach and organizing. Who cares about the issue? Within that broad potential, which individuals and organizations add the most value to your effort, based on everything from the strength of their numbers to their status in the policy debate? Whom can you reach easily within the complement of groups who would be valuable supporters?

Cycle of Organizing. The ongoing work of building a base, building power, ensuring that people have a voice on issues, requires an ongoing cycle of activity

FIGURE 13.3. ADVOCACY AND ORGANIZING CYCLE.

Source: Grassroots Solutions (www.grassrootssolutions.org). © 2009 Grassroots Solutions, Minneapolis, MN. Reprinted by permission.

(see Figure 13.3). In organizing for public policy advocacy and in organizing for civic engagement, nonprofits target those who will support and advance their work, recruit supporters, often with initial personal contact, and ensure that supporters are engaged, informed, and trained for their role. Once supporters have been engaged, then it is possible to do authentic grassroots mobilizing, calling upon people to do the work that you have been getting ready for over time. The action is not the end. It is a step along the way. Every action deserves a debriefing session and evaluation. Each support can be applauded and thanked. And then: reengage.

Media Advocacy
Checklist: Elements of Media Advocacy

- Learn about the media available to you, traditional and new media.
- Identify and build working relationships with members of the media who cover your issue area, government, and politics.
- Present your organization as a resource to the media on issues in which you have expertise.
- Prepare your key messages and adapt them for many forms of earned media: letters to the editor, opinion editorials, YouTube or Facebook postings, Web postings, and other available outlets.
- Provide the media with contacts 24/7. Their deadlines may not coincide with your usual working hours.
- Build and maintain good media lists and communications systems for reaching media.

Public policy advocacy, lobbying, and civic engagement depend on building solid working relationships, and this is true in media advocacy. Nonprofits strive to have their issues and activities portrayed positively in all media forms. Often having an editorial or feature story about the value of your organization's issues and programs provides a spotlight that will gather the attention that you seek from supporters.

Nonprofits work with both earned media and paid media. In all instances, the challenge is to convey key messages to target audiences using media that they use and respect. For elected officials, newspaper coverage matters. Most political leaders pay close attention to opinion pieces, editorials, letters to the editor, online or in newspapers, especially in their districts. Supporters are encouraged by supportive news coverage and excited by the opportunity to participate in the public debate on the radio or TV. Social media can be especially effective in providing up-to-date information, commentary, and calls to action to the base, thus giving them knowledge and building momentum for their action.

Message development and media strategies are key components of advocacy, and much has been written to guide nonprofits. Large coalitions often work with media consultants who can shape the messages and media used in an advocacy or organizing campaign. Polling and focus groups can strengthen message development. In an information-overloaded society, selecting the most compelling and user-friendly ways to reach target audiences is a priority.

Regardless of the scale of the effort, relationships with target audiences matter. To get media attention, to be consulted by the media for your point of view on your issues, to establish your organization as an interesting and reliable source of news and feature stories, study the media available to you. Who covers your issues? Who vets opinion pieces for news and radio outlets? Which blogs have legitimacy with target audiences? Which radio producers program policy debates? Once you identify the media useful for your effort, introduce your organization to members of the press and producers in brief meetings that demonstrate that you are a resource to them.

Plan media components to your advocacy work as part of your overall advocacy strategy and prepare the groundwork so that you have access when needed and your role in the public debate and promotion of civic engagement is elevated.

Evaluating Public Policy Advocacy, Lobbying, and Civic Engagement

As with all initiatives, policy, lobbying, and civic engagement work should be evaluated relative to the project goals and objectives to the extent possible. For all forms of advocacy, however, many projects move slowly and in increments. Some work—engaging the broad public in increased civic activity—is never done. Some issue-related work advances only when the political landscape and public will are ready. Therefore:

Nonprofits should rely on quantitative and qualitative tools to assess progress.

Questions to consider include measures of gains and continuing needs in organizational capacity, the extent of base building in progress, the quality and nature of relationships with elected officials and the media, progress on increasing voter turnout or moving the needle on an issue in decision-making areas, and the satisfaction of those organizations and individuals in their experience with your organization.

Design evaluation as part of the initial work plan and capture stories as well as data throughout the work. The sector needs case stories from which to learn more about this ever-growing field of advocacy, and your organization and others will benefit from what you can measure and what you learn from stories about signs of progress or concern. Your assessment of this work is ongoing and can direct your organization to make timely and strategic course corrections, as well as build on your strengths.

Advancing Advocacy as a Field

No significant social change has ever taken place without the energy and perseverance of movements and advocates.

GARA LAMARCHE, ATLANTIC PHILANTHROPIES (2008)

As more and more nonprofits engage in civic life and draw their constituencies into the public decisions in our society, nonprofits are increasingly a force for change. Collective action, collective power, commitment to sustained effort in advocacy, lobbying, and civic engagement strengthen the nonprofit sector and position it for increasing power.

As your organization strives for excellence in meeting its mission, include public policy advocacy in your strategic planning. The information included here will provide you with a sound starting place, and there are an increasing number of information resources, training opportunities, and partners available to help you with your advocacy initiatives. As you initiate or enhance your nonprofit's work in advocacy, these key lessons should drive your work.

1. Advocacy and lobbying are legal nonprofit activities, encouraged by the Congress and expected by elected officials.
2. Nonprofits need to be part of the public policy dialogue. The sector and its specific activity areas have the expertise and experience needed for a fully informed policy dialogue. In this sense, nonprofits are a critical resource for policy shapers and for the community. Those who count on nonprofit programs and services, also count on nonprofits to be a voice in shaping decisions in public arenas.
3. Nonprofit advocacy requires strategic planning. A basic framework for advancing issues allows you to define a need, propose a specific solution, determine where the issue is decided, and influence those decisions.
4. The three primary tools for nonprofit advocacy are organizing, lobbying, and media advocacy. Your organization can build its capacity in these skill areas with existing talent, the advocacy training materials available in the sector, and through training.

5. Nonprofits are a vehicle through which people participate in public life. One key role for nonprofits is to engage people through organizing and civic engagement initiatives. Doing this work on an ongoing basis builds power for your organization, your issue, and the people you represent and serve.

In a democratic society, nonprofits have the potential to level the playing field in policy arenas. Nonprofits have information and organized power that can offset the influence of other powerful groups in setting policies that have an impact on people and communities. For dedicated nonprofit leaders and managers, public policy engagement is an extraordinary leadership opportunity.

Advocacy work can position your nonprofit as the lead organization in an issue area, and it can secure your organization's place in leadership circles. Most important, advocacy can make an enormous difference in your organization's ability to serve people well for the long term. Advocacy can get to the root causes of basic social problems and, over time, redefine the context within which people and communities strive for fairness, equity, and an acceptable quality of life.

Change sometimes takes a long time. The dedicated and determined leaders in the nonprofit sector who are committed to change need to be advocates for needed change.

There has rarely been a more important time for nonprofits to insist that the voices of people in communities are heard. It is important for nonprofits to recognize the value of their deep knowledge of issues and people's needs and experience. And it is important for nonprofits to insist that that knowledge is included in public dialogue.

Advocacy is important and it is exciting. Be the person to encourage the nonprofits with which you work to begin or expand their commitment to advocacy. When the choices are between angst and action, nonprofits are charged with being the steady hand and the strong voice that speaks to community needs and advocates for change.

Begin now to do your part. Start the conversation. Help plan the work. Join with others to build a strong base of support and a meaningful role in shaping public policies.

Note

1. It is important to keep in mind that the nonprofit law explained in this chapter applies to active 501(c)3 charitable organizations. Community foundations are permitted to lobby in similar ways. But other nonprofits and foundations are governed by different rules. The Alliance for Justice and the Council of Foundations are two good resources for the rules applicable to foundations and other nonprofit organizations that are not public charities.

References

Arons, D. F., "Lobbying, Advocacy, and Nonprofit Management." In V. Futter, J. Cion, and G. W. Overton (eds.), *Nonprofit Governance and Management* (2nd ed.). Chicago, American Bar Association Section of Business Law and American Society of Corporate Secretaries, 2002.

Bass, G. D. "Advocacy in the Public Interest." *Essays on Excellence: Lessons from the Georgetown Nonprofit Management Executive Certificate Program.* Washington, D.C.: Georgetown University, 2009.

Berry, J. M., and Arons, D. F. *A Voice for Nonprofits.* Washington, D.C.: Brookings Institution Press, 2003.

Ganz, M. *Why David Sometimes Wins.* New York: Oxford University Press, 2009.

LaMarche, G. "Building Capacity for Maximum Impact." www.theatlanticphilanthropies.org. Feb. 28, 2008.

Obama, B. "Why Organize? Problems and Promise in the Inner City." In P. Knoepfle (ed.), *After Alinsky: Community Organizing in Illinois.* Chicago: Institute for Public Affairs, 1990.

Reid, E. J. "Advocacy and the Challenges It Presents for Nonprofits." In E. T. Boris and C. E. Steuerle (eds.), *Nonprofits and Government: Collaboration and Conflict.* Washington, D.C.: The Urban Institute Press, (2nd. ed). 2006.

Smucker, B. "Nonprofit Lobbying." In R. D. Herman (ed.), *The Jossey-Bass Handbook of Nonprofit Leadership and Management.* San Francisco: Jossey Bass, 2005, 230–253.

CHAPTER FOURTEEN

COLLABORATION AND STRATEGIC ALLIANCES

John A. Yankey and Carol K. Willen

The trend toward partnering in the nonprofit sector traces its origins to the 1980s, when social service agencies and health care providers, facing increased competition from for-profit entities, began forming alliances in order to respond to community needs and ensure their own institutional viability (Bailey and Koney, 2000). Nonprofits in other subsectors, following the lead of organizations in the human service and health fields, soon adopted the practice of developing alliances as a way of addressing competitive forces and challenges of their own. New types of relationships began to emerge as organizations devised creative ways of building capacity; sharing costs, benefits, and risks; achieving synergies; competing successfully; accomplishing common goals; and fulfilling their individual missions. Salamon's 1999 call for "an explicit acknowledgment of the modern reality of collaborative problem-solving" and his vision of "*nonprofit organizations working collaboratively with government and the business sector to respond to societal needs,*" offer a prescient forecast of the dynamics of interorganizational relationships in the first decade of the twenty-first century (Salamon, 1999, p. 179, emphasis in the original).

By the beginning of the 2008 recession, the number of tax-exempt organizations registered with the Internal Revenue Service (excluding chambers of commerce, civic leagues, and religious congregations) had risen to well over 1.5 million (National Center for Charitable Statistics, 2008). The steep economic downturn not only produced the "perfect storm" for nonprofit organizations—a reduction in available resources conjoined with an increased demand for services—but has also focused even greater attention on the need for collaborative solutions. A March 2009 survey of over 1,100 nonprofit leaders nationwide conducted by the Nonprofit Finance Fund indicated that in order to weather challenging economic circumstances, 42 percent either had collaborated with another organization in the last twelve months to provide programs or anticipated doing so in the coming year; moreover, 13 percent had collaborated or planned to do so as a means of reducing administrative expenses (Nonprofit Finance Fund, 2009). In other parts of the United States, the tendency to seek or pursue collaborative opportunities as a means of coping with economic pressures was even more pronounced.[1] For their part, grantmakers, too, emphasized the need for collaboration as a response to the economic crisis; funders surveyed by the Foundation Center in September 2009 called it a "key to solving problems, meeting the needs of constituents, and delivering lasting impact" (Lawrence, 2009, p. 4).

Strategic Alliances and the Collaborative Process

While collaborative activity, including the exploration and formation of mergers and other alliances, has been called "the new strategic planning for the 21st century" (McLaughlin, 1998, p. xxii), there is neither a consensus on the selection of an all-encompassing name for partnering relationships nor a common nomenclature for the types of alliances or structures that can be formed. The absence of both a standard lexicon and a generally accepted theoretical base presents challenges for those who would seek to define and categorize such arrangements.[2]

A number of researchers and practitioners have created taxonomies and frameworks for organizing and categorizing alliance configurations by type, but these schema are based on conceptual variations. To further complicate matters, identical terms are employed by various authors to mean different things. A word used in an overarching or everyday sense by one author may, in the lexicon of another, refer to a specific alliance type.

When the term *collaboration* is employed to refer to the partnering relationship, it can be used in many different ways. For example, McLaughlin (1998) and the team of Mattessich, Murray-Close, and Monsey (2001) use *collaboration* as a general term encompassing the full array of alliance configurations. Bailey and Koney (2000) employ it to refer to one of four different "strategic alliance processes," specifically a process in which the partners are united by a common strategy, as in the case of consortia, networks, and joint ventures. While *collaboration* appears on the La Piana Partnership Matrix (La Piana, 1999), it is not considered to be a form of strategic restructuring.

In the context of this chapter, *collaboration* refers to the *process* of partnering, while the general name *strategic alliance* refers to the interorganizational relationship (IOR) itself. Strategic alliances, of which there are many types, are understood to be capacity-building mechanisms that enable partnering entities to achieve results exceeding those that might be attained on the basis of each participant's individual resources and efforts. Within this broad context, the partners can align themselves in any number of ways and with varying degrees of integration—an array of possible models ranging from the loosely connected to the highly integrated. For those who view such configurations through an IOR lens, a key feature of the collaborative process is the boundary-spanning aspect of the interaction between the partnering organizations (Alter, 2009, p. 436).

The choice of the adjective *strategic* underscores the purposeful quality of relationships in which two or more entities come together in a planned way in order to accomplish a mutually valued goal. For example, Bailey and Koney (2000), in defining strategic alliances, emphasize their intentional quality. Fosler (2002), whose focus is *intersectoral* collaboration involving government, business, and nonprofit organizations, speaks of "consciously undertaken joint activity among entities that would not ordinarily be expected to work intentionally together" (p. 19).

What is most important at this juncture is the recognition that both within the nonprofit world itself and across the sometimes blurry boundaries of the nonprofit, corporate, and public sectors, entities of various types are engaging in collaborative activity with increasing frequency in order to achieve mission enhancement and greater organizational effectiveness.

Driving Forces of Strategic Alliance Formation

Strategic alliances come into being for a host of different reasons, variously referred to as "driving forces," "drivers," or "motivations." Some authors emphasize conditions in the external environment that provide impetus for the formation of alliances, while others focus on the individual organization's internal rationale for seeking the benefits of partnering. Both sets of causes are important, and in some instances, an external force and an internal motive may be viewed as two ways of describing the same reality. Understanding the context for strategic alliance development requires examining *environmental* issues and trends as well as intraorganizational factors—*financial, managerial,* and *programmatic* considerations—for the kind of thinking required of nonprofit leaders and managers when contemplating an alliance is closely related to the process of strategic planning (Arsenault, 1998).

Environmental Drivers

"Turbulent" is a term frequently used to characterize the environment in which nonprofit organizations must operate. Powerful forces such as new technologies, globalization, regionalization, increased competition, the redefinition of performance, and the demand for greater accountability, along with other social, political, and cultural shifts, have affected government, business, and nonprofit organizations alike (Fosler, 2002). Besides competing for consumer attention and market share, nonprofits must vie for a diminishing pool of human and financial resources.

While competition has long been recognized as an environmental driver of alliance formation, in recent years the concept of collaborating with one's own competitors, an accepted notion in the for-profit world, has received increasing attention in the nonprofit literature. The neologism "co-opetition," attributed to Novell founder Raymond Noorda and later adopted by Brandenburger and Nalebuff in their book of the same name, refers to "a mind-set that combines competition and cooperation" (Brandenburger and Nalebuff, 1996). Building upon game theory, the authors demonstrate how to identify the players and their interdependencies, then "change the game." La Piana's *Play to Win: The Nonprofit Guide to Competitive Strategy* (2005) introduces nonprofit leaders to ways of creating "an optimal mix of collaborative and competitive relationships." In a rapidly changing environment, "being able to recognize when to collaborate and when to compete—and having the capacity to move with confidence between the two—will be key to nonprofits' ability to survive and thrive" (Gowdy, Hildebrand, La Piana, and Campos, 2009, p. 22). "Organizations must become more facile around all sorts of dynamics, from 'co-opetition' . . . to understanding joint ventures, mergers, and acquisitions activities," states David Eisner, former CEO of the Corporation for National and Community Service, in describing this critical skill (quoted in Gowdy et al., 2009, p. 22). For the Plexus Consulting Group, collaborating with a rival organization "is perhaps the epitome of strategic partnering" (Plexus, 2008, p. 34).

Changes in the funding climate are also critically important environmental factors. The economic events of 2008, leading to the most severe recession since the Great Depression, have had a profound effect on funders and nonprofits alike. The March 2009 policy report *The Quiet Crisis: The Impact of the Economic Downturn on the Nonprofit Sector* clearly describes the new funding environment:

> The economic recession has dramatically affected the nonprofit sector. The demand for services that nonprofits traditionally provide has increased significantly. Additionally, Americans have less disposable income to continue

giving at the levels they have in previous years . . . . In a survey conducted of 800 nonprofits at the end of 2008, 75 percent of nonprofits reported already feeling the effects of the downturn, with 52 percent already experiencing cuts in funding . . . . Across the country, nonprofits are feeling the pinch, particularly those that rely on government funding (with 61 percent of nonprofits reporting cuts in government funding) and those that rely on foundations for monetary contributions (with 48 percent of nonprofits reporting cuts in foundation funding). (Reed and Bridgeland, 2009, p. 6)

"The turbulent economy is creating new incentives for charities to cooperate," notes *The Chronicle of Philanthropy* in March 2009 under the headline "Economic Woes Bring More Charities Together: Nonprofit Organizations Look to Mergers and Collaborations as a Way of Surviving in Tough Times" (Wallace, 2009, p. 30). Not only are charity leaders seeking each other out in order to explore potential alliances, but in addition, funders themselves are fostering such conversations. Shifts in the flow of public dollars and cuts in government support, conjoined with a reduction in the availability of private funding for nonprofits due to the shrinkage of foundation endowments and the drop in corporate profits, have resulted in lower contribution levels and more intense competition for scarce resources. Under these circumstances, both public and private funders, intent on achieving maximum impact with finite resources while simultaneously promoting nonprofit efficiency and effectiveness, have encouraged, or even pressured, organizations to form alliances.

Two related developments in the philanthropic community merit attention in this regard. The first is an increase in the number and visibility of grantmaking initiatives specifically aimed at stimulating collaboration among grant recipients. This approach is illustrated by the Nonprofit Transitions Fund of The San Francisco Foundation, which was established in 2009 "to help organizations rethink and regroup in response to the downturn in the economy" (San Francisco Foundation Web site),[3] and the Fund for Financial Restructuring of The Columbus Foundation, also established in 2009, which will "support nonprofit leaders and their organizations as they adapt to the new economic reality facing the sector" (Columbus Foundation Web site). One of the areas for which The Columbus Foundation will provide funding is the "assessment of strategic partnerships and other forms of doing business, including shared services, formal affiliations, and mergers." Perhaps the most visible example of an effort by a grantmaker to recognize and reward collaboration, however, is the creation of the Collaboration Prize by the Lodestar Foundation, whose mission— "to maximize the growth and impact of philanthropy"—is "fulfilled, in part, by supporting collaborations that increase impact and eliminate duplication of efforts among nonprofits that would otherwise compete" (Collaboration Prize Web site). To build an information base of effective practice models, the Foundation collaborates with the AIM Alliance ©, which is itself a partnership among academic institutions in three states.[4]

A second noteworthy development in the philanthropic community is the rise in collaborative activity among grantmakers, accompanied by a growing literature on how funders can work together successfully, maximizing the impact of their limited dollars and at the same time achieving their own goals through partnering. It should also be noted that some funder collaboratives have assembled for the express purpose of stimulating collaboration on the part of their grantees. One such example is the Strategic Alliance Partnership in Toledo, Ohio, created in 1996 as a funding alliance of The Stranahan Foundation, the Toledo Community Foundation, and United Way of Greater Toledo in order to "challenge themselves and community institutions to find innovative ways to work collaboratively" (Toledo Community Foundation Web site).[5] Another example is the Nonprofit Alliance Support Program, an initiative of The Dayton (Ohio) Foundation, Montgomery County, the Dayton Power and Light Foundation, and the consulting firm Leadership Associates, which seeks to "help nonprofits develop new, more efficient ways to structure their organizations through partnerships, alliances or mergers" (Dayton Foundation Web site). Funder collaboratives, particularly those intentionally created to foster strategic alliance formation and restructuring among grantees, represent a unique opportunity for grantmakers and grantseekers to span the traditional boundaries between donor and recipient, experiment with new ways of working together, and in the process learn with—and from—their nonprofit partners, notes Denise San Antonio Zeman, President and CEO of the Saint Luke's Foundation (personal communication, Dec. 8, 2009).

Interorganizational alliances and collaborative approaches to problem-solving and service delivery are also vitally important in the realm of government funding, where potential partners may include public and private entities as well as other nonprofit organizations. President Barack Obama's February 5, 2009 Executive Order amending the January 29, 2001 order creating the White House Office of Faith-Based and Community Initiatives substitutes the name "White House Office of Faith-Based and Neighborhood Partnerships" for the original title of the office and underscores the critical role of the Federal Government in strengthening the ability of faith-based and other nonprofit providers "to deliver services effectively in partnership with Federal, State, and local governments and with other private organizations."

In the current economic environment, the capacity to form strategic relationships with other entities seeking government support and the ability to successfully operationalize funded projects with both new and traditional partners are skills that will serve the organization well. For example, under the aegis of the American Recovery and Reinvestment Act of 2009, while some economic stimulus funds are being distributed through direct federal competitive grants, other monies are flowing to—and through—state and local governments. Local officials may, in turn, "spend" those dollars by contracting with, or providing grants to, nonprofit organizations that will be engaged in direct service delivery. Throughout the process, nonprofits interested in securing ARRA dollars through grants or contracts have been advised to consider partnering with state or local governments and with other nonprofit organizations, especially with those agencies that have a positive track record as recipients of public funding. "Collaboration is the key to securing funding as well as meeting the very explicit requirements set out by most ARRA funding opportunities" (Massachusetts Nonprofit Network, 2009).

Another external driver of alliance formation is the performance culture that arose in the business world and has since spread to the public and nonprofit sectors (Fosler, 2002). Government interest in managed care and the adoption of a system of outcome assessment by United Way of America are but two examples of the growing emphasis on results. Private funders, too, are calling for evidence of a return on investment, establishing evaluation criteria for grants and tying future allocation decisions to the attainment of performance standards.

Strategic alliance formation can also be influenced by external factors such as political pressures and other dynamics in the environment that may cause organizations to reposition themselves. For example, proposed legislative, regulatory, or policy changes that may adversely affect a group of organizations, their funding, their tax-exempt status, or the population or cause that they serve can drive like-minded nonprofits to align themselves in coalitions so as to focus their advocacy efforts more effectively. Finally, real or perceived external threats, such as the discovery or the perception that funders are reevaluating their own strategic directions, may trigger preemptive actions on the part of nonprofits.

Internal Drivers

Because of the ominous implications of some of these external forces, it would not be difficult to conclude that alliance formation is tantamount to circling the wagons. However, by behaving *strategically*—that is, by joining together intentionally with one or more carefully selected partners—an organization can exercise a substantial measure of control over its own destiny. There are many benefits, both individual and collective, to be gained through involvement in such alliances. As positive motivations for alliance participation, these considerations provide the internal rationale that a nonprofit might use to explain or justify its actions to stakeholders. Yankey, Jacobus, and Koney (2001) categorize these driving forces as *financial, managerial,* or *programmatic.*

Financial drivers are among the most frequently cited reasons for pursuing a strategic alliance. By partnering, nonprofits can often achieve greater efficiency through economies of scale, gain access to increased (or more reliable or stable) external funding, leverage their strengths to increase purchasing power, obtain a better return on investment, improve cash flow, and enhance their bottom line. In fact, recent research has shown a positive relationship between the involvement of more collaborative partners (within certain limits) and the likelihood of obtaining financial support (Berardo, 2009).

Closely related to the financial forces that give impetus to alliance formation are the *managerial* drivers. Alliance participation enables nonprofits to acquire intellectual capital, expertise, and professional competencies, thus enriching their human resources. Organizations can also strengthen their strategic positions, solidify their service niche, gain increased visibility, and expand political influence. In addition, research suggests that under specific conditions, collaborative behavior can positively affect organizational performance (Berardo, 2009), and that interorganizational relationships can be related to organizational innovativeness (Jaskyte and Lee, 2006).

The final set of organizational drivers is *programmatic* in nature. Here the focus is on the "deliverables"—the organization's products and services. Partnering enables participating organizations to improve the quality of their offerings, diversify or expand their product or service mix, and extend their geographic market. In this way, strategic alliances help organizations realize their missions and at the same time demonstrate a commitment to social responsibility (Bailey and Koney, 2000).

From a programmatic perspective, alliances offer the potential for significant public benefit, for they build community capacity as well as organizational capacity and provide a way of ensuring the survival and increasing the availability of valued and important programs and services. In addition, alliances can "provide the resources necessary to sustain research and development of new tools, processes, and services" (Hoskins and Angelica, 2005, p. 8). Finally, if they are multisectoral in nature, they can help to foster systems change (Hoskins and Angelica, 2005).

Types of Strategic Alliances

As indicated, *strategic alliance*, *collaboration*, and *strategic restructuring* are terms frequently used by those who have conducted research in this area to describe intentional relationships aimed at maximizing the use of resources to advance the mission and goals of the organizational participants.

The various types of strategic alliances are typically arrayed along a continuum of progressively increasing levels of formalization or integration (Bailey and Koney, 2000) or mutual involvement (Girl Scouts of the USA, 1997). In their representation of strategic alliance options, Yankey, Jacobus, and Koney (2001) associate the degree of autonomy relinquished with a concomitant level of risk, while Arsenault (1998), in a pyramid depicting what is termed the Consolidation Continuum, incorporates three factors: autonomy, risk, and cost.

Figure 14.1 is a useful device for graphically depicting and differentiating alliance types proposed by various authors along parallel continua. The range of mutual involvement described by the national organization Girl Scouts of the USA (1997) identifies a series of key elements that are represented in the strategic alliances continuum. As one moves to the right on the continuum, incremental changes occur along seven dimensions:

- The intensity, scope, and duration of the joint efforts increase.
- There is greater unity of mission and purpose.
- The legal linkage of the organizations tends to become more complex and permanent.
- A greater amount of authority is ceded to the alliance.
- A higher degree of trust is necessary.
- A greater measure of change is required.
- The potential for resistance increases.

Cross-sectoral strategic alliances can be characterized in a similar manner. Austin (2000, p. 35), writing of collaboration between nonprofits and businesses, depicts a continuum reflecting progressive movement along the following dimensions:

- Level of engagement
- Importance to mission
- Magnitude of resources
- Scope of activities
- Interaction level
- Managerial complexity
- Strategic value

FIGURE 14.1. STRATEGIC ALLIANCE CONTINUA.

Girl Scouts of the USA *Alliance Strategies*	COORDINATE	COLLABORATE	JOINTLY OPERATE	UNITE
		Range of Mutual Involvement		
	Lesser →			→ Greater
Yankey, Jacobus, and Koney *Strategic Alliance Continuum*	Co-sponsorships	Federations Coalitions Consortia	Joint Ventures Networks Parent-subsidiaries	Mergers Consolidations
		Amount of Autonomy Relinquished/Level of Risk		
	Low →			→ High
Bailey and Koney *Strategic Alliance Processes and Models Along a Continuum*	COOPERATION Affiliations	COORDINATION Federations Associations Coalitions	COLLABORATION Consortia Networks Joint Ventures	COADUNATION Mergers Consolidations Acquisitions
		Formalization/Integration		
	Low →			→ High
Arsenault *Consolidation Continuum*	Joint Venture or Partnership	Management Service Organization	Parent Corporation	Merger Consolidation
	Lower risk Lower cost Autonomy maintained →			→ High risk High cost to create Reduced autonomy

Sources: Girl Scouts of the USA, 1997, pp. 13–14, 17; Yankey, Jacobus, and Koney, 2001, p. 6; Bailey & Koney, 2000, pp. 9–10 (Copyright © by Sage Publications, Inc. Reprinted by permission of Sage Publications, Inc.); and Arsenault, 1998, p. 34.

Each of the frameworks shown in Figure 14.1 seeks to encompass virtually every type of strategic alliance. Due in large measure to the absence of a generally accepted terminology and classification system, each framework uses a somewhat different set of names for the types that are displayed. In instances where the same word or phrase appears in more than one framework, its placement on each of the continua may be different.

Stages of Strategic Alliance Development

Despite the challenges posed by differences in language and taxonomy, one finds striking similarities among various descriptions of the stages of development of strategic alliances. Although scholars and practitioners who have written most recently on this topic have applied a variety of names to the evolutionary stages of alliance development—and have divided the process into differing numbers of steps—there is a consistency to the way in which they portray the sequence and nature of these stages. Commonalities among authors who envision a four-stage approach are apparent in Figure 14.2.

Every alliance, regardless of type, follows a "developmental path" which begins with one or more individuals conceiving of the possibility of partnering.

FIGURE 14.2. STAGES OF STRATEGIC ALLIANCE DEVELOPMENT.

	1	2	3	4
Girl Scouts of the USA	Exploration	Planning	Implementation and Integration	Evaluation
Yankey, Jacobus, and Koney	Making Decisions	Planning	Implementation	Reviewing or Evaluating
Bailey and Koney	Assembling	Ordering	Performing	Transforming
La Piana	Inspiration	Formalization	Operation	Institutionalization or Termination
Austin	Making Initial Connection	Ensuring Strategic Fit	Generating Value	Managing the Relationship

Sources: Girl Scouts of the USA, 1998, pp. 14–18; Yankey, Jacobus, and Koney, 2001, p. 17; Singer and Yankey, 1991, p. 358; Bailey & Koney, 2000, p. 33; La Piana, 2001, p. 7; and Austin, 2000, pp. 41–146.

Regardless of how it is labeled, the initial stage typically involves the following activities:

- Self-examination on the part of at least one organization (sometimes conducted in conjunction with a strategic planning process)
- A decision to explore the possibility of an alliance
- Identification of potential partners
- Initial contacts between representatives of the organizations
- Efforts to assess the degree of mutual interest

Before the parties agree to form an alliance, they must learn more about each other. The process known as "side-by-side analysis" entails the joint development of full-blown organizational profiles (Yankey, Jacobus, and Koney, 2001). Dimensions investigated include mission, vision, values, organizational culture, governance, programs and services, human resources (both paid and volunteer), facilities and equipment, financial management, fund development, and communications. In less formal alliance types in which the parties surrender very little autonomy, prospective partners do not ordinarily take the time to scrutinize one another's operations in minute detail. However, the more highly integrated the proposed alliance type and the more permanent the relationship is intended to be, the more important it is to do a multifaceted examination of the potential partner's background, current situation, and future potential. Although the phrase "due diligence" is sometimes used to refer in a broad sense to the systematic examination of a potential partner's operations (McLaughlin, 1998), as if it were synonymous with "side-by-side analysis," the primary foci of a due diligence investigation are the legal status and financial condition of the organizations (Bailey and Koney, 2000). When viewed in this narrower context, due diligence represents the final step in the exploratory process and entails careful scrutiny by attorneys and accountants.

Although experts may differ in drawing the boundaries between the stages of development, the second stage generally begins when the organizations, having agreed to engage in a strategic alliance, begin to formalize their relationship. A negotiation process, often involving legal counsel, culminates in an agreement. Depending upon the alliance type, this may be as simple as a memorandum of understanding or as complex as a full set of legal documents detailing the dissolution of a number of nonprofit corporations and the creation of a new one. In this stage, future partners also focus their attention on "operational issues involving the differentiation and integration of systems, strategies, and structure" (Bailey and Koney, 2000, p. 42), as they plan how the alliance will function. It is also important at this point that the partners determine the criteria and measures that will be used to gauge the success of the newly formed alliance.

The third stage of the four-stage process is marked by the transition from planning to action as the alliance begins to operate. This stage has been variously titled "implementation" (Singer and Yankey, 1991), "implementation and integration" (Girl Scouts of the USA, 1998), "performing" (Bailey and Koney, 2000), and "operation" (La Piana, 2001). Systems and procedures designed by the planners are now activated. As those who are performing the work of the alliance discover areas that require fine-tuning, modifications may be made. During the implementation stage, the anticipated benefits of the alliance begin to accrue to the participants. Data gathered on activities and their outcomes will lay the groundwork for the next stage, which involves reflection and evaluation.

In the fourth and final stage, the partners assess the experience of the alliance to date and determine how to proceed in the future. If an evaluation of the track record shows that the alliance has been generally successful, the participants may agree to continue along established lines, or they may modify the nature of the arrangement to ensure even greater effectiveness, take measures to make it more permanent, or seek additional resources to expand it programmatically or geographically. Alternatively, this review may lead to the conclusion that the alliance has *not* achieved the anticipated results and should therefore be disbanded. La Piana, in *Real Collaboration* (2001), thus refers to the final stage as "institutionalization or termination."

The work of Austin (2000), who examines strategic alliances between nonprofit organizations and businesses, offers an interesting set of parallels to this four-stage process. In language characteristic of the field of *for-profit* management, he speaks of making the connection with the right organizational partner; ensuring strategic fit by aligning mission, strategy, and values and achieving environmental (as well as organizational) fit; generating value, thus providing benefits to the participants as well as to society as a whole; and managing the relationship to ensure sustainability through the continued generation of value (pp. 16–17).

Although this four-stage process provides a useful conceptual framework, it is not the only way to describe the sequence of steps in alliance formation. McCormick, in *Nonprofit Mergers* (2001), does not speak of stages per se but suggests a similar sequence of activities through chapter titles such as "Deciding to Merge," "Selecting a Merger Partner," "Laying the Groundwork with Staff and Volunteers," "Negotiating and Determining Structure," "Transitioning to Merge," and "Evaluation and Stewardship."

Even among those who segment the process into a greater number of steps, the flow of activities is comparable. For example, McLaughlin (1998) identifies seven tasks of alliance development, referring to each activity as a stage. Fosler (2002), who explores boundary-spanning alliances involving government, business, and nonprofit organizations, identifies seven elements of cross-sector collaboration that in some respects parallel the tasks of alliance development cited by McLaughlin.

However helpful it may be to portray alliance formation as a series of stages, any linear representation is an oversimplification. As Bailey and Koney (2000) note, the process, although evolutionary, is also iterative, and "the fact that an alliance has been together for a long time does not necessarily mean that it will have reached a late phase of development" (p. 32). As in all human interactions, an element of unpredictability is ever-present, for the path taken by the participants as they journey toward alliance formation is influenced not only by environmental factors and intra- and interorganizational considerations but also by interpersonal dynamics.

The complexity and challenge of these endeavors, particularly the intricacy and delicacy of interorganizational negotiations, should not be underestimated. Throughout the strategic alliance formation process, measures must be taken to build trust among participants. Some phases require confidentiality, while others call for communication; and determining what to communicate, when, and to whom can be of critical importance. External assistance, which can be extremely valuable in a variety of areas, is virtually imperative in the more technical aspects of alliance development. Unbiased consultants with specialized expertise can be engaged to conduct research and gather data, facilitate the process, and offer advice on public relations and communication strategies. Professionals such as attorneys and certified public accountants, particularly those whose practice focuses on the nonprofit sector, can play an indispensable role, most notably during the due diligence step, in helping to ensure that the partnering organizations do not encounter avoidable problems of a legal or financial nature.

The development of boundary-spanning relationships—because it involves power and the need to share it—is at its core a political process (Alter, 2009). Recent research has focused on the power dynamics of interorganizational restructuring (Campbell, 2008), the roles played by organizational representatives "who act as agents in boundary interchanges," the importance of the "boundary spanner's ability to build trust," the "embedded interpersonal ties [that] have an impact on interorganizational collaborative relations," and the intimate connection between interpersonal and interorganizational trust (Tsasis, 2009, pp. 10, 14, 16). There is much at stake in a process in which individual actors are charged with communicating broader organizational interests, power dynamics are in play, and the eventual outcome can hinge upon the degree to which interpersonal trust can be sustained. Even the slightest misstep can alter the course of events. David Bergholz, retired executive director of the George Gund Foundation, wisely observes that deliberations having to do with alliance exploration and development can be nothing short of high drama (personal communication, Aug. 4, 2003).

Partner Selection

Once a nonprofit organization has identified reasons to explore the possibility of forming a strategic alliance, the most critical decision to be made is the selection of one or more potential partners. In some instances, this may be a simple matter of turning to a known entity with which one's own organization has had a successful partnering experience. An existing arrangement can also evolve into one that is more fully integrated. For example, organizations engaged in a loose affiliation may decide to further intensify and more completely formalize their relationship—or to create a new one. Such variations in the prototypical alliance formation process help reinforce the point that any representation of a stage-by-stage linear sequence can only be considered a framework for understanding the vagaries of these interorganizational dynamics.

Yankey, Jacobus, and Koney (2001) explain how to initially assess the degree of fit between one's own organization and other nonprofits. Although the following set of considerations was developed for use in evaluating the attractiveness of potential merger partners, a number of items on this comprehensive checklist pertain to other forms of proposed alliances as well. Given the variability and distinctiveness of individual alliance situations, it must be emphasized that determining what makes for the most effective matches is not an exact science. These elements should therefore be regarded as considerations rather than criteria:

- History of previous relationships
- Mission and values compatibility
- Consistency of vision of future direction
- Receptivity to giving up some degree of autonomy
- Program strengths and weaknesses (The potential for success is enhanced when the strengths of one partner help to compensate for the weaknesses of another.)

- Organizational size (There is no convincing evidence of a positive correlation between the relative sizes of the prospective partners and the likelihood of alliance success; moreover, the optimal size relationship may vary from one type of strategic alliance to another.)
- Complementarity of organizational culture
- Board and trustee compatibility
- Organizational management and staff leadership
- Human resource integration complexities
- Potential for operating efficiencies
- Financial status (including endowment/cash reserves)
- Predicted long-term survival
- Funders' support of partnership
- Community and stakeholder perceptions
- Other special assets

McCormick (2001) also focuses on mergers when enumerating factors that bear upon the choice of a potential partner. He articulates four possible types of connection that can help lay the foundation for future success: mission relatedness, organizational relatedness, constituency relatedness, and geographical relatedness.

Regardless of the type of strategic alliance being explored, there are ways in which the respective parties can ensure that their best interests, both individually and collectively, will be served. During exploratory negotiations, individual organizations should "read the signs," states Arsenault (1998), and utilize impressions gleaned by their representatives to "draw conclusions about the [potential] success of the relationship based on the observed behavior or unspoken messages from members of the other team" (pp. 101, 103). They can also make a conscious effort to build trust so that the potential partners are willing to discuss the proposed alliance and their qualifications for participation both candidly and completely. Underscoring the relationship between trust and the partner selection process, Yankey, Jacobus, and Koney (2001) observe that the level of trust between organizational leaders influences not only which organizations are approached as potential alliance partners but also the final decision about whether to proceed.

It is becoming increasingly clear that in both the corporate world and the nonprofit domain, "managing partnerships, alliances and other forms of inter-organizational collaborative arrangements is now a major aspect of most managerial jobs so that the ability to do so effectively has become a seriously important managerial skill" (Advanced Institute of Management Research

Web site). Developing alliances and overseeing their implementation is not, however, a task for managers alone. A distinct new *governance* responsibility—whose broad parameters encompass such activities as assessing the readiness of one's organization to engage in strategic alliances, making partner selection decisions, guiding the development of collaborative processes, monitoring the implementation of interorganizational relationships, and evaluating the outcomes and success of such endeavors—is beginning to emerge. Abundant and varied resource materials—publications, readiness assessments, toolkits, evaluation instruments, and worksheets—are now available in both print and electronic forms to assist the directors and staff of nonprofit organizations in making strategic decisions related to collaborative processes and partnerships.[6]

Challenges to Strategic Alliance Formation And Implementation

Creating strategic alliances is both an art and a science. Although every situation is different—and the influence of intangibles is often difficult to anticipate—there are clearly identifiable challenges to the formation and implementation of alliances as well as a number of proven factors that foster success.

The literature reveals general agreement among authors with regard to the primary challenges facing organizations that elect to enter into a partnering relationship. These include the following:

- *Incompatible mission, vision, and values.* The conditions for alliance formation and operation are unfavorable when the parties are divided by substantial ideological differences, a history of disagreement, or debates that leave little room for flexibility.
- *Egos.* Both the egos of individual leaders and the generally positive tendency of group members to demonstrate pride in their own team can be sources of active or passive resistance to alliance formation (McLaughlin, 1998).
- *Turf issues.* Organizational "turf issues" can be a major obstacle. An agency that perceives itself to be preeminent in a specific domain because of its size, scope, or program quality may expect to play a dominant role in the new configuration and may be less likely to treat potential partners as equals. Failure to place the partners' shared mission and the good of the community above loyalty to one's own agency will imperil the alliance.
- *Cost: time required.* Alliance formation requires a significant amount of two precious commodities, time and money. Whereas less formal alliances can

be mounted or disbanded fairly quickly, more complex alliances may require twelve to eighteen months from the moment of their conception to the date on which they become operational.

- *Cost: funds required.* The more integrated the alliance, the more expensive it will be to develop and implement. Expenditures will frequently be required for facilitation, organizational analyses, and due diligence (legal fees, financial auditing, and so on). The expenses do not stop there. Opportunity costs may be involved as well because substantial amounts of energy, attention, and time are likely to be directed to the development of the relationship between the partnering organizations, possibly at the expense of programmatic activities or administrative functions. Once a merger or consolidation is up and running, costs may be incurred for any or all of the following: accrued salaries, severance pay, legal judgments, systems integration (management information systems, human resources, payroll, fund development, and so on), lease-related payments, mortgage financing, new taxes, signage, printing, and promotional and public relations materials to reposition the entity in the marketplace.

- *Cultural differences.* The role of cultural differences between organizations is of major importance. Most of the authors writing about alliance formation and implementation emphasize both the importance and the magnitude of this challenge. Cartwright and Cooper (1996) have shown that rumors or announcements of impending alliances raise concerns and cause stress for employees as they begin to anticipate the changes in culture that they may experience and the impact of the new organizational structure on their careers. As Arsenault (1998) indicates, although certain parallels can be drawn between for-profit and nonprofit consolidations, cultural integration poses a special set of challenges for nonprofits. Because nonprofits typically use volunteers as well as paid personnel, human resource issues are more complex. Moreover, as value-driven entities operating in a world of intangibles, nonprofits employ many well-educated people in nonroutine jobs who perform their work with higher degrees of individual autonomy than their counterparts in the corporate world (Arsenault, 1998). Failure to correctly assess one's own organizational culture and that of potential partners, coupled with inattention to the need for cultural integration, can endanger board and staff morale and jeopardize the success of a strategic alliance.

Other concerns stem from fears of perceived threats to personal and professional security or, at the institutional level, the potential loss of independence, control, identity, volunteers, funding, or public support. Such fears are often the result of misapprehensions or misperceptions. They rest on assumptions that are partially, if not completely, erroneous, such as the following:

- Organizational survival should be pursued at any cost.
- To be viable, an organization must remain totally independent.
- Joining an alliance is tantamount to going out of business.
- An organization loses everything by giving up its name.
- The safest course is to preserve the status quo.
- Reductions in force are inevitable.
- Public and philanthropic support will necessarily erode.

Accurate information is often the best way to dispel personal concerns and overcome sources of organized resistance.

Because risk is an inherent element of any form of collaborative activity, adopting a risk management perspective can be a prudent approach to addressing the challenges of strategic alliance formation and implementation. (Chapter Twenty-Three of this handbook presents a complete overview of the subject of nonprofit risk management.) A sample "Risk Management Checklist for Collaboration" recommends that prospective partners confirm compatibility, understand motivations, conduct due diligence, interpret the message (to constituents and stakeholders), clarify expectations, and put agreements in writing (Herman, 2002, pp. 5–6).

Factors Contributing to Alliance Development Success

The likelihood of alliance success is influenced by many factors, but there is broad agreement on those that appear to be among the most important. Although these consistently recurring themes are described in the literature in different terms, they include a shared vision, a sound process, open communication, an atmosphere of trust, effective leadership, and hard work.

Shared Vision

The possibility of success is greatly enhanced when there is clarity of purpose and a congruency of mission, strategy, and values (Austin, 2000). Strategic alliances enable the partnering organizations to harness their collective resources and capacities in the pursuit of a mutually desired outcome. Because organizations with varying missions may be drawn together for different reasons, it is vital that they agree upon a shared vision and purpose and develop a set of concrete, attainable goals and objectives (Mattessich, Murray-Close, and Monsey, 2001). Both the aspirations and the limitations of the partnering arrangement must be clearly articulated and mutually understood.

Sound Process

The process through which the alliance is developed and operationalized has a significant impact on the likelihood of its success. Care must be taken to ensure that the strengths and contributions of all parties are recognized and validated and that more powerful organizations and individuals do not suppress the views of others. A skilled convener (Mattessich, Murray-Close, and Monsey, 2001) or an external facilitator can help to create an environment that is conducive to success by streamlining management of the process and reducing feelings of anxiety and uncertainty (Arsenault, 1998). Based on their review of the research literature, Mattessich, Murray-Close, and Monsey (2001) recommend that alliance members share in both the process and the outcome, that clear roles and policy guidelines be developed, and that there be multiple layers of decision making. Continual learning, which Austin (2000) considers to be essential to the success of collaborations between nonprofits and businesses, is applicable to intrasectoral alliances as well.

Open Communication

Honest and open communication is consistently cited as a critical element of successful partnering (La Piana and Kohm, 2003; Yankey, Jacobus, and Koney, 2001; Mattessich, Murray-Close, and Monsey, 2001; Austin, 2000). The sharing of accurate and objective information by potential partners, including the disclosure of negative as well as positive features of each organization, enables board and staff members to make sound, reasoned, and clear-sighted judgments about the benefits and risks of entering an alliance. Creating and adhering to a communications plan will enable the prospective partners to keep key internal and external stakeholders apprised of developments in a timely fashion and will help ensure that an appropriate level of confidentiality is maintained.

Atmosphere of Trust

Trust, perceived by some as the "glue" of strategic alliances, is based upon shared expectations, mutual obligations, and a commitment to accountability—as well as a recognition of possible risk (Yankey, Jacobus, and Koney, 2001). The establishment of trust promotes successful alliance development by helping to lower the barriers between individuals and organizations, foster the growth of positive relationships, discourage hidden agendas, and promote good-faith negotiations. In a climate of mutual respect, understanding, and trust (Mattessich, Murray-Close, and Monsey, 2001), prospective partners are better able to take the leap of faith that entering into an alliance requires and better prepared to manage the challenges that will inevitably arise during implementation. Since trust involves disclosure and consultation, open and candid communication is essential to its development (McLaughlin, 1998).

Effective Leadership

Successful alliances cannot be created without strong and effective leadership on the part of at least one of the partnering organizations. Every alliance needs to be championed by individuals who are capable of articulating a vision and inspiring others to follow. Leaders set the tone for their coworkers and colleagues (including board members) by modeling such behaviors as mutual respect, candor, fairness, and flexibility. They convene and guide the teams that will develop and operationalize the alliance, continually promoting the concept of mission-focused rather than ego-based decisions (La Piana and Kohm, 2003).

Hard Work

The formation of a strategic alliance is a labor-intensive undertaking and there is a great deal of hard work to be done at each stage of the process. The initial spark—the inspiration for partnering—may be kindled during the intensive organizational self-examination and thorough, extensive environmental scanning performed in conjunction with a strategic planning exercise. The exploration and assessment of various options, the identification of potential partners, and the investigation of their suitability through a side-by-side analysis and a due diligence examination are research steps that require considerable effort and care.

After the organizations agree to formalize their relationship, they must negotiate arrangements, define a structure, and resolve operational issues relating to systems and procedures. Personnel, facilities, and technology must be addressed, along with internal and external communications. Mutually understood expectations need to be articulated and an evaluation mechanism established. Once implementation begins, the delivery of programs and services must be monitored and evaluated so that a decision to maintain, modify, or terminate the alliance at some future time can be made on the basis of sound data.

In summary, throughout the process, either the prospective partners or their agents must perform essential activities such as research, analysis, planning, monitoring, and assessment. The hard work that is a necessary condition for strategic alliance success clearly demands energy and commitment as well as time and other resources.

Lessons from the Field

The key components of success—a shared vision, a sound process, open communication, an atmosphere of trust, effective leadership, and hard work—are important considerations for nonprofits that are contemplating the possibility of entry into a strategic alliance. In addition to the lessons implicitly contained in these success factors, there is much wisdom to be gleaned from the experience and observations of practitioners. The following insights and recommendations, representing "a view from the field" (Yankey, Jacobus, and Koney, 2001) emerged from answers given by respondents from sixty-five organizations who participated in a national study of nonprofit strategic alliance development:

- There is no such thing as a "zero defects" strategic alliance.
- The size of a nonprofit organization is not positively correlated to success.
- Organizations should proactively pursue strategic alliances rather than waiting to be pursued.
- Strategic alliances usually should not be presented as an approach or strategy that will yield short-term cost savings.
- The criteria and process for evaluating the success of a strategic alliance should be established prior to its implementation.
- Strategic alliances are often more successful when funders are partners and provide financial support for both planning and implementation.
- A change in leadership in one or more of the organizations may represent an opportune time for exploring a merger or consolidation.
- The challenges in creating a new corporate culture following a merger or consolidation can be more significant than the challenges presented in the exploring and planning phases of strategic alliance development.
- Merger and consolidation processes must include opportunities to grieve and to celebrate.

Conclusion

As the conditions in which nonprofits operate rapidly change, the dynamic field of strategic alliance development also continues to grow and evolve, accurately reflecting what Salamon (1999) termed "the modern reality of collaborative problem-solving" in response to societal needs. Describing the new competitive environment for nonprofit organizations, the authors of a recent report on trends reshaping the social sector observe that the "blurring of sector boundaries creates opportunities for a growing number of public-private and corporate-nonprofit collaborations to share learning and innovation" (Gowdy et al., 2009, p. 16). Cross-sectoral alliances, although not new, are likely to become increasingly common in the emerging "sector-blind" environment. "What is new is the range of structural options available to individuals and organizations" seeking to achieve social benefit (p.16), including, for example, the low-profit limited liability company (L3C).

Perhaps of equal importance are the new ways in which work is being done, "ways of *working wikily*" that are "dramatically reducing traditional barriers to coordination and collaboration" (Kasper and Scearce, 2008; Scearce, Kasper, and Grant, 2009). As a consequence of "the advent of new technologies and new norms for working collaboratively, the potential impact of networks is increasing exponentially" (Gowdy et al., 2009, p.12).[7] Adopting a futurist's lens, these authors conclude that successful nonprofits will not only "be proactive and adept in leveraging both collaborative and competitive strategies to fulfill their mission" (p. 17), but will also "expand their reach and deepen their impact through networks and coalitions of both organizations and individuals," and "organize their work as a collaborative, evolving process, rather than as something they can completely control internally" (p. 13).

The need to engage in collaborative processes and create strategic alliances, not only with other nonprofits but also across sectoral boundaries, has never been more apparent. Monitoring social and technological trends as well as political and economic developments will help organizations remain adaptive—and competitive—in this complex and constantly changing environment. As new types of partnering arrangements emerge, and as nonprofit entities—and their public, private, and hybrid partners—continue to experiment with systems, structures, and strategies, the capacity to advance one's organizational mission will increasingly depend on the ability of both leaders and managers to participate thoughtfully and strategically in collaborative interorganizational activities and alliances.

Notes

1. For example, a similar survey conducted in Northeast Ohio by the Nonprofit Finance Fund and Business Volunteers Unlimited in August 2009 revealed even higher levels or expectations of collaboration: 55 percent in the programmatic area and 26 percent for administrative purposes (Nonprofit Finance Fund, 2009).

2. Alter (2009) captures the challenges associated with terminology and taxonomy by examining both the nouns employed to describe interorganizational relationships and the verbs that are commonly used to refer to the act of creating and sustaining them.

3. "The goal of the Nonprofit Transitions Fund is to help nonprofits reduce costs and time spend on administrative work, as well as increase productivity." According to the Foundation's Web site, included among the activities that will be supported are planning efforts, consultants, due diligence, and other expenses related to: back office collaborations; merger/acquisition/consolidation; dissolution; bankruptcy; post-merger integration or closure costs; and service delivery joint ventures. [www.sff.org/about/whats-new/nonprofit-transitions-fund-launches-to-support-intentional-change].

4. The three academic partners in the AIM Alliance are: The Lodestar Center for Philanthropy and Nonprofit Innovation at Arizona State University, The Center on Philanthropy at Indiana University, and The Johnson Center for Philanthropy and Nonprofit Leadership at Grand Valley State University (Michigan).

5. Grants made by the Strategic Alliance Partnership "support the exploration and formation of alliances that will enable Toledo area nonprofits to enhance program delivery and/or achieve more effective and efficient use of financial and human resources" (Toledo Community Foundation Web site).

6. Examples include the "Board Members' Guide to Partnership Planning" (Ramanath and Van Eyk, 2009); *The M Word: A Board Member's Guide to Mergers* (Vergara-Lobo, Masaoka, and Smith, 2005); and the "Partnership Self-Assessment Tool" (Center for the Advancement of Collaborative Strategies in Health, 2006).

7. Gowdy et al. (2009) define networks as traditionally including "coalitions, alliances, partnerships, learning communities and various other collections of individuals and organizations working toward a common goal" (p. 12).

References

Advanced Institute of Management Research. Retrieved from www.aimresearch.org/index.php?page=the-theory-and-practice-of-collaborative-advantage.

Alter, C. F. "Building Community Partnerships and Networks." In R. Patti (ed.), *The Handbook of Human Services Management*. (2nd ed.) Thousand Oaks, Calif.: Sage, 2009.

Arsenault, J. *Forging Nonprofit Alliances: A Comprehensive Guide to Enhancing Your Mission Through Joint Ventures and Partnerships, Management Service Organizations, Parent Corporations, and Mergers*. San Francisco: Jossey-Bass, 1998.

Austin, J. E. *The Collaboration Challenge: How Nonprofits and Businesses Succeed Through Strategic Alliances*. San Francisco: Jossey-Bass, 2000.

Bailey, D., and Koney, K. M. *Strategic Alliances Among Health and Human Services Organizations: From Affiliations to Consolidations*. Thousand Oaks, Calif.: Sage, 2000.

Berardo, Ramiro. "Processing Complexity in Networks: A Study of Informal Collaboration and its Effect on Organizational Success." *The Policy Studies Journal*, 2009, *37*(3), 521–539.

Brandenburger, A. M., and Nalebuff, B. J. *Co-opetition.* New York: Currency Doubleday, 1996.

Campbell, D. A. "Getting to Yes . . . or No: Nonprofit Decision Making and Interorganizational Restructuring." *Nonprofit Management and Leadership*, 2008, *19*(2), 221–241.

Cartwright, S., and Cooper, C. L. *Managing Mergers, Acquisitions, and Strategic Alliances: Integrating People and Cultures.* Oxford, England: Butterworth-Heinemann, 1996.

Center for the Advancement of Collaborative Strategies in Health. "Partnership Self-Assessment Tool," 2006. Retrieved from www.cacsh.org/psat.html.

The Collaboration Prize. Retrieved from www.thecollaborationprize.org/About-the-Prize.aspx.

The Columbus Foundation. Retrieved from www.columbusfoundation.org/media/press/09022009_c.aspx.

The Dayton Foundation. Retrieved from www.daytonfoundation.org/041909dn.html.

Fosler, R. S. *Working Better Together: How Government, Business, and Nonprofit Organizations Can Achieve Public Purposes Through Cross-Sector Collaboration, Alliances, and Partnerships.* Washington, D.C.: Three Sector Initiative, 2002.

Girl Scouts of the USA. *Exploring Strategic Alliances in Girl Scouting.* New York: Girl Scouts of the USA, 1997.

Girl Scouts of the USA. *Combining Our Strengths in Girl Scouting: Merger and Consolidation.* New York: Girl Scouts of the USA, 1998.

Gowdy, H., Hildebrand, A., La Piana, D., and Campos, M. M. "Convergence: How Five Trends Will Reshape the Social Sector." James Irvine Foundation, November 2009.

Herman, M. L. "Managing Collaboration Risks: Partnering With Confidence and Success." Nonprofits' Insurance Alliance of California and Alliance of Nonprofits for Insurance, Risk Retention Group, 2002. Retrieved from www.InsuranceforNonprofits.org.

Hoskins, L. and Angelica, E. *Forming Alliances: Working Together to Achieve Mutual Goals.* Saint Paul, Minn.: Fieldstone Alliance, 2005.

Jaskyte, K. and Lee, M. "Interorganizational Relationships: A Source of Innovation in Nonprofit Organizations?" *Administration in Social Work*, 2006, *30*(3), 43–54.

Kasper, G., and Scearce, D. "Working Wikily: How Networks Are Changing Social Change," 2008. Retrieved from www.monitorinstitute.com.

La Piana, D. "The Partnership Matrix," La Piana Associates. Retrieved from www.lapiana.org/defined/matrix.html. 1999.

La Piana, D. *Real Collaboration: A Guide for Grantmakers.* New York: Ford Foundation, 2001.

La Piana, D, with Hayes, M. *Play to Win: The Nonprofit Guide to Competitive Strategy.* San Francisco: Wiley, 2005.

La Piana, D., and Kohm, A. *In Search of Strategic Solutions: A Funders' Briefing on Nonprofit Strategic Restructuring.* Washington, D.C.: Grantmakers for Effective Organizations, 2003.

Lawrence, Steven. "Foundations' Year-end Outlook for Giving and the Sector" (Foundation Center Research Advisory). New York: Foundation Center, November 2009.

Massachusetts Nonprofit Network. "Stimulus and Nonprofits," Vol. 4. MNN's ARRA Newsletter, May 27, 2009.

Mattessich, P. W., Murray-Close, M., and Monsey, B. R. *Collaboration: What Makes It Work.* (2nd ed.) St. Paul, Minn.: Amherst H. Wilder Foundation, 2001.

McCormick, D. H. *Nonprofit Mergers: The Power of Successful Partnerships.* Gaithersburg, Md.: Aspen, 2001.

McLaughlin, T. A. *Nonprofit Mergers and Alliances: A Strategic Planning Guide*. New York: Wiley, 1998.

National Center for Charitable Statistics. *Nonprofit Almanac 2008: Public Charities, Giving, and Volunteering*. Washington, D.C.: The Urban Institute, 2008.

Nonprofit Finance Fund. "Nonprofit Finance Fund Survey: America's Nonprofits in Danger." New York, April 2009. Retrived from www.nonprofitfinancefund.org/content.php?autoID=166.

Nonprofit Finance Fund and Business Volunteers Unlimited. "Survey: Northeast Ohio Nonprofits Brace for Tough 2010; Turn to Collaboration and Financial Planning." Cleveland, October 8, 2009. Retrieved from www.nonprofitfinancefund.org/content.php?autoID=205.

Plexus Consulting Group, LLC. *The Power of Partnership: Principles and Practices for Creating Strategic Relationships Among Nonprofit Groups, For-Profit Organizations, and Government Entities*. Washington, D.C.: ASAE and The Center for Association Leadership and the U.S. Chamber of Commerce, 2008.

Ramanath, R., and Van Eyk, J. A. "Board Members' Guide to Partnership Planning," 2009. Nonprofit Good Practice Guide of the Johnson Center at Grand Valley State University. Retrived from www.npgoodpractice.org/Topics.Boardmembersguidetopartnership planning.

Reed, B., and Bridgeland, J. M. "The Quiet Crisis: The Impact of the Economic Downturn on the Nonprofit Sector." Retrieved from www.dlc.org/documents/Quiet_Crisis.pdf. 2009.

Salamon, L. M. *America's Nonprofit Sector: A Primer*. (2nd ed.) New York: Foundation Center, 1999.

The San Francisco Foundation. Retrieved from www.sff.org/about/whats-new/nonprofit-transitions-fund-launches-to-support-intentional-change.

Scearce. D., Kasper, G., and Grant, H. M. "Working Wikily 2.0: Social Change with a Network Mindset." The Monitor Institute. July 2009. [http://www.monitorinstitute.com].

Singer, M. I. and Yankey, J. A. "Organizational Metamorphosis: A Study of Eighteen Nonprofit Mergers, Acquisitions, and Consolidations." *Nonprofit Management and Leadership*, 1991, *1*, 357–369.

Toledo Community Foundation. Retrieved from www.toledocf.org/index.php?src=new&srctype=detail&category=Toledo%20Community%20Foundation%20News&refno=27.

Tsasis, P. "The Social Processes of Interorganizational Collaboration and Conflict in Nonprofit Organizations." *Nonprofit Management and Leadership*, 2009, *20*(1), 5–21.

The Urban Institute, National Center for Charitable Statistics, Master File; Internal Revenue Service, Exempt Organization Business Master File, 1995–2009.

Vergara-Lobo, A., Masaoka, J., Smith, S. L. *The M Word: A Board Member's Guide to Mergers: How, Why & Why Not to Merge Nonprofit Organizations*. CompassPoint, 2005.

Wallace, N. (2009, March 26). "Economic Woes Bring More Charities Together: Nonprofit Organizations Look to Mergers and Collaborations as a Way of Surviving in Tough Times." *Chronicle of Philanthropy*. Retrieved from http://philanthropy.com/free/articles/v21/i11/11003001.htm.

Yankey, J. A., Jacobus, B. W., and Koney, K. M. *Merging Nonprofit Organizations: The Art and Science of the Deal*. Cleveland, Ohio: Mandel Center for Nonprofit Organizations, 2001.

CHAPTER FIFTEEN

OUTCOME ASSESSMENT AND PROGRAM EVALUATION

John Clayton Thomas

Nonprofit organizations need to know how effectively they are performing their jobs. Are their programs achieving the desired results? How could programs be modified to improve those results? Because the goals of non-profit programs are often subjective and not readily observable, the answers to these questions may be far from obvious.

These questions have grown in urgency in recent years as a consequence of new external pressures. As perhaps the watershed event, "the Government Performance and Results Acts of 1993 . . . placed a renewed emphasis on account-ability in federal agencies and nonprofit organizations receiving federal support" (Stone, Bigelow, and Crittenden, 1999, p. 415). More specific to nonprofit organizations, funders increasingly demand evidence of program effectiveness, as exemplified by the United Way of America's outcome measurement initia-tive of recent decades and its more recent Outcome Measurement Resource Network (see, for example, United Way of America Web site for the Outcome Measurement Resource Network). As Ebrahim describes in Chapter Four of this volume, there is today a major press for nonprofit organizations to be highly accountable in all sorts of ways. Yet research on contemporary practice indicates that many nonprofit agencies still perform relatively little assessment of program performance (Carman, 2007; Morley, Hatry, and Cowan, 2002).

To address these needs nonprofit organizations need, at a minimum, to engage in systematic outcome assessment—that is, regular measurement and monitoring of how well their programs are performing relative to the desired outcomes. (The terms *outcome assessment* and *performance assessment* will be used interchangeably in this chapter.) Nonprofit executives may want, in addition, to employ the techniques of program evaluation in order to define the specific role their programs played in producing any observed beneficial changes. Used appropriately, outcome assessment and program evaluation inform a wide range of decisions about whether and how programs should be continued in the future and satisfy funder requirements.

This chapter introduces the techniques of outcome assessment and program evaluation as they might be employed by nonprofit organizations. These techniques are not designed for more general evaluations of organizational effectiveness which, as Herman and Renz (2008, pp. 411–412) have observed, seldom "could be legitimately considered to equal" program effectiveness (see Chapter Sixteen in this volume for a detailed discussion of organizational effectiveness). The emphasis here is on how these tools can be useful to organization executives by providing information that speaks to decisions those executives must make. To make that case, we will first provide a step-by-step description of how to conduct outcome assessment, before turning to how that assessment can be incorporated into more advanced program evaluations processes.

Planning the Process for Outcome Assessment

For outcome assessment to have maximum value, the process for that assessment must be well planned and executed. The first step in that regard is for the organization's leaders to be committed to the effort. Ideally, an initiative of this kind will begin with the chief executive of the nonprofit organization but, in any event, the chief executive and the organization's board should understand and support the initiative. Support includes recognizing and accepting that outcome assessment could uncover unwelcome truths about program performance. There is no point in taking the time to develop and obtain performance data if those in charge are not committed to using the data.

Assuming this support is assured, outcome assessment should be undertaken on a program-by-program basis. For a nonprofit organization with multiple programs, that guideline means that each program will require separate outcome assessment planning. A specific individual should be assigned primary responsibility for that planning for each program, preferably as part of a small team. (The discussion below will use the term *decision makers* to encompass both possibilities.)

Regardless of whether a team is used, the planning process should entail extensive involvement of staff and perhaps even clients who are involved with the program. That involvement serves at least two functions. First, it assists in information gathering. Since those who are involved with a program know it from the inside, they can provide valuable intelligence on the program's desired outcomes and possible means for measuring their achievement. Second, involvement can build ownership in the outcome assessment process. If program staff and clients have the opportunity to speak to how the program will be assessed, they are more likely to buy into the eventual results of the assessment.

Finally, the process should also be linked to the organization's information technology. Improved information technology, by facilitating the recording and analysis of performance data, is a major factor underlying the recent push for better performance assessment in both the nonprofit and public sectors. Building a strong performance assessment system requires that the system be planned in conjunction with the organization's technology.

Defining Program Goals

Outcome assessment is a goals-based process; programs are assessed relative to the goals they are designed to achieve. Defining those goals can prove a difficult task since the project leader or team must define and differentiate several types of goals while navigating the often-difficult politics of goal definition. This section first explains several goal types and then discusses how to define them in a political context.

Types of Goals

A first type of goal refers to the ultimate desired program impact. United Way of America, in its outcomes assessment Web site, defines *outcome goals* as "benefits or changes for individuals or populations during or after participating in program activities." Here we prefer a broader definition of outcome goals as the final intended consequences of a program for its clients and/or society. An outcome goal has value in and of itself, not as a means to some other end, and is usually people-oriented because most public and nonprofit programs are designed ultimately to help people. This broader definition probably fits better the new United Way interest in measuring the success of programs based on both "client-level outcomes" and "achievement of measurable community outcomes" (Minich et al., 2006, p. 183).

Activity goals, by contrast, refer to the internal mechanics of a program, the desired substance and level of activities within the program. These specify the actual work of the program, such as the number of clients a program hopes to serve. How the staff of a program spend their time—or are supposed to spend their time—is the stuff of activity goals.

The distinction between outcome and activity goals can be illustrated through a hypothetical employment-counseling program. An activity goal for this program might be "to provide regular employment counseling to clients," with an outcome goal being "to increase independence of clients from public assistance." The activity goal refers to the work of the program, the outcome goal to what the work is designed to achieve. As this example also suggests, outcome goals tend to be more abstract, conceptual, and long term; activity goals are more concrete, operational, and immediate.

Understanding the distinction is crucial if outcome assessments are to resist pressures to evaluate program success in terms of activity rather than outcome goals. Program staff often push in that direction for several reasons. First, activity goals are easier for them to see; they can more readily see the results of their day-to-day work than what that work is designed to achieve sometime in the future. Second, activity goals tend to be more measurable; it is easier to measure the "regularity" of counseling than "independence from welfare." Finally, activity goals are usually easier to achieve. Police working in a crime prevention program, for example, can be much more confident of achieving an activity goal of "increasing patrols" than an outcome goal of "reducing crime."

Outcome assessment planning often can sidestep pressures of this kind by including both types of goals in the goal definition. As a practical matter, both outcome and activity goals must be examined in most outcome assessments in order to know how different parts of a program link to eventual program outcomes.

Sometimes a program will have so many activity goals that it could be too much work to attempt to define much less measure all of them as part of the outcome assessment system. A good guideline in such cases is to define activity goals only for key junctures in the program, that is, only at the major points in the program sequence where information is or might be wanted (see also Savaya and Waysman, 2005, p. 97).

Falling between activity and outcome goals are *bridging goals*, so named because they supposedly connect activities to outcomes (Weiss, 1972, pp. 48–49). Bridging goals, like outcome goals, relate to intended consequences of a program for society, but bridging goals are an expected route to the final intended consequences, rather than being final ends in and of themselves. In an advertising campaign designed to reduce smoking, for example, a bridging goal between advertising (activity) and reduced smoking (outcome) might be "increased awareness of the risks of smoking." That increased awareness would be a consequence of the program for society but, instead of being the final intended consequence, it is only a bridge from activity to outcome.

Bridging goals can be important for outcome assessment systems for a variety of reasons. For one thing, because they are often essential linkages in a program's theory of change—the hypothesized process by which program inputs lead to outcomes—their achievement may be a prerequisite to demonstrating that program activities have produced the desired outcomes. Thus, to confirm that a program works, it may be necessary to establish first that the bridging goal is achieved before any change on the outcome goal would even be relevant. Bridging goals also may provide a means to obtain an early reading on whether a program is working. Effects may be observable on a bridging goal when it is still too early to see any impact on final outcome goals.

Outcome assessment systems may also occasionally incorporate *side effects*. Side effects, like outcome and bridging goals, are also consequences of a program for society, but *unintended* consequences. They represent possible results other than the program's goals. For example, a neighborhood crime prevention program might displace crime to an adjacent neighborhood, producing the side effect of increased crime there. A side effect can also be positive, as when a neighborhood street cleanup program induces residents to spruce up their yards and homes, too.

Given the potential for any given program to have a wide range of side effects, where should an assessment draw the line? An outcome assessment for a nonprofit agency program should incorporate side effects only to the extent that the chief executive, staff, and other key stakeholders view specific possible side effects as important program aspects. Is there an interest in examining a possible negative side effect, perhaps with an eye to changing the program so as to reduce or eliminate that result? Agency decision makers must make that judgment based on whatever data they believe are necessary for a full outcome assessment. In most cases, given a principal interest in activity and outcome goals, the executive may not want to spare limited resources to monitor possible side effects, too. On occasion, though, possible side effects may loom as so important that they must be addressed.

Whatever the type of goal, its definition should satisfy several criteria:

1. Each goal should contain only one idea. A goal statement that contains two ideas (for example, "increase independence from welfare through employment counseling") should be divided into two parts, with each idea expressed as a distinct goal.
2. Each goal should be distinct from every other goal. If goals overlap, they may express the same idea and so should be differentiated.
3. Goals should employ action verbs (for example, "increase, improve, reduce"), avoiding the passive voice.

Goal definitions can be derived from two principal sources: (1) program documentation, including initial policy statements, program descriptions, and the like, and (2) the personnel of the program, including program staff, the organization's executive, and possibly other key stakeholders such as clients. These personnel should always be asked to react to draft goals before they are finalized.

The Politics of Goals Definition

Understanding the different types of goals and where to find them may be the easy part of goal definition. The difficult part can be articulating those definitions in a manner that satisfies all important stakeholders. To do that may require navigating the perilous politics of goal definition.

As a first difficulty, many programs begin without clearly defined goals. Initial program development focuses on where money should be spent to the neglect of defining what the program is expected to achieve. Second, as programs adapt to their environments, goals sometimes change and, in the process, depart from the program's original intent. "Policy drift" can result wherein programs move away from that original intent, and once-distinct goals become fuzzy or inconsistent (for an example, see Kress, Springer, and Koehler, 1980).

More difficulties can arise when planning for outcome assessment begins. The commonly perceived threat from any kind of assessment may prompt some program staff or other stakeholders, when they are asked, to be evasive about goals. Or, those staff or other stakeholders from their different vantage points inside and outside the program may simply have different views, resulting in conflicting opinions about a program's goals.

A variety of techniques is available to cope with these problems. Fuzzy or inconsistent goals may be accommodated by including all of the different possible goals in a comprehensive goals statement. If some perspectives appear too contradictory to fit in the same statement, a goals clarification process might be initiated (for an illustration, see Kress, Springer, and Koehler, 1980). Working with staff and stakeholders to clarify the goals of a program could be the most important contribution of an outcome assessment planning process since it may build a cohesiveness previously lacking in the program.

Disagreement over goals can also sometimes be sidestepped as irrelevant. Patton (2008, pp. 238–241) recommends asking stakeholders what they see as the important *issues* or questions about the program. These issues, because they represent areas where information might be used, should be the focus of most eventual data analysis anyway. And, there may be more agreement about issues than about goals. Decision makers might then be able to express these issues in terms of the types of goals outlined earlier.

The agency's chief executive can play any of several roles in the definition of program goals. At a minimum, the executive should oversee the entire process to ensure the necessary participation, lending the authority of her or his position as necessary. Ideally, the executive should review proposed goals as they are defined, both for clarity and for conformity to the agency's overall focus. Finally, if conflicts over goals arise, the executive may need to intervene to achieve resolution.

The Impact or Logic Model

As part of the process of goal definition, a program's various goals should be combined into a visual *impact* or *logic model*—an abstracted model of how the various goals are expected to link to produce the desired outcomes (see Savaya and Waysman, 2005; McLaughlin and Jordan, 2004; W. K. Kellogg Foundation, 2004). Such a model should have several characteristics. First, it should be an abstraction, removed from reality but representing reality, just as the goals are. Second, the model should simplify matters, reducing substantially the detail of reality. Third, as the "logic" component, the model should make explicit the significant relationships among its elements, showing for example how activity goals are expected to progress to outcome goals. Fourth, the model may involve formulation of hypotheses—the suggestion of possible relationships not previously made explicit in program documents or by program actors. Indeed, a principal benefit of model development often lies in how program stakeholders are prompted to articulate hypotheses they had not previously recognized. Exhibit 15.1 shows an impact model for a hypothetical nonprofit training program.

EXHIBIT 15.1. AN IMPACT MODEL FOR A TRAINING PROGRAM FOR EXECUTIVES OF LOCAL BRANCHES OF A NATIONAL NONPROFIT

1. Determine developmental needs of local executives (AG).
2. Develop training materials to address these needs (AG).
3. Screen and select executives for training (AG).
4. Conduct training of executives (AG).
5. Executives formulate individualized plans for development of their organizations (BG).
6. Executives attend follow-up training (AG).
7. Local organizations increase volunteer membership (OG).
8. Local organizations increase volunteer giving (OG).

Key: AG = activity goal; BG = bridging goal; OG = outcome goal.

The model links the various goals from the initial activity goals through the bridging goals to the ultimate outcome goal. As the model illustrates, bridging goals sometimes fall between two activity goals, but still serve as links in the chain from activity goals to outcome goals. This model may be atypical in that the goals follow a single line of expected causality, where the more common model may fork at one or more points (as, for example, if different types of executives received different kinds of training). Should staff or stakeholders disagree about the likely impact model, decision makers must determine whether the disagreement is sufficiently important to require resolution before further outcome assessment planning can proceed.

Development of an impact model can help staff and stakeholders clarify how they expect a program to work and the questions they have about its operation, in the process perhaps suggesting how to use assessment data once it becomes available. As Savaya and Waysman (2005, pp. 85–86) have documented, impact models can be useful for a variety of other purposes, too—from "assessing the feasibility of proposed programs" to "developing performance monitoring systems." To date, however, these models still appear to be used only infrequently by nonprofit organizations (Carman, 2007, p. 66).

Measuring Goals

Once the goals have been defined, attention must turn to how to measure them. Before thinking about specific measures, decision makers should become familiar with some basic measurement concepts and with the various types of measures available.

Concepts of Measurement

Measurement is an inexact process, as suggested by the fact that social scientists commonly speak of "indicators" rather than measures. As the term implies, measurement instruments indicate something about a concept (that is, about a goal), rather than provide perfect reflections of it. So, crime reported to police constitutes only a fraction of actual crime; and scores on paper-and-pencil aptitude test reflect the test anxiety and cultural backgrounds of test takers as well as their aptitudes.

The concepts of *measurement validity* and *measurement reliability* rest on recognition of the inexactness of measurement. Measurement validity refers to whether or to what extent a measure taps what it purports to measure. More valid measures capture more of what they purport to measure. Measurement reliability refers to a measurement instrument's consistency from one application to another.

Reliability is higher if the instrument produces the same reading (a) when applied to the same phenomenon at two different times or (b) when applied by different observers to the same phenomenon at the same time. Obviously, the better measures are those that are more valid and reliable.

Executives and staff of nonprofit agencies need not become experts on how to assess the validity and reliability of measures, but they should know to keep at least two points in mind. First, given the fallibility of any particular measure, multiple measures—two or more indicators—are desirable for any important goal, especially any major outcome goal. (One measure each may prove sufficient for many activity goals.) Once data collection begins, the different measures should then be compared to see if they appear to be tapping the same concept. Second, if there are concerns about reliability, taking multiple observations is recommended. Any important measure should, if possible, be applied at a number of time points to see if and how readings might fluctuate. (Multiple observations are also useful for other aspects of research design, as explained below.)

Decision makers must also consider *face validity;* that is, whether measures appear valid to key stakeholders. Measurement experts sometimes discount the importance of face validity on the grounds that measures that appear valid sometimes are not. However, the appearance of validity can be crucial to the acceptance of a measure as really reflecting program performance. As a result, decision makers should be concerned about whether recommended measures appear valid, but they must try to avoid using any seemingly attractive measures that may *not* actually tap the relevant goal.

In selecting measures, the ability of program staff to assess measurement validity should not be underestimated. By virtue of their experience with the program, staff often have unique insights into the merits of specific measures, insights that trained outside experts might miss.

Types of Measures

Outcome assessments can employ several types of measures, and to achieve the benefit of multiple measures, will typically utilize two or more of the types. The different types are briefly introduced below in terms of what nonprofit executives and staff may need to know about each.

Program Records and Statistics. An obvious first source for data is the program itself. Records can be kept and statistics maintained by program staff for a variety of measures. Almost every evaluation will employ at least some measures based on program records (for a detailed treatment, see Hatry, 2004).

These measures must be chosen and used with caution, however. For one thing, program staff ordinarily should be asked to record only relatively objective data such as numbers of clients served, gender and age of clients, dates and times services are delivered, and the like. Staff usually can record these more objective data with little difficulty and high reliability; they should not be expected, without training, to record more subjective data such as client attitudes, client progress toward goals, and so on.

In a similar vein, although program records can serve as an excellent source of measures of activity goals—the amount of activity in the program—they should be used only sparingly as outcome measures and probably never as the *sole* outcome measures. Program staff are placed in an untenable position if they are asked to provide the principal measures of their own effectiveness, especially if those measures include subjective elements.

That concern not withstanding, the staff who will record the measures should be involved in defining the measures. In addition to offering insights about measurement validity, staff can speak to the feasibility of the proposed record keeping and help ensure that the record keeping process will not be so onerous that staff must choose between spending their time on the evaluation or on the actual program. If that were to happen, either the evaluation would interfere with the program because staff give too much time to record keeping, or the measures will produce poor data because staff slight record keeping in favor of working on the program's activities.

Client Questionnaire Surveys.

Any program serving client populations, including most nonprofit programs, should include some measures of client perceptions and attitudes. These perceptions could include ratings of the program's services and service providers, client self-assessments, and other basic client information. The obvious means for obtaining these measures is a questionnaire survey, of which there are several forms. Each has its own advantages and disadvantages (see also Newcomer and Triplett, 2004; Rea and Parker, 1997).

Phone surveys can produce good response rates (that is, responses from a high proportion of the sample), assuming respondents are contacted at good times (usually in the evening) and interviewed for no more than ten to fifteen minutes. However, phone surveys can be expensive due to interviewer costs and the need for multiple phone calls in order to reach many respondents.

The desire for a lower-cost procedure often leads to consideration of *mail surveys*. Here questionnaires are mailed to respondents, who are asked to complete and return by mail. Any reduction in costs through using a mail survey can be more than offset, however, by the frequent poor response rate, typically lower and less representative than with a phone survey. Questions on mail surveys must also be structured more simply since no interviewer is available to guide the respondent through the questionnaire. Mail surveys work best when sent to groups that are both highly motivated to respond (as sometimes with clients of nonprofit programs) and willing and able to work through written questions independently. Even then, obtaining a high response rate usually requires sending one or two follow-up mailings to nonrespondents.

E-mail surveys represent a contemporary variation on the mail survey. Relatively inexpensive online options are now available, too, for recording and summarizing responses. Obviously, though, this technique will work only with a computer-literate population, and, as with mail surveys, the population must be motivated to respond. As another alternative, e-mail surveys might be combined with traditional mail surveys, an approach that can often produce excellent response rates (see, for example, Thomas, Poister, and Ertas, 2009).

The best choice for many programs will be the so-called *convenience survey*, a survey of respondents who are available in some convenient setting such as when they receive program services. A program can capitalize on that availability by asking clients, while on site, to complete and return a brief questionnaire. As with mail surveys, the questionnaires must be kept simple and brief to permit easy and rapid completion. To reassure respondents about the confidentiality of their responses, receptacles similar to ballot boxes might be provided for depositing completed questionnaires. A well-planned convenience survey can produce a good response rate at a cost lower than that of any of the alternatives.

Construction of any kind of questionnaire requires some expertise. Agency executives wishing to economize might share the construction process with an outside consultant. The outcome assessment planners might draft initial questions for the consultant to critique before another review by staff and again by the consultant. This collaborative procedure can both reduce the organization's costs and provide training in questionnaire construction to program staff.

Formal Testing Instruments. With many programs, the outcomes desired for clients—self-confidence, sense of personal satisfaction—are sufficiently common that experts elsewhere have already developed appropriate measurement instruments. Some formal testing instruments are available free in the public domain; others may be available at a modest per-unit cost. In either case, it is sometimes wiser to obtain these instruments than to develop new measures.

Trained Observer Ratings. These ratings can be especially useful "for those outcomes that can be assessed by visual ratings of physical conditions," such as physical appearance of a neighborhood for a community development program (Hatry and Lampkin, 2003, p. 15). As that example suggests, these ratings work best for subjective outcomes that are not easily measured by other techniques. These ratings can be expensive in terms of both time and money, however, since their use necessitates development of a rating system, training of raters, and a plan for oversight of the raters. It may also be difficult in a small or moderate-sized nonprofit agency to find raters who do not have a personal stake in a program's effectiveness.

Qualitative Measures. Outcome assessment will typically be enhanced by use of some qualitative measures, measures designed to capture nonnumerical in-depth description and understanding of program operations. After long disdaining these measures as too subjective to be trusted, most experts now recognize that programs with subjective goals cannot be evaluated without qualitative data.

Qualitative measures can be obtained through two principal techniques, observation and in-depth interviews. Observation can provide a sense of how a process is operating, as, for example, in evaluating how well group counseling sessions have functioned. By observing and describing group interaction, an evaluator could gain a sense of process unavailable from quantitative measures.

In-depth interviews have a similar value. In contrast to questionnaire surveys, relatively unstructured interviews are composed principally of open-ended questions designed to elicit respondent feelings about programs without the constraints of the predefined multiple-response choices of structured questionnaires. These interviews can be extremely useful as, for example, in assessing the success of individualized client treatment plans.

Still, nonprofit agencies should use qualitative measures with caution, taking care to avoid either over- or underreliance on them. Evaluation of most nonprofit programs calls for multiple measures, including both quantitative and qualitative measures. Outcome assessment planners should be sure that both perspectives are obtained.

Finally, outcome assessment planners should be prepared for the possibility that discussion of measures may rekindle debate about goals. Perhaps staff paid too little attention to the earlier goal definition, or maybe thinking about measures prompts staff to see goals differently. When that happens, planners should be open to a possible need to reformulate goals.

Data Collection, Analysis, and Reporting

Once the necessary measures have been defined, decision makers should plan for data collection, analysis, and reporting. They must ensure first that procedures are established for recording observations on the measures. They must also determine how the new data collection process will be integrated with the agency's information technology, including evaluating whether new software will be needed for the effort.

Before putting the full outcome assessment in place, the agency should pilot test the measures and the data collection procedures to see how well they work. Measures sometimes prove not to produce the anticipated information. Convenience surveys, for example, sometimes elicit only partial responses from program clients, which could require either improving or abandoning that instrument. Problems can also arise in the recording of data, perhaps necessitating rethinking the recording procedures.

Decision makers, certainly including the agency's chief executive, should also establish a schedule for regular reporting and review of the data. Depending on agency preferences and perceived needs, reviews might be planned as frequently as weekly or as infrequently as annually. Or, less intensive reviews might be planned more often with more intensive reviews scheduled only occasionally (for example, on a quarterly or annual basis).

The details of the schedule are probably less important than that a schedule is established and implemented. Judging from the findings of one study (Morley, Hatry, and Cowan, 2002, p. 36), many nonprofit agencies that collect outcome information do not systematically tabulate or review the data, instead "leaving it to supervisors and caseworkers to mentally 'process' the data to identify patterns and trends." Agencies unnecessarily hamstring themselves when they make such choices. If systematic outcome data are available, agencies should ensure that the data are tabulated and reviewed.

Growing numbers of governments and some nonprofit agencies (see Carman, 2007, p. 65) are taking the additional step of putting program effectiveness and efficiency data into comprehensive performance management systems and then reporting the data through summary "scorecards" or "dashboards." Popularized by Kaplan and Norton, the so-called "balanced scorecards" are designed to present a 360-degree picture of an organization's performance at any given time. With their growing popularity among governments (see, for example, Edwards and Thomas, 2005), these scorecards seem likely to become increasingly common among nonprofit agencies in the coming years.

Actual review of the data can go in a number of directions depending on what the data look like and what questions the agency has about the programs. At the outset, initial data on any new measures can be at once the most interesting, yet the most difficult to interpret. Novelty accounts for the likely high interest: agency executives and staff may be looking at outcome readings they have only been able to guess at before. However, with initially only one data point to analyze, those readings may seem uninterpretable. Interpretation becomes easier as readings accumulate over time, permitting comparisons of current performance to past performance.

To increase interest and potential utilization of the data, agencies should consider asking key staff to predict results in advance. Poister and Thomas (2007) have documented that asking for such predictions (albeit on a limited number of measures) increased interest among state administrators in the results of stakeholder surveys. Prediction questions can be asked relatively simply, too (for example, "What proportion of program clients will say they are satisfied with the program?").

The focus of the interpretation depends on a variety of factors. If the data show an unexpected trend or pattern—such as an unanticipated decline on an outcome measure from one quarter to the next—attention may focus on explaining that pattern. More generally, though, the analysis of the data should be driven by the questions and concerns of the agency. Is there a concern about whether a program is working at all? Or, might the concern instead be whether a new program component is achieving desired improvements?

At the same time, care should be taken not to *over-interpret* outcome data. In particular, outcome data should not by themselves be read as implying causality—that is, to conclude that any observed changes resulted from a specific program or programs. Such changes could have resulted from other factors (a change in the economy, for example) that are wholly independent of the program. Outcome assessment data by themselves speak to important questions of whether progress is being made on key agency objectives, but cannot explain the part the agency has played in inducing those changes.

When questions about program performance turn toward these issues of causality, agency executives must move a step beyond outcome assessment to conduct a full program evaluation. Program evaluations, in essence, start from a foundation of strong outcome assessment and add the techniques of comparison and control necessary to speak more definitively to the role of specific programs in producing desired outcomes.

Two Approaches to Program Evaluation

Program evaluation can seem a frightening prospect, raising the specter of outside experts "invading" the organization, seeking information in a mysterious and furtive manner, and ultimately producing a report that may contain unexpected criticisms. Such fears are not ungrounded. The traditional approach to program evaluation, sometimes termed the "objective scientist" approach, often proceeds along those lines.

Borrowed from the natural sciences, the objective scientist approach entails several elements. To begin with, objectivity is valued above all else. To achieve objectivity, the evaluator seeks to maintain critical distance from the program being evaluated in order to minimize possible influence by program staff, who may be biased in the program's favor. The objective scientist also strongly prefers quantitative data, recognizing qualitative data to be subjective by nature—the antithesis of objectivity. Finally, the usual purpose of an evaluation for the objective scientist is to determine whether or to what extent the program has achieved its goals. Is the program sufficiently effective to be continued, or should it be terminated? The objective scientist takes little interest in how a program's internal mechanics are functioning.

Two decades of experience have revealed shortcomings to this approach. Evaluators who insist on keeping their distance miss the unique insights staff often have about their programs. Disdaining qualitative data further limits the ability to assess a program because the goals of most public and nonprofit programs are too subjective to be measured only by quantitative techniques. Finally, the insistence on critical distance combined with an exclusive focus on program outcomes can result in evaluations that fail to answer the questions decision makers have.

Recognition of these problems led to the development of an alternative, the approach that Michael Quinn Patton has termed *utilization-focused evaluation*. As Patton (2008, pp. 451–452) has explained, this approach begins with the goal of balance rather than objectivity. Where objectivity implies taking an unbiased view of a program by observing from a distance, balance recommends viewing program operation from up close as well as from afar, thus to discern important details as well as broad patterns. Achieving balance also requires qualitative as well as quantitative data because the latter are unlikely to capture all that is important about programs whose goals are subjective. A balanced assessment necessitates multiple perspectives.

The balanced approach also rejects outcome assessment—"did the program work?"—as the only purpose of an evaluation. A utilization-focused evaluation seeks information for use in modifying and improving programs, too. Getting close to the program helps by putting the evaluator in contact with the program administrators who have questions about how programs should be modified as well as the authority to implement those modifications.

The balanced approach is not appropriate for every program, every evaluator, or every nonprofit executive. In getting close to a program, an evaluator can risk being "captured" by the program and, at the extreme, becoming only a "mouthpiece" for those who are vested in the program. For that reason, if there are serious questions about the quality of a program or about the competence of its staff, the nonprofit executive may prefer an evaluation performed from the critical distance of the objective scientist.

For the most part, though, nonprofit executives will find that the utilization-focused evaluation approach promises both a more balanced assessment and information more likely to be useful in program development. As a consequence, the following discussion assumes a utilization-focused approach to evaluation.

Who Does the Evaluation?

A first question, when planning a program evaluation, is who should conduct the evaluation. Here the principal options are (a) an internal evaluation performed by the organization's staff, (b) an external evaluation performed by outside consultants, and (c) an externally directed evaluation with extensive internal staff assistance.

An internal evaluation is possible only if the organization has one or more staff members with extensive training and experience in program evaluation. Unlike outcome assessment, full-scale program evaluation is too technical a task to attempt without that expertise. An internal evaluation also requires that the nonprofit executive give essentially a free rein to the evaluation staff. Since inside evaluators may face strong pressures to conform their findings to the predispositions of program staff, standing up to those pressures is possible only if the nonprofit executive has made an unequivocal commitment to an unbiased evaluation.

As a practical matter, although many nonprofit organizations prefer to conduct evaluations internally (see, for example, Carman, 2007, p. 70), most appear to lack sufficient in-house expertise to produce high-quality evaluations. They are probably better advised to seek outside assistance from United Way or private-sector consulting firms, management assistance agencies for the nonprofit sector, or university faculty (often found in public administration, education, or psychology departments).

Hiring an outside consultant carries its own risks. Perhaps the greatest risk is that the external evaluators, perhaps trained in the objective scientist tradition, may resist getting close to the program and consequently conduct the evaluation with insufficient concern for the organization's needs. A preference for critical distance may blind them to the questions and insights the agency has about the program.

To minimize this risk, the nonprofit executive should discuss at length with any prospective evaluators how the evaluation should be conducted, including whether they are capable of taking a utilization-focused approach. It is also wise to negotiate a contract that specifies in detail how the nonprofit organization will be involved in the evaluation.

Perhaps the best means for conducting an evaluation is through a combination of outside consultants and internal staff. In this mode, outside consultants provide technical expertise plus some independence from internal organizational pressures while internal staff perform much of the legwork and collaborate with the consultants in developing the research design, collecting data, and interpreting findings. The idea, as documented in one study of successful evaluations (Minich et al., 2006, p. 186), is to "not expect program staff to be researchers" and, in that spirit, to "shift measurement tasks to full-time evaluators."

There are several advantages to this approach. First, it provides the necessary technical expertise without sacrificing closeness to the program. Second, greater staff involvement should produce greater staff commitment to the findings, increasing the likelihood that findings will be utilized. Third, the evaluation can be used to train staff to serve a greater role in future evaluations. Finally, having staff implement much of the legwork could reduce the out-of-pocket costs for the outside consultants. This reduction is possible, however, only if care is taken that working with the staff does not require too much of the consultants' time.

That time commitment can be limited by creating a small advisory team to oversee the evaluation. This team should include the outside evaluators, the nonprofit executive (or the executive's representative), and at least one to three other staff members in the nonprofit organization. The team should serve as the central entity to which the evaluator reports, reducing the time necessary for working with program staff. Keeping its size small (in the range of three to five members) facilitates the team ability to provide clear and prompt feedback to the evaluation process. A team of this kind is probably desirable for wholly internal or external evaluations, too.

The only way to assure that the chief executive's concerns about the program are addressed is for that executive to be personally involved in the evaluation, optimally as a member of the evaluation advisory team. In addition, as the literature on organizational change attests (see, for example, Fernandez and Rainey, 2006), programmatic change is unlikely to occur through an evaluation unless the chief executive is involved and committed to the process.

The goal of this involvement should not be to obtain the "right" answers—answers that conform to the executive's predispositions—but to ensure that the right *questions* (the questions crucial to the program's future) are asked. The chief executive should emphasize this distinction to the evaluator(s) up front, and then monitor to be sure the distinction is observed as the evaluation proceeds.

Determining the Purpose of the Evaluation

The first task of an evaluation is to define its purpose. That is, what sort of information is desired and why? How will the information be used? Answers to these questions will be crucial in determining the other elements of the evaluation.

Discussion of evaluation purposes typically begins with a dichotomy between *summative* and *formative* purposes (see Rossi, Lipsey, and Freeman, 2004, pp. 34–36). A *summative* purpose implies a principal interest in program outcomes, in "summing up" a program's overall achievements. A *formative* purpose, by contrast, means that the principal interest is in forming or "reforming" the program by focusing the evaluation on how well the program's internal operations function. In reality, though, the purposes of evaluations are much more complex than a dichotomy can convey. Saying an evaluation has a formative purpose, for example, does not indicate which of the program's internal mechanisms are of interest.

An evaluation's purpose should reflect the concerns key stakeholders have about the program. The process of defining this purpose thus should begin with the nonprofit organization's executive: What questions does he or she have about how the program is working? What kinds of information might speak to anticipated decisions about the program? Opinions of other stakeholders, including funders, may also be solicited.

In the end, a number of purposes is possible, depending on the perceptions of stakeholders and the specific program. An evaluation performed primarily for funders, who may be most interested in whether the program is having the desired impact, is likely to have a summative purpose. By contrast, a program that has only recently been implemented may be a good candidate for an *implementation assessment*—an evaluation of how well a program has been put into operation—but a poor candidate for a summative evaluation because the program has not been operating in the field long enough to expect an observable impact. Evaluations designed mainly for program staff are likely to have principally formative purposes to help staff modify and strengthen the program.

Because this purpose will guide decisions at all subsequent steps in the evaluation, a mistake at this stage can hamper the entire effort. The nonprofit executive should consequently review this purpose and make certain it reflects his or her concerns as well as the concerns of other key stakeholders. It is also true, though, that an evaluation's purpose may become clearer as the evaluation progresses. Stakeholders may be able to articulate their questions about programs only as they consider program goals and measures. Evaluators should be open to this possibility.

Evaluators and nonprofit executives must also be alert to the possibility of so-called *covert purposes,* unvoiced hidden purposes for an evaluation (Weiss, 1972, pp. 11–12). Program managers, for example, sometimes have an unspoken goal of "whitewashing" a program by producing a favorable evaluation. The responsible chief executive will reject such an evaluation as unethical as well as incapable of producing useful information.

It is at this stage that the evaluator and the organization's chief executive should also consider whether the evaluation is worth doing. Revelation of a dominant covert purpose would provide one reason to bow out. Or, it may be impossible to complete an evaluation in time to inform an approaching decision about the program. The resources necessary for a program evaluation are difficult to justify unless the results can be meaningful and useful.

Outcome Evaluation Designs

Most program evaluations will be concerned to some extent with assessing program impact—whether or to what extent a program has produced the desired outcomes. To achieve that end, evaluators can employ a number of outcome evaluation designs. Nonprofit executives and staff usually will neither need nor desire to become experts on these designs. However, to participate intelligently in the evaluation process, they need to understand at least their basic structure and underlying principles. This section will explain those principles and then briefly survey the most important of the designs. (For a more detailed discussion of the designs, see Rossi, Lipsey, and Freeman, 2004, Chapters 8–10.)

Causality

The goal of any outcome evaluation design is to assess causality—whether a program has caused the desired changes. To do so, the evaluation design must satisfy three conditions:

1. *Covariation*: Changes in the program must covary with changes in the outcome(s). Changes in outcome measures should occur in tandem with changes in program effort.
2. *Time order*: Since cause must come before effect, changes in the program must *precede* changes in the outcome measures.
3. *Nonspuriousness*: The evaluator must be able to rule out alternative explanations of the relationship between the program and outcome. The evaluator must demonstrate that the relationship is not spurious, that it is not the result of a joint relationship between the program, the outcome, and some third variable.

An evaluation design has *internal validity* to the extent that it satisfies these three conditions. Internal validity, in other words, refers to how accurately the design describes what the program actually achieved or caused.

Evaluation designs can also be judged for their *external validity*: the extent to which findings can be generalized to contexts beyond that of the program being evaluated. Ordinarily, nonprofit organizations will have little or no concern for external validity; nonprofit executives usually will be interested only in how their own program works, not with how it might work elsewhere. External validity becomes a major concern only if, for example, a program is being run as a pilot to test its value for possible broader implementation. Even then, internal validity must still take first priority. We must be sure that findings are accurate before considering how they might be generalized.

Threats to Internal Validity

The difficulties of satisfying the three conditions for causality can be illustrated relative to three so-called pre-experimental designs, designs that are frequently but often carelessly used in program evaluations:

1. One-shot case study: X 01
2. Posttest only with comparison group: X 01 02
3. One-group pretest/posttest 01 X 02

In each case, X refers to treatment, 01 to a first observation, and 02 to a second observation (on the comparison group in item 2, on the experimental group in item 3).

The one-shot case study satisfies none of the conditions of causality. As the most rudimentary design, it provides no mechanism for showing whether outcomes and program covary, much less for demonstrating either time order or nonspuriousness.

The posttest only with comparison group design can establish covariation since the comparison of a program group to a nonprogram group will show whether outcomes and program covary. However, this design can tell us nothing about time order; we cannot tell whether any outcome differences occurred *after* the program's inception or were already in place beforehand.

The one-group pretest/posttest design can satisfy the first two conditions for causality since taking observations before and after a program's inception tests for covariation and time order. The weakness of the design—and it is a glaring weakness—lies in its inability to establish nonspuriousness.

Take, for purposes of illustration, a rehabilitation program for substance abusers as evaluated by the one-group pretest/posttest design. This design can establish covariation, whether substance abuse decreases with program involvement, and it can establish time order, since substance abuse is measured both before and after the program intervention. But it does not control for such threats to nonspuriousness as the following:

1. *Maturation*: Decreased substance abuse could have resulted from the maturing of participants during the time of the program, a maturation not caused by the program.
2. *Regression*: Extreme scores tend to "regress toward the mean" rather than become more extreme. If program participants were selected on the basis of their extreme scores (that is, high levels of substance abuse), decreased abuse could be a function of irrelevant statistical regression rather than a program effect.
3. *History:* Events concurrent with but unrelated to the program can affect program outcomes. Perhaps a rise in the street price of illegal drugs produced a decline in substance abuse, which could mistakenly be attributed to the program.

These flaws make the pre-experimental designs undesirable as the principal design for most evaluations. Stronger designs are necessary to provide reasonable tests of the conditions of causality.

Experiments

Experimental designs offer the strongest internal validity. The classic experimental design takes this form:

$$R \; 01 \; X \; 02$$
$$R \; 03 \;\;\;\; 04$$

R refers to *randomization,* meaning that subjects are assigned by chance—for example, by lot or by drawing numbers from a hat—to the experimental or control group in advance of the experiment.

Randomization is a crucial defining element of experimental designs. With the inter-group and across-time components of this design testing for covariation and time order, randomization establishes the final condition of causality, nonspuriousness, by making the experimental and control groups essentially equivalent. As a consequence of that equivalence, the control group provides a test of "change across time"—the changes due to maturation, regression, history, and so forth, which could affect program outcomes. Comparing the experimental and control groups can thus separate program effects from other changes across time, as this simple subtraction illustrates:

Program effects + change over time (02 − 01)
− Change over time (04 − 03)
= Program effects

Unfortunately, many practical problems work against the use of experimental outcome designs in evaluations. In particular, randomization poses a number of difficulties. First, it must be done prior to the beginning of an intervention; participants must be randomly assigned before they receive treatment. Second, ethical objections may be raised to depriving some subjects of a treatment that other subjects receive, or political objections may be raised to providing treatment on anything other than a "first come, first served" basis. Experiments can also be costly, given the need to establish, maintain, and monitor distinct experimental and control groups. Since many programs are still changing as they begin operation, it sometimes proves impossible to (as an experiment requires) maintain the same program structure throughout the length of the experiment.

But the possibility of conducting an experiment should not dismissed too quickly. The need for prior planning can sometimes be surmounted by running an experiment not on the first cohort group of subjects, but on a second or later cohort group, such as a second treatment group of substance abusers. Ethical and political objections often can be overcome by giving the control group a traditional treatment rather than no treatment. That choice may make more sense for the purpose of the evaluation anyway, since the ultimate choice is likely to be between the new treatment and the old, not between the new treatment and no treatment.

Quasi-Experiments

If an experimental design cannot be used, the evaluator should consider one of the so-called *quasi-experimental designs*. These designs are so named because they attempt, through a variety of means, to approximate the controls that experiments achieve through randomization. The strongest of these designs come close to achieving the rigor of an experiment.

A first quasi-experimental design is the *nonequivalent control group*:

01 X 02

03　 04

Here, in lieu of randomization, a comparison group is matched to the experimental group in the hope that the pre-post comparison of the two groups will furnish an indication of program impact.

This design is as strong—or weak—as the quality of the match. The goal of matching is to create a comparison group that is as similar as possible to the experimental group, except that it does not participate in the program. A good match can be difficult to achieve because the available comparison groups often differ in crucial respects from the experimental group.

Consider a hypothetical job-training program for the unemployed that takes participants on a first come, first served basis. The obvious candidates for a comparison group are would-be participants who volunteer *after* the program has filled all of the available slots. The evaluator might select from those late volunteers a group similar to the experimental group in terms of race, sex, education, previous employment history, and the like—similar, in other words, on the extraneous variables that could affect the desired outcome of employment success.

The difficulty arises in trying to match on all of the key variables at once. Creating a comparison group similar to the experimental on two of those variables—say, race and gender—may be possible, but the two groups are unlikely then also to have equivalent education levels, employment histories, and other characteristics. In addition, the two groups may differ on some unrecorded or intangible variable. Perhaps the early volunteers were more motivated than late volunteers, accounting for why they volunteered sooner. If that difference were not measured and incorporated in the analysis, the program could erroneously be credited for employment gains that actually stemmed from the differences in motivation. In cases such as this, no match is preferable to a bad match.

A second kind of quasi-experimental design is the *interrupted time series design*, diagramed as follows:

01 02 03 X 04 05 06

The defining elements of this design are three or more observations recorded both before *and* after the program intervention. Multiple observations are important because they provide a reading on trends, thereby controlling for most changes over time (maturation, regression, and so on), which experimental designs achieve through randomization. Those controls give this design relatively good internal validity.

History is the principal weakness of this design, with respect to internal validity. There is no control for any event that, by virtue of occurring at the same time as the program, could affect program impact. A program to improve the situation of the homeless could be affected, for example, by an economic upturn (or downturn) that began at about the same time as the program.

Obtaining the necessary multiple observations can also prove difficult. On the front end, preprogram observations may be unavailable if measurement of key outcome indicators began only when the program itself began. On the back end, stakeholders may demand evidence of program impact before several post-program observations can be obtained.

One of the strongest of the quasi-experimental designs is the *multiple interrupted time series*:

$$01 \quad 02 \quad 03 \text{ X} \quad 04 \quad 05 \quad 06$$
$$07 \quad 08 \quad 09 \quad \quad 010 \quad 011 \quad 012$$

The strength of this design results from combining the key features of the interrupted time series and the nonequivalent group design. The time series dimension controls for most changes across time; the nonequivalent control group dimension controls for the threat of history.

The problems with this design derive from the possible weakness of its component parts. A bad match can provide a misleading comparison; the lack of longitudinal data can rule out use of this design at all.

Other Designs and Controls

The realities of many programs preclude the use of either experimental or quasi-experimental designs. Perhaps no one planned for an evaluation until the program was well under way, thereby ruling out randomization and providing no preprogram observations. Finding a comparison group may also prove too diffi-cult or too costly. Under these conditions, the evaluator may be forced to rely on one or more of the pre-experimental designs as the principal outcome evaluation design, leaving the evaluation susceptible to many threats to internal validity.

Fortunately, means are available to compensate for if not to eliminate these design weaknesses. A first possibility is to use *statistical controls*. If their numbers and variability are sufficient, the subjects of a program can be divided for comparison and control. For example, a one-group pretest/posttest might be subdivided into those receiving a little of the program (x) and those receiving a lot (X). The resulting design becomes more like the stronger nonequivalent control group design:

$$01 \text{ X} \ 02$$
$$03 \text{ x} \ 04$$

There remains the question of whether the two groups are comparable in all respects other than the varying program involvement. If that comparability can be established, the design can provide a reading on whether more program involvement produces more impact, substituting for the unavailable comparison of program versus no program. The option to strengthen designs through statistical controls can also be useful with quasi-experimental and experimental designs. When a nonequivalent control group design is used, the evaluator may want to subdivide and compare subjects on variables on which the matching was flawed. If the two groups were matched on race and gender but not on education, the experimental and control groups might be compared while statistically controlling for education. Or, where a time series design is employed, additional data might be sought to control for threats of history. In a study of how the 55-mile-per-hour speed limit affected traffic fatalities, researchers examined data on total miles traveled to test an alternative explanation that fatalities declined as a consequence of reduced travel (amid the 1974–1975 energy crisis), not as a consequence of reduced speed (Meier and Morgan, 1981, pp. 670–671). The data added to the evidence that reduced speed was the cause.

Combining several outcome evaluation designs can also add to the strength of the overall design. Many evaluations will employ multiple designs, each for a different measure. Stronger designs on some measures might then help to compensate for the weaker designs necessary for other measures.

Assuming an outside evaluator is involved, these design decisions will be made principally by that individual. Still, to the extent that executives and staff understand these basic principles of evaluation design, they will be able to advise evaluators on these decisions. The nonprofit executive can perform an even more important role by monitoring the design planning to assure its fit to the purposes of the evaluation. The most rigorous design will be of no use unless it speaks to the issues of concern to the organization's board, executive and stakeholders. It is up to the executive to ensure that the evaluation remains relevant and appropriate to the organization's needs.

Process Evaluation

With most program evaluations, nonprofit executives will want to evaluate the program process as well as its ultimate impact. Outcome evaluation designs usually indicate only whether a program is working, not why. Process evaluation may be able to discern what steps in a program's process are not working as intended, perhaps pointing to how a program can be changed to increase its effectiveness. These suggestions will often prove the most useful.

The techniques of process evaluation are both simpler and less systematic than those for outcome evaluations (see also Thomas, 1980). In essence, process evaluation entails examining the internal workings of a program—as represented largely through activity goals—both for their functioning and for their role in producing the desired outcomes. It usually begins with the development of a good logic model (see Savaya and Waysman, 2005), then progresses to an examination of specific parts of that model.

The executives and staff of nonprofit organizations should be key actors in any process evaluation. To begin with, they should attempt to define at the outset the specific questions they have about the program's process. Conceivably, they may already feel adequately informed about performance as it pertains to some activity goals, and so may not desire new information there. They will then want to be certain that the evaluation includes the questions they do have about program process.

The basics of a process evaluation can be illustrated by the case of an affirmative action program designed to increase the hiring of minority firefighters by a municipal government. The activity goals of interest in this evaluation included the following:

1. Increase the number of minority applicants.
2. Increase the success rate of minority applicants on the written examination.
3. Increase the success rate of minority applicants on the physical examination.

These activity goals are designed to lead to this outcome goal (among others):

4. Increase the proportion of minority firefighters in the fire department.

The several activity goals can illustrate how a process evaluation can be useful. Data on these various activities could indicate where, if at all, the program might be failing. Are too few minorities applying? Or are minorities applying only to be eliminated disproportionately by written or physical exams? Answering these questions could help a program administrator to decide whether, or how, and where to change the program.

A good process evaluation often can help to compensate for weaknesses in the outcome evaluation designs. When the difficulty of controlling for all threats to internal validity in an outcome evaluation design leaves unanswered questions about the linkage of program to outcomes, the process evaluation could provide an additional test of this linkage by documenting whether the program activities have occurred in a manner consistent with the observed outcomes. If an impact evaluation shows significant gains on the outcome measures *and* the process evaluation shows high levels of program activities, the evaluator can argue more convincingly that the program caused the impact. By contrast, evidence of low activity levels in the same scenario would cast doubts on the possibility that the program is responsible for outcome gains.

Most program evaluations should contain some form of process evaluation. Though less systematic than outcome designs, process evaluation techniques will often provide the more useful information for nonprofit executives.

Data Development, Report Writing, and Follow-Up

Nonprofit executives should plan to involve themselves and the program staff extensively in analysis and review of evaluation findings. This involvement is necessary first for accuracy: staff review of data and reports minimizes the risk of outside evaluators reporting inaccurate conclusions. Staff members also are more likely to utilize findings and implement recommendations that they helped to develop.

When outside evaluators are used, the best approach to this involvement may be to ask for the opportunity to review and comment on interpretations and reports while still allowing the evaluators to retain final authority on the substance of reports. Most evaluators should welcome this arrangement for self-protection; no evaluator wants to go public with conclusions that are subsequently shown to be erroneous. Staff might also be involved in basic data interpretation as, for example, by meeting with evaluators to review data printouts. As suggested earlier, interest among staff might be heightened by asking them to predict some of the results before the findings are in (Poister and Thomas, 2007).

The chief executive must also decide what final written products to request. A comprehensive evaluation report is usually desirable, both for the historical record and as a reference in case questions arise, along with a brief executive summary of one to three pages for broader distribution and readership. Other reports may be desirable for particular types of clients.

The job of the outside evaluator customarily concludes at this point, but the agency's chief executive and program staff should consider if and how the program should be changed in light of the evaluation. A program evaluation can provide both a direction and an impetus for change, but often with a limited window of opportunity to achieve any change. The agency's chief executive should take advantage of that window by discussing the evaluation with staff and, where appropriate, developing plans for what changes to make and how. Since the evaluation data presumably came from the agency's outcome assessment system, this is also a good time to consider any need to change that system. Only through such efforts can a nonprofit agency gain the full value of a program evaluation.

Summary

Nonprofit agencies today confront increasingly strong demands to demonstrate that their programs work. To meet these demands, contemporary nonprofit agencies must engage in systematic outcome assessment, measuring and monitoring the performance of their programs. In some cases, these agencies must take the additional step of subjecting particular of their programs to systematic program evaluation.

Outcome assessment data can speak to important questions of whether progress is being made on key agency objectives. As a result, every nonprofit agency, if it has not already done so, should consider if and how it can develop, collect, and analyze these data on a continuing basis.

Outcome assessment data alone can *not* speak to issues of causality, that is, to whether any observed changes resulted from a specific agency program or programs. Agency executives who wish to investigate those kinds of causal connections should consider taking a step beyond outcome assessment to conduct a program evaluation, too. Program evaluations build from a foundation of strong outcome assessment, adding the techniques of comparison and control necessary to speak to the role of specific programs in producing desired outcomes.

Success in these efforts may not come easily. For one thing, nonprofit agencies often need to find additional funds to support new initiatives in either outcome assessment or program evaluation. Yet as Carman (2007, p. 71) has observed, "although funders and other stakeholders may be asking [nonprofit agencies] to report on evaluation and performance information, most are not receiving separate funds or additional grants to collect this information." In the long term, the solution may lie in these agencies "investing in their own evaluation capacity," as Carman (2007, p. 73) recommends, but that strategy offers no help in the near term.

Even if the necessary funding can be found, success in either outcome assessment or program evaluation also requires a delicate balance of analytic and scientific expertise with group process skills. On the analytic side, nonprofit executives and staff should acquire at least a basic expertise, which can be supplemented as necessary with the talents of skilled consultants. On the group process side, nonprofit executives must ensure that any outcome assessment planning or program evaluation includes extensive participation of the agency's stakeholders, including at least the program staff and funders. Achieving that balance can give the executives and staff of nonprofit organizations the knowledge necessary to provide better programs and services.

Useful Internet Resource Sites

United Way of America resources on nonprofit outcome assessment: www.liveunited.org/outcomes/

W. K. Kellogg Foundation resources on program evaluation, logic models, and theories of change: www.wkkf.org/knowledge-center/Resources-Page.aspx (click on *Evaluation Handbook and Logic Model Guide.*)

References

Carman, J. G. "Evaluation Practice Among Community-Based Organizations: Research into the Reality." *American Journal of Evaluation*, 2007, *28*(1), pp. 60–75.

Edwards, D. J., and Thomas, J. C. "Developing a Municipal Performance Measurement System: Reflections on the *Atlanta Dashboard.*" *Public Administration Review*, 2005, *65*(3), 369–376.

Fernandez, S., and Rainey, H. G. "Managing Successful Organizational Change in the Public Sector." *Public Administration Review*, 2006, *66*(2), 168–176.

Hatry, H. P. "Using Agency Records." In J. S. Wholey, H. P. Hatry, and K. E. Newcomer (eds.), *Handbook of Practical Program Evaluation*, 2nd ed. San Francisco: Jossey-Bass, 2004.

Hatry, H., and Lampkin, L. *Key Steps in Outcome Management*. Washington, D.C.: The Urban Institute, 2003.

Herman, R. D., and Renz, D. O. "Advancing Nonprofit Organizational Effectiveness Research and Theory: Nine Theses." *Nonprofit Management & Leadership*, 2008, *18*(4), 399–415.

W. K. Kellogg Foundation. "Logic Model Development Guide." Battle Creek, Mich.: Author, 2004.

Kaplan, R. S., and Norton, D. P. *The Balanced Scorecard: Translating Strategy into Action*. Boston: Harvard Business School Press, 1996.

Kress, G., Springer, J. F., and Koehler, G. "Policy Drift: An Evaluation of the California Business Enterprise Program." *Policy Studies Journal*, 1980, *8*, 1101–1108.

McLaughlin, J. A., and Jordan, G. B. "Using Logic Models." In J. S. Wholey, H. P. Hatry, and K. E. Newcomer (eds.), *Handbook of Practical Program Evaluation*, 2nd ed. San Francisco: Jossey-Bass, 2004.

Meier, K. J., and Morgan, D. P. "Speed Kills: A Longitudinal Analysis of Traffic Fatalities and the 55 MPH Speed Limit." *Policy Studies Review*, 1981, *1*, 157–167.

Minich, L., Howe, S., Langmeyer, D., and Corcoran, K. "Can Community Change Be Measured for an Outcomes-Based Initiative? A Comparative Case Study of the Success by 6 Initiative." *American Journal of Community Psychology*, 2006, *38*, 183–190.

Morley, E., Hatry, H., and Cowan, J. *Making Use of Outcome Information for Improving Services: Recommendations for Nonprofit Organizations*. Washington, D.C.: The Urban Institute, 2002.

Newcomer, K. E., and Triplett, T. "Using Surveys." In J. S. Wholey, H. P. Hatry, and K. E. Newcomer. *Handbook of Practical Program Evaluation*, 2nd ed. San Francisco: Jossey-Bass, 2004.

Patton, M. Q. *Utilization-Focused Evaluation*, 4th ed. Thousand Oaks, Calif.: Sage, 2008.

Poister, T. H., and Thomas, J. C. "The 'Wisdom of Crowds': Learning from Administrators Predictions of Citizen Perceptions." *Public Administration Review*, 2007, *67*(3), 279–289.

Rea, L. M., and Parker, R. A. *Designing and Conducting Survey Research: A Comprehensive Guide*, 2nd ed. San Francisco: Jossey-Bass, 1997.

Rossi, P. H., Lipsey, M. W., and Freeman, H. E. *Evaluation: A Systematic Approach*, 7th ed. Newbury Park, Calif.: Sage, 1993.

Savaya, R., and Waysman, M. "The Logic Model: A Tool for Incorporating Theory in Development and Evaluation of Programs." *Administration in Social Work*, 2005, *29*(2), 85–103.

Stone, M., Bigelow, B., and Crittenden, W. "Research on Strategic Management in Nonprofit Organizations: Synthesis, Analysis, and Future Directions." *Administration & Society*, 1999, *3*, 378–423.

Thomas, J. C. "'Patching Up' Evaluation Designs: The Case for Process Evaluation." *Policy Studies Journal*, 1980, *8*, 1145–1151.

Thomas, J. C., Poister, T. H., and Ertas, N. "Customer, Partner, Principal: Local Government Perspectives on State Agency Performance in Georgia." *Journal of Public Administration Research and Theory*, advance online 2009.

United Way of America. *Outcome Measurement Resource Network*. Retrieved from www.liveunited .org/outcomes. December 17, 2009.

Weiss, C. H. *Evaluation Research: Methods of Assessing Program Effectiveness*. Englewood Cliffs, N. J.: Prentice-Hall, 1972.

CHAPTER SIXTEEN

EVALUATING THE EFFECTIVENESS OF NONPROFIT ORGANIZATIONS

Vic Murray

In these increasingly difficult economic times, nonprofit organizations are increasingly under pressure from funders, clients, and others to "prove" that they are achieving their missions effectively and efficiently. Aside from greater external pressure, better-trained managers and board members are also more likely to want improved information on how the organization is performing. All this means an increased demand for more and better evaluation.

However, formal evaluation at the level of the organization as a whole is a complex and costly task. Furthermore, it is usually very difficult to carry out in a way that is completely objective. Thus, there is a "political" element to it that requires evaluators, evaluatees, and other interested parties to "negotiate" the process and how its results are to be interpreted and used.

In spite of the problems with formal evaluation systems, the process of evaluation always goes on. Decisions are constantly being made about the introduction or change of programs, funding allocations, and a myriad of policy matters. To some extent, these are based on an assessment (however subjective) of past performance. Therefore, there are always new tools and guidelines for evaluation being offered to nonprofit leaders to make their decisions better.

This chapter addresses the challenges of organizational effectiveness evaluation by looking at the following questions:

What is organizational effectiveness?

What is organizational effectiveness evaluation?

Why is it important?

How *should* it be done, ideally?

How is it actually done?

How can it be done better?

What Is Organizational Effectiveness?

As Herman and Renz have pointed out (2004, 1997), the concept of organizational effectiveness arises from a theoretical perspective which posits that formal organizations are created to achieve one or more consciously identified goals. Measures of effectiveness, therefore, seek to ascertain how well these goals have been achieved. There are several problems with this "goal attainment" model of effectiveness, however:

- Goals are often vague and difficult to measure (for example, "It is the goal of Any Town Art Gallery to enliven and enrich the human spirit through the visual arts").
- There are sometimes several goals which might be mutually contradictory such that achieving one might inhibit achieving another (for example, "It is the purpose of the Liver and Spleen Society to support patients with, find a cure for, and educate the public in the prevention of, diseases of the liver and spleen").
- No organization can exist without human and financial resources to support it. These resources exist outside the organization. If people will not join it as staff or volunteers and if they will not contribute to, or pay for, the organization's services, it will cease to exist. However, these and other critical stakeholders may have differing ideas as to what the organization's goals should be and, especially, how it should go about achieving them.

Because of these difficulties with the goal achievement model of organizational effectiveness, various theorists over the years have advanced alternatives to it (see Baruch and Ramallho, 2006; Shilbury and Moore, 2006). For example, Yuchtman and Seashore (1967) suggested that, because of the importance of external stakeholders in determining organizational survival and growth, the best indicators of effectiveness should be those showing how successful the organization is in attracting external resources in the larger system of which it is a part (the "systems resource model"). Others have asserted that, because of the difficulties of the goal attainment model with its emphasis on the "ends" of the organization, it is more useful to identify and measure a variety of management practices ("means") which, if followed, lead to successful organizations.

This is known as the "internal process approach" to organizational effectiveness (Steers, 1977).

In the final analysis, however, there is now substantial consensus among organizational behavior researchers around the conclusion that there is no such thing as organizational effectiveness in any absolute sense nor is there any single indicator that will unambiguously reveal the degree of effectiveness at any one time. Instead, effectiveness is thought of as a "social construction." It exists in the minds of the organization's diverse internal and external stakeholders. In so far as they interact and need to make joint decisions based on an assessment of the effectiveness, the definition of it must be "negotiated" at that time and renegotiated as times change (Ospina et al., 2002).

In spite of this consensus by researchers, however, those actually responsible for making the decisions that affect the future rarely think of themselves as' negotiating reality' with other stakeholders. Generally they aspire to make decisions that will move the organization toward what *they* define the organization's aims to be and are interested in assessing how well this is happening. This leads to their interest in organizational effectiveness evaluation.

What Is Organizational Effectiveness Evaluation?

Evaluation is the process of gathering information on the results of past activities for the purpose of making decisions about them. Organizational effectiveness evaluation (OEE) occurs when this process is applied to assessing the state of the organization as whole. As noted above, this refers to how well it is achieving what its stakeholders define to be its goals. (This is different from program evaluation, wherein the focus is on one specific program within the organization. It is discussed in Chapter Fifteen of this handbook.)

Evaluation can occur in a formal, systematic way through the application of a professionally designed evaluation program, or it can be carried out with varying degrees of informality ranging from gathering a few reports to completely impressionistic estimates about how things have been going.

Why Is Organizational Effectiveness Evaluation Important? The Accountability Movement

Ever since the beginning of the movement to make government organizations more efficient and responsive (see Hatry, 1999; Osborn and Gaebler, 1992), pressure has been growing for nonprofit organizations to do so also. This general tendency has sometimes been called the "accountability movement" and refers to the belief that nonprofits, and those who run them, should be more "accountable" to those they are created to serve and those who provide the money to operate them. It is this pressure from the environment of the sector—funders, clients, regulators, and other stakeholders—that has been the primary cause of the growing interest in organizational evaluation (Zimmerman and Stevens, 2006).

Before providing some illustrations of these recent pressures, it is necessary to first clarify what the concept means. In essence, accountability is "the obligation to render an account for a responsibility which has been conferred" (Cutt and Murray, 2000, p. 1). This definition presumes the existence of at least two parties, one who allocates responsibility and one who accepts it and undertakes to report on the way it is being discharged. It is also necessary to understand that there are two basic forms of accountability: "legal" and "moral." Legal accountability occurs when the parties formally and officially accept their relationship and commit to some form of explicit reporting. Moral accountability exists when reporting is not legally required but the parties believe there is an obligation for one to be accountable to the other. (Chapter Four of this handbook presents an extensive discussion of the nature of nonprofit accountability, and Chapter Seven offers further consideration of the ethics of accountability.) For example, the board of directors of a nonprofit organization may not be legally accountable to the organization's clients; however, clients may expect, and the board may agree, that it should report to clients on how well the organization is serving them. Conversely, a funder who stipulates in a grant agreement the nature of the reports it expects regarding how its money is to be used would be an example of a legal accountability relationship.

In an accountability relationship, much of the information produced is derived from formal evaluations of past activities. However, it must be noted that this is not the *only* source of information. Those expecting accountability reports from others might also want, for example, reports on planned *future* activities.

As noted, the demand for both legal and moral accountability has been growing significantly. Currently, there are at least eight organizations in the United States created to act as "watchdogs" over nonprofit organizations. They purport to assess (in various ways) how efficiently charitable organizations use the money they obtain. The pros and cons of their services are discussed later in this chapter.

Within the sector itself, umbrella organizations such as The United Way of America (United Way of America, 1996 and online), The Independent Sector (Morley, Vinson, and Hatry, 2001), and the Aspen Institute (Light, 2000) have felt the need to respond to what they perceive to be the growing public concern over inefficient or unethical charities by launching major initiatives aimed at improving and increasing evaluation especially emphasizing the measurement of outcomes (see definition below). In Canada, sector leaders created a high-profile body known as the Panel on Accountability and Governance in the Voluntary Sector for the very same reasons. It traveled the country gathering information on the sector's accountability practices and produced an influential report before it disbanded (PAGVS, 1999).

As for *why* these external pressures have been growing so substantially, one of the best explanations comes from Light (2000) who looks at the phenomenon in terms of institutional theory (DiMaggio and Powell, 1983). It posits that a great deal of organizational behavior can be accounted for by the pressure put on the organization by other organizations (stakeholders, allies, competitors, regulators). These pressures can be coercive (involving the use of power), mimetic (the tendency to want to be "with it" by imitating what others do) or normative (unconscious adoption of group norms). All three of these pressures can be seen in the accountability movement with funders and regulators applying coercive pressure ("evaluate or you won't be funded"), business corporations becoming models to imitate ("we must be more businesslike"), and professional and trade associations creating normative pressure on their member groups to adopt certain standards.

The call for more and better evaluation in accountability relationships has been growing steadily along with the availability of tools for helping with this process. What is *not* known are the answers to three very important questions:

1. Have these developments led to more organization-wide evaluation actually taking place?
2. To what extent is the information generated by evaluations being used in an effort to improve the performance of nonprofits?
3. To the extent that it is being used, how much are nonprofits being improved as a result?

Before looking at these questions, however, we must first briefly review how the evaluation process works in theory and practice.

The Ideal Evaluation Process and Its Problems

In an ideal world, the process of evaluating the impact of an organization's efforts in the voluntary sector would be rational and objective. Everyone involved—those asking for the evaluation, those carrying it out and those being evaluated would be seeking valid information so they could make better decisions for the benefit of all. The only problem might be the occurrence of some technical difficulties in developing the measurement instruments which first class, professionally trained, evaluators should be able to overcome.

Unfortunately, the world is far from ideal and the fact is that the evaluation process is rarely rational and objective. And once matters become subjective, they quickly become political.

Why Politics Is Inevitable in Evaluation[1]

Politics is inevitable in evaluation because there is so much room for subjectivity that differences can easily arise between the parties involved. All evaluation processes go through four distinct stages and, at each, decisions are required that evaluators, evaluatees, and other interested stakeholders may often may disagree about, thus giving rise to political behavior. These stages and the trigger questions that lead to differences are discussed below. The bases of these disagreements lie in inherent problems with the technical elements of evaluation methods and very common frailties in many human beings.

The Subjectivity of Each Stage of the Process

The design stage. The key question here is: What is the purpose of organizational evaluation? The usual answer is "to learn more about the strengths and weaknesses of the organization in order to make better decisions in the future." But what if those being evaluated believe the "real" purpose is to increase efficiency by uncovering ways to cut costs by eliminating jobs? Also in this phase there is the question of what, exactly will be measured—inputs, activities or processes, outputs or outcomes (these terms are discussed under the next heading).

The implementation stage. Turning the design into an implementable process raises the important question of how the information will be gathered—for example, by collecting statistics, administering questionnaires, creating focus groups, conducting personal interviews. Differences galore can arise over what should be measured and whether the measurements will accurately get the information they are supposed to get.

The interpretation stage. Once information is gathered as a result of evaluation, there arises the question of how to interpret it. What will be considered a "success" or a "failure"? Even more important, if an evaluation measure reveals problems, there is the question of drawing conclusions about *why* these occurred in order to make decisions about the future. Was it because those being evaluated were poorly selected or trained? Was it due to poor management? Or was it due to a series of external events that were beyond anyone's control? Most evaluation processes are not sophisticated enough to "prove" what caused what, which leaves all interested parties free to come up with their own differing explanations.

The application stage. This is the "so what" stage. Given that evaluations produce reports, statistics, and so on regarding how something worked out, there remains the question of how that information will be used in subsequent decision making. The more it is used to make tough decisions, such as whether to keep, drop or change programs, increase or decrease funding and terminate, promote or transfer staff, the greater the chances will be that one or more of the involved parties will disagree with the decisions.

Clearly, then, differences can arise between evaluators, evaluatees and other interested parties around many decision issues. There are two reasons that make it almost inevitable that one or more of these differences will, in fact, occur. One is because of technical problems and the other because of human foibles.

Technical Problems of Evaluation Methods. There would be few problems if all evaluations clearly measured the results of whatever they were supposed to measure and led to unambiguous conclusions about what changes are needed for the future. But that is rarely the case. Here are some of the places where evaluations have technical weaknesses and therefore give rise to the differences that lead to political behavior.

Evaluation works best when the measurements can be compared to clearly stated goals, objectives, or standards that a given organization is trying to achieve. But, as noted earlier, goals are often, at best, vague and ambiguous. How does one evaluate the goal of the Scout movement to develop the potential in youth and create better citizens? It is not *impossible* to measure such goals, but it is easy to see how any given set of measures might be seen to be inadequate. And developing valid measures of these kinds of things is technically very challenging, often costly, and certainly subjective.

Then there is the question of deciding what to focus the evaluation on. The work of individuals, programs, or organizations proceeds in a recurring cycle. It begins with an objective—the reason for the work being done. This leads to the first phase of the cycle—obtaining the resources needed to carry out the work (commonly called inputs). It then proceeds to the actual production of goods or services. This is called the process, activity, or output phase. The cycle concludes with the work actually having some kind of impact. This is the outcome phase. Some evaluation systems just measure inputs (for example, how much money was invested and how was it spent?). Some systems measure the numbers of activities that were engaged in (for example, number of clients served, number of interviews carried out, number of staff training sessions held). These are called process or output measures. Finally, some systems focus on the actual impact that the program or organization has had, that is, the extent to which it achieved its objectives. These are outcome measures.

A good evaluation system will always attempt to make explicit the underlying assumptions (or "logic model" as it is called by professional evaluators) that link one part of the cycle to the others. This articulation of assumptions need not be elaborate or complex. The main thing is to make them explicit before the evaluation gets under way so potential conflicts can be identified before it is too late. Regrettably, few evaluation systems articulate their logic models. This leads to situations in which one stakeholder, say a funder, may want to see outcome information, for example, whereas others inside the organization think that information on the need for funds (inputs) and the numbers to be served (outputs) should make it "obvious" that funds should be supplied.

Another common technical problem in design is that of measuring one level of an organization but generalizing to another. Again, this causes problems when there is no logic model worked out showing the links between the performance of individuals, programs, or functions and the organization as a whole. It is *assumed* that organizations are performing well if it can be shown that individuals are performing well or that specific programs are performing well. At the organization-wide level of analysis a unique problem is how to compare the results of one program as against another. When programs have different goals, this becomes a problem of comparing "apples and oranges" and it raises immense technical difficulties (Cutt and Murray, 2000).

Even when everyone focuses on outcomes and agrees on what should be evaluated, there are inevitable difficulties over the extent to which outcome measures really capture the goals they are intended to measure. Take, for example, an organization created to teach English as a second language to recent immigrants. An outcome measure in its evaluation system might be the number of its clients who achieve a certain level on a standard test of English proficiency at the end of their program. Is this a clear, unambiguous indicator of the organization's mission? What if those in charge of this organization, in an effort to score well on this indicator, select only clients who are already quite proficient in English or who have certain characteristics that make it more probable that they will succeed in the program? Some might argue that this is a distortion of the "real" mission which is to provide this service to all those in need of it, not just those who are most likely to pass a test.

Finally, as noted earlier, most evaluation systems are unable to provide conclusive analyses of *why* the results they produce came out as they did. Most outcomes have multiple causes and opinions can easily differ over which are the most important ones.

Human Foibles in Evaluation Processes. In addition to the inevitable technical difficulties that make it easy for differences to arise among those involved in evaluation, there are several common psychological tendencies that increase the likelihood of political game playing. These are the "LGAB," "SIR," and trust factors (Cutt and Murray, 2000).

Most people prefer to succeed and, if there is a failure, prefer not to be seen as responsible for it. This is the "look-good-avoid-blame" (LGAB) mindset. Managers embarking on a formal evaluation process often proclaim that it is not being carried out for the purpose of judging those responsible. The intent is simply to reveal any problems that might exist and provide information so everyone can learn how to overcome them. The difficulty is that, in spite of all the assurances to the contrary, many evaluatees believe in their hearts that, if an evaluation reveals problems, they will be blamed; or, conversely, if the evaluation results are positive, they can take the credit. The behavior of elected officials when there are reports of economic conditions improving or worsening is only one of the more vivid examples of this tendency.

Therefore, when an LGAB attitude prevails, the evaluation process likely will be a "political" one. The evaluators will tend to focus on whatever the evaluation indicators are and will do what they can to show the desired results. If the results look bad in spite of their efforts, the temptation is to go to whatever lengths are necessary to explain them as being beyond their control.

The other key psychological tendency that creates major problems for evaluation systems is called the subjective interpretation of reality (SIR) phenomenon. It arises when evaluation data must be interpreted and explained. We have already seen how frail most logic models are. When it comes to analyzing almost any aspect of human behavior, there are too many variables and too little control over those variables to permit solid conclusions about causal connections. For every human behavior, there are usually many theories that can be presented to explain it, few of which can be conclusively proven. This is one of the reasons for the constant flow of new ideas in fields such as child rearing, managing people, education, how to handle chronic welfare dependency and the treatment of mental illness.

In spite of the lack of fully proven theories, however, decisions about complex social problems must be made. Those who make such decisions would usually say they make them on the basis of empirical evidence, but since such evidence is inevitably inconclusive, they also base them on their preexisting beliefs and attitudes about "what works." In other words, in keeping with the "social constructionist" perspective, most evaluation results are interpreted subjectively and different people can interpret the same data many ways.

One additional factor is vital in triggering both the LGAB and SIR phenomena in evaluation: the extent to which the parties involved in the evaluation process trust one another (Ring and Van de Ven, 1994). Trust is the feeling that one can rely on others to be honest and supportive. In the context of evaluation and accountability, it is the belief that others will not intentionally do them harm. It is a complex concept with many levels ranging from total distrust through varying degrees of partial trust (for example trusting someone only in certain contexts or about certain matters) to full trust in all things. The lower the level of trust, the more likely that the LGAB and SIR phenomena will result political game playing during evaluation activities.

Research into Real-Life Evaluation Experiences

It would be a pleasure to report that a number of large-scale studies of nonprofit organizational evaluation activities have been carried out. Studies which would provide data from many different kinds of nonprofits with a wide range of missions that would tell us how their performance was measured, what responses occurred during and after these assessments and, most important, the nature and extent of any improvements that occurred as a result of these evaluations. Unfortunately, these kinds of large-sample, comparative, longitudinal studies do not exist as yet.

What has appeared instead is a series of smaller studies, usually of one or a few organizations, often based on case study methodology. This makes it difficult to generalize across the whole nonprofit sector but, when most report similar findings, it is tempting to start drawing some tentative conclusions about what is likely to happen when organizational evaluation occurs under various circumstances.

One large-scale study of evaluation practices was carried out in Canada in 2002 (Hall et al., 2003). This research was based on a stratified random sample of 1,965 voluntary sector organizations of all types and sizes from across the country. In addition, 322 funders of these organizations were surveyed. They included various government bodies, federated funding organizations, private foundations and others. The study produced a number of very interesting findings. Among them are these:

- 41 percent of funders reported that they expected more evaluation-based information from their fundees than three years ago and 50 percent said they wanted more outcome-based information than three years ago. This confirms the assertion at the beginning of this chapter regarding the increased pressure for evaluation from the environment of the nonprofit sector.
- Though expectations may be higher, only half the funders said they provide their fundees with tools or resources to help them with this process (53 percent provided no funding and did not allow their funds to be used to pay for the

costs of evaluation). Sixty percent claimed they offered "evaluation advice" but only 38 percent of the nonprofit organizations reported actually receiving such advice. (A similar finding is reported by Light [2000].)

- Though 77 percent of the nonprofit organizations surveyed said that they had carried out some type of evaluation in the previous year, only 18 percent reported that the evaluation was focused on "organizational goals and objectives," that is, on the performance of the organization as a whole. The other foci of evaluation were programs and projects (25 percent), staff or volunteer performance (14 percent), services or products (e.g. workshops, courses) (12 percent), client or community satisfaction (10 percent), and events or activities (e.g. fundraising) (11 percent).

- Of those who reported carrying out some kind of evaluation in the previous year, 73 percent claimed that they evaluated outcomes. However, post-survey follow-up interviews with a small sample of respondents revealed that "when asked how they actually measured outcomes, many gave examples of output measures" (Hall et al., 2003, p. 17).

- In spite of this, the great majority (95 percent) of respondents claimed that they were satisfied with their evaluation efforts and that they used the results of evaluations in making a variety of decisions. By contrast, less than half (47 percent) of the funders reported making effective use of the evaluation information provided to them in evaluation reports. More than a third (36 percent) said the information they received was not what they asked for and more than a quarter (26 percent) reported they had no capacity to review the information they received.

- Though overall satisfaction with evaluation practices was high, this did not keep both funders and the nonprofits themselves from admitting it could be better and identifying several barriers that prevent them from improving. Chief among them were: "lack of internal capacity, such as staff or time" (67 percent of voluntary organizations, 81 percent or funders); "unclear expectations from funders about what is wanted in an evaluation" (31 percent and 64 percent); "lack of skills and knowledge in conducting evaluations" (31 percent and 64 percent). Note that funders identified all barriers as posing problems to a greater extent than did voluntary organizations, which suggests that funders may have greater concerns about evaluation (Hall et al., 2003, pp. 31–33).

Turning to more in-depth case studies, they can be roughly categorized in terms of those which have tried to follow the entire evaluation process through all the stages discussed above, those that have focused primarily on the design and results-interpretation phase and those that have focused primarily on the results-application phase.

Overall Process Studies. When researchers attempt to observe the behavior of evaluators, evaluatees, and other interested stakeholders over time, the results all seem to support the "social constructionist" model (Herman and Renz, 2008). Time and again, we see the parties bringing their own attitudes, perceptions, values, and agendas to the process and engaging in some form of negotiation of their differences at each stage of the process. For example, Herman and Renz (2004) conducted one of the more sophisticated studies in that it looked at 44 nonprofit organizations in a single community over two points in time (1993 and 1999). At both times they found that key stakeholders such as funders or client groups all had opinions as to how the studied nonprofits were doing but all had differing criteria for judging and utilized different "data" to make up their minds about this.

In a similar vein, Cutt and Murray reported a series of case studies of eight nonprofit organizations in two Canadian cities (Cutt and Murray, 2000, Tassie et al., 1996). They too focused on the relationship between funders and fundees. Although both the funders and nonprofit managers subscribed wholeheartedly to the rhetoric of evaluation—that there should be more of it, that it should be objective and emphasize outcomes—in fact they behaved quite differently. Funders did not demand that much in the way of formal evaluation data; that which was provided rarely attempted to measure outcomes and both funders and fundees attempted to influence one another's behavior in many informal ways outside of the evaluation process. In the end, funders came to definite conclusions about the performance of the organizations they funded but it was heavily influenced by their preexisting values and the organization's informal reputation in the funder's broader information network. And, in spite of these opinions, their eventual decisions about whether to increase, decrease, or terminate funding to these organizations was scarcely influenced at all by their evaluations. Other matters such as economic conditions and political pressures to favor one set of social issues over another proved much more important. Similar conclusions to these were reached by Forbes (1998) and Scotch (1998).

More recently Balser and McClusky (2005) looked directly and in depth at how executive directors of highly regarded nonprofits managed their relationships with stakeholders. It was found that they projected a consistent image of good management to all. Conversely, Tassie et al. (1998) reported on eight case studies in which executive directors (EDs) who were more successful in obtaining funds from external agencies were more likely to present their organizations diversely in ways that met the differing expectations of the funders. Balser and McClusky reconcile these apparent differences by pointing out that in the first case the external stakeholders formed a close network whereas in the second they did not. Clearly further research is needed into how organizational leaders "tell their stories" to key external stakeholders.

Studies of Evaluation Design and Interpretation Processes. Several case studies have looked in detail at the questions of what will be evaluated, how it will be done and how the results will be interpreted. For example, Campbell (2002) studied eight local economic development projects in Northern California with an emphasis on the negotiations over evaluation criteria between funders and project leaders. Lindenberg (2001) reported on a detailed case study of the efforts of the head of CARE (the international relief and development organization) to implement a variety of modern management practices drawn from business such as the practice of benchmarking. Ebrahim (2002) looked at efforts by funders of two major NGOs in India to control the information coming to them and the resistance they encountered. Ospina et al. (2002) document even more complex patterns of negotiation between organization leaders, funders, and clients in four successful Latino nonprofits in the New York area.

Finally, Paton (2003) describes a wide range of evaluation practices in some twenty-seven "social enterprises" primarily in Britain. Among them are ten organizations required to report Administrative Cost to Expenditures (ACE) ratios to external evaluation bodies, five organizations that implemented various forms of Total Quality Management systems, four that subjected themselves to external performance audits such as ISO 9000, three that attempted to implement outcome measurement systems and one that conducted a social audit to assess its impact on the community it served.

The conclusions from all of these studies are neatly summarized by Paton (2003, p. 160):

> The limitations, difficulties and pitfalls associated with the various forms of performance measurement are very clear, if hardly a great surprise. Thus, it is probable that, if taken literally, outcome measurement will be impracticable for many social enterprises. More generally, the features that managers hope to find in measurement systems—such as both focus and comprehensiveness, or reliable validity and non-intrusive simplicity—are incompatible and so cannot be realized simultaneously. Moreover, for both internal and external reasons, 'measurement churn' [constantly changing indicators] seems increasingly to be a fact of life in social enterprises, as it is elsewhere. So the stability on which much of the logic of measurement depends is unlikely to be realized.

These conclusions are also well supported by Cairns et al. (2005) in their in-depth look at the adoption of quality management systems in thirty-four U.K. nonprofit organizations.

Studies of the Use of Evaluation Data. When evaluators do obtain information on organizational performance by whatever means, there is the question of what they will do with it—the extent to which it will be considered in making decisions about the future. In theory, formal evaluations of what has worked and how efficient a nonprofit organization has been *should* play a prominent role in the making of these kinds of major decisions. The question is: do they?

Research into this question remains skimpy but what there is suggests that it often has only a minimal influence at best, except when the evaluation was carried out as part of a special investigation of a crisis situation. Gebelman et al. (1997), Cutt and Murray (2000), Holland (2002), and Miller (2002) all report studies revealing that many boards of directors in particular are prone to: (a) not proactively seek more and better evaluation systems; and (b) ignore or willfully misinterpret evaluation information that presents "bad news" until a crisis arises. The same tendencies are probable among CEOs though, surprisingly, there is much less research available on them. A similar pattern also prevails when looking at funders as revealed in the work of Hall et al. (2003), Cutt and Murray (2000), and Lohman (1999).

This brief review of research into "what actually happens" in organizational evaluation tends to confirm the conclusion that it is a subjective, "political" process involving a negotiated interpretation of reality by all interested parties.

In spite of these conclusions, several points must be remembered:

1. Those who make the decisions affecting an organization will continue to make them and often they wish for more information. Sometimes they genuinely feel that they don't know what to do and want as objective information as can be obtained to shed light on the problem. But, at other times, what they really want is information that will back up what they already believe to be the truth so it will help them "tell their story" to influential stakeholders.
2. At other times, both the users of evaluation information and those being evaluated may manage to agree that carrying out a formal evaluation is a desirable thing and both may wish to find a process that is as thorough, fair and objective as is possible.
3. There has developed over the past fifty years an entire occupational group of professional evaluators many of whom are always looking for more useful and valid evaluation systems to offer their clients. The universities and colleges who offer training in evaluation methods do the same.

What all this means is that new evaluation tools are always being developed and welcomed by nonprofit managers. Therefore, the final section of this chapter will look briefly at some of the better-known evaluation tools that have achieved prominence in recent years. The chapter will conclude with a few remarks aimed at practicing executives regarding what can be done to give organization performance assessment efforts a chance of succeeding in the real world politics of evaluation.

Recent Tools for Improving Organizational Effectiveness Evaluation

In general, applied methods for assessing organizational effectiveness can be grouped in two categories: Those that focus on *ends*, or outcomes such as the attainment of organizational goals, and those that focus on the *means* for achieving outcomes, that is, inputs and processes. The latter are based on the assumption that use of correct means will lead to better ends.

Outcome-Based Performance Assessment: The United Way Approach[2]

This evaluation system focuses exclusively on the identification and measurement of outcomes for United Way–funded agencies. The system starts by evaluating results at the program level, and these are to be aggregated at the organizational level to provide a report on overall effectiveness.

This outcome information is intended to be used by the United Way to help member agencies improve their performance, identify and achieve United Way priorities (funding allocation criteria) and broaden the base of financial and volunteer support (fundraising).

Implementation of the outcome measurement system is divided into six stages:

- Building agency commitment and clarifying expectations
- Building agency capacity to measure outcomes
- Identifying outcomes, indicators, and data collection methods
- Collecting and analyzing outcome data
- Improving the outcome measurement system
- Using and communicating outcome information

The United Way has developed a set of guiding principles and specific steps to help member agencies complete each stage of the implementation process. Rather than advocate one particular way to develop outcomes or collect outcome data, the United Way uses a checklist approach to encourage agencies to think more broadly and critically about its measurement processes. For example, agencies are asked to think about their proposed data collection methods in terms of their validity, reliability, sensitivity to client characteristics, and ability to capture longer-term results, but they are not told which methods to use.

The outcome measurement system does not specify the type of evaluation standards to be used but does suggest that target-based absolute standards and time-based relative standards are best. Agencies are not expected to establish targets until they have at least one year of baseline data. The system discourages the use of benchmark-based standards until accurate outcome data are available. It is generally understood that in the first few years of an outcome measurement system, the data often say more about what is wrong with the evaluation system than what is taking place in the programs so the advice is to take the time to get the system working well.

Research reported on the United Way Web site suggests that there is general satisfaction with the six-stage process it recommends and its approach to developing an outcome measurement system. Of all the tools we discuss, this tool is also the most sensitive to the importance of the implementation process.

Means-Based Performance Assessment: The Balanced Scorecard[3]

The Balanced Scorecard is a multi-attribute system for conceptualizing and measuring performance designed originally for business organizations and adapted for non-profit organizations (Kaplan, 2001). In its original form, it assumes that the primary goal of a business is long-run profit maximization. It argues that this will be achieved through a "balanced scorecard of performance attributes" grouped around four "perspectives":

- The *financial perspective* measuring various financial performance indicators of primary interest to shareholders
- The *customer perspective* comprising measures of customer satisfaction
- The *internal business perspective*, which measures internal efficiency and quality
- The *innovation and learning perspective*, which attempts to measure the organization's ability to adapt to changes required by a changing environment

In the case of nonprofit organizations, their mission statement, rather than the profit statement, becomes the endpoint to be reached through these perspectives. The process starts with defining what that is and identifying outcome indicators that will reveal the extent to which it is being achieved. "Customers" must be replaced by "clients" or "users" of the organization's services and the "financial perspective" becomes that of the funders or potential funders.

To date, in spite of considerable reported use of the BSC in nonprofit organizations, there is little in the way of systematically designed empirical research into its long-term value.

Another approach related to the Balanced Scorecard model is that presented by Paton of the Open University in Britain (Paton, 2003). Called "the dashboard for social enterprises," it is more specifically designed for nonprofit organizations and focuses on two sets of questions about the organization's activities: "Do they work?" and "Are they well run?" These questions are then asked in two contexts, the short-term operational context and the longer-term, strategic context.

Best Practice Benchmarking

One of the most frequently cited tools in recent years is the application of benchmarking to the evaluation of nonprofit organizations (see especially Letts, Ryan et al., 1999). Benchmarking is a system that compares the organization's practices with those of others doing similar things but who are deemed to be doing it very well. It is usually applied to specific programs or functions of the organization so is not, strictly speaking, a tool for evaluating the organizations as a whole. However, it is assumed by those that advocate it that a thorough program of benchmarking will "roll up" to provide a good indicator of how well the organizations is doing overall.

Paton (2003) is one of the few who have actually carried out research into how well benchmarking works for nonprofits in practice. He found that though there was considerable enthusiasm for the idea of benchmarking, it was not actually implemented very frequently (in Britain, at least). In part, this is because it is extremely time-consuming and costly. It may also be because, in the nonprofit sector, it can be particularly difficult to identify the better-performing organizations with which to compare oneself (unlike the situation in many industries where trade associations facilitate the exchange of information about who is succeeding and why). There is also a problem with what Paton calls "measurement churn"—the tendency to frequently change measurement tools so the same data is rarely gathered over long periods. This makes it difficult to compare performance with others over time. A final difficulty with "best practice" comparisons is that there is no way of knowing if they are the reason for other organizations being more successful. It is possible that practices that "work" for one organization may not work for one's own due to unique situational characteristics of history, culture, personalities, and economic conditions.

Other Means-Based Performance Assessment Tools

In addition to the specific tools mentioned above, there are a large number of organization performance "checklists" available on the Internet. They vary greatly in their length, quality and sophistication, but many can be useful to executives and managers as ways to stimulate critical thinking about current management practices. Examples of these more general tools are those posted by the Charity Commission of the United Kingdom (www.charity-commission.gov.uk/ publications/cc10.asp#c) and that of Authenticity Consulting's free management library (www.managementhelp.org/aboutfml/diagnostics.htm).

Charities Rating Services

As noted earlier, one result of the accountability movement affecting the nonprofit sector has been the emergence of a new genre of nonprofit organizations devoted to assessing the performance of other nonprofits so as to inform potential donors and others about their effectiveness and efficiency. Two of the largest and best-known of these organizations are

> Guidestar (www2.guidestar.org/)
> Charity Navigator (www.charitynavigator.org/)

> Smaller and less well known are

> Charity Watch (www.charitywatch.org/)
> Charities Review Council of Minnesota (www.smartgivers.org/)
> Give Well (www.givewell.net/)
> Great Nonprofits (greatnonprofits.org/)
> Philanthropedia (myphilanthropedia.org/)
> Wise Giving Alliance (www.bbb.org/us/Wise-Giving/)

These performance information organizations vary greatly. None cover *all* American nonprofits but two of them, Guidestar and Charity Navigator, cover a large number. Guidestar includes all those nonprofits that file Form 990 with the U.S. government (that is, those that are registered charities eligible to give tax deductions to donors). These forms provide financial and programmatic information on the filing organizations. Guidestar provides, to those who register (for free), access to the information contained in these reports and, for a fee, more detailed information on the filer from other government sources as well as special reports on such matters as executive compensation. It does not attempt to pass any judgments on the organizations in its database, leaving that up to the user of the information. It does, however, offer general comments about how to interpret the information it provides.

The largest organization that attempts to play a "watchdog" role by rating charities on their effectiveness is Charity Navigator. It too looks at Forms 990 but only those that report over $500,000 in public donations and are four or more years old. (It excludes hospitals, universities and colleges, land trusts and community foundations). From the Form 990 data, it calculates organizational performance on seven criteria. Four are deemed to measure efficiency: program expense as a percentage of total expenses, administration expenses as a percentage of total expenses, the costs of fund raising as a percentage of total budget and fund raising efficiency (the cost of raising $1 in donations). Three criteria are applied to gauge an organizations "capacity," that is its ability to sustain its services over time and make changes in the face of environmental threats or opportunities. These are: revenue growth over time (four years), growth in program expenses, and working capital ratio.

All of the five smaller "watchdog" organizations review three thousand or fewer charities, most of which are large national organizations. Some of them take the initiative in deciding who to review while others respond to requests to be reviewed by organizations that wish to obtain their stamp of approval. Since doing their ratings, some use the same criteria as Charity Navigator but not entirely. The Better Business Bureau's Wise Giving Alliance, for example, includes an assessment of the quality of an organization's governance based on such criteria as board size, board compensation and the existence of conflict of interest policies. They and others also examine "transparency"—the nature and extent of communications to the public on the organization's activities and performance. Philanthropedia, which assesses five-hundred organizations, bases its judgments on the opinions of "experts" in the four subsectors of the nonprofit world in which it is interested.

Many of the caveats about organization evaluation already discussed in this chapter apply when considering the value of charity rating services. Because they attempt to create criteria that are generalizable across a broad spectrum of nonprofits, they end up assessing inputs and processes but not *outcomes*. Whether those organizations that meet the various financial criteria established by Charity Navigator and others actually achieve their stated mission more effectively is not known. Such criteria also may be of more interest to some external stakeholders such as donors but less so to others such as clients. Even popular criteria such as administrative overhead ratios and the cost of fundraising have come under criticism by scholars such as Steinberg and Morris (2010) and Sargeant and Jay (2009).

Interestingly, the inherent complexity of assessing organizational effectiveness and the potentially misleading nature of engaging in an overly narrow set of characteristics has been recognized by some of the watchdogs themselves as this chapter is being written in 2010. In a recent press release through philanthropyaction.com, Charity Navigator, Guidestar, Philanthropedia, Give Well, and Great Nonprofits jointly announced that they were revising their criteria to place less emphasis on financial ratios and more on effectiveness. Details on how they would do this were not available at the time.

Another problem with all of the evaluation tools except the United Way approach is that very little attention is paid to how the evaluation system is to be implemented. As previously noted, a great deal of research has concluded that unless all those to be affected by an evaluation system trust the evaluators, have a strong voice in its design, and accept the final product, there is a high probability the system will be dominated by the LGAB phenomenon discussed earlier in this chapter (Cutt and Murray, 2000; Mark et al., 2000; Sonnichsen, 2000).

Do these criticisms of charity rating services mean that they should not be used by potential donors or others wishing to make better-informed decisions about where to direct their money for greatest effect? The answer to this is no. *But* it would be unwise to use them alone. For truly informed giving, effort must be made to estimate impact as well. (See Brest and Hall, 2008, for a full discussion of "smart philanthropy.")

To summarize, it appears that there is still a long way to go before there will be available a tried and tested evaluation system that can be applied by most nonprofit organizations to reveal valid pictures of how well the organization is performing. Some would argue there is no point in trying, yet decisions are made every day based on untested assumptions and idiosyncratic perceptions of performance. Therefore, the goal of trying to improve the dialogue around this process in a way that takes account of the research into the everyday reality of OEE processes discussed in the first part of this chapter is worthwhile pursuing.

Conclusion

How can nonprofit organization leaders make practical use of the tension between the results of the empirical research and the promises of the new tools?

I have argued that politics in evaluation is almost inevitable because of the frailties in evaluation techniques and simple human foibles: The LGAB, SIR, and trust phenomena. Many political games can be destructive in that they distort the information produced or result in it being ignored or misused in the way it is applied to future decision making. They can also create major motivational problems among the evaluatees that can, paradoxically, damage their productivity.

Since one cannot avoid the political dimension in evaluation, therefore, attention has to be focused on what can be done to make the differences among the parties constructive rather than destructive. Conflict is not inevitably bad. Indeed, when handled constructively, it can often result in a product that is better than if there were no conflict at all.

In an ideal world, each phase of the evaluation process—its design, implementation, interpretation, and application—would be characterized by open discussions among all interested parties during which differences would be aired and resolved by mutual consensus. Unspoken beliefs and assumptions would be made explicit in logic models and standards. Even if some people cannot change their beliefs to make them congruent with the other parties', at least all parties would be conscious of where each is "coming from" and why they hold the positions they do. This could lead to greater understanding, if not acceptance, of these positions. What has to be done to move toward this ideal of constructive conflict resolution?

Trust Building

The basic secret for creating openness is the creation of an atmosphere of trust among the interested parties. If one of them believes the other is concerned only with their own interests, there is little chance of avoiding destructive game playing. The only approach then becomes one of trying to win the games more often than the opponents.

How is this trust built? Unfortunately for those seeking a "quick fix," it is usually built over time through many encounters between the parties. During these interactions each must show concern for the other, each must commit fully to communicating reasons for their actions, each must allow the other to have a voice in decisions that affect them, and each must keep their word when actions are promised or provide explanations if they can't. Paradoxically, though trust takes time to build, it can be destroyed in an instant with only one or two violations of the above rules.

If a prior relationship of trust does not exist before evaluation begins, it must consciously be worked on as the process is developed. This means involving all interested parties in that process, particularly those who are to be evaluated. All must have a voice in deciding the following six questions:

1. What is the purpose of the evaluation?
2. What should be measured?
3. What should be the evaluation methods used?

4. What standards or criteria should be applied to the analysis of the information obtained?
5. How should the data be interpreted?
6. How will the evaluation be used?

Is there a time when this kind of consultation is *not* advisable? Probably the only occasion is when there is strong evidence of malfeasance or willful ineptitude among the evaluatees. This would suggest that there is a high probability that they will consciously suppress or distort information. In such cases, external evaluation by professionals trained in looking for reporting errors, (for example, forensic accountants) would have to be used.

Logic Model Building

Many evaluation systems founder in destructive politics simply because those designing them fail to articulate the underlying logic models. This allows all parties to unconsciously apply their own answers to the above questions, which gives rise to differences that are not confronted. Two basic logic models need to be discussed among the parties: measurement based and level based. These are illustrated in Figures 16.1 and 16.2.

Measurement logic models (see Figure 16.1) try to articulate the links between inputs, activities/outputs, outcomes, and goals. They recognize that inputs create the basis for how much and what kind of outputs will occur but that *other* influences can also affect this linkage so it is not possible to argue, for example, that more inputs alone will improve performance. Similarly, this logic model lays out the connections between activities/outputs and outcomes, again trying to consciously identify what *else* can affect outcomes. Finally, they recognize that the link between outcome measures and the actual objectives they are trying to

FIGURE 16.1. GENERIC MEASUREMENT LOGIC MODEL.

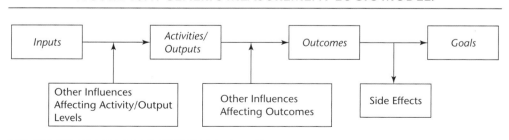

FIGURE 16.2. GENERIC LEVEL-BASED LOGIC MODEL.

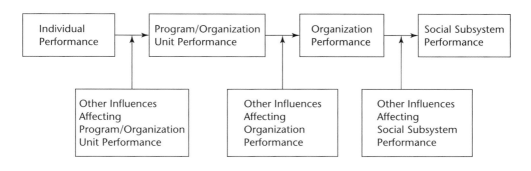

measure is not always perfect and that unanticipated side effects can occur when an organization is trying to reach a given objective.

A logic model based on the level of evaluation is illustrated in Figure 16.2. It attempts to articulate the links between the performance of individuals, programs/units within the organization, the organization as a whole, and (if this is of interest) between the organization and any system of organizations of which it is a part. It also tries to identify the other influences that intervene between these links so that no one will try to argue, for example, that good or bad evaluations of individuals reveals how well a program is doing or that good or bad evaluations of a program reveals how well the organization is doing.

The time to develop such logic models is during the design phase of the evaluation process. For example, if the top management of an organization wants to evaluate how well the organization is performing, it would sit down with representatives of those who are on the front line of program delivery and representatives of program users to discuss the six questions noted above. When it comes to the question of what to measure and how (methods), the outline of the Measurement Logic model could be distributed and these kinds of questions asked: Can we measure outcomes, and, if so, how? How well will outcome information reveal goal achievement? Is there any chance the organization's activities might be causing unanticipated side effects beyond the stated goals? Assuming we can get good indicators of program outcomes, what input, activity, and output measures are needed to track the possible factors that could influence them?

Similarly, the Level-Based Logic model could be used as the basis for discussing the links between individuals, programs or organizational units, and the organization as a whole. Applying it, these kinds of questions could be raised: If program evaluation reveals problems, what implications does this have for the organization as a whole? Do we need to reconsider the strategic priorities of the organization? To what extent are problems with a program due to performance problems of individuals or other influences such as funding levels? How do we compare the evaluations of very different programs in order to get a sense of their contribution to the organization's overall performance?

By addressing these kinds of questions with the aid of logic model frameworks, it is possible to surface a lot of potentially conflicting assumptions and beliefs before they can cause problems once the evaluation process gets started. The resulting design will usually be stronger and better supported by all interested parties.

Some Practical Problems in Certain Relationships

The general guidelines of trust building, participant involvement, and logic model creation will help create constructive political climates in evaluation. However, they are more or less difficult to apply depending on who are the evaluators and who the evaluatees. The most straightforward situation is where the evaluator is the management of the organization (or some part of it) and the evaluatees are those running a particular program, function, or department within it. Evaluation in this situation is known as "internal evaluation" (Love, 1991; Sonnichsen, 2000). The decisions about the evaluation process are under the control of the management who are in a position to ensure that consultation with evaluatees occurs and logic models are thought through before the process starts.

But what if the evaluator is the organization's board of directors? This group is legally responsible for seeing that the organization achieves its mission, so the management team is accountable to the board. As the earlier discussion of empirical research shows, however, many boards make little time for, and feel they have no skill in, carrying out evaluations. Many also do not know what to evaluate and feel that probing too deeply into how the organization is doing would suggest that they do not trust the executive director (who is usually well known to them and often is considered as a friend by some of them). As a result, many boards fail badly in their fiduciary duty to hold management accountable for its actions. Special effort must be devoted to training boards in these duties and providing them with the expertise they need to develop evaluation systems that meet their information needs (Cutt et al., 1996). However, if the board wants to minimize political game playing with management, the guidelines presented here suggest that the design process should be consultative. In most situations, the best approach would be a board task force on evaluation working together with staff representatives and a professional evaluator (if possible).

An even more difficult relationship exists when the evaluator is an external funder or contractor (for example, United Way, community foundation, government department). Usually funders or contractors have *many* organizations as their clients. How can they follow the recommended participative model in developing systems for evaluating the performance of these clients? They often express the wish for more and better accountability reporting from them but the participative approach takes time and usually involves intense face-to-face interactions that are difficult to arrange when there are so many clients. Because of this, as the review of the empirical literature shows, many of these external organizations go to one of two extremes. Some require little or no evaluation other than regular budget and financial reports on how money was spent. As a result, they get no real idea what impact their funds have had.

Alternatively, other funders and government contractors arbitrarily impose requirements for complex and numerous progress reports as well as final reports. Since many evaluatees in this situation don't see the point in this reporting, a climate of frustration and cynicism develops and, along with it, incomplete or inaccurate reporting practices. The only way to overcome these kinds of problems is for those who seek better accountability to invest the time and money needed to bring their clients together to design mutually satisfactory accountability frameworks.

In practical terms, this means that whenever a funding arrangement is made the discussion of it should include a detailed look at the evaluation system that will be used in reporting results. The recipient organization needs to know what kind of information the funder wants. If, for example, it wants only statistics that obscure important outcomes that can only be assessed qualitatively, the fundee should have an opportunity to influence that decision. It also should have the opportunity to raise beforehand the question of how reported information will be interpreted or used. For example, if measurements reveal low levels of participation or higher-than-expected costs, will there be an opportunity to conduct research into the reasons for this?

One of the more innovative approaches to conducting the kinds of open dialogues between the parties in an evaluative process is that known as Appreciative Inquiry. This is not specifically a model of evaluation but rather a model for organizational change developed initially by David Cooperrider and Suresh Srivasta (Srivasta and Cooperrider, 1990; Cooperrider and Whitney, 2000). It posits an alternative to the conventional "problem-solving approach" which lies at the base of traditional evaluation methods. The AI approach focuses primarily on appreciating the best of "what is," envisioning "what might be," and conducting a dialogue on "what should be." Emphatically a collaborative process, it requires the involvement of all stakeholders in an organization's future. Also, evaluation does not occur for its own sake. It is part of the larger change process, and it occurs only *after* the much more positive discussion of what is done well and what a better future would look like. In order to overcome barriers to progress toward a future vision, all parties would then, and only then, apply evaluation techniques in looking at how performance could have been better. As with so many approaches to management and decision making that consultants and others put forward, the AI approach has not been itself carefully evaluated as to its impact beyond the level of case studies of success reported by its adherents.

Organizational effectiveness evaluation will never be free of politics. In the final analysis, there will always be a subjective element that will lead to differences among those involved. It is only when these differences can be confronted and talked through in a nonthreatening, trusting environment that we can avoid destructive game playing and realize the benefits that can be obtained from a well-designed organizational evaluation process.

Notes

1. It is necessary to explain what is meant by the terms "politics" and "political." As used here the term does not refer to the intrusion of government-style politics—parties, campaigning, right-wing/left-wing politics—into nonprofit organizations. Small 'p' politics refers to behavior that occurs when conflict is perceived to exist by at least one party in a relationship (Tassie et al., 1996). Once differences are seen to exist, any subsequent actions taken to deal with them can be called "political." These actions can bring the perceived differences out into the open and try to resolve them (overt politics) or other parties can be kept unaware of them (covert politics). Applied to the world of evaluation, whenever one of the parties involved disagrees with the reasons for the evaluation, the type of evaluation to be undertaken, the methods used, the interpretation of the results or the way the results are used, there will be a political element to the evaluation.
2. See United Way Web site at www.unitedway.org/outcomes
3. See Balanced Scorecard Web site at www.balancedscorecard.org

References

Balser, D., and McClusky, J. "Managing Stakeholder Relationships and Nonprofit Organization Effectiveness." *Nonprofit Management and Leadership*, 2005, *15*, 295–316.

Baruch, Y., and Ramallo, N. "Communalities and Distinctions in the Measurement of Organizational Performance and Effectiveness." *Nonprofit and Voluntary Sector Quarterly*, 2006, *35*, 6–39.

Brest, P., and Hall, H. *Money Well Spent: A Strategic Plan for Smart Philanthropy*. New York: Bloomburg Press, 2008.

Cairns, B., Harris, M., Hutchison, M., and Tricker, M. "Improving Performance? The Adoption and Implementation of Quality Systems in UK Nonprofits." *Nonprofit Management and Leadership*, 2005, *16*, 135–151.

Campbell, D. "Outcomes Assessment and the Paradox of Nonprofit Accountability." *Nonprofit Management and Leadership.* 2002, *12*, 243–260.

Cooperrider, D., and Whitney, D. *Collaborating for Change: Appreciative Inquiry.* Cleveland: Barrett-Koehler, 2000.

Cutt, J., and Murray, V. *Accountability and Performance Evaluation in Non-Profit Organization.* London: Routledge, 2000.

Cutt, J., et al. "Nonprofits Accommodate the Information Demands of Public and Private Funders." *Nonprofit Management and Leadership* 1996, *7*, 45–68.

DiMaggio, P., and Powell, W. W. "The Iron Cage Revisited: Institutional Isomorphism and Collective Rationality In Organizational Fields." *American Sociological Review*, 1983, *48*, 147–160.

Ebrahim, A. "Information Struggles: The Role of Information in the Reproduction of NCO-Funder Relationships." *Nonprofit and Voluntary Sector Quarterly*, 2002, *31*(1), 84–114.

Forbes, D. P. "Measuring the Unmeasurable." *Nonprofit and Voluntary Sector Quarterly*, 1998, *27*(2), 183–202.

Gebelman, M., Gilman, S. R., and Pollack, D. "The Credibility of Nonprofit Boards." *Administration in Social Work*, 1997, *21*(2), 21–40.

Hall, M. H., Phillips, S. D., Meillat, C., and Pickering, D. *Assessing Performance: Evaluation Practices and Perspectives in Canada's Voluntary Sector.* Ottawa: Voluntary Sector Evaluation Project, Centre for Voluntary Sector Research and Development, Carleton University, 2003.

Hatry, H. P. *Performance Measurement.* Washington, D.C.: Urban Institute, 1999.

Herman, R. D., and Renz, D. O.. "Multiple Constituencies and the Social Construction of Nonprofit Organization Effectiveness." *Nonprofit and Voluntary Sector Quarterly*, 1997, *26*, 185–206.

Herman, R. D., and Renz. D. O. "Doing Things Right and Effectiveness in Local Nonprofit Organizations: A Panel Study." *Public Administration Review*, Nov.-Dec. 2004, *64*, 694–704.

Herman, R. D., and Renz, D. O. "Advancing Nonprofit Organizational Effectiveness Research and Theory: Nine Theses." *Nonprofit Management and Leadership*, 2008, *18*, 399–416.

Holland, T. P. "Board Accountabilities: Lessons From the Field." *Nonprofit Management and Leadership.* 2002, *12*(4), 409–428.

Kaplan, R. S. "Strategic Performance Measurement and Management in Nonprofit Organizations." *Nonprofit Management and Leadership*, 2001, *11*(3), 353–370.

Letts, C., Ryan, W. P., and Grossman, A. *High Performance Nonprofit Organizations: Managing Upstream for Greater Impact.* New York: Wiley, 1999.

Light, P. *Making Nonprofits Work.* Washington, D.C.: The Aspen Institute and Brookings Institution Press, 2000.

Lindenberg, M. "Are We at the Cutting Edge or the Blunt Edge: Improving NGO Organizational Performance With Private and Public Sector Strategic Management Frameworks." *Nonprofit Management and Leadership*, 2001, *11*(3), 247–270.

Lohman, R. A. "Has the Time Come to Reevaluate Evaluation?" *Nonprofit Management and Leadership*, 1999, *10*(1), 93–101.

Love, A. *Internal Evaluation: Building Organizations from Within.* Thousand Oaks, Calif.: Sage, 1991.

Mark, M. M., Henry, G. T., and Jules, G. *Evaluation: An Integrated Framework for Understanding, Guiding and Improving Policies and Programs.* San Francisco: Jossey-Bass, 2000.

Miller, J. "The Board as a Monitor of Organizational Activity." *Nonprofit Management and Leadership*, 2002, *12*(4), 429–450.

Morley, E. E., Vinson, E., and Hatry, H.P. *A Look at Outcome Measurement in Nonprofit Organizations*. Washington, D.C.: Independent Sector and The Urban Institute, 2001.

Osborne, D., and Gaebler, D. *Reinventing Government*. New York: Plenum Press, 1992.

Ospina, S., Diaz, W., and O'Sullivan, J. F. "Negotiating Accountability: Managerial Lessons From Identity-Based Nonprofit Organizations." *Nonprofit and Voluntary Sector Quarterly*, 2002, *31*(1), 5–31.

Panel on Accountability and Governance in the Voluntary Sector (PAGVS). *Building on Strength: Improving Governance and Accountability in Canada's Voluntary Sector*. Ottawa: Voluntary Sector Roundtable, 1999.

Paton, R. *Managing and Measuring Social Enterprises*. London: Sage, 2003.

Ring, P., and Van de Ven, Andrew H. "Developmental Processes of Cooperative Interorganizational Relationships." *Academy of Management Review*, 1994, *19*, 90–118.

Scotch, R. K. "Ceremonies of Program Evaluation." *Conference Proceedings*. Association for Research on Nonprofit Organizations and Voluntary Action, 1998.

Sargeant, A., Lee, S., and Jay, E. "Communicating the 'Realities' of Charity Costs: An Institute of Fundraising Initiative." *Nonprofit and Voluntary Sector Quarterly*, 2009, *38*, 333–342.

Shilbury, D., and Moore, K. "A Study of Organizational Effectiveness for National Olympic Sporting Organizations." *Nonprofit and Voluntary Sector Quarterly*, 2006, *35*, 5–38.

Steers, R. M. *Organizational Effectiveness: A Behavioral View*. Santa Monica, Calif.: Goodyear, 1977.

Steinberg, R., and Morris, R. "Ratio Discrimination in Charity Fundraising: The Inappropriate Use of Cost Ratios Have Harmful Side Effects." *Voluntary Sector Review*, 2010, *1*, 77–95.

Sonnichsen, R. C. *High Impact Internal Evaluation*. Thousand Oaks, Calif.: Sage, 2000.

Srivasta, S., Cooperrider, D., and Associates. *Appreciative Management and Leadership*. San Francisco: Jossey-Bass, 1990.

Tassie, B., Murray, V., Cutt, J., and Bragg., D. "Rationality and Politics: What Really Goes On When Funders Evaluate the Performance of Fundees?" *Nonprofit and Voluntary Sector Quarterly*, 1996, *25*(3), 347–363.

United Way of America. *Measuring Program Outcomes: A Practical Approach*. Alexandria, Va.: United Way, 1996 and online at www.liveunited.org/outcomes.

Yuchtman, E., and Seashore, E. S. "A Comparison of Multiple Constituency Models of Organizational Effectiveness." *Academy of Management Review*, 1967, *9*, 606–616.

Zimmerman, J. A., and Stevens, B. "The Use of Performance Measurement in South Carolina Nonprofits." *Nonprofit Management and Leadership*, 2006, *16*, 315–328.

DEVELOPING AND MANAGING NONPROFIT FINANCIAL RESOURCES

Essentially all nonprofit managers and leaders understand the importance of financial resources to the success of their organizations, yet all too often they view financial aspects of the nonprofit enterprise too narrowly. The chapters of Part Four collectively address essentially all facets of the process of developing and managing financial resources. Jeanne Bell introduces Part Four with a discussion in Chapter Seventeen of the most strategic level of financial management, financial leadership. Dennis R. Young then addresses a similarly strategic yet oft-overlooked dimension of nonprofit financial management with a comprehensive discussion in Chapter Eighteen of the options for securing financial resources, including a useful approach by which to evaluate a nonprofit organization's revenue choices.

Of course, raising money through philanthropic channels is a time-honored approach for nonprofits, and fundraising has become more competitive and sophisticated. Nonetheless, nonprofit organizations do not exist to raise money; they exist to pursue a mission or cause. Robert E. Fogal emphasizes in Chapter Nineteen how to develop the fundraising effort so that it fits with and flows from the mission and culture of the organization. The extent to which nonprofit organizations rely on donations varies substantially, and an increasingly large number of nonprofits seek to generate financial revenues via social enterprises that produce earned income. In Chapter Twenty, Scott T. Helm discusses social enterprise and shows how nonprofit organizations can make better decisions about enhancing various types of earned income, including ventures that generate unrelated business income. Of course, one of the most common of earned-income strategies for many nonprofits involves contracting with government. In Chapter Twenty-One, Steven Rathgeb Smith discusses the key benefits, challenges, and dynamics inherent in nonprofit-government contracting.

Although fundraising is sometimes overemphasized as at the heart of non-profit financial management, the principles, practices, and applications of management accounting are often underemphasized. This part of the hand-book includes an extensive chapter by David W. Young on financial accounting and management, including a discussion of how nonprofit managers can use financial ratios and other accounting tools to enable effective financial and pro-grammatic performance. In the final chapter of Part Four, Melanie Lockwood Herman provides a thorough guide by which nonprofit leaders can effectively assess and manage their organization's risks.

CHAPTER SEVENTEEN

FINANCIAL LEADERSHIP IN NONPROFIT ORGANIZATIONS

Jeanne Bell

Nonprofit executives need to exercise strong financial leadership to sustain their organization's impact over time. In finance, there is an important distinction between management and leadership. Financial *management* is about collecting and *producing* financial data; financial *leadership* is about *consuming* financial data and making good decisions that strengthen an organization's financial position. Financial management can be outsourced; financial leadership cannot. Executives who embrace their financial leadership responsibility recognize that virtually all decisions they make have financial implications: hiring and firing, investing in technology, choosing consultants, closing down a program, launching a major donor campaign, and the list goes on. Indeed, nonprofit leadership is essentially about sustaining deep mission impact by acquiring and deploying resources strategically.

Financial leadership is (1) ensuring that the nonprofit's decision makers have *timely and accurate* financial data; (2) using financial data to *assess* the financial condition of your activities and the nonprofit organization overall; (3) *planning*

The focus of this chapter is explicitly on public charities, although the concepts apply to other types of tax-exempt organizations as well. Many of the key themes and concepts presented in this chapter are drawn from the author's books on financial leadership and strategy: *Financial Leadership: Guiding Your Organization to Long-Term Success* (2005) written with Elizabeth Schaffer, and *What Next: Decision-Making for Financial Sustainability* (2010) written with Jan Masaoka and Steve Zimmerman, and reprinted here with permission.

around a set of meaningful financial goals; and (4) *communicating* progress on these goals to your staff, board, and external stakeholders. It is not about being a trained accountant, or having an MBA, or even having run a business in another lifetime. Although none of these things can hurt, they are not requirements for providing financial leadership.

Assessment, planning, and communication—these familiar leadership skills are the same skills you would use to develop a new community-based program, or even achieve a personal goal such as physical fitness or getting out of debt. I do not mean to downplay the unique vocabulary or concepts of nonprofit finance, yet I do want to suggest that financial leadership is integral to organizational leadership. As such, it requires the same set of skills as programmatic or fundraising leadership. Six key concepts and perspectives are central to successful nonprofit financial leadership:

- Creating a healthy culture of money
- Recognizing the nonprofit business model
- The profitability assumption
- Planning and real-time financial projection
- Talent as an investment
- From planning to deciding

Creating a Healthy Culture of Money

Many people think of nonprofit organizations as having organizational cultures distinct from business and government: mission-driven, community-engaged, collaborative and consensus-oriented, and so on. An aspect of nonprofit organizational culture that gets less attention is the culture of money. It is easier to see and feel the culture of money in a for-profit setting, where profitability goals are clear and routinely referenced and people are rewarded for reaching specific financial targets. But every nonprofit has a culture of money too. It may be unspoken or unrecognized, but it is there nonetheless. It is the executive's job to create a healthy organizational culture around money. When the culture of money is healthy, it fosters a deep understanding across the organization of its business model—or how its particular core activities have an impact and attract financial resources—resulting in a staff and board better able to contribute to the organization's financial success.

The foundational aspect of a healthy culture of money is transparency: the consistent sharing of meaningful financial information with all staff and board members. Among the most toxic problems that can plague an organization is a leader who won't share financial information. The motivation is often one of two things, or both at once: financial illiteracy or the fear of how people will react to the financial truth. Some executives are not as financially literate as they need to be to effectively run a nonprofit business and thus are uncomfortable sharing and discussing financial information. This is easily corrected through an intentional investment in their own professional development. Some executives worry that sharing less than optimal financial results with staff will scare them unduly and hurt morale. But staff members have the right to know if an organization is struggling financially, even if it means they will opt to leave. In fact, staff members may have good ideas for ways to improve the situation if only they were engaged in the problem solving. Further, morale is never maintained when layoffs and program cuts happen in a seemingly sudden fashion because staff members weren't informed along the way of financial trouble.

Some executives don't want to share full financial information with their boards because they fear they will be judged or blamed for poor financial results. Of course, they very well may be. Yet it is delaying the inevitable (not to mention unethical) to keep a board in the dark about serious financial problems. And again, how can the board help if it doesn't understand the problem? Financial transparency is fundamental to a healthy culture of money. Given the choice, executives should overshare rather than undershare financial information. In so doing, they educate and empower their staff and board colleagues to share responsibility for the financial health of the organization.

Of course, in order to be transparent, leaders have to have something to share. And so another contributing factor to the culture of money is the quality of the financial management systems that leaders put in place. Nonprofit tendencies to underinvest in administrative infrastructure can yield inadequate financial systems. The result is late, inaccurate, or unhelpful financial reporting, leaving staff and board members with little to go on as they make decisions. Obviously, over time, this jeopardizes the financial sustainability of an organization. Poor systems also create chronic inefficiencies and frustration among staff. Taking two weeks rather than two hours to cobble together a grant report to a funder because expenses have not been well coded to the grant all year is the kind of frustrating recurrence that drives talented people to leave poorly led nonprofits. Quality financial information also needs to be shared with funders, auditors, the Internal Revenue Service (IRS), and other regulators. Doing what an organization is supposed to do financially—what it promised or is regulated to do—feeds into a healthy culture of money.

A third key aspect of the culture of money is the degree to which leadership models a balanced view of mission and money. Effective leaders do not allow a mission *or* money culture to take root but insist instead on a mission *and* money culture. Dysfunctional cultures of money often find executives and senior staff who claim "not to be numbers people," preferring to pretend that it's the bookkeeper and the board treasurer who run the business side of the house while the mission people "do the real work." This ignores the reality that, just as in a for-profit business, it's the performance of everyone on staff that drives the business. For instance, if the program staff at a youth services organization don't deliver an exceptional tutoring program with measurable results, parents will eventually choose another provider of these services. An imbalanced view of mission and money can also lead to romanticizing a culture of scarcity, wherein it's acceptable or even noble to work without the essential technology, systems, and staffing to get the work done effectively. In fact, an underinvestment in an organization's management and infrastructure has a strong negative impact on the quality of programming over time. It's unfortunate that some donors, funders, and even some "watchdog groups" continue to correlate low overhead costs with program efficiency, when the opposite is actually true. Great programs thrive in thriving organizations with the right people and adequate resources to invest in them.

Recognizing the Nonprofit Business Model

In order to intentionally build an organization's financial strength over time, it is critical that all nonprofit leaders recognize that they are, in fact, running a business. Further, each nonprofit business has a particular business model; that is, a particular way that the organization's programmatic and support activities work together to attract resources and deliver community impact. As with any business, there are people to pay, resources to secure, investments to make, savings to build, and risks to mitigate. The fact that this is all done in pursuit of a mission bottom line does not lessen the urgency of the financial bottom line. If anything, it heightens it. It is these dual bottom lines—mission and money—that nonprofit executives and boards must continuously monitor. Moreover, a typical human service organization in the United States—a youth services nonprofit with a $1.5 million dollar annual budget, for instance—is likely a more complex financial entity than a typical $1.5 million for-profit corporation, such as a restaurant or a boutique. The complexity comes from the variety of revenue sources and types that most nonprofits assemble: a mix of contributed and earned income streams that all need to be solicited and managed differently. While a restaurant has one source of income—cash from its customers—the youth services organization may have six distinct types of income: fees from parents, contracts with the school district, grants from private foundations, in-kind donations from corporations, an annual donor campaign, and a gala dinner event. The organization not only has to have the systems and staffing to acquire and manage this variety of income streams, but leadership has to be savvy enough to weather their respective ebbs and flows and continuously refine the mix to cover expenses, if not grow the organization. And again, all of this complex business management has to be done while maintaining programmatic relevance and impact (see Chapter Eighteen of this handbook for an extensive discussion of the range and implications of various types of funding and financing).

Nonprofit financial leadership requires maintaining a healthy mix, or portfolio, of core activities. Core activities are the primary programmatic, fundraising, and administrative efforts of the nonprofit. So the $1.5 million youth services organization might have seven core activities: tutoring, arts, sports, gala dinner, annual campaign, general fundraising, and administration. From a financial management perspective, an accountant creates a cost center for each of these and reports financial results monthly. From a financial leadership perspective, the executive and her team must ensure that each activity is financed as well as it can be—in most nonprofits not every activity will be self-sustaining—and that together the seven-activity portfolio results in both mission impact and financial health.

Though many nonprofits receive large programmatic grants and contracts from foundation and government agencies, it is critical to recognize that these funding sources are *not* core activities. Again, the three programmatic core activities in the hypothetical youth services organizations are tutoring, arts, and sports. The tutoring program has three funding sources: a school district contract and two foundation grants. A very common mistake that nonprofit leaders make is to treat each of these sources as their own core activity rather than having them all "roll up" to one core activity, which is tutoring. Each source does need to be tracked and reported upon on in the financial *management* system, yet the *leadership* should be analyzing whether tutoring as an activity is delivering exceptional impact and—with its three funding sources—meeting financial projections. In other words, grant and contract tracking is financial management; analyzing the mission and money performance of core activities is financial leadership.

The activity portfolio's contents will vary along the mission and money continua. By design, not everything a nonprofit does has high mission impact, just as not everything has high financial return. Figure 17.1—a dual bottom line matrix—captures this idea.

On the one hand, the tutoring program for the youth services organization is a "star." They have the evaluation data to demonstrate its impact on kids finishing high school, and the school district contract, combined with loyal foundation

FIGURE 17.1. THE DUAL BOTTOM LINE MATRIX.

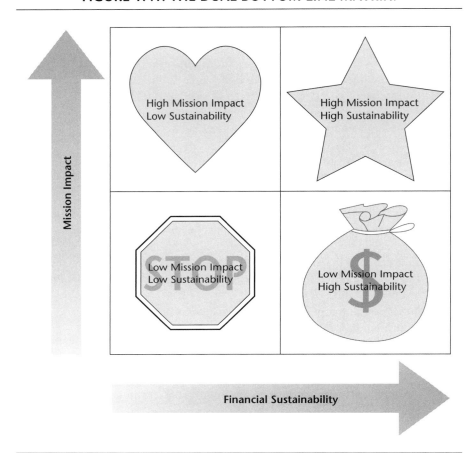

support, results in the program covering all of its costs. On the other hand, the arts program is a "heart." It, too, has measurable impact on youth social and academic outcomes, but the program has no dedicated funding source, so it is being subsidized by the annual dinner gala. In turn, the annual dinner gala is a "money bag." Despite the inclusion of youth art in the silent auction and moving client stories during the program, it is a classic fundraiser with modest mission impact. However, it nets $125,000 a year for the organization, partially offsetting the arts program losses. And so it goes in most nonprofit business models: an alchemic mix of money losers and money makers leveraging one another to achieve the organization's overall programmatic and financial position.

The nonprofit activity portfolio is dynamic rather than static. Strong financial leadership involves continuously monitoring and, to the degree possible, anticipating the migration of activities along the dual bottom-line axes. The tutoring program is a star now, but next year's state budget cuts could mean a 30 percent reduction in the school district contract. Suddenly a star becomes a heart through no fault of staff and board. Will leadership immediately cut expenses and services by 30 percent? Will it quickly seek an additional foundation grant? Will it raise gala dinner prices to increase the event's net to $175,000 for greater subsidy of its programs? If they choose to maintain services and increase income, will it work? What if they continue spending as though the increased income plan will work, but then it doesn't? These are the questions and anxieties of nonprofit financial leadership.

The Profitability Assumption

There remains in too many quarters of the nonprofit sector a persistent and dangerous misperception that nonprofits cannot or should not be profitable. The "cannot" is easy to counter. There is nothing in the tax code that forbids nonprofits from generating profits from their mission-related activities; the requirement is that any profits be reinvested in the organization rather than being paid to shareholders or used to excessively compensate interested parties (see Chapter Two of this volume for a more complete discussion of the legal aspects of nonprofit financial management). It is the "should not" that is harder for nonprofit staff and board—and the general public—to get past. And our sector's nomenclature doesn't help; *nonprofit* implies an absence of profit and *charity* or *public charity* also connotes giving away and retaining nothing. Of course, all of this defies logic. It isn't possible to sustain impact over time without adequate capital. If an organization breaks even every year—meaning income matches expenses exactly—it will have not a penny to its name to withstand changes in funding, let alone invest in its growth or improvement.

Executives who are strong financial leaders are comfortable and skilled at pursuing profitability. This is just as true for a grassroots social justice organization as it is for the mainstream opera or ballet company. Financial leaders recognize that the sustained health of their organizations requires working capital for flexibility and investment. Profitability means generating surpluses—income in excess of the operating needs for the year. It does not necessarily mean earned income, though it might. Nonprofit profitability can come from successful fundraising, from successful earned-income strategies, or from both. The only requirement is that the funds generated are in excess of what is needed to meet current obligations, and that the organization has control over them. This means, for instance, that restricted grants from foundations do not help with profitability because they have to be spent on particular activities rather than retained for the nonprofit's own use. Most government contracts don't lend themselves to profitability either, because they tend to reimburse for actual costs or limit allowable costs such that nonprofits are fortunate if the full cost of the purchased service is even covered (though there are some exceptions).

By and large, to achieve a profit a nonprofit needs unrestricted contributions, which typically come from individuals; or earned income such as fees, tuition, or the sale of goods; or both. Because of the misguided inattention to generating profit in our sector, many nonprofit organizations are operating without substantial access to either of these sources of profit. That is, leaders—often with collusion from institutional funders—have set up business models that by design will not achieve profit, and thus, their organizations will never achieve financial health. This, for example, is true of many human service organizations that rely entirely on government and foundation support, never building an individual donor base or developing earned-income channels. Such organizations have very little "agency," or financial autonomy, to invest in themselves for greater efficiencies and deeper impact. Too many nonprofits find themselves at twenty years old without even a month's operating cash to their names. This can be the direct result of a flawed business model and ill-informed assumptions about profitability. Chapters Eighteen and Twenty of this handbook provide additional information about the options and issues inherent in funding and financing nonprofits, including the merit and challenges of pursuing earned income.

Why do nonprofits need to be profitable? Simply put: so that they can have a savings account with their own money in it—their own money to fix the real or proverbial roof, or withstand a 30 percent contract reduction until replacement funds can be raised, or to build on online giving program. A healthy organization has a cash savings or reserve. Strong financial leadership results in profitability, at least some years, so that a cash reserve can be built. Effective leaders educate and impress upon their staffs and boards that the health of their organizations depends on this. Just the way a financially healthy family has three months of living expenses in savings, ideally a nonprofit has three months of operating expenses invested. Again, depending on whether an organization has access to individual donors or earned income, this goal will be relatively easier or harder to achieve. The leadership issue is that the executive must set the expectation of organizational savings, be disciplined in the building and preserving of that savings, and help everyone in her organization understand why and how the business model is working to achieve them.

Planning and Real-Time Projection

It is critical for nonprofit executives and other leaders to get very specific about what it takes to lead an organization to financial health. The approach to annual budgeting is critical here. Too often in nonprofit organizations, the executive and board approach building next year's budget as though they had a clean slate, as though they were starting all over again. In fact, there is no starting over; leaders bring the financial results of December 31 with them to January 1, or wherever the fiscal year change may be on the calendar. What leadership should do is assess the *current* financial condition of the organization, and based on that assessment, set a financial goal for the coming year—and *then*, build a budget to meet that financial goal. Certainly there should be no built-in assumption that a break-even budget is a good budget; that assumption is the anti-profit bias at work.

When a board of directors approves a budget, they are approving a net financial result for the coming fiscal year. There are three potential financial outcomes: build net worth through a surplus budget, invest (deplete) net worth through a deficit budget, or maintain net worth through a break-even budget. Any one of these could be the right decision for financial health depending on the mission and state of the organization. When would depleting net worth be a good financial decision? For instance, the youth services organization could determine that spending down one week of its four month cash reserve is financially prudent if it allows them to purchase an outside evaluation of their tutoring program. The perspective might be that, with a reputable evaluation, new opportunities for program replication and funding will be available in future years. So while purchasing the $40,000 evaluation means that in the coming twelve months they will spend $40,000 more than they bring in—and thus will have a deficit for this fiscal year—the investment of a small portion of their reserve, they believe, will ultimately more than pay for itself with new and larger funding. Less financially sophisticated leaders don't think about how to build up—or how to invest—their nonprofit's own money during the annual budgeting process.

Financial leadership is also crucial in how the budget is monitored throughout the year. It is critical that all staff and board members remember the ultimate aim of the budget: its net result. There is no such thing as "spending on budget" if income isn't coming in on budget; if the net is out of whack, the budget is out of whack. It is typically fairly easy for nonprofits to anticipate expenses—salaries, rent, and so forth—but income is rarely fully raised or even identified in nonprofits as the fiscal year begins. In other words, leaders begin spending on day one of the fiscal year as if income will come in as planned but without any reasonable basis for making this assumption. It takes judgment and discipline to rethink expenditures if it becomes clear that income isn't coming in as expected. Among the questions to consider:

- How soon do we change expenditures?
- If the first quarter's income wasn't on target, should we give ourselves another quarter to catch up?
- Are we being overly optimistic?
- Are we reading the environment and our constituents and funders accurately?

These questions must be asked year-round, not just during annual budgeting. Income typically is dynamic and, to a real degree, beyond the control of leadership throughout the year, so engaging in annual budgeting is simply not enough to ensure good financial decision making all year. Instead, as the year progresses, effective financial leaders shift from a budget variance orientation to a rolling projection orientation. This means regularly generating and using financial data that updates everyone's understanding and expectations about what is happening financially in real time.

Talent as an Investment

For most nonprofits, people—represented financially in the form of salaries, benefits, consultant and contractor fees, and volunteer management—are by far the largest expense item. For this reason, the approach a nonprofit takes to recruiting, deploying, developing, and retaining talent is in very large part a question of financial leadership (for more on the design and management of compensation and benefits programs, specifically, see Chapter Twenty-five of this volume).

In for-profit companies, executives make an explicit link between employee investment and financial return. This is less true in the nonprofit culture, and it is a major sector weakness. Too many nonprofit leaders do not consider the financial drain that underperforming or underutilized staff represent. They see these as human resource or supervision problems but not also as the very real financial problems that they are. Moreover, nonprofit staff members typically are not forced to consider how their performance—or lack thereof—impacts the organization's bottom line. Consider the case of the employee who is constantly yet unexpectedly out of the office, requiring management to secure costly temporary help to keep a drop-in center open. Or consider the case manager whose salary is paid by a deliverables-based government contract and who regularly does not meet minimum client service hour targets. Fundraising positions often can be the exception to this rule, although even in this overt income-generating role there is rampant misunderstanding and underenforcement of performance expectations across the sector. Effective nonprofit financial leaders live with the daily reality that people are their single largest investment—their largest expense *and* their primary source of community impact—and therefore see effective talent management as central to building the financial health of their organizations.

When the renowned business writer Jim Collins (2001) turned his attention to the nonprofit sector in his monograph, *Good to Great and the Social Sectors* (2005), he acknowledged that organizational culture and relative underpay (compared to other sectors) pose talent management challenges for nonprofit executives. In his view, the nonprofits that never achieve greatness are those that invest time and resources trying to fix underperformance rather than aggressively pursuing and retaining exceptional performers:

> The comparison companies in our research—those that failed to become great—placed greater emphasis on using incentives to "motivate" otherwise unmotivated and undisciplined people. The great companies, in contrast, focused on getting and hanging on to the right people in the first place—those who are productively neurotic, those who are self-motivated and self-disciplined. . . . Lack of resources is no excuse for lack of rigor—it makes selectivity all the more vital. (p. 15)

Talent is an investment, so extra care and strategic thinking should be integral to developing and maintaining the staffing and compensation plan during each annual budgeting process. Every staff person should be reevaluated in terms of which core activity, or activities, they will be deployed in during the coming year. Among the questions leaders should ask themselves: How will we maximize our organization's return on investment in this staff person this year? If people clearly are in the wrong jobs, they should be moved or, if necessary, let go. If people could contribute more, they should be provided the supervision and support to do so—that is, to become even more valuable to the organization. Financial leaders recognize that retaining talent is their primary talent management objective and, therefore, performance-based compensation is essential. Cost-of-living increases may be employed uniformly, but retaining what Collins (2005) called the "productively neurotic" requires intentional investment in them through competitive compensation, benefits, and professional development opportunities. Moreover, effective financial leaders make periodic market corrections to ensure that long-tenured high performers' compensation does not fall so far behind what similarly talented people are securing in the marketplace today that they are tempted to move on (see Chapter Twenty-Five for extensive guidance on effective planning and management of compensation and benefits programs).

From Planning to Deciding

For too long in the nonprofit sector there has been an overemphasis on planning, to the neglect of decision making and execution. Making matters worse, much of the strategic planning that goes on in the sector lacks any real financial basis; nonprofit leaders and their consultants define strategies and goals and objectives, but nowhere in the planning do they do the hard work of determining how they will actually fund or finance them. The current economic recession has proven, as all recessions do, that predicting the future is a very dicey proposition. Periodic organizational planning, wherein board and staff work together to ensure that everyone shares an understanding of the current operating context and the essential direction of the organization, is certainly valuable. Nonetheless, the day-to-day work of financial leadership involves making the best business decisions possible given the information at hand at the time. Three-year strategic plans are very unlikely to anticipate a recession, or an employee lawsuit, or a market opening caused by the closure of a competitor, or (often) even the resignation of a longtime leader. These unplanned factors mandate real-time decision making, and the leaders who get more of those decisions right than wrong are the ones who sustain and grow mission impact over time.

The practice of business planning is gaining traction in the nonprofit sector, yet it, too, often focuses only on earned-income strategies rather than holistically on the entire business model that the vast majority of nonprofits employ. Further, it tends to downplay mission impact as a critical component of the nonprofit business model. That is, it neither assumes nor plans for the dual bottom line reality in which nonprofits operate. And finally it, too, tries to predict the future and assure people that documented plans are somehow highly likely to come true. Thus, just like traditional strategic planning, it runs the risk of providing a false sense of security and "doneness" (that is, all the big decisions have been made and now staff "simply" have to implement the plan).

It's not overstating the case to say that leadership is to a great degree about decision making. And further, all important decisions have some kind of financial implications, whether immediate or eventual. What does it look like to shift from a predominantly planning orientation to a predominantly financial decision-making and execution orientation? Of great importance is that all decision making is based on an explicit consideration of mission and money factors. If the organization is trying to decide whether to have a live receptionist or just a voicemail system, for instance, executive leaders should frame the mission and money factors for the decision-making group's consideration. On the mission side: will the youth clients, including those for whom English is a second language, navigate a voice mail system or will they be discouraged and hang up (thus limiting our impact with them)? On the money side: exactly how much (with full benefits) does a live receptionist cost us? Is there a way we could deploy those dollars in service of mission with greater return, or is this expenditure essential? Perhaps the group could consider using youth volunteer receptionists as employment training. However, what would it cost to recruit, train, and supervise these volunteers, and who on staff would do that and at what opportunity cost? The point here is that good decisions are not made from a mission-only or money-only perspective; the factors must be considered holistically. In the end, judgment will be required to make a decision; there is always subjectivity. Financial leadership is about framing the decision in mission and money terms and about a focus on decisive execution.

The Practice of Financial Leadership

Informed by the six perspectives just covered, the day-to-day *practice* of financial leadership is ensuring that decisions makers have *timely and accurate* financial data; using financial data to *assess* the financial condition of your activities and nonprofit business overall; *planning* around a set of meaningful financial goals; and *communicating* progress on these goals to your staff, board, and external stakeholders. The financial leadership model's elements are both interdependent and cyclical. Without accurate financial data, one cannot assess financial health. Without quality assessment, one cannot set meaningful goals. Without shared goals, communicating about process is flat and unengaging, and so on. Moreover, financial leadership does not occur once a year (for instance, solely during the annual budgeting process), but all year long, every year. Decisions as varied as whether to begin or end a program, to hire your first development director, or to enter into a partnership with another nonprofit organization, if made effectively, draw on the skills presented in this model. Therefore, effective financial leadership involves the four elements of

- Securing financial data you can trust
- Assessing your organization's financial health
- Engaging in financial planning
- Communicating financial progress

Securing Financial Data You Can Trust

As executive director and financial leader, your primary interest is in the programmatic and financial *performance* of your nonprofit business activities.

But the leadership model outlined here requires that appropriate financial *processes* be in place. To exercise your assessment, planning, and communication leadership roles, you need accurate financial data, and you need it in a format you can understand. Clearly, inaccurate data would cause you to set potentially unrealistic goals and would also undermine your ability to communicate progress. But ensuring that the appropriate processes are in place can be a challenge for an executive who does not have a background in finance. Executives often ask us, "How am I supposed to know if my finance person knows what he or she is doing when I don't speak the language of accounting?" People sometimes compare this feeling to the vulnerability most of us feel when we take a car to a mechanic. Who are we to argue with a mechanic's $1,500 diagnosis when we don't know the difference between a carburetor and an alternator?

Despite these challenges, the first step toward exercising financial leadership has to be determining whether or not the financial information you have is credible. There are three key factors to consider here: staffing, accounting practices, and the accounting system.

Staffing. You need to be confident that you have adequate financial staffing before you put your full trust in the financial statements being provided to you. Whether your financial people are employees, contract bookkeepers, or consulting CPAs, the most important question you have to answer is, Do they understand and have experience with *nonprofit* accounting? However you staff your finance function, to have confidence in the accuracy of your financial statements, you need to feel assured that the producers of the statements are not undertrained, overworked, or inappropriately isolated.

I have found it helpful to consider finance staffing in three categories: strategic, operational, and transactional. Table 17.1 defines these categories and provides examples of the tasks and qualifications for each category.

As your organization's leader, you are looking for finance staff members that share your attitude that finance is an essential part of infrastructure and that it should be done in the spirit of supporting programs and mission. The quality of financial information you receive will suffer if the people preparing it aren't interested in your organization's work. It will suffer if they are not responsive to your needs to evaluate the financial performance of your activities. Producers of financial data who are inflexible or indifferent to the needs of their consumers can represent a huge roadblock on your path to strengthening financial leadership in your organization. Too many nonprofit leaders feel held hostage by unresponsive finance staff because they are insecure about their own finance knowledge or afraid they won't find an adequate replacement. We encourage you to remember

TABLE 17.1. FINANCE FUNCTIONS, TASKS, AND QUALIFICATIONS

Finance Functions	Specific Tasks	Qualifications
Strategic Perform the planning and oversight role for the finance department; guide accounting activities as needed	Conduct general financial planning and provide oversight Develop a cost allocation framework Analyze financial reports on a monthly basis and submit reports to the board and executive director on a monthly basis Monitor financial activities; conduct a periodic comparison to the budget Lead the annual budgeting process Serve as the main point of contact with the auditor	Strong analytical skills Excellent communication skills Exposure to nonprofit financial statement analysis Program planning and nonprofit budgeting
Operational Pay bills, invoice contracts, follow up on accounts receivable, prepare bank deposits, process payroll, and perform other accounting duties as assigned	Prepare A/P, A/R, and 1099 forms Make cash disbursements Complete contract invoicing (including the preparation of monthly reports to funders) Report hours by program to the payroll processing agency Perform journal entries Assist with budget and financial statement preparation Monitor cash flow Allocate all expenses (code checks) to the appropriate programs and grants based on the established cost allocation methodology Respond to ad hoc analytic requests from the finance director	Strong skills in Microsoft Excel Strong nonprofit accounting experience (A/R, A/P), and experience in accounting for restricted grants Experience in preparing financial statements from an accounting software system
Transactional Support the accounting function by performing clerical and administrative tasks	Write checks once they are coded Distribute financial statements to program managers Photocopy checks, invoices, and other documents as required, and maintain check and invoice files Make bank deposits Maintain grant binders (obtain grant agreements, copies of monthly reports, and other necessary grant documentation) Maintain personnel files Collect time sheets	Quick, accurate worker Exposure to basic accounting principles Strong attention to detail

that you are a financial leader, which means you are entitled to ask questions and receive helpful answers from the people you hire to support you in that role.

Accounting Practices. Just as appropriate staffing is a requirement for accurate financial data, so too is implementation of certain accounting practices. Even though you are not an accountant, your awareness and understanding of several key accounting practices will allow you to get a good sense of how accurate and well presented your financial data are. The following are the six accounting practices that you need to ensure are in place before you rely on the financial statements provided to you:

1. Treatment of restricted contributions
2. Function classification of expenses
3. Employee time tracking
4. Allocation of common costs
5. Accrual basis accounting
6. Capitalization and depreciation

A very complete explanation and discussion of the managerial aspects of nonprofit financial accounting, with more detail and financial operations and the use of each of these six practices, is presented in Chapter Twenty-two.

Accounting Systems. Many hear the term "accounting system" and think immediately of software, yet the heart of an accounting system actually is what's called the *chart of accounts*. The chart of accounts is the set of labels or categories that your organization uses to organize the description of its assets, liabilities, net assets, income, and expenses. In a chart of accounts, you also assign separate categories to your core program, administration, and fundraising activities. Many organizations also assign separate categories to their key funding sources such as grants and contracts. Nonfinance staff members, including the executive director, typically interact with the chart of accounts in two ways. First, they use the categories to code the expenses they authorize. Second, all of the reports that an accounting system can produce are based on the chart of accounts. Therefore, it is critical that the financial leaders of a nonprofit organization understand the chart of accounts for their organization and influence its design or organization to ensure that the system is capable of meaningful financial reporting. (Chapter Twenty-two provides examples and detail on the use of the chart of accounts in the process of financial planning and reporting.)

Choosing accounting software—for the first time or as an upgrade from the system you have now—is a seemingly technical event in which executives should nonetheless play a role. As a financial leader of the organization, you should be concerned with the following issues when purchasing an accounting system:

1. Do we actually need new software or are we merely inadequately trained to maximize the use of our current system?
2. Are we buying a product that is consistent with our needs and staff capacity?
3. Are we using the purchase process as a platform for updating and streamlining our financial tracking procedures (based on the chart of accounts)?
4. Is the staff person coordinating the purchase adequately involving the key consumers of the system's reports—people such as the program managers and executives, development managers, board treasurer, and executive director?

If your organization is large enough to have paid finance staff, you should make the senior finance staff person the project manager on an accounting software purchase. She or he can convene key consumers to learn what reporting needs are currently unmet, restructure the chart of accounts accordingly, investigate appropriate products in your price range, and work on setup and implementation. As the financial leader, you should be involved in the process, including the final decision of what to buy. You will not actually use the accounting system in a hands-on way, yet on behalf of yourself and the other key consumers of financial information on your board and staff you need to exercise leadership to help ensure that the quality of your accounting system meets your organization's needs.

Further, although you as a nonprofit executive may not typically be involved in a hands-on way with your organization's finance systems, you must ensure that those systems are in place and operating effectively. Proper staffing, appropriate accounting practices, and a strong accounting system are the foundation upon which you can develop financial leadership. Together they ensure that the right processes are in place to generate accurate and meaningful financial data for the organization's decision makers.

Assessing Your Organization's Financial Health

When you have determined that you can trust the financial data you have about your nonprofit business, you can move on to assessment. Among nonprofit leaders who don't bring a finance background to their work, assessment is typically the weakest part of their financial leadership skill set. This is because it requires the ability to read and understand financial statements—something that is a scary proposition for many nonfinance people. Nonetheless, assessment is critical to doing good planning and communicating, and the information provided throughout this and the next chapters of Part Four of the book provide the fundamental information that a nonprofit leader needs to know.

As a financial leader, you have three overarching questions to examine as you assess the financial health of your organization:

1. What are our immediate financial strengths and vulnerabilities?
2. What are our long-term financial strengths and vulnerabilities?
3. Do our constituents perceive us as efficient and competitive?

A nonprofit financial leader and his or her key partners on the board and staff need to be able to evaluate the financial strengths and weaknesses of the organization from a variety of perspectives. They should be constantly aware of the immediate financial issues facing the organization, such as cash flow challenges or major variances in income and spending compared with the year's budget. They should also look at trends and how well the organization is positioned to thrive in future years. And finally, they also have to assess perceived efficiency from the point of view of potential donors and funders, competitor organizations, and watchdog groups. All of this assessment work will inform the kinds of financial goals (budget and work plan) that a well-led organization sets for itself for the following year.

Engaging in Financial Planning

The next aspect of financial leadership is financial planning, which takes place largely through the annual budgeting process. In order to lead a successful annual budgeting process, a financial leader must embrace two fundamental budgeting principles: first, a budget is a tool for *planning* and *monitoring*; and second, a good budgeting process is *inclusive* of many voices and perspectives. For many nonprofit executives, budgeting is the most comfortable and interesting part of financial leadership. Done correctly, the budgeting process actively engages many staff and board members who are otherwise uninterested in accounting or even monthly financial reporting. It becomes an opportunity for these stakeholders to contribute to the organization's work plan. For most organizations, the annual budgeting cycle also offers the best (if not only) time to set meaningful financial goals. As your organization's financial leader, you want to ensure that the process results in a useful tool—one that will be used to guide decisions, anticipate problems, and provide a baseline against which actual program and financial performance can be monitored.

In years when the organization is not undergoing a strategic planning process, the budgeting process is typically the only formal vehicle for strategic thinking and planning. The effective financial leader ensures that the process includes all voices: program, development, finance, and governance (board). When it is responsive to a thorough assessment of strengths, weaknesses, opportunities, and threats, the budget becomes a true reflection of the organizational goals and work plan. Once approved, a good budget becomes an instigator of discussions and a means for helping everyone understand and own the financial progress of the organization.

Communicating Financial Progress

The final element of financial leadership is communicating progress toward the established goals with the organization's key stakeholders. Communicating about finance is a high art. It requires engaging people who are untrained in finance in meaningful financial discussions, sharing financial information that may at times be uncomfortable or unflattering, and demonstrating financial accountability to the people and institutions that use, fund, and regulate your work as a nonprofit. But the most important outcome of ongoing, clear communication is the ability of the executive director, the board, and staff to anticipate financial challenges, revise plans, and avoid uninformed or ill-informed decisions that could lead the organization into financial crisis.

Financial reports are the primary tool for communicating financial progress. Some financial reports come right out of an accounting system. Others, such as an annual report to the community and the IRS Form 990, use figures from the accounting system but are created outside of it. As the financial leader, you may or may not be responsible for the actual creation of these reports, but you are responsible for ensuring that they are well done and that each of your key financial audiences receives the information it needs and wants. Moreover, it is in your best interests that these audiences get useful financial information because you seek their partnership in monitoring progress and continually evaluating organizational goals and objectives.

Depending upon how you are staffing the financial function at your nonprofit organization, you will be working with a staff finance manager, an independent bookkeeper, or a CPA to develop your financial reports. In any case, it's important to remember your leadership role. In our work with community-based nonprofits, we often encounter executive directors, program managers, and boards of directors who are very unhappy with the financial reporting they receive but who feel unable to change it. You may know nothing about the accounting software being used or about bookkeeping per se, yet it is your role and responsibility to work with your producer of financial reports to get the information that your key audiences need—in the format they need it. This can take time and negotiation, but it is critical. If in the end the person you are working with is unable or unwilling to prepare the documents or make the improvements to the reporting that you seek, it is probably time to look for someone new who can carry out these functions.

And remember: *Match the message to the audience.* There are five primary audiences that a financial leader should keep informed and communicate with about the organization's financial progress:

- Staff (all staff and the management team)
- Board (full board and finance committee)
- Funders (governmental and nongovernmental)
- Constituents (clients or beneficiaries, donors, community partners, and other external stakeholders)
- Regulators, especially the Internal Revenue Service

These five audiences vary in terms of the financial information they need or require and the frequency with which they need or require it. They also vary in terms of the financial story that you, as the leader, want them to read and understand. For instance, a program manager who is running a single program at your organization needs to read and understand a financial story different from the one your board treasurer does. The IRS mandates a detailed annual financial report (Form 990), whereas clients and community supporters want to read a more basic overview of your financial progress each year. Chapter Twelve addresses the subject of strategic communications and provides information that may be very useful regarding communication of financial information and results.

Nonprofit leaders who go beyond assessment and budgeting to year-round communication about the organization's financial progress with staff, board, and key stakeholders are at an enormous advantage over their peers who do not. Though it takes more time and means answering more questions, this approach creates buy-in from staff and board and serves to develop them professionally; it ensures their assistance in responding to unanticipated financial challenges and opportunities; and it demonstrates a transparency that sustains people's faith in the organization and its leadership. This last advantage has important ripple effects—from improved staff retention to the increased confidence of your funders.

Conclusion

Few nonprofit executives were drawn to their work by a love of financial assessment, planning, or communication. For most, these are acquired skills and acquired tastes. As trainers and consultants, we have seen the difference a strong financial leader can make in the health and impact of a nonprofit organization over time. Indeed the most dangerous thing a nonprofit executive can do is to put his or her head in the sand about money. In our experience, relying completely on a bookkeeper or board treasurer simply does not work. It is not an exaggeration to say that the very healthy nonprofits with which we have worked all have executives who view themselves as the financial leaders of their organizations.

Growing or changing an organization's financial culture and systems is almost always a multiyear process. For instance, improving the way your organization does financial planning and budgeting will happen over several budget cycles (years) while staff and board become oriented to what it takes to approach the process inclusively and strategically. Similarly, reaching the quality of financial reporting that is suggested in this chapter may take a year or more when you consider any necessary changes in staffing or board or in training, system redesign, or the conceptual work of identifying core programs and activities that need to be tracked and analyzed. In short, if you have a lot to do to improve the financial practices of your nonprofit organization, don't expect it to happen in one quarter or even one fiscal year. Instead, talk with your key staff and board partners about your needs and priorities, develop a plan for who will work on them, and determine a realistic time line.

Strong financial management—the production of accurate, timely financial statements—is essential but insufficient for financial sustainability. It is what leaders *do* with that information each and every day that leads to sustained mission impact or not. Strategic plans and business plans can help to clarify and document direction, but in the end it's the decisions that leaders make in real time that are the difference between financial weakness and strength over time. Those decisions will be stronger if they start from an assumption that nonprofits in fact have a business model and that the model must yield both mission impact and profit in order to be sustainable.

References

Bell, J., and Schaffer, E. *Financial Leadership: Guiding Your Organization to Long-Term Success.* St. Paul, Minn.: The Fieldstone Alliance, 2005.

Bell, J., Masaoka, J., and Zimmerman, S. *What Next: Decision-Making for Financial Sustainability.* San Francisco: Jossey-Bass, 2010.

Collins, J. *Good to Great.* New York: Harper Business, 2001.

Collins, J. *Good to Great and the Social Sectors: A Monograph to Accompany Good to Great.* Boulder, Colo.: Jim Collins, 2005.

CHAPTER EIGHTEEN

NONPROFIT FINANCE

Developing Nonprofit Resources

Dennis R. Young

Nonprofit organizations finance themselves through a wide variety of sources that provide both monetary and in-kind resources. This is one way in which nonprofits distinguish themselves from business or government organizations. Nonprofit sources include fees revenues, charitable contributions, government funding, investment revenues, and volunteer and in-kind contributions. Thus nonprofit finance involves much more than traditional charitable fundraising. Rather it requires cultivation of several of these sources, as well as finding the right mix of sources for organizations in different fields of service, with different missions, and in different circumstances. This chapter explores the conditions under which nonprofits can pursue these alternative sources, as well as the factors that may determine their proportions of total income. The discussion is guided by economic theory, especially the idea of public and private goods and the notion of economic benefit that can be tied to finance through the concept of demand by individuals, groups, and organizations that are willing to pay for nonprofit services.

Sources of Nonprofit Income

We use the term *income* to include both monetary and in-kind sources of support. However, most available data are confined to monetary support that is commonly referred to as "revenue." In this chapter I distinguish between these two terms but primarily focus on revenue for which data are most readily available and with which nonprofit management practice is most heavily concerned. Data on nonprofit finance are generally aggregated into broad categories. For example, data from IRS 990 forms distinguish broadly between charitable contributions (called public support), government grants, program revenues, and investment returns. These categories blur important distinctions among individual versus institutional philanthropy, government grants versus contracts, and fee revenue from sales versus government reimbursements. In this chapter I make finer distinctions among alternative sources of revenue. Still, a review of the broad categories of income provides a useful general picture of finance of U.S. nonprofit organizations in different fields of service. Table 18.1, for example, shows that among broad fields of service, as reported by nonprofits that file IRS 990 forms for the year 2005, there is considerable variation among sources of support. (Note that these data do not include churches or nonprofits with annual income less than $25,000. Moreover, these data apply only to charitable nonprofits under section 501(c)3 of the IRS code, not to various other categories of nonprofit corporations and associations.)

Table 18.1 demonstrates that over broad fields of service, the revenue bases of nonprofit organizations vary substantially. Education, health, and human services nonprofits are most heavily dependent on fee revenue, whereas arts, environmental, and international nonprofits depend more substantially on charitable contributions. Investment income tends not to dominate any particular field but is quite important in education and the arts. Table 18.1 tends to mask the importance of government revenues, however. In the fields of health and human services, for example, and for the charitable sector as a whole, much of the fee revenue ultimately derives from government through insurance and reimbursement programs such as Medicare and Medicaid.

TABLE 18.1. SOURCES OF REVENUE FOR ALTERNATIVE NONPROFIT SUBSECTORS

	Fees (%)	Private Gifts (%)	Government Grants (%)	Investment Income (%)	Other (%)
All	70.3	12.3	9	5.4	2.9
Arts	31.3	40.8	12.5	7.7	7.7
Education	55.9	14.9	11.9	14.1	3.1
Environment	25.1	48	14.1	5.8	6.9
Health	87.5	4	3.4	2.9	2.2
Human Services	53.1	16.4	22.7	2.9	4.9
International	7.6	67.3	21.9	2.2	1

Source: Wing, Pollak, and Blackwood, 2008.

TABLE 18.2. SELECTED ARTS AND CULTURE NONPROFITS IN ATLANTA

	Gifts (%)	Government Grants (%)	Earned Income (%)	Investment Income (%)	Other Revenue (%)	Total Revenue ($ millions)
Zoo	39	8	46	7	0	19.6
Botanical Garden	64	0	23	13	0	13.9
Children's Museum	32	0	64	4	0	2.2
Ballet	37	0	60	1	1	7.3

Source: Computed from IRS 990 forms; www.guidestar.org

The aggregate numbers of Table 18.1 obscure considerable variation within broad categories of nonprofits. For example, Table 18.2 displays a few organizations in the city of Atlanta that are broadly categorized within the "Arts and Culture" field. Here it may be observed that dependence on fee revenue runs from a high of 64 percent for the children's museum to a low of 23 percent for the Atlanta Botanical Garden, whereas dependence on charitable gifts runs from 64 percent for the botanical garden to 32 percent for the ballet. Meanwhile, investment income varies from one percent for the ballet to thirteen percent for the botanical garden, and only one of these organizations, the Atlanta Zoo, exhibits any significant government (grant) income. Similar results would obtain for most other nonprofit subfields. Such data clearly demonstrate that although field of service is an important determinant of the sources of nonprofit income, variations are substantial and many other factors come into play.

Another way in which such aggregate data can be misleading is their implication that particular types of income—for example, fee income, charitable gifts, or government funding—are homogeneous in nature. This is far from true, although it is often analytically convenient or necessary to treat them as such. To illustrate, charitable contributions may consist of gifts from individuals or from institutions such as foundations or corporations, they may come in the form of annual giving or gifts for capital projects, and they may be gifts from living donors or bequests from estates, or they may derive from income from special fundraising events such as golf tournaments or running or bicycling marathons. So, too, earned (fee income) may come in the form of fees for service, royalties, and license fees for intellectual property or from rental income. A particularly interesting category of revenue is memberships, which may represent fee income (such as the cost of belonging to a YMCA) or essentially a charitable contribution with some benefits (such as membership in a museum) (Steinberg, 2007). Similarly, government income may come in the form of grants (which are essentially gifts), contracts (which are essentially fee for service), and insurance reimbursements, credits, and vouchers (which is revenue routed through clients and looks like fee income). Even investment income is multifaceted. It may take the form of returns on permanent endowment funds, interest on operating accounts, returns on commercial ventures, or returns on so-called "program-related investments" designed to produce both social benefits and financial returns (for example, microloans to social enterprises designed to employ challenged populations).

Finally, in-kind income can be particularly important to nonprofits in various circumstances. In arts institutions such as museums, for example, contributions of works of art are critical to success. And in many human services, such as homeless shelters, food banks, youth organizations, or emergency relief, volunteering is critical. Organizations such as the Girl Scouts and the Red Cross depend overwhelmingly on volunteer labor, more so than on paid staff. For that matter, many of the smaller nonprofit organizations that fly under the radar of the datasets that we have available are based primarily on volunteer effort. Some scholars characterize the part of the nonprofit sector that we can count and measure and whose finances we can analyze as only the tip of an iceberg that may include vastly more entities in the United States than those we know about (Smith, 1997).

Given the wide variations in financing of nonprofit organizations, it is clear that nonprofits require some integrating concepts to guide how they should be financed in any particular case. In this chapter I examine each source of potential finance from the viewpoint of microeconomic theory, focusing on the benefits, beneficiaries, and beneficiaries' willingness to pay that characterize alternative nonprofit services, leading to different combinations of finance appropriate to particular circumstances. First, I delineate the economic concepts that will aid in this analysis. Then I examine each potential source of nonprofit finance individually. Finally, I discuss the considerations that go into combining different sources of income into a mix or portfolio appropriate for a given organization.

Economic Concepts Underlying Nonprofit Finance

The economic concept of "demand" is tied to the notion of "willingness to pay" (Young and Steinberg, 1995). In the commercial marketplace, consumers express their demand for private goods and services by paying the market price. This price represents the marginal benefit they receive from purchasing the good. Some nonprofits produce goods that are largely private in nature (that is, goods or services for which consumers receive personal benefits not shared by others and from which they can be excluded if they refuse to pay for them). Attendance at a concert, enrollment in a training program, or treatment for an illness are illustrations. In these cases, consumers receive personal benefits for which they may be willing to pay some direct fees.

Nonprofits also produce goods and services that are public in nature (that is, goods whose benefits are shared widely by others and for which it is difficult to exclude people if they are unwilling to pay). Such goods include research, public art, and advocacy for a social cause. In this case there is some group of people who intrinsically value the good and would theoretically pay for it, but they have no market incentive to do so through fees. In economists' terms, there is a "free rider" problem, since the good will presumably be available to them whether or not they pay for it. Thus, financing depends on another mechanism, for example charitable contributions made by members of the beneficiary group who feel particularly strongly about its provision or are driven by other motives such as a sense of social responsibility or pressure or a "warm glow" from the act of giving. Alternatively, if the benefits of the public good are particularly widespread and diffused among a large group of beneficiaries, it may be necessary for government to finance the good through taxation (Olson, 1965).

In addition, many nonprofits produce goods or services that are mixtures of public and private. Such goods may be characterized as having significant "positive externalities." For example, inoculating a child to prevent contraction of a contagious illness provides direct private benefits to that child and her family, as well as widespread benefits to the community because of the smaller likelihood that the disease will spread to others. In such case, there two are groups of beneficiaries—direct recipients of the good who are probably willing to pay something for the personal benefits through fees, and a wider community that should be willing to subsidize the good through charitable contributions or government support.

Moreover, nonprofits also produce goods that may be characterized as "distributional" in nature. That is, they produce private goods that are deemed desirable or necessary for the recipients to consume, whether or not they are able to pay for them. Distributions from a food bank, vaccinations for children from low-income families, work training for former felons, and homeless shelters fit this description. For all practical purposes, distributional goods may be treated as public goods. They depend on the charitable motivations of groups of people who care about particular distressed populations and they may be considered to be of such widespread importance to society as to warrant government support.

Finally, let's consider another variation on private and public goods with which nonprofits are commonly involved—"transactions goods" that produce "trade" or "exchange" benefits. For example, nonprofits often enter collaborations or partnerships with other organizations or groups with which services and benefits are exchanged. These goods can be peripheral to a nonprofit's mission but they may be integral to its ability to garner the financial or material support to carry out that mission. For example, American health charities have entered collaborations with major pharmaceutical companies to support products such as tobacco patches that are considered beneficial to the cause the nonprofits promote (such as, smoking reduction). In such arrangements, the corporate partners are willing to support the nonprofits through grants and in-kind services (such as enhanced publicity) because they receive strategic corporate benefits such as increased product sales and improved public relations.

The concepts of private, public, distributional, and transactions goods, and the associated mechanisms through which to pay for private, public, distributional, and trade benefits, support the rationales under which nonprofits can pursue particular forms of income support. These are considered in greater depth in the next section.

The Role of Different Forms of Nonprofit Income

There are many forms of income that a nonprofit could employ, including fee or earned income, individual gift income, institutional gifts, governmental support, investment income, and volunteer and in-kind support. Each form has unique characteristics, benefits, and challenges that must be considered.

Fee (Earned) Income

It comes as a surprise to many that fee income is the dominant source of revenue for reporting charitable nonprofits in the United States, given the traditional association between charity and gifts. However, the United States is not alone in this pattern; many other countries' third sectors are dependent primarily on fee income (Salamon et al., 2004). Nor does this pattern hold for all nonprofit subsectors, as previously noted. Still, fee income is sufficiently dominant as to warrant its examination for most operating nonprofit organizations in the course of their resource development and planning deliberations. The issue of fees breaks down into several parts: For any given service offered by a nonprofit, one can ask whether a price should be charged at all. If the answer is positive then the question becomes how to appropriately design the price structure. The latter question is contingent on the nature of the service itself. If the service entails public as well as private benefits then the price will need to reflect that, perhaps only partially covering the cost of the service in order to ensure that an efficient level of externalities or distributional benefits are produced. However, if the service produces fully private benefits, and is perhaps even intended solely for financial support rather than mission impact, then prices should be designed to maximize net revenue.

Given a salience of private benefits, the issue of whether to charge a fee involves several considerations (Oster, Gray, and Weinberg, 2002). First, implementing a fee for a previously free service will entail investment in what economists call "transactions costs"—a new cost of doing business. An historically free museum will need to build and staff ticket booths, implement a system to collect, track, and reconcile these new revenues, and implement fraud prevention measures, or contract with an outside firm that knows how to do these things. Thus, the nonprofit needs to determine if the additional net fee revenue would offset the additional transactions costs associated with putting in place a fee system.

In addition, the museum may have to overcome cultural resistance from a community or donor base that feels entitled to free access or believes that open access is historically mandated or required by the original benefactors. The recent experience of a Salvation Army Homeless Shelter whose management wanted to implement a fee for extended stays illustrates the dilemma (Associated Press, 2004). Although the purpose of the shelter was short-term relief, representatives of the community objected in principle to the idea of charging homeless people for lodging.

The question of how the fee will affect the ability of the nonprofit to accomplish its mission is, of course, central to the decision. In the case of the museum or the homeless shelter, one has to ask whether the fee system would reduce usage by those people the organization is intended to serve. This is partly a matter of *how* the fee system is implemented. For example, sliding scales or special periods of time when access is made free (for example, free Wednesdays at the museum) can allow fee revenues to be collected without seriously impinging on mission impact. In fact, properly designed fees can sometimes increase mission impact. In particular, aside from providing more revenue, fees can create constructive incentives. In the case of the homeless shelter, the proposed fee might have freed up space for serving day-to-day homeless emergencies while generating funds for longer-term programming. In other cases, a fee can add a dignity factor that may make it more likely for targeted populations to participate. For example, a free transport service for elderly residents to travel to their senior center might be viewed as "charity" whereas a nominal fee might preserve self-respect and increase usage.

Once a decision to implement a fee is reached, there are a variety of considerations that go into determining the fee structure. Much stems from the goals of the service involved. If the service is purely a commercial venture intended to generate maximum profit for the organization, which can then be devoted to supported mainline mission-related services, then prices should be set for that purpose. If, however, the service serves a mission-related social purpose, the fees must be gauged to what targeted recipients are willing to pay for the private benefits they receive. Here is where sliding scales and other approaches can be helpful. In such cases, the goal is not full cost recovery or the generation of net financial surpluses but rather some level of off-setting revenues that can help pay for the service, or extend its volume or reach, in combination with other forms of support.

Finally, it is worth addressing the option of "membership" fees or dues in connection with overall fee revenue alternatives (Steinberg, 2007). One conception of membership dues is that they are a form of "package pricing" under which it may be more effective to charge consumers for several services under a single price than to charge them separately for each component service. For example, memberships in YMCAs are more efficient than charging clients separately for the weight room, the swimming pool, and towels. Savings accrue in the form of convenience and lower transactions costs. In addition, package pricing can help advance the mission of the organization by inducing clients to use included services that they might not otherwise do if they had to pay separately. Thus, clients of the Y are more likely to use the diet counseling service if it is included in the membership price, thus advancing the Y's mission to improve personal health.

Overall, the key to determining whether fee revenue should be a component of a nonprofit's revenue mix is to assess whether there is a strong component of private benefit to an identifiable beneficiary group to whom prices can be feasibly and effectively charged. For a variety of reasons, many nonprofits produce services for which there is a strong private benefit component. One reason is that they are capable of offering certain commercial products at a profit because of some competitive advantage, the revenues from which can support the charitable mission. Universities are good at offering public lecture programs and arboreta are well suited to provide attractive facilities for private weddings and bar mitzvahs. Moreover, nonprofits' mainline missions often justifiably entail private goods and benefits because of their competitive advantage in producing sensitive services, such as child day care or elderly care, in which consumers can comfortably place their trust. In such cases, it is entirely sensible for nonprofits to pursue fee income as an important component of their revenue portfolio.

Gift Income Contributed by Individuals

When nonprofits offer services that entail a significant component of public or redistributional goods or externalities it makes sense to look for other sources to supplement fee revenues. This is because the benefits associated with these goods are such that beneficiaries can enjoy them without paying for them. For example, it is difficult to charge people in a community for the benefits of lower contagion risk associated with inoculating their neighbors' children. Similarly, the benefits of cleaner air, lower crime, or more informed citizens that may result from the programs of particular nonprofit organizations accrue collectively to various groups of beneficiaries whose individual members would be difficult to identify or charge. As a result, substantial "free riding" occurs when people are asked to pay voluntarily.

Nonetheless, people do contribute voluntarily to nonprofits for services they care about. The challenge to nonprofits is to find ways to overcome free riding as much as possible so that beneficiary and donor groups come as close to contributing levels commensurate with the benefits they receive. Those benefits, related to the reasons that people do give, are severalfold. Research shows that people are both altruistic and self-serving in their giving behavior, that is, they value both public and private benefits from giving (Vesterlund, 2006). To the extent that donors care directly about the level of output a nonprofit provides, they are being altruistic, giving simply to ensure that those services are provided in sufficient quantity. Donors also receive personal satisfaction from the act of giving itself, sometimes called "warm glow." In this case, donors give irrespective of the nonprofit's level of service.

In order for nonprofits to be effective in raising charitable contributions from individual donors, they must build strategies based on these diverse motivations. They can appeal to altruism by measuring, describing, and communicating the level, quantity, and effectiveness of the services they perform, and they can appeal to warm glow by communicating the virtue of their work, the good reputation of the organization, and by recognizing donors' particular contributions. Long ago, Mancur Olson (1965) identified several distinct strategies for overcoming free riding in the case of public goods. One of these strategies, which he called "selective incentives," would appeal to the warm glow and other selfish motives of donor and beneficiaries by tying private rewards (special gifts, naming rights, membership privileges, and so on) to gift giving. Another strategy, social pressure, would exploit the power of small groups and public exposure to encourage, perhaps intimidate, donor and beneficiaries to give their fair share. Such strategies are common in church congregations and on boards of directors of prestigious or well-respected nonprofit institutions.

In sum, there are several steps nonprofit managers and development officers can take in order to enhance individual giving as much as possible. These include identifying those groups of beneficiaries and potential donors who care about the collective (public and redistributional) benefits the organization is producing, understanding and appealing to the motivations of these groups, and devising strategies to overcome the tendency to free ride on the contributions of others. Just as fee revenue has its transactions costs, development efforts to secure individual contributions involve fundraising costs. A sensible way for a nonprofit to view its fundraising program is to conceive of it as a profit-making business whose purpose is to maximize net revenues. Like any business, this entails some investment in the form of fundraising expenses to identify and communicate with current and potential donors. An important question is how much a nonprofit should spend on its fundraising operation. Viewed as a profit-maximizing business, an economist would say: continue to invest until the last dollar of expense produces at least a dollar in raised revenue (Young and Steinberg, 1995). Spending any less would forfeit potential additional net contributed revenue; spending any more would entail spending some (marginal) dollars for less than a dollar in return.

As simple as the above rule is, nonprofits commonly violate it because of certain commonly accepted practices. One such practice is to set an arbitrary fundraising goal and spend whatever it takes to reach that goal. Obviously if that goal is not carefully calibrated it can cause the nonprofit to over- or underspend on fundraising, perhaps even spend more on fundraising than the goal itself. Another practice is to adhere to specified ratios of fundraising expenses to total expenses (sometimes identified as "good practice" by watchdog agencies such as Charity Navigator or the Wise Giving Alliance) or, worse, to attempt to minimize average fundraising cost within some range of revenue generation. The problem here is that the point of maximum net revenue generation does not necessarily correspond to the point at which specified ratio standards are met. Indeed, the level of optimal fundraising expense will vary widely with the circumstances (for example, field of service, age, size, location) of the nonprofit in question. Thus, nonprofit managers need to use careful judgment and basic economic principles to determine how much they can raise in the form of individual charitable contributions, rather than strictly adhere to arbitrarily specified watchdog guidelines.

Institutional Giving

More than 80 percent of charitable giving comes from individuals, yet the remaining 20 percent from foundations and corporations can be very important to nonprofit organizations. Although there are more than seventy-thousand foundations in the United States, and many additional corporate giving programs not formalized as separate foundations, the largest of these institutional philanthropies are the most visible, focused, and assertive in their giving. Thus, they are the natural targets for nonprofits seeking charitable support. However, institutional givers are not entirely similar to individual donors, although there are some common attributes. In particular, the many small foundations (including family foundations) and some larger ones are essentially the institutional personifications of their benefactors, who have found it to be efficient to channel their giving through the foundation structure. Moreover, much of the funding by community foundations takes place through "donor-advised funds" that essentially manifest the giving preferences of their individual donors. The same observation applies even more strongly to giving by the charitable funds administered by securities firms such as Fidelity or Schwab.

One variety of institutional philanthropy takes the form of foundations that can be viewed essentially as nonprofit organizations with their own articulated missions but which have chosen to pursue those missions by making grants. In some sense, these are nonprofits that simply outsource the implementation of their missions through operating nonprofit grantees. As a consequence, nonprofits seeking support from such philanthropies need to propose projects and programs that promulgate those missions, hopefully without distorting their own missions. Many institutional funders, however, have broad missions and programs that may accommodate a wide variety of nonprofit proposals. Nonetheless there are again serious transactions costs associated with searching for appropriate potential institutional funders, cultivating relationships with program officers, staff consultants, or board members, and engaging in the procedures, negotiations, and implementation and evaluation processes required by those funders. These costs vary widely from funder to funder.

Given the relatively small role that institutional philanthropy plays in the overall financing of nonprofit organizations in the United States (roughly 20 percent of the 15 percent of nonprofit funding that is accounted for by charitable giving, or approximately 3 percent of the total), it is not surprising that institutional funders prefer to make strategic grants rather than be relied up on as sources of ongoing operational support. Thus, foundation grants tend to be time limited and focused on particular project initiatives, and contingent on an overall plan for the nonprofit to sustain the initiative over the longer run from other sources. There are many exceptions to this pattern of course, and foundations have been criticized for failing to provide ongoing infrastructure support for nonprofits. One variant that addresses some of this criticism is an approach called "venture philanthropy" under which institutional funders make intensive and ongoing investments in selected nonprofit organizations, and maintain intensive oversight and support of those organizations at least until it is clear that they can make it effectively on their own or are judged to have failed.

An important distinction should be made between funding by private independent foundations or public charities such as community foundations on the one hand, and corporate philanthropy on the other. Internal corporate giving programs and many separately incorporated corporate foundations that maintain close ties to the mother corporation must be understood within the overall context of corporate strategy. There are many benefits that corporations can derive from their relationships with nonprofits and charitable causes, and most corporations have these in mind as they engage in charitable giving. Such benefits include improved public and community relations, enhanced employee morale, greater effectiveness in marketing their products and services, opportunities to cultivate new markets among nonprofit stakeholders, obtaining access to expertise and knowledge that the nonprofit may harbor, and tax benefits. These are the kinds of "exchange" benefits corporations can derive for themselves by supporting nonprofits.

The trick to securing corporate support is to find a corporate relationship with the right "strategic fit" wherein the needs of the nonprofit and those of the corporation are both met (that is, a mutually satisfactory exchange of benefits can be arranged). Nonprofits may receive monetary and valuable in-kind support, including, for example, valuable public exposure through a corporation's marketing program, in exchange for some combination of the above-mentioned benefits to the corporation. In this negotiation the nonprofit needs to think about what exchange benefits are of value to the corporation and to pitch its proposals accordingly. There is risk in this exchange, of course, if the negotiated arrangements damage the reputation of the nonprofit or somehow undermine its mission. For example, nonprofits must be wary of endorsing corporate products that may be harmful or fail to best serve their stakeholders. Thus, the American Cancer Society or the American Lung Association can be comfortable associating themselves with manufacturers of tobacco patches but they would err by endorsing a particular brand because other brands may ultimately prove to be superior.

In summary, support from institutional philanthropy requires awareness of the needs and goals of the funders. In the cases of independent and community foundations, the issues are likely to be compatibility with the charitable missions of those institutions and planning for long-term sustainability once the initial grants are expended. For corporate funding the objective is to find the appropriate strategic partnership that serves the purposes (provides the exchange benefits) to both parties in the transaction.

Government Funding

Approximately a third of nonprofit funding derives from government in the form of contracts and grants of various kinds. Like charitable giving, the rationale for government funding derives from the public or redistributional nature of some of the goods and services delivered by nonprofit organizations. In particular, a third strategy for overcoming the free rider problem in providing collective goods is for the government to apply coercion through taxation. For goods and services that entail widespread public benefits or widely supported redistributional goals, there may be a political (majority) consensus for government to support these services through legislation. Ultimately, government may choose either to deliver these services itself or to outsource them to private delivery agents, commonly nonprofit organizations. This is the American system of "third-party government" described by Salamon (1987), which permits government to exploit efficiencies and diversity in private provision while assuring adequate resource support.

From the nonprofit viewpoint, seeking government funding is appropriate for support of programs and services for which there are widespread public benefits and existing or potential statutory programs available for funding. This is largely the case in areas such as human services, education, health care, and environmental conservation but less so for expressive activities such as the arts or religion, where there is less consensus.

As with other sources of funds, government support comes with certain risks, challenges, and costs. Substantial transactions costs are often associated with building and maintaining the necessary capacity, skills, and political acumen to navigate governmental systems of funding eligibility and maintaining mandated reporting and evaluation procedures. Governments also have a reputation for slow payment of their bills, requiring nonprofits to set aside working capital to manage cash flows.

A number of other, more subtle, risks are also sometimes associated with government funding. For example, given the substantial investment that nonprofits receiving government funding must make in administrative infrastructure and in meeting government service standards, there is the risk that a nonprofit will become heavily professionalized and lose some of its voluntary spirit and indeed become less attractive to volunteers or effective paid workers who lack the formal credentials that government may require. Moreover, government funding may "crowd-out" private contributions if donors perceive that the recipient nonprofits no longer require as much in charitable assistance (Steinberg, 1991). There is also the possibility, however, that government funding, especially if it is properly structured in the form of matching requirements, can induce a "crowd-in" of additional private contributions. Finally, substantial dependence on government funding may run the risk of "mission drift" wherein the nonprofit essentially loses its own sense of direction and assumes the role of a government contractor, foregoing its own autonomy and independence (Smith and Lipsky, 1993). One manifestation of this may be increased reluctance of the nonprofit to engage in advocacy work if such activity causes friction with its government benefactors.

Of course, the foregoing risks are likely to vary with the different forms of government support. The strings are looser on grants than contracts, and payments in the form of vouchers, tax credits, or per capita subsidies attached to service consumers are likely to be even less constraining. In general, it makes sense for nonprofits to seek out government assistance when it provides services with widespread public or redistributional benefits or positive externalities that are supported by government programs, and where fee income and private charitable contributions are unlikely to support efficient levels of service provision.

Investment Income

Income from investments constitutes a category of support for nonprofits somewhat different from other sources, because it is not generally directly associated with particular services and benefits. Investment income comes in the form of interest and dividends on nonprofit funds, ranging from interest on operating funds to investment returns on endowments or other restricted funds (Bowman, Keating, and Hager, 2007). As such, funds from investments provide flexibility for nonprofits because they do not generally require appealing to a particular beneficiary group or providing a particular kind of service or benefit. However, this statement requires a number of qualifications. First, the principals or corpuses of investment funds from which returns are derived must come from somewhere. For example, they may accrue from accumulated operating surpluses derived from fee income and annual charitable contributions. Typically, endowments are put in place through capital gifts by living donors or through bequests. As such, the building of investment income requires appealing to the beneficiaries of these sources of capital, along the lines discussed above.

In addition, there are some forms of investment income that are tied more directly to services, benefits, and beneficiaries—namely program-related investments (PRIs). PRIs are generally the domain of grantmaking foundations. They entail loans or other investments of the corpus of foundation funds in activities that have a direct mission impact but that also provide a financial return. For example, a foundation can provide low-interest loans to nonprofits starting up a new commercial venture, say a restaurant, intended to employ inner-city youth. PRIs may also be appealing for larger operating nonprofits. For example, a large children's hospital may wish to loan funds to the local children's museum for a project that educates children and families about nutrition and preventive health practices, on the theory that such an investment contributes both revenue to the hospital and advances its mission of improving children's health.

As discussed below, investment income can have an important role to play in a nonprofit organization's overall income portfolio, especially in connection with managing risk and covering shortfalls that may occur because of large fixed costs (Bowman, 2007). For example, costs associated with maintaining large physical plants or core staff may be difficult to fully finance from other forms of operating income that depend more directly on the level of output that the organization can produce. Frequently, nonprofits restrict use of returns on endowment funds to particular long-term fixed costs, such as building maintenance, student scholarship support, endowed chairs for professorships or curator positions, and so on.

Endowments intended to generate steady streams of operating income also entail some challenges and risks. First, as recent experience has shown, investment revenues, despite their presumed immunity from the day-to-day volatility of service provision, can exhibit substantial instability over time. They also entail transactions costs in the form of competent investment management, and they are subject to the systemic risks associated with downturns in the stock market and the economy at large. Moreover, endowments are often raised for specific projects and facilities that can involve significant additional operating costs. In particular, it is often attractive for donors to contribute endowments for a new building or program facility, or for hiring a prestigious new professorship named in their honor. These projects entail ongoing maintenance and support costs that the donor is often uninterested in covering. Indeed, sometimes donors prefer to give "challenge grants" that require nonprofits to raise additional capital from other donors, let alone cover the increased operating costs of the new project. For nonprofits, this is a matter of looking gift horses in the mouth. What can appear to be an attractive, prestigious, and generous gift can easily become an albatross that threatens the entire organization. Prudent negotiations with donors of endowment capital require that the ancillary fixed costs associated with capital projects are part of the financing package.

Volunteer and In-Kind Contributions

A major portion of the income support for nonprofit organizations in the United States comes in the form of nonmonetary or in-kind contributions, most of that in the guise of volunteer labor. It is reasonably estimated that the value of such labor is roughly equal to the value of monetary charitable contributions to nonprofit organizations. Thus, although these forms of income do not normally appear in the financial statements or tax forms of nonprofit organizations, they do constitute significant resources that nonprofits should take into account in developing, managing, and planning their finances.

As with other sources of income, in-kind support entails substantial transactions costs. For material contributions such as art collections, real estate, automobiles, furniture, computers, or perishables such as food or supplies, there are several issues: maintenance and operating costs, compatibility of use in the organization's operations, and liquidity (Gray, 2007). In short, gifts-in-kind are not necessarily net gains to the organization unless their benefits exceed their maintenance or operating costs, or they can be easily used without excessive adjustment or loss of quality in operations, or they can be profitably sold for cash. Still, handled well, gifts-in-kind can be valuable contributions to nonprofit income.

Appropriate contributions of art can add substantially to a museum's mission, contributed real estate in areas where real estate values are rising can become an important part of an organization's asset portfolio or might contribute directly to the mission of an environmental organization wishing to protect a rural area from overdevelopment, and receipt of used cars can provide a source of resale income or economical replacements for cars in a nonprofit's existing fleet. Motivations of individual donors vary from needing to dispose of unwanted but functional items to seeking to preserve cherished collections to receiving tax benefits more or less equivalent to selling items directly. (As to the latter, it is important for nonprofits to be prudent in offering donors a fair market estimate of the value of the gift to avoid the taint of a tax scam.) For corporate gifts there is the additional motivation for companies to provide visibility to their products, with the possible benefit of expanding future markets. Gifts of pharmaceuticals to health clinics or computers to schools allow manufacturers to expose future paying consumers to their products. In this sense, generation of in-kind income, particularly from corporations, involves the generation of exchange benefits wherein both donor and recipient nonprofit purposes should be well served.

Similar considerations apply to volunteering (Leete, 2006). People volunteer with nonprofit organizations for a variety of reasons, and nonprofits must employ them prudently if volunteering is to be an effective addition to an organization's income. Here again, nonprofits may be viewed as exchanging various benefits to secure the resources that volunteers provide. For volunteers these benefits may span the range from pure altruism in wanting to advance the charitable work of the organization to various private benefits including warm glow, experience gained that may prove useful in future paid work, social benefits of interaction with other individuals in the workplace, free or reduced-cost access to the organization's services (such as the opportunity to hear concerts or attend classes), and nonmonetary recognition of a job well done.

The transactions costs associated with volunteering are also multidimensional. Resources must be devoted to managing volunteers, including their recruitment, screening, assignment to tasks, training, monitoring, evaluation, and coordination with other members of the workforce. (See Chapter Twenty-six of this volume for a substantive discussion of the process of volunteer management.) Preston (2007) makes an interesting distinction between two classes of volunteers—those whose work complements those of paid workers and those whose work can substitute for that of paid workers. In the latter case, volunteers offer a financial savings to the organization and do not require extensive coordination with other (paid workers). In the former case, volunteers can increase the productivity of paid workers; however, they may also generate extra costs associated with properly coordinating them with the paid work staff. (This can be problematic if volunteer schedules are irregular or unpredictable.) In short, volunteers are not free and nonprofit managers must ensure that they are accepted and utilized prudently in order for their contributions to represent net additions to the organization's resources.

Portfolio Issues

Nonprofit organizations necessarily finance themselves with different mixes of fee, gift, government, investment, and in-kind income because, fundamentally, even nonprofits with very similar missions produce different combinations of public and private goods and services and their associated classes of benefits. If nonprofit finance is necessarily transactional (that is, that resource support is forthcoming in rough exchange for the kinds of benefits produced), then different missions, program and service combinations, and consequent benefits and beneficiaries will lead to different income portfolios. We argue here that a productive way to approach nonprofit finance is to begin with mission, analyze the programs and services that follow from this mission, consider the public and private benefits that are generated by these services, and develop a strategy for securing payments that exploit the willingness to pay of the various sets of beneficiaries.

The forgoing sounds very straightforward and logical and perhaps obvious. However, it tends to turn conventional nonprofit development strategy on its head. Rather than figure out how to increase one or another form of income, given a nonprofit organization's overall financial needs, a "benefits approach" to nonprofit finance emphasizes mission and program as the key to finance. Thus, ensuring adequate financing of a nonprofit organization necessarily involves two basic questions: (1) Are the benefits accruing to particular individuals and groups being captured through appropriate forms of finance, such as fees, contributions or government support? and (2) What adjustments in programs and services might lead to a stronger mix of benefits and beneficiaries and associated payments toward a stronger financial position for the organization?

It is the rare nonprofit that produces only one kind of benefit and is restricted to one source of income. Examples of such may include the following:

• A health charity that funds research on a rare disease and depends solely on charitable contributions from individuals at risk of contracting the disease or families and friends of the afflicted. If the disease is rare it may not draw sufficiently widespread interest to warrant government support, volunteer involvement, or a market for any kind of fee income.

- An offender rehabilitation program entirely funded by government, reflecting its widespread public benefits of citizen safety and redistributional benefits to low-income communities, but which generates little empathy among potential donors and produces no particular marketable product or service.
- A church whose operations are financed solely on the basis of a Sunday collection plate to whom regular worshippers contribute.

Even in these cases, it is not hard to imagine additional sources of income tied to broader benefits and beneficiary groups. The health charity might emphasize the fundamental nature of its research (such as genetic), hence drawing on a wider pool of donations and possible corporate sponsors and government support. The offender rehabilitation organization might incorporate a social business enterprise, such as a restaurant or a landscaping service, as a means of teaching its clients market skills, thus drawing on fee income from consumers of that enterprise. The church could provide religious instruction or social programs for which fees could be charged, it could hold bake sales or other special events to generate additional contributions, or it could package its services into memberships for which dues can be charged.

More generally, nonprofits depend on multiple sources of income, prompting economists such as Estelle James (1983) to model them as "multi-product firms." Consider the following examples:

- A thrift shop that provides used clothing at low cost to needy citizens depends on a combination of in-kind donations, volunteer labor, and fee income from sales.
- A theater that offers experimental works of new artists depends on a combination of ticket revenues and charitable gifts from the local community of theater lovers.
- A preschool center charges tuitions for its services, perhaps on a sliding scale basis, and receives government support in recognition of the societywide benefits (greater economic productivity, reduced crime, and so on) associated with early childhood education.
- An organization that monitors environmental quality receives government funding, reflecting its contributions to a cleaner and healthier environment, and charitable contributions from a community of nature lovers, scientists, and conservationists.
- A university supports itself on tuition income, recognizing the private benefits accruing to its students, charitable contributions from alumni who care about

the institution and benefit from its reputation, government funding that supports its research and contributions to a more informed and productive citizenry, and capital gifts from alumni who enjoy the special benefits of naming rights and prime seats at football games.

The possible combinations are manifold and particular to each institution. Moreover, any given institution can entertain a variety of ideas for additional sources of income. It does not follow, however, that every nonprofit should increase the number of its income sources without limit. In particular, as we have noted, each additional source of income comes with its own transactions costs. Hence, nonprofits must always consider the possible trade-offs between the transactions costs of pursuing an additional source of income and the potential net income benefits that might derive from the addition. There are also a number of other considerations that go into deciding the appropriate number and mix of income sources in a nonprofit portfolio.

Mission Effectiveness

The advantage of analyzing benefits and beneficiaries is that it will help nonprofits avoid leaving money on the table from beneficiaries who might provide the resources to allow them to expand to an optimal scale at which they are providing maximum net social benefits. This applies to both the private and public benefits a nonprofit may produce and may finance through alternative mechanisms. In theory a nonprofit should continue to expand as long as the marginal benefits, as reflected in additional revenues from beneficiaries, at least offset additional costs of expansion.

Solvency

As previously noted, some sources of support are more difficult to garner than others. In particular, free-rider effects may preclude a nonprofit from fully exploiting the willingness to pay of beneficiaries of the public benefits it provides. In order to finance those benefits, adjustments may be needed in its finance portfolio, such as the generation of investment revenues or the undertaking of commercial ventures that can compensate for free-rider losses. Essentially, non-profits are private organizations producing a combination of private and public benefits. As such they must ensure that their financial bottom lines are sound.

One additional factor affecting solvency is the problem of cash flow. If the nonprofit depends on revenues that are episodic in nature it will need ways to even the flow of income so as to be able to pay its expenses on a regular basis.

There are various ways of addressing this issue, including prudent borrowing and building up of a working capital fund that can be depleted and replenished as income flows permit. Another approach is to seek alternative sources of income with different time profiles. For example, tuition payments and alumni gifts may flow into a nonprofit school at different times, thus helping smooth the flow of income over the course of a year.

Income Interactions

By pursuing benefit-related income from one source, losses may be incurred in another—this is the so-called "crowding out" or "crowding in" noted above in connection with government funding. Crowding effects may also manifest themselves with other combinations of income, such as fee revenues crowding out charitable contributions (Kingma, 1995). This requires awareness on the part of nonprofit managers as they pursue one source of income at the possible expense of another. As such it may limit the degree to which additional sources of income can be productively pursued, or it may require an educational initiative to explain to resource providers why substitutions are undesirable. Alternatively, revenue interactions may provide opportunities for synergy if, for example, donors are encouraged by organizational efforts to increase earned income, or if government programs match income from other sources.

Organizational Capacity

The seriousness of transaction-cost issues associated with administering different sources of income may depend on the maturity, size, and sophistication of the particular nonprofit organization. A small or young organization may not be capable of handling more than one type of income source. For example, it may know how to collect donations from individuals through an annual campaign or special event but may be clueless in applying for a government grant. As organizations grow and mature they can acquire additional capacities and skills to enable effective administration of multiple sources of income. In general, larger nonprofit organizations tend to have more diversified income portfolios, partly for this reason.

Risk Management

In the management of financial investments, diversification is a key strategy of risk management. So-called *unsystematic risk* can be reduced for any given level of investment return by diversifying investments whose fluctuations are uncorrelated or weakly correlated over time. The same principle applies to nonprofits, since fee, gift, government, investment, and in-kind income do not vary exactly in tandem over time (that is, they are imperfectly correlated). This can provide a measure of safety for nonprofits that would be at greater risk if they depended on only a single source. Thus, within the parameters and limitations discussed above, it is desirable for nonprofits to diversify their sources of income, both among broad categories of income such as fees versus contributions, and also within categories, for example, by engaging a variety of different donors or corporate sponsors.

There are limits to this strategy, however. First, not all financial risk to nonprofit organizations is unsystematic. The economic downturn of 2008–2009 illustrates that when there is a fundamental deterioration of the overall economy, multiple sources of support can be affected deeply and simultaneously. This has been the case with charitable contributions, government funding and investment income, and to a certain extent earned income as well. However, these sources have not been perfectly correlated, so that delays in reductions in foundation funding and other charitable contributions have helped ease the initial shocks to nonprofits. Moreover, the crisis has led to a rise in volunteering and to increases in certain manifestations of fee income, such as tuitions to lower-cost educational institutions as a result of people going back to school or moving from higher- to lower-cost colleges and universities.

There is also an argument that diversification may undermine another source of potential stability for nonprofits—the development of deep relationships with funders. The premise here is that putting most of your eggs in the right basket, such as government social service programs that are unlikely to be diminished (such as Medicare or Medicaid), can be an effective risk management strategy (Gronbjerg, 1993). Recent experiences with struggling state government budgets will certainly put this strategy to the test.

In addition to income diversification, nonprofits can manage their financial risk in other ways. For example, developing various types of funds can help provide stability (Bowman, 2007). A reserve fund that socks away six months or a year of operating income in anticipation of a future period of scarcity is a wise precaution assuming it is invested in safe securities. More generally, endowment funds, although they are intended for other purposes, can provide a modicum of stability. Endowments offer a steady source of income unconnected with the success of the nonprofit's program side (and sources of income associated with those programs). However, even a prudent investment strategy may not withstand the kind of market turmoil recently experienced. Even the financial investment wizards at Harvard and Yale experienced 30 percent to 40 percent losses of endowment value in the recent downturn. Still, endowments provide other safety features as well, including an increased capacity to borrow in hard times, given the asset value that endowments represent. In dire circumstances, it may be assumed that endowments can be invaded to secure debt or cover operating deficits. This is a dangerous practice, however, which has led to the demise of once healthy and prestigious institutions such as the New York Historical Society (Guthrie, 1996).

Conclusions

This chapter has focused on the various ways in which nonprofit organizations finance their operations. We have not given particular attention to financing of capital needs, which would entail examination of a variety of technical strategies (including capital campaigns, tax-free bonds, and various other debt, equity, and governmental financing approaches). Nonetheless, with the exception of borrowing, the sources of nonprofit capital are mirrored by the main sources of nonprofit operating income support—charitable giving, government financing, and retained (earned) income. As such, the general approach that we have taken here—connecting the benefits of a nonprofit's programs to its sources of finance—applies as well to capital financing. In fact, the two dimensions of nonprofit finance are intimately related. In particular, the capital structure of a nonprofit, especially its degree of reliance on fixed assets, helps determine the kinds of operating income it needs to generate. Fixed costs associated with the maintenance of capital assets such as real estate and physical facilities, for example, require steady sources of income independent of service output—such as investment income or steady sources of charitable gifts, including capital gifts from donors who appreciate being associated with named facilities.

The main premise of this chapter is that nonprofits produce unique mixes of public and private and benefits, which through appropriate financial mechanisms can be paid for by the recipients of those benefits. By matching financing strategies to benefits and beneficiaries, nonprofits can approach efficient levels of financing that allow them to produce maximum net social benefits within acceptable bounds of organizational stability and remain true to the missions for which they are established.

References

Associated Press. "Homeless Advocates Criticize Shelter Fees." June 24, 2004.

Bowman, W. "Managing Endowment and Other Assets." In D. R. Young (ed.), *Financing Nonprofits*. Lanham, Md.: AltaMira Press, 2007, 271–289.

Bowman, W., Keating, E., and Hager, M. A. "Investment Income." In D. R. Young (ed.), *Financing Nonprofits*. Lanham, Md.: AltaMira Press, 2007, 157–181.

Gray, C. M. "Gift-in-Kind and Other Illiquid Assets." in D. R. Young (ed.), *Financing Nonprofits*. Lanham, Md.: AltaMira Press, 2007, 227–241.

Gronbjerg, K. A. *Understanding Nonprofit Funding: Managing Revenues in Social Services and Community Development Organizations*. San Francisco: Jossey-Bass, 1993.

Guthrie, K. M. *The New-York Historical Society: Lessons from One Nonprofit's Long Struggle for Survival*. San Francisco: Jossey-Bass, 1996.

James, E., "How Nonprofits Grow: A Model." *Journal of Policy Analysis and Management*, Spring 1983, 350–365.

Kingma, B. "Do Profits 'Crowd-Out' Donations or Vice Versa? The Impact of Revenues from Sales to Local Chapters of the American Red Cross." *Nonprofit Management and Leadership*, 1995, *6*, 21–38.

Leete, L. "Work in the Nonprofit Sector." In W. W. Powell and R. Steinberg (eds.), *The Nonprofit Sector: A Research Handbook* (2nd ed.). New Haven, Conn.: Yale University Press, 2006, 159–179.

Olson, M. *The Logic of Collective Action: Public Goods and the Theory of Groups*. Cambridge, Mass.: Harvard University Press, 1965.

Oster, S. M., Gray, C. M., and Weinberg, C. "Pricing in the Nonprofit Sector." In D. R. Young (ed.), *Effective Economic Decision Making by Nonprofit Organizations*. New York: The Foundation Center, 2004, 27–45.

Preston, A.E., "Volunteer Resources." In D. R. Young (ed.), *Financing Nonprofits*, Lanham, Md.: AltaMira Press, 2007, 183–204.

Salamon, L.M., "Partners in Public Service: The Scope and Theory of Government-Nonprofit Relations." In W. W. Powell (ed.), *The Nonprofit Sector: A Research Handbook*. New Haven Conn.: Yale University Press, 1987, 99–117.

Salamon, L. M., Sokolowski, S. W., and Associates. *Global Civil Society: Dimensions of the Nonprofit Sector*, vol. 2. Bloomfield, Conn.: Kumarian Press, 2004.

Smith, D. H. "The Rest of the Nonprofit Sector: Grass Roots Associations as the Dark Matter Ignored in Prevailing 'Flat Earth' Maps of the Sector." *Nonprofit and Voluntary Sector Quarterly*, *26*(2), 1997, 114–131.

Smith, S. R., and Lipsky, M. *Nonprofits for Hire: The Welfare State in the Age of Contracting*. Cambridge, Mass.: Harvard University Press, 1993.

Steinberg, R., "Does Government Spending Crowd Out Donations? Interpreting the Evidence." *Annals of Public and Cooperative Economics*, 1991, *62*, 591–617.

Steinberg, R. "Membership Income." In D. R. Young (ed.), *Financing Nonprofits*. Lanham, Md.: AltaMira Press, 2007, 121–155.

Vesterlund, L. "Why Do People Give?" In W. W. Powell and R. Steinberg (eds.), *The Nonprofit Sector: A Research Handbook* (2nd ed.). New Haven, Conn.: Yale University Press, 2006, 568–587.

Wing, K.T., Pollak, T.H., and Blackwood, A., *The Nonprofit Almanac 2008*, Washington, D.C.: The Urban Institute Press, 2008.

Young, D. R., and Steinberg, R. *Economics for Nonprofit Managers*. New York: The Foundation Center, 1995.

CHAPTER NINETEEN

DESIGNING AND MANAGING THE FUNDRAISING PROGRAM

Robert E. Fogal

Fundraising is essential to charitable organizations. For their organizations to be successful, boards and senior management must give substantial attention to philanthropic support as an income generator. This chapter provides a guide to thinking about fundraising and addresses ways to *integrate fundraising into an organization's life*. These emphasized words are central to the perspective called "philanthropic fundraising," understood as the philosophy and practice that fosters voluntary giving to achieve public good. This author supports the view that philanthropic fundraising will substantially assure the future of nonprofit organizations and the good work that they aim to accomplish. Three themes amplify this view: fundraising as a management concept, fundraising as a management process, and issues in fundraising management.

Fundraising as a Management Concept

Fundraising is important to nonprofit leaders for many reasons. The first, which is the most obvious and practical, is that fundraising generates essential income for charitable organizations. As a percentage of nonprofit outlays, private giving in recent years has ranged from a low of 24.8 percent in 1995 to a high of 34.2 percent in 2000, remaining in that range during subsequent years (Wing, Pollack, and Blackwood, 2008, p. 69). (This statistic is an aggregate number for the sector. A specific organization's experience may be outside these aggregate numbers—that is, less than or greater than the range indicated.) Private support in 2009 declined for the first time since 1974; charitable contributions dropped to $307.7 billion from $314.1 billion in 2007. This 5.7 percent decline (measured in inflation-adjusted dollars) was the deepest decline since 1956, when *Giving USA* began estimating giving. The only other decline of similar magnitude was the 1974 drop of 5.4 percent from the previous year (Wasley, 2009). How giving from all three donor markets—individuals, corporations, and foundations—recovers will be a source of much analysis in subsequent years. Discussions will be an integral aspect of how the world economy is faring after the "great recession" and stock market decline that began in 2008.

An equally important but typically less obvious reason for fundraising to be a priority for nonprofit leaders is that fundraising success measures the degree to which an organization's purpose is affirmed. Donors' support for a particular organization or institution reflects their perception of that entity as an effective vehicle in meeting a community or human need. The responsibility of a nonprofit's board and senior managers to clearly articulate their organization's mission and document its effectiveness in fulfilling that mission—that is, to provide a strong case for support—is critical to successful fundraising. Through their contributions, donors show their regard for an organization's mission, trust in its leadership, and confidence in the nonprofit's financial future. Conversely, low response to fundraising appeals can suggest that an organization's purpose may not be well accepted and may not benefit from such trust and confidence.

An organization's need for gift income and its style of engaging prospective donors correlates with various attitudes toward fundraising. Henry A. Rosso, the founding director of The Fund Raising School (now a program at the Center on Philanthropy at Indiana University), developed a succinct grid that characterizes these organizational attitudes (see Table 19.1). Rosso titled this grid "Three Stages of Fundraising Development" because it represents the steps through

TABLE 19.1. THREE STAGES OF FUNDRAISING DEVELOPMENT

Stage	1: Formative Stage	2: Normative Stage	3: Integrative Stage
Who	Vendor	Facilitator	Strategist
What	Product	Relationships	Growth partnerships
Skills	Selling	Soliciting	Building and maintaining philanthropic relationships
Result	Making sales	Relationships with donors	Assured organizational growth

Source: H. A. Rosso, personal communication; terminology adapted by the author.

which nonprofits often progress in developing their fundraising programs. The idea is that most begin at the formative stage, when fundraising is a new activity. Organizations potentially reach the integrative stage, when fundraising is a fully developed component of an organization's life and work.

The *formative stage* views fundraising as an appendage to organizational life—something we do because we have to, a "necessary evil." It is characterized by an emphasis on fundraising techniques that generate needed income, such as mass appeals through direct mail and telephone solicitation.

Fundraising in the formative stage is motivated by the simple need to have more money. The objective is to "sell" the organization and what it does (the products) to donors who want to "purchase" the idea or service that the nonprofit represents. Success is measured by how often asking for gifts results in "making a sale." In this stage, fundraising is commonly carried out by personnel who are hired to perform as a sales staff, with their primary role being to interact with prospective donors and persuade them to contribute to the nonprofit. When volunteers participate in this style of fundraising, they also view their work as sales activity.

The *normative stage* often employs the image of family, applying fundraising techniques largely to prospective donors whose connections to the nonprofit have been established through some other relationship, such as those who receive services (for example, clients, students, audience members, or patients) or volunteer leaders and workers. Leaders and managers typically concentrate on the operation of the institution. Fundraising in this stage is commonly staff-centered also, with a small number of others, usually the chief executive and a handful of volunteers, participating selectively in the process of engaging a prospect's interest, soliciting a contribution, and maintaining good relationships with donors.

The *integrative stage* places philanthropy at the center of who we are and what we do. That is, it is central to the building of a human community that achieves a common good. Donors are regarded as thoughtful participants in the organization's life and work, filling a role that is appropriate to them and essential to the well-being of the nonprofit. In the integrative stage, volunteer leaders are vocal advocates of the nonprofit and its work, and they participate fully in the process of building constituencies who can financially support the organization.

In addition, senior staff, board members, and other volunteer leaders work at sustaining healthy relationships (or growth partnerships) with those who have made philanthropic commitments to the organization, responding to donors' needs and interests that relate to the nonprofit and its mission and its activities. There is a high level of communication between the nonprofit and those who make "leadership gifts." These donors know the organization well.

Their gifts reflect values that are important to them. Furthermore, because they are known for their generous commitments, their views are valued by others, and they are often articulate advocates of the organization. In the integrative stage, organizational leaders are capable of looking at their institution or agency from the perspective of important donors whose views may help assure an organization's continued growth.

The three stages are not mutually exclusive. Fundraising principles and techniques are important to all three. But how they are used reflects the organization's style of management and institutional philosophy. Philanthropic fundraising strives to achieve the integrative stage of fundraising practice, which incorporates voluntary giving as one of the nonprofit's core values.

The original intent of the three-stage model was to describe a somewhat linear developmental process that organizations and their leaders undergo as they build fundraising experience. An equally useful concept that also advocates for philanthropic fundraising, or the integrative stage, adapts the economics terminology of supply and demand to fundraising practice.

> The demand-side approach emphasizes that donors are hesitant givers and so must be pushed in more or less aggressive ways to separate themselves from their money. In the extreme, obtaining charitable dollars is a process of stealthy extraction at worst and shrewd persuasion at best. The supply-side approach emphasizes that donors are inclined to donate to charity and are motivated to do so by having excess financial resources and a desire to identify with and affect the fortunes of others. They do not so much need to be pushed into giving as helped to discern how to make wise decisions about their wherewithal. (Schervish, 2000, p. 6)

The demand-side approach is how many organizational leaders perceive fundraising, thus leading to their reluctance to participate in fundraising. The approach is reinforced by the need to obtain specific amounts of money within a given time frame, and engenders the use of fundraising tactics and techniques that, at their worst, accommodate an attitude of "the ends justify the means." Even while articulating how gifts will achieve specific objectives that fulfill an organization's mission, the language used commonly focuses on the organization's needs.

In contrast, a supply-side attitude and approach invites prospective donors to participate in giving by engaging their moral sense along with their self-perception of financial capacity to give. Drawing upon their own psychic and spiritual resources, donors desire to partner with those organizations that provide a conduit for carrying out the donor's personal goals of human betterment. Interacting with donors from a supply-side perspective, especially those with greater financial capacity, is the foundation for the integrative stage of philanthropic fundraising.

Fundraising as a Management Process

Classic management practice consists of five activities: analysis, planning, execution, control, and evaluation. Fundraising as a management process uses all these activities. The most effective fundraising staff are managers who discipline the fundraising process through these five activities.

Through *analysis*, a nonprofit assesses whether or not it is ready for fundraising. Analysis is guided by questions such as these: What is the fundraising history? How many donors contributed at what levels? Are constituencies and gift markets well defined and responsive? Are internal resources adequate to meet the costs of fundraising? Is the case for support valid and compelling?

An essential tool in analyzing fundraising performance is the gift range chart, which organizes information about past giving by the number of philanthropic gifts and grants received at defined dollar levels. Consider, for example, a human services organization with a $2.5 million budget. (A nonprofit of this size is in the cohort with 11.4 percent of public charities having expense budgets from $1 million to $4.99 million. About 6.3 percent of public charities have expenses of $5 million or more; the expenses of 82.3 percent of public charities are less than $1 million. See Wing, Pollack, and Blackwood, 2008, p. 142.) In the past fiscal year, our sample organization received $299,500 in gifts and grants, with the balance of revenue derived from government contracts and service fees. Table 19.2 shows a distribution of gifts and grants that reflects an established fundraising effort: two-thirds of gift revenue came from about 10 percent of donors, another 24 percent was contributed by 42 percent of donors, and the final 10 percent of gifts came from 48 percent of the donors. Such information about the distribution of donors among gift levels is essential to answering the kinds of analysis questions articulated in the preceding paragraph.

Planning grows out of analysis. Too little planning impedes success; too much planning leads to inaction. Good planning encourages prudent risk taking and helps nonprofits respond to opportunities that will advance their purposes. Answers to the following questions will facilitate good planning: How should the case for support be articulated? How many gifts in what amounts are needed? From whom? How should donor prospects be solicited? By whom? When should the gift be solicited? What training is required for volunteers to engage prospects and ask for gifts? How much money should be invested to accomplish fundraising objectives?

TABLE 19.2. GIFT RANGE CHART ANALYZING THE PREVIOUS YEAR'S GIVING

Gift Level($)	Number of Gifts	Subtotal ($)	Cumulative Total ($)
25,000	1	25,000	25,000
10,000	2	20,000	45,000
5,000	5	25,000	70,000
2,500	12	30,000	100,000
1,000	30	30,000	130,000
500	75	37,500	167,500
250	120	30,000	197,500[a]
100	350	35,000[b]	232,500
50	720	36,000[b]	268,500
25	1,240	31,000[c]	299,500
Totals	2,555		299,500

[a] Sixty-six percent of the total philanthropic gifts and grants received ($197,500) is from 244 donors, or about 10 percent of the 2,554 donors (those who gave $250 or more).

[b] Twenty-four percent of the total gifts and grants received ($71,000) is from 1,070 donors, or about 42 percent of total donors ($50 and $100 donors).

[c] Ten percent of the gifts and grants received ($31,000) is from 1,240 donors, or 48 percent of total donors (those who contributed $25).

As in analysis, the gift range chart undergirds fundraising planning by focusing the attention of staff and volunteers on the number and size of gifts needed to reach a fundraising goal. (Gift range charts were used historically only for capital campaigns, but their use is now commonly accepted in annual campaigns for funds as well.) Continuing with the example of a $2.5 million human services organization, Table 19.3 is an example of a planning gift range chart to reach an annual giving goal of $500,000.

The planning gift chart, when compared with current patterns of voluntary contributions, helps nonprofit leaders understand the potential of the donor base (and the work that will be required to grow giving) by comparing "what is" with "what we want to be achieve." Comparing the charts (Tables 19.2 and 19.3) makes clear how many new prospective donors at what gift levels need to be identified, and how many additional donors at each level have to be successfully invited to give, to reach the desired fundraising goal of $500,000. Planners can assess if the desired goal is feasible by identifying the prospects for each gift level and evaluating the likelihood of their giving at the proposed level.

The number of prospects for each gift level varies. At the higher levels, more prospects are required for each gift simply because these gifts and grants are usually more difficult to obtain. Since gifts at the lower levels are easier to obtain,

TABLE 19.3. GIFT RANGE CHART FOR A $500,000 ANNUAL FUNDRAISING GOAL

Gift Level ($)	Number of Donors	Number of Prospects	Subtotal ($)	Cumulative Total ($)
25,000	2	10	50,000	50,000
10,000	5	20	50,000	100,000
5,000	10	40	50,000	150,000
2,500	20	60	50,000	200,000
1,000	50	150	50,000	250,000
500	100	300	50,000	300,000
250	200	600	50,000	350,000[a]
100	500	1,500	50,000[b]	400,000
50	1,000	3,000	50,000[b]	450,000
25	2,000	5,000	50,000[c]	500,000
Totals	3,877	10,680		500,000

Note: The arithmetic for creating an annual giving gift chart is based on the top gift range being 5 percent of the goal, with two gifts required at that level. Subsequent gift levels are simply defined as conventional gift amounts that donors are accustomed to considering. Subtotals for each range are usually the same amounts or amounts that do not vary widely. The number of donors required for each gift level is determined by calculating how many are needed at each level to achieve the desired subtotal (in this example, the subtotal of $50,000).

[a]Seventy percent of the goal ($350,000) is projected from 387 major or leadership gifts, or 10 percent of the 3,887 donors (those who will give $250 or more).

[b]Twenty percent of the goal ($100,000) is projected from 1,500 donors, about 40 percent of total donors (those who will give $50 and $100).

[c]Ten percent of the goal ($50,000) is projected from 2,000 donors, about 50 percent of total donors (those who will give $25) .

fewer prospects are required. Also, many prospects at higher gift levels may give at lower levels, thus adding to the prospective donor pool at lower levels.

Gift charts for capital campaigns are built on the same principles, with the difference that the top gift range is at least 10 percent of the goal and may even equal 20 to 25 percent, with only one gift anticipated at the top level. Capital campaigns are typically characterized by a fairly small number of donors committing to substantially larger gift pledges that are paid over three to five years.

For example, presuming that the two donors of $10,000 gifts in the previous year (Table 19.2) renew their giving at the same level, the planning chart (Table 19.3) requires three more gifts or grants at this level (a total of five gifts of $10,000 each) than the analysis chart indicates to reach the $500,000 goal. Since four prospects for each donor are suggested for this level (the planning chart indicated twenty prospects for the five gifts desired), the organization needs to identify twelve additional prospects for $10,000 gifts or grants to ensure the likelihood of obtaining the three additional gifts. Implementing this planning process for all gift levels will determine whether or not the $500,000 is feasible. It may be that only four $10,000 gifts are likely but enough prospects for seven or more $5,000 gifts are identifiable, thus compensating for the lower number of $10,000 donors. In this way, fundraising managers and volunteer leaders can prepare a planning gift chart that provides a sound basis for the year's fundraising activity.

Effective planning requires that a nonprofit's leaders, both board and staff, take ownership of fundraising activities. Given the importance of planning, it is also important to recognize that plans can be changed, and should be, to take advantage of giving opportunities when they occur or to respond to other unanticipated situations.

Execution means carrying out the plan. Tasks are assigned and responsibilities are accepted, individuals are trained and empowered, time lines are established and respected, and follow-up ensures that tasks have been completed. A high-performance fundraising executive is guided by the following question: What should I do to ensure that everyone involved in our fundraising is successful in our behalf? Fundraising managers have the challenge of directing the energy and activity of people to whom they are responsible (senior staff, board members, and other volunteers) in their fundraising tasks. This requires a high level of mutual respect and a firm commitment from all participants to their common success.

Control depends on information systems that enable fundraising staff to implement the plan. A multitude of details and tasks must be monitored and coordinated. Gift processing must be timely, gift records must be accurate, and gifts must be acknowledged. Reports must be generated. Volunteer and staff time must be used effectively. Time lines should be honored. Budgets have to be well utilized. Interpersonally, fundraising executives have to exercise control on a daily basis by diplomatically asserting their leadership to ensure that tasks are accomplished and the fundraising plan is fulfilled.

Evaluation enables leaders and staff to grow and become more effective. The key question for fundraising is this: What factors enabled (or prevented) us from meeting our objectives for each level in the planning gift chart? It is as important to assess what worked well and why as it is to determine how to improve. By reflecting on its fundraising practice, as well as all its management and programs, a nonprofit's leadership determines whether or not resources are maximized, constituents' needs are served, and the mission is fulfilled. Good evaluation depends on a spirit of cooperation and a sense of common purpose. It combines objectivity with sensitivity, and fosters organizational integrity that leads to a more productive future. As a result, voluntary giving in support of the nonprofit's mission will be enhanced.

In addition to these classic areas of management, fundraising for nonprofits is substantially enhanced by a solid professional stance that is distinguished by integration and integrity. First, sound fundraising is highly integrated and synergistic. For example, effective direct marketing solicitations broadly promote an organization's mission and help create the climate for engaging leadership giving. Also, major donors are typically leaders in many areas of community life, and their support includes their gifts as well as their advocacy on behalf of the organizations they support. Although such dynamics occur in ways that are distinctive to each organization, fundraising leaders need to foster a sense of connection among fundraising practices so that all participants focus on a shared outcome—accomplishing the organization's mission—that is greater than the sum of the parts.

Connecting the parts also produces feelings of integrity that have immeasurable value in a philanthropic organization. An organizational sense of wholeness or completeness—a broadly shared purpose—energizes everyone from board members and other volunteers to every employee on the payroll. Such cohesiveness communicates to prospective donors that the organization has its act together, thus adding value to the community and meriting philanthropic support.

Nonprofits that are successful in philanthropic fundraising apply all these activities to three dimensions of institutional life: at the department level, throughout the organization, and in its interaction with the environment that surrounds it. In each dimension, specific fundraising management activities are required. Table 19.4 shows how the tasks of fundraising pertain in all three dimensions.

Within the fundraising office or department, fundraisers implement several technical tasks for which they are solely responsible. Alongside these are several organizational tasks that fundraising staff may foster and coordinate but that involve other staff and board leadership and may require some compromise to accomplish. Finally, a number of activities are directed beyond the nonprofit and require that fundraising managers exercise considerable judgment and negotiation in their realization. The responsibilities and tasks listed in Table 19.4 are not mutually exclusive. Nor does the figure list all possibilities. It does indicate, however, how the management of philanthropic fundraising intersects with various dimensions of a nonprofit's life.

Issues in Fundraising Management

Fundraising as a management concept provides the large frame of reference for fundraising as a management process. Together, they inform how nonprofit leaders and mangers become engaged in various aspects and issues of fundraising practice.

TABLE 19.4. FUNDRAISING MANAGEMENT GRID

Fundraising Management Tasks	Organizational Dimensions		
	Departmental	Organizational	External
Analysis	Fundraising history/gift range chart Gift vehicle productivity Data systems Office space Staff resources	Communicating the case for support	Market needs and social needs Constituencies and gift markets Volunteer resources Feasibility study
Planning	Fundraising budget Gift range chart Gift market identification Gift vehicle selection Timelines	Fundraising goals Internal case statement Gift vehicles and donor markets Expressing the case for support Public information	Leadership training. Gift solicitation: to whom, by whom, how much, when Gift incentives
Execution	Communication: letters, phone Staff relationships and tasks	Marketing fundraising internally Staff relationships Staff solicitation	Expressing the case for support Volunteer and donor relationships Donor engagement and solicitation Public information
Control	Gift processing Gift acknowledgment Gift records Gift reports Fundraising costs	Gift reports	Volunteer recognition Donor recognition Time lines Major donor prospect system
Evaluation	Gift vehicles Fundraising budget Staff performance	Effectiveness of programs being supported	Gift markets Volunteer leaders Effectiveness of the case for support
Professional stance	Integrity of judgment about fundraising practices and information reported	Integrity of leadership among program and administrative colleagues in meeting organizational commitments	Integrity of mission in achieving public good

Volunteer Leadership and Giving

Fundraising will be most successful when leadership for fundraising is shared among many people. Core leadership includes the board chair, the chair of the development committee, the chief staff officer, and the chief fundraising officer, working together to develop fundraising policies and plans. Their work together sets the tone for the entire organization and its commitment to building effective partnerships with leadership donors whose gifts (as illustrated in the gift chart) are major contributions.

The involvement of board members and other key volunteers reinforces the philanthropic character of nonprofit organizations. Their voluntary service demonstrates their commitment to the values that the nonprofit serves, providing an example and setting the standard for others' participation as volunteers and as donors. If board members, who are the volunteers most closely related to the organization, do not support it financially, it is unrealistic to expect others to contribute to the nonprofit's mission and work. When board members are recruited to serve, expectations regarding their financial support should be made clear. One of the most effective statements of standards for board giving is the following: "After your contributions to your religious community, we expect that our organization will be among your highest charitable priorities." This allows for people of differing financial ability to demonstrate their commitment in the manner most appropriate for them while still emphasizing that their giving is an essential responsibility of being a board member. This standard also encourages broad diversity on a board, along with the philanthropic commitments of time, service, and money.

It is worth noting that volunteer service has a direct relationship to contributions. Independent Sector studies show that people who volunteer are more generous in their giving. In Independent Sector's most recent survey, households that both gave and volunteered averaged annual giving of $2,295, or 4.0 percent of household income. In contrast, households that only contributed and did not volunteer gave an average $1,009, or 2.4 percent of income (Toppe, Kirsch, and Michel, 2002, p. 107).

Organizational Readiness

As noted earlier, nonprofits too often pursue fundraising solely on the basis of their need for additional revenue. When this occurs, fundraising is characterized by the use of techniques designed to acquire as much money as possible in the shortest possible time. To succeed in the long-term development of philanthropic support, nonprofits must be internally prepared for fundraising. Leaders and managers must fully understand and be able to articulate the case for support. A compelling statement of the case for support will draw prospective donors to an organization's mission by answering the following questions persuasively (Seiler, 2003, p. 25):

1. Why does the organization exist? The answer lies in the human or social problem or need addressed by the nonprofit. This is the organization's mission, its raison d'être.

2. What services or programs does the nonprofit provide to meet the need or solve the problem?
3. Why should prospective donors (individuals, corporations, foundations) provide gifts, and what benefits accrue to donors who make gifts?

The answers to these questions will clarify the value of an organization to the community it aims to serve. They will explain how community life is enhanced because the nonprofit meets community needs; what specific goals, objectives, and programs the nonprofit plans to implement in response to the identified needs; and what constituencies will be served by those who support the organization. A nonprofit cannot exist in isolation from its environment. Its programs and activities must be valued, not only by the clients it serves but also by potential donors who view the nonprofit as contributing to the quality of community life. Fundraising success will depend on how well a nonprofit responds to its environment, adapts to changing conditions in the environment, and builds constituencies who believe in its value. An effective case is the foundation on which to build philanthropic support.

Stewardship and Investment

The cost of raising money and the effectiveness of fundraising programs are critical issues for nonprofit leaders. Nonprofits that merit philanthropic support are able to justify fundraising costs. One study pointed out, however, "that 59 percent of non-profits receiving direct public contributions did not report any fundraising expense at all" (Sargeant and Jay, 2004, p. 302). Although some giving may be spontaneous, this fact seems quite incredible, since fundraising typically involves the management of asking donors to contribute along with gift collecting, processing, and acknowledging—all of which require staff time (and therefore cost).

Although standards of fundraising costs are not widely established, experienced fundraisers accept certain guidelines as reasonable (see Table 19.5). These guidelines are best understood in the context of a nonprofit's own giving history, measuring each year's results against previous years' outcomes and costs. A well-established program is likely to have costs that are lower than a new fundraising program. Introducing a new component of fundraising will be more expensive than maintaining or expanding a current program component. The guidelines in Table 19.5 also show that different fundraising strategies require different levels of investment. The more expensive forms of fundraising reflect the need to constantly renew the donor base with large numbers of smaller gifts. The less expensive strategies involve smaller numbers of larger gifts, commonly received from donors who have long giving histories with an organization. These people,

TABLE 19.5. SUGGESTED GUIDELINES FOR FUNDRAISING COSTS

	Cost per Dollar Raised
New donor acquisition	Up to $1.50
Special events	Up to $0.50
Donor renewal (general donor programs)	Up to $0.25
Major gifts and capital campaigns	Up to $0.10
Planned giving	Up to $0.15[a]
Corporate and foundation grant seeking	Up to $0.20

[a]After at least five years of initial investment.

whose donations are variously identified as "major gifts," "leadership gifts," or "strategic gifts," provide important credibility for an organization through the example they set for others.

Another important consideration in budgeting for fundraising is efficiency (the cost per dollar raised) versus effectiveness (the net total amount raised). One nonprofit, for example, might raise an annual fund of $400,000 with a fundraising budget of $100,000. The annual fund nets $300,000 by spending $0.25 for each dollar raised. Another nonprofit might raise $600,000 with a fundraising budget of $200,000, netting $400,000 at a cost of $0.33 per dollar raised. The first organization would be considered more efficient because it spent less money per dollar raised, but the second would be considered more effective because it raised more money. The balance between fundraising efficiency and effectiveness is an issue that nonprofit boards must consider when setting their organizational budgets. Occasionally boards must decide to increase their fundraising investment so their organizations can achieve higher levels of philanthropic giving. Fundraising managers are responsible for showing how such investment can yield new levels of contributions.

Stewardship and Providing Public Benefit

Stewardship, defined as how we exercise ethical accountability in the use of resources, applies to an organization's general success in fulfilling its mission as much as it does to its fundraising. Nonprofit boards carry ultimate responsibility for the fiduciary well-being of their organizations. This includes ensuring that all resources are used both efficiently and effectively. The board of directors has the right to be fully informed by staff about how resources are being used. Along with program evaluation, which is an essential part of this process, fundraising managers have a key role to play in helping volunteer leaders meet their stewardship responsibilities.

Obtaining the status of a 501(c)(3) nonprofit in the United States requires that the organization be committed to and demonstrably provide a public benefit. This requirement challenges the trend among many nonprofits to meet revenue needs by operating "more like a business" and focusing on service areas that will generate greater earned income. Earned income is certainly critical, but sound judgment among institutional leaders calls for a careful balance between generating operating margins and sustaining the core mission. One consequence of this trend is that the organization's mission may unintentionally become diverted or diluted. If commercialization of their services becomes a dominant priority, nonprofits run the risk of losing their identity as agents for community good and stewards of community resources.

Other potential distortions that can result from using business metaphors to characterize nonprofits are that "(a) donors are spoken of as customers; (b) fundraising is spoken of as marketing; and ... (c) donors are likened to stockholders" (Clohesy, 2003, p. 134). Certain technical aspects of each of these perspectives may relate to fundraising practice: sales techniques in gift solicitation; opinion gathering to position a nonprofit's message; and the notion of investing in a nonprofit's cause. The fundamental fallacy in all of these, however, is that the imagery presupposes a private interest or a private gain, which contrasts with the public benefit and common good that are the hallmarks of philanthropy and of nonprofit organizations and institutions.

Technology and Fundraising

In 2000, predictions were that "within two decades, real-time transactions will be common in direct response fundraising. . . . By authorizing a gift in the course of an online videoconference . . . a donor may instantaneously transmit funds from her bank account to the charity. . . . " (Warwick, 2000, p. 5). Real-time giving occurred in less than ten years—much more quickly than anyone predicted. Many people see technology advances, and especially social media, as easy vehicles to grow giving. When considering the use of any technologies, however, the following questions raise fundamental considerations for nonprofit managers.

1. *What is the scale of the proposed effort relative to our overall fundraising program?* What is the relative level of investment involved, and what impact might the proposed diversion of investment in this new direction have on meeting our committed goals?
2. *Is our fundraising audience—the folks giving our organization money today—ready for this new approach?* Are they users of the technology or tools involved? Based

on what evidence? Are we aware of any results from like organizations trying similar approaches?

3. *What do we actually know about the new channel or technology?* Who on our team will be in charge? Do we have pertinent skills? Do we need outside expertise?

4. *Are there any opportunity costs?* There are still issues of mind share, workload, timing, integration with other fundraising efforts, and donor reactions (including not responding). Have these operational issues and contingencies been thought through?

5. *What value will we get from this, and how will we measure success?* By definition, what's proposed is an experiment. So I wouldn't expect the exercise to make us rich and famous. But *some* ROI analysis should be presented.

> [The] fundraising team's job is to protect and nurture our existing donor base; to raise the funds projected for this year; to make prudent investments to grow that base using proven methods and current response data; and to scan the horizon for new opportunities and ways to grow. In that order! (*The Agitator,* October 1, 2009)

Too often, even though e-mail and Web sites are ubiquitous, many nonprofits still manage Internet use as an inexpensive substitute for print media such as direct mail appeals and newsletters. At the other extreme, excessive "creativity" leads to Internet communications that demonstrate the latest graphics but have little impact on the potential audience. Organizational managers (who usually are not "techies") need to remember some key criteria regarding Web sites: the specific goals of the Web site; simplicity and ease in navigation (finding the balance between effective communication and strong graphics); content that is pertinent to and beneficial to visitors (including different categories of visitors); asking for a gift and telling how to contact the organization on every page; evaluation of the Web site's impact; and respecting professional and legal standards for Web sites (Sargeant and Jay, 2004, pp. 277–282).

Managing technology effectively is essential to building and sustaining effective philanthropic fundraising. E-mail use is not limited to any particular age groups. Web sites are the organizational front door for anyone who visits. Social media are creating fascinating opportunities for new kinds of relationships with constituents. Taken together, communication technologies potentially open every nonprofit to the multicultural and multiethnic world in which we live. Leaders and managers must be smart users in order for technology policies and goals to fully support the organization's mission and vision.

Ethics in Fundraising

Nonprofits play a special role in our country because they address diverse public needs and enable people to participate in meeting those needs. Fundraising managers play a critical role in both of these outcomes. Their work leads to additional resources by helping articulate the good that is to be achieved and by facilitating donors' contributions. They ask donors "to become engaged in an activity of great importance to specific people in their community or somewhere in the world.... Donors are invited to act publicly, to make a difference, and to enjoy the satisfaction that comes with public action on behalf of a worthwhile cause" (Clohesy, 2003, p. 136).

In the daily activity of fundraising, unfortunately, evaluation is too often based on the precept that "what works is what is right." As indicated at the beginning of this chapter, fundraising can be narrowly regarded as simply a means to obtain revenue. How a nonprofit raises funds, however, is a powerful index of the degree to which its leaders grasp the moral dimensions of the nonprofit's purposes.

We all live according to the customs, traditions, and values that have been handed down to us, and we apply this heritage to the decisions we make each day. The advances of technology and the challenges of a changing world, however, increasingly cause people to reflect on their purposes and think about how they should conduct their lives. Nonprofit leaders who think about philanthropic fundraising, supply-side giving, organizational readiness, efficiency and effectiveness, and technology in fundraising will probably find themselves reflecting on ethical matters on behalf of their organizations.

The most comprehensive statement on ethics in fundraising is the Association of Fundraising Professionals (AFP) Code of Ethical Principles and Standards of Professional Practice. Members of the AFP agree to abide by these standards, and nonprofits that hire AFP members should expect to support the standards as well. Nonprofits whose fundraising staff members do not belong to AFP will do well to apply these principles as guidelines for professional performance. The complete text of AFP's Code of Ethical Principles and Standards of Professional Practice, along with additional materials on ethical fundraising, can be found at www.afpnet.org/ethics.

The AFP code implies that fundraising staff bring appropriate technical and managerial competency to their responsibilities. Such competency, and the commitment to continually strengthen it, is an ethical provision of fundraising that is an integral part of staff professionalism. Successful nonprofit organizations will serve as vehicles for fundraising that is ethical and professional.

In addition to the AFP ethics code, organizations do well by adopting the Donor Bill of Rights (Exhibit 19.1). Originally developed by a group of leading professional associations (included in the Additional Resources below), countless organizations have now adopted these standards of care that donors have the right to expect from organizations they support.

EXHIBIT 19.1. THE DONOR BILL OF RIGHTS

Philanthropy is based on voluntary action for the common good. It is a tradition of giving and sharing that is primary to the quality of life. To ensure that philanthropy merits the respect and trust of the general public, and that donors and prospective donors can have full confidence in the nonprofit organizations and causes they are asked to support, we declare that all donors have these rights:

  I. To be informed of the organization's mission, of the way the organization intends to use donated resources, and of its capacity to use donations effectively for their intended purposes.

  II. To be informed of the identity of those serving on the organization's governing board, and to expect the board to exercise prudent judgment in its stewardship responsibilities.

  III. To have access to the organization's most recent financial statements.

  IV. To be assured their gifts will be used for the purposes for which they were given.

  V. To receive appropriate acknowledgement and recognition.

  VI. To be assured that information about their donation is handled with respect and with confidentiality to the extent provided by law.

  VII. To expect that all relationships with individuals representing organizations of interest to the donor will be professional in nature.

  VIII. To be informed whether those seeking donations are volunteers, employees of the organization, or hired solicitors.

  IX. To have the opportunity for their names to be deleted from mailing lists that an organization may intend to share.

  X. To feel free to ask questions when making a donation and to receive prompt, truthful, and forthright answers.

Summary

"Fund raising is an essential part of American philanthropy; in turn, philanthropy as voluntary action for the public good is essential to American democracy" (Payton, Rosso, and Tempel, 1991, p. 4). This observation affirms the reality that fundraising cannot be an isolated activity in a successful nonprofit organization. Fundraising practices reflect what we are as organizations. The values, style, and commitment that undergird fundraising are likely to be the same as those that characterize the rest of an organization's work.

Philanthropic fundraising is mission driven. That is, funds are sought to enable a nonprofit to serve the community good that the organization exists to address. Philanthropic fundraising is also volunteer centered. Over the long term, the involvement of volunteers in governance, advocacy, and giving is essential to healthy nonprofits.

Successful fundraising is also the result of disciplined management. When fundraising professionals provide leadership to other staff and to volunteers, a productive collective effort results. Just as disciplined fundraising management is important to obtaining resources, it is also important in exercising accountability for resources. Nonprofits must ensure that they use contributed income for the purposes for which it was sought. Although they are privately controlled, mission-driven nonprofits are publicly accountable.

The public good that fundraising supports is essential to the wellbeing of our communities and our nation. Weaving philanthropic fundraising into the fabric of their existence is integral to the moral purpose of ethical nonprofits.

Five professional organizations provide key leadership to the fundraising profession, dating back to 1935. These organizations and their Web sites are the following:

Association of Fundraising Professionals (originally the National Society of Fund Raising Executives)

> www.afpnet.org

Association for Healthcare Professionals

> www.ahp.org

Council for Advancement and Support of Education

> www.case.org

Giving Institute (originally the American Association of Fundraising Council)

> www.aafrc.org

Partnership for Philanthropic Planning (originally the National Committee on Planned Giving)

> www.pppnet.org

References

The Agitator. "Want to Try Something New?" http://wwwtheagitator.net/dont-miss-these-posts/want-to-try-something-new. Downloaded October 1, 2009.

Clohesy, W. H. "Fund-Raising and the Articulation of Common Goods." *Nonprofit and Voluntary Sector Quarterly*, 2003, *32*, 128–140.

Payton, R. L., Rosso, H. A., and Tempel, E. R. "Toward a Philosophy of Fund Raising." In D. F. Burlingame and L. J. Hulse (eds.), *Taking Fund Raising Seriously: Advancing the Profession and Practice of Raising Money.* San Francisco: Jossey-Bass, 1991.

Sargeant, A., and Jay, E. *Fundraising Management: Analysis, Planning and Practice.* New York: Routledge, 2004.

Schervish, P. G. "The Material Horizons of Philanthropy: New Directions for Money and Motives." In E. R. Tempel and D. F. Burlingame (eds.), *Understanding the Needs of Donors: The Supply Side of Charitable Giving.* New Directions for Philanthropic Fundraising, No. 29. San Francisco: Jossey-Bass, 2000.

Seiler, T. L. "Plan to Succeed," In H. A. Rosso (ed.), *Achieving Excellence in Fund Raising.* San Francisco: Jossey-Bass, 2003.

Toppe, C. M., Kirsch, A. D., and Michel, J. *Giving and Volunteering in the United States in 2001.* Washington, D.C.: Independent Sector, 2002.

Wing, K. T., Pollack, T. H., and Blackwood, A. *The Nonprofit Almanac 2008.* Washington, D.C.: The Urban Institute Press.

Warwick, M. "Introduction: Heads Up! Eyes on the Future!" In M. Johnston (ed.), *Direct Response Fund Raising.* New York: Wiley, 2000.

Wasley, P. "Giving Takes a Beating." *The Chronicle of Philanthropy*, June 18, 2009. http://philanthropy.com/premium/articles/v21/i17/17002801.htm.

Additional Resources

Dove, K. E. *Conducting a Successful Capital Campaign.* San Francisco: Jossey-Bass, 2000.

Fischer, M. *Ethical Decision Making in Fund Raising.* New York: Wiley, 2000.

Grace, K. S. *Over Goal!* Medfield, Mass.: Emerson & Church Publishers, 2003.

Greenfield, J. M. *Fund Raising: Evaluating and Managing the Fund Development Process.* New York: Wiley, 1999.

Hopkins, B. R. *The First Legal Answer Book for Fund-Raisers.* New York: Wiley, 2000.

Jordan, R. R., and Quynn, K. L. *Planned Giving: Management, Marketing, and Law.* New York: Wiley, 2000.

Pettey, J. G. *Cultivating Diversity in Fundraising.* New York: Wiley, 2002.

CHAPTER TWENTY

SOCIAL ENTERPRISE AND NONPROFIT VENTURES

Scott T. Helm

One of the leading trends to capture the attention of many nonprofit leaders during the past two decades is that of social enterprise—the development and operation of nonprofit earned-income ventures. This trend emerged as part of the larger interest in the overall phenomenon of social entrepreneurship (discussed by Matthew Nash in Chapter Ten of this handbook) and reflects the interaction of several significant forces and challenges. Central is the impact of the growing competition for limited funding from both governmental and philanthropic sources, and, as Nash describes, the search for alternative sources of revenue has encouraged a growing number of nonprofits to "explore market-driven approaches and experiment with practices drawn from the business sector, including the launch of earned-revenue ventures, both mission-related social enterprises and unrelated businesses"(p. 264). Similarly, in Chapter Three, Lester Salamon reports that one of the drivers of growth of the U.S. nonprofit sector has been "the vigor with which nonprofit America embraced the spirit and the techniques of the market." He observes that a clear indication of the success of this approach is the substantial rise in nonprofit income from fees and charges, which he characterizes as "indicative of the success with which nonprofit organizations succeeded in marketing their services to a clientele increasingly able to afford them" (p. 91). Social enterprise continues to grow in practice, even as its legitimacy is challenged by some, and it promises to play a significant role in the twenty-first-century nonprofit sector.[1]

Many nonprofits generate significant commercial revenues in the course of their everyday activities. Salamon reports "fees and charges accounted for nearly half (about 47 percent) of the growth in nonprofit revenue between 1977 and 1997—more than any other source" (p. 91). Blackwood et al. (2008) report that health care organizations and educational institutions, the two largest income generating nonprofit classifications, comprise 32 percent of all public charities yet account for 75.2 percent of public charity revenue. They also report that more than 70 percent of all public charity revenue was generated from fees-for-service or government contracts.

A related trend among nonprofit organizations is the growth in unrelated business income. Unrelated business income refers to income generated from any nonprofit business activity that is outside the scope of the charitable purpose for which the organization received its tax exempt status. Unrelated business income is reported separately and, because it is generated from activity outside the scope of the organization's tax-exempt mission, it is subject to income tax (and social enterprises that involve unrelated business fall in this category, too). According to the U.S. Internal Revenue Service (IRS), the number of nonprofits filing unrelated business income tax (UBIT) returns increased 52 percent between 1990 and 2006. Further, the amount of unrelated business income reported over the same period increased 184 percent (IRS, 2010). This growth is especially interesting in light of the fact that U.S. nonprofit law limits the amount of unrelated business income that a nonprofit may generate without jeopardizing its tax-exempt status.

As the statistics illustrate, the lure of social enterprise can be very enticing to nonprofit leaders. In times of economic stress, such as that the nonprofit sector has experienced the last several years, the development of a social enterprise can appear to be a panacea. Especially to a financially desperate nonprofit leader, social enterprise may seem to be a sure-fire way to stabilize financials and maintain programming. Unfortunately, nonprofit leaders past and present can tell many tales of ill-conceived enterprises that exhausted already-limited funds. Foster and Bradach, for example, tell the story of a nonprofit organization that decided to make and sell salad dressing (2005). The intent was to develop revenues that could subsidize the nonprofit's mission-relevant operations. However, a failure to recognize or account for indirect costs and an inaccurate assessment of direct costs led the organization to severely underestimate total costs of salad dressing production. Using the inaccurate numbers, the organization set the price for the dressing with the expectation that each bottle of salad dressing would earn $0.35—a nice profit for the organization. In fact, their later assessment determined each bottle cost the organization approximately $86.50 to produce—a terrible and dramatic loss! Not every case of financial failure is this dramatic, yet such mistakes illustrate the need for nonprofits to fully understand the implications (financial and otherwise) of operating social enterprises. This is especially true when the social enterprise is expected to be a profit generator.

Horror stories notwithstanding, many nonprofits have generated significant benefits from their enterprise activities. Consider, for example, the YMCA of Greater Kansas City, which is regionally recognized as a successful enterprising nonprofit organization. YMCA leaders engaged in an analysis of the fitness center market in the metropolitan area and determined that there was a demand for more fitness centers, and the leadership team also recognized that every YMCA had a very valuable (and often less than fully utilized) asset—weight rooms. Perceiving an opportunity to meet this need and generate additional revenue in the process, the YMCA set out on a very aggressive expansion plan. Using their existing network of facilities as an anchor, they developed new locations and merged with other independent YMCAs in the region to achieve the level of scale needed to serve the metro market. The result was exceptional growth in revenues. Today the Kansas City YMCA system generates 85 percent of its annual revenue from fitness center membership fees. As YMCA leaders are quick to explain, this enhanced revenue base enables them to provide access to all youth who wish to participate in Y programs regardless of their ability to pay—a true mission-relevant value.

The purpose of this chapter is not to promote or discourage the use of social enterprise strategies but to provide nonprofit leaders with a broader understanding of the issues and opportunities associated with social enterprise and help them prepare to examine them. Rather than duplicate the content of the many existing "How-to" volumes on social enterprise, this chapter is designed to serve as an orientation to help nonprofit leaders make sense of key elements of the overwhelming volume of literature on the topic and understand key concepts that will be important to consider as they explore options for enterprise development. I encourage every nonprofit leader considering social enterprise options to discuss the relevant issues identified in this chapter with their board and executive colleagues and collaborators. The Internet resource site for this handbook includes a number of tools and resources that may be helpful to nonprofit leaders as they facilitate such conversations and weigh their options. Many of the important elements of the social enterprise development process fall under the bailiwick of other chapters in the handbook, and it will be important to link the insights of this chapter with function-specific methods and tools presented in the associated chapters (see Chapter Nine for further information on the strategy and planning process, and Chapter Eleven for specific information about market research and planning).

Social enterprises develop within the larger context of the nonprofit organization and even the nonprofit sector, and this context differs from region to region of the world. Therefore, I begin this chapter with a brief discussion of the cultural context of social enterprise. Culture shapes and influences the ways we perceive and understand the value of a strategy such as pursuit of social enterprise. Next I address the questions, Who should launch a social enterprise? What are the implications of this choice? I describe knowledge acquisition and resources likely to be useful in the process of enterprise development. I then discuss who ventures into social enterprises, and the options that exist for engaging in a social enterprise. Finally, I talk about planning, the planning process, and the relationship between planning and social enterprise.

Culture and the Context of Social Enterprise

As the field of nonprofit inquiry expands and takes on a more global dimension, we gain additional insights into the role that culture and national context play in the creation of various forms of nonprofit enterprise. This is illustrated by the variation in the types of social enterprises described in the European literature versus those described in the American literature. There are several differences of interest and relevance and, taken together, they offer important insights into the reasons and ways that such enterprises develop and function.

Generally speaking, European scholarship describes social enterprise as it develops in the context of a strong welfare state. Typically, European social enterprise exhibits the following characteristics:

1. It takes the form of a collaborative or association.
2. Its legal status differentiates it from more traditional nongovernmental activity in many countries; in many it is a special class of organization.
3. It is focused primarily on the creation of social benefit, not economic ends.
4. It operates in the niche of human services.
5. It is funded or heavily supported by government (Kerlin, 2006).

United States social enterprises, which develop in the context of capitalism, differ in some relatively significant ways. Typically, U.S. social enterprise exhibits the following characteristics:

1. Social enterprise is a strategy, not an organization category.
2. It comprises both for-profit and nonprofit organizational forms (Dart, 2004).
3. It focuses on revenue generation as well as social benefit (LeRoux, 2005).
4. It operates in many different service niches or "industries" (Kerlin, 2006).
5. It is privately funded (Kerlin, 2006).

This chapter focuses on U.S. social enterprises and, as such, the reader will note a strong emphasis on the purpose of commercial revenue generation. Equally important from this perspective is that social enterprises are often funded privately (that is, by foundations, individuals, nonprofit lenders, and banks). Both of these have important implications for how U.S. social enterprises are planned and implemented.

Who Should Establish a Social Enterprise?

Unlike Hamlet's quandary, "To be or not to be, that is the question," the decision to establish a social enterprise venture is less existential and more pragmatic. As noted earlier, in many European countries social enterprise is a special class of organization designed to serve particular purposes; in the United States it is a strategy. Therefore, in the United States, the choice to operate a social enterprise (like any strategy choice) is available to any nonprofit organization regardless of its particular mission niche.

Social enterprise may be an option to any nonprofit, yet that does not mean every nonprofit should launch a commercial venture. Then how should a nonprofit begin to decide? The answer to this question requires significant deliberation, particularly regarding four core areas:

- Mission impact and relevance
- Characteristics of the nonprofit's operating environment
- Financial and revenue implications
- Organizational capacity to implement the enterprise

Each of these four areas offers a different and complementary lens through which to examine your enterprise's possibilities.

At the core, it is essential to have clarity regarding who you are as an organization and how a potential enterprise strategy might relate to this. Typically, when asked to define their organization, nonprofit leaders will recite their mission. Mission is important, so this is an important starting point, but I would assert that mission only begins to describe the true nature of a nonprofit. In what ways might a potential enterprise be relevant to mission? What are the organization's core values or guiding principles and what guidance do they offer when it comes to exploring enterprise options? Will the development of an enterprise add value to the organization or might it distract us? It is essential that nonprofit leaders develop a shared sense of why they might explore an enterprise option, the results they seek, the risks they are willing to incur as a part of the process (and why they would be warranted), and whether an enterprise option will in fact offer appropriate benefits and results.

The second of the key areas of consideration and deliberation is that of operating environment. Later in this chapter, I discuss the implications for assessment of the operating environment as it relates to planning. At this early phase in exploring enterprise ideas, there are two basic areas to examine with regard to operating environment. First is the category of legal environment; the second is that of normative environment. When nonprofits take actions that conflict with either the legal or normative expectations of their environments, the ramifications can be grave—and both environments place constraints on the options that will be acceptable for nonprofit enterprise. In the United States, for example, legal environment parameters include constraints on

- The amount (percentage) of unrelated earned income an organization can generate
- The use of funds for (mission) unrelated activities
- The demonstration of charitable purpose in the normal business of the organization

Normative elements are less formal and usually vary by the mission of the organization, the location of the organization, and the constituencies of the organization. Normative elements are primarily about expectations and the sense of what is and is not acceptable for a nonprofit to do, and it is essential that nonprofit leaders consider these dimensions at the very outset of their exploration of enterprise options. Even though a given enterprise option may be legal, it may be dangerously inconsistent with the expectations and values of an organization's key stakeholders. It may be inconsistent with (or even threaten) the overall culture of the nonprofit itself. For example, the decision of a volunteer center to charge people for their volunteer placement might conflict with the values of traditional volunteer center operations or the norms of the communities in which they operate. These are critical issues that have great potential to damage the legitimacy, credibility, and even sustainability of the nonprofit.

The third area of initial deliberation focuses on the business model or revenue model of the nonprofit and how it may change (or need to change) if an enterprise is developed. At core, the idea of revenue model involves understanding the sources of revenue for the organization and why and how they provide financial resources. Nonprofits need to make explicit and informed choices about the potential of various types of revenue sources that might be available to finance their operations. This topic is fundamentally a marketing and economics discussion—beginning with an understanding of the demand for the nonprofit's services and the nonprofit's relationships with its current customers, and consideration of alternative ways that customers might be willing to engage in commercial exchanges with the organization. The topic of markets and market relationships is thoroughly examined in Chapter Eleven of this volume; the focus of this chapter to underscore that these central choices must be examined again by a nonprofit considering the development of an enterprise.

Similarly, in Chapter Eighteen, Dennis Young explores nonprofit finance and addresses another facet of the revenue model—the critical relationship between source of revenue and beneficiary of the provision of services. Framing revenue generation in economic terms, Young's model connects commercial revenues with the value a client places on a service. The question is one of value and the overall value proposition: Do potential clients consider the value commensurate to the cost? This is central to any consideration of social enterprise. For example, an opera house may provide multiple programs to their community. The main line of business is the production of operas. Opera enthusiasts view purchasing a ticket to a show as a value transaction. The consumers receive a good (in this case the ticket to the opera), and they are willing to pay a price commensurate to the value they place on an experience. In economic parlance this is the essence of private good markets; social enterprises must operate successfully in private good markets.

More generally, nonprofits providing a good or service that directly benefit the client and only that client may be well-advised to examine that relationship as social enterprise. A few examples of this type of venture include

- Counseling
- Medical care
- Education
- Business consulting
- Fitness services
- Performance art productions

Each of these types of services has individual clients (even though some may involve third parties, such as insurance companies) who pay for the value they receive for the respective service.

Finally, nonprofits exploring social enterprise will be well served by an analysis of organizational capacity and assets. Similar to environmental and revenue model issues, capacity issues are examined in great depth as part of the enterprise planning process, but they must be given initial general consideration at an early stage in any dialogue about the potential to develop an enterprise. In addition to financial capacity, the organization's leaders need to assess the organization's capacity with regard to the knowledge and competence required to move forward with enterprise development and the availability of other key resources needed to develop the enterprise—particularly human capital and assets.

Each of these "lenses" provides nonprofit leaders with a framework to help initiate an assessment of their organization and their enterprise options. Because social enterprise is a strategy that, at least in principle, can be employed by any type of nonprofit, the insights that you can gain from this examination will not necessarily encourage or discourage your decision to develop an enterprise. But it is important to understand these dimensions of your organization; having a better understanding of who you are as an organization will make it easier to recognize future obstacles and opportunities if you choose to develop an enterprise.

Access to Knowledge and Expertise About Social Enterprise

Google the phrase "social enterprise" and you will find there is no shortage of information on the topic. The sheer volume of social enterprise information may present a different problem for the busy nonprofit executive, since sifting through the many sources may seem an insurmountable task. However, nonprofit leaders beginning to explore social enterprise options may need to do so as an internally developed process. These "Do-It-Yourselfers" will probably seek resources for two types of information: the enterprise planning process and options for enterprise strategies. The vast range of literature derives from one of three general categories: social enterprise management books, information Web sites, and planning templates.

Management books on social enterprise target the nonprofit practitioner. As a whole, the genre introduces nonprofit leaders to key social enterprise concepts and provides instruction on how to use these concepts. Topics include market analysis, organization structure, and financial management. Some are organized as workbooks with exercises for the nonprofit to complete as they plan their enterprise (for example, Dees et al., 2001); others are more conceptual and help nonprofit leaders frame their enterprise (for example, Lynch and Wall, 2009). In addition to these volumes, which take a holistic approach, practitioners can draw on the wisdom of books on specific functional areas of social enterprise management (such as technology, marketing, financial management). (When selecting specific books, remember that books of different nations are unlikely to work from a consistent definition of social enterprise. Therefore, select books that are relevant to the nation where you wish to develop the enterprise.)

New Internet media also provide an abundance of information sources for the Do-It-Yourselfers. Using the Internet as a research medium has both positives and negatives, of course, but there is much that the careful user can glean. Among the promising are information Web sites with enterprise case studies (such as, Social Enterprise Alliance), reference materials on legal and managerial considerations (for example, National Center for Nonprofit Enterprise and Social Enterprise Magazine-Online), and interactive venues such as chats and blogs (such as, The Skoll Foundation). There is also a variety of planning tools and templates available on the Internet. Of course, Internet sources also have shortcomings. The most significant shortcoming is the reliability of some information sites. (References and links to useful Internet sites and resources are provided to readers via the handbook resource site.)

Nonprofit leaders considering the development of a social enterprise may debate whether to go it alone or work with a consultant. When making this decision, these questions and observations may help clarify the answer:

1. Do you have the time to plan in addition to your existing workload? Many nonprofits hire consultants as a time management tactic—their leaders simply do not have time to do all that is needed. The saying, "The urgent crowds out the important," speaks to the potential danger of trying to develop a social enterprise internally: Will the process of developing the enterprise create interference that undermines other leadership or management work? Consultants can offer process organization, process facilitation, research assistance, and guidance. All of these services can reduce the time demands on executives and board leaders.

2. Do the existing information resources (books, electronic materials, and templates) provide adequate support to equip you and your team with the knowledge you need to implement the enterprise development process?

3. Will the absence of a consultant hamper full involvement by all necessary parties? Effective planning processes are contingent on diverse participation. Each member of the planning team brings a unique perspective. If a current leader assumes the role of facilitator, one of two potentially negative scenarios may occur. One, the facilitator dominates planning, essentially creating their own plan instead of a plan that draws upon the full range of diverse expertise in the room; or two, the facilitator takes care to remain in the facilitation role and therefore does not provide information or input even when they have important information to share. As a result, the plan may lack the insights of a key organization leader (often the executive director or a board member).

4. Can you afford the cost of assistance? Although consultants may bring important value to the social enterprise development process, they also bring cost. Consultant fees vary by region and expertise. When investigating consultants, consider their background with social enterprise and familiarity

with your industry in addition to their price tag. It may be useful to do a cost-benefit analysis to compare the cost of a consultant to the cost of internal development.

Structure Options for Social Enterprises

One of the first questions many nonprofit leaders consider when organizing a social enterprise is, How should I structure it? Structures need to be chosen based on the purpose and conditions under which the enterprise will operate, and the appropriate answer will be influenced by a number of factors:

- Who is to be served by the enterprise?
- Will the enterprise be implemented within an existing organization or will the enterprise be established as a new nonprofit?
- What are the social, political, and other environmental considerations?

Social enterprises typically take one of three general forms (Alter, 2009):

- The social enterprise is constituted as a discrete organization
- The social enterprise is part of the organization
- The social enterprise is a subsidiary or affiliate of the organization

I describe each of these forms in the following sections (based on the typology of Alter, 2009). At the outset, it is important to note that no form is inherently superior to another and each form offers potential merits (and drawbacks). Further, no model is automatically consistent with an organization's external environment. Instead these organizational forms should be evaluated as strategic options.

Discrete Organization

Nonprofit organizations that implement their sole or core "business" as a revenue-generating social enterprise are common throughout the sector. Hospitals, day care centers, and schools all charge fees-for-services and use these fees to finance the cost of providing their services. Operating in environments with norms (and laws) supportive of the generation of earned income, these organizations implement earned-income programs that are completely aligned with their charitable missions. Their enterprise programs are central to their organization's charitable purpose, so the organization does not need to be concerned with questions of mission relevance or the threat that the enterprise might lead to mission drift.

When a social enterprise constitutes the organization's primary business, it is most likely to be implemented as a new organization. (Existing nonprofit organizations that are not already social enterprises are unlikely to appear in this category since they obviously have revenue sources other than fees-for-service.) When an existing nonprofit chooses to shift its design to make a social enterprise its primary business, one of two scenarios is likely to have caused the change:

1. The organization's operating environment changed and, for whatever reason, the primary enterprise now can be (or maybe even needs to be) funded by fees-for-service.
2. The nonprofit has chosen to discard its previous primary program design and create a new social enterprise business.

Part of the Organization

A second structural arrangement is the operation of a social enterprise as one part or unit of an organization. Unlike the first structural form, these social enterprises are considered related but not necessarily central to mission fulfillment. Depending on the relevance of the enterprise to the organization's mission, the earnings of this form of social enterprise may be subject to unrelated business income tax (UBIT). However, more often than not, a program's activities will be sufficiently related to mission to avoid this. For example, a typical program of a sheltered workshop includes work activities to be implemented by their developmentally disabled clients. The workshop then sells the products of their work to the public. For the sheltered workshop, the work opportunities for the developmentally disabled population are central to the mission. Therefore, the earnings of the work products are directly related to the mission and thus not subject to UBIT. We often see this second structural form in existing organizations. A nonprofit may realize there is a revenue generation opportunity, closely related to their mission, that they could implement. Consequently, they establish this mission-relevant program to generate additional revenues

Subsidiary or Affiliated Organization

Social enterprises structured as subsidiaries or affiliates of the nonprofit are a third structural option. The subsidiary structure allows a nonprofit to achieve legal separation between an enterprise and the parent organization. This may be useful or even essential as the nonprofit implements an enterprise that may not be feasible or appropriate to operate internally, usually for reasons of tax or other legal liability. The subsidiary organization may take either the nonprofit or for-profit form of organization. I discuss the implications of both next.

Nonprofit Subsidiaries. Social enterprise subsidiaries that take a nonprofit form often exist because an organization wants to pursue a charitable purpose without opening itself to UBIT or other legal liability (see Chapters Two and Twenty-three of this volume for extended discussions of legal and risk management issues). For example, this option might be chosen because a nonprofit wishes to address a new need or opportunity that is tax-exempt and charitable but is not within the scope of its own tax exemption as granted by the IRS. Or it might be chosen to ensure a legal separation so that risks and liabilities associated with the new venture could not result in losses of the new venture being assessed against the parent organization (for example, a church that creates a low-income housing redevelopment agency and wants to keep its church assets separated from the riskier work of the redevelopment agency). The subsidiary is a separate nonprofit corporation with its own legal status. The subsidiary organization will have a separate governing board, but it will be under the control of the parent nonprofit (for example, the parent organization board would appoint or approve the membership of the subsidiary organization's board). Therefore, the board of the parent organization will be the primary governing body for the parent nonprofit *and* will either oversee or itself serve as the board of a subsidiary.

For-Profit Subsidiaries. The for-profit subsidiary approach appears more often in the U.S. social enterprise literature. Prescribed as a revenue generation model, the for-profit subsidiary is a taxable entity that can pursue financial opportunities outside of traditional charitable constraints. Since its earnings are taxable but it pays tax on them (just as any other for-profit would do), it has no limits associated with tax-exempt status. Of course, the use of the for-profit subsidiary status can bring some of its own problems. Thus, prior to creating or spinning off a for-profit subsidiary, a nonprofit would be wise to consider the implications of the following potential issues.

- New places, new faces

    Entering a profit-oriented marketplace means a different set of competitors. In particular, when nonprofits enter for-profit markets they will be met by competition from for-profit organizations already in that market. These for-profits may well have more experience in this operating environment, giving them certain competitive advantages. Further, it is likely existing organizations in this new market will have developed at least some form of an established customer base. In order to be profitable in such an environment, nonprofits will need to make up significant ground in both of these areas.

- Capacity 2.0

Management and staff of the parent nonprofit organization may need to develop new or additional skills that will be required to succeed in the new business in the new operating environment. The extent of the adjustment will be partially dictated by staffing decisions for the subsidiary. If staff and management of the parent will be redeployed to work in the new subsidiary, they will need to adjust to the orientation of working in a for-profit environment—and this may be a major adjustment. The employees of the for-profit will need to have the capacity to address what are likely to be different marketing techniques, financial management systems, and sales processes. Of course, the specific skills needed for each of these areas will be determined by the subsidiary's type of business; some will be highly transferable and others will not. Further, if staff members are redeployed from the nonprofit to the subsidiary, will important functions in the parent organization be in danger of being shortchanged or ignored? I have seen nonprofit executive directors invest so much time in their new subsidiaries that their core nonprofit activities have suffered from inattention and neglect—to the detriment of the parent's performance. If new staff are hired and will run the new venture autonomously, top management also should determine how the two entities will connect and coexist. Will the subsidiary develop a unique culture or adopt the parent organization's culture? How will compensation and benefits need to differ? How much, if any, collaboration or coordination is to take place between the nonprofit and for-profit subsidiary? Appropriate answers to these questions will be critical to success.

Other Enterprise Options

Nonprofit social enterprises are not confined to program activities. Many nonprofit social enterprises have successfully generated revenues from activities that are not directly involved with their programming. Three increasingly common enterprise opportunities of this type are

- Cause-related marketing (CRM)
- Licensing
- Asset reappropriation

Each of these strategies involves the utilization of an organization's assets in a new way. CRM and licensing leverage a nonprofit's brand through relationships with for-profit organizations. Asset reappropriation involves the use of organizational assets for commercial revenue generation. Each of these is described below.

Cause-Related Marketing (CRM)

How many times have you visited a grocery store around Thanksgiving or another holiday and, at the checkout counter, the cashier asks if you would like to make a donation to the local food pantry? If you answered more than zero, then you have experienced a form of CRM. The question for a nonprofit leader is, When does CRM make sense?

Cause-related marketing is defined as "a mutually beneficial collaboration between a corporation and a nonprofit in which their respective assets are combined to: create shareholder and social value, connect with a range of constituents,...and communicate the shared values of both organizations" (Foundation Center, 2010). Research on CRM has validated the potential value of a mutual-benefit relationship as described in the definition and, more specifically, research has found that CRM between organizations with similar purposes improves customer perceptions of the for-profit organization (Pracejus and Olsen, 2004; Barone et al., 2000).

There are a multitude of examples of CRM success. The initial example cited by the Foundation Center was between American Express and the Statue of Liberty. American Express launched a campaign in 1983 that donated to the restoration of the Statue of Liberty one cent for every purchase on one of their credit cards. As a result, usage increased 28 percent (Foundation Center, 2010). In a more recent CRM type of collaboration, telecommunications firm Sprint Nextel donated two dollars to the Nature Conservatory for each Samsung reclaimed phone that was sold (http://causerelatedmarketing.blogspot.com/).

These examples demonstrate two critical points for nonprofits considering a CRM strategy. First, to attract for-profit partners, the nonprofit needs strong brand identity. A strong brand is critical so the for-profit's customers identify (and value) the nonprofit cause. Second, it is more useful for a nonprofit to seek for-profit partners whose businesses have some mission or service commonality. For example, the link between recycled telephones and an environmental organization offered such synergy for the Sprint-Nature Conservancy relationship. The key here is that not every for-profit will be a good CRM partner. A mutually beneficial relationship is contingent on some form of common purpose.

Brand Licensing

Let's go back to the grocery store setting we described in the CRM section. As you fill your cart with your favorite items you recognize that some of the items you have selected have the American Heart Association brand and logo. This is illustrative of another form of partnership, brand licensing. Under such relationships, nonprofits license the use of their brand in a business's marketing for a fee.

Similar to CRM, the success of brand licensing is contingent on a strong nonprofit brand and consistency between the nonprofit's mission and the for-profit product. This may appear to be a sure-fire social enterprise strategy, but it is important to remember that connecting your nonprofit brand and identity with a for-profit organization can open the door to problems. If the for-profit product performs poorly or the business misrepresents an aspect of a product that carries the nonprofit brand, the damage affects the nonprofit. Even in cases of no impropriety, failure of the nonprofit to conduct due diligence may lead to a partnership that conflicts with the core values of the nonprofit. In these cases, the nonprofit appears to "sell out" for money and the result can be loss of trust, credibility, or worse.

Asset Reappropriation

Unlike CRM and brand licensing, which are enterprising strategies using a nonprofit's soft assets, asset reappropriation involves finding alternative uses for tangible assets. Too often nonprofits look at their assets through overly narrow lenses: a building, for example, is only a place to implement core mission activities, or land is merely green space that adds to the aesthetic quality of the campus.

A strategic look at these same assets may uncover a possible revenue opportunity or stream not previously considered. For example, Drumm Farm is a Missouri nonprofit originally started as a boys' home in the early 1900s. As the founding family passed away and perceptions of the roles of boys' homes in society changed, Drumm experienced a significant decline in clients. What at one point was a robust campus with extensive acreage and buildings full to capacity began to wither away. Hampered with severely depreciating assets leading to ever-greater cash flow problems, the Drumm Farm executive director and board of directors revaluated their use and began to redeploy their property assets. Instead of leaving their buildings empty, they created a social service campus and rented the buildings to local nonprofits. Further, realizing that their greatest asset was property, they developed a lease agreement with a local golf course management company. The management company converted a segment of the Drumm Farm land into a golf course, operates the new course, and pays the nonprofit an annual fee (that is, lease). This venture has provided a significant source of new income that Drumm has been able to use to help fund its core mission operations.

Of course not every nonprofit has an abundance of land and empty buildings. But almost all nonprofits do have some assets that may have potential as a source of additional revenue. It is important to ensure that redeployment of the assets should generate income that will exceed (by some significant margin) the expense involved in redeploying the asset. For example, if it takes $1,000 of time to negotiate the use of the asset, you should require the venture to generate profit exceeding that $1,000 by an appropriate margin. Further, you may not need to manage the use of the asset to generate revenues. In the Drumm Farm example, Drumm staff did not manage the golf course or the organizations in the buildings. Lease agreements included management responsibilities. This allowed Drumm Farm to earn revenues without incurring the expense of management or oversight.

Enterprise Planning

Thus far, this chapter has discussed in relatively broad terms some of the options for social enterprise. Of course, to take these options and develop them into a useful social enterprise that benefits the nonprofit organization requires additional planning and development, and that is the focus of this section of the chapter. It is important to understand that effective enterprise planning and development flows from and builds on the broader organizational strategizing and planning processes explained by John Bryson in Chapter Nine of this handbook. In many cases, the development and implementation of a new enterprise would constitute a strategy from the nonprofit's overall strategic plan. The planning and development process explained in this chapter will be most useful if it is implemented as an outgrowth of such a strategic plan.

Prior to beginning enterprise planning, nonprofit leaders need to recognize the preconceptions and commitments associated with the process. A quick survey of any group of individuals who have participated in planning exercises in the past will reveal that many have had less than positive experiences. Common among planning complaints are, "It's a lot of talk with no action" and "There are more important things I could do with my time." It is essential that the planning process be planned and organized well, and that it make effective use of participants' time and input. As discussed earlier in the chapter, the amount of time demanded of participants and (especially) executives will be influenced by the decision to use a consultant or process facilitator. However, even with external help, it is essential to recognize that a well-developed process will require that key participants devote an adequate amount of time to the process, time that will be in addition to their existing work responsibilities.

The enterprise planning process must begin with consideration of the current state of the organization. Organization leaders must have the answer to the question, Where are we today? In an earlier section of this chapter, I outlined the key elements of this type of initial discussion—discussion about mission impact and relevance, characteristics of the nonprofit's operating environment, financial and revenue implications, and organizational capacity to implement the enterprise. The decision to proceed with enterprise planning assumes that those initial deliberations resulted in a conclusion that the context for enterprise development is positive and that a social enterprise strategy has potential for benefiting the nonprofit.

Overall, there are three levels of planning that are germane to the process of evaluating and planning a social enterprise: strategic planning, feasibility assessment, and business planning. A summary of the three levels is provided in Table 20.1. Each of these levels of planning has its own focus, and each adds its own unique value to the development of the enterprise.

TABLE 20.1. LINKING ENTERPRISE PROCESS AND PRACTICE

Planning Type	Purpose	Role in Enterprise Development Process
Strategic planning	Disciplined effort to produce fundamental decisions and actions shaping the nature and direction of an organization's (or other entity's) activities within legal bounds (see Bryson, Chapter Nine of this volume).	An organization with no specific direction would begin with strategic planning. This comprehensive approach would identify multiple organizational strategies, including options for social enterprise.
Feasibility study	Assess the viability of an opportunity, and usually serves as a precursor to a business plan.	Explore an enterprise idea (usually from the strategic planning process) and assess how well it would fit and operate within the organization (or linked to the organization, if developed as a subsidiary). The idea is formed and needs to be examined through a feasibility process.
Business planning	The final type of planning that leads to implementation, the business plan specifies in relatively great detail how the enterprise will be organized, managed, financed, staffed, and operated. It specifies goals and provides time-based projections of financial, market, and operational performance for the enterprise.	Assuming the feasibility study process suggests that the idea is viable and attractive, the nonprofit would develop a business plan for the enterprise. This will serve as a guiding document for the initial three to five years of operation.

The remainder of this section of the chapter explains the sequence and key elements that comprise the seven stages of activity that will be important to a successful enterprise planning process. These seven stages or elements are

- Planning your planning
- Organizational assessment
- Environmental assessment
- Strategy design
- Financial considerations
- Implementation
- Evaluation

Planning Your Planning

The beginning of the planning process starts with an organizing stage. Similar to the themes Bryson describes in his Chapter Nine outline of the planning-to-plan process, critical questions to address during this stage include

1. Who will be on the planning team?
2. What is the purpose and goal(s) of the planning process?
3. What is the time line and what are the target dates for the process?
4. How often will the planning team meet?

The composition of the planning team is critical to the overall success of the process. The key is to bring to the table the people who have important knowledge to inform the planning of the potential enterprise. Inclusion of executive leadership plus a mix of board and staff is important because it combines the strategic leadership and perspective of the board and senior executive(s) with the operational and tactical organizational knowledge of staff. The exact mix will vary by organization and opportunity. Regardless, board members provide a valuable perspective and should be included in the planning process; often board members bring knowledge, skill sets, and experiences that staff do not possess. In addition to board and staff, some organizations also invite selected key stakeholders to participate on the planning team. These stakeholders may be previous board members, past clients, or close collaborators. It should be noted that involving individuals outside the organization may require additional norming processes to ensure the team comes together and is "pulling" in the same direction.

After the planning team is created, the plan-to-plan shifts focus to aligning the intentions of all the members. The first step in this process is developing a goal. The goal of the planning process will be defined by the purpose of the proposed social enterprise. For example, if the process is the result of a collaborator approaching your organization with a social enterprise idea, the planning process goal would be to assess the viability of the idea. Alternatively, if the process is the result of a strategic plan strategy that directs the organization to create a new earned-income enterprise, the planning process goal would be to develop enterprise options and then proceed to feasibility assessment. The key purpose of the goal definition is to provide a standard by which planning progress can be assessed and to help ensure all team members are working toward a common purpose.

Based on the planning goal, the planning team should establish milestones and timelines for the planning process. The planning process as a whole should have a finite end point. One pitfall many nonprofits encounter as they plan a social enterprise is perpetual planning. Seeking a level of certainty not feasible, some nonprofits continue to plan with no end date. Planning team fatigue eventually sets in and the process fizzles with no outcome. The long-term impact of these endless processes is evident when the organization begins to plan again. Team members and other stakeholders will be reticent to engage in a process they fear will have no end.

In order to avoid this trap, establish decision-making deadlines at the beginning. The deadlines should include the timing of a final decision on whether or not to pursue the enterprise, as well as intermediate deadlines for completion of stages such as the situational analysis. When considering time lines, it is important to achieve a balance between enough time to complete your work and time frames short enough to maintain planning momentum. No rule of thumb exists on how long an enterprise planning process should last. However, your plan will be built on certain assumptions and if your processes extend for too long those assumptions may change.

Finally, the plan-to-plan addresses the frequency of team meetings. The number of team meetings is not as important as how the meeting time is spent. Research should be conducted and summarized outside of meetings. This allows meeting time to focus on interpretation and analysis of the data. After broad enterprise strategies are developed, it may be useful to break the full team into a set of smaller subproject work teams. These work teams (composed of fewer members) will investigate specific areas of a strategy and bring information back to the full planning team for further analysis and planning. The work team model maybe useful for making effective use of specialized skill sets of individual planning team members.

Organizational and Environmental Assessments

The foundation of successful planning is research. Research enables nonprofit leaders to have a full understanding of the organization's capacities, effectiveness, and efficiencies. In an organizational context, research is often referred to as assessment. During a social enterprise planning process, assessment has dual foci: internal and external. Because the motivations for each are unique I will deal with them separately.

Internal Assessment. Internal assessment, sometimes taking the form of an organizational audit, is designed to identify organizational capacity and assets and identify organizational weaknesses. Operating a social enterprise requires specific capacities, capacities unique from traditional nonprofit activity. It is important that these capacity needs be clearly identified at the outset of this process. Then the organizational assessment should take care to assess whether the necessary organizational capacities and systems are in place to support the enterprise.

There are a multitude of assessment tools available to nonprofit organizations, and some will be more relevant or useful than others (for an overall discussion of various tools available for organization capacity assessment, see Bartczak, 2005). Assessment value needs to be judged on the basis of the information the organization needs to know in order to evaluate its capacity for the specific enterprise in question. Some types of enterprise call for very specific capacity, others do not. General assessments, such as the McKinsey Capacity Assessment (Bartczak, 2005), focus on an overall set of organizational capacity elements. The McKinsey assessment provides a vehicle for an organization's leaders to assess seven general categories:

1. Organization mission and vision (aspirations)
2. Strategy
3. Organizational skills
4. Human resources
5. Systems and infrastructure
6. Organizational structure
7. Culture

Tailoring an assessment such as McKinsey to a social enterprise process often requires a nonprofit leader to add additional assessment areas. However, every process should provide a systematic basis by which to assess each of the following capacity elements:

• Financial management

Social enterprise management requires cost accounting, breakeven analysis, and revenue projections. Running a social enterprise involves accounting for transaction revenues. Unlike grants and donations, transaction revenues are collected directly from the client (or a third party in some cases). Consequently your assessment should examine whether or not staff members are knowledgeable about transaction receivables management, breakeven analysis, and unit cost analysis (see the other chapters of Part Four of this handbook and especially Chapter Twenty-two for a substantive discussion of these and related processes).

- Customer relationships

  Traditional nonprofit management has a focus on quality that at least equals that of a for-profit business. However, equal does not mean the same. The relationship with and behavior of a client who seeks services from a soup kitchen is different from the relationship and behavior of a free-market customer who may purchase services. The free-market customer presumably has options from which to choose, and this creates a need for the supplier (that is, the enterprise) to develop a relationship with the customer. The assessment process for a nonprofit considering a social enterprise must evaluate existing capacities for customer relationship management. In addition, it will be very important to determine staff's ability to engage in market research and analysis (for example, to collect and synthesize information about customer characteristics; see Chapter Eleven of this volume for in-depth discussion on markets, market research, and market decision making.)

- Human resources

  The human resource functions of a nonprofit focus on recruiting, retaining, and motivating qualified personnel, board members, and volunteers. Comparable to the comments regarding the financial management and customer relationship topics, social enterprise makes demands relevant to the field of human resources. Enterprise planners should consider the ability of human resource personnel and systems to attract new employees for the enterprise with backgrounds in transactional businesses. For example, a social enterprise program director should have some background in financial management and marketing, and the agency's human resources systems will have to adapt to meet the needs of people with these (potentially) new capabilities. (See the chapters in Part Five of this handbook for substantive discussion of the functions and capacities of human resource systems.)

- Strategic leadership

  Even as it implements a social enterprise, mission must be the primary focus of a nonprofit organization. Nonetheless, the elevated importance of transactional revenues in the social enterprise process demands that members of the nonprofit's executive leadership team (executive and key board leaders) have some capacity in this area. Related to this, at least some members of this group should have knowledge of and experience in providing oversight of commercial activities of the type that would be central to the proposed enterprise.

The four capacity areas discussed above do not constitute an exhaustive list. Other areas of concern will relate to the focus of the proposed enterprise. For example, will the enterprise operate in an area governed by professional regulatory or licensure authorities (for example, admission to practice law or medicine)? It is essential to identify the additional areas of capacity that are likely to be relevant to your enterprise and implement relevant assessments in these areas.

External Assessment. An external organizational assessment for a social enterprise does not vary dramatically from external assessments any nonprofit would conduct, although a new enterprise idea may require a nonprofit to go back and redefine its relevant "external environment." During an external assessment the planning team will collect data on competitors (often similar service providers), pricing models and practices, client characteristics, key stakeholder perspectives, and other factors (such as legislation) that are relevant to the venture. The goal of the external assessment is to identify and understand the implications of the opportunities and threats in the new enterprise environment. In order to develop a successful strategy, the planning team must be apprised of environmental influences that will support or mitigate performance of the new venture.

Following the completion of both assessments, the planning team will analyze the information by using practices similar to those Bryson discusses in Chapter Nine. Many nonprofits will use processes such as SWOT (that is, strengths, weaknesses, opportunities, and threats) analyses for the analysis process. Such analyses provide the initial sense of the implications for enterprise viability or acceptability, and development of this information into strategic decisions is the essence of the next stage of the enterprise planning process. The most promising venture ideas will capitalize on synergies between existing organizational capacities and environmental opportunities. Of course the real world rarely affords us such utopian scenarios. More likely, analysis will reveal a couple of options where some capacity exists and potential threats are minimized. The next stage of planning, strategy formulation, takes these ideas and develops plans to move forward.

Strategy Formulation

Strategy formulation is the stage during which key strategic choices are made—choices about which options to pursue and how best to organize and pursue them. In the context of enterprise planning, this is the point in the process at which the nonprofit's decision makers weight the relative merits of the enterprise options and determine whether or how to proceed. In the previous stage the planning team identified a couple of possible broad directions or opportunities.

During strategy formulation the planning team develops broad programmatic maps to guide the new enterprise.

Other chapters in this book explain in significant depth the key facets of strategy development, so little space will be allocated to those topics in this chapter. For example:

- The legal and regulatory implications of social enterprise options are discussed in Chapter Two by Bruce Hopkins and Virginia Gross.
- The processes for strategy development and strategy decision making are discussed in two chapters in Part Two of this book, Chapter Eight on strategic management (by William Brown) and Chapter Nine on the strategy cycle (by John M. Bryson).
- The processes by which nonprofit leaders examine and make decisions about market opportunities (including issues of market positioning and pricing issues) are explained in detail by Brenda Gainer (Chapter Eleven), and key questions associated with portfolio analysis and enterprise development also are explored in a special section of Jeanne Bell's chapter on financial leadership (Chapter Seventeen).
- The overall topic of social entrepreneurship and the range of entrepreneurship options that exists for nonprofit organizations are discussed by Matthew Nash in Chapter Ten.

Financial Implications Planning

The next stage in the enterprise planning process involves aligning the financial dimensions of the enterprise with the strategic choices to be made. Far too many nonprofits adopt courses of action without ever making any systematic assessment of the financial implications of their choices—choices about where and how revenues are generated, and choices about where and how these resources are managed. The results of ignoring these financial aspects of our choices can range from underperformance in important mission-centric projects to an outright diversion of resources from mission to a relatively less valued activity. This stage of the planning process calls for the nonprofit's leaders to examine and prepare to make decisions regarding three key areas:

- Financing the start-up of the social enterprise, including determination of the amount of money needed to effectively start and capitalize the initial phases of operation of the new enterprise and also assessing the costs and implications of securing these essential financial resources from various sources (such as, banks, key donors, foundations, government funders, and so on)

- Financing the ongoing operations of the enterprise, including covering all ongoing operating costs, securing sources of additional operating capital, managing the costs of ongoing operations, and servicing the debt as you repay the sources of the start-up financing
- Documenting and accounting for the financial operations of the enterprise and ensuring the necessary levels of accountability and transparency for both the social enterprise and its relationship (overlap and separation) with the host nonprofit

The actual methods by which these assessments, plans, and decisions are made are explained in great depth in Part Four of this handbook. The essential point I wish to make in this chapter is that these all are important elements of the initial social enterprise planning process, and there are critical decisions to be made—decisions that can have lasting implications for both the social enterprise *and* the larger nonprofit organization that is the host or parent entity for the enterprise.

Financial discussions can be difficult for nonprofit leaders. Because mission is (and must be) the central focus for a nonprofit organization's executives, financial discussions often end up being of secondary concern (if they even receive that much consideration). However, when it comes to social enterprises, ignoring financial matters can have disastrous results. At worst, social enterprise financial problems can end up undermining all that the organization is doing to maximize mission accomplishment! I previously described the story of a nonprofit organization that decided to make salad dressing and the terrible costs the organization incurred because it failed to account for indirect costs and inaccurately understood its direct costs. Such mistakes underscore the need for nonprofits to ensure careful financial planning as they evaluate prospective social enterprises. This is especially true when the social enterprise is expected to be a profit generator.

A critical financial concern for a new social enterprise and its host organization is that of "capital structure." A nonprofit's capital structure is the mix and distribution of an organization's assets, liabilities, and net assets (Miller, 2003); a nonprofit's capital structure can create significant problems with a nonprofit's ability to develop a viable social enterprise. Capital structure essentially defines the ability of a nonprofit to undertake new projects and absorb risks (both conventional projects and potential enterprises). Stated plainly, organizations with more liquidity have more flexible capital structures that are going to be more flexible in accommodating the financial dimensions of a new social enterprise. Analysis of capital structure helps the planning team appraise fixed assets available for the new enterprise (and if there is no one on the planning team with the ability to assess this aspect of the nonprofit's capacity, the organization should secure external talent to ensure that this can be done).

In the enterprise planning process, it is essential to acknowledge that all new ventures require start-up capital. Social enterprise planning must plan for start-up funding, including attention to the amount needed to initiate the venture and to the debt service necessary to recover start-up costs. Flexible budgets (which map multiple scenarios) and breakeven analysis can provide organization leaders with insights that inform necessary cash-reserve decisions. Armed with this information, the planning team can identify potential funders for their new enterprise. When it comes to nonprofit social enterprises, the most common start-up funders tend to be the nonprofit hosts themselves (using cash reserves), individual donors, and charitable foundations. On a less frequent basis, nonprofits may find start-up support from government grants or banks.

Strategy Implementation Plan

Moving from strategy development and financial implications to strategy implementation planning can be much more involved than many nonprofits expect. At this stage, the process moves from one of assessment to one of decision and—assuming that the decision to proceed is affirmative—to the creation of the actual operational or business plan that will take the information from the earlier stages of the planning and integrate it into an operational document. The process of evaluating the feasibility of an enterprise strategy and, ultimately, creating the implementation plan requires decisions on the key issues that have been examined throughout the process, including the following:

- What services will you provide? This is an obvious question, but one that requires detail and specificity. In addition to describing the services, you must also outline the service delivery pattern. At what times of the day will you provide the services? Will the services be provided on site or at a remote location?
- Who will you sell this to? Who is the target market for the program? Understanding the demographics of the target market will inform marketing strategies, pricing, and service delivery. For example, if you will be providing clinical services, your price will be influenced by reimbursement schedules of third-party payers. In addition, it is important to clarify whether the target market demands the services or whether you are providing services that will require you to create awareness. The two scenarios will require differing marketing approaches.
- How will these services be delivered and sold? Is this place-based, Internet-based, or some combination? Where will the actual business be located and what kinds of facilities will be needed?

- How will the program be structured? Will the venture be a program of the existing organization or will the venture be a separate subsidiary?
- Who will manage and who will staff the enterprise? This decision is grounded in the internal assessment. How many people will you need, and will you hire new staff or use (or redeploy) existing staff? Implicit in this discussion is the issue of capacity. If you use existing staff, what additional capacities will you need to develop? If you hire new staff, what will you pay them (for example, comparable to nonprofit salaries or to for-profit market rates)?
- What are the financial plans for the enterprise? For example, what are the revenue projections for the first three years? What is your profit estimate for the first three years? When will the enterprise break even? How much money do you need, and why? How will the money be repaid?

In order to develop the strategy implementation plan, the planning team may need to involve other key staff members (if they are not already on the planning team). Knowledgeable input from key staff is critical in this process.

The strategy implementation plan often is created in the form of a business plan for the new social enterprise. Business plans are documents that bring all of this information together and present it in a well-organized and complete manner—one single place that leaders and managers can use as the key reference point as they proceed with the implementation process. There are many formats for business plans, and the Internet resource site for this handbook provides examples and a number of resources and links. A typical business plan will include the following specific information (drawn from Massarsky, 2005; the list below could serve as the table of contents for such a document):

- Executive summary
- Description of the business (including a mission statement)
- Industry and market analysis (including forecast of demand)
- Marketing plan
- Governance and management plan
- Operations plan (including staffing)
- Financial plan (including projections and forecasts)
- Risk assessment and contingency plan
- Appendix (supporting documents)

There are a number of books and guides that have been written specifically for nonprofit enterprises. These can be especially useful because they contain sections that are not typically found in traditional business plans, such as a description of the mission of the nonprofit, its purpose and goals for the social enterprise, and the operational, financial, and legal relationships between the nonprofit and the new enterprise (Massarsky, 2005).

Evaluation

Similar to any planning process, the enterprise planning process should include a process for evaluation and refinement of plans and operations. It is important to note that evaluation plans should be developed before the social enterprise planning process concludes. In addition to program metrics, metrics of enterprise financial performance also must be included (examples of financial metrics are profit and loss, marginal costs, and unit costs for both outputs and outcomes). Evaluation is addressed in depth in two chapters in this volume: John Clayton Thomas explains program evaluation and outcomes assessment in Chapter Fifteen, and Vic Murray explains the process of assessing organizational effectiveness in Chapter Sixteen. Both chapters offer important guidance regarding processes that are appropriate to enterprise evaluation, and the reader is encouraged to incorporate their information as they develop the evaluation part of the enterprise plan.

Moving Forward

Social enterprise continues to be a source of both excitement and intimidation to nonprofit leaders as they explore the most useful ways to ensure that their organizations remain viable and responsive for years to come. Implemented effectively in appropriate contexts, social enterprise is another important strategy that the nonprofit sector has to use to address the needs of its clients and communities. Used less appropriately, social enterprise has the potential to derail an organization and undermine the trust it has earned. As discussed throughout this chapter, social enterprise simply is one unique strategic option among many strategic options.

Nonprofits should not begin their consideration of enterprise strategies with the assumption that they "ought to" create a social enterprise. Legitimate enterprise development requires thorough and thoughtful assessment and deliberation and due diligence by nonprofit governing boards and executives. The process begins with an accurate assessment of the organization's mission and critical issues, and a thorough understanding of markets, structure, and culture is imperative to the successful development of a viable social enterprise.

The content of this chapter serves two purposes. First, the framework of social enterprise is intended to be useful to academics and practitioners as they pursue their equal yet diverse interests. For both groups, the discussion of markets, structure, and strategy is intended to help organize the diverse aspects of social enterprise in a meaningful way that will enhance understanding. Second, the chapter is designed to serve as a reference tool to guide thinking as practitioners consider social enterprise options.

As we, academics and practitioners alike, continue to grow and develop with the sector, we have much to learn and share regarding social enterprise. Academics will continue to explore issues of structure, finance, markets, and culture through carefully constructed research. Practitioners will also conduct their own form of research and development as they explore enterprising new ways to fulfill their missions and sustain their organizations. Together we can add to the growing knowledge of the sector as we help ensure that nonprofits remain vital and viable as they provide the critical services their clients and communities need.

Note

1. Consistent with the definitions in Chapter Ten, "social enterprise" and "social entrepreneurship" are *not* used as synonymous terms in this chapter.

References

Alter, K. *Social Enterprise Typology*. Retrieved February 5, 2010, from http://www.virtueventures.com/setypology. 2009.

Barone, M. J., Miyazaki, A. D., and Taylor, K. A. "The Influence of Cause-Related Marketing on Consumer Choice: Does One Good Turn Deserve Another?" *Journal of the Academy of Marketing Science*, 2000, *28*(2), 248–262.

Bartczak, L. (ed.) *Funder's Guide to Organizational Assessment: Tools, Processes, and Their Use in Building Capacity*. St. Paul, Minn.: Fieldstone Alliance, 2005.

Blackwood, A., Wing, K., and Pollak, T. H. Retrieved February 10, 2010, from http://www.urban.org/url.cfm?ID=411664. 2008.

Dart, R. "The Legitimacy of Social Enterprise." *Nonprofit Management and Leadership*, 2004, *14*(4), 411–424.

Dees, J. G., Emerson, J., and Economy, P. *Enterprising Nonprofits*. New York: Wiley, 2001.

Foster, W., and Bradach, J. "Should Nonprofits Seek Profits?" *Harvard Business Review*, 2005, *83*(2).

Foundation Center. "Frequently Asked Questions." Retrieved February 10, 2010, from http://foundationcenter.org/getstarted/faqs/html/cause_marketing.html. 2010.

Internal Revenue Service. *Nonprofit Charitable Organization and Domestic Private Foundation Information Returns, and Exempt Organization Business Income Tax Returns: Selected Financial Data. Expanded Version*. Retrieved from http://www.irs.gov/taxstats/article/0,,id=175876,00.html. May 15, 2010.

Kerlin, J. "Social Enterprise in the United States and Europe: Understanding and Learning from the Differences." *Voluntas: International Journal of Voluntary and Nonprofit Organizations*, 2006, *17*(3), 247–263.

LeRoux, K. M. "What Drives Nonprofit Entrepreneurship? A Look at Budget Trends of Metro Social Service Agencies." *American Review of Public Administration*, 2005, *35*(4), 350–362.

Lynch, K., and Wall, J. *Mission, Inc.: The Practitioners Guide to Social Enterprise*. San Francisco: Berrett-Koehler, 2009.

Massarsky, C. W. "Enterprise Strategies for Generating Revenue." In R. D. Herman (ed.), *The Jossey-Bass Handbook of Nonprofit Leadership and Management* (2nd ed.). San Francisco: Jossey-Bass, 2005.

Miller, C. "Hidden in Plain Sight: Understanding Nonprofit Capital Structure." *The Nonprofit Quarterly*, 2003, Spring, 1–8.

Pracejus, J. W., and Olsen, G. D. "The Role of Brand/Cause Fit in the Effectiveness of Cause-Related Marketing Campaigns." *Journal of Business Research*, 2004, *57*(6), 635–640.

CHAPTER TWENTY-ONE

MANAGING THE CHALLENGES OF GOVERNMENT CONTRACTS

Steven Rathgeb Smith

During the last forty years, government contracting with nonprofit organizations for the delivery of important public services has risen sharply. The widespread interest in the United States and other countries in contracting with nonprofit organizations reflects many factors: pressure to reduce the costs of public service; broad interest in voluntarism, social innovation, and citizen and community engagement; and the influence of the New Public Management and "reinventing government" movements which seek to improve the efficiency and effectiveness of public services through privatization, more competition, individual choice, and decentralization (Hood, 1991; Rhodes, 1996; Lynn, 1998; Kettl, 2005; Smith and Smyth, 2010). The community connections and roots of many nonprofit organizations also are attractive to government as a vehicle for reaching politically valuable and important constituencies. From the perspective of the nonprofit organization, government contracting also can be attractive by offering greater resources, improved legitimacy in the community, and the potential to have broader and deeper impact on urgent social problems or concerns.

The author would like to gratefully acknowledge the support of the Center for Public and Nonprofit Leadership at the Georgetown Public Policy Institute and the Nancy Bell Evans Center on Nonprofits & Philanthropy at the Evans School of Public Affairs at the University of Washington in the preparation of this chapter.

Nonetheless, government contracting can have profound effects on nonprofit organization governance, program innovation, and the relationship of agencies to their local communities and the citizens using their services (Smith and Smyth, 2010; Smith, 2010a). Moreover, political, economic, and organizational trends are creating much greater uncertainty for nonprofit organizations receiving contracts: competition for contracts is growing; many governments are reducing funding (sometimes quite drastically); policymakers are expecting much higher levels of performance and accountability from nonprofits; and citizens are demanding more choice and responsiveness from nonprofits providing contracted services.

The management challenges for nonprofit agencies created by contracting in the context of an era of greater competition and uncertainty are the subject of this chapter. These challenges are discussed in detail, as are potential strategies nonprofit agencies may adopt to effectively cope with the higher accountability demands of government while successfully maintaining a sustainable, effective organization with an ongoing commitment to community building and citizen engagement. The chapter is based upon extensive research on the impact of government contracting on nonprofit organizations, primarily in the fields of social services and health care, although many of the findings and management recommendations are applicable to other types of nonprofit organizations (Smith and Lipsky, 1993; Smith, 2006, 2010a).

Background and History

Prior to the 1960s, nonprofit service agencies in the United States were primarily dependent upon private revenue from client fees, charitable donations, and endowment income. Some agencies such as child welfare organizations received public subsidies, but these agencies were nonetheless largely reliant on private funds. This funding mix changed dramatically in the 1960s with the rise of the federal role in social policy. As part of the War on Poverty, the federal government created a host of new programs and initiatives, including neighborhood health centers, community mental health centers, community action agencies, youth service agencies, and drug and alcohol treatment programs. Most of these new programs were implemented through government contracting with local nonprofit service organizations. Some of these agencies were entirely new. Existing agencies such as Catholic Charities and Lutheran Social Services also expanded their service offerings in response to the dramatic increase in federal funding support for social and health services (Smith and Lipsky, 1993).

Many existing nonprofit agencies were initially reluctant to accept government contracts due to concern that government funding might undermine the mission and autonomy of private agencies (Coughlin, 1965; Perlmutter, 1969). However, many agencies eventually accepted government contracts. This shift occurred for several reasons. First, some federal programs were matching programs so a private agency might be able to use a 25 percent private match to obtain a 75 percent matching grant from the federal government. So at least initially, federal revenues essentially allowed the expansion of existing services. Second, some of the early federal grant programs had very loose accountability requirements so nonprofit agencies could accept the funds without onerous compliance requirements. Third, federal grants offered many agencies far more money than they could reasonably expect from private philanthropy and fees. Fourth, and related, federal funding allowed nonprofit agencies to reduce their dependence on private donations and fees, allowing agencies in some cases to increase their services to disadvantaged and very needy clients. And fifth, many federal programs were structured as grants to state and local governments who then contracted with local agencies. Often, state and local government officials already had established relationships with private agencies such as Catholic Charities. With the advent of federal funding, these government officials tended to simply continue these relationships and, at least initially, did not change the terms of the existing agreements between the nonprofit agency and government (Smith, 2010a).

Thus, federal social service spending soared in the 1960s and 1970s, primarily through contracts with nonprofit human service agencies. Federal expenditures for social welfare services almost tripled between 1965 and 1970, from $812 million to $2.2 billion. Federal funding continued to expand throughout the 1970s. By 1980, federal funds accounted for 65 percent of total government spending at all levels on social welfare services, compared to 38 percent in 1965. State and local spending also rose, spurred in part by the increase in federal spending. Total spending at all levels of government (in constant 1995 dollars) for social welfare services rose from $45.2 billion in 1965 to $104.79 billion in 1980 (Bixby, 1999, pp. 92–93). A large percentage of the increase in public funding of social services was channeled through nonprofit agencies in the form of government contracts. Many state agencies relied almost exclusively on nonprofit agencies to provide services, especially new and innovative services such as community residential programs, respite care, and day treatment (Smith and Lipsky, 1993).

This increased federal role changed dramatically when the Reagan administration came to power in 1981 with a commitment to reduce federal spending. During his first year in office, President Reagan successfully achieved the enactment of the Omnibus Budget Reconciliation Act (OBRA). Key features of the legislation included an approximate 20 percent reduction in federal spending on social services, the consolidation of many different categorical federal social programs into block grants, and the decentralization of administrative responsibility for the expenditure of federal funds to state and local governments (Gutowski and Koshel, 1982).

Over time, though, federal spending rebounded. Through a variety of changes to existing law, as well as new program initiatives, funds for social and health services provided by nonprofit agencies rose again in the late 1980s and 1990s. One increasingly important source of funding of social services was Medicaid, the program created in 1965 as the health program for the poor. Until the 1980s, Medicaid was a very limited source of funding for traditional social services such as individual and family services or residential care for foster children. But starting in the 1980s, Medicaid grew in prominence as a revenue source for social services, as evident in community programs for the developmentally disabled and mentally ill. In 1980, most government funding for services for the developmentally disabled was state funding (primarily for institution-based programs). Most of this spending is now devoted to community-based programs that are typically provided by nonprofit community agencies funded primarily by Medicaid. In essence, Medicaid has supported the shift from a public institutional system for the developmentally disabled (operated by state government with state employees) to a community-based system provided by nonprofit (and to a lesser extent, for-profit) service agencies that receive government contracts (Braddock and others, 2005; Smith, 2006; Vladeck, 2003). To an increasing degree, Medicaid also funds mental health, child welfare, home care, hospices, counseling, residential foster care, drug and alcohol treatment, and services for the mentally ill (although the extent of coverage varies depending upon the state) (Geen, Sommers, and Cohen, 2005; Holahan and Yemane, 2009; Kaiser Family Foundation, 2009; Vladeck, 2003).

In addition, contracting with nonprofits grew in the aftermath of the landmark welfare reform legislation of 1996, Temporary Aid to Needy Families (TANF). As part of this legislation, the federal government created new funding for services and gave greater administrative discretion to state and local governments to spend the new money, including much greater flexibility by local administrators to shift money from cash assistance to services. With these new requirements and funding streams, the welfare rolls and the expenditure of funds on welfare-related programs dropped sharply, whereas federal funding for welfare related services rose significantly (Ways and Means Committee, 2004, pp. 7–3, 7–4; Winston and Castaneda, 2007). Overall, a large percentage of this additional service funding was spent in support of services provided by nonprofit organizations, including in day care, welfare to work, job training, and counseling. In addition to Medicaid and TANF-related funding, other federal programs for at-risk youth, community service, drug and alcohol treatment, prisoner reentry, and community care also witnessed substantial rises in funding during the 1990s and in the early 2000s.

Yet the economic crisis that began in 2008 has led to severe cutbacks in public funding of many nonprofit agencies, especially in states such as California that have been hard hit by the recession. Sources of private funding for nonprofit agencies, such as the United Way and private foundations, have limited capacity to substitute for declining government funds, especially given the sometimes-severe decrease in their own assets. This competitive and austere funding climate, though, is likely to encourage continued reliance on government contracting with nonprofit agencies. Many state and local governments, eager to save money, view contracting as a less costly way of providing needed public services. Moreover, the percentage contribution of government revenues to many nonprofit organizations remains high despite the public cutbacks. Indeed, even many of the newer entrepreneurial nonprofits such as City Year and YouthBuild depend substantially on government contracts.

A Changing and Challenging Policy and Fiscal Environment

Even before the economic crisis, nonprofit agencies receiving government contracts were facing important shifts in their funding and their relationship with other government, nonprofit, and for-profit organizations, as well as their host communities. These important developments have profoundly affected the contracting relationship, as well as the staffs and clients of nonprofit agencies. It is significant, however, that even though it had increased such funding until 2008, government has moved away from the traditional contracts that were the hallmark of the initial period of widespread government contracting in the 1960s and 1970s. In this earlier period, most nonprofit agencies did not really compete with other agencies for contracts. Most contracts were cost-reimbursement contracts that paid agencies for their costs based upon the contract terms and budget. Reimbursement was not linked to outcomes and most agencies recovered their costs (at least as specified in the contract). Little incentive existed for agencies to compete with other agencies, since contracts were unlikely to be moved from one agency to another unless egregious problems existed.

The current contracting environment is much more competitive. Contracts are increasingly performance-based, with government specifying contract goals and priorities that nonprofits are required to meet in order to receive reimbursement for their services (Behn and Kant, 1999; Blalock and Barnow, 2004; Heinrich and Choi, 2007; D. Smith, 2009; Krauskopf, forthcoming). Since the mid-1990s, performance contracting with nonprofits (and for-profits) has risen rapidly. This is due in part to the "reinventing government" and New Public Management movements, which have sparked extensive interest in improving the performance of public services, especially through more market-based strategies (Osborne and Gaebler, 1992; Hood, 1991; Lynn 1998; Behn, 2002; Behn and Kant, 1999; Smith, forthcoming 2010b). Over time, performance contracting spread to a wide variety of service categories. New York City, for instance, has restructured hundreds of millions of dollars of its contracts with social service and health agencies as performance contracts (D. Smith and Grinker, 2004; D. Smith, 2009). Some state governments have "privatized" at least some of their child welfare services by shifting public services provided by state or county staff to performance-based contracts with nonprofits with the goal of improving the efficiency and effectiveness of child welfare services (McCullough and Schmitt, 2000).

From the perspective of the nonprofit agency, performance contracts are especially consequential because they increase organizational and revenue uncertainty and because these contracts offer at least the threat of contract termination for poor performance (although in practice losing contracts is still relatively rare). Nonprofit service agencies also have an incentive to compete with their fellow agencies, since they could potentially grow through additional contracts. Also, performance contracts are usually structured so that agencies receive graduated payments as they hit their performance targets; therefore, agencies may receive less revenue than planned, thus reducing their available cash flow.

Increased competition for funding is also a direct and indirect effect of the restructuring of government support itself. In the big build-up of government contracting with nonprofits, government funding primarily flowed to nonprofits through block contracts for certain levels of service. However, many current forms of government support are tied to the client rather than the agency. The most vivid example is Medicaid, which functions like a "quasi-voucher" because eligibility is tied directly to the client (Steuerle, 2002). Agencies are reimbursed for providing qualifying services to eligible clients; their reimbursement rate is a vendor rate, whereby government will pay a certain amount for a specific service regardless of the actual costs incurred by the agency. In general, Medicaid vendor rates encourage competition for clients, since it may only be possible to generate surpluses at high levels of service volume (because each new Medicaid eligible client is more revenue for the agency at only marginally more cost). This financing arrangement is dramatically different from the traditional cost-reimbursement contract. Under the latter, agencies actually faced disincentives for service expansion because additional services added to an agency's cost without any certainty that these costs would be reimbursed.

The diversification of government support—or policy tools (Salamon, 2002; Smith, 2006)—is also evident in the growing use of vouchers for child care and housing, and tax-exempt bond money to support the capital needs of nonprofit agencies. Access to bond funding can be very competitive, although the economic crisis has greatly reduced the willingness of state and local government to support the issuance of these bonds. Nonetheless, the overall popularity of such bonds among many nonprofits and government officials means that the utilization of these bonds is likely to increase as the economy recovers.

Increased competition for contracts has also been fueled by growing competition from for-profit social and health services firms, although this competition tends to vary tremendously by the service category. Many traditional social services such as foster care, youth services, and emergency assistance remain dominated by nonprofits. However, for-profit firms now compete with nonprofit agencies in several key service categories, such as child care, home care, and community programs for the mentally ill and developmentally disabled. Many for-profits possess some notable advantages vis-à-vis nonprofits in competition for government contracts (and private fees). For example, for-profit chains have access to capital and operate at a sufficient size to enable substantial economies of scale, thus allowing them to operate at least some programs more efficiently. Further, since nonprofits are mission-based and many are small and unwilling to serve certain types of clients or certain regions, the opportunities for them to cross-subsidize their operations through growth or a diversified client mix are reduced. Many community-based nonprofits may also be very ambivalent about expansion (or even lack the capacity for expansion.) For-profits typically do not have these types of mission constraints and are thus more willing to serve a more diverse mix of clients (including controversial clients). Finally, larger for-profits may be able to use their size and bargaining power to obtain higher rates than the small community-based nonprofits (Smith, 2010).

Contracting as a Regime

This changing and more competitive environment for contracting has disrupted—or has the potential to disrupt—many longstanding relationships between government and nonprofit agencies. During the development of extensive contracting in the 1960s and 1970s, contracting tended to evolve through patterned relationships and expectations between government and nonprofit agencies that could be characterized as a "contracting regime" (that is, "a set of stable relationships that transcend simple common practice and reveal assumptions about the way the world works" [Smith and Lipsky, 1993, p. 43]). The nonprofit-government contracting relationship can be characterized as a "regime" for the following reasons. First, regimes tend to have accepted means of resolving disputes and addressing particular problems. This is evident in the tendency to rely on nonprofit organizations funded by government to address current social problems, and in the existence of accepted norms governing the interaction between nonprofit organizations and government. Second, the regime concept is helpful in illuminating the regularized patterns of interaction between government and nonprofit agencies, even when these nonprofit organizations are opposed or resistant to particular government regulations and mandates. Third, regimes are marked by continuity, and participants in regimes are mutually dependent. If participants depart from the regime norms, they are penalized, either by the dominant party or by third parties. Fourth, regimes are usually sustained and dominated by a powerful party. (For example, in international relations, this role is performed by a country whose policies and norms are accepted by other countries in the regime [Krasner, 1985]). The government-nonprofit relationship is similar; despite the mutual dependency of government and nonprofit organizations, government tends to be the more powerful in the relationship. Thus nonprofit organizations are often in the position of being forced to accept or follow the norms and policies of government (Smith and Lipsky, 1993; Considine, 2000).

The implications of the contracting regime for nonprofit management are profound. Managers of nonprofit agencies receiving government contracts are not free agents but are linked in an ongoing relationship with government, which at once constrains their behavior as well as provides certain incentives for managerial action. As Considine (2000) observes, the specific characteristics of the contracting regime also may vary by country, depending upon the prevailing public policies.

In part, the vulnerability of nonprofit agencies within the context of the contracting regime reflects the particular features of nonprofit finance, especially in the fields of social and health services. Nonprofit agencies, especially grassroots community organizations such as battered women's shelters, poverty agencies, and youth organizations, emerge through the collective efforts of like-minded individuals interested in addressing a particular social problem. Typically, these organizations are dependent on a mix of small cash and in-kind donations. As a result, they tend to be significantly undercapitalized. Overcoming the capitalization dilemma is hampered by the preference of private donors for specific programs and projects. This undercapitalization can be exacerbated by many banks' reluctance to loan money to nonprofits, especially smaller agencies. Such constraints on building an adequate capital base make it difficult to weather disruptions in cash flow. When nonprofit organizations are young, mostly volunteer, and small, a cash flow interruption may represent a minor problem. But when a nonprofit becomes involved in a contractual arrangement with government, the implications of cash flow disruptions often are more serious. Contracting typically requires more resources, such as more paid staff with higher salaries for the agency—hence much greater cash flow demands. Thus, shortfalls in client censuses, management miscues, payment delays, or unexpected expenses are much more disruptive and problematic. This is especially true in the current recessionary economic climate.

The cash flow problem, as well as the more general challenge of generating adequate revenue, is exacerbated by a common characteristic of the contracting regime: the inability to secure contracts that fully fund the agency's costs. The current economic crisis has definitely aggravated this already serious problem. Given the current revenue shortfalls faced by the public sector, government officials across the country routinely set rates for nonprofit providers at levels insufficient to cover their costs. Indeed, even before the current recessionary crisis, rates were often inadequate. This may be because over a period of years the contract amount has lost ground to inflation and government budget cuts. Or a nonprofit manager may have underestimated the costs of implementing a contract or agency expenses may rise unexpectedly and exceed contract revenues.

Underfunded contracts put nonprofit managers in a delicate position: give up the contract, with its implications for staff layoffs and shrinkage of the agency, or continue with the contract, albeit at an underfunded level. Since nonprofit executives are rarely rewarded for staff layoffs and the accompanying organizational turmoil, most nonprofit executives elect to keep the contract. To compensate for revenue shortfalls from contracts, nonprofit managers often try one or more of several strategies: (1) diversify their government contracts so they can obtain greater economies of scale; (2) seek private donations from individuals or corporations; (3) obtain foundation grants; and (4) increase earned income from more commercial revenue sources (for example, from rental income or technical assistance services).

Obtaining additional revenue in the current economic climate is especially challenging, particularly given the sharp increase in the number of nonprofit organizations in existence (NCCS, 2009). Given this increase, intense competition exists for private donations and government contracts. Public and private funders also expect contract agencies to be much more performance-oriented, and this places additional demands on the capacity of agencies to provide services. The desirability of a diversified revenue base and a sophisticated administrative infrastructure is a major reason that large agencies may have a competitive advantage in the current contracting environment. Only the large agencies have the credit lines, the endowments, or the fundraising capacity to compensate for the inevitable revenue shortfalls and cash flow difficulties experienced by nonprofit agencies (Smith and Smyth, 2010).

One other important change in the contracting environment is the advent of managed care in many government contracted social and health services. Managed care has been widely employed with hospital services since the 1970s. Managed care is where a third-party organization (for-profit or non-profit) such as a health maintenance organization "manages" the health care for a population of patients with the goal of improving the efficiency and delivery of care. Beginning in the 1990s, many state and local governments started to contract with third-party organizations to manage the services provided by government in areas such as child welfare or mental health (Frank, McGuire, and Newhouse, 1995; Burns et al., 1999; Frank and Glied, 2006; Courtney, 2000). For instance, a county government that had previously contracted directly with local nonprofit agencies for community mental health services now may provide a fixed sum of money to a "managed care organization" that will be responsible for managing the mental health services for a specified number of clients. The managed care organization then subcontracts with local nonprofit (and for-profit) service agencies to provide the actual community mental health services. From the perspective of the nonprofit agency, this contractual arrangement is inherently more uncertain and less reliable than traditional contracting relationships.

The greater uncertainty of the contracting environment for nonprofits has exacerbated longstanding problems that may occur in the contract renewal process. Delays and problems in contract renewal occur for many reasons: a state legislature may be deadlocked, requiring that the state agencies suspend final action on contract renewals until the available funding for contracts is known; key government contract administrators may have left or been replaced; an election may be under way, generating funding uncertainty and job insecurity with resultant ripple effects on the contracting process.

Other reasons for delay may be more strategic. For example, government contract administrators may delay the process of contract renewal in order to gain greater compliance by nonprofit agencies with contract terms and expectations. Alternatively, government administrators may use their ability to expedite the contract-renewal process, to at least some degree, as a way of currying favor with nonprofit contract agencies. This assistance may then be remembered in future negotiations.

The uncertainties of the contract renewal process are masked somewhat by the relatively high rate of contract renewal. A domestic violence agency awarded a contract in 1995 is likely to still have a contract in 2005, barring serious quality problems or major shocks to the provider system. Nonetheless, the renewal process can be highly frustrating. Nonprofit managers may be unclear as to the exact amount of the new contract. And due to government funding cutbacks, a renewed contract might well be for a lower amount than the previous one. Also, government officials may decide to rewrite the contract upon renewal. For instance, a child welfare agency might have a contract for several years to provide counseling services to children. But a change in political priorities might lead state administrators to use contract renewal as an opportunity to restructure the agreement so that the child welfare agency, if it wants to keep the contract, would be required to provide (for example) intervention services to abused and neglected children. Other examples of substantive changes in contracts by state officials include requiring nonprofit agencies to serve a larger geographical area, giving part of a contract to another agency, reducing the administrative costs allowed on the contract, or adopting new policies on client referrals and reimbursement.

Nonprofit managers, at least theoretically, have the option of refusing to accept the terms of the contract or to abide the long delays often accompanying contract renewal. But this can be very problematic. First, the proliferation of nonprofit (and for-profit) service agencies gives government administrators more service options (although the number of agencies varies tremendously across geographic areas). Thus, nonprofit managers know that if they resist the renegotiation of a contract, many other agencies are likely to be eager to take the contract on the terms stipulated by government. Second, competition for private charitable funds, which might serve as alternatives to contract funds, is fierce. Moreover, most foundation and United Way grants tend to be short-term and for much smaller amounts than government funds. And raising private funds with appeals to individuals is a long-term process that usually cannot substitute for lost government funds. Third, nonprofit agencies often find that the only way they can fulfill their mission to address a particular problem, such as juvenile delinquency or child abuse, is through government funding; private funding is either unavailable or inadequate for the agency's needs.

Strategic Management in an Era of Competition and Accountability

Despite the increasingly uncertain and competitive environment for nonprofits contracting with government, many nonprofit executives are nonetheless successful in managing their agencies and their relationships with government. Their success requires sustained attention to agency governance, effective leadership, broad and sustained community support, and ongoing advocacy on behalf of the agency and its clients. These strategies are discussed in more detail in the following pages.

Rethinking Agency Governance and Management

An effective board of directors of a nonprofit agency serves as a key connecting link between the organization and the local community. This board role is especially critical if community-based service agencies are to effectively represent their communities and service users. Yet contracting poses serious problems for many boards. Most board members tend to be unfamiliar with contracting and the intricacies of the contracting process. Consequently, board members may be unable or unwilling to exercise effective oversight over agency contracts.

Significantly, contracting also requires the agency to develop and maintain effective new systems of accountability to document and report on expenditures and clients, and this almost inevitably requires greater staff specialization and a more formal structure and organization. Thus, the administrative staff needs to expand and become more professionalized (Hwang and Powell, 2009). Given the increased emphasis on performance contracting and outcome measurement, nonprofits also need to invest in sophisticated data collection and information technology (IT) capacity. As the paid staff expands and the demands on the agency's resources grow, the board may not be well positioned to set the agenda for the agency, especially if they are highly dependent on contract revenues. The board may be relegated to a position of supporting the executive's initiatives, rather than the executive implementing the board's directives and policies. The danger for the organization inherent in this kind of shift is that the board may encounter some unpleasant surprises. The executive, in the pursuit of contract revenues, may obligate the agency to contracts that are underfunded or ill-advised. Board involvement in the agency may wither as board members find that their governance roles are quite restricted. And as board involvement declines, management mistakes or morale problems may go undetected until a crisis develops.

Other types of management problems may develop from conflicts over agency mission. For example, the board of a relatively young nonprofit may comprise the founding members of the organization who are deeply committed to a specific mission and vision. In some cases, to secure additional contract funds, the executive may try to steer the organization in a direction that is quite different from the board's vision for the agency. The result may be protracted negotiations between the board and staff about the agency's future. Sometimes the outcome is the resignation of some board members or the ouster of the chief executive as the board and staff compete to define the agency's future mission. Alternatively, the executive may serve in the key role in agency governance until a crisis develops, such as inadequate cash flow, staff discontent, or lost contracts. Then, in response, the board may intervene to exert greater control and oversight over agency operations. Although the board often withdraws to its previous role as the crisis eases, in other cases the board simply may be unable to find an appropriate executive director and so the board will retain a major role in day-to-day agency management, as well as the overall agenda setting for the organization.

There is a general tendency among nonprofits with substantial contracts to see a shift in influence from the board to the executive director and his or her staff, although the extent of this change will differ with organizations' individual circumstances. This kind of change, and the organizational problems it can create, can be especially visible in new community-based organizations with roots in the informal sector of community members, neighbors, and social movements. For these organizations professional management often represents values and policies antithetical to the original purposes of the organization (Wilson, 1973; Smith and Lipsky, 1993).

To a certain extent, the enhanced role of the executive and the professionalization of the staff is part of the natural process of organizational growth and development (Carlson and Donahue, 2003; Chait, Ryan, and Taylor, 2005). However, many boards have successfully addressed the organizational challenges of contracting in ways that strengthen board governance and productive board-staff relations. First, the board can recruit individuals with knowledge of contracting for board membership. Second, the board can become more engaged in advocacy on behalf of the agency with government officials—a process that can help provide board members with valuable information and contacts on the agency's contracts and important public policy matters that affect the agency. Third, the board can broaden its membership to include more consumer or community representatives. These individuals can supply useful feedback to the rest of the board on agency performance and provide very valuable input on the quality and impact of agency programs. Indeed, community participation can be critical to effective management and governance (Smith, 2010; Crosby, 2003). Chapter Five of this book provides important additional information on development and maintenance of effective nonprofit boards.

Finding the Right Executive

Given the changing environment for contracting, the quality of executive leadership in nonprofits is more important than ever to the ability of nonprofits to provide effective and efficient programming. In the current era of budget scarcity, even a relatively small management mistake can create a financial crisis for the agency. This new environment places significant pressure on the executive director to effectively manage both the internal operations and the external network of public and private funders. Ideally, agency executives should be very knowledgeable of government contracting and financial management, as well as sensitive to the agency's mission. Given the multiple economic and organizational challenges facing executive directors, the process of selecting an executive director can often reveal underlying differences among members of the board and staff about the agency's future. Moreover, many individuals with the credentials necessary to cope with the management complexities of contracting may not be well attuned to the subtleties of the agency's relationship with its surrounding community or consumers. This may be exacerbated in the current era of funding cutbacks, when executive directors may need to make difficult programmatic or administrative decisions.

The ideal type of executive for a nonprofit service agency cannot be determined without understanding the particular characteristics and needs of the organization. Although it may no longer be sufficient to have a respected clinician with relatively little management training or experience as an executive, it is equally true that a board of directors would be in error if it simply sought an executive whose primary qualification was a management background. Individuals with a business background may bring a new focus on efficiency to an agency, yet over the long run ineffective executive leadership may result in very high costs in terms of staff turnover, morale, and client dissatisfaction. An agency needs to strike a balance between a concern for the efficient utilization of resources, due in part to the demands of the contracting regime, and the commitment to agency mission that exists outside market-driven imperatives.

Arguably, the current contracting environment also places a primacy on the ability of nonprofit executives to work collaboratively, both internally and externally. Competition and scarcity of funding mean that executive directors need to be able to work closely and productively with government contract administrators. In addition, agency executives need to be able to partner with local foundations, United Way chapters, and local businesses. Agency executives with government contracts also have a major incentive to work with other nonprofit agencies in support of shared public policy goals on funding and regulatory issues. Further, given the challenges of staff recruitment and retention, effective nonprofit executives are able to share leadership throughout their organization (Grant and Crutchfield, 2007). Chapter Six of this volume presents an extensive discussion of the challenges of effective executive leadership.

Broadening the Agency Constituency

Nonprofit agencies, as noted, typically represent at their founding the efforts of like-minded people to address a particular problem. Often these organizations are not representative of their community as a whole; many agencies are directed by people from a particular political, ideological, ethnic, or income group in a community. Indeed, many nonprofit organizations are valued in part because of their ability to represent specialized or minority constituencies (Weisbrod, 1988; Smith and Lipsky, 1993). This narrowness can become a handicap as an agency develops and obtains contracts from the government: the board may be small; broader community connections may be weak; political support may be lacking; and clients and services provided by the agency may be at variance with the expectations of government.

Successful and sustainable nonprofits with government contracts are able to transcend the initial targeted focus of the agency without compromising their mission or programmatic priorities. This effort requires a diversification and broadening of the organization's constituency. Toward this end, an agency may create an affiliate organization that can help with fundraising, community support, and program visibility. Typically, these organizations are directed by the paid staff of the parent organization but are operated primarily by volunteers. A nonprofit also may alter the composition of its board in order to engage key supporters in the oversight and governance processes of the organization. Further, an agency might join community organizations, such as the Chamber of Commerce. The regular presence of a nonprofit agency at Chamber meetings can go a long way toward creating a role for the agency as a vital and important member of the community.

An agency may also alter its rules for membership. As noted earlier, many nonprofit organizations were established by a relatively small number of people who formed the core of the initial board of directors; no official membership in the organization apart from the board and staff existed. Often, in these situations, the board of directors is self-perpetuating rather than elected by the membership. Such a board structure can work against wide and sustained community engagement. Thus, a nonprofit agency may be well served by rethinking the concept of membership and consider engaging community members and service users as voting members of the organization. This approach can offer important friends of the organization a stake in the agency and help recruit new supporters and volunteers for the agency. Over time, these new members could be very helpful in mobilizing community and political support on behalf of the agency. This type of constituent engagement also can help promote greater accountability (Smith, 2010b). To be sure, this type of membership is not appropriate for all nonprofit agencies. For example, some drug treatment agencies are located in remote locations and work with a difficult client population. Nonetheless, service agencies with roots in a local community might benefit from rethinking their membership structure.

One strategy to engage the community that may achieve some of the same goals as changes in membership is the creation of advisory committees (or other more informal governance entities) as complements to the board of directors. Advisory structures can be especially helpful for specialized purposes such as strategic planning, advocacy, and a new capital campaign for the organization (Saidel, 1998; Smith, 2010b).

Constituency development can also be achieved through strategic partnerships and collaborations with other nonprofit, public, and for-profit organizations. Partnerships with local businesses can help with private fundraising, political support for the agency, and the recruitment of volunteers and board members. Collaborations with other nonprofits can yield potential savings on administrative costs and potentially help win new grants and contracts, given the current emphasis of public and private funders on collaboration among nonprofit service agencies. The subject of nonprofit partnerships and collaboration is discussed in more depth in Chapter Fourteen.

Enlarging an agency's constituency is not without risks. New members or supporters may try to change the agency's mission and lead it in new directions. An agency may trade dependency on state contract administrators for dependency on a powerful donor or group of donors. More community members may make the organization more risk-averse. For example, a community residence program for the developmentally disabled might avoid developing an innovative apartment program if it was aware of substantial community opposition. Clarity about an organization's mission and the role of new constituency groups is absolutely critical if an agency is to develop and sustain effective programs.

Engaging the Policy Process

Prior to the advent of widespread government contracting, nonprofit service agencies tended to operate quite apart from the political process. Dependent primarily on private revenues, management decisions and the fate of the organization were relatively disconnected from decisions made by state and local legislatures, the federal government, or governors and mayors. The practice of government contracting fundamentally changed this situation; nonprofit agencies with contracts are now inextricably connected to the political process.

Important political decisions, legislation, and administrative rulings can have a very profound impact on the success of nonprofits and their leaders. For example, if a legislature refuses to allocate sufficient funds for a contract rate increase the nonprofit may be forced to cut staff, with the resultant implications for morale and program quality. Accountability requirements instituted by the legislature or government administrators also may have a major impact on staff priorities and activities. Contract requirements or funding cutbacks or both may require agencies to collaborate, merge, or go out of business entirely. Even relatively minor or technical changes to eligibility requirements or rate levels can have an enormous impact on the capacity of local nonprofit agencies to deliver quality services. Sometimes nonprofits providing contract services may need special zoning permits in order to house their facilities. And some nonprofits receive various cash and in-kind subsidies from municipalities. Special linkages also may exist, such as nonprofit child welfare agencies that are required to have close connections with local school districts, or the need for nonprofit clients and consumers to use local public transportation to access agency services.

A nonprofit agency can also encounter political difficulties if it disagrees with a major decision of a state or local contracting agency (for example, changing the geographic scope of agency services). In response, state contract administrators may want to refer different types of clients to the agency. Or the state may want to restrict or curtail certain contract expenditures. Perhaps the state may even want to end the contract altogether and award it to another agency. Personal appeals by the executive, the board of directors, or intervention by community political supporters may produce a reversal of unfavorable rulings, although many nonprofit agencies (especially smaller or newer agencies) can lack the political clout to get such decisions overturned.

In short, the success of nonprofits now hinges, at least in part, on decisions made in the political arena. This changed relationship between nonprofits and the political world requires nonprofit executives and their boards to be actively engaged with policymakers on an ongoing basis. Successful engagement in the policy process means that nonprofit executives and their boards need to increase their agency's political visibility and support. Thus, nonprofit boards and staff should enlist the support of local political figures, including municipal leaders and state legislators. This goal may be accomplished in part by enlisting key community leaders (including political figures, where appropriate) as agency board members. More routinely, nonprofit staff and boards should make local leaders aware of agency activities through e-mail announcements, an agency's home page, mailings, and articles in the local newspaper. (Chapter Twelve of this volume explains in more depth the process of nonprofit strategic communication.) Over time, even modest efforts can create a positive public image of the agency and garner favorable political support. If an agency does not have good relations with its surrounding community and its political leaders, implementing the agency's programs may prove very difficult. These actions may also help prevent the adoption by government of arbitrary or ill-advised policies.

As nonprofit staff and volunteers engage in advocacy, they should also strive to represent the needs of their clients and communities, broadly defined. Nonprofit agencies receiving government contracts tend to be most involved in policy issues such as funding and regulations directly relevant to the agency itself.

However, while advocacy in support of higher contract funding may help with eligibility and funding for clients, it usually needs to be accompanied by agency advocacy on the remediation of the social problems that affect agency clients (for example, the lack of affordable housing, inappropriate regulations, persistent joblessness).

Despite the incentives for political engagement, many nonprofit staff and board members are very reluctant to engage in advocacy on behalf of their agency or their clients. In particular, many nonprofits are very wary of advocacy because they fear that it might spur scrutiny from the Internal Revenue Service or other government regulators, perhaps leading to threats to their tax-exempt status or serious fines (Berry and Arons, 2003; Bass et al., 2007). Further, many agencies are quite small and lack the staff resources to actively participate in the political process. The board members of many nonprofits tend to be attracted to board service due to their commitment to the agency's mission and services such as child welfare or homelessness; consequently, most board members possess little experience with government policy. Nonprofit contract agencies may also be averse to advocacy due to concern that such efforts may alienate government contract officials and lead to retribution against the agency at a later date (Smith and Smyth, 2010).

Nonprofit agencies can be effective advocates in spite of these obstacles, but to do so does require persistence and a multipronged strategy. And executives and boards need to be much more aware of the legal issues surrounding advocacy and lobbying, including sustained efforts to educate board members and staff regarding what is permissible and effective (Berry and Arons, 2003; Bass et al., 2007). The topic of nonprofit advocacy and lobbying is addressed more fully in Chapter Thirteen.

The Role of Associations

Nonprofits also should work collaboratively with other nonprofits, as well as through local and statewide associations to influence government policy. Indeed, many nonprofit agencies have participated in associations for decades. The Child Welfare League of America and the Alliance for Families are just two examples of the many national associations of nonprofit organizations. Associations have not generally been involved in issues of contracting. More recently, though, many nonprofit associations have been organized at the state and local levels, and these organizations tend to be more directly involved in government contracting policies.

The new associations are typically of two types. The first are mission- or service-specific associations, such as the North Carolina Association of Home

Care Agencies and the Massachusetts Association of Community Mental Health Centers. The second type are statewide associations comprising nonprofit agencies of many different missions and services. Prominent examples include the California Association of Nonprofits and the Maryland Association of Nonprofits. Indeed, thirty-seven states and the District of Columbia currently have associations of nonprofit organizations that advocate for their members with state legislatures. Further, the National Council of Nonprofits advocates for the state associations at the federal level and throughout the United States on important policy concerns of direct relevance to nonprofits (National Council of Nonprofits, 2010).

Overall, both types of nonprofit associations can be helpful to nonprofits on policies relating to agency contracts, including rates, funding levels, programmatic priorities, and contracting procedures. At times, these associations may also be helpful in advocating for agencies in specific disputes between a state and individual organizations. Statewide associations can also be highly useful to nonprofit contract agencies in less direct ways. For instance, statewide associations can call attention to the organizational difficulties nonprofits face due to state cutbacks and regulatory changes. Statewide associations can also assist member agencies with more operational concerns such as insurance, liability issues, human resource problems, and bulk purchasing.

The capacity of nonprofit associations to be effective advocates for their members may be constrained at times by internal issues. Some associations are forced to be very cautious in their advocacy work because of their members' concerns about alienating government policymakers. Other associations are divided on issues such as funding levels, contract requirements, and rates. Some associations with diverse memberships may also need to focus on issues of concern to every member, such as broad contracting policies or higher wages for nonprofit employees, rather than address policies of interest to subsectors. Further, many of these associations are themselves small and struggle financially. Nonetheless, in an era when state and local governments are increasingly important in the funding and monitoring of nonprofit programs, nonprofit associations are increasingly important to the overall effectiveness of nonprofit agencies receiving government contracts.

Innovation and Reform in Contracting

The sharp expansion of contracting with nonprofits in the United States and beyond has been accompanied by persistent nonprofit complaints about the contracting process itself. These include a lack of transparency, overly burdensome regulations, and a general lack of accountability for results and outcomes.

Response to these problems has led to important changes in the contracting process, although the extent of these changes has varied substantially across different jurisdictions.

First, many government administrators have adopted policies to make contracting a more equitable process with detailed expectations on performance and the selection of contract agencies (Smith and Grinker, 2004; Behn and Kant, 1999). Second, many governments and nonprofit agencies are experimenting with strategies to "rationalize" the regulation of contract agencies. For instance, performance contracting can be conceptualized at least in part as an effort to ease the regulatory burden on nonprofits. A persistent lament among nonprofits pertains to the perceived excessive regulation of line items in an agency's budget, which reduces program and budgetary flexibility that can be essential in a time of fiscal stress. Line item accountability also creates heavy reporting requirements that, in turn, require the diversion of resources from program services to administration. Thus, effective performance contracting at least has the potential to hold agencies accountable for outcomes while giving them the flexibility to achieve these outcomes, providing agencies with some programmatic decision-making authority, and reducing reporting requirements and expectations. As noted earlier, the practice of performance contracting has increased sharply in recent years in a wide variety of service categories, including welfare-to-work, mental health, workforce development, foster care, and counseling (Behn and Kant, 1999; Blalock and Barnow, 2004; Heinrich and Choi, 2007; Smith and Grinker, 2004; Smith, 2010b).

In practice, though, performance contracting in the current environment often means much greater attention to outcomes without the reduction in paperwork and staff time. Consequently, there is a growing interest among government officials and nonprofit agencies for reforms in contracting that might reduce regulatory burdens and at the same time achieve positive outcomes. Strategies to help with this include enhanced accreditation, self-regulation, and technical assistance and capacity building.

The accreditation movement is a worldwide movement to adopt practices to improve performance without the need to resort to traditional forms of government regulation. In this context, accreditation policies typically mean a specified minimum standard of care detailed by the accrediting body. For example, nonprofit organizations in Herefordshire in the United Kingdom created their own accreditation system, which is administered by a third-party organization; government agrees to only contract with accredited agencies (Smith and Smyth, 2010). In the United States, examples of such accrediting bodies include the Commission on the Accreditation of Rehabilitation Facilities (CARF) and the Joint Commission (which accredits health care organizations).

Increasingly, governments are looking to these accrediting bodies to certify minimum standards of quality in services provided by nonprofit service providers in social and health care.

Also, growing interest exists in the United States and abroad in developing quality frameworks specifically tailored for nonprofit organizations. Thus, the Maryland Association of Nonprofits has developed its Standards of Excellence program, which details a set of standards for excellence in the governance and management of nonprofits (Maryland Association of Nonprofits, 2009). Another example is the work of the Panel on the Nonprofit Sector (2007), which is sponsored by the national organization, Independent Sector; it has issued its *Principles of Good Governance and Ethical Practice* document as a guide for self-regulation by nonprofits and foundations. These standards are designed to apply to nonprofit organizations more broadly than simply those nonprofits receiving contracts, but they also have prompted extensive discussion on contractual quality standards. Their long-term impact remains to be determined.

A growing recognition exists among policymakers and nonprofit leaders that investment in nonprofit capacity also is essential for the delivery of sustainable and quality programs. Indeed, since so many nonprofit organizations are now "agents" of government, one could argue that government has an obligation to support training and education and, more generally, capacity building among nonprofit agencies providing public services. Several different strategies exist. Government can provide funding to intermediary organizations such as consulting firms or technical assistance organizations that then can help nonprofits address the complexities of government funding. For example, the federal government's Compassion Capital Fund was designed to help faith-based and community organizations obtain government grants and contracts. Many state and local governments have provided similar types of support to intermediary organizations to assist nonprofits. Government officials can provide direct help to nonprofits through information sessions and direct capacity-building assistance to nonprofits, and they can indirectly assist nonprofits by their willingness to work collaboratively with organizations and their representative associations on issues of mutual concern (such as rates and regulations). Of course, a sustained collaborative effort requires an ongoing commitment of resources by government.

In support of improved nonprofit capacity, government can structure contracts to include support for reasonable administrative costs. This effort is especially important given the constant challenge faced by nonprofits to find sufficient funds to support their administrative infrastructure. Underfunded infrastructure is a common problem, since many government and private funders focus on program-related funding. Without sufficient funds to pay for an adequate administrative structure, agencies are at a disadvantage as they raise private funds and compete for public grants and contracts. Insufficient infrastructure also contributes to program instability, especially among smaller community-based organizations. More generally, state and local governments can strive to more fully fund contracts to reflect reasonable costs of nonprofits, even though the current fiscal crises of state and local governments create imposing obstacles to reaching this goal (Smith, 2008).

Government can also play an important role in directly and indirectly helping nonprofit contract agencies with their capital costs. Before the financial crisis hit in 2008, many states and localities expanded the access of nonprofit contract agencies to tax-exempt bonds to help them with their capital needs, such as the purchase and renovation of their facilities and new equipment (Smith, 2006). To the extent that nonprofits can improve their capital position, they will be in a better position to manage their cash flow effectively and be able to develop productive relationships with government contract officials.

Government administrators, especially at the state and local level, can also help improve governance and performance among nonprofit organizations through their support of appropriate mergers and collaborations. As discussed earlier, many nonprofits are small and struggle with capacity and funding issues, thus creating problems with board and executive leadership. Mergers of some of these organizations could be quite helpful in resolving some of these governance problems. Nonetheless, nonprofits are often resistant to mergers, so support from government (and private funders) is often essential if mergers are actually to occur.

These steps to enhance performance in nonprofits will be insufficient to improve the overall quality and effectiveness of publicly funded services provided by nonprofit agencies unless government takes steps to invest in its own management team and structure. In the case of contracting with nonprofits, state and local government will most assuredly fail to realize the benefits of contracting if government contract administrators are unable to monitor nonprofit performance or work effectively with nonprofits. Consequently, government agencies need contract managers with skills in negotiation and bargaining and knowledge of management, finance, budgeting and the organization of nonprofits. Government managers could thus benefit from executive education and training opportunities focused on contract management, nonprofit management, financial management, program evaluation, and negotiation (Van Slyke, 2007; Smith, 2008; 2010).

Government contract managers with these skill sets would also promote more effective relationships with nonprofits, as well as support working groups and more formal arrangements among nonprofits and government, to address important sector policy and management issues. Toward this end, government and nonprofit organizations in the United Kingdom have negotiated and revised a formal agreement, called "The Compact," outlining key principles and practices to guide their interactions at all levels of government (United Kingdom, 2009). The U.K. Compact has generated broad attention among governments and nonprofit organizations throughout the world. Some countries such as Australia have experimented with local level compacts (Casey and Dalton, 2005). Nonetheless, the basic principles of The Compact (such as regular communication and dialogue between government and the nonprofit sector), as well as standards of practice, can be developed through more informal relationships and partnerships at any level of government.

Nonprofits for their part should strive to invest in their administrative and programmatic infrastructure, including new technology and qualified administrative staff (Light, 2004). This effort can also include new or innovative ways to infuse the board and local community members with specific expertise in support of the organization. The development of a private donor base can also be essential to building capacity, especially given the competition for scarce public contracts. Fundraising may not produce large benefits for the organization in the short term but, in the long term may become very important as a way of cross-subsidizing programs inadequately funded by government contracts.

Conclusion

Government contracting with nonprofit agencies is in the midst of an important transition phase that is likely to continue, although local forces and circumstances will certainly affect the character and pace of this transition. Nonprofit agencies will continue to grapple with the twin pressures of demands for more collaboration while coping with a more competitive contracting environment. Collaboration will be encouraged by pressure to reduce costs, the need to be more influential politically, and the continuing demands by public and private funders for agencies to share costs and programmatic expertise.

The widespread interest among funders for more collaboration reflects their concerns for the large increase in the number of nonprofit agencies that are relatively small and undercapitalized. These agencies, in particular, face daunting problems of sustainability in an austere funding environment. Given this situation, government and private funders also are understandably reluctant to support the creation of new agencies. Indeed, many funders are actively trying to promote agency consolidation, especially between larger, more stable agencies and financially weak agencies. However, since nonprofit mergers are difficult and fraught with potentially unexpected complications, the pressure for collaboration is likely to lead to a variety of other strategies for organizational cooperation—strategies such as co-location of services and formal agreements to merge some services but retain separate organizations.

This pressure for collaboration is greatly complicated by the increasingly competitive environment for government contracts. It reflects the growth in the number of agencies, coupled with the intense interest of government and many private donors in accountability, efficiency, and results. Further, over time, the broad interest in implementation, better service targeting, and outcome evaluation is likely to lead to more extensive comparisons among nonprofit organizations, as well as between nonprofits and for-profits, particularly in service fields (such as home care) where these agencies directly compete. In the process, the monopoly now enjoyed by many nonprofits in their local communities is likely to be eroded or threatened by for-profit agencies or upstart nonprofit agencies. Further, government is likely to continue to shift at least some of its contract funding away from traditional contracts and into other less direct funding strategies and policy tools such as vouchers, "quasi-vouchers," and tax credits.

Given these trends, larger nonprofit (and for-profit) contract agencies with proven track records and capacity are likely to have an edge in the competition for contracts. However, these agencies often have difficulty connecting with service users and community members (Smith and Smyth, 2010). Thus, a central challenge for nonprofit agencies that seek contracts is to adapt their management and organizational structure to emphasize flexibility, nimbleness, and efficiency while retaining a commitment to equity, social justice, and community support and engagement. Nonprofit agencies will need to be innovative in their organizational structure and willing and able to invest resources necessary to comply with government regulations and performance expectations. More broadly, agencies should develop—with government encouragement and support—new ways to engage clients in agency governance as the staff and board strive to adapt their organizations to foster greater client choice and input. Through such internal investments in capacity and good governance, coupled with sustained engagement of local citizens, the promise of nonprofits as effective providers of vital public services may be realized.

References

Bass, G. D., Arons, D. F., Guinane, K., and Carter, M. F. *Seen But Not Heard: Strengthening Nonprofit Advocacy*. Washington, D.C.: Aspen Institute, 2007.

Behn, B. *Rethinking Democratic Accountability*. Washington, D.C.: Brookings Institution Press, 2002.

Behn, R. D., and Kant, P. A. "Strategies for Avoiding the Pitfalls of Performance Contracting." *Public Productivity and Management Review*, 1999. *22*(4), 470–489.

Berry, J. M., with Arons, D. *A Voice for Nonprofits*. Washington, D.C.: Brookings, 2003.

Bixby, A. K. "Public Social Welfare Expenditures, Fiscal Year 1995." *Social Security Bulletin*, 1999, *62*(4), 86–94.

Blalock, A. B., and Barnow, B. S. "Is the New Obsession with Performance Management Masking the Truth About Social Programs." In D. Forsythe (ed.), *Quicker, Better, Cheaper? Managing Performance in American Government*. Albany, N.Y.: The Rockefeller Institute Press, 2004.

Braddock, D., and others. *The State of the State in Developmental Disabilities: 2005*. Preliminary Report. Washington, D.C.: American Association of Mental Retardation, 2005.

Burns, B. J., Teagle, S. E., Schwartz, M., Angold, A., and Holtzman, A. "Managed Care Behavioral Health Care: A Medicaid Carve-Out for Youth," *Health Affairs*, 1999, *18*(5), 214–225.

Carlson, M., and Donohoe, M. *The Executive Director's Survival Guide: Thriving as a Nonprofit Leader*. San Francisco: Wiley, 2003.

Casey, J., and Dalton, B. "The Best of Times, the Worst of Times: Community-Sector Advocacy in the Age of 'Compacts.'" *Australian Journal of Political Science*, 2005, *41*(1), 23–28.

Chait, R., Ryan, W. P., and Taylor, B. E. *Governance as Leadership: Reframing the Work of Nonprofit Boards*. San Francisco: Wiley, 2005.

Considine, M. "Contract Regimes and Reflexive Governance: Comparing Employment Service Reforms in the United Kingdom, the Netherlands, New Zealand, and Australia." *Public Administration*, 2000, *78*(3), 613–638.

Coughlin, B. J. *Church and State in Social Welfare*. New York: Columbia University Press, 1965.

Courtney, M. E. "Managed Care and Child Welfare Services: What Are the Issues?" *Children and Youth Services Review*, 2000, *22*(2), 87–91.

Crosby, A. "Community Purpose Means Community Involvement." *Nonprofit Quarterly*, 2003, *10*(3), 24–28.

Frank, R. G., McGuire, T. G., and Newhouse, J. P. "Risk Contracts in Managed Mental Health Care." *Health Affairs*, 1995, *14*(3), 50–64.

Frank, R., and Glied, S. A. *Better But Not Well: Mental Health Policy in the United States Since 1950*. Baltimore Md.: Johns Hopkins University Press, 2006.

Geen, R., Sommers, A., and Cohen, M. *Medicaid Spending on Foster Children*. Brief No. 2. Washington, D.C.: The Urban Institute, 2005.

Grant, H. M., and Crutchfield. L. R. "Creating High-Impact Nonprofits." *Stanford Social Innovation Review*, 2007, 32–41.

Gutowski, M. F., and Koshel, J. J. "Social Services." In J. L. Palmer and V. Sawhill (eds.), *The Reagan Experiment*. Washington, D.C.: Urban Institute. 1982, 307–328.

Heinrich, C. J., and Choi, Y. "Performance-Based Contracting in Social Welfare Programs." *American Review of Public Administration*, 2007, *37*(4), 409–435.

Holahan, J., and Yemane, A. "Enrollment Is Driving Medicaid Costs—But Two Targets Can Yield Savings." *Health Affairs*, 2009, *28*(5), 1453–1465.

Hood, C. "A Public Management for All Seasons." *Public Administration*, 1991, *69*, 3–19.

Hwang, H., and Powell, W.W. "The Rationalization of Charity: The Influences of Professionalism in the Nonprofit Sector." *Administrative Science Quarterly*, 2009, *54*, 268–298.

Kaiser Family Foundation. *Medicaid Home and Community-Based Service Programs: Data Update.* http://www.kff.org/medicaid/upload/7720−03.pdf. 2009.

Kettl, D. *The Global Public Management Revolution.* Washington, D.C.: Brookings, 2005.

Krasner, S. D. "Structural Causes and Regime Consequences: Regimes as Intervening Variables." *International Organization*, 1982, *36*, 185−205.

Krauskopf, J. "Administering and Managing Contracts: The Dual Role of Government Human Service Officials." *Journal of Policy Analysis and Management*. Forthcoming.

Light, P. C. *Sustaining Nonprofit Performance: The Case for Capacity Building and the Evidence to Support It.* Washington, D.C.: Brookings, 2004.

Lynn, L. E. Jr. "The New Public Management: How to Transform a Theme into a Legacy." *Public Administration Review*, 1998, *58*(3), 231−237.

Maryland Association of Nonprofits. "The Maryland Budget and Tax Policy Institute." http://www.marylandnonprofits.org/html/policy/02_04.asp. Downloaded May 20, 2010.

McCullough, C., and Schmitt, B. "Managed Care and Privatization: Results of a National Survey." *Children and Youth Services Review*, 2000, *22*(2), 1117−130.

National Center of Charitable Statistics (NCCS). *Number of Nonprofit Organizations in the U.S. 1996−2006; 2008.* www.nccs.urban.org/statistics/index.cfm. 2009.

National Council of Nonprofits. "What We Do." http://www.councilofnonprofits.org/who-we-are#programs. Downloaded on May 10, 2010.

Osborne, D., and Gaebler, T. A. *Reinventing Government: How the Entrepreneurial Spirit Is Transforming the Public Sector.* New York: Plenum Press, 1992.

Panel on the Nonprofit Sector. *Principles of Good Governance and Ethical Practice.* Washington, D.C.: The Independent Sector, 2007.

Perlmutter, F. "The Effect of Public Funds on Voluntary Sectarian Agencies." *Journal of Jewish Communal Service*, 1969, *45*(4), 312−321.

Rhodes, R.A.W. "The New Governance: Governing without Government." *Political Studies*, 1996, *44*, 652−667.

Saidel, J. R. "Expanding the Governance Construct: Functions and Contributions of Nonprofit Advisory Groups." *Nonprofit and Voluntary Sector Quarterly*, 1998, *27*, 421−436.

Salamon, L. M. (ed.) *The Tools of Government.* New York: Oxford University Press, 2002.

Smith, D. "Making Management Count: A Case for Theory- and Evidence-Based Public Management." *Journal of Policy Analysis and Management*, 2009, *28*(1), 497−505.

Smith, D. C., and Grinker, W. J. *The Promise and Pitfalls of Performance Based Contracting.* New York: Seedco, 2004.

Smith, S. R. "Government Financing of Nonprofit Activity." In E. Boris and C. Steuerle (eds.), *Nonprofits and Government: Collaboration and Conflict.* Washington, D.C.: Urban Institute, 2006, 219−256.

Smith, S. R. "The Challenge of Strengthening Nonprofits and Civil Society." *Public Administration Review*. 2008, 132−145.

Smith, S. R. "Nonprofits and Public Administration: Reconciling Performance Management and Citizen Engagement." *American Review of Public Administration*. 2010a, 129−152.

Smith, S. R. "The Political Economy of Contracting and Competition." In Y. Hasenfeld (ed.), *Human Services as Complex Organizations*, 2nd ed. Thousand Oaks, Calif.: Sage, 2010b.

Smith, S. R., and Lipsky, M. *Nonprofits for Hire: The Welfare State in the Age of Contracting.* Cambridge, Mass.: Harvard University Press, 1993.

United Kingdom. *The Compact*. London: The Crown, 2009. Available for download at www.thecompact.org.uk.

Smith, S. R., and Smyth, J. "The Governance of Contracting Relationships: 'Killing the Golden Goose,' a Third Sector Perspective." In S. Osborne (ed.), *The New Public Governance? Critical Perspectives and Future Directions*. London: Routledge, 2010.

Steuerle, C. E. "Common Issues for Voucher Programs." In C. E. Steuerle, V. D. Ooms, G. E. Peterson, and R. D. Reischauer (eds.), *Vouchers and the Provision of Public Services*. Washington, D.C.: Brookings, 2000, 3–39.

Van Slyke, D. M. "Agents or Stewards: Using Theory to Understand the Government-Nonprofit Contracting Relationship." *Journal of Public Administration Research and Theory*, 2007, *17*(2), 157–188.

Vladeck, B. C. "Where the Action Really Is: Medicaid and the Disabled." *Health Affairs*, 2003, *22*(1), 90–100.

Ways and Means Committee, U. S. House of Representatives. *The Green Book*. Washington, D.C.: Governmental Publications Office, 2004.

Weisbrod, B. *The Nonprofit Economy*. Cambridge, Mass.: Harvard University Press, 1988.

Wilson, J. Q. *Political Organizations*. New York: Basic Books, 1973.

Winston, P., and Castaneda, R. M. *Assessing Federalism: ANF and the Recent Evolution of American Social Policy Federalism*. Washington, D.C.: The Urban Institute, 2007.

CHAPTER TWENTY-TWO

FINANCIAL MANAGEMENT AND ACCOUNTING

David W. Young

Financial management and accounting are concerned with the information needs of both external readers of an organization's financial statements and individuals within the organization, principally the organization's managers, planners, and staff analysts. This chapter focuses on internal users.[1] Much of this focus is on costs and cost behavior. With *full cost accounting*, the concern is with each service's or each program's direct costs plus its fair share of the organization's overhead costs. By contrast, *differential cost accounting* focuses on how costs change as circumstances change (such as when an outsourcing opportunity is being considered). With *responsibility accounting*, costs (and sometimes revenues) are analyzed from the perspective of the individuals in an organization who can control them.[2]

Because of these different approaches, the central theme of this chapter is that *different costs are used for different purposes*. There is nothing illegal or unethical about looking at costs differently for different purposes. Rather, as managers' decision-making needs change so do the relevant costs.

This chapter is a condensed and abridged version of several separate chapters contained in David W. Young, *Management Control in Nonprofit Organizations* (Cambridge, Massachusetts: The Crimson Press), 2008.

Full-Cost Accounting

Arriving at an answer to the question "What did it cost?" can be more difficult than it might first appear. Obviously, it is rather easily answered if we are discussing the purchase of inputs (supplies, labor, and so on) for the service-delivery process. Even calculating the full cost of a "unit" produced—whether it is a dialysis procedure or 50 minutes of psychotherapy—is relatively easy as long as the organization provides completely homogeneous goods or services. Complications arise when an organization provides multiple goods and services, and uses different kinds and amounts of resources to provide each of them.

Uses of Full-Cost Information

Information on the full cost of carrying out a particular endeavor has four basic uses: pricing, profitability assessment, comparative analyses, and external reporting. Most managers use cost information for all of these purposes at different times and under varying decision-making scenarios.

Pricing

Clearly, cost information is not the only information that is used for setting prices, but it is an important ingredient. Some nonprofit organizations are paid on the basis of their full costs, thereby creating the need for a full-cost analysis that effectively establishes the "price." Many nonprofits engage in such an effort, including such disparate entities as the TVA, the U.S. Postal Service, hospitals, and universities.

Profitability Assessments

In some situations, an organization is a price-taker, and a full-cost analysis is not used in setting prices. Nevertheless, the organization must calculate full costs if management is to know whether a particular product is financially viable.[3] If a product is not covering its full costs, it is, by definition, a "loss leader." Since an organization cannot have all its products be loss leaders, full-cost accounting serves to highlight where cross subsidization is taking place.

Comparative Analyses

Many organizations compare their costs with those of similar organizations that deliver the same sorts of products. Although full-cost information can assist in this effort, comparative analyses can be complicated. For example, before undertaking such an analysis, we would need to know whether the organizations used for comparison measure their costs in the same way we do. There can be a variety of complexities in undertaking a comparative analysis.

Example

Northern College, a small private liberal arts college, is interested in comparing its cost per student with the cost per student in some similar colleges. In making this comparison, the college must consider issues such as average class size, the existence of specialized programs in athletics, art, music or other subjects, special services (such as career counseling), whether it wishes to include room and board and/or the library costs in the comparison, and, if so, the method used to calculate the cost (for example, whether it amortizes its library collections and over what time period), and a variety of similar matters.

Because there is such a wide range of choices embedded in an organization's cost accounting system, many managers simply make comparisons over time for their own organization. This way, they can be certain that the methodology has remained consistent from one year to the next.

External Reporting

In situations where a third party pays on the basis of cost, an organization usually must calculate its full costs according to certain guidelines. It then must submit the resulting cost report to the third party before receiving payment. When the U.S. government contracts with a university to do research, for example, the university's cost accounting must abide by the principles in the Office of Management and Budget's *Circular A-21, Cost Principles for Educational Institutions*.[4] These principles provide for direct costs plus "an equitable share" of overhead costs. Overhead costs include items such as depreciation of buildings and equipment, operations and maintenance of plant, general administration, departmental administration, student services, and the library.

The Full-Cost Accounting Methodology

Conceptually, the goal of full-cost accounting is to measure as accurately as possible the resources consumed in producing a particular product. In some instances, the measurement process is quite easy. For example, an organization that produces a single product usually has little difficulty in calculating the full cost of each unit. All costs associated with the organization, and hence the product, can be added together and divided by the number of units produced during a particular accounting period to arrive at a full cost per unit. By contrast, organizations that produce a variety of products, each requiring different amounts of resources, will have a more difficult time determining the cost for each unit sold.

Examples

In a freestanding dialysis clinic, computing the full cost of a dialysis procedure is relatively easy. The clinic can add together all of its costs for an accounting period, such as a month, and divide by the number of procedures provided during the month. Since all procedures are more or less identical, this average cost figure is quite accurate. By contrast, in a freestanding ambulatory surgery center that performs several different types of surgical interventions, computing the full cost of an operation is considerably more complicated than for a procedure in the dialysis clinic. Since each operation consumes different kinds and amounts of resources, an average cost per operation would likely be misleading.

For organizations with a heterogeneous mix of outputs, such as the above ambulatory surgery center, the full-cost accounting effort typically goes through two stages. In Stage 1, the accounting staff undertakes several steps, at the end of which all costs reside in the organization's mission centers. During Stage 2, each mission center's costs are attached to its outputs (or products). Combined, the two stages constitute the full cost accounting methodology.

Stage 1

Stage 1 entails four activities: (a) defining the organization's cost objects, (b) selecting the cost centers that will be used to collect costs, and dividing them between service centers and mission centers, (c) assigning all costs to one or more cost centers, and (d) allocating service center costs into mission centers.

Defining Cost Objects

Final cost objects are the units of output for which we wish to know the full cost. In a hospital, for example, the final cost object might be an all-inclusive day of care. As such, it would include all surgical procedures, laboratory tests, radiology exams, pharmaceutical usage, and so on. When this is the case, calculating the full cost of a day of care is as simple as was calculating the cost of a dialysis procedure in the above example: total costs divided by total days of care provided.

In most hospitals, the final cost objects are more complex than an all-inclusive day of care. In some instances, for example, one cost object is a day of "routine" care (for example, room, dietary, housekeeping, laundry, and nursing costs), with separate cost objects for other activities, such as a day of intensive care, a laboratory test, a radiological procedure, and so on. In other hospitals, the final cost object is something broader than a day, such as a discharge. If a discharge is the cost object, the hospital includes all costs associated with the patient's entire stay (that is, for all days of care, rather than just an average single day). Here, too, however, computing the average cost per discharge would be quite easy: total costs divided by total discharges.

Complications arise only when we decide that different cost objects use resources differently, such as when we want to know the cost of a discharge according to the patient's diagnosis or diagnosis-related group (DRG).[5] In this case, the *final cost object*, a DRG, is computed by summing a variety of *intermediate cost objects*. The final cost object is used for billing payers (or for a comparison with the payment the hospital receives from its payers), and the intermediate cost objects are smaller units needed to produce the final cost object.

Example

If a hospital wants to know the cost of a patient with DRG 200 (the final cost object), it must add the costs of all resources provided to the patient during his or her stay (the intermediate cost objects). These include operative procedures, laboratory tests, radiological procedures, pharmaceuticals, intensive care days, routine care days, and so forth. This means that it needs to determine the cost of each intermediate cost object.

When the final cost object becomes more heterogeneous than a single procedure (such as a dialysis) or an all-inclusive day, the focus shifts to the intermediate cost objects that were used to produce it. Different combinations of intermediate cost objects will affect the cost of the final cost object, even though the final result (or "product")—the discharge of a patient—is the same. Thus, our real interest is in the cost of the intermediate cost objects, or the "intermediate products," as they sometimes are called.

Example

The annual cost of caring for a child in the Western Home for Children (the final cost object) depends on the services the child receives (intermediate products). There are four basic types of services: foster home care, psychological testing, social work counseling, and psychotherapy. Each of these services is also a mission center, where a variety of costs are accumulated. The psychological testing center, for example, includes the costs of part-time psychologists, testing materials, and the fee the agency pays to an outside organization to have the tests processed and scored. The costs in the psychological testing mission center are accumulated for the year, and are divided by the number of children tested to give a cost per child tested. Each child who was tested has this cost added to his or her other costs to arrive at the total cost of caring for him or her for the year.

Selecting Cost Centers

To calculate the cost of the intermediate products, we first assign all costs to cost centers. These can be thought of as "buckets" where an organization's costs are accumulated for the Stage 1 analysis. Frequently, an organization's cost centers are identical to its departments. For example, in a hospital, the department of radiology might be one cost center, the social work department another, the housekeeping department a third, and so on. However, some departments are a collection of several cost centers. For example, a department of radiology might be divided into the cost centers of CT scanning, angiography, magnetic resonance imaging, and so on. If this is done, radiology's intermediate cost objects will be produced in several different cost centers.

Mission Centers Versus Service Centers

An organization's cost centers are divided between mission centers and service centers. Mission centers are associated with the organization's main focus (or mission). In a hospital, mission centers provide care to patients and usually charge (or are reimbursed) for their services. Because of this, they sometimes are called "revenue centers."

Service centers, by contrast, accumulate the costs of activities the organization carries out to support its mission centers. In a hospital, housekeeping, laundry, dietary, administration, and the like would be considered service centers, while inpatient care, radiology, pathology, pharmacy, and so forth would be classified as mission centers. In some instances, a service center may charge both mission centers and other service centers for their support activities, but they do not charge patients (or clients) directly.

Assigning Costs to Cost Centers

After an organization's cost centers have been defined, all costs then must be assigned to them. This usually is not difficult, although it can become somewhat complicated at times. For example, if a radiology department has several separate costs centers, as described above, it must find a way to assign the salary of, say, its scheduler to each center. The scheduler is easily assigned to the overall radiology cost center, but not so easily assigned to individual cost centers within radiology. The assignment can be carried out by either developing techniques that measure cost usage in considerable detail, or establishing a distribution formula.

Example

A social worker in the foster home department of Western Home for Children is supervised by a person who also supervises the psychologists in the testing department. The supervisor's salary must be distributed between the two departments. To do so, the accountants might develop a formula, using, say, relative hours of service or number of personnel in each cost center as the assignment mechanism. Alternatively, the supervisor might be asked to maintain careful records of time spent in each cost center, which the accountants then could use to distribute the salary. In this latter case, the cost accounting effort would be more precise since the cost (time) would be directly traceable to each cost center. Obviously, doing so is more costly than using a formula.

Allocating Service Center Costs

The full cost of a mission center includes its *fair share* of the organization's service center costs. To allocate service center costs to mission centers, we must choose an allocation basis for each service center, that is, a unit of output that measures its use by the other cost centers as accurately as possible. For example, the allocation basis for the housekeeping service center might be square feet. We can measure the number of square feet in each cost center and divide total housekeeping costs by total square feet to get the housekeeping cost per square foot. We then multiply that rate by the number of square feet in each cost center to determine its fair share of the housekeeping center's costs.[6]

Precision of Allocation Bases. When selecting allocation bases, it is important to keep in mind that increased precision generally requires greater measurement efforts, giving rise to higher accounting costs. For example, not all square feet in an organization are equally easy to clean. Therefore, rather than using number of square feet to allocate housekeeping costs, we might allocate them on the basis of hours spent. While hours spent is a more accurate basis, and would give us a more accurate cost figure, its use requires an ongoing compilation of the necessary data. As a result, less accurate approaches occasionally are adopted in response to time, staffing, and technical constraints.

Allocation Methodology. Three methods of varying complexity and accuracy are available for allocating service center costs to mission centers: *direct, stepdown,* and *reciprocal.*

With the *direct* method, service center costs are allocated only to mission centers and not to other service centers. This is the simplest method of the three, and is used by many organizations. It is the least precise, however, in that it excludes the cost effects associated with one service center's use of another service center.

The *stepdown* method allocates service center costs into both other service centers and mission centers. Because it allocates a service center's costs to other service centers, as well as to mission centers, the stepdown method is more complicated than the direct method. It also is more accurate in that it includes the cost effects associated with one service center's use of another. However, once a service center's costs have been allocated, it cannot receive an allocation. Thus, for a given service center, the stepdown method includes only the cost effects of its use of the service centers that precede it in the allocation sequence, and not those that follow it.

With the *reciprocal* method, all service centers make and receive allocations to and from each other, as well as to mission centers. The allocation amounts are determined by a set of simultaneous equations, which are solved on a computer. Because all service centers both make and receive allocations, the reciprocal method is the most accurate of the three, but also the most complicated to use.

An Example Using the Stepdown Method. Despite the greater accuracy of the reciprocal method, many organizations find that the stepdown method strikes about the right balance between accuracy and ease of use. Thus, we will use it here for illustrative purposes.

Choosing a Service Center Sequence. When the stepdown method is used, the sequence followed in allocating the service centers can have an impact on the costs in each mission center. Conceptually, the approach to choosing a sequence is to rank service centers in order of their use by other service centers. That is, the service center that uses other service centers the *least* is allocated *first,* and the service center that uses other service centers the *most* is allocated *last.* Clearly, considerable judgment is required to determine this sequence, and, even then, there is no such thing as the "right" sequence.

Conducting the Allocations. After we have chosen the sequence for service centers, the allocation effort can begin. To illustrate, assume that a small hospital has the

FIGURE 22.1. THE STEPDOWN METHOD.

	Cost Centers	Assigned Costs	Administration (# Employees)	Housekeeping (Square Feet)	Medical Records (# Records)	Total Costs
Service Centers	Administration	100				
	Housekeeping	20	25			
	Medical Records	30	10	10		
Mission Centers	Inpatient Services	1,000	40	20	30	1,090
	OPD Clinics	500	25	15	20	560
	Total Costs	1,650	100	45	50	1,650

--------------------Allocations--------------------

three service centers and two mission centers shown in Figure 22.1. The service centers are Administration (assigned costs of $100), Housekeeping (assigned costs of $20), and Medical Records (assigned costs of $30). The mission centers are Inpatient Services (assigned costs of $1,000) and the Outpatient Department (OPD) Clinics (assigned costs of $500). The hospital's total costs are thus $1,650, as shown at the bottom of the Assigned Costs column.

The allocation process begins with the first service center in the sequence (here, we have chosen Administration), which, as the note in parentheses under its column indicates, is allocated on the basis of number of employees. Each remaining cost center will receive its share of Administration costs based on its proportion of employees.

The next service center to be allocated is Housekeeping. The amount to be allocated is its assigned costs of $20 *plus* the $25 that was allocated to it from Administration. As a result, a total of $45 must be allocated. As the parentheses under the Housekeeping column indicate, it is allocated to the remaining centers on the basis of square feet, such that the more space a receiving cost center has, the greater its share of Housekeeping costs.

The final service center to be allocated is Medical Records, which, as Figure 22.1 indicates, has a total of $50 to be allocated: $30 of assigned costs, plus $10 allocated from Administration, and $10 allocated from Housekeeping. It is allocated to the remaining cost centers on the basis of the number of medical records.

We now can add up the costs of the two mission centers. Inpatient Services has $1,000 of assigned costs, plus $40 of allocated Administration, $20 of allocated Housekeeping, and $30 of allocated Medical Records, for a total of $1,090. The OPD Clinics have $500 of assigned costs, plus $25 of Administration, $15 of Housekeeping, and $20 of Medical Records, for a total of $560.

Note that our total costs of $1,650 remained the same as they were prior to allocating service center costs. However, we now have fully allocated the service center costs to the two mission centers. The full cost of a mission center includes its assigned costs, plus the costs allocated to it from the organization's service centers.

Key Aspects of the Stepdown Method. There are several important points to keep in mind about the stepdown method.

1. Only service center costs are allocated. Mission center costs are not. Mission centers receive costs from service centers, but once a cost has been allocated to a mission center it stays there.
2. The *allocation basis* chosen for a service center attempts to measure the use of that center's resources by the other cost centers—both service centers and mission centers. For example, in a hospital's laundry, "pounds washed" frequently is used as the allocation basis. Each cost center receives a portion of the laundry center's costs in accordance with its proportion of the total pounds of laundry washed. If a particular cost center sent no laundry to be washed, it would not receive an allocation.
3. The amount of a service center's allocation to other cost centers depends, in part, on its position in the sequence. If it is allocated late in the sequence, it will contain some costs from service centers allocated earlier in the sequence. If it is allocated early, it will not.
4. Total costs do not change. Different allocation bases and stepdown sequences only change the distribution of total costs among the mission centers. Thus, the effect of any change in methodology is solely one of making shifts among cost centers.

Stage 2

At the end of Stage 1, all costs reside in mission centers. Stage 1 can have some flaws, but with minimal effort, it usually can provide a reasonably accurate depiction of mission center costs. It is during Stage 2, when a mission center's costs are attached to its cost objects, that more serious difficulties can arise.

There are two approaches used to attach mission center costs to cost objects. The first is a *process system*, which typically is used when all units of output are roughly identical. All mission center costs for a given accounting period are simply divided by the total number of units produced to give an average cost per unit. This approach would be appropriate for the dialysis clinic discussed earlier, and for many other situations where all output units are roughly identical.

By contrast, a *job order system* is used when the units of output are quite different. Consider, for example, a repair garage for a municipality's waste collection vehicles. Adding all costs for a given accounting period, such as a month, and dividing by the number of vehicles repaired to determine an average cost per repaired vehicle, would provide quite misleading information. Instead, the garage would use a job ticket, on which the time and parts associated with each repair effort would be recorded separately, and costed out by means of hourly wage rates, unit prices, and so on. Many nonprofits face similar situations with heterogeneous output units.

Examples

- The research department at a university may work on several different research projects, and each project must be costed out individually.
- The counseling department of a social service agency comes into contact with many clients, and wishes to know the cost associated with each client.
- The special education department of a junior high school provides services to many students, and wishes to know the cost for each student.
- The internal medicine department of a rural group practice sees many patients each day and wants to know the cost of each patient's visit.

As the above examples illustrate, the mission centers of many nonprofit organizations have units of output whose diversity requires a job order system. Implementing such a system requires understanding the nature of a mission center's costs. These are shown in Table 22.1.

As Table 22.1 indicates, a mission center's costs fall into two categories: *direct* and *indirect*. Direct costs are those that can be attached to a cost object unambiguously; they typically comprise direct labor and direct materials. There is no big problem here. A job ticket (or its equivalent) can be used to record their use, and unit rates can be used to cost them out.

The problem arises with a mission center's *indirect costs*, that is, those costs that cannot be unambiguously associated with a cost object. As shown in Table 22.1, these costs fall into four categories: (a) indirect labor, such as supervisory time; (b) indirect materials, that is, materials that cannot be directly associated with a cost object, such as cleaning solvents for machines; (c) other indirect costs, such as

TABLE 22.1. ELEMENTS OF FULL PRODUCTION COST

Type of Cost	Description	Examples
Direct	Costs that are unambiguously associated with the mission center where the cost objects are produced, and that can be attached rather easily to any given cost object by using ...	
Direct labor	... time and motion studies.	Technicians in a radiology department; nurses on an inpatient ward
Direct materials	... material usage studies.	Reagents in a laboratory; medical supplies on an inpatient ward
Other direct	... machine and/or equipment studies.	Depreciation on a piece of equipment that is used for a single cost object
Indirect		
Indirect labor	Costs that also are unambiguously associated with the mission center where the cost objects are produced, but that cannot be attached directly to a given cost object.	Quality inspectors, supervisors
Indirect materials		Cleaning solvents for machines, recordkeeping supplies
Other Indirect		Depreciation on the mission center's computers
Allocated service center costs	Service center costs that are allocated to the mission center during Stage 1. They also cannot be attached directly to a given cost object.	Maintenance, laundry, housekeeping, and general administration costs.

depreciation on administrative computers; and (d) service center costs that were allocated to the mission center during Stage 1.

In a typical job order context, indirect costs are "attached" to products through the use of one or more "overhead rates." The *absorption process*, as this effort is called, can be a little tricky, and can give misleading results on occasion. For example, when only one overhead rate is used, as frequently happens, the implicit assumption is that the unit used in that rate (for example, direct labor hours), drives the use of all indirect costs. But indirect costs generally arise from a more complex array of forces, such that an absorption process using a single overhead rate can give management misleading information about the full cost of a cost object. As we'll see below, this can lead to an inaccurate full-cost analysis, and hence poorly informed pricing decisions and profitability analyses.

Enter Activity-Based Costing

Activity-based costing, or ABC, is now used in many settings to correct for this deficiency. Designers of ABC systems use several "indirect cost pools," and try to design each pool so that the resources in it are relatively homogeneous as possible. They then identify the activity that drives the use of the pool's resources, and use it to compute the pool's overhead rate. For example, an indirect cost pool in a laboratory might be the labor and supervisory time needed to set up the machines for processing a batch of tests. In this case, the appropriate cost pool would be everything associated with setting up the machines (such as cleaning and adjusting tolerances), and the appropriate unit of activity for the pool would be a single machine setup. As a result, a unit of output (a test in this case) in a small batch would get a higher share of the setup costs than one in a large batch.

Many nonprofit organizations have developed fairly sophisticated Stage 1 accounting systems, but few have developed ABC systems for the Stage 2 effort. As a result, they have limited or—perhaps worse—incorrect information about the cost of their intermediate cost objects (such as laboratory tests).[7] If the costs of their intermediate cost objects are wrong, then so too are the costs of their final cost objects.

Developing an ABC System

To use ABC, an organization begins by identifying the activities that cause the indirect costs for one product or batch of products to differ from those of another. To see the how an ABC system can improve Stage 2 of a full-cost analysis, let's use a relatively simple example.[8] Table 22.2 shows an abbreviated stepdown cost report for Stage 1 for Owen College.

TABLE 22.2. ABBREVIATED FULL-COST REPORT FOR OWENS COLLEGE (STAGE 1)

	Assigned Costs 1	Allocated Costs 2 = 4 + 5 + 6 + 7	Costs to Be Allocated 3 = 1 + 2	Allocations				Full Cost 8 = 1 + 2
				Depreciation (sq ft) 4	Maintenance (hours) 5	Housekeeping (sq ft) 6	Administration (salary $) 7	
Service Centers								
Building depreciation	600,000	0	600,000	52,500				
Building maintenance	475,000	52,500	527,500	47,500	29,777			
Housekeeping services	150,000	77,277	227,277	78,000	79,125			
Admin & General	650,000	190,812	840,812			33,687		
Mission Center								
Chemistry Department	855,000	415,877		114,000	73,850	59,865	168,162	1,270,877
Math Department	675,000	394,406		80,000	86,273	34,747	193,387	1,069,406
English Department	765,000	293,717		84,000	58,025	33,978	117,714	1,058,717
History Department	700,000	326,563		72,000	79,125	32,500	142,938	1,026,563
Economics Department	786,064	444,436		72,000	121,325	32,500	218,611	1,230,500
Total cost	5,656,064			600,000	527,500	227,277	840,812	5,656,064

TABLE 22.3. COURSE BREAKDOWN BY DEPARTMENT

	Number of Sections 1	Credit Hours per Student per Section 2	Average Enrollment per Section 3	Average Student Credit Hours per Section $4 = 2 \times 3$	Total Student Credit Hours $5 = 1 \times 4$	Full Cost (from Stage 1) 6	Cost per Student Credit Hour $7 = 6 \div 5$
Mission Centers							
Chemistry Department	16	4	25.6	102	1,638	$1,270,877	$775.68
Math Department	13	4	30.2	121	1,570	1,069,406	680.98
English Department	18	4	40.6	162	2,923	1,058,717	362.18
History Department	21	4	20.3	81	1,705	1,026,563	602.02
Economics Department	20	4	23.8	95	1,900	1,230,500	647.63
Totals	88				9,737	$5,656,064	$580.87

Assume that during the period covered by the cost report, the five departments taught 88 sections of courses, with the resulting cost per credit hour shown in Table 22.3.

Assume now that there are two students, each of whom enrolled in one section of a course in the Economics Department. Using the department's cost per student credit hour of $647.63 (shown in Table 22.3), we might conclude that the full cost per student in each section was the same, as shown below:

Student	Course	Credit Hours	Cost per Credit Hour	Total Cost
A	Economics 101	4	$647.63	$2,590.52
B	Economics 501	4	$647.63	$2,590.52

This analysis would be reasonably accurate only if all sections had the same enrollments, were taught by faculty earning the same salaries, and used the same amount of departmental administrative resources and allocated service center costs.

The department offers several different courses, however, and some have several sections. In addition, each section uses a different faculty member and draws on different department resources. All of these costs are included in the $786,064 assigned cost figure in Table 22.2 (that is, the amount that is listed in column 1 for the Economics Department). Some of them, such as the salary of the faculty member teaching a section, are also a direct cost of the section. Others, such as the administrative costs of the department, cannot be unambiguously associated with a section. They are direct costs of the department, and are in the $786,064 figure, but they are *indirect* with regard to any given section. And yet, if we are to know the full cost of a section, we must find a way to attach some portion of these costs to it.

In addition, the $444,436 of service center costs that were allocated to the department during Stage 1 also are *indirect costs*—here with regard to both the department and any given section. We also must attach a portion of these costs to each section.

Let's begin with an analysis of the costs that are direct for each course, namely the salary of the faculty member, and let's relax the assumptions that all courses have the same enrollment and are taught by faculty earning identical salaries. Assume the department's 20 sections were distributed as shown in Table 22.4.

TABLE 22.4. COURSE BREAKDOWN IN THE ECONOMICS DEPARTMENT

Course Number	Number of Sections	Credit Hours per Student per Section	Total Enrolled Students	Average Enrollment per Section	Total Student Credit Hours	Average Student Credit Hours per Section
101	6	4	183	30.5	732	122
102	5	4	124	24.8	496	99
301	4	4	74	18.5	296	74
302	4	4	84	21.0	336	84
501	1	4	10	10.0	40	40
	20	4	475	23.8	1,900	95

Assume that Student A took Section 1 of Economics 101 (an introductory course), and that the course's enrollment was 30 students, for a total of 120 credit hours (30 × 4). Assume it was taught by a junior faculty member (comparatively low paid), such that the faculty salary component of the course's cost was $17,500. By contrast, Economics 501 (a doctoral seminar) had an enrollment of only 10, resulting in a total of 40 credit hours. Assume it was taught by a senior faculty member at a cost of $45,000.

The resulting faculty cost per credit hour is $145.83 ($17,500 ÷ 120) for Section 1 of Economics 101, and $1,125.00 ($45,000 ÷ 40) for Economics 501. Therefore, the direct cost per student for each section is as follows:

Student	Course	Credit Hours	Cost per Credit Hour	Total Cost
A	Economics 101 (Section 1)	4	$145.83	$583.33
B	Economics 501	4	$1,125.00	$4,500.00

However, in addition to attaching the direct costs (faculty, in this instance) to a student enrolled in the section, we also must attach a portion of the department's administrative costs plus a portion of the costs that were allocated to the department. Here is where ABC comes into play.

ABC in the Economics Department

Let's begin by assuming that the department does not have an ABC system. Instead, to determine the full cost of each section, we use a single overhead rate. This rate will give each section its share of the department's administrative costs plus the costs that were allocated to the department in Stage 1. Assume the Economics department's direct costs are as follows:

Administrative Salaries	$150,000
Utilities	8,530
Depreciation	8,910
Supplies	8,650
Travel and lodging	64,000
Other direct expenses	10,974
Department administrative costs	$251,064
Faculty salaries	535,000
Total department direct costs	786,064 (The same as the assigned costs in Table 22.2)

The faculty salaries already have been included as direct costs of each section. What remains is to attach the department's administrative costs, plus the $444,436 of allocated costs (from Stage 1) to each section.

A typical unit that some organizations use for computing an "overhead rate" is salary dollars (although there could be many others). If we used salary dollars, we would have an overhead rate of $1.30, computed as follows:

Department Administrative Costs	$251,064
Allocated costs (see Table 22.2)	444,436
Total indirect costs	$695,500
Divided by total faculty salary dollars	535,000
Equals indirect costs per faculty salary dollar	$1.30

The total cost per student then would be as follows:

		Cost per Student		
Student	Course	Faculty Cost	Indirect Cost at $1.30	Total
A	Economics 101 (Section 1)	$583.33	$758.33	$1,341.70
B	Economics 501	$4,500.00	$5,850.00	$10,350.00

The problem with this approach is that it assumes all indirect costs are a function of faculty salary dollars. But that is unlikely. ABC relaxes this assumption

TABLE 22.5. OVERHEAD COST POOLS, DRIVERS, AND UNIT COSTS IN THE ECONOMICS DEPARTMENT

Indirect Cost Pool	Total Cost	Cost Driver	Cost/Unit
Departmental administrative costs	$251,064	Enrolled student	$528.56 (a)
Allocated depreciation (from Stage 1)	72,000	Square foot	$1.44 (b)
Allocated housekeeping (from Stage 1)	32,500	Square foot	$0.65 (c)
Allocated maintenance (from Stage 1)	121,325	Maintenance hour	$18.00 (d)
Allocated administration costs (from Stage 1)	218,611	Faculty salary dollar	$0.41 (e)
Total	$695,500		

Calculations:
(a) $251,064 ÷ 475 enrolled students (from Table 22.4)
(b) $72,000 ÷ 50,000 square feet (from engineering records)
(c) $32,500 ÷ 50,000 square feet (from engineering records)
(d) $121,325 ÷ 6,740 hours (from maintenance records)
(e) $218,611 ÷ $535,000 faculty salary dollars

and attempts to develop multiple overhead cost pools that will more accurately attach the department's indirect costs to its sections.

To apply ABC to the Economics Department, we first determine the department's overhead cost pools—relatively homogeneous collections of indirect costs—and identify a cost driver for each pool. One possible arrangement is shown in Table 22.5. There are several important aspects that should be noted about this example.

In this example, there are five indirect cost pools, with a separate cost driver for each. The driver allows us to assign a portion of the pool's costs to each of the department's sections. For the college's service centers, this example uses the same bases that were used to allocate the costs into the department (such as square feet for depreciation and housekeeping). It then computes the amount of space, maintenance hours, and salary dollars associated with each of the cost centers (sections), and uses the resulting unit costs to distribute the indirect costs among them. The results are shown in Table 22.6.

Although the specific results would change depending on the indirect cost pools and cost drivers selected, Table 22.6 makes it clear not only that the average cost of $2,590.52 per student is quite misleading, but so too are the figures that were computed using faculty salary dollars to attach the indirect costs: $1,341.70 for a student in Section 1 of Economics 101 and $10,350.00 for a student in Economics 501. With the more precise attachment of indirect costs under the ABC system, the cost per student for Section 1 of Economics 101 increased to $1,842.34, and the cost per student for Economics 501 fell to $7,197.67. As Table 22.6 shows, this is because Section 1 of Economics 101 received more indirect costs from every cost pool except administration—which was attached to a section based on the faculty salary.

TABLE 22.6. ACTIVITY-BASED COSTING IN THE DEPARTMENT OF ECONOMICS

Reference Number / Course/Section	Faculty Salary	% of Students Enrolled	Dept. Admin Cost	% of Space	Depreciation Cost	House-keeping Cost	% of Maint. Hours	Maintenance Cost	% of Faculty Salaries	Administration Cost	Total Cost	Cost per Student for 4-Credit Course	Overhead Cost
	1	2	3	4	5	6	7	8	9	10	11	12	13
Course/Section													
Economics 101, Section A	$17,500	0.06	$15,857	0.06	$4,320	$1,950	0.07	$8,493	0.03	$7,151	$55,270	$1,842.34	$37,770
Economics 501, Section A	$45,000	0.02	$5,286	0.02	$1,440	$650	0.01	$1,213	0.08	$18,388	$71,977	$7,197.67	$26,977

Reference Numbers

1. Computed based on faculty salary
2. Computed based on information from college registrar's records
3. Total obtained from department records. Assigned to section based on % of students enrolled
4. Obtained from college maintenance department, based on classroom size
5. Total from Stage 1 (see Table 22.2). Assigned to section based on % of space occupied.
6. Same as column 5
7. Obtained from maintenance department records
8. Total from Stage 1. Assigned to section based on % of maintenance
9. Computed with information from department records
10. Total from Stage 1. Assigned to section based on % of faculty salary dollars
11. Sum of columns 1. 3. 5. 8. and 10
12. Column 11 divided by course enrollment
13. Column 11 minus column 1

Summary of Stage 2

Outside the nonprofit world, ABC has led many managers to revise their thinking about the full cost of their products. It is likely that similar conclusions would be reached in a nonprofit organization that undertook an ABC effort. Indeed, in an era of intense pressures for cost control, a nonprofit that does not have an ABC system may lack essential information for decision making.

Example

The Internal Revenue Service used ABC to guide managers in decision making. In one office, the activity pools were (1) managing accounts, (2) informing, educating, and assisting, (3) ensuring compliance, and (4) resourcing. The cost drivers included volume and cycle time.[9]

Complicating Factors

In practice, the full-cost accounting effort in Stages 1 and 2 has many variations and nuances. Most of these "complicating factors," are dealt with more appropriately in a cost accounting textbook. There are a few worth noting, however.

Defining Direct Costs

There are differences in the ways that different organizations draw the line between direct and indirect costs. For example, in calculating the cost of university research projects, one university may count pension and other fringe benefits of researchers as direct costs, while another may count these items as indirect costs; one may charge secretarial assistance directly to a project, but another may charge all secretarial help to a common pool (a service center), allocate it to different mission center, and then attach it to each project using a cost driver, much as we did with the administrative costs at Owens College. Similarly, if electricity, heat, and other utilities are metered for each mission center, they are direct costs; if not, they must be allocated to mission centers. Because of these differences in accounting practices, comparisons of indirect costs among different universities (or other nonprofits) are likely of little use.

Appropriateness of Indirect Costs

Frequently, the issue is not one of distinguishing between direct and indirect costs, but of the appropriateness of the cost item itself. For example, some people claim that university indirect costs have been rising unchecked for years. University officials contend that such costs are needed to run the university. At issue are several questions: (1) What kinds of costs should be allowed? (2) Which projects should help to pay for these costs? (3) What kinds of efficiency standards should be used (such as how many librarians are needed to run the library)?

Example

Much university research is supported by the federal government through contracts and grants. If the support comes in the form of a contract, the university is paid in accordance with the principles contained in Circular A-21 of the Office of Management and Budget. These principles provide for direct costs plus an equitable share of indirect costs, including a use allowance for depreciation of buildings and equipment, operations and maintenance of plant, general administration and general expenses, departmental administration, student administration and services, and library.

Despite the OMB's principles, claims of overcharging for indirect costs are frequent. In some instances, the debate has reached the faculty ranks, with faculty expressing concern that high indirect rates impede a university's ability to obtain research funding.

Similar claims have surfaced in other nonprofit organizations, as well. In health care, for example, concerns have been voiced about the indirect costs that teaching hospitals charge Medicare for medical education. Teaching hospitals claim that these costs are appropriate in that, over the long term, they benefit Medicare's beneficiaries. This, of course, is not a debate that will be resolved by improved cost accounting alone.

Imputed Costs

In certain situations, many would argue that imputed costs also need to be incorporated into the cost accounting system. The cost of polluting water is such an example. In the U.S., companies have not been charged for the social cost of the rivers they pollute, whereas in the Ruhr Valley in Germany, polluters pay a charge based on the effect of the effluent on the river's biochemical oxygen demand. The revenue derived from this charge is used to help pay for water treatment.

Example

The Dutch government developed a system of national accounting to reflect the damage done to the air, water, soil, and animal and plant life, and to account for the cost of maintaining or restoring them. Sweden, France, and Norway also have engaged in similar efforts, or what is now called "green accounting."[10]

Differential Cost Accounting

The full-cost accounting principles discussed above are useful for activities such as pricing, profitability analysis, and reimbursement. They are inappropriate, however, for a variety of decisions—called alternative choice decisions—made regularly in an organization. The contrast between full- and differential-cost accounting, as well as between these two and responsibility accounting, is shown in Exhibit 22.1. As this exhibit indicates, alternative choice decisions include (a) retaining or discontinuing a program or service that is unprofitable on a full-cost basis, (b) performing an activity in-house or outsourcing it, (c) offering a special price for one of the organization's products in exchange for, say, a large volume of business, and (d) selling or disposing an obsolete asset.

EXHIBIT 22.1. DIFFERENT COSTS FOR DIFFERENT PURPOSES.

	Full-Cost Accounting	Differential-Cost Accounting	Responsibility Accounting
Costs Used	Direct versus indirect	Fixed versus variable	Controllable versus noncontrollable
Activities Performed	Assignment of costs to cost centers	Analysis of cost behavior	Programming
	Choice of allocation bases	Cost-volume-profit analysis	Budgeting
	Allocation of service center costs to mission centers	Contribution analysis	Variance analysis
			Reporting and evaluation
Management Uses/Decisions	Pricing	Retain or discontinue an unprofitable program	Program additions and modifications
	Product line profitability		
		Outsource an activity	Cost control
	Strategic decisions concerning which products and services to offer	Offer a special price	Performance measurement
		Sell or dispose of an obsolete asset	

The Nature of Cost Analysis for Alternative Choice Decisions

A key question in an alternative choice decision is: "How will costs (and sometimes revenues) change under the proposed set of circumstances?" That is, which costs (and revenues) will be *different?* For example, if an organization outsources an activity, some existing costs will be eliminated but some new costs will be incurred. If a product or service line is discontinued, some costs will be eliminated, but so (usually) will some revenues. In the special-price and obsolete-asset situations, some revenue will be received but costs will change only minimally or not at all.

Assessing differential revenues ordinarily is easy, but determining how costs will change can be tricky. Indeed, using full-cost information as a basis for assessing cost behavior can lead managers to make decisions that are financially detrimental to their organizations.

Example

The full cost of educating a child in a certain public school system is $7,500 a year. This figure includes teachers' salaries, curriculum supplies and materials, a fair share of individual school overhead expenses (such as the principal's salary) and a fair share of the school system's overhead expenses (such as the school system superintendent's salary). The decision to reduce enrollment by 10 students clearly would not save $75,000 (10 × $7,500), since it is unlikely that teacher salaries, individual school overhead, or school system overhead would change with a reduction of 10 students.

Even the decision to close an entire school would not save $7,500 per student since it is unlikely that the school system's overhead expenses would be reduced. Moreover, if closing a given school resulted in shifting some tax revenues that had been assigned to the school system to some other use, and these revenues exceeded $7,500 per student, the school system would be worse off as a result of the closing—its revenues would have declined by more than its costs.

Cost Behavior

The first section of this chapter distinguished between direct and indirect costs. This section uses a different distinction—dividing costs between those that are relatively fixed and those that vary with changes in volume. This fixed/variable distinction lets us see more clearly how a change in the volume of activity of a particular program or service line will affect its costs. These different types of costs, as well as the refinements of step-function and semi-variable costs, are shown schematically in Figure 22.2.

FIGURE 22.2. TYPES OF COST BEHAVIOR.

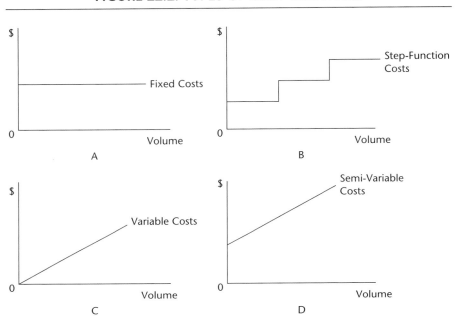

Fixed Costs

Fixed costs are independent of the number of units that are produced. While no costs are fixed if the time period is long enough, the relevant range for fixed costs (that is, the span of units over which they remain unchanged) generally is quite large, so they can be viewed graphically as shown in Segment A of Figure 22.2. An example of a fixed cost in most organizations is rent for a building. Regardless of the volume of activity in the building, the amount of rent remains the same.

Step-Function Costs

Step-function costs are similar to fixed costs except they have a much narrower relevant range. As such, they do not change in a smooth fashion, but are added in "lumps," or "steps." The result is that, graphically, they take the form shown in Segment B, where the dotted lines represent discontinuous jumps. A good example of a step-function cost in many organizations is supervision. In a social service agency, for instance, as the number of social workers, and other professionals increases, supervisory personnel must be added. Since it is difficult for most organizations to add part-time supervisory help, supervisory costs will tend to behave in a step-like fashion. Similarly, in a school system or university, new faculty are added in step-like increments when the number of students (either in the school or in a given course) reaches a certain level.

Variable Costs

Variable costs, shown in Segment C of Figure 22.2, change in a roughly linear fashion with changes in volume, such that, as volume increases, total variable costs increase in constant proportion. The result is a straight line whose slope is determined by the amount of variable costs associated with each unit of output. In a hospital laboratory, for example, reagents would be a variable cost, increasing in direct proportion to increases in the number of tests processed. Some organizations will have relatively high variable costs per unit, resulting in a line that slopes upward quite steeply; others will have relatively low variable costs for each unit of output, resulting in a line with a more gradual slope.

Semi-Variable Costs

Semi-variable costs (sometimes called mixed costs) share features of both fixed and variable costs. There is a minimum level that is fixed, and the cost line then rises linearly with increases in volume. The result is a line that begins at some level above zero, and slopes upward, as shown in Segment D of Figure 22.2. A good example of a semi-variable cost is electricity. Typically, there is some base cost each month for electrical service that an organization must incur even if it uses no electricity at all. Costs then increase in accordance with the number of kilowatt hours used. Similar cost patterns exist for other utilities such as telephone, gas, and water.

Total Costs

Total costs are the sum of the fixed, step-function, variable, and semi-variable components. Because cost analyses combining all four types of costs are quite complex, however, most analysts generally classify all costs as either fixed or variable. For semi-variable costs, this can be accomplished by incorporating the fixed element into total fixed costs and adding the variable element to the variable costs. For step-function costs, an assumption is made about the volume range, and the cost is added to fixed costs.

Example

The Abbington Youth Center has annual rent and other fixed costs of $100,000, and variable supply and material costs of $100 per student. Its annual meal costs are semi-variable. They have a fixed element (a part-time dietitian) of $14,000, and a variable component (food and beverage) of $500 per student.

In computing Abbington's total costs, we can divide semi-variable costs into their fixed and variable components. The result is the following breakdown of costs:

Cost Element	Fixed Amount	Variable Amount (per student)
Rent and other fixed	$100,000	$0
Supplies and materials	0	100
Meals	$14,000	500
Total	$114,000	$600

Abbington also has a student-teacher ratio of 15:1. Faculty salaries currently are $30,000 per year. The step function relationship for teacher salaries is shown in Figure 22.3:

FIGURE 22.3. STEP-FUNCTION COSTS FOR ABBINGTON YOUTH CENTER.

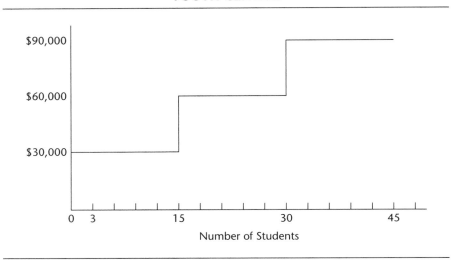

Once teacher salaries have been simplified in this manner, they can be added to the fixed cost totals. If we assume enrollment of 30 to 45 students, our total costs would be as follows:

Cost Element	Fixed Amount	Variable Amount (per student)
Rent and other fixed	$100,000	$0
Supplies and materials	0	100
Meals	$14,000	500
Teachers (30 to 45 students)	90,000	0
Total	$204,000	$600

Note that the fixed costs are only valid within a range of 30 to 45 students. Above 45 students, they jump to a higher step. Below 30, they would drop to a lower step.

Cost-Volume-Profit Analysis

Once costs have been classified as either fixed or variable, we can analyze how they will vary with changes in the volume of activity. One technique used in such situations is *cost-volume-profit (CVP) analysis*. The intent of CVP analysis is to determine either (a) the volume of activity needed for an organization to achieve its financial surplus (or profit) goal, (b) the price that it needs to charge to achieve its surplus goal, or (c) the cost limits (fixed and/or variable) it needs to adhere to if it is to achieve its surplus goal.

A CVP analysis usually is conducted for a particular activity within an organization—such as a product line or program. It begins with the basic equation for profit:

$$\text{Profit} = \text{Total revenue (TR)} - \text{Total costs (TC)}$$

Total revenue for many activities is quite easy to calculate. If we assume that price is represented by the letter p and volume by the letter x, then total revenue is price times volume, or

$$TR = px$$

Total costs are somewhat more complicated. CVP analysis requires a recognition of the different types of cost behavior in a organization: fixed, step-function, variable, and semi-variable. Let's begin with the simplest of cases, where there are no step-function or semi-variable costs. In this instance, the formula would be quite simple:

$$\text{Total costs} = \text{Fixed costs} + \text{Variable costs}$$

Fixed costs can be represented by the letter a, and variable costs per unit by the letter b. Thus, total variable costs is bx, where, as before, x represents volume. The resulting cost equation is

$$TC = a + bx$$

This means that the fundamental profit equation can be shown as: Profit = px − (a + bx), which can be represented graphically as shown below. On this graph, point x1 is the *breakeven volume*—it is the point at which total revenue, px, equals total costs, a + bx. With volume in excess of x1, the organization earns a surplus; below x1, it incurs a loss.

FIGURE 22.4. GRAPHIC REPRESENTATION OF REVENUE, FIXED COSTS, AND VARIABLE COSTS.

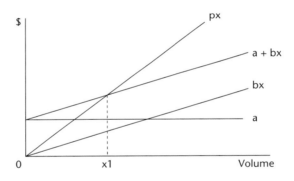

Example

The Alberta Chamber of Commerce (ACOC) publishes a monthly magazine for its members. The publication department has fixed costs of $100,000 a month, variable costs per magazine of $.80, and charges $1.80 per magazine. To determine breakeven volume (number of magazines per month), we can begin with the CVP formula, and substitute the known elements. We then solve for the unknown, which in this case is volume, or x.

$$Profit = px - (a + bx)$$

At breakeven, profit = 0, and px = a + bx, or

$$1.80x = 100,000 + .80x$$
$$1.00x = 100,000$$
$$x = 100,000$$

Breakeven therefore is 100,000 magazines. To confirm:

Revenue: $1.80 \times 100,000$	=	$180,000
Less costs:		
Variable costs: $0.80 \times 100,000$ = 80,000		
Fixed costs: $100,000 per month = 100,000		$(180,000)
Profit		$ 0

Unit Contribution Margin

An important aspect of CVP analysis is unit contribution margin. This is the contribution to fixed costs that comes about as a result of each additional unit sold, or the difference between price and unit-variable cost. By rearranging the terms of the CVP formula, we can see that breakeven volume is simply fixed costs divided by unit contribution margin, as follows:

$$px = a + bx$$
$$px - bx = a$$
$$x(p - b) = a$$
$$x = \frac{a}{(p - b)}$$

Stated somewhat differently, price minus unit-variable cost tells us how much each unit sold *contributes* to the recovery of fixed costs. When this amount is divided into fixed costs, the result is the volume needed to recover all fixed costs, that is, the breakeven volume.

Example

The ACOC publication department has a unit contribution margin of $1.00 ($1.80 − $.80). When we divide this amount into its fixed costs of $100,000, we arrive at its breakeven volume of 100,000 magazines.

Incorporating Other Variables into a CVP Analysis

Thus far, we have been using CVP analysis to solve only for breakeven volume. Clearly, if we knew (a) how many units of our product we were likely to sell,

(b) our fixed costs, and (c) our unit-variable costs, we then could determine the price needed to break even. Similarly, if we were in an environment where price was given, and we knew approximately how many units we could sell at that price, we could set up either fixed costs or unit-variable costs as the unknown and solve for it.

We also could incorporate a need for a financial surplus into a CVP analysis simply by adding the amount of desired surplus to our fixed costs. We then could calculate a "breakeven point" with the new level of "fixed costs."

CVP Analysis with Semi-Variable Costs

As discussed earlier, incorporating semi-variable costs into a CVP analysis is relatively easy. Since semi-variable costs have fixed and variable components, we simply need to add the fixed component to the fixed cost total, and the variable component to the unit-variable cost amount.

CVP Analysis with Step-Function Costs

The analysis of step-function costs can be a little tricky. Ideally, we would like to be able to assume that, for any given volume level, we could simply add together the step-function costs and the fixed costs to give us the total applicable fixed costs. We then could use the CVP formula. Unfortunately, since volume is the unknown in the equation, the process is not quite that simple, as the following example illustrates.

Example

Assume that, in addition to its $100,000 in fixed costs, ACOC's publication department has some supervisory costs. These costs behave as follows:

Volume	Costs
0–50,000	$10,000
50,001–100,000	$20,000
100,001–150,000	$30,000
150,001–200,000	$40,000

If we use the first level of step-function costs in the breakeven formula, we have the following equation:

$$
\begin{aligned}
1.80x &= (100{,}000 + 10{,}000) + .80x \\
1.00x &= 110{,}000 \\
x &= 110{,}000
\end{aligned}
$$

The problem with this solution is that, while the breakeven volume is 110,000 magazines, the relevant range for the step-function costs was only 0–50,000 magazines. Thus, a breakeven of greater than 50,000 magazines is invalid. Only when we get to the third level do we encounter a valid solution, as follows.

$$
\begin{aligned}
\mathbf{1.80x} &= \mathbf{(100{,}000 + 30{,}000) + .80x} \\
1.00x &= 130{,}000 \\
x &= 130{,}000
\end{aligned}
$$

The conclusion we can draw from this analysis is that the incorporation of step-function costs into the CVP formula requires a trial-and-error process to reach the breakeven volume.

Complicating Factors

In addition to step-function costs, there are several other factors that can complicate a CVP analysis. Some of these relate to the occasional need to use full-cost reports as the source of cost information. In particular, two potential problems arise when information for a differential-cost analysis is obtained from full-cost reports: cost distinctions and the behavior of allocated costs. Each of these potential problems calls for the analyst to exercise caution in working with full-cost data.

Cost Distinctions

The analysis of differential costs would be simplified if, as occasionally is assumed, all indirect costs are fixed and all direct costs are variable. But this is rarely the case. Exhibit 22.2 contains examples of four different cost types and their fixed/variable, direct/indirect distinctions. Note that each of the four cells in the matrix contains a possible cost, leading to the conclusion that the direct and indirect costs in a full-cost accounting system must be analyzed individually to determine how they can be expected to behave as volume changes.

EXHIBIT 22.2. COST EXAMPLES: FIXED/VARIABLE VERSUS DIRECT/INDIRECT IN THE FOSTER HOME PROGRAM OF A SOCIAL SERVICE AGENCY.

	Fixed	Variable
Direct	Supervisor's salary in the foster home care program	Payments to foster parents for room and board
Indirect	A portion of the executive director's salary, which is a fixed cost, and is part of administration—a support center whose costs are allocated to the foster home program	Electric bills, which are mainly variable costs, and are part of administration—a support center whose costs are allocated to the foster home program

Behavior of Allocated Costs

Additional complexities are introduced into a cost analysis when overhead costs are involved. Two such complexities involve allocation bases and the stepdown sequence.

Misleading Allocation Bases. Although an organization may attempt to measure the use of service center costs very precisely, there nevertheless can be many instances where a given service center's basis of allocation does not accurately reflect the actual use of its services by receiving cost centers. If, for example, a product line is discontinued, the organization may be able to reduce some of the service center costs that were allocated to the mission center in question. In most instances, however, only the variable costs in the service center (plus, perhaps, some step-function costs) will be reduced. The remaining costs will be allocated to other cost centers.

Example

Consider the administration and general (A&G) service center. A reduction of staff in a given mission center will lead to a reduction in total salaries in that mission center. If A&G costs are allocated on the basis of salaries, there will be a reduction in the amount of A&G allocated to this mission center. It is highly unlikely, however, that there will be a reduction in the staff or other costs in the A&G cost center. Thus, more A&G costs will be allocated to those cost centers that did not reduce their salaries.

The reverse may happen as well. That is, a reduction in a mission center's activity may lead to a decrease in a service center's costs, but the mission center may not realize the full effect.

Example

Consider a housekeeping service center whose costs are allocated on the basis of square feet. A change in the activities in a given mission center may reduce the center's need for housekeeping services, which may permit the manager of the housekeeping service center to reduce some costs. Yet, unless the space used by the mission center is reduced, the cost report (that allocates housekeeping on a square-footage basis) will not show an equivalent reduction in the housekeeping costs allocated to the mission center. The costs allocated to the mission center will fall slightly as a result of the lower housekeeping costs *overall,* but the reduced allocation will be much less than the actual cost savings that took place in the housekeeping service center. The rest of the savings will accrue to those cost centers that continue to receive the same amount of housekeeping as before.

Effects of the Stepdown Sequence. Recall that the total cost allocated from each service center includes both its assigned costs plus the costs that were allocated to it from previous service centers (or "steps") in the stepdown. Therefore, costs of those service centers lowest in the stepdown sequence will include allocations from all the service centers above them.

Example

In a hospital, if the social work service center is far down in the stepdown sequence, the social work costs allocated to a particular mission center will have a significant allocated component (for example, administration, housekeeping, laundry, and so on). It may be possible to reduce the use of social workers in a mission center by reducing the number of patients receiving social services, or by changing the nature of the treatment plans. However, the full impact of that change on the costs in the social services cost center will be overstated if one uses the fully allocated social service amount. This is because the social services cost center contains costs that have been allocated to it from a variety of other service centers. The costs in these service centers will not be affected at all by the change in a mission center's use of social workers.

Differential Costs Versus Fixed and Variable Costs

With an understanding of costs according to the nature of their behavior, and with some background in the elements of CVP analysis, we are in a position to undertake a differential-cost analysis. A differential-cost analysis attempts to identify the behavior of an organization's costs under one or more alternative scenarios. These scenarios are related to the decision under consideration. To illustrate, consider the following:

Example

Clearwater Transportation Service operates two minivans that transport senior citizens on errands and shopping trips. It charges $2.00 a mile for each service mile driven. Last year, Van 1 drove 60,000 service miles, and Van 2 drove 30,000 service miles. The variable cost per mile (gasoline, tires, wear and tear) for each van was 80 cents. Each driver (both were part-time) was paid a salary of $20,000 per year. Rent and administration totaled $60,000, and were allocated to each van on the basis of the number of service miles driven. As a result, total revenues and expenses for the year were as follows:

Item	Van 1	Van 2	Total
Revenue	2.00 × 60,000 = $120,000	2.00 × 30,000 = $60,000	$180,000
Expenses:			
Variable costs	.80 × 60,000 = 48,000	.80 × 30,000 = 24,000	$72,000
Drivers	20,000	20,000	40,000
Overhead costs (rent and admin.)	40,000	20,000	60,000
Total expenses	$108,000	$64,000	$172,000
Surplus (deficit)	$12,000	($4,000)	$8,000

Would Clearwater's financial performance would have improved if Van 2 (which lost money) had been discontinued at the beginning of the year? To answer this question, we must structure the data in terms of differential costs. The question is not whether Van 2 lost money on a *full-cost* basis (as it did), but rather the nature of its differential costs and revenues; that is, how would Clearwater's revenues and costs have changed if Van 2 had been discontinued?

Although the data are not as good as we might like, we nevertheless can see that discontinuing Van 2 would have eliminated its revenue and its variable costs, as well as the fixed cost of the driver. From all indications, however, the overhead costs (rent and administration) would have continued (that is, they were not differential). The result would have been a shift from an $8,000 surplus to an $8,000 deficit, as the analysis below indicates:

Item	Van 1
Revenue	2.00 × 60,000 = $120,000
Expenses:	
Variable costs	.80 × 60,000 = 48,000
Driver	20,000
Overhead costs (rent and administration)	60,000
Total expenses	128,000
Surplus (Deficit)	($8,000)

This example illustrates several important principles.

Principle #1. Full-Cost Information Can Be Misleading

The kind of information available from a full-cost system can produce highly misleading results if used for differential-cost decisions. This is due mainly to the apparent behavior of overhead costs when they are allocated, as contrasted with their true behavior. Note that the overhead allocated to Van 2 did not go away when we eliminated the vehicle; it simply was reallocated to Van 1.

Principle #2. Differential Costs Can Include Both Fixed and Variable Costs

Although initially counterintuitive, differential costs can include both fixed and variable costs. In the Clearwater case, the driver's salary, while a fixed cost of Van 2, was eliminated when we eliminated the van. However, as long as we operate the van, we have the fixed cost of the salary; it does not fluctuate in accordance with the number of miles driven (within the relevant range). But when we eliminate the van, we also eliminate this cost in its entirety; thus, it is differential in terms of a decision to eliminate or retain the service.

Principle #3. Assumptions Are Needed

Differential-cost analyses focus on the future. As such, they require the analyst to make assumptions about many factors, from unit prices to staff efficiency. For example, inflation will affect an organization's costs, and perhaps its prices. The general state of the economy along with a wide variety of other matters will affect volume. For many managers, these factors raise concerns about the reliability of a differential-cost analysis. Despite these concerns, however, since we do not have perfect knowledge of the future, we must make assumptions as best we can about how costs and revenues will behave.

Principle #4. Sensitivity Analysis Is Essential

Because assumptions play such a crucial role in a differential analysis, we must attempt to identify and document them as completely as possible, and to explore how changes in them would affect the conclusions of the analysis. This activity is called *sensitivity analysis.*

If we were doing a sensitivity analysis for the Clearwater scenario, we might try to determine how many more miles Van 1 would need to drive for the organization to maintain its $8,000 surplus. Or, if we thought we might be able to reduce our rent and administrative costs with an elimination of Van 2, we might ask by how much they would need to fall to maintain the $8,000 surplus. For example, if we could reduce them by $16,000 by eliminating Van 2, we would be indifferent. That is, with administrative costs reduced to $44,000 ($60,000-$16,000), Van 1 would earn a surplus of $8,000—the same as we were earning with both vans. As a result, any reduction in overhead beyond $16,000 that resulted from the elimination of Van 2 would favor the decision to eliminate it.

Principle #5. Causality Must Be Present

A key aspect of differential analysis is causality—for an item to be included in a differential analysis, it must be *caused* by the alternative under consideration. For example, if we assume there will be an increase in the miles driven by Van 1, we would need to be certain that it was *caused* by the elimination of Van 2. If Van 1 would have driven more miles anyway, the increased mileage is irrelevant for the differential analysis. If, on the other hand, we assume that the elimination of Van 2 means that some people who would have used it now will use Van 1, then the increased mileage is relevant for the differential analysis. We would need to include that additional mileage in computing Van 1's revenue and variable expenses under the alternative scenario.

The same is true for cost items such as rent and administration. If we were planning to decrease our administrative costs with or without Van 2, then the change is irrelevant for the differential analysis. If, by contrast, the elimination of Van 2 would allow us to decrease administrative costs (such as to eliminate a portion of the dispatcher wage expenses), then we would need to include this decrease in the differential analysis.

Principle #6. Information Must Be Structured Appropriately

An analysis of differential costs is most easily performed when the fixed and variable costs of the particular activity are analyzed separately from the allocated overhead costs. An analysis that separates costs in this way usually is structured in terms of *contribution to overhead*. The difference between a unit's revenue and its variable, semi-variable, fixed, and step-function costs is its contribution to the organization's overhead costs.

A *contribution income statement*, which is the term given to this analysis, has a different format from a more traditional income statement. One typical construction is as follows:

> Total Revenue (net)
>
> Less: total variable costs
>
> Equals: margin (for fixed and overhead costs)
>
> Less: the product's or program's fixed costs
>
> Equals: the product's or program's contribution to the organization's overhead costs
>
> Less: allocated overhead costs
>
> Equals: surplus (deficit) on a full-cost basis

Table 22.7 shows how a contribution income statement would look for Clearwater. As it illustrates, while Van 2 was losing money on a full-cost basis, it was contributing $16,000 toward paying for overhead.

The general principle is that, in the short-run, it is unwise to eliminate an activity that is contributing to the coverage of overhead, even if is losing money

TABLE 22.7. EXAMPLE OF A CONTRIBUTION INCOME STATEMENT

Item	Van 1	Van 2	Total
Revenue	2.00 x 60,000 = $120,000	2.00 x 30,000 = $60,000	$180,000
Less: Variable expenses	0.80 x 60,000 = 48,000	0.80 x 30,000 = 24,000	72,000
Contribution to fixed expenses	$72,000	$36,000	$108,000
Less: Fixed expenses (Drivers)	20,000	20,000	40,000
Contribution to overhead	$52,000	$16,000	$68,000
Overhead (rent and admin.)	40,000	20,000	60,000
Profit (loss)	$12,000	($4,000)	$8,000

on a full-cost basis. This is because eliminating the activity will reduce the total contribution to overhead costs and thus will either reduce the organization's surplus or increase its deficit.

The Outsourcing Decision

Until now, the discussion of differential costs has been in situations where the alternative choice decision involved a change in volume. This is the characteristic of most keep/drop and special price situations. Many other types of alternative choice decisions do not involve a change in volume, however. Perhaps the most common of these is an outsourcing decision. For many government and nonprofit entities, outsourcing has involved *privatizing* the service (that is, contracting with a private, for-profit entity to provide it).

In federal, state, and local governments, outsourcing has become increasingly popular during the past twenty-five years. It has touched on a wide variety of services that previously were seen as the exclusive domain of government, and in almost all instances, the principal driving force has been cost savings. The diversity of privatization initiatives has been impressive, ranging from prison operations to animal control.

Examples

Butte, Montana, saved $600,000 a year by contracting with a private firm to run its municipal hospital. Newark, New Jersey, used a private firm to collect about one-third of its refuse, at a reported annual savings of over $200,000. It also hired private contractors to provide services such as tree trimming, building demolition, snow plowing, and street cleaning. Farmington, New Mexico, contracted with an independent firm to run its airport control tower at a cost savings of almost $200,000 a year. Scottsdale, Arizona—the first U.S. city to use a private company for fire protection—boasted better than average fire response times, at less than half the cost to cities of comparable size.[11]

Outsourcing Principles

Although each outsourcing opportunity is unique, and must be analyzed separately to decide on the relevant costs and other matters, there are a few general principles that are pertinent to almost all such decisions.

Time Period. The longer the time period involved, the more costs are differential. For example, if the alternative being considered is to outsource a single printing job rather than use in-house facilities, the only reduction in costs might be the savings in paper and ink; the printing presses remain, payment to employees probably would not be reduced, and no overhead costs would be affected. If, however, the proposal is to discontinue the in-house print shop permanently, all the direct costs associated with operating it would be saved, as might be some of the relevant overhead costs.

Role of Depreciation. A common error in calculating differential costs for outsourcing decisions (and other alternative choice decisions) is to include depreciation on plant and equipment as a cost that would be saved if the organization used an outside contractor to provide the service. Depreciation is not a differential cost, however. Once assets have been acquired, the costs to purchase them have been incurred.[12] Depreciation is simply the mechanism that charges each accounting period with the expense associated with "using up" the asset. Since the past cannot be undone, and money spent cannot be recovered, there are no cash effects associated with depreciation.

Of course, if the asset can be sold, the amount realized is a differential cash inflow associated with the outsourcing decision, but this amount is based on the asset's *market* value, not its *book* value (purchase price less accumulated depreciation). Moreover, it is a one-time cash inflow only, and therefore applies only to the first year of outsourcing.

If the outsourcing time frame is sufficiently long, such that the acquisition of new assets would be required under the "in-house" option, but not under the "outsource" option, then depreciation might be used as a surrogate for the costs associated with replacing the assets as they wear out. However, the replacement cost rarely will correspond to the original purchase cost. It might be lower in the case of assets whose replacement cost is falling (such as computers), or higher if the replacement cost is increasing (such as medical technology).[13]

Nonquantifiable Factors. In any outsourcing decision (in fact, in any *alternative choice decision*) there are a variety of factors that cannot be quantified easily, if at all, and that can easily tip the balance in one direction or another, frequently overriding the financial analysis. This is especially true if the financial analysis indicates that all options under consideration have roughly similar cost and revenue implications.

Nonquantitative considerations typically include factors such as quality, service, delivery, and reputation of the vendor. They also may include market considerations, such as the difficulty and/or cost of switching from one vendor to another if a particular relationship does not work out to management's satisfaction.

Examples

A university that contracts for snow plowing services for its parking lots typically has an easy time switching from one vendor to another. There are many people with pickup trucks and snow plowing blades who can provide the service. By contrast, a hospital that outsources its social services may have a difficult time switching vendors since the number of such vendors may be quite small.

A related consideration is the cost of switching back to internal service provision. After outsourcing a service, an organization will likely eliminate the facilities, equipment, and trained personnel needed to provide it. Obtaining replacement facilities and equipment, and training new personnel, may be quite costly. If the market for vendors is not very competitive, and the organization therefore will have a difficult time finding a replacement vendor, it may find itself in difficulty.

Finally, nonquantitative factors can include stakeholder sensitivity. If a municipality outsources a service, such as waste collection and disposal, and the service is not performed according to expectations, the citizenry generally looks to the municipality, not the private contractor, as the responsible party. Depending on the service and its importance to the community, this can have an impact on how the citizenry votes in the next election.

Example

If a municipality outsources the printing of a brochure for a summer youth program and the vendor performs badly, the mistakes can be corrected before the citizenry is aware of them. By contrast, if the municipality outsources snow removal, and the streets are not plowed within a reasonable time after a heavy snowstorm, the citizenry will be acutely aware of the problem, even if corrective measures are taken later.

The combination of stakeholder sensitivity, the nature of the market for vendors, and the difficulty of either switching vendors or returning to internal service provision are shown schematically in Figure 22.5. As Figure 22.5 indicates, if stakeholder sensitivity to service quality is high, if the market is not especially competitive, and if switching costs are high, the outsourcing activity is high risk.

Example

From a patient's or physician's perspective, a hospital's laundry service clearly is much more important than, say, its publications department. Patients and physicians are very concerned about the availability of clean linens and scrubs, but only minimally concerned about printing quality.

FIGURE 22.5. THE THREE DIMENSIONS OF OUTSOURCING RISK.

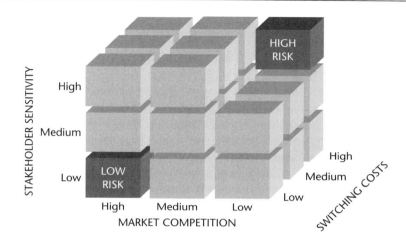

The low-risk cube in Figure 22.5 embodies services such as the publication department with a combination of low stakeholder sensitivity, high competition, and low switching costs—situations with a high probability of successful outsourcing without the need for careful vendor management. A service such as snow removal might be in the northwest front corner, where stakeholder sensitivity is high but where a poorly performing vendor can be replaced easily and quickly. By contrast, with high-risk outsourcing an organization must give very careful consideration to how a vendor will be managed.

Example

Some years ago the Commonwealth of Massachusetts outsourced its Medicaid Management Information System, a system that mailed several hundred thousand checks each month to indigent citizens. Citizen sensitivity was high, and there were almost no vendors with computer systems of sufficient size and sophistication to undertake the various activities (only one of which was sending out checks). Moreover, due to the need to transfer software (or rewrite code in some instances), plus the difficulty of moving data files from one vendor to another and performing the needed audits, the switching costs were high. When the vendor went bankrupt, several hundred thousand Medicaid recipients learned, quite painfully, the true meaning of "high-risk" outsourcing.

Managing High-Risk Outsourcing

Even though a service may fall into the high-risk area of Figure 22.5, it still may have considerable cost-saving potential. To achieve this potential, however, the organization must manage the vendor carefully. As Figure 22.6 indicates, for a high-risk outsourcing contract to be successful, there must be a high level of output measurement, a great deal of ongoing communication and cooperation, and a full linkage with the organization's responsibility accounting system.[14]

This latter requirement is especially important. For example, the various results measures for the outsourced services need to be reported on a regularly. Otherwise, managers may learn about a problem too late to do anything about it.

In short, when an organization engages in high-risk outsourcing, and wishes to assure its stakeholders that the savings realized from the outsourced activity are not matched by a reduction in service quality, it must develop an appropriate set of activities to manage the vendor. Given that many outsourcing arrangements

FIGURE 22.6. THREE KEY ACTIVITIES FOR MANAGING HIGH-RISK OUTSOURCED SERVICES.

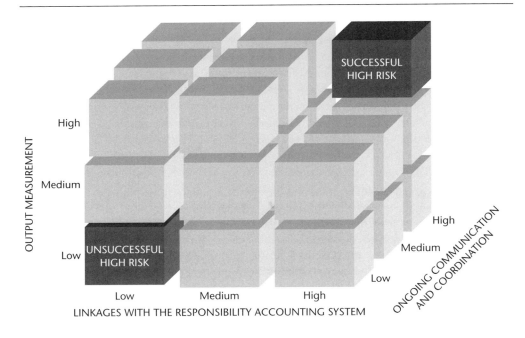

are of a high-risk nature, a focus on these activities is essential for organizations that wish to assure their stakeholders of effective services at a reasonable cost.

Responsibility Accounting

A nonprofit organization is affected by many forces in its *external environment*, but the forces vary greatly among organizations. For example, one nonprofit might have relatively certain revenues, almost no competition, and programs that are essentially unchanged from one year to the next; a good example is a school. Another, such as a museum, might have relatively uncertain sources of funding, numerous competitors, and programs whose emphases shift rapidly. Similarly, government organizations, as well as organizations that receive substantial funds from government sources, are subject to a variety of pressures and scrutiny from legislative bodies and the general public. In these cases, the desires of the press and the public for information constitute an important responsibility accounting issue.

An organization also has an *internal environment*, and senior management must give careful consideration to the fit among its elements. These elements include the authority and influence structure, the program structure, the account structure, and a variety of behavioral and cultural factors. In addition, all organizations except the tiniest have a recurring set of activities—called the responsibility accounting process—that also are important.

The Authority and Influence Structure

Organizational structure refers to the *formal* reporting relationships among managers and other individuals in an entity.[15] Senior management weighs many factors in determining the best formal structure. These considerations involve questions such as the most appropriate division of tasks, the activities that should be carried out by specialized staff units versus those that should be the responsibility of line managers, and the decisions that should be made at or near the top of the organization versus ones that should be delegated to lower levels.

An organization's formal structure can take one of several basic forms: functional, divisional, or matrix. In a matrix, the most complex structure—and the one that characterizes many nonprofit organizations—individuals have two supervisors: a divisional or program supervisor and a functional supervisor. Social workers might report to a team manager for their day-to-day activities, for example, and to a director of social work for their professional development and training. In a hospital, nurses might have similar dual reporting responsibilities. In some universities, faculty report to both a department chair and a program director

Responsibility Centers

The formal structure for responsibility accounting purposes is defined in terms of a network of responsibility centers, each of which is headed by a manager who is in charge of its activities. There are five different types of responsibility centers. Exhibit 22.3 lists them and the responsibility accounting implications of each.

EXHIBIT 22.3. TYPES OF RESPONSIBILITY CENTERS AND ASSOCIATED RESPONSIBILITIES.

Type	Responsible for ...
Revenue center	Revenue earned by the center
Discretionary expense center	Total expenses incurred by the center regardless of the volume of activity
Standard expense center	Expenses per unit of output, but not total expenses, incurred by the center
Profit center	Total revenues minus total expenses of the center
Investment center	Total revenues minus expenses of the center, computed as a percent of the center's assets, i.e. the center's return on assets (ROA)

From the viewpoint of senior management, the whole organization is an investment center; it must obtain a satisfactory return on assets (ROA) if it is to remain financially viable. This is true for nonprofit as well as for-profit organizations.[16] The role of senior management is to decide how best to decentralize ROA responsibility throughout the organization. As a result, in any organization except a very small one, there is a hierarchy of responsibility centers. Senior management's objective in choosing a given type of responsibility center is to hold the center's manager accountable for those inputs and outputs over which he or she can exercise a reasonable degree of control. As a result, all five types of responsibility centers can be found in some nonprofit organizations.

As Exhibit 22.3 indicates, the focus in a discretionary expense center is on *total expenses* regardless of the volume and/or mix of activity. By contrast, because the manager of a standard expense center cannot control the volume or mix of the center's output, the focus is on *expenses per unit of output* rather than total expenses. A standard expense center's budget is "flexed" each reporting period using the actual volume and mix of output. The manager is expected to spend no more than the flexed amount. In a profit center, the focus is on both revenues and expenses.

Potential Dysfunctional Incentives of Profit Centers. The competitive spirit that a profit center fosters can have dysfunctional consequences.[17] For instance, a profit center manager may place too much emphasis on the revenue side of the equation, or cut expenses without concern for the longer term consequences of the cuts. Moreover, senior management's desired degree of cooperation with other responsibility centers may not occur—profit center managers may make decisions that add to the profit of their own units to the detriment of other units in the organization. They may be reluctant to incur overtime costs, for example, even though their centers' services may be badly needed by other responsibility centers.

Despite the potential for dysfunctional consequences, profit centers generally are desirable if their managers have a reasonable amount of influence over both the revenues and expenses of their centers. In many nonprofit organizations, managers who carry out identifiable programs, especially ones that are geographically separate, have their units designated as profit centers.

Managerial Autonomy. Organizations vary considerably in the autonomy they give to their profit center managers. In most organizations, although a profit center may operate almost as if it were an independent entity, its manager does not have all the autonomy of a chief executive officer. This is because profit centers are part of a larger organization, and their managers are subject to the organization's policies. Profit center managers rarely have the authority to initiate new programs or commit to major capital expenditures, for example. Those decisions, like others that influence the organization's overall strategy, usually are made by senior management.

Apart from these restrictions, profit center managers should be able to exert *reasonable* influence over their centers' revenues and expenses. That is, they should be able to exercise some control over their centers' volume of activity, work quality, unit variable costs, direct fixed costs, and, sometimes, the prices charged. Nevertheless, there may be unwritten rules concerning, for example, what decisions may be made independently by a profit center manager versus those that require approval of higher authority or consultation with (but not necessarily approval of) staff offices. In general, chief executives tend to give more autonomy to subordinates whom they know well and whose judgment they trust. As a result, some profit center managers may have considerably more decision-making latitude than others.

Fairness. Despite these restrictions, a profit center manager should perceive that the profit reported for his or her unit fairly measures its financial performance. This does not mean that the reported profit is completely accurate, or that it encompasses all aspects of performance, for no profit measure does this.

Transfer Prices. When one profit center receives goods and/or services from another and is charged for them, the charge is called a *transfer price*. A transfer price is used exclusively for transactions *within* an organization, as contrasted with an external price, which is used for transactions between an organization and its clients.

In general, transfer pricing provides a mechanism for encouraging the optimal use of an organization's resources. This is because the behavior of profit center managers (and to a lesser extent standard expense center managers) frequently is influenced considerably by the way the transfer prices are structured.[18]

The Program Structure

Most nonprofit organizations exist to carry out programs. Fixing responsibility for control over programs would be relatively easy if each program (1) sold its services, (2) were staffed by personnel who worked in no other program, and (3) were run by a manager who had reasonable control over hiring, other personnel decisions, and decisions on program supply purchases. Under these circumstances, each program could be designated as a profit center.

Most nonprofits are not organized in a way that permits such tidy and well-defined control structures. Many operate over large geographic areas, and must consider this fact when designing their structure. For example, does a multihospital system have one director of alcoholic rehabilitation services with broad geographic responsibilities, or several area directors, each with responsibility for all programs in his or her area, including the alcoholic rehabilitation program?

In other organizational settings, the program and functional lines become similarly blurred. Does the director of the summer festival program for a symphony orchestra have control over the number of personnel taking part in the festival or their salaries? Does the director of a master's degree program in a large university control the number of applications received, the tuition charged, or the salaries of the faculty who work in the program? Moreover, while performers in the orchestra or faculty in the university may take part in a particular program, their reporting relationships within the organization may be to several programs, and perhaps to a functional manager (such as a department chair) as well.

In summary, a separate program structure is needed when responsibility for a program involves more than one responsibility center. A municipality organized so that each responsibility center performs a defined type of service (for example, public safety, highway maintenance, education, and so on) does not need a separate program structure. By contrast, a federal government agency that runs many separate programs through several regional offices does. So does a research organization that draws on the resources of several departments to carry out its research projects.

Many organizations have found that devising a good program structure is not easy. Indeed, it generally is quite difficult to align responsibility with control, and to overlay an appropriate set of responsibility centers on the broad organizational structure. Therefore, senior management must devote considerable time and effort to the task.

Components of a Program Structure

In a large organization, the program structure usually consists of several layers. At the top are a few major programs, and at the bottom are a great many program elements—the smallest units in which information is collected in program terms. A program element is a definable activity or a set of related activities that the organization carries out—either directly, to accomplish its objectives, or indirectly, to support other program elements.

Between programs and program elements are summaries of related program elements, or "program categories," and, perhaps, "program subcategories." In a relatively flat organization, there may be no need for program categories or subcategories; program elements can be aggregated directly into programs. In a more hierarchical organization, there may be several levels of program categories. Exhibit 22.4 contains an example of programs, program categories, program subcategories, and program elements in a public school system.

Types of Programs. In general, programs can be classified as either *mission* or *support*. Mission programs relate to the organization's objectives and usually are focused on clients. Support programs provide services to other programs but usually don't work directly with clients. In making decisions about the allocation of resources, management usually focuses its attention on mission programs. Within limits, the amount of resources required for support programs is roughly dependent on the size and character of the mission programs.

EXHIBIT 22.4. HIERARCHY OF PROGRAMS, PROGRAM CATEGORIES, AND PROGRAM ELEMENTS.

Program	100. Formal Education
Program Categories	101. Pre-Elementary School Service
	102. Elementary and Secondary School Service
	103. Post-Secondary School Education Service
	104. Special Education Service For Exceptional Persons
Program Subcategories (for Program Category 102)	1. Kindergarten
	2. Primary or Elementary School Education
	3. Secondary or High School Education
	4. Vocational and/or Trade High School
Program Elements (for Program Subcategory 2)	a. Language instruction
	b. Music instruction
	c. Art instruction
	d. Social sciences instruction

Example

In a college or university, mission programs would be related to instruction and research. Support programs would include buildings and grounds maintenance, publications, and financial aid.

Criteria for Selecting a Program Structure

Since the primary purpose of the classification of programs is to facilitate senior management's judgment on the allocation of resources, the program structure should correspond to the principal objectives of the organization. It should be arranged so as to facilitate decisions having to do with the relative importance of these objectives. Stated another way, it should focus on the organization's outputs—what it achieves or intends to achieve—rather than on its inputs—the types of resources it uses or the sources of its support. A structure that is arranged by types of resources (for example, personnel, supplies, services) or by sources of support (for example, tuition, legislative appropriations, and gifts in a university setting) is not a program structure.

The designation of major programs helps clarify the objectives of the organization. The development of the program structure may also clarify the organization's purpose, and thus suggest improvements in its overall structure. Therefore, the program structure should correspond to those areas of activity that senior management expects to use for decision-making purposes.

Matrix Organizations. Although the program structure need not match the organization structure, there should be some person who has identifiable responsibility for each program (as well as each program category and each program element in large organizations). This need for a fit between the organizational structure and the program structure often results in a matrix organization. The matrix consists of program managers along one dimension and functional managers along the other.

Example

Faculty members of a business school typically have a home base in a subject-area department (such as organizational behavior, accounting, or marketing). They also may be assigned to one or more programs, such as undergraduate education, graduate education, or executive education. Program managers call on departments for work to be done on their programs. Under these circumstances, responsibility is divided between the department chair and the program heads.

An example of a matrix structure is contained in Figure 22.7. This is for a large agency—the Department of Mental Health in a state government. As it shows, complexity exists along several dimensions that affect the agency's responsibility accounting structure. Some of those dimensions include the following:

- The agency does not generate revenues. Therefore it is an expense center. Since its budget probably cannot be changed with changes in volume during the year, the agency quite likely is a discretionary expense center.
- Resource allocation is along two dimensions. One is field operations and facilities, which corresponds to the agency's organizational structure (the left side of the matrix). The other is the agency's major programs, such as community mental health (the right side of the matrix). The major programs correspond to appropriation accounts in the state's budget, and are the responsibility of "account executives" (program managers).
- Both field operations and the major programs have several layers of responsibility. The field operations activity is comprised of regions at the highest level, followed by facilities, areas, and units within the facilities. The major programs are comprised of subprograms.
- Overall program control is the responsibility of the account executives, who may not spend more than the amount allotted to their appropriation accounts. Programs cut across all regions, although not all regions or all facilities have all programs or all subprograms. Thus, an account executive must determine the regions and facilities that can best meet the needs of each major program and its various subprograms.

FIGURE 22.7. MATRIX STRUCTURE IN A LARGE STATE AGENCY.

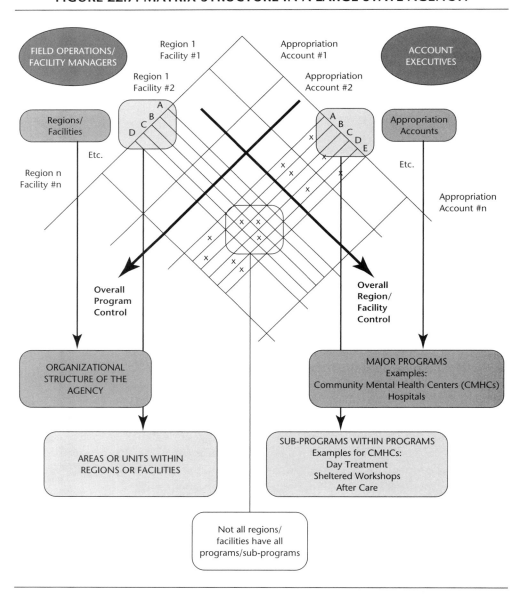

- Control over the activities in regions and facilities is the responsibility of the field operations and facility managers. They receive budgets from the account executives, and must adhere to them while striving to meet the objectives of the programs and subprograms that the budgets fund.
- Although the agency is a discretionary expense center, some of its units might be set up as standard expense centers. This is because the managers of these units have no control over the number or mix of individuals who need their services. Since the appropriation account budgets are fixed, account executives should assure that increases in one region or facility are matched by decreases in other regions or facilities.

The Account Structure

To provide information needed by all relevant parties, the accounting system should contain an account structure that is responsive to multiple demands. In addition to providing information to program planners, analysts, and operating managers, the account structure must provide information to two other groups:

- *Senior managers and governing bodies.* These parties make policy decisions regarding the division of resources among programs and the relation of programs to organizational objectives. Both groups need information on how the organization is performing.
- *Resource providers,* including contributors, legislative bodies, grantors, dues-paying members, taxpayers, third-party payers, oversight bodies, and regulatory agencies. These groups need information about what the organization did with the resources they provided. The needs of some resource providers can be met by general-purpose financial statements, but others, particularly legislatures and grantors, often request reports prepared according to their own specifications.

Conflicts Among Information Needs

Since the needs of these diverse parties frequently conflict with one another, the accounting system must strike a balance. A well-designed account structure should be able to reconcile most needs. This is especially important since senior management usually is interested in summaries of information provided to all other groups.

The Need for Articulation

Ideally, all the accounts in the account structure make up a single, coordinated system. Technically, such a system is called an articulated system; each account is related to all other accounts. Serious responsibility accounting problems can arise if program accounts are not linked with responsibility accounts, or if the actual costs in each set of accounts cannot be compared to the budgeted costs.

In some systems, a good program structure is used for planning and budgeting purposes, but after the program has been planned and the budget approved, the structure is not rearranged according to the responsibility centers that must carry out the program. Instead, a separate budget is prepared for responsibility centers, often without any relationship to the program budget. As a result, both budgets and actual spending are recorded by responsibility centers but not by programs. When this happens, actual or planned results cannot be compared in any meaningful way.

There are two problems with systems that don't articulate. First, since the system cannot ascertain costs by program, program planners do not have the information they need to estimate future program costs. Second, without program-based costs, senior management has no adequate way of determining whether its program decisions are actually being implemented. If senior management decides that $1 million should be spent on a certain program, it needs to know whether the organization is in fact carrying out the program at the level of effort that $1 million represents. It cannot find this out unless the records classify actual spending in terms of programs.

Behavioral Factors

Responsibility accounting involves interactions among human beings. The behavior of people in organizations is therefore an important element of the internal environmental. The major issue that senior management must address here is the congruence between the *personal* goals of managers and professionals, and the goals of the *organization* itself.

Goal Congruence

An organization's goals are determined by its board of trustees and senior management. Unfortunately, these goals are not always congruent with the personal goals of operating managers and professionals. Because participants tend to act in their own self-interest, the achievement of organizational goals may be frustrated.

This distinction between organizational and personal goals suggests that a central purpose of a responsibility accounting system is to assure that the actions participants take in accordance with their perceived self-interest are also actions that are in the best interests of the organization. That is, the incentives inherent in the responsibility accounting system should encourage *goal congruence*.[19] If this condition exists, a decision that a manager regards as sound from a personal viewpoint also will be sound for the organization as a whole.

Clearly, perfect congruence between individual and organizational goals cannot exist. For example, many individuals want as much compensation as they can get, whereas from the organization's viewpoint there is an upper limit to salaries. At a minimum, however, the responsibility accounting system should not encourage individuals to act against the best interests of the organization.

Example

An organization has a goal of low-cost, high-quality services, but its responsibility accounting system rewards managers exclusively for reducing costs. If some managers decrease costs by reducing the quality of service, there is an absence of goal congruence.

The Motivation and Reward Structure

An important factor in attaining goal congruence is the reward structure. Ideally, managers should be rewarded on the basis of actual performance compared with expected performance under the prevailing circumstances. This ideal frequently cannot be achieved for two basic reasons. First, the performance of a responsibility center is influenced by many factors other than the actions of its manager. As a result, the performance of the manager usually cannot be cleanly separated from the effects of these other factors. Second, managers are supposed to achieve both long- and short-run objectives, but the responsibility accounting system often focuses primarily on the short-run. This is because the system can only report what has happened; it cannot report what will happen in the future as a consequence of the manager's current actions. As a consequence, responsibility center and program managers are motivated to focus on achieving short-run goals. Indeed, a lack of knowledge about how best to measure and reward a manager's performance for achieving long-term results is probably the most serious weakness in responsibility accounting systems in nonprofit organizations.[20]

Cooperation and Conflict

Generally, the lines connecting the boxes on an organization chart imply that organizational decisions are made in a hierarchical fashion. Senior management makes a decision, which is communicated down through the organizational hierarchy, and operating managers at lower levels proceed to implement it. Clearly, this military model is not the way most organizations actually function.

Operating managers react to an instruction from senior management in accordance with their perception of how it affects their responsibility centers. Interactions between managers also affect what actually happens. For example, the manager of the maintenance department may be responsible for maintenance work done in all departments, but maintenance work in one operating department may be slighted if there is friction between the maintenance manager and the operating manager. Also, actions that a manager takes to achieve personal goals may adversely affect other managers. For these and many other reasons, there is organizational conflict.

Clearly, an organization will not achieve its objectives unless managers work together with some degree of harmony. Thus, there also must be cooperation in an organization. As a result, senior management must maintain an appropriate balance between the forces that create conflict and those that create cooperation. Some conflict is both inevitable and even desirable. It results from the competition between participants for resources, and, within limits, such competition is usually healthy. Conflict also arises because different members of an organization see the world differently, and believe that different actions are in the organization's best interests. For example, conflict arises in museums over the most appropriate exhibits, in colleges over the most appropriate courses, and in hospitals over the most appropriate treatment patterns for patients. To a certain extent, this sort of conflict is beneficial in that it frequently brings out the best ideas of an organization's members. Thus, if undue emphasis is placed on fostering a cooperative attitude, the most able managers and professionals may be denied the opportunity to use their talents fully.[21] Senior management must seek to foster the right balance.

Cultural Factors

Every organization has a culture—a climate or atmosphere in which certain attitudes are encouraged and others are discouraged. Cultural norms are derived in part from tradition, in part from external influences, such as unions and societal norms, and in part from the attitude of the organization's senior management and trustees. They are extremely important in that they explain why each of two entities may have an adequate responsibility accounting system but one has much better performance than the other.

Cultural norms are almost never written down, and attempts to do so almost always result in platitudes. Instead, norms are transmitted partly by hiring practices and training programs. They also are conveyed by managers, professionals, and other organization members using words, deeds, and body language to indicate that some types of actions are acceptable and others are not.[22]

The Responsibility Accounting Process

The responsibility accounting process takes place in the context of an organization's goals and responsibility center structure. Much of the process is informal. It occurs by means of memoranda, meetings, conversations, and even such signals as facial expressions—control devices not amenable to systematic description. Most organizations also have a formal system, however, in which the information consists of planned and actual data on both outputs and inputs. Prior to a given operating period, decisions and estimates (budgets) are prepared, which specify desired levels of outputs and inputs. During the operating period, records of actual outputs and inputs are collected. Subsequent to the operating period, reports are prepared that compare actual outputs and inputs to their planned levels. If necessary, corrective action is taken on the basis of these reports.

The four phases of the formal responsibility accounting process are shown in Figure 22.8. As the figure indicates, the phases occur in a regular cycle, and together they constitute a closed loop.

FIGURE 22.8. PHASES OF THE RESPONSIBILITY ACCOUNTING PROCESS.

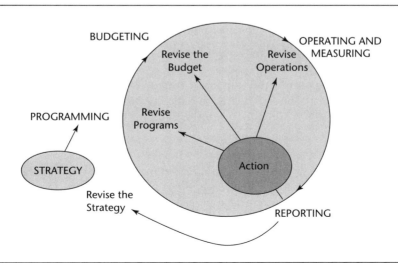

Programming

In the programming phase, senior management determines the major programs the organization will initiate during the coming period and the approximate revenues and expenses associated with each. These decisions are made within the context of the organization's strategy and goals. If a new program represents a change in strategy, the decision to initiate it effectively is part of strategic planning, rather than the responsibility accounting process. Strategic planning and responsibility accounting merge in the programming phase.

Some organizations state their programs in the form of a *long-range plan* that projects outputs and inputs for several years ahead, sometimes, in the case of public utilities, for as many as twenty years. Other organizations do not have a formal mechanism for describing their overall future programs. They rely instead on annual proposals for new programs or amounts to be invested in new fixed assets. Nevertheless, in a nonprofit organization, programs effectively define the types of services the organization has decided to provide, and hence provide considerable insight into its strategy.

To the extent feasible, decisions about new programs are based on economic analyses, which compare estimated revenues or other benefits from a proposed program with the program's estimated costs. In many instances, however, reliable estimates of a program's benefits cannot be made. Decisions about these programs tend to rest on senior management's ability to exercise sound judgment in the face of some persuasive program advocates, political considerations, and the frequently parochial interests of external constituencies.

Budgeting

A budget is a plan, expressed in quantitative (usually monetary) terms, that covers a specified period, usually a year. In the budgeting phase of the responsibility accounting process, each program's objectives are translated into terms that correspond to the spheres of responsibility of the managers charged with implementing them. Thus, during the budgeting phase, plans made in program terms are converted into responsibility terms.

Example

In a university, a program on medieval art may have several objectives: train a certain number of students, provide some cross-cultural experiences, raise a designated amount of support from alumni, and so forth. During the budgeting phase, the university determines the faculty and staff resources that are to be committed to the program, the necessary operating expenses (such as travel) for the program, and, perhaps, some program objectives (for example, to admit a certain number of international students to the program). The manager of the program assumes responsibility for accomplishing these objectives within some specified amount of resources (the budget), and the department chairs assume responsibility for providing the requisite faculty to teach in the program. The program manager also may obtain commitments from his or her subordinates to achieve certain objectives (such as to send three newsletters to 90 percent of alumni or to initiate a fundraising campaign).

The process of arriving at the budget is essentially one of negotiation between responsibility center managers and their superiors. The end product of these negotiations is a statement of the outputs expected during the budget year and the resources (inputs) that will be used to achieve these outputs. As such, the agreed-on budget is a *bilateral commitment*. Responsibility center managers commit to producing the planned output with the agreed amount of resources, and their superiors commit to agreeing that such performance is satisfactory. Both commitments are subject to the qualification "unless circumstances change significantly."

Operating and Measuring

During the period of actual operations, managers supervise what is going on and the accounting staff keeps records of actual resources consumed and actual outputs achieved. Ideally, the records of resources consumed (costs) are maintained in such a way to reflect the costs incurred by both programs and responsibility centers. Program cost records are used as a basis for future programming; responsibility cost records are used to measure the performance of responsibility center managers.

Reporting and Evaluating

Accounting information, along with a variety of other information—some of it nonfinancial and even nonquantitative—is summarized, analyzed, and reported to those individuals who are responsible for knowing what is happening in the organization, as well as those charged with attaining agreed-on levels of performance. The reports enable managers to compare planned outputs and inputs with actual ones. The information in these reports is used for three purposes: operational control, performance assessment, and program evaluation.

Operational Control. The reports help managers to coordinate and control the organization's current operations. Using this information, together with information obtained from conversations or other informal sources, managers attempt to identify situations that may be "out of control," investigate them, and initiate corrective action where necessary and feasible.

Performance Assessment. The reports also are used by senior management to assess operating performance. Such assessments lead to actions related to responsibility center managers: praise for a job well done, constructive criticism, promotion, reassignment, or, in extreme cases, termination. Such information is also used to guide managers of responsibility centers in the development of improved methods of operating.

Program Evaluation. For any of a number of reasons, the plan for a program may be suboptimal. If so, a program evaluation may reveal that the program needs to be revised or perhaps discontinued.

The reporting and evaluating phase thus closes the loop of the responsibility accounting process. Evaluation of actual performance can lead back to the first phase, a revision of the program, or to the second phase, a revision of the budget, or to the third phase, a modification in operations. It can also lead to senior management reconsidering the organization's approaches to achieving its goals, or even to a revision of the organization's strategy.

Role of the Controller

In most organizations, the controller is responsible for the operation of the responsibility accounting system. The controller department is a staff unit, in contrast with the responsibility accounting function itself, which is a line function. The responsibility of this staff unit is similar to that of a telephone company: it assures that messages flow through the system clearly, accurately, and promptly. It is not responsible for the content of these messages, however, or for the way managers act on them.

The controller ordinarily works with senior management to design the responsibility accounting system in such a way that fairness and goal congruence are maximized. Most of this effort is associated with designing the responsibility center structure and transfer pricing arrangements. The controller also works with senior management to design the phases of the responsibility accounting process. Because of the major impact that design choices can have on managers' and professionals' behavior, senior management should be heavily involved in these choices. In many organizations, senior management completely delegates these choices to the controller, which is a mistake since the controller typically does not have a sufficiently broad perspective of the organization and its goals.

Senior Management's Challenges

One of the most difficult aspects of designing a responsibility accounting system is defining the system's structure—its network of responsibility centers. In determining what sort of responsibility center a given manager's unit will be, senior management needs to pay careful attention to the resources the manager can control. This is the driving force behind responsibility center design.

Beyond this, senior management needs to consider ways to attain goal congruence between the personal goals of each responsibility center manger and its goals for the organization as a whole. In part, a responsibility center manager's goals are determined by the incentives that senior management creates to reward certain forms of behavior.

In addition to these considerations, senior management also must pay close attention to the fit between programs and responsibility centers. Programs represent the operational definition of an organization's strategy, and each aspect of a program must be assigned to a responsibility center. Thus, the responsibility accounting system must be designed in such a way that it can provide information on both program and responsibility center activities. This calls for a careful design of the account structure, a task that ordinarily is carried out by the accounting staff but needs considerable guidance from senior management.

Senior management must constantly bear in mind that responsibility accounting is fundamentally behavioral. The various control tools are effective only to the extent they influence behavior, and they will influence behavior only to the extent that the culture of the organization is conducive to their doing so. In addition, a delicate balance must be struck between cooperation and conflict so that individuals—both managers and professionals—work together toward the attainment of organizational goals and yet are able to have legitimate and healthy conflicts over the best ways to attain them.

Notes

1. Readers interested in knowing more about financial management from the perspective of external users, should go to the Crimson Press Curriculum Center, at www.TheCrimsonGroup.org. Click on the Finance/Financial Management link, and scroll to the Notes area. There are several background notes on a variety of topics related to external users.
2. This chapter is a condensed and abridged version of several separate chapters contained in David W. Young, *Management Control in Nonprofit Organizations* (Cambridge, Mass., The Crimson Press), 2008.

3. Technically, the term *product* refers to either a good or a service. It could refer to a lab test, a museum exhibit, an opera, a served client, or a discharged client. This is not meant to suggest that a client or patient is a product, but rather to clarify a shorthand that will make it easier to discuss the concepts without excessive verbiage.

4. To see these principles, go to www.access.gpo.gov/nara/cfr/waisidx_07/2cfr220_07.html

5. A *diagnosis-related group* is a collection of several related diagnoses. There are several hundred DRGs.

6. It is important to distinguish between *assignment* and *allocation*. Assignment precedes allocation, and serves to place costs into service and mission centers. By contrast, *allocation* distributes service center costs among mission centers. This terminology can be confusing. *Allocation* is sometimes called *apportionment*, and vice versa. Moreover, the terms *assignment*, *distribution*, *allocation*, and *apportionment* occasionally are used interchangeably. In addition to these differences in terminology, service center costs that are allocated to production centers often are called *indirect* or *overhead costs*. The context usually clarifies the meaning, but because of these terminology differences, it is important to understand the activities taking place rather than to memorize definitions of the terms.

7. Some hospitals argue that they can determine the cost of their intermediate cost objects by using ratios of costs to charges (RCCs) or relative value units (RVUs). However, both of these methods are flawed. For a discussion of the flaws, see David W. Young, "The Folly of Using RCCs and RVUs for Intermediate Product Costing," *Healthcare Financial Management*, April 2007.

8. Additional details about this process are discussed in many cost accounting texts, and are beyond the scope of this chapter. A particularly good source for additional information is R. Cooper and R. S. Kaplan, *The Design of Cost Management Systems*, 2nd edition, (Englewood Cliffs, N.J., Prentice Hall), 1998. Also see *Note on Activity-Based Costing*, available from the Crimson Press Curriculum Center.

9. John B. MacArthur, "Cost Management at the IRS," *Management Accounting*, November 1996.

10. Marlise Simons, "Europeans Begin to Calculate the Price of Pollution," *New York Times*, December 9, 1990.

11. Neil A. Martin, "When Public Services Go Private," *World*, May-June 1986, pp. 26–28.

12. Accountants call these "sunk costs."

13. If asset acquisition is a significant aspect of the decision, that is, if assets must be acquired in order to pursue the *make* option, then depreciation alone is insufficient. Instead, a technique known as *net present value* is required.

14. For additional details on high-risk outsourcing, see Emanuele Padovani and David W. Young "Managing High Risk Outsourcing," *Public Management*, Jan/Feb 2006, and Federica Farneti and David W. Young "A Contingency Approach to Managing Outsourcing Risk in Municipalities," *Public Management Review,* 2007.

15. There also is an *informal* structure that is unwritten and perhaps unintended. The informal structure encompasses a network of interpersonal relationships that has important implications for management. Because it is unwritten, however, the informal structure is difficult to identify and describe. For this reason, the focus here is on the formal structure.

16. For a discussion of the issues, see *Note on Financial Surpluses in Nonprofit Organizations* (Cambridge, Mass.: Crimson Press Curriculum Center).

17. For a discussion of dysfunctional consequences in a hospital context, see David W. Young, "Profit Centers in Clinical Care Departments: An Idea Whose Time Has Gone," *Healthcare Financial Management*, March 2008.

18. Transfer pricing is used widely in the corporate sector but relatively little in nonprofit organizations. It could be a powerful tool for many nonprofits, however. For general information on transfer pricing, see *Note on Transfer Pricing*. For a health care application, see *Note on Transfer Pricing in Health Care*. Both documents are available from The Crimson Press Curriculum Center at www.TheCrimsonGroup.org.

19. Senior management can *influence* the personal goals of the organization's managers and professionals by using its hiring, promotion, and termination policies to select and retain individuals who have personal goals that are closely aligned with the organization's goals.

20. For-profit organizations sometimes use stock options as a way to motivate managers to think about the long-term consequences of their decisions. Some nonprofit organizations have used sabbatical leaves as a form of long-term incentive, but it is difficult to link leave time to long-run performance.

21. For further discussion on conflict and its benefits, see *Note on Conflict Management*, available from The Crimson Press Curriculum Center.

22. One of the most thorough descriptions of culture is Edgar H. Schein, *Organizational Culture and Leadership* (San Francisco: Jossey-Bass), 2004. For additional information on culture, see *Note on Cultural Maintenance*, available from The Crimson Press Curriculum Center, and David W. Young, "The Six Levers for Managing Organizational Culture," *Business Horizons*, September-October 2000.

CHAPTER TWENTY-THREE

RISK MANAGEMENT

Melanie Lockwood Herman

The discipline of risk management too often inspires fear and dread among nonprofit leaders. These reactions can be understood if we take a closer look at how leaders perceive the discipline. Many leaders believe that

- The more informed they are about the risks facing their organization the greater the likelihood that these now known risks will materialize
- Responsibility for managing risk lies with the administrative staff of the nonprofit
- Purchasing insurance will insulate the organization from most risks and if the organization were able to afford all of the insurance it needs and wants there would be little remaining to do in the area of risk management
- The greatest risks facing the organization revolve around the safety of clients, in particular vulnerable clients receiving services from the nonprofit

Each of these myths about risk management creates disincentives to increase awareness about an organization's risk profile and elevate the discussion about risk to the highest level in an organization. Despite the continuing prevalence of these myths, a growing number of nonprofit executives and volunteer board members are asking questions that lead them to risk management. These questions include

- How can we protect our mission and "brand" in a competitive environment where we can't control what people say about us?

- What steps should we take to ensure the financial sustainability of the organization and help us cope with fluctuations in contributions and other forms of support?
- What strategies should be considered to reduce the frequency of turnover in our professional and administrative ranks?
- What can we do to better engage our board and help them discharge their legal responsibilities?

Contrary to what has become a popular view, risk management is not about mopping up spills on the linoleum floor in the break room. Risk management is about helping an organization—for the purpose of this book, a nonprofit organization—advance its mission. Truly effective risk management efforts free resources for mission-related projects. The dollars and hours spent on cleaning up in the wake of an accident, incident, or donor complaint can be redirected to the activities and programs of the nonprofit that move its mission forward.

Key Elements of an Effective Risk Management Program

In the paragraphs that follow we explore essential components of a risk management program. Each of these components can be scaled to fit the needs of a nonprofit organization, from the smallest, all-volunteer effort run from a home office to a large, multimillion dollar agency with multiple facilities and a complex governing structure. The most important thing to keep in mind as you review these elements is the need for customization to fit the environment and culture of the nonprofit you serve. "What works" in one organization could be disastrous in another.

1. Bring risk discussion to the board room.

The first essential element of effective risk management is making certain that a discussion of risk taking and risk management occurs in the board room. Countless nonprofits have attempted to manage risk by assigning the "task" to professional staff or outside advisors. Nonprofit boards bear ultimate responsibility for mission fulfillment and therefore they should shape the organization's understanding of risk, define its appetite for risk taking, and feel confident about the nonprofit's strategies for managing its risks. A board that is kept in the dark or that relies fully on staff or consultants to "take care of risk issues" will be unable to develop a full understanding of the risks the organization does and should take. A board that ignores risk is arguably incapable of discharging the legal duty of care. As I wrote in the Nonprofit

Risk Management Center's book *Pillars of Accountability: A Risk Management Guide for Nonprofit Boards*:

> The *duty of care* asks a director to be reasonably informed, participate in decisions, and to act in good faith and with the care of an ordinarily prudent person in similar circumstances. Ways to assess a board member's commitment include asking if the person participates actively in decisions, attends meetings, uses independent judgment, and seeks reliable information to make informed decisions. (Herman, 2009, p. 6)

2. Commit to the development of a risk management plan.

   Every nonprofit takes steps to manage the risks it faces. From writing an advertisement for a position that helps job-seekers determine whether they are a good "fit" for the organization to showing new volunteers "the ropes" before they are assigned to classrooms, job sites, or KP duty, steps to increase the chances of success while minimizing the likelihood of harm or loss are visible and often well documented in most nonprofits. What is often missing, however, is a cohesive plan that describes
   - The nonprofit's risk taking appetite and philosophy about risk
   - The agency's goals for its risk management programs and activities
   - A description of the respective roles of key players in risk management, including the board, staff, service volunteers, contractors, and in some cases, clients/service recipients
   - A compilation of all of the policies and procedures that have been put in place to help manage the risks the agency faces

   Developing a risk management plan in a nonprofit organization requires, at a minimum, a commitment of time and human resources. In some organizations, the implementation of some strategies outlined in the plan will require the expenditure of financial resources. By developing a cohesive plan that describes both an organization's risk-taking appetite and its principal strategies for managing risk, the agency increases the chance of a shared understanding of and appreciation for its policies and procedures. Instead of viewing a policy requiring background checks as a nuisance, volunteers will learn to see that the requirement is essential to increasing the likelihood of matching the best suited applicant with a key position and positioning the nonprofit as an agency that all prominent carriers would want to insure.

   There is no single best approach to developing a risk management plan. Many leaders have found the Web tool *My Risk Management Plan* helpful in developing a plan. The tool is available at www.myriskmanagementplan.org.

3. Strive for sign-on versus sign-off.

Nonprofit leaders often are policy development experts. With a few simple clicks of the mouse and a relatively quick Web browser it is possible to find (and copy) any number of policies that seem ready-made for a nonprofit. Yet finding what appears to be a reasonable policy (for example, a participant code of conduct or a conflict of interest policy for the board and staff) is only a small part of the process. Distributing the written policy (now containing the nonprofit's name and logo at the top) requires only minutes of time followed by additional time pestering busy professionals to return their "signed" policy statement. New employees and volunteers are easily coerced by explaining that they need to "sign off" on the nonprofit's policies before they can begin work. The problem with this approach is that it puts the emphasis on "signing off" on a policy rather than where it belongs: understanding the rationale for the policy and the role of the policy in protecting the vital assets of the nonprofit, including its brand, reputation, and mission. Sound risk management requires a commitment to helping staff and volunteers understand the role of policies in the areas of financial management, human resources, facility safety, governance, and program supervision to help advance the mission of the nonprofit and explain why their support and participation are vital to protecting those essential assets.

4. Revisit and revise.

Unfortunately, many risk management policies outlive their usefulness and appropriateness long before they are excised from the voluminous manual of "volunteer policies" or "facility guidelines." There is a tendency to emblazon the rules in permanent ink and let them gather dust while an agency takes advantage of the latest technology to engage and serve clients. The harm that might occur in the gymnasium when the "no hitting" rule is violated pales in comparison to the harm caused by the bully who sends threatening text messages to a peer. Every nonprofit leader who seeks to improve his or her agency's risk management efforts should begin with a commitment to revisiting long-standing rules and policies. The following questions may be helpful in determining whether changes are in order:

- Is the rule or policy relevant given our current circumstances? If so, how does the rule or policy protect the mission of the organization? What assets (people, property, income, or goodwill) are protected as a result of this rule of policy?
- Is the rule or policy understood by those who must follow or enforce it? If not, why not? What training, orientation, or education is required to ensure understanding by those who "need to know"?

- Is the rule or policy consistently enforced? If not, why not? Is the culprit lack of understanding or a belief that the rule is unnecessary? What changes are needed to improve enforcement of the policy? If the rule is dated or unnecessary are there any reasons *not* to eliminate or repeal it?

Integrating Sound Risk Management in Your Nonprofit

The starting point for developing and sustaining a risk management program in a nonprofit is assigning responsibility for the development, implementation, and monitoring of the risk management goal setting and activities.

Assigning Responsibility for Risk Management

There are two contrasting schools of thought with respect to assigning responsibility for risk management activities in a nonprofit. According to the first, it is important to assign responsibility for risk management to a single paid or volunteer staff member who can coordinate the organization's risk management efforts, document policies or programs developed, track losses and "near misses," and provide periodic reports to the board on the success or failure of ongoing loss prevention efforts. This individual also serves as the point of contact with staff, volunteers, contractors, and vendors (including insurance providers) who have questions about risk management policies or activities. Using this approach, a nonprofit can hold a single person accountable for the development of risk management activities.

The second school of thought suggests that a nonprofit is best served by involving a diverse group of people in the design and implementation of a risk management program. According to this school of thought, bringing a diverse group of people together early in the process not only increases the creativity of the risk identification and strategy development but also creates a road map for obtaining buy-in from key personnel. In some organizations, this approach is selected through the designation of a risk management committee, whereas other nonprofits add responsibility for various risk management tasks to the job descriptions of a handful of employees. Most nonprofits that have made a commitment to risk management fashion an approach that contains elements of both schools of thought. For example, a nonprofit social services agency might decide to create a volunteer risk management committee consisting of staff members, outside professionals, and representatives of the board, client community, and corps of volunteers. The committee might be staffed by the nonprofit's chief financial officer, who serves as coordinator of the group's activities.

Small, all-volunteer or principally volunteer nonprofits are most likely to rely solely on a volunteer risk management committee, whereas large, established, and mature nonprofits are more likely to add the position of risk manager to their organizational charts. The vast majority of nonprofits will select a strategy for staffing risk management that is compatible with the organization's culture. At a minimum, however, a decision about who will coordinate the design and implementation of risk management activities should be made before the nonprofit launches a vigorous risk identification exercise. Consider people with expertise in a broad area as you form the team or group that will coordinate risk management in your nonprofit. Some excellent candidates are

- People with working knowledge of the risks the nonprofit encounters on a day-to-day basis, such as representatives in the human resources, technology, service delivery, maintenance, and finance areas
- Outside advisers who bring expertise in finance, legal matters, and insurance buying
- Volunteers who have expressed concerns about safety or liability issues
- Individuals familiar with the governance structure and rules of the nonprofit
- People with knowledge of the nonprofit's communications strategies, challenges, and opportunities
- Key staff and volunteers who raise restricted and unrestricted support for the nonprofit

A nonprofit's risk management committee is often responsible for all phases of an organization's risk management program, from development through implementation and monitoring. In a committee with wide-ranging responsibility, a work plan may include any or all of the following:

- Developing, for board approval, an organizational risk management policy that affirms the organization's commitment to safeguarding its assets
- Establishing the nonprofit's risk management goals (for example, ensuring its survival, maintaining essential operations, or providing humanitarian services)
- Identifying the organization's risks and establishing the risk management priorities
- Selecting the best risk management techniques (avoidance, modification, retention, or sharing) for the priority risks
- Recommending appropriate risk financing alternatives
- Communicating the agency's risk management plan and loss control procedures to the board of directors, employees, volunteers, clients, and the other stakeholders

- Selecting an insurance adviser (broker, agent, or consultant) and negotiating insurance arrangements
- Overseeing loss prevention and control activities
- Providing an annual risk management report to the board of directors

Once a nonprofit's leaders have decided who will coordinate the organization's risk management activities, these key designees can begin the process of developing a program that suits the nonprofit's unique circumstances, exposures, concerns, and resources. This work should generally begin with a discussion of the nonprofit's goals and aspirations for its risk management effort.

Setting Risk Management Goals

As in other disciplines, it is important for a nonprofit to establish goals before moving too far along with any effort to realize changes in attitudes and outcomes. Establishing goals before engaging in risk identification and strategy development will provide the nonprofit with a yardstick against which it will be able to measure its results.

Although there are common threads in the risk management goals of diverse nonprofits, each organization should take the time to articulate what it hopes to accomplish by integrating risk management into its operations. Here are some examples of risk management goals:

- Reducing the frequency and severity of injuries suffered by volunteers working at site-based projects
- Planning appropriately for communitywide disasters to enable a nonprofit to resume mission-critical operations within two days of a crisis
- Ensuring the adequate protection of a nonprofit's financial assets by developing a sound operating budget, implementing a thoughtful investment policy, developing and instituting thoughtful internal controls, and ensuring capable fiscal oversight by active but separate finance and audit committees

Although taking a broad approach is admirable, establishing narrow goals for a nonprofit's first risk management program increases the odds of success. An overly ambitious program, such as one established to "prevent all accidents" is more likely to fail over time because the task at hand is disproportionate to the resources the nonprofit is able to marshal.

Acknowledge Existing Risk Management Efforts

Many nonprofits report that they have few, if any, risk management activities in place. Yet even a small, all-volunteer program is likely to have risk management policies and safeguards—including some activities that the nonprofit's leaders regard as "common sense" or simply good management. These existing assets should be recognized and noted by the risk management committee as it goes through the risk management process described in the next section. As the risk management effort matures, the committee will be encouraged by all that the organization is already doing to protect its vital assets.

There are various ways to go about examining a nonprofit's operations for risks that threaten its mission. And there are at least an equal number of ways to formulate strategies that will enable an organization to address major and minor risks. A multistep risk management process offers one approach to this important task. One approach is outlined in the pages that follow.

The Risk Management Process

Once the team that will tackle the assignment of integrating risk management into the culture, governance, and operations of a nonprofit has been identified and formed and the broad goals of the effort have been articulated, it's time to focus on the process or steps the committee will follow to achieve its goals. The five-step process described here is a continuous loop. As soon as the committee reaches step 5, it's time to return to the beginning and reexamine the environment in which the organization operates. There is no set time frame in which the steps should be followed. Some organizations will try to come full circle in a year's time, while others will strive to begin at step 1 at least every two years. And in some cases, a shorter time frame will be required, due to the nature of the nonprofit's operations. Other organizations work to build risk management into the non-profit's day-to-day planning and operational activities. For example, when the planning team for a fundraising event meets, it automatically includes a discussion of safety issues on its planning meeting agenda without a reminder to do so.

Step 1: Consider the Context

Before discussing the risks the nonprofit faces, the risk management committee should focus its attention on the environment in which the nonprofit operates. For example, the nonprofit's staff expertise, funding outlook, appetite for risk taking, past experience with losses and risk management, and economic and political circumstances are all aspects of the context in which any future risk management activities will take place. These contextual factors should be considered as the committee brainstorms risks and considers what strategies will work for the nonprofit.

The risk management committee should consider a wide range of factors as it discusses the environment in which future risk management activities will take place, including the following:

- *Personnel:* The attitudes and availability of staff members should be examined.
- *Financial resources:* Determine what funds, if any, are available to implement the committee's recommendations.
- *Past experience:* Past losses, crises, and risk management should be reviewed, as they will be instructive about the potential for future success.
- *Requirements:* Any changes that have been mandated by regulators, funders, and other bodies should be discussed.

The following questions may be helpful in unearthing the risk management context:

- What is the nonprofit's experience with accidental losses? If the organization has faced frequent or severe losses in the past, how well has it handled these events? What changes in operations were made as a result of these losses?
- What attitudes about risk prevail at the nonprofit? Do the organization's leaders support thoughtful risk taking in pursuit of its mission, or has an overly cautious approach led to the cancellation of mission-critical activities? (Some boards and executives may feel that they should be cautious, seeing themselves as stewards of the community's assets. This issue must be periodically discussed and agreed on.)
- What level of interest in risk management and loss prevention has been expressed by paid and volunteer staff? Is the organization likely to face resistance from key personnel when it tries to implement new risk management policies and procedures?
- Are there outside pressures to implement risk management from groups such as funders, regulators, and business partners?
- Have there been developments in the nonprofit's insurance program, such as the cancellation of coverage, new restrictions on coverage, or unprecedented premium increases, that have led to a greater interest in risk management?

Step 2: Identify Risks

During the second step of the risk management process, the committee works to identify the risks the organization faces. One approach is to encourage open brainstorming, during which every risk is written down without discussion about its merits or the nonprofit's level of exposure. A committee with diverse perspectives is in the best position to identify a wide range of risks, including those related to finance and administration as well as service delivery, collaborations, special events, governance, employment practices, and the nonprofit's reputation among stakeholders and in the community at large. This step works best when the committee members name specific rather than general risks. For example, during a brainstorming session, the members of a risk management committee for a nonprofit after-school tutoring program might come up with a list that includes the following risks:

- The risk that a child will be picked up from the program by a noncustodial parent or another unauthorized person
- The risk that the reading levels of program graduates will not be markedly improved from their levels at the time of enrollment and that lack of change will be perceived as the organization's fault
- The possibility that two children enrolled in the program will have a physical confrontation
- The risk that parents of a participant will accuse one of the program volunteers of inappropriately touching their child
- The possibility that a volunteer tutor will establish inappropriate, out-of-program contact with a child or the child's family

The detail in such a list will be immeasurably helpful as the committee moves on to evaluating and addressing the risks it has identified. Risks stated in unspecific terms, such as "the risk that a client will be harmed," will be difficult, if not impossible, to quantify.

One of the concerns that is likely to be expressed by the members of the committee is the fear that it will not "cover the bases" in its risk identification efforts. A suggested approach for addressing this concern is to identify categories of exposure and then place identified risks within these categories. Some groups will do this by separating risks according to asset categories within the nonprofit: people, property, income, and goodwill or reputation. Others prefer to use the existing structure of the organization as a framework for identifying subcategories. For example, one national nonprofit social services organization used its organizational chart as the basis for the risk identification exercise. Risks that were articulated during the brainstorming exercise were listed under the nonprofit's six department headings: finance and administration, communications, development and special events, education programs, recreation programs, and facilities management.

This approach allows the committee to quickly see whether it has identified a least a minimum number of risks in each functional area. If the committee has difficulty naming risks in a particular area, this may signal the need to involve others who bring knowledge of day-to-day operations to the committee's deliberations.

Step 3: Evaluate Risks

The third step in the risk management process moves the committee from an exhaustive "laundry list" of risks to a more concise list of short-term and long-term risk management priorities for the nonprofit. There is no single best or preferred way in which to analyze, review, or rank the list of risks identified in step 2. Nonprofits that operate informally may prefer to simply discuss the list and provide committee members with an opportunity to weigh in on the relative importance or urgency of the risks that have been identified. One guiding principle for an informal approach to risk evaluation is to single out recurring downside risks that can be avoided through simple or inexpensive means. For example, the committee at a shelter for homeless families may determine that several times each winter at least three clients slip on ice that has formed on the walkway in front of the shelter. This recurring event is a top candidate for risk management intervention because it is predictable and exposes the organization to financial loss. Another guiding principle for ranking risks is to give special notice to risks that rarely occur but would seriously threaten the mission and sustainability of the nonprofit if they did occur. The same shelter might identify the physical abuse of a family member by a paid or volunteer counselor as such an event. The organization expects that such event may never happen, yet it recognizes that the aftermath of an incident—including media reports that a shelter intended to provide haven for homeless families is exposing clients to danger—could result in the loss of community support, public and private funding, and the ability to sustain the organization.

Another approach to evaluating or ranking the risks identified in step 2 is to assign scores or grades to each risk in terms of *frequency* (how likely it is to occur) and *severity* (how costly such an occurrence would be). Scoring systems of 1 to 10 (1 being extremely rare or inexpensive, 10 meaning likely to occur or costly) or A to F may provide the tools the committee needs to separate risks that deserve immediate attention from those for which no action is recommended.

Exhibit 23.1 illustrates how the committee for the hypothetical tutoring program might score the risks listed in the text. Given these results and assuming that the tutoring program must make choices about what risks will be most important to address in the upcoming year, organization is likely to focus on preventing pickup by noncustodial parents and preventing the abuse of children in the nonprofit's care.

EXHIBIT 23.1. RATING THE RISKS IDENTIFIED BY AN AFTER-SCHOOL TUTORIAL PROGRAM.

Risk	Frequency	Severity	Score	Rank
The risk that a child will be picked up from the program by a noncustodial parent or another unauthorized person	2	9	11	1
The risk that the reading levels of program graduates will not be markedly improved from their levels at the time of enrollment and that lack of change will be perceived as the organization's fault	1	4	5	5
The possibility that two children enrolled in the program will have a physical confrontation	3	5	8	3
The risk that parents of a participant will accuse one of the program volunteers of inappropriately touching their child	1	9	10	2
The possibility that a volunteer tutor will establish inappropriate, out-of-program contact with a child or the child's family	3	4	7	4

Notes: Frequency and severity were rated on a scale of 1 (low) to 10 (high). Scores are the sum of the frequency and severity ratings.

Step 4: Decide What to Do and Take Action

The fourth step of the risk management process requires the greatest commitment of time. During this step, the committee makes decisions about the actions the nonprofit will take to address its priority risks. These actions can range from simple operational changes, such as requiring visitors to wear name tags while on the nonprofit's property or conducting a monthly fire drill, to potentially costly policy changes, such as requiring the rigorous screening of all volunteers seeking positions in a youth-serving organization. One way to approach this task is to create a table listing the organization's top risks—the risks that the committee has determined deserve immediate attention. Columns indicating the proposed action steps, due dates for implementation, and staff assignments are then added to the matrix. A sample is presented in Exhibit 23.2.

EXHIBIT 23.2. SAMPLE ITEM ON A RISK MANAGEMENT ACTION PLAN.

Risk	Rank	Action Steps	Due Date	Staff
Child picked up from the program by a noncustodial parent or another unauthorized person	1	Modify application to include verification of persons allowed to pick up client	Jan. 1	Mary
		Draft new procedure and add to operations handbook	Jan. 5	Bob
		Brief all staff on new procedure, including importance to safety of nonprofit and clients	Jan. 15	Bob

Step 5: Monitor and Adjust

Various outcomes are possible when a nonprofit adopts new risk management measures, including the following:

- The new policy, procedure, or practice is widely accepted as a practical way to reduce exposure to serious claims or other forms of harm to the nonprofit's assets.
- The new practice proves impractical and is followed inconsistently, thereby undermining its effectiveness.
- The new policy proves too difficult to follow or is communicated ineffectively, resulting in unintended policy violations.
- The new practice proves too costly in light of the risk to the organization or in the face of budget retrenchment at the nonprofit.
- The new risk management activity appears to have a neutral effect—it is unclear that it is making a difference with respect to preventing losses or increasing confidence among key stakeholders.

Most nonprofits are to some extent guardians of outdated, impractical, or ineffective policies and procedures. Like their counterparts in the business and government sectors, nonprofit managers find it difficult to spend time reviewing long-standing policies and practices and weed out those that no longer serve the organization well. Risk management activities that no longer serve the interests of the nonprofit should be modified to meet the nonprofit's needs or else be abandoned. Ironically, the failure to do this could increase the nonprofit's exposure to liability claims. For example, a nonprofit that adopts a policy requiring the completion of fingerprint-based criminal history background checks for all staff is likely to discover that implementing the policy is very costly. An organization might be tempted to obtain such checks on only a small fraction of applicants in order to save time and money—perhaps those applicants whose appearance or demeanor generate suspicion among screening personnel. This practice could be potentially damaging evidence in a case against a nonprofit stemming from the hiring of an individual who wasn't subjected to the nonprofit's adopted screening procedure. Furthermore, an individual who was singled out for rigorous screening might pursue a claim alleging discrimination.

In addition to making changes to the existing risk management program based on the committee's analysis of the effectiveness of various strategies, the committee should also discuss changes in the nonprofit's environments, circumstances, and programs that warrant a new look at the exposures the organization faces. An important facet of step 5 is reexamining the nonprofit's exposure to risks and identifying new areas that deserve priority attention. For example, the hypothetical homeless shelter may, after an assault that resulted in the hospitalization of a young client, decide that addressing the risk of client-on-client violence deserves top attention.

Applying the Risk Management Framework

The risks nonprofits face vary with mission, clientele, geographical location, funding sources, and many other factors. For example, some of the risks identified by a nonprofit recreation program located on the coast of North Carolina will be quite different from those identified by a church located in rural Iowa. Yet many nonprofits will identify risk exposures that are common to nonprofits with polar-opposite missions. For example, a conservation nonprofit that takes children on wilderness hikes will face some of the same risks as a nonprofit organization that teaches adults and children how to hunt safely.

Here are some examples of these common exposures:

- Protecting vulnerable clients from harm
- Avoiding the theft of financial resources by insiders
- Minimizing disruptive and costly claims alleging wrongful employment practices

- Ensuring that the nonprofit is prepared to cope with a wide range of crisis situations, including those caused by natural hazards or events, as well as human-caused events such as workplace violence or equipment failure
- Minimizing the potential liability of volunteers for services delivered on the nonprofit's behalf and the apprehension of volunteers concerning their personal liability

All of these issues—in addition to the unique exposures a nonprofit faces—can be addressed by involving a group of people who understand and appreciate the organization's resources, operations, and constraints and following the steps in the risk management process.

Next we discuss the specific issue of volunteer liability and risk management. We single out this area because it is a common concern among a large number of nonprofits. It is also an area that continues to generate misunderstanding.

Volunteer Liability and Risk Management[1]

The topic of volunteer liability remains an important concern for nonprofit leaders. Some of the concerns that are raised under the volunteer liability umbrella include the following:

- Can we be sued and held liable for the mistakes or negligence of our volunteers?
- Can our volunteers sue us?
- What should I tell a volunteer who is concerned about his or her personal liability?

Volunteer Negligence. The simple answer to the first question is yes, an organization that deploys hundreds of thousands of volunteers who perform services, interact with clients and the general public, and represent the organization in other ways has a substantial exposure to the risk of being held liable for the actions of volunteers. Yet there is no need for the use of volunteers to cause alarm. As is discussed later in this chapter, there are many things a nonprofit can do to enhance the safety of volunteer service and thereby reduce the risk of claims by volunteers. In addition, it is important to recognize that when a client or other participant is injured while participating in a nonprofit's program, a finding of liability is not automatic. Determining whether a nonprofit will be liable for harm resulting from the organization's acts or omissions depends on the confluence of various factors, including whether the nonprofit had a duty of care with respect to those who were harmed, the nonprofit breached its duty of care, harm actually occurred, the harm that occurred was foreseeable, the breach of the duty of care was a proximate cause of the harm that occurred, and there were reasonable measures available to the nonprofit that would have prevented the harm from occurring.

Each of these issues will be considered, along with the laws of a particular jurisdiction and the perspective and biases of the judge or jury who review the facts in a particular case. It is difficult, if not impossible, to predict whether liability will be imposed. Legal counsel representing the nonprofit, with full knowledge of all of the circumstances and facts at hand, will try to make this prediction and advise the nonprofit accordingly. Some commentators have observed that when children are hurt while participating in a nonprofit's programs, the imposition of liability on the nonprofit is increasingly likely and seemingly automatic. Under the legal concept of *respondeat superior* ("let the master answer"), a nonprofit is responsible for the acts and omissions of its agents. Volunteers—people who work on the nonprofit's behalf and whose labor benefits the nonprofits—are agents. There are some exceptions to this principle. For example, in some cases, a nonprofit may avoid responsibility for the negligent acts of a volunteer who is clearly acting outside the scope of his or her authority or whose actions are a direct violation of the nonprofit's rules and requirements.

Claims by Volunteers. Nonprofit leaders may also be concerned about the possibility of lawsuits filed by volunteers. The good news on this topic is that suits against nonprofits by volunteers continue to be rare events. The bad news, however, is that a claim by a volunteer—even one without legal merit—can be costly to a nonprofit. Two scenarios are most likely in regard to this exposure: (1) a volunteer suffers an injury and seeks compensation for it, or (2) a volunteer alleges nonphysical harm (such as defamation, discrimination, or wrongful termination). Injuries suffered by paid staff of the nonprofit are insured under mandatory workers' compensation coverage, which is triggered regardless of the fault of the employer and covers medical expenses and provides income replacement. The vast majority of nonprofits do not cover volunteers under their workers' compensation policies—it is generally cost-prohibitive to do so. Another option is to purchase an accident policy that ensures the availability of funds to cover medical expenses (up to a predetermined limit) following injury to a volunteer.

At a minimum, an accident policy is a goodwill gesture by a nonprofit that conveys its concern for the safety of volunteers. A nonprofit should consider how it will react when a volunteer is injured and consider steps that will reduce the likelihood of a legal claim by the volunteer. Occasionally, a volunteer will seek redress for nonphysical harm, accusing the nonprofit of wrongful termination or discrimination. Although a number of such cases have reached the courts in recent years, most have ruled consistently that volunteers do not have standing to sue for wrongful employment actions. Although a nonprofit may prevail in the long run, the cost of defending such a claim can take a toll on the organization. Claims alleging defamation may be addressed on the merits. To guard against these claims, nonprofits must be cautious when screening, supervising, disciplining, and terminating volunteers: information that portrays the volunteer in a negative light should be shared only with persons who need to know it.

Fear of Liability Among Volunteers.   During the years leading up to the adoption of the federal Volunteer Protection Act of 1997 (VPA), the legislation's supporters argued that large numbers of prospective volunteers had become increasingly fearful of being sued and that this widespread fear had a negative effect on the size of the pool of persons willing to volunteer for charitable organizations. Yet between 1980 and 1995—a long period in which volunteers' enthusiasm was allegedly dampened due to the fear of liability—the number of volunteers in the United States grew from 80 million to 93 million, an increase of 16 percent, and a record 90 percent of individuals volunteered when asked.

The recurring theme found in the federal and state volunteer protection laws is that certain volunteers serving nonprofit or government programs should, under certain circumstances, be protected from personal, civil liability for harm that results from their volunteer service. One of the recurring misconceptions about the protection afforded under the VPA (and the comparable state laws) is that the laws protect nonprofits as well as volunteers. The opposite is true. The proponents of the VPA argued forcefully that the new law would not leave victims of negligence by nonprofit personnel without recourse but instead ensure that the nonprofit, and not its volunteers, is responsible for negligent acts stemming from operations.

There have been positive benefits of the fear of personal liability among current or prospective volunteers as well as the fear that liability will be imposed on a nonprofit due to the actions of volunteers, including the following:

- Greater receptivity to policies adopted by the nonprofit pertaining to the screening of volunteers as well as operational policies and procedures related to safety
- Awareness and appreciation of the need to take care when providing service to a nonprofit
- Increased awareness by the paid staff and leaders of a nonprofit concerning the importance of carefully screening, selecting, and supervising volunteers

State Volunteer Protection Laws.   Every state has a law that pertains specifically to the legal liability of some volunteers. These laws differ greatly. Some state volunteer protection laws protect only directors and officers serving nonprofits; others protect narrow categories of volunteers, such as firefighters or other emergency service personnel. The exceptions contained in the state statutes eliminate protection for volunteers in many circumstances. The most common exceptions in the various state statutes are the following:

- Willful or wanton conduct by the volunteer
- Gross negligence on the part of the volunteer
- Wrongful acts committed while operating a motor vehicle

These are some other exceptions featured in some of the state laws:

- Fraud or fiduciary misconduct
- Actions brought by an attorney general or other state official
- Delivery of certain professional services
- Knowing violation of the law

In addition to exceptions, there are various requirements that must be met in order for the limitation on liability to apply. Examples of conditions found in some of the various laws include these:

- The requirement that the nonprofit retaining the volunteer carry liability insurance at a specified level
- The requirement that the nonprofit amend its articles of incorporation or bylaws to specifically indemnify volunteers
- The requirement that certain volunteers receive training from the nonprofit
- The requirement that volunteers receive prior written authorization to act

The conditions are consistent with the federal law's intent: to ensure that the nonprofit, not the volunteer serving the nonprofit, is financially responsible for negligent acts or omissions committed by an uncompensated volunteer. However, there is great irony in these conditions. For example, the insurance requirement often means that volunteers serving the smallest nonprofits—those with only meager resources—may not receive protection under the state volunteer protection law, whereas those volunteering for larger organizations, which can arguably afford liability insurance, will enjoy protection.

The three other conditions lead to a similar outcome: volunteers who are serving smaller, more informal organizations are at greatest risk, because the lack of sophistication and resources of the nonprofits they serve removes the protection the volunteers would otherwise enjoy under the state volunteer protection law.

In short, state and federal volunteer protection statutes provide volunteers with a defense to counter claims that a volunteer should be legally responsible for harm stemming from his or her service for a nonprofit. They *do not* insulate volunteers from claims, provide protection or immunity for nonprofit organizations, or provide volunteers with a defense to many common claims, including those alleging negligence in the operation of a motor vehicle or wrongful employment practices.

When volunteers express concern about personal liability stemming from their service, a nonprofit should respond by providing information and resources that enable volunteers to better understand the exposure and protect themselves. For example, a nonprofit can direct its volunteers to an analysis of the state and federal volunteer protection statutes, and caution volunteers about the importance of acting within the scope of their authority and not exceeding the instructions and guidelines provided by the nonprofit. Insurance coverage that the nonprofit has purchased for the benefit of its volunteers, including directors' and officers' liability or volunteer liability policies, should be explained to concerned volunteers.

Risk Management for Volunteer Programs.   Every nonprofit that engages volunteers at the governance or service delivery level should examine the risks posed by the deployment of volunteers and identify practical measures available to address these risks. It is neither necessary nor advisable to exhaust an organization's financial resources in an effort to foreclose the possibility of missteps or harm. Every proposed risk management activity should be evaluated in relation to its role in preventing foreseeable harm or increasing the organization's prospects of realizing success.

Several principles for managing volunteer-related risks can provide guidance.

1. *Apply common sense before dollars and cents.* Although nonprofit leaders continue to view insurance as a primary risk management response, the truth is that many risk management measures cost little, if anything, to implement. For example, prohibiting volunteers from establishing out-of-program personal relationships with clients is a commonsense strategy for reducing the risk of out-of-program abuse of a client by an agent of the nonprofit. Yet this commonsense strategy is of little value unless the nonprofit carefully communicates the policy (and its rationale) to volunteers as well as clients and their parents or guardians.
2. *Involve volunteers in risk management planning.* On occasion, risk management programs are developed at the management level of a nonprofit and imposed on the people required to implement new procedures or adhere to new policy. In some cases, the top-down approach is necessary and appropriate. But

in other cases, this approach leads to a lack of commitment and support that jeopardizes the policy. It is prudent to involve volunteers in the design of strategies intended to protect them, as well as activities that keep the nonprofit's clients and financial assets safe from harm.

3. *Provide explicit direction.* Some nonprofits shy away from providing explicit direction to volunteers out of fear of offending these unpaid but essential workers. Providing explicit instructions (including dos and don'ts) helps volunteers succeed. It also helps a nonprofit avoid potentially costly circumstances when a volunteer claims, "I didn't know we weren't supposed to do that." For example, you may require an ongoing commitment of a certain number of service hours per week for volunteers working with vulnerable clients or that your volunteers attend a defensive driving course before driving your minibus. Don't forget to include prohibited activities when you provide instruction—including topics that may be difficult to discuss, such as your prohibition against volunteers dating or engaging in sexual acts with clients of any age or inviting clients into their homes.

4. *Maintain standards.* Directors of volunteers are generally well versed on the importance of recognizing and rewarding outstanding volunteer service. Yet it is sometimes difficult to acknowledge the need, from time to time, to discipline and even remove volunteers who fail to measure up. This is required when a volunteer performs at a level below your standards, does something prohibited by your program, or otherwise fails to meet your minimum requirements. It is critical that every nonprofit prepare for the day when it must remove a volunteer whose continued participation poses too great a risk to the health and safety of the organization, its clients, or other volunteers. Firing a volunteer, though never an easy task, may be absolutely necessary to protect the vital mission of an organization.

5. *Discuss responsibilities openly with partners.* Nonprofits often collaborate to achieve results that wouldn't be possible if the organizations operated alone. The greater an organization's reliance on volunteers, the more likely it is to partner with other organizations. Reduce the risk of these valuable collaborations by never assuming that the other organization has something covered. Every collaboration should begin with a frank discussion of who will do what, when, and where, including who will be responsible (and how) if harm to persons or property results from the collaboration.

6. *Establish and monitor policies.* Policies and procedures are crucial to the success of volunteer risk management. State-of-the-art eye protection, for example, is useless if volunteers aren't instructed that they must wear the protection before picking up a power tool. As a nonprofit develops policies that it requires its volunteers to follow, it must pay particularly close attention to the way in

which these policies are communicated to all personnel. Using overlapping forms of communication and providing an opportunity for questions will reduce the risk that a key policy will go unnoticed or be misinterpreted.

7. *Guard client privacy.* Volunteers engaged in service delivery should be instructed about their responsibility for guarding client privacy. These instructions should include direction about the steps a volunteer should take to report accidental violations of privacy or concerns they may have about the organization's practices.

8. *Put expectations and duties in writing.* A growing number of nonprofits that rely on volunteers have adopted the use of written job descriptions or volunteer agreements. These resources serve several purposes, including making it easier to determine and account for who is serving as a volunteer in your organization and what their responsibilities are; clearly establishing the terms of appointment and reappointment (for example, for one year, renewable by mutual agreement an unlimited number of times); reminding volunteers that they are serving at the discretion and will of the organization; and establishing a sense of accountability of the volunteer to the organization and its rules.

9. *Cast a wide net by making risk management a shared responsibility.* Strive to engage volunteers in all phases of your risk management program, and seek feedback from these valuable personnel as you work to integrate safe practices in the culture of your organization.

Insurance and Risk Management

A small percentage of nonprofit leaders continue to equate risk management with the purchase of insurance. When asked about their organization's risk management program, they reply, "We purchase insurance!" Yet even though insurance is an important risk financing option—a way to pay for losses that result despite the nonprofit's attempt to avoid them—insurance plays no role in reducing the likelihood that harm will result from operations. In addition, there are many exposures faced by the vast majority of nonprofits for which no insurance is available. The best example is risk to reputation: no coverage is available to restore a nonprofit's sullied reputation following an attention-grabbing scandal reported on the front page of the local newspaper.

Insurance Market Cycles. Like other consumers of commercial insurance, nonprofits are subject to conditions in the insurance marketplace. One of the conditions that often has a dramatic effect on nonprofits is the cyclical nature of the industry. During the "soft market" phase of the cycle, insurers compete aggressively for new business. "Bells and whistles" may be added to commonly purchased policies, such as directors' and officers' liability, and insurers are willing to compete on price and coverage in order to retain customers and write new accounts. During the "hard market" phase of the cycle, nonprofits face a "seller's market." Typical hard market conditions include premium increases unrelated to an insured's loss history, restrictions in coverage, the requirement that buyers agree to higher deductibles, and the refusal of some carriers to offer the limits of liability that consumers wish to purchase.

Insurance Dos and Don'ts. Although nonprofits have been purchasing commercial insurance for decades, the process has become only marginally simpler during this time. The insurance world remains a strange and daunting environment for most nonprofit managers. Before discussing various forms of coverage that nonprofits often purchase, I present the following list of dos and don'ts that should be considered as a nonprofit sets about procuring insurance.

Do

- Find a competent insurance intermediary (broker, agent, or consultant) whom you trust to advocate for your nonprofit.
- Take the time to read your insurance policies.
- Investigate the financial stability of your insurers.
- Ask your broker or agent to respond to your questions in writing.
- Seek multiple bids for your insurance coverage at least every three to five years. If relying on your broker or agent to do this, request documentation of their efforts.
- Give thoughtful consideration to how much risk your nonprofit can afford to retain.
- Provide your board of directors with a copy of your directors' and officers' liability policy.
- Discuss risk management and insurance issues at the board level.

Don't

- Delegate responsibility for your insurance program to a junior staff member.
- Simply renew your coverage each year without considering whether your needs have changed.
- Wait until the last minute to submit completed applications.
- Be evasive about your operations or risk exposures on your application.
- Be shy about asking questions concerning your coverage or the process.
- Regard your insurance coverage as your risk management program.

What's Appropriate Insurance Coverage? Nonprofit managers and executives cope with many complex challenges on a regular basis. One of the perennial questions is whether the nonprofit's insurance program (the total of all coverage you purchase) is adequate. Unfortunately, there are no easy answers to what seems like a simple question. Every nonprofit must evaluate its exposures, risk-taking appetite, and budget constraints to determine how much insurance it can and should buy. Some experts urge nonprofits to purchase as much insurance as they can afford. Yet insurance is probably most economically efficient when it is an organization's risk financing method for unexpected or catastrophic exposures. Costs that can be readily predicted on the basis of past experience should be financed internally. During hard market conditions, the limits available to your nonprofit may be declining or the broadly worded coverage you purchased during the 1990s may be restricted through wording changes and new exclusions.

The following are some of the common property and casualty policies nonprofits purchase.

- *Commercial general liability* (CGL) coverage protects against third-party legal claims alleging bodily injury, property damage, and personal injury. There are numerous standard forms and a wide range of variations. For example, the CGL policy may include miscellaneous professional liability and improper sexual conduct, or it may explicitly exclude coverage of these claims.
- *Commercial auto liability and physical damage* coverage protects against claims and damage stemming from use of the nonprofit's owned vehicles, including cars, vans, minibuses, buses, and trucks.
- *Directors' and officers' liability* (D&O) coverage protects against claims alleging wrongful management acts. Most nonprofits that purchase D&O purchase nonprofit-tailored forms that provide broad protection for the nonprofit itself in addition to volunteer directors, other volunteers, and paid staff. Most nonprofit D&O policies also include coverage for claims alleging wrongful employment practices, although this coverage can also be purchased separately or as part of another policy.
- *Professional liability* coverage protects against claims alleging negligence in the delivery of professional services. Nonprofits providing medical, legal, counseling, consulting, and many other services that require special training may be exposed to professional liability claims. This coverage can be purchased in a stand-alone policy or as part of a CGL or D&O policy.
- *Improper sexual conduct or sexual abuse* coverage protects against claims alleging improper sexual contact. This policy may provide a defense for claims alleging improper contact between clients, or such conduct may be specifically excluded. Coverage may be purchased on a stand-alone basis or as part of another line of liability coverage.

- *Nonowned or hired auto* policies provide excess coverage for damages and medical expenses that exceed the limit of the coverage on a car owned by a volunteer or employee acting on the nonprofit's behalf.
- *Property* insurance covers property owned or leased by the nonprofit, including buildings and equipment.
- *Business interruption and extra expense* coverage helps out in emergencies. The business interruption portion of the policy covers loss of income if premises are completely shut down for a period of time due to a covered property loss (such as a fire or a hurricane). Income from funding sources and participant fees are included, and the policy provides dollars for continuing expenses such as rent or salaries. The extra expense portion provides funds for additional costs a nonprofit might incur due to its inability to use its regular facilities, such as the cost of renting alternative space from which to deliver services.
- *Fidelity and crime* insurance covers claims alleging theft of financial assets by an insider or a third party.
- *Umbrella* insurance provides additional and even excess coverage over several primary policies, such as CGL, auto liability, and employers' liability. The policy increases the amount of liability coverage beyond that of the basic policies carried by the nonprofit and covers some areas that are missing from the basic insurance policy.
- No-fault *workers' compensation* coverage is required by state law to cover medical expenses and lost income stemming from employee injuries. In some cases, volunteers can be insured under workers' compensation, although most nonprofits find this option to be cost-prohibitive.
- *Accident* insurance is additional insurance that covers medical expenses (up to a preset limit) for volunteers or participants who are injured while serving the nonprofit or participating in the nonprofit's activities. Accident insurance covers any excess over the individual's health insurance and provides primary coverage for persons who are uninsured.

Summary

Risk management is gradually being embraced by nonprofit board members and executives as an important management discipline that can enable an organization to more effectively advance its mission. As leaders learn more about risk management, the myths associated with the discipline are beginning to dissipate. A growing number of staff and volunteer leaders are recognizing that a risk management program is vital to mission fulfillment and fully within their grasp. The risk management process can be coordinated by a task force consisting of paid and volunteer staff as well as outside advisers—only the largest nonprofits can afford to hire a full-time risk manager. Yet in every organization it is essential that risk-taking and risk management be on the board's radar screen. It is never appropriate to expect staff and advisors to "handle" the risks facing a nonprofit. Decisions about risk taking and risk management should be strategic as well as tactical. The risk management process consists of the following steps:

Step 1: Consider the context

Step 2: Identify risks

Step 3: Evaluate risks

Step 4: Decide what to do and take action

Step 5: Monitor and adjust

The most important goal for risk management in a nonprofit organization is integrating the identification of risks and strategies to address them into the governance and day-to-day operations of the organization so that the practice becomes intuitive and seamless.

Note

1. The material in this section is based on the guidance contained in the Nonprofit Risk Management Center's book, *No Surprises: Harmonizing Risk and Reward in Volunteer Management*, 4th edition, available at www.nonprofitrisk.org.

References

Herman, M. L. *Pillars of Accountability: A Risk Management Guide for Nonprofit Boards*. Washington, D.C.: Nonprofit Risk Management Center, 2006.

Herman, M. L. *No Surprises: Harmonizing Risk and Reward in Volunteer Management*, 5th ed. Washington, D.C.: Nonprofit Risk Management Center, 2009.

Additional Resources

An extensive set of nonprofit risk management readings, references, and resource materials, including checklists and Web-based planning tools, is available at the Web site of the Nonprofit Risk Management Center: www.nonprofitrisk.org.

The *My Risk Management Plan* risk management plan development tool is available at www.myriskmanagementplan.org.

PART FIVE

LEADING AND MANAGING PEOPLE IN NONPROFITS

The three chapters of Part Five of this book discuss leadership and management from the perspective of the most significant assets of any nonprofit organization: the people who, whether as employees or volunteers, make the organization what it is. Regardless of employment status, every nonprofit must be able to attract, retain, and motivate people. Mary R. Watson and Rikki Abzug, in Chapter Twenty-four, the first chapter of this final part of the book, explain the process of strategic human resource management and detail the human resource processes and systems that are essential to any well-functioning nonprofit organization. Nancy E. Day then follows with Chapter Twenty-five, which explains the design and operation of a Total Rewards approach to compensation and benefits that is appropriate to the nonprofit environment. In the final chapter of Part Five, Chapter Twenty-six, Jeffrey Brudney presents a comprehensive explanation of effective volunteer management and how a nonprofit can systematically and strategically implement an effective program to attract, organize, lead, and manage volunteers. All three chapters take care to attend to the legal dimensions of personnel and volunteer management while emphasizing the importance of accomplishing the mission and vision through ethical and effective human resource management strategies and practices.

CHAPTER TWENTY-FOUR

EFFECTIVE HUMAN RESOURCE PRACTICES

Recruitment and Retention in Nonprofit Organizations

Mary R. Watson and Rikki Abzug

The attraction, selection, and retention of staff are among the most important processes that managers in organizations undertake. After all, the people of the organization are the architects and agents of everything that ultimately gets accomplished. Yet processes that are seen to be related to increased overhead, such as the funding of human resource practices, tend to garner woefully inadequate attention and support (Gregory and Howard, 2009) in many nonprofits. Overcrowded schedules, underfunded programs, endless client needs, irregular financial cycles, and demands for reports of accountability are among the never-ending pressures that crowd out the organization's ability to focus on the critical human dimensions of nonprofit management. With too little time, information, and money, not to mention staff needed yesterday rather than tomorrow, how can leaders learn how to plan a human resource system, much less implement one and then evaluate whether it is reaching the desired outcomes?

The purpose of this chapter is to help executive directors and staff at all levels build a system of human resource practices that is both effective and realistic in the contexts of their own organizations. Toward this end, we have organized the chapter around two goals. Our first goal is to demonstrate the advantages of thinking systemically about the role that people play in organizations, showing how better human resource practice leads to better long-term outcomes. Not only is it possible to save time and effort in recruitment, selection, and staff retention programs, but building an effective human resource culture is also key to long-term success. Our second goal is to provide an overview of the most critical human resource processes, demonstrating how they can be accomplished in settings without significant formal human resource structures and staff in place. We also discuss important legislation related to various aspects of finding and keeping the right people that enable each nonprofit to reach its own unique objectives. Although it is not possible to be comprehensive in every aspect of human resource management—volumes have been written on this subject—this chapter provides the essential knowledge necessary to find staff prospects, interview and evaluate applicants, keep staff motivated, and manage the circumstances under which staff will ultimately leave the organization. The next chapter in this handbook, prepared by Nancy Day, provides complementary information about the design and management of compensation and benefits programs.

Staff and leaders might wonder what is different about our approach to nonprofit human resources. In fact, one might simply pick up a current practitioner article on the "top ten tips for recruitment," for example, and conclude that the answers are stated there. The difference lies in our deliberate recognition that nonprofit organizations are values driven, and so must be their approach to human resources (Ridder and McCandless, 2010). Yet there is no universal approach to nonprofit human resource management because of the variety of contexts, structures, and conditions in which social sector organizations operate. Further, there are no simple rules: contingency approaches that argue a simple set of "if . . . then" recommendations (for example, if an organization is in a rural area, then it must have a local recruitment strategy) are not sufficient. Outcome measures like return on investment (Bartel, 2000; Fitz-enz, 2000) can be useful, but they are not sufficient unless systems are considered holistically and in context. Instead, we propose that "configurational" (Toh, Morgeson, and Campion, 2008) approaches are best because they recognize that there are unique synergies gained through human resource systems and that these synergies differ depending on the context in which they exist. Executives who capitalize on the relationships among human resource approaches, the organization's environment, the mission and goals of the organization, and knowledge management principles are the ones who are successful in building momentum toward the organization's desired state. To aid in this endeavor, throughout this chapter, we remind executives of the key questions that should be asked regarding elements of the human resource system in their organizations.

Why Put People First?

Given the humanistic missions of most nonprofit organizations, it is paradoxical that nonprofit leaders need to be reminded of the importance of the people in the organizations. Yet across organizations and time, multiple constituencies demand attention from nonprofit leaders (Kanter and Summers, 1987). Nonprofit mission statements typically do focus on people, but people who are external to the organizations—the clients—rather than internal staff. The attention paid to internal staff issues is scant in many nonprofit settings.

The primary focus of nonprofits is typically to ensure that the organization delivers on mission. Most staff are attracted to nonprofits because they are motivated by their organization's mission. Thus compared to their for-profit counterparts, nonprofits have an extremely powerful advantage in all aspects of their human resource systems. Studying the nonprofit workforce, Paul Light (2004, p. 7) has suggested that "the nonprofit sector survives because it has a self-exploiting work force: wind it up and it will do more with less until it just runs out." A 2006 American Humanics report underscored Light's findings that nonprofit employees are comparatively highly motivated, hard working, and deeply committed (Halpern, 2006). Even in treacherous economic times, the motivations of nonprofit staff are precisely what enable their organizations to thrive (Block, 2003; Light, 2002), if they avoid the pitfalls of adopting for-profit approaches without first considering their suitability for nonprofits (Beck, Lengnick-Hall, and Lengnick-Hall, 2008). How can they do this?

We emphasize here that the nature of nonprofits makes them ideally suited to maximize their outcomes through the people of the organizations. This focus on people results in additional organizational capacity, effective succession planning, engaged and motivated staff, and improved client service delivery. These are not just effectiveness outcomes; they are also the keys to the time, money, and information organizations need to survive and thrive. They also lead to reputation effects that attract staff and funders through positive profiles featured in outlets like *The 100 Best Nonprofits to Work For* (Hamilton and Tragert, 2000) and awards given by entities like the New York Times with its Nonprofit Excellence Awards (www.npccny.org/info/awards.htm).

Successful nonprofit organizations recognize that organizational success lies in the creative engagement of the human resources of the organization. They regard human resources not as a staff function outside the organization's operation but rather as the central conduit through which organizations succeed. They capitalize on the power of mission to attract and motivate staff. They recognize the critical nature of staff synergies in selecting new staff members. They leverage technology, where appropriate, to reduce recruitment costs and administer standardized human resource functions. They encourage diversity on many dimensions, and they enact cultures that are constituted by diverse groups working well together. They design motivation and retention systems that recognize both the intrinsic motivators that brought staff to the organization (such as mission focus or client focus) as well as the extrinsic motivators (such as pay, health care, or retirement) that are necessary for staff financial and physical health. They retain and develop talented staff whenever possible, and they manage terminations in humane and positive ways when layoffs are unavoidable.

Human Resources Is a System, Not a Set of Tasks

Our approach is a systems approach to human resources that considers the unique complement of the configuration of human resource practices. The activities of human resources cannot be thought about independent of one another, and effective leaders develop an overarching set of integrated human resource goals to guide their day-to-day decision making. Effective nonprofit managers avoid staffing decisions that come about as part of an immediate crisis: for example, needing to hire quickly to scale up and deliver on outcomes expected from additional funded projects, or reacting to the sudden departure of a crucial staff person who needs to be replaced immediately. Instead, effective nonprofit organizations keep an eye on their future, anticipating stages where the mission will be broadened and additional talent will be needed, conducting succession planning to identify needs to develop internal staff before there is a crisis, and monitoring the external environment to determine what new funding sources will be coming its way.

Avoiding immediate crises can circumvent unintended long-term outcomes. For example, government contractors who consistently add and delete staff based on variable levels of program funding can inadvertently create a climate of insecurity and distrust. Organizations that vary staff levels can develop a reputation as an unstable employer, thus discouraging qualified and committed applicants to apply when new staff are needed. Individual human resource decisions, seemingly isolated, can cause reverberations inside and outside the organization, many of which may be unintended and unwanted.

Not only are human resource functions interconnected, but in the aggregate they also represent the experienced culture of the organization. The organization's human resource goals are very important because they define the day-to-day quality of work life enjoyed by staff. Because of their centrality, informed executives engage all staff in imagining their ideal collective human resource culture. In this way, they begin at the desired end. First they figure out, collectively in their organization, where they want to go. Then they do a needs assessment of their current culture of human resources, assess their planning needs, engage staff at all levels in designing human resource processes, and later evaluate their progress toward the desired end. All along the way, effective nonprofits keep in mind where they are trying to go as they take the small steps that will get them there.

Some examples will illustrate the point. Affirmative businesses, incorporated as or created by nonprofits, with goals of providing jobs and job training for mentally, physically, or economically disadvantaged individuals, often center human resources in their sustainability and growth plans. For organizations serving the mentally ill or the homeless, for example, the line between clients and staff can be amorphous, and best practices suggest an integrated approach that emphasizes job design, career pathing, motivational compensation, and respect for individual choice. Organizations from New York's Housing Works Bookstore to Seattle's Boomtown Café find they can do good by doing well (Kanter and Summers, 1987) if they stand by all of their people.

If You Build It, They Will Come (and Stay)

There are two key concepts to keep in mind while imagining the end state of an effective nonprofit human resource system: fit and embeddedness. These two concepts make clear that whereas successful executives design human resource systems, these systems are continually re-created by everyone associated with the organization. Therefore, in successful nonprofits, all staff are continually rebuilding their human resource culture. There is no true end result: human resource culture is a never-ending exercise in coevolution.

In two decades of studies on person–organization fit and person–job fit (see Chatman, 1989; O'Reilly, Chatman, and Caldwell, 1991; Ostroff and Judge, 2007), a consistent finding is that staff are attracted to organizations with which they perceive an alignment between the goals of the organization and their own values and objectives. This is one explanation as to why recruiting by internal referral is so successful (Barber, 1998): individuals who know insiders are much more likely to understand what the organization is about and accurately assess whether or not they would like to work there. Thus self-selection on the part of prospective and current staff plays a huge role in shaping the ultimate human resource culture. This notion of perceived fit has also been shown to apply to the person and the job, as well as the person and the work group (Kristof-Brown, Jansen, and Colbert, 2002; Resnick, Baltes, and Shantz, 2007).

Nonprofit executives should keep in mind that these perceived fit processes are going on in all aspects of the human resource system (attracting, recruiting, selecting, retaining, and staff turnover). One productive task is to engage all staff in a dialogue around what constitutes fit in their organization. Effective nonprofits work to make explicit what the fit dimensions are, beginning by examining the mission statement. A second task is to investigate perceptions of your organization held by those in similar and different organizations. Knowing how the culture of the organization is perceived by outsiders will provide key information about who might be attracted to the organization and who might be approaching staff to recruit them away. Once these dimensions are clearer, the human resource strategy of the organization can recognize the power and limitations of the notion of fit. Whether an organization makes it explicit or not, perceived fit (or lack thereof) is always an element of the human resource system success.

One important clarification needs emphasis here. Fit is not a synonym for homogeneity. Successful organizations tend to seek and engage diverse viewpoints. In fact, one might have as an element of the mission an explicit goal of nourishing a culture of diversity. In this case, fit means attracting staff who share the value of honoring difference, not attracting similar staff. One useful interpretation of diversity is articulated by scholar Taylor Cox (1994), who acknowledges and embraces the wide variety of social characteristics held by people who work together. Successful nonprofits shape their human resource systems around a broad and diverse set of views, using their historical, community, and mission contexts to define their diversity goals.

The second key element of an effective nonprofit human resource system is the notion of embeddedness. This refers to the extent to which the staff and their families are engaged in the organization and its community. Embeddedness is a broader concept than organization satisfaction and commitment, which have been argued to account for less than 5 percent of actual turnover (Hom and Griffeth, 1995). Drawing on Kurt Lewin's field theory (1951), research on embeddedness (Lee, Mitchell, Holtom, McDaniel, and Hill, 1999) suggests that staff who are more embedded in their organizations are less likely to leave voluntarily. There are three dimensions to embeddedness: the extent to which individuals have links to other people, the extent to which their job and community fit with other aspects of their lives, and the perception of what would be lost if the individual left his or her job (Mitchell, Holtom, Lee, Sablynski, and Erez, 2001).

For successful nonprofits, embeddedness is a powerful concept. Nonprofit organizations can increase their human and social capital by remembering what embeds staff into their organizations (Holtom, Mitchell, and Lee, 2006). Not only is it desirable that staff share a passion for the organization's mission, but they must also be motivated by the way in which their role facilitates reaching part of that mission. Further, the more extensive the networks of relationships they and their families have within the organization and the community, the more likely they are to stay with the organization. Finally, the understanding of what would be lost if they left the organization ("sacrifice," in embeddedness terms) helps leaders guide human resource systems closer to the ideal state that staff would imagine. Here a good exercise for executive directors would be to encourage open dialogue around human resource systems, eliciting from staff a shared understanding of the really unique elements of the nonprofit and the community it serves. Note that discussion of human resources includes all aspects of work, including the design of jobs themselves.

In addition to shared values, it is also important to recognize individual needs of staff, which will differ from person to person and family to family, and vary considerably by generation (Kunreuther, 2003). The quality of the relationship that staff members have with leaders is a key factor in their intention to stay with the organization. Informal dialogue, or more formalized 360-degree performance appraisals systems, in which staff give constructive feedback to the executive staff (and vice versa), can help keep positive communication open across levels. Staff families matter too. Offering cafeteria-style benefits, allowing staff to choose from an array of human resource benefits what best fits their family needs, is one example of engaging with the "whole person." Flexible work schedules might also help in this area. At a minimum, open dialogue between staff and managers must be encouraged to keep shared lines of communication open.

First Things First: Make It Legal

It is always wise to begin any discussion of the processes involved in human resource systems with a discussion of the existing law related to these human resource processes. Many nonprofit managers are unfamiliar with current legislative statutes, and the consequences of decisions that violate the law can be dire, particularly for smaller organizations without the resources to engage in lawsuits or absorb fines.

The United States has a century-long tradition of creating policy to protect workers. Starting around the turn of the twentieth century with the birth of the union movement following the shirtwaist workers' strike, employment law emerged during the civil rights movement of the 1960s around race and equity, through advances in workplace safety in the 1970s, and today's work issues of HIV/AIDS, family-friendly policies, and procedures to reduce terrorism. We shall review the essential laws that all nonprofit professionals must know, whether "human resources" is part of their job title or not.

It is important to note that nonprofits are typically held accountable for actions taken by their staff, vendors, clients, and contractors. In general, actions that managers knew about, as well as those the courts deem they should have known about, are deemed to be the responsibility of the nonprofit's leadership, not the individual who committed the discriminatory action. The best defense against discrimination charges is the existence of clear policy that spells out the nature of discriminatory actions and a system through which all staff are educated about fair employment practice.

There are a variety of legislative frameworks around the world, made up of varying combinations of national, regional, and local legislation. Knowing how these levels of legislation interact in one's own country is important. For instance, in Canada, federal labor code covers less than ten percent of the nation's employees, so most employment legal issues are determined by laws created by the various provinces (Bernier and Lajoie, 1986). In the United States, by contrast, federal regulations apply to all organizations with staff above a certain size (which varies, depending on the particular law). There are also state and local laws that provide more stringent standards than the federal legislation, and each nonprofit must familiarize itself with the laws of its own state and the states in which it operates. Due to space limitations, we review only U.S. federal law here. State and local laws vary considerably.

This section provides a general overview of the U.S. federal legislative framework, with particular emphasis on discrimination law. Using this chapter as a starting place, you may find that a user-friendly legal guide to U.S. federal employment law, like the one published by the American Bar Association (Fick, 2006), can help clarify key questions. However, general legal knowledge is not to be substituted for appropriate legal advice from qualified counsel. It is always necessary to consult an attorney for specific applications to your organization.

Title VII: The Civil Rights Act of 1964

Title VII of the Civil Rights Act, arguably the most influential piece of legislation regarding employee treatment, was passed into law in 1964. Building on energy from the civil rights movement that garnered more attention than previous civil rights bills, the Civil Rights Act was signed into law under Lyndon Johnson's administration. Title VII of that act focuses on employment, and it specifically prohibits employment discrimination based on race, skin color, religion, sex, and national origin. In addition, it established the Equal Employment Opportunity Commission (EEOC), a federal agency empowered with the enforcement of discrimination violations. Other sections of the Civil Rights Act relate to education and public facilities contexts. Here we focus only on the employment dimensions of the law specified in Title VII.

The prohibition of discrimination provided under Title VII applies to all aspects of the work relationship: recruiting, hiring, promoting, performance evaluation, access to training, discharging, and so on. A common misperception is that the coverage is narrowly applicable to hiring decisions. All organizations with fifteen or more employees are required to adhere to nondiscriminatory practices in all aspects of their treatment of employees. Furthermore, any organization of any size that receives substantial federal government funds or contracts (the dollar value varies by program) must comply. Also, any employment agency, labor organization, or joint labor-management committee controlling apprenticeship or other training or retraining must comply, regardless of size. Title VII was amended by the Civil Rights Act of 1991 to include the opportunity of compensatory and punitive damages for intentional discrimination, enable litigants to collect legal fees, and allow for jury trials.

There is one particularly notable exception to enforcement of anti-discrimination categories. In general, religious organizations have been considered exempt from the religion category and supported in their right to make employment decisions based on faith. However, some federal social programs (the Workforce Investment Act, for example) contain language explicitly prohibiting religious discrimination, others (such as community development block grants and Head Start) might be interpreted as prohibiting employment decisions based on religion, and some other states and localities require religious organizations not to discriminate on the basis of religion in order to be eligible for funding. In 2004, the Bush administration's Office of Faith and Community Based Initiatives considered legislation that would clarify the legality of existing practice that allows religious organizations to make employment decisions based on faith when they are receiving federal money. At the time of the writing of this chapter, the Obama administration has made clear it intends to expand the White House faith-based initiatives already in place, but the legality of the religious exception is still common practice, although not yet officially clarified by law.

Disparate Treatment Versus Adverse Impact. Understanding what human resource practices constitute discrimination requires reading the legal text of Title VII. Discrimination, as defined under Title VII, falls into two categories. What is termed "disparate treatment" is sometimes also called deliberate or direct discrimination. Under a charge of disparate treatment, a litigant who is a member of a protected group (race, color, religion, sex, or national origin) would argue that he or she was treated differently because of his or her protected class. A litigant might argue that the interviewer indicated racial or national origin bias during the interview, for example. In addition to evidence of direct discrimination, disparate treatment charges require not only that the litigant has been denied access to the employment benefit but also that another person who is not a member of the protected class was chosen. Fortunately, most organizations have put human resource practices and staff training programs in place to alleviate many of the intentional discrimination charges.

Lesson

Make sure all staff members are aware of the organization's intolerance of deliberately discriminatory practices, and ensure that training around these issues is provided. Many issues are subtle.

Determining the much more common charge "adverse impact" is more complex. Sometimes called indirect or unintentional discrimination, adverse impact occurs when the aggregate outcomes for a protected group are less advantageous than for the majority group. The landmark case in this instance is *Griggs* v. *Duke Power* (401 U.S. 424, 1971). Griggs, an African American employee of the Duke Power Company in North Carolina, was denied promotion to a supervisory position because he did not hold a high school diploma. At that time in North Carolina, the high school graduation rates for blacks and whites were significantly different, with blacks earning diplomas at a lower rate (this disparity has since been corrected). The U.S. Supreme Court ruled that the high school diploma requirement discriminated against blacks because they had a lower graduation rate. Further, the organization failed to demonstrate why a high school diploma was necessary to do the job effectively. In fact, some supervisors promoted earlier did not have diplomas.

The *Griggs* case makes two things clear for nonprofit leaders. First, it is necessary to examine your own human resource practices to ensure that the outcomes for protected groups are not different from the outcomes for majority groups. Second, be certain that you can demonstrate the job-relatedness of any human resource criterion, regardless of whether you think it might be correlated with protected class. For example, imagine that you regularly select staff to attend a leadership development program. To encourage fairness, you make it a practice to choose individuals from across your organization's geographical locations to attend, and you make these decisions one by one over time. Imagine, however, that in compiling an analysis of your decisions in the past year, you discover that in the aggregate, women have been chosen less frequently than men, despite the fact that your workforce is balanced by gender. How would you know if you have enacted a discriminatory selection for training?

The first test is to see whether you have what is called a *prima facie* ("on its face") case of discrimination. The legal test is what is called the four-fifths rule: Was the rate of selection of the women at least four-fifths (80 percent) of the rate of selection for the men? Assume that there are ten women and ten men from whom you might have chosen. If you have chosen five men, you must also have chosen at least four women to diffuse a prima facie case. In the event that there appears to be discrimination after application of the four-fifths rule (in this example, if you chose fewer than four women), can you defend the decisions you made by arguing that the criteria on which you based the selection of trainees are related to job performance? Numerous court decisions based on gender, including well-publicized ones argued by airlines to defend female-only flight attendant positions, have established that gender is not a valid job criterion. You have a problem.

Lesson

Remember that under Title VII, discrimination does not have to be intentional to be illegal. The aggregate outcome of your organization's decisions can be used as evidence of discrimination even if it was not intentional.

Consider another example. Imagine you are choosing among applicants for a counseling position where the clients speak English. Among your applicant pool are ten U.S.-born native English speakers and ten Chinese-born immigrants with Mandarin as their native tongue. If five of the Americans pass the initial English language test you use for prescreening but only one of the Chinese applicants does, is there discrimination based on national origin? Superficially, there is a prima facie case of discrimination (50 percent of the U.S.-born make the cut, compared to only 10 percent of the Chinese-born, which fails the four-fifths test). In this situation, however, you may be able to successfully muster a job-relatedness defense that the skill on which you screened (language) is essential to performing the job (counseling clients). Although there are other defenses in the case of prima facie discrimination (seniority system, bona fide occupational qualification), job-relatedness is the best defense (Fick, 2006). Nonprofits need to be careful to use selection criteria that are quantifiable and empirically proven to be related to job performance. General impressions of candidates and their attitudes do not hold up well in court.

Lesson

Use only human resource criteria that your organization can demonstrate are directly related to job performance. Do not rely on opinions or assumptions; collect hard data.

Interpretations of Title VII. An interpretation of Title VII surrounds the issue of sexual harassment. Although Title VII did not specifically identify sexual harassment as part of its domain, subsequent court cases have interpreted sexual harassment as discrimination based on gender. According to law, there are two kinds of sexual harassment. The first is called *quid pro quo,* Latin for "something in exchange for something." To meet the criteria under this category, a staffer (or in some legal findings, clients or board members) must have been the unwanted recipient of an advance that is sexual in nature, where the "submission to or rejection of this conduct explicitly or implicitly affects an individual's employment," including employment decisions (Equal Employment Opportunity Commission, 2002b). Most organizations have mechanisms in place to ensure that deliberate sexual harassment does not occur, as well as channels for safely reporting incidents.

The category of "hostile work environment" is more subtle. In general, a staffer must have been subjected to either sexual advances or other verbal or physical conduct of a sexual nature that either "unreasonably interfered with an individual's work performance" or created "an intimidating, hostile, or offensive working environment" (Equal Employment Opportunity Commission, 2002b). Courts typically consider whether the staffer made it known to the alleged harasser that the advances or behaviors were unwelcome, and the advances or behaviors must have been repeated. However, in some circumstances, courts have interpreted an act as so egregious as to not warrant meeting the conditions of notice and readvance.

Supreme Court cases clarify that both men and women are protected, and harassment can be perpetrated by individuals of the same sex regardless of the sexual orientation of either party (for example, *Oncale* v. *Sundowner Offshore Services, Inc.*, 523 U.S. 75, 1998). Further, the harasser can be connected to the organization in many capacities: as a supervisor, employee, agent of the organization, coworker, or nonemployee. Employers can be held liable even if the employee does not complain about the harassment (*Faragher v. Boca Raton*, 524 U.S. 775, 1998). Finally, the harassed does not need to be the direct recipient of the unwanted sexual behavior. A charge can be filed by anyone affected by the conduct. Court decisions on legal standards for behavior have shifted from those of a "reasonable person" to those of a "reasonable woman" or "reasonable victim."

Lesson

Make sure all staff members understand what constitutes sexual harassment, how to avoid harassing incidents, and the channels they should follow to report unwanted behaviors. Extend your training to clients, vendors, and other related staff.

Legislation Protecting the Disabled

Other legislation has extended nondiscriminatory practices to other protected groups. For example, the Age Discrimination in Employment Act of 1967 (and amendments in the Older Workers Benefit Protection Act) applies to employers with twenty or more employees and protects workers over age forty (younger in some states) against discrimination based on age. The Pregnancy Discrimination Act (an amendment to Title VII) protects women who are pregnant against refusals to hire, requires treatment of pregnancy that interferes medically with the employee's ability to work to be treated as any other disability, requires that any health insurance offered by the employer include pregnancy coverage (but not abortion coverage), and requires that employees be given leave, vacation calculation, and pay under the same practices that are afforded to other employees on leave.

One final group deserves special explanation: the disabled. The Council for Disability Rights estimates that 43 million Americans have physical or mental disabilities (Council for Disability Rights, 2009). The employment rate of those with disabilities is half that of those without, despite the fact that two-thirds of those unemployed with disabilities say they would prefer to be working (National Council on Disability, 2007).

The Americans with Disabilities Act of 1990 (ADA) protects those with physical and mental disabilities, whether perceived or real, from discrimination in employment (and public access). The act covers all employers with more than fifteen employees, as well as all state and government programs and activities. The ADA defines a person with a disability as "someone with a physical or mental impairment that substantially limits a major life activity, has a record of such an impairment, or is regarded as having such an impairment" (Equal Employment Opportunity Commission, 2002a).

Clarifications of the ADA by the EEOC indicate that the use of items like medications or prostheses does not disqualify a disabled person. Mental and emotional characteristics such as thinking and concentrating are covered, and short-term impairments are generally interpreted as less life-altering (Equal Employment Opportunity Commission, 2000). Active drug use is not a disability, although prior drug use can qualify if the person is discriminated against based on a record or perception of prior use. Although the ADA and its amendments do not specify the disabilities that qualify, case law has upheld such diverse conditions as mobility, vision, speech, and hearing impairments, asymptomatic HIV status, learning disabilities, and mental illness.

The passage of the ADA changed employment screening practices directly. Under the ADA, no employer may require a medical examination prior to extending a job offer. Further, where applicants or employees request "reasonable accommodation" of the physical workplace, the design of their jobs, or their benefits, employers are required to comply to the extent to which the accommodations do not cause the employer undue financial or logistical hardship. Examples of accommodations under ADA might include modifying work schedules, purchasing special equipment to facilitate reading or translation, physical alteration of the work site, or job reassignment.

Lesson

Be open to making accommodations to employees who might have disabilities. Encourage open dialogue so that staff members with "invisible" disabilities feel free to come forward to request accommodation. Do not screen based on disability; ask only if the employee can do the essential functions of the work required.

Legislation Protecting Individuals Based on Sexual Orientation

Progress toward federal legislation that protects individuals from discrimination based on sexual orientation, sexual preference, or transgendered status has been slow in its development. The Employment Non Discrimination Act (ENDA) has been considered by Congress multiple times since its introduction in 1994. ENDA would extend nondiscrimination based on sexual orientation in ways similar to the Title VII and the ADA. As the legislation currently stands, ENDA would provide protection for "lesbian, gay, bisexual, or heterosexual orientation, real or perceived, as manifested by identity, acts, statements, or association." Support for a protection of transgendered individuals has been controversial, and thus this category was dropped from the ENDA definition. In 2009 ENDA was considered in House and Senate committees; no resolution has been reached as of this writing.

Some protection does exist based on sexual orientation, but the coverage is inconsistent across the U.S. At the state level, twenty-one states and the District of Columbia have discrimination protection based on sexual orientation in place, and twelve states and the District of Columbia have discrimination protection based on sexual identity. More than 180 cities and counties have laws protecting the rights of individuals based on sexual orientation. For employees of the Federal Government, Executive Order 11478, signed by President Bill Clinton, prohibits employment discrimination based on sexual orientation.

Lesson

Although there is currently no federal law protecting individuals based on sexual orientation, state and local coverage exists in many locations. Ensure that your staff members are well versed in nondiscriminatory practices based on sexual orientation, sexual identity, and transgendered status.

Legislative Protection for Genetic Information

Title II of the Genetic Information Nondiscrimination Act of 2008 prohibits discrimination in employment based on genetic information. This protection extends to all conditions of employment (hiring, promotion, pay firing, and so on), as well as prohibiting sharing of genetic information. Included in protected data is family medical history, which may be seen as a proxy for genetic predisposition. Harassment and retaliation based on genetic information are prohibited. Except in certain specific cases, the law prohibits the collection of genetic information. Among the exceptions are information needed to support Family Medical Leave (FMLA) requests, voluntary wellness programs, and information obtained inadvertently.

Role of the EEOC in Discrimination Cases

Under federal law, discrimination charges must be filed with the EEOC within 180 days of the incident or awareness that the incident might have caused discrimination. Most state laws allow up to 300 days. Charges can be brought against an individual or any organization on behalf of the individual. No private lawsuit can be filed until the EEOC evaluates the case. Where EEOC investigation warrants, and where individuals request an EEOC "right to sue," private lawsuits can be started within a period of 90 days after the right to sue finding (Equal Employment Opportunity Commission, 2003).

Additional Legislation of Interest to Nonprofit Managers

In addition to the antidiscrimination legislation just described, there are many other major laws that affect your organization. Details about the key legal frameworks are listed here, and the U.S. government's official Web portal (www.firstgov.gov) is a great place for nonprofit managers to find resources to answer questions.

- Fair Labor Standards Act of 1938, which covers wages and hours standards, as well as overtime, for employees who work interstate. This act covers large employers (with $500,000 in annual revenue) and small employers whose employees operate across state borders. Of particular interest in this legislation is the determination of which staff are exempt from overtime pay for work in excess of forty hours per week. "Professionals," "executives," and "outside salespeople" are the official exempt categories, but interpretations are more complex.
- Equal Pay Act of 1963, which prohibits sex-based wage discrimination and applies to most organizations with one or more employees. Exceptions include seniority, merit pay, and job performance. The Lilly Ledbetter Fair Pay Act of 2009 extended the time allowed for filing pay discrimination claims.
- Executive Order 11246, which requires nondiscrimination and affirmative action plans of federal government agencies and government contractors. At

the time of this writing, the status of affirmative action in various states and at the Supreme Court level was in flux.

- Family and Medical Leave Act of 1993, which guarantees up to twelve weeks of unpaid leave to employees in organizations with more than fifty employees to welcome a natural or adoptive child into the family, to care for an immediate relative, or to recover from an illness.

- Homeland Security Act of 2002, which contains provisions regarding the hiring of foreign workers. The act created the Department of Homeland Security and transferred the processing of work authorizations from the Immigration and Naturalization Service to the Bureau of Citizenship and Immigration Services, a division of the Department of Homeland Security.

- Immigration Reform and Control Act of 1986, which requires employers to verify employee identity and legal eligibility to work in the United States.

- Occupational Safety and Health Act of 1970, which was designed to reduce workplace injuries and illnesses and resulted in the creation of the Department of Labor's Occupational Safety and Health Administration.

- USA Patriot Act of 2001, which broadens government ability to review employment records, conduct surveillance of employees and employers, and monitor financial flows.

- The Health Insurance Portability and Accountability Act of 1996 (HIPAA), which is designed to ensure that new staff can obtain health care benefits without being subjected to preexisting conditions clauses. This legislation is complex, and the reader can find details at the Health and Human Services Web site (www.hhs.gov).

- The Patient Protection and Affordable Care Act of 2010 (PPACA) and the Health Care and Education Reconciliation Act of 2010, both enacted just as this chapter is being written, are part of a broad initiative to reform health care in the United States. This complex legislation includes significant provisions and requirements related to employers and workplace health insurance. The process for implementation of this legislation is only now becoming clearer. The reader can find current information on this legislation and associated regulations and policies at www.healthcare.gov.

- All state and local laws related to the workplace. Many of these follow the spirit of the federal laws but are likely to cover more organizations of smaller size. They may also cover groups not protected by federal legislation.

Make It Legal, Make It Fair

There is a sometimes a paradox in legality and fairness: What is legal is not always perceived as fair, and what is perceived as fair is not always legal. It is, of course, necessary to meet legal standards in all human resource decisions, and the law is relatively clear on what those specifics might be. However, a higher and more complex standard is establishing human resource approaches that are perceived by everyone inside and outside the organization as fair. Promoting antidiscrimination, following legal hiring procedures, and creating legal wages and benefits are all important signals of the centrality of human resources to the nonprofit. Yet despite consensus on these concepts, implementation can often lead to staff feeling that they are not being treated fairly. Creating open communication channels to bring issues of fairness—and perceived unfairness—to everyone's attention is important. Finally, going beyond simply what is legal to embracing what staff feel is fair takes an organization a long way toward building trust and commitment.

This is especially true for small or religious organizations that may be exempted from the requirements of many of these legislative initiatives. Small or religious organizations that do not respect the spirit of the law (even if not required to respect the letter of the law) do so at their own risk. They run the risk of disengaging the funding community, government opportunities, and local labor markets and talent pools, as well as segments of the giving public. With exemptions for religion-based discriminatory hiring for faith-based organizations seeking public support currently under contention, all organizations need to weigh the mission fulfillment and community needs argument in favor of exclusionary human resource practices against legal and public norms and expectations of fairness and diversity.

Putting It All Together: The Processes of Human Resources

This section of the chapter reviews effective approaches to recruiting and retaining motivated nonprofit staff. We begin by reinforcing the idea of beginning with the desired end state, and we recall the concepts of fit and embeddedness. We discuss how recruitment and selection affect the culture of any nonprofit. We address legal pitfalls. Finally, we raise awareness about what elements of the organization's context must be taken into consideration.

The Human Resource Audit

Earlier in the chapter, we introduced the idea of "starting at the desired end," that is, figuring out where the organization stands with respect to human resources and where it wants to go. Every nonprofit organization should regularly engage in systematically evaluating where it stands with respect to human resources. Exhibit 24.1 suggests the kinds of questions to be asked and answered.

EXHIBIT 24.1. SAMPLE HUMAN RESOURCE AUDIT CHECKLIST.

Organization and Job Structure

How accurate is the organization chart? Does it reflect both formal and informal reporting relationships? Is it current? Do staff at different levels agree that it is accurate?

How up-to-date are job descriptions and statements of knowledge, skills, and abilities (KSAs)? Do hiring, performance appraisal, and promotion standards support applicant matching and staff skill development for these jobs and KSAs?

Do the existing organization structure and distribution of work responsibilities match future operational plans? Which aspects of the structure seem appropriate for the next three to five years, and which will need modification?

Human Resource Planning

What skills are required for current projects? Do existing staff have the needed skills? What training might be needed?

What skills are anticipated to be needed for future projects? Does the organization have these skills on staff at this time? If not, how will they be required?

What turnover is anticipated within the next year? Will it likely be voluntary or involuntary? What gaps will this create in the organization's ability to meet its goals? What capacity may be lost due to turnover?

How strong is the internal promotion ladder? Are internal promotions a goal for this organization? If so, for what positions? How complete is the leadership succession plan?

What future hiring plans currently exist? Are there resources in place to fund these openings? What recruitment strategies have been developed in anticipation of upcoming recruitment?

How competitive is the organization in its labor market with organizations of similar size and purpose? Are salaries and benefits offered that will attract desired applicants? How does the organization's reputation affect potential recruitment success?

Organization Culture

What characteristics were identified in the organizational fit analysis as important? How well has fit been accomplished?

What were the outcomes of the internal embeddedness analysis? Which staff are embedded, and which staff are not committed? Are the more highly desired staff the more embedded? If not, how will the organization work to achieve this?

What is the state of staff motivation? What makes working in this organization desirable for staff? What are the negative aspects of the work environment? How and why do individuals vary in their motivation?

What characterizes the existing human resource culture? Is this culture consistent with the organization's mission? What values are central to the operation? What dimensions of diversity are desired?

Once the answers to the human resource audit questions are understood, the organization is ready to begin the process of adding staff in a way that will enhance the organization's movement toward its desired state. The goal is that every hiring and retention decision is made in the context of an overall plan for where the organization is headed. All staff should be involved in the human resource audit process as well as in developing plans for bridging any identified gaps.

The Staffing Plan

Nonprofits are likely to address the issue of staff planning within the broader context of the organization's strategic plan, although all nonprofits would do well to strategically consider the staffing mix at start-up, at present, and for a future desired state. The motivating question for any staffing plan is, "What are the continuing activities that need to be performed to help the organization meets its goals (and, ultimately, its mission)?" The staffing plan involves determination of the complement of staffers (full-time or full-time equivalent, part-time, volunteer, consultant, and outsourced) that will most effectively contribute to achieving the organization's purpose. It is likely that planning such levels will involve careful review of state and federal laws around fair labor standards and the designation of employees as exempt versus nonexempt. The staffing plan will also likely designate staffing positions as belonging to central administration, general operations, or program staff.

Especially in the case of small grassroots organizations transitioning to professionally staffed entities, the staffing plan must address the shift in day-to-day operations from a founding board or executive director to a supervised staff. Funding exigencies, growth projections, community and subsector expectations, and size and scope of expected service provision will all play a role in motivating or constraining the staffing levels set by organizational leaders. Staffing levels and complements for individual program areas may be set by constituent demands and supply for those services, while staffing levels and complements for central administration are likely to vary with the coordination and planning needs of the organization as a whole.

One of the most important yet most overlooked areas in staff planning in the nonprofit sector remains succession planning. In 2003, the United Way of New York City's study of CEOs, board members, and pipeline leaders confirmed sectoral fears that almost half of all New York executive directors were planning to leave their positions within five years at the same time that only one-third of all directors stated that they had a succession plan in place (Birdsell and Muzzio, 2003). Given demographic changes and likely competition for talent from other organizations and sectors, nonprofit leaders can give their organizations a leg up by engaging in reflective succession planning as well as thoughtful leadership development and training. Staffing, succession, and training and development planning will also make staff retention a less daunting challenge.

Recruitment

The first step in recruitment is figuring out what kind of staff the organization is seeking. Typically, a search is initiated by the creation of a new staff position or by the departure of staff in an existing role. In either case, it is important to begin any search with a clear idea of the characteristics the organization is seeking in a candidate. Increasing competition, especially for candidates of color, makes recruiting qualified and appropriate candidates challenging (Salamon and Geller, 2007).

Identifying Job Characteristics. In human resource terminology, these characteristics are called KSAs, for *knowledge, skills, and abilities. Knowledge* encompasses the content knowledge a staff person needs to know prior to being hired. Proficiency in many positions presumes a specific body of knowledge. Is an understanding of how arts management organizations are funded essential to the position? Is a knowledge of state laws related to nonprofit status required? When thinking about the term *knowledge,* it is useful to think about what facts an individual *should know.* The term s*kills* refers to proficiency in doing things with objects or ideas. Is operating a computer necessary for this job? Does the applicant need to be able to calculate tax credits on a loan? When defining the term *skills,* think about what the applicant *needs to do.* Finally, *abilities* refers the capacity to undertake certain work responsibilities. Does the individual need to be able to communicate effectively? Are supervisory abilities paramount? When defining *abilities,* think about what the individual *has the capacity to accomplish.*

KSAs are similar to, but not the same as, *competencies* (which are defined as capacities to act). KSAs have long been in use in government settings and made their way into the private sector nearly two decades ago. Although the term is somewhat less commonly used in the nonprofit sector, the KSA concept has an important legal distinction. In the event the nonprofit organization is required to demonstrate that a job requirement is related to the ability to perform the job, the organization will be asked to demonstrate what KSAs were used for hiring and how those KSAs are related to job performance. Thus they serve as the underpinnings for any legal and fair recruitment process.

Effective managers begin by determining what KSAs are desired for the available position through a process called job analysis. This process of discovery usually includes interviewing current and former staff incumbents (if any), dialogue among those who will work with the individual about what they feel is needed for success in the position, and strategic planning about what is needed for the organization in that role. Job analysis is a process of uncovering various perspectives on what the staff position is, might, and should encompass.

Writing Job Descriptions. After the job analysis phase, most organizations write job descriptions. The job description serves three purposes: to help those who will select among applicants consider what is needed for the position, to advertise to potential staff what the job will entail, and for use in legal defense against discrimination charges. It is important that the job description be both comprehensive and flexible. No candidate will meet all desired aspects, and the position's requirements will be fluid over time as needs arise. The effective nonprofit manager strikes a balance, articulating clearly what the organization is seeking without writing an unrealistically rigid characterization.

There are commercially available products for job analysis and the writing of job descriptions, as well as technical assistance available from a variety of consulting firms who specialize in these tasks. Each organization must decide how it will undertake this responsibility. For larger organizations, crafting job descriptions in-house may be easier, as there may be numerous other similar positions. Conversely, it may be easier for outside consultants to compare positions with others in other organizations. For smaller organizations, the task is more difficult and is often best accomplished with outside advice from peer networks combined with sample job description materials found on the Internet.

Searching

Once the job description is in hand, the organization should consider how it will search for applicants. There are many sources of potential employees, grouped for the purpose of discussion here into external and internal types.

The primary consideration when drafting a recruitment strategy is determining the goal of the recruitment program. Is the organization trying to attract a large applicant pool? Is diversity of applications a major objective? Is promotion from within the desired outcome? What are implications of hiring from without versus hiring from within? Are the candidates likely to be available locally, or will a national search be required? Answers to these questions can help inform choices about recruitment strategies. There is significant evidence that recruitment practices do matter to organizations. For example, there is a broad and extensive literature on the effect of different recruitment strategies on applicant perception (Barber, 1998). Less is known directly about recruitment strategies and organizational effectiveness, but anecdotal research suggests there is good fodder for investigation.

External Approaches. Under some circumstances, searching for potential staff from outside the organization is deemed desirable. Several types of sources can be used, depending on the applicant pool targeted.

Newspaper Ads. Running ads in newspapers or magazines is a broad recruitment approach: it will generate a large applicant pool with a wide range of general skills—all the more so given the huge audience that online versions of these periodicals attract. Advertising in newspapers is a good idea when the organization is entering a new market, needs a large number of staff, wants to broaden its contacts, and has the capacity to review a large number of applications. The cost is related to the advertising rates of the newspaper or magazine itself and the staff to review applications that are generated. The typical urban newspaper ad can generate as many as one thousand applicants, so be prepared to manage the volume. Most newspapers have a local readership, so newspapers allow a geographically targeted search (national newspapers will attract a national pool), although this is increasingly changing as the news goes online and worldwide. As such, this is a good approach for attracting a diverse applicant pool, as a wide array of individuals will be exposed to the advertising.

Online (Web-Based) Recruitment and Social Networking. Popular and very inexpensive, posting job listings through online databases and clearinghouses like Idealist.org enables nonprofits to reach out for applicants worldwide. Estimates have suggested that recruitment costs can be reduced by as much as 95 percent through online recruiting (Cappelli, 2001). Services differ, but they generally allow the nonprofit to specify the characteristics they are seeking and to screen out applicants who lack requisite qualifications. One related issue is that Web recruiting acts as a stimulus for applicants to visit the hiring organization's Web site. There is evidence that Web site information is used by applicants to assess whether they fit with the organization or not (Dineen, Ash, and Noe, 2002), suggesting that nonprofits should make sure that their Web materials contain accurate information about the organization's mission and purpose. Also increasingly popular is the use of social networking tools (Facebook, LinkedIn, Plaxo, and YouTube Nonprofit Partners, and so on) for recruiting staff, volunteers, and donors. Nonprofits that can identify the general user characteristics of these different online social networks can target their recruitment efforts for maximum yield.

Professional Publications, Associations, and Conferences. Releasing a job posting through a professional association or advertising in a professional journal is a good idea when the position the organization is seeking to fill is closely related to a specific profession. For example, if the organization is seeking a licensed social worker, advertising in professional social work outlets will attract a large proportion of qualified applicants. Conference listings are good when the organization can identify key conferences where applicants of interest would be in attendance.

College Recruiting and Internship Programs. Appropriate for positions requiring a college education, college recruiting is effective for reaching that market of applicants. For nonprofits, education about opportunities in the nonprofit sector needs to be part of on-campus recruitment efforts. Internships are particularly useful to test out staff before making a permanent hire and to allow students exposure to the organization. American Humanics (soon to become The Nonprofit Leadership Alliance), a nonprofit organization dedicated to developing the next generation of nonprofit staff and leaders through a nonprofit management certificate program delivered through college and university programs across the United States, is another source of talent for nonprofits.

Government Job Services Offices and Placement Agencies. These options are appropriate for locating entry and mid-level staff with little to some experience. Both types of agencies prescreen candidates, which can be a cost-saving measure for nonprofits with little time to cull through candidate files. Services are usually free to the organization; government-funded job services work for no fee, while placement agencies usually charge a fee to the applicant.

Professional Search Firms or Executive Recruiters. Usually the most expensive of the options, professional search firms are a good source of high-level applicants with a specific skill set. Search firms usually offer expertise in identifying applicants with specific experience. They also offer the advantage of confidentiality, as they can make inquiries between the organization and potential applicants without identifying either party. Many search firms charge the hiring organization, not the applicant, and fees typically range from 10 to 25 percent of the first year's salary. Increasingly, search firms and recruiters are specializing in nonprofit placements, and in some cases, these services may be both less expensive and more targeted for the nonprofit sector.

Specific Career Fairs, Conferences, Showcases. During the first decade of the new millennium, there was an explosion of nonprofit-specific venues for nonprofit recruiting. Since 2001, Idealist.Org has been hosting local nonprofit career fairs in cities across the United States. Job seekers attend for free, while recruiting organizations pay a small fee to help cover costs. State and local associations of nonprofits (along with their national federation) also provide nonprofit career services to help match nonprofit professionals with nonprofit recruiters. Even Youtube.com has jumped into the mix, providing a special nonprofit program so allow third sector organizations to tell their story to a wide audience including job seekers.

Internal Approaches. In some cases, filling staff vacancies from inside the organization is the better strategy. The following are internal approaches that may be undertaken.

Employee Referral. As mentioned earlier, internal referral programs have advantages. Typically, employee referrals are relatively low in cost. Some nonprofits create staff incentive programs that give financial rewards to staff who recruit others who are hired and work successfully in the organization. Employee referrals lead to the identification of potential employees who know quite a bit about the organization and whose interest in the organization is therefore typically high. Employee referral programs tend to generate a geographically local applicant pool, and prospects are limited to candidates who are connected somehow to individuals already in the organization. One downside is that this can make diversifying the nonprofit more difficult.

Internal Postings and Promotion. Making opportunities available to current staff is a critical dimension of a successful nonprofit. When hiring is consistently done from the outside for positions above the entry level, a signal is sent to staff that their opportunities are limited. Ensure that all staff are aware of upcoming openings, and give them access to ample information about the positions. Managing decisions to hire from the outside when there are qualified internal candidates can be difficult, but seriously considering insiders as applicants tends to lead to better perceptions of fairness, even if the internal candidates are not ultimately chosen.

Client and Volunteer Recruitment. A rich source of candidates for nonprofits is the client and volunteer base of individuals who already have a relationship with the organization. These sources offer the benefits of familiarity with the organization and understanding of its basic operations. Many successful nonprofits make the boundaries between volunteers and paid staff permeable. Organizations with client bases can improve services by hiring clients as staff members. As already noted, many nonprofits and affirmative businesses, by mission and strategy, choose to hire mostly or exclusively from within client and volunteer ranks.

In general, what recruitment sources are most effective? Meta-analyses of studies of recruitment sources have found that individuals hired through internal sources are as much as 24 percent more likely to stay on the job for the first year (Zottoli and Wanous, 2000) and tend to be more satisfied than those recruited from the outside. Among the competing explanations for this effect: applicants have a realistic preview of the job; there is better person-job and person-organization fit for inside referrals; internal candidates are of higher quality; and employees are more credible as sources of job information.

Finally, what information should be included in the recruitment process? Effective and accurate communication is always a goal; candidates not hired by the organization will nevertheless learn a lot about it and should be left with a good impression. More information and accurate information both lead to positive outcomes. Friendliness and timeliness on behalf of everyone in the recruitment process leads to perceptions of a fair and friendly organization that is interested in the applicant (Breaugh and Starke, 2000). Inclusion of women and people of color in the recruitment process signals an organization open to diversity (Highhouse, Stierwalt, Bachiochi, Elder, and Fisher, 1999).

Choosing a Candidate

Perhaps the most challenging human resource task is determining which candidate or candidates from the pool of applicants should be chosen. As briefly described earlier, it is important that any applicant be evaluated on whether or not he or she has the ability to perform the required tasks. In nonprofits, the needs for flexibility of staff are often paramount; thus structured approaches are often not practical and are arguably less desirable.

Most nonprofit organizations are also particularly interested in the notion of fit—in many cases, this is interpreted as the extent to which the applicant shares a commitment to the mission. Mission drift is sometimes seen as one result of hiring key staff who do not share the organization's view on its future direction. In all selection decisions, the premiere challenge is finding a qualified, motivated, and adaptable candidate on whom various staff can agree.

Particularly applicable in large nonprofit contexts, staff selection can include highly technical procedures. For example, there is a plethora of well-established selection instruments, including personality, cognitive ability, and honesty testing;

assessment centers that evaluate leadership and team performance; and work sample tests that replicate actual portions of the job to be performed. We will review each of these approaches briefly (more extensive details on these topics can be found in Gatewood, Feild, and Barrack, 2007).

Once the recruitment pool has been identified, the first selection step is to determine which of the applicants merit further consideration. Now is the time to apply what has been determined by the job analysis, examining which potential staff members hold the best promise based on the KSAs previously identified for the position. It is best to review a variety of applicant materials, including résumés, letters of interest, and application forms (see Table 24.1).

TABLE 24.1. THE CANDIDATE SELECTION PROCESS

Questions	Aspects to Consider	Details Needed	Action to Be Taken
Is the candidate qualified?	What required qualifications does the candidate clearly meet?	Degrees, certifications, credentials, past job titles, dates of employment	*If yes:* Verify facts from sources after candidate has reached the finalist pool. *If no:* Send rejection letter.
Is the candidate among the best available?	What evidence of past performance looks applicable to this position in this organization? What limitations does past experience suggest?	Statements of accomplishments, key positions held, experience in related organizations.	*If yes:* Investigate or probe into in the interview; administer selection tests, if used. *If no:* Send rejection letter.
Can this candidate (with job and organization) be verified?	Who are the key references for the applicant?	Extent to which listed references can evaluate various qualifications, experiences, motivation, and limitations; candidate consent to check other references not listed.	*If yes:* Conduct reference checks after the candidate has reached the finalist pool. *If no:* Send rejection letter.
Should this candidate be selected?	What do various staff sources say? How does all the evidence collected so far add up? (Consider using a team selection process.)	Candidate who best fits the job and the organization at this time.	*If yes:* Tender an offer. *If no:* Wait until an offer has been accepted before rejecting other candidates, politely, in writing.

Step 1: Determine Which Applicants Have the Required Qualifications. Candidates who do not have the required qualifications should be immediately rejected from the pool. Most organizations write a polite letter to the candidate indicating that many other applicants who are more qualified for the position are being considered. It is important to thank candidates for their interest in the organization and to encourage them to apply for future openings as they become available. If possible, keep on file information about applicants who look promising but do not meet the organization's current needs.

For candidates who meet the required qualifications, the organization typically moves on to determine whether this is the best candidate for the position. Although the qualifications must eventually be verified (degrees actually awarded, employment checked, and so on), it is usually best to wait to verify these details after the candidate has shown interest through the interview.

Step 2: Assess Which Candidates Are Among the Best for the Position. In this stage of the selection process, it is necessary to choose a pool of candidates whom the organization will consider further. The size of the reduced pool will be determined by the number of qualified candidates available, the organization's resources for further investigation, and the timetable under which the decision must be made. Most organizations will reduce the qualified candidate pool to between three and five candidates.

If the organization has the available resources and assessment instruments are considered appropriate for the position being considered, at this stage the organization may ask the candidates to submit to these tests. Many organizations (particularly in the private sector) use psychological tests, the most common of which is called the "Big Five" personality test. The five characteristics, identified through either the Five Factor Index instrument (Goldberg, 1990) or the NEO-PI instrument (Costa and McCrae, 1997) are based on decades of psychological research that suggests that the stable elements of personality include openness to experience, conscientiousness, emotional stability, agreeableness, and extroversion. Of the five, conscientiousness has been shown to be the best predictor of performance overall, and extroversion best for external relations positions like sales or fundraising (Gatewood, Feild, and Barrick, 2007). Tests of general cognitive ability, which research has shown to be among the best predictors of job performance for complex jobs across the United States, with even stronger relationships across Europe (Salgado, Anderson, Moscoso, Bertua, and De Fruyt, 2003), are also widely used. In recent years, honesty tests have become popular. Research findings about the general efficacy of integrity tests exists, but questions remain about the appropriateness of their use, the ability of individuals to fake the results, the underlying conceptual reasons why integrity tests might work, and the cultural contexts in which they are appropriate (Berry, Sackett, and Wiemann, 2007).

Psychological testing has been shown to be a good predictor of future performance and to have high "predictive validity," as there is empirical evidence that the traits they test are indeed related to some kinds of job performance. Thus such tests have generally been upheld in most court cases as legal, particularly where the organizations have tested the relationship between test scores and performance in their own organizations. However, personality tests often have low "face validity," that is, candidates may perceive the tests as inappropriate or invasive, and this sometimes gives rise to perceptions of inequity. Other organizations use work sample tests, and/or "realistic job previews" (RJPs) to assess requisite skills such as financial management, software proficiency, or industry expertise. One challenge in using work sample tests is to identify appropriate tests available for commercial sale or to develop one's own instruments in-house, an expensive undertaking that sometimes requires particular expertise. However, RJPs can take a wide variety of forms, from "homemade" videos providing "realistic" observations of typical work days/assignments to more in-depth trial assignments that may range from a few minutes to whole days on an assortment of tasks. Supporters of RJPs point to the two-way-street aspect of evaluation they provide: organizations observe how the candidate actually handles the work expected, and candidates observe how the organization is actually managed. For organizations interested in "fit," RJPs provide an opportunity for both sides of the recruiting equation to test out values and work congruence.

Another popular selection tool, assessment centers, is very effective if the position requires leadership or team management skills, but their design and administration are expensive. In general, the advantage of work sample tests is that they assess work qualifications directly. Thus they tend to have high face validity and are usually perceived by applicants as fair since they are directly related to the work to be performed.

Perhaps the holy grail in selection is the personal interview. Historically conducted face-to-face, some organizations are finding that resource constraints and large applicant pools make preliminary telephone, video, or Web-based interviews an important first screening test. Empirical evidence about selection interviews is mixed. Research shows that interviews have low predictive validity for job performance but high face validity, as they are perceived as desirable by both interviewers and interviewees (Macan, 2009). Despite limitations, interviews are nearly universally conducted in selection.

We offer the following guidelines to help interviewers do a better job at conducting effective interviews.

- *Use a structured interview format.*

  A consistent finding in the selection literature is that the same questions should be asked of all candidates for the position. Thus rather than using a free-flowing conversation to assess candidate appropriateness, determine ahead of the interview what questions will be asked of all candidates. This helps the organization keep the interview tied to the relevant KSAs being assessed, it encourages managers to consider carefully the characteristics they are seeking *before* the interview, and it ensures that each candidate is asked to address the same issues.

- *Stick with behaviors.*

  Successful interviewing relies on conversations that focus on the behaviors candidates have exhibited in past work settings. Interview questions should ask what the candidate *did* in past situations, as past behavior has been shown to be the best predictor of future performance.

- *Keep it legal.*

  As covered in detail earlier, there are many categories of protected employees. No interview questions should explore any protected category, either deliberately or inadvertently. For example, it is never appropriate to ask candidates if they have made child-care arrangements or if they have spousal coverage on benefits (implying gender or parental status); instead, ask if the candidate is able to work the hours required. Never ask candidates when they graduated from high school or college or earned a professional certification (implying age); instead, ask if the degree has been obtained or if the certification is currently valid. Do not ask whether a candidate is a U.S. citizen; ask instead whether the candidate is authorized to work in the United States or can gain authorization if selected for the position.

- *Consider a team interview.*

  A relatively new development in selection involves team-based selection. Research suggests that conducting a team interview (with two to five members in diverse positions who are savvy about employment practices) and using a team selection process can enhance fit and improve commitment to selection decisions (Stewart, 2003). Team interviews also enhance the likelihood of a realistic job preview that outlines both the strengths and weaknesses of the position, making it more likely that the candidate will be informed about what the position will really entail, enhancing early commitment to the organization and encouraging self-selection out of the process for candidates who feel they would not be a good match. Realistic job previews also have the advantage of setting appropriate expectations for those accepting the position (Morse and Popovich, 2009).

Step 3: Verify Candidate Qualifications and Match. Once a candidate has passed the interview stage, it is time to check references. The candidate will have provided references in writing or listed names to be contacted. In either case, it is advisable to follow up with a telephone call with specific questions. These questions should be designed to probe information already obtained from other sources and to facilitate more detailed understanding of the candidate's qualifications.

The reference-checking process is fraught with difficulties. Many former employers will provide only very basic information, including dates of employment and whether the employee is eligible for rehire. This reluctance is sometimes due to personal preferences and at other times is the result of legal counsel's advice to avoid possible slander or libel suits. Yet reference checking is a step that should never be skipped: it is imperative to show "due diligence" in the hiring process. A legal concept called "negligent hiring" can be invoked by staff members who feel that adequate precautions were not taken to ensure that the candidate does not prove dangerous to the other staff (Gatewood, Feild, and Barrick, 2007).

Step 4: Make the Selection Decision and Tender the Offer. Once all information has been collected, it is time to make an offer to the leading candidate. Ideally, there is agreement among those involved in the selection process as to who the best candidate is. Often there is more than one leading candidate. It is a good idea to keep all top candidates in the pool until a final offer is accepted. The offer should be given by phone, followed up with details in writing. The offer letter should include the name of the position, annual (or hourly) salary, benefits to be included in the package, starting date, and terms of employment (full-time permanent, part-time temporary, and so on). The letter should include a deadline, usually within two weeks, by which the candidate must reply. Salary level should be discussed with the candidate before tendering the final offer.

Summary of the Selection Process

To summarize, the selection process should be designed to attract and hire qualified candidates who fit both the job and the organization. Throughout the process, attention must be paid to the overall hiring strategy and staff and succession planning of the organization. Performance standards must always be kept in mind during the selection process. A thorough job evaluation should help guide the criteria on which decisions are made. It is advisable to involve multiple staff members in the selection process to ensure an open dialogue among current and future staff. Legalities should be considered, and each step of the selection process should be valid in that it leads to the selection of a staff member who can succeed in the organization.

Retention Through Motivation

Once the organization has selected the right staff and the right complement of staff to achieve organizational goals, the next (ongoing) steps involve motivating and retaining (good) people. For-profit organizations and traditional business schools have spent the better part of a century trying to understand and enact the elusive motivation of staff that brings organizational effectiveness. The good news, as we noted at the beginning of this chapter, is that motivation of staff is one area where nonprofit organizations seem to have the inherent advantage. Indeed evidence shows that mission attachment of nonprofit workers enhances their satisfaction and increases their intention to stay, especially for younger and part-time workers (Brown and Yoshioka, 2003).

Study after study has demonstrated that nonprofit employees are more engaged, more motivated, and sometimes even more satisfied in and by their work than employees in other sectors (see, for example, De Cooman, De Gieter, Pepermans, and Jegers, 2009). Yet turning that motivation into productivity and guarding against burnout remain confounding issues for nonprofit leaders. Developing work-life balance policies, like flexible scheduling and family leaves, is key to retaining nonprofit staff (Pitt-Catsouphes, Swanberg, Bond, and Galinsky, 2004), especially for nonprofits with more than 100 staff members. And retaining experienced workers when pay and benefits are not competitive can be difficult. Furthermore, assuming that all nonprofits have the motivation advantage is misleading. Small nonprofits motivate employees toward goal achievement differently from larger nonprofits, and great variability in motivational techniques and organizational cultures exist across (and within) nonprofit subsectors. Indeed, motivating employees in large urban hospital systems may take a very different organizational culture and set of tools than motivating employees in a small rural community development corporation.

There are any number of theories that purport to explain how organizational actors are motivated. These include needs theories that emphasize how organizational life can help satisfy individual desires (Maslow, 1943) and process approaches like equity (Adams, 1963) and expectancy theories (Vroom, 1964), which emphasize the cognitive analyses and choices that individuals make in deciding how much exertion of effort is worth their while. These concepts have then been differentially applied by the generic management literature to construct techniques and programs aimed at increasing employee motivation and concomitant productivity. In the for-profit world, management flavors of the month have included the recognition of individual differences in designing motivation programs, managing by objectives (using goal setting to spur effort), basing rewards on performance, and enhancing opportunities for participation in decision making. Many of these theories and applications start with the assumption that human resources need to be aligned with organizational goals, and motivation techniques exist to do just that. (Compensation strategies and designs are discussed in depth in Chapter 25.)

These theories and applications are variably useful to nonprofit leaders as suggested by the review work of Schepers, De Gieter, Pepermans, Du Bois, Caers, and Jegers (2005). Indeed, Schepers, et al. (2005) underscore our point that nonprofit employees might be differentially motivated from for-profit employees at the same time that nonprofit employees in different subsectors may also be uniquely motivated. Robert C. Clark (2006) of the Harvard Law School is quietly shopping around his potential answer to the riddle of nonprofit motivation—a strong moral system that sustains and enhances nonprofit participation through internalized values and norms and the threat of sanctions including social disapproval and guilt.

In the end, though, it might be most helpful to reconceptualize motivation in nonprofits as part of the larger human resource system embedded within the organization's culture, always with an eye toward the power of the mission. In nonprofit (and in particular service) organizations, human resources are not so much aligned with the organization as they *are* the organization. Further, it is often the case that nonprofits do not have to align employee goals with organizational goals because the selection process and the draw of the mission have already done that.

For nonprofits, then, activity around motivation might best be spent nourishing an organizational culture that values all constituencies, respecting each participant's contribution to fulfillment of mission. While such motivation may be complemented by compensation and benefit programs, it is also enacted by the management of organizational symbols, rites and rituals, and affirmative events and recognition (Bolman and Deal, 2008). Progressive nonprofit cultures motivate employees through fair and humane compensation and benefits but also affirm people's value and commitment to the organization's mission in an ongoing fashion.

Discharge, Layoffs, and Voluntary Turnover

Although we hope, and textbooks infer, that organizations can motivate people to stay goal-focused and loyal, we know that organizational turnover is a fact of life. Getting a handle on voluntary turnover seems especially important to nonprofit organizations that are, indeed, defined by their human resources. Costs of voluntary turnover, even in organizations not so dependent on labor, can be staggering, if not debilitating. Immediately, turnover means starting the recruiting, selecting, and even training processes all over and incurring their concomitant costs. There is also the disruption to the organization's processes, culture, and other constituents when old faces disappear.

Traditional advice to managers suggests a correlation between job satisfaction and voluntary turnover. However, many of the causes of turnover are varied and often not directly under the control of the organization. These include, most conspicuously, labor market conditions and alternative job (and life) opportunities. Recent literature has sought to explore how even these external factors might be addressed by organizational leaders eager to retain their most valued and valuable employees. A wave of literature in the for-profit sector cited earlier posits that "job embeddedness" is an even better predictor of staying the organizational course than job satisfaction, organizational commitment, job alternatives, and job search (see Mitchell, Holtom, Lee, Sablynski, and Erez, 2001). As noted earlier, these researchers define job embeddedness as a multifaceted construct that includes three core components: links between individuals and coworkers, perceptions of fit with both organization and community, and the sense of sacrifice if the position were to be relinquished.

This line of thinking takes organizational leaders out of the realm of the "at work-only" context and suggests that leaders need to take a more holistic approach to employees' well-being. Encouraging employees' links to coworkers, boards, and clients might elevate employees' feelings of embeddedness, as would encouraging employees' connections to community activity. In many ways, these suggestions may be second nature to leaders of community-based organizations, but their value to organizational human resources has not been so acutely supported in the past. We suggest that in the nonprofit context, job embeddedness often morphs into organizational embeddedness, which is often overlaid with a sense of community embeddedness. If organizational leaders ignore the reality of embeddedness, within a job, an organization, or a community, they do so at their own peril. Conversely, finding organizationally sanctioned ways to encourage cross-linkages and social networks, as well as community involvement, will likely result in more embedded and then committed staffers and may go a long way toward supporting organization and community missions.

Particularly in the relatively dismal current economic conditions (at the time of this writing), some organizations inevitably find it necessary to lay off staff involuntarily. Inconsistent funding streams, failure to obtain grants or grant renewals, or a general downturn in demand can all lead to these difficult decisions that challenge the very fabric of a nonprofit's culture. Our general advice for downsizing (as it is bloodlessly called) is to avoid it where possible and, where it is unavoidable, to enact it mindfully. This includes careful performance-based identification of those to be eliminated, sufficient advance warning, adequate explanation of rationale, and assistance in outplacement (Cascio, 2002). Perhaps paradoxically, handling these issues with a personal touch is important. Although an executive's instincts may be to avoid face-to-face conversations with those being terminated or to delegate this responsibility to staff, handling these issues openly, honestly, and directly is the best approach. Legal considerations are also important. Many downsizings in the 1990s tended to target high-paid workers as a cost-cutting measure, resulting in class action lawsuits for discrimination based on age. Finally, managers also must not forget the remaining staff, termed "survivors" (Brockner, Grover, Reed, and De Witt, 1992). Research suggests that those who retain their jobs are often haunted by stress, fatigue, and guilt.

Make or Buy? Outsourcing Human Resources

One contemporary trend is toward the outsourcing of human resource functions. For small nonprofits in particular, the attraction of delegating human resource functions to external experts may be strong: often there is little internal capacity to perform what are viewed as specialized tasks. Indeed, the outsourcing of recruitment, applicant screening, relocation services, payroll, and benefits is common in some subsectors.

Nonetheless, each organization must decide which human resource functions are core to its approach. For many organizations, this makes deciding to outsource payroll and benefits delivery (but not design) a clear choice: external vendors often have software and specialized expertise in delivering these services, and the cost can be advantageous. However, for human resource functions more central to the organization's mission, such as attracting and selecting staff, it often makes sense to keep these functions in-house. Although there can be economic benefits of scale when outsourcing recruitment and selection in small organizations, these reduced costs can sometimes also translate into loss of control of attraction of staff who fit the organization's culture. Outsourcing human resource functions that play critical roles in identifying and retaining staff who share the organization's mission are often best left inside.

One notable exception is the idea of collaborating across organizations to provide health care and retirement benefits. For small nonprofits in particular, purchasing power for health care packages and investment power for retirement are in short supply. Joining a benefits collaborative, or creating one, can dramatically decrease the cost of such services per individual employee.

When a decision to outsource is ▮▮▮▮▮ ▮o follow up with thorough management of the outsou▮▮▮ ▮▮▮▮▮ valuation of the efficacy of those relationships after ▮▮▮▮ ▮ to considering administrative costs, organizations a▮▮ ▮▮▮ staff satisfaction with outsourced services.

One last outsourcing trend wo▮▮▮ ▮▮▮ving industry of "rent an ED" for nonprofits in tr▮▮ ▮ whole field has developed to supply transitioni▮▮ ▮▮terim Executive Leaders). Consulting and headhunti▮▮ ▮ aspiring EDs to become IELs to serve nonprofits tha▮ ▮ talk of a coming crisis in nonprofit leadership (brougl▮ ▮▮rements of baby-boomer EDs) has proliferated, so h▮▮ ▮ nonprofit, that specialize in outsourcing the ED fu▮

Summary: Effective Human Re▮

If the more humanistic aspects of th▮ ▮▮ent to jump-start a reluctant nonprofit human resou▮ ▮▮arch suggests that human costs (payroll, benefits, tra▮ ▮ntensive nonprofit organizations can account for m▮ ▮ costs, compared to under 15 percent in capital-i▮ ▮cpherson, 2001). Obviously, inattention to the maj▮ ▮ion is a recipe for trouble. And this chapter has reco▮ ▮tention.

We began with the suggesti▮ ▮which we define broadly as "the organization"—▮ ▮ systems dynamic. Successful nonprofit leaders wo▮ ▮ganizational goals around human resources as ▮ ▮. The parts are interconnected—breakdowns in ▮ ▮(a disintegration of organizational culture, a spate of ▮ ▮ on) will likely lead to disrupted service delivery, whi▮ ▮ninish the ability to get funds, and cause harm in my▮ ▮nning organization will devote executive-level atten▮ ▮an resources.

We recognize that one size ▮ ▮gue around human resource goals is highly depende▮ ▮nd life cycle (not to mention cultural and industry o▮ ▮ that value-creating and value-diffusing nonprofits ▮ ▮are well advised to engage the whole of their labor ▮ ▮process at all stages of the organization's growth. Ex▮ ▮will necessarily face different human resource decisi▮ ▮evant questions. To

TABLE 24.2. RELEVANT HUMAN RESOURCE QUESTIONS AS A REFLECTION OF ORGANIZATION SIZE AND LIFE CYCLE

Matter Under Consideration	Small or Start-Up	Large or Established
Culture	Do our mission, vision, and strategy support our culture? Should our human resource systems be professionalized? If so, how? Should human resource responsibilities be part of existing staff roles, or are separate positions warranted?	Do our mission, vision, and strategy support our culture? Is our staff culture consistent with the values of our mission? Has human resources remained an integral part of our strategic thinking, or has becoming functionalized make it separate? Does our large organization feel small?
Legal	At what staff size do state labor and employment laws apply? At what staff size do federal labor and employment laws apply? Are we above those levels? Is our subsector subject to further labor regulation?	Are we compliant with state labor and employment laws? Are we compliant with federal labor and employment laws? Are we superseding legal standards in promoting an equitable workplace? Is our subsector subject to further labor regulation?
Human resource audits	When and how should we allocate funds to human resource audits? Where can we find sample materials and benchmarks?	What are the goals of our human resource audits? Do our audits meet those goals? Are our human resource audits comprehensive? Are we using a variety of metrics?
Staffing Plan	Do we need to grow our staff to meet our mission? If so, how will we identify the resources to grow our staff?	Do we have the right complement of staff to meet our mission? Are we planning growth, transition, or downsizing?
Selection	Does our small size allow growth from inside, or is external recruitment more likely? Do religious orientation, regional culture, industry subsector, or other factors delimit our selection?	Does our culture promote growth from the inside? Have we identified appropriate channels through which to search for unique skills? Do religious orientation, regional culture, industry subsector, or other factors delimit our selection?
Retention and motivation	How much does our small size contribute to the culture we have developed? If we are growing, how is this affecting our culture?	What motivates our staff? How do we allocate resources to motivate and retain our proven staff? Which staff are leaving voluntarily, and why are they leaving?
Discharge, layoff, and turnover	Absent large size or long-term community track record, how do we embed our employees?	How do we leverage our size, standing, and reputation to help embed our proven employees?
Make or buy?	Do we "buy" to attempt to keep permanent staff size small?	Does our choice to "buy" alienate or support permanent internal staff?

illustrate how some of these co_____ ut, a sampling of how size and life cycle of the _____ ıman resource questions should be asked is pres_____ questions might be periodically reviewed to take sto_____ _____anization is doing in developing and maintaining their hum____ ____roach.

Certainly, some subsectors (and wi_____ ____ctor, particular organizations) of the nonprofit universe are marred by ____ss than stellar labor records, and so we underscore the importance of rethinking the organization from the standpoint of those who make it work. All nonprofit leaders can be guided by the basic questions raised by this chapter, and the answers, of course, will vary: What motivates employees? What embeds them in their jobs, organizations, and communities? What laws model best practices even when size or subsector exempt an organization? What staffing plans best support an organization's human resource goals? What recruitment and selection processes are most likely to result in an augmentation of the most laudable components of the organization's unique culture? And finally, what are all of our goals for the people of the organization?

Since the process of answering the questions is likely to be as important as the actual answers, it is through the continuous re-creation of human resource goals that an effective nonprofit human resource culture is designed.

References

Adams, J. S. "Toward an Understanding of Inequity." *Journal of Abnormal and Social Psychology*, 1963, *67*, 422–426.

Barber, A. E. *Recruiting Employees: Individual and Organizational Perspectives*. Thousand Oaks, Calif.: Sage, 1998.

Bartel, A. P. "Measuring the Employer's Return on Investments in Training: Evidence from the Literature." *Industrial Relations*, 2000, *39*, 502–524.

Beck, T. E., Lengnick-Hall, C. A., and Lengnick-Hall, M. L. "Solutions Out of Context: Examining the Transfer of Business Concepts to Nonprofit Organizations." *Nonprofit Management and Leadership*, 2008, *19*(2), 153–171.

Bernier, I., and Lajoie, A. *Labor Law and Urban Law in Canada*. Toronto: University of Toronto Press, 1986.

Berry, C. C., Sackett, P. R., and Weimann, S. "A Review of Recent Developments in Integrity Test Research." *Personnel Psychology*, 2007, *60*(2), 271–301.

Birdsell, D. S., and Muzzio, D. "The Next Leaders: UWNYC Grantee Leadership Development and Succession Management Needs." unitedwaynyc.org/pdf/the_next_leaders.pdf, 2003.

Block, S. R. *Why Nonprofits Fail: Overcoming Founder's Syndrome, Fund-Phobia, and Other Obstacles to Success*. San Francisco: Jossey-Bass, 2003.

Bolman, L., and Deal, T. *Reframing Organizations* (4th ed.). San Francisco: Jossey-Bass, 2008.

Breaugh, J. A., and Starke, M. "Research on Employee Recruitment: So Many Studies, So Many Remaining Questions." *Journal of Management*, 2000, *26*, 405–435.

Brockner, J., Grover, S., Reed, T. F., and De Witt, R. L. "Layoffs, Job Security, and Survivors' Work Effort: Evidence of an Inverted-U Relationship." *Academy of Management Journal*, 1992, *35*, 413–425.

Brown, W. A., and Yoshioka, C. F. "Mission Attachment and Satisfaction as Factors in Employee Retention." *Nonprofit Management and Leadership*, 2003, *14*(1), 5–18.

Cappelli, P. "Making the Most of On-Line Recruiting." *Harvard Business Review*, 2001, 139–146.

Cascio, W. F. "Strategies for Responsible Restructuring." *Academy of Management Executive*, 2002, *3*, 80–91.

Chatman, J. A. "Improving Interactional Organizational Research: A Model of Person-Organization Fit." *Academy of Management Review*, 1989, *14*, 333–349.

Clark, R. C. "Moral Systems in the Regulation of Nonprofits." The Hauser Center for Nonprofit Organizations, Harvard University: Working Paper 33.6, 2006.

Costa, P. T., and McCrae, R. R. "Stability and Change in Personality Assessment: The Revised NEO Personality Inventory in the Year 2000." *Journal of Personality Assessment*, 1997, *68*, 86–95.

Council for Disability Rights. "Frequently Asked Questions." www.disabilityrights.org/adafaq. htm#general, 2009.

Cox, T. *Cultural Diversity in Organizations: Theory, Research, and Practice*. San Francisco: Berrett-Kohler, 1994.

De Cooman, R., De Gieter, S., Pepermans, R., and Jegers M. "A Cross-Sector Comparison of Motivation-Related Concepts in For-Profit and Not-For-Profit Service Organizations." *Nonprofit and Voluntary Sector Quarterly*, 2009, 1–22.

Dineen, B. R., Ash, S. R., and Noe, R. A. "Web of Applicant Attraction: Person-Organization Fit in the Context of Web-Based Recruitment." *Journal of Applied Psychology*, 2002, *87*, 723–734.

Equal Employment Opportunity Commission. "Section 902: Definition of the Term *Disability*." www.eeoc.gov/policy/docs/902cm.html, 2000.

Equal Employment Opportunity Commission. "The Americans with Disabilities Act." www.eeoc.gov/ada/adahandbook.html, 2002a.

Equal Employment Opportunity Commission. "Facts About Sexual Harassment." www.eeoc.gov/facts/fs-sex.html, 2002b.

Equal Employment Opportunity Commission. "Filing a Charge of Employment Discrimination." www.eeoc.gov/charge/overview_charge_filing.html, 2003.

Fick, B. J. *The American Bar Association Guide to Workplace Law: Everything You Need to Know About Your Rights as an Employee or Employer* (2nd edition). New York: Times Books/Random House, 2006.

Fitz-enz, J. *The ROI of Human Capital: Measuring the Economic Value of Employee Performance*. New York: AMACOM, 2000.

Gatewood, R. D., Feild, H. S., and Barrick, M. *Human Resource Selection*. (6th ed.) Fort Worth, Tex.: Harcourt, 2007.

Goldberg, L. R. "An Alternative Description of Personality: The Big Five Factor Structure." *Journal of Personality and Social Psychology*, 1990, *59*, 1216–1230.

Gregory, A. G., and Howard, D. "The Nonprofit Starvation Cycle." *Stanford Social Innovation Review*, 2009, *7*(4), 49–54.

Halpern, R. P. *Workforce Issues in the Nonprofit Sector: Generational Leadership Change and Diversity*. American Humanics, 2006. Retrieved January 17, 2009, from http://humanics.org.

Hamilton, L., and Tragert, R. *100 Best Nonprofits to Work For*. (2nd ed.) Lawrenceville, N.J.: ARCO, 2000.

Highhouse, S., Stierwalt, S. L., Bachiochi, P., Elder, A. E., and Fisher, G. "Effects of Advertised Human Resource Management Practices on Attraction of African American Applicants." *Personnel Psychology*, 1999, *52*, 425–442.

Holtom, B., Mitchell, T., and Lee, T. "Increasing Human Capital by Applying Job Embeddedness Theory." *Organization Dynamics*, 2006, *35*(4), 316–331.

Hom, P. W., and Griffeth, R. W. *Employee Turnover*. Cincinnati: South-Western, 1995.

Kanter, R. M., and Summers, D. V. "Doing Well While Doing Good: Dimensions of Performance Measurement in Nonprofit Organizations and the Need for a Multiple-Constituency Approach." In W. W. Powell Jr. (ed.), *The Nonprofit Sector: A Research Handbook*. New Haven, Conn.: Yale University Press, 1987.

Kristof-Brown, A., Jansen, K. J., and Colbert, A. E. "A Policy-Capturing Study of the Simultaneous Effects of Fit with Jobs, Groups, and Organizations." *Journal of Applied Psychology*, 2002, *87*, 985–993.

Kunreuther, F. "The Changing of the Guard: What Generational Differences Tell Us About Social-Change Organizations," *Nonprofit and Voluntary Sector Quarterly*, 2003, *32*(3), 450–457.

Lee, T. W., Mitchell, T. R., Holtom, B. C., McDaniel, L., and Hill, J. W. "The Unfolding Model of Voluntary Turnover: A Replication and Extension." *Academy of Management Journal*, 1999, *42*, 450–462.

Lewin, K. *Field Theory in Social Science*. New York: HarperCollins, 1951.

Light, P. C. *Pathways to Nonprofit Excellence*. Washington, D.C.: Brookings Institution Press, 2002.

Light, P. C. *Sustaining Nonprofit Performance: The Case for Capacity Building and the Evidence to Support It*. Washington, D.C.: Brookings Institution, 2004.

Macan, T. "The Employment Interview: A Review of Current Studies and Directions for Future Research." *Human Resource Management Review*, 2009, *19*(3), 209–213.

Macpherson, M. "Performance Measurement in Not-for-Profit and Public-Sector Organizations." *Measuring Business Excellence*, 2001, *5*(2), 13–17.

Maslow, A. H. "A Theory of Human Motivation." *Psychological Review*, 1943, *50*, 370–396.

Mitchell, T. R., Holtom, B. C., Lee, T. W., Sablynski, C. J., and Erez, M. "Why People Stay: Using Job Embeddedness to Predict Voluntary Turnover." *Academy of Management Journal*, 2001, *44*, 1102–1121.

Morse, B. J., and Popovich, B. M. "Realistic Recruitment Practices in Organizations." *Human Resource Management Review*, 2009, *19*(1), 1–8.

National Council on Disability. *Empowerment for Americans with Disabilities: Breaking Barriers to Careers and Full Employment*. Washington, D.C.: National Council on Disability, October, 2007.

Ostroff, C. and Judge, T. A. (eds.), *Perspectives on Organizational Fit*. New York: Lawrence Erlbaum Associates, 2007.

O'Reilly, C. A., Chatman, J., and Caldwell, D. F. "People and Organizational Culture: A Profile Comparison Approach to Assessing Person-Organization Fit." *Academy of Management Journal*, 1991, *34*, 487–516.

Pitt-Catsouphes, M., Swanberg, J. E., Bond, J. T., and Galinsky, E. "Work Life Policies and Programs: Comparing Responsiveness of Nonprofit and For Profit Organizations." *Nonprofit Management and Leadership*, 2004, *14*(3), 291–312.

Resnick, C. J., Baltes, B. B., and Shantz, C. W. "Person Organization Fit and Work-Related Attitudes and Decisions." *Journal of Applied Psychology*, 2007, *92*(5), 1446–1455.

Ridder, H-G., and McCandless, A. "Influences on the Architecture of Human Resources Management in Nonprofit Organizations." *Nonprofit and Voluntary Sector Quarterly*, 2010, *39*(1), 124–141.

Salgado, J. F., Anderson, N., Moscoso, S. C., Bertua, C., and De Fruyt, F. "International Validity Generalization and Cognitive Abilities: A European Community Meta-Analysis." *Personnel Psychology*, 2003, *56*, 573–605.

Salamon, L. M., and Geller, S. L. "The Nonprofit Workforce Crisis: Real or Imagined?" *The Listening Post Project*, 2007, Communique no. 8, Johns Hopkins University.

Schepers, C., De Gieter, S., Pepermans, R., Du Bois, C., Caers, R., and Jegers, M. "How Are Employees of the Nonprofit Sector Motivated? A Research Need." *Nonprofit Management & Leadership*, 2005, *16*(2), 191–208.

Stewart, G. L. "Toward an Understanding of the Multilevel Role of Personality in Teams." In M. R. Barrick and A. M. Ryan (eds.), *Personality and Work*. San Francisco: Jossey-Bass, 2003.

Toh, S. M., Morgeson, F. P., and Campion, M.A. "Human resource configurations: Investigating fit with the organizational context." *Journal of Applied Psychology*, 2008, *93*(4), 864–882.

Vroom, V. *Work and Motivation*. New York: Wiley, 1964.

Zottoli, M. A., and Wanous, J. P. "Recruitment Source Research: Current Status and Future Directions." *Human Resource Management Review*, 2000, *10*, 353–382.

CHAPTER TWENTY-FIVE

TOTAL REWARDS PROGRAMS
IN NONPROFIT ORGANIZATIONS

Nancy E. Day

Many nonprofit organizations, particularly those that are smaller and less sophisticated, consider employee compensation an onerous and expensive obligation on which as little time as possible should be spent. All too often, salaries and benefits may be set haphazardly, based on "gut feelings" about how much certain jobs bring on the general market or on the difficulty of attracting qualified people to key positions. These organizations view compensation as extraneous to their organization's overall mission or strategy. This is unfortunate and unwise, given that labor costs make up over 50 percent of total costs for many U.S. employers (Milkovich and Newman, 2008).

Total Rewards: Integral to Organizational Strategy

It is essential that the compensation system attracts and rewards the best quality workforce it can afford, since the organization's human resources are indeed its most important resources. Without them, the organization's goals cannot be achieved and its values cannot be enacted. As Louis Mayer, of Metro Goldwyn Mayer, said, "The inventory goes home at night" (Choate, 1990). This is especially true for nonprofits.

In addition to these considerations, the contemporary view of pay and benefits has become an integrative one that is more appropriately conceptualized as "total rewards" (Christofferson and King, 2006). Whereas compensation includes anything of monetary value that the organization provides its employees in exchange for their services (pay and benefits, including perquisites), "total rewards" includes all those things that will motivate workers to be attracted to the nonprofit, join it, perform well in it, and remain with it. This definition includes not only the "basics" such as base salary, incentive pay, and benefits, but also those work environment characteristics that create a "workplace of choice": good supervision, safe and attractive facilities, access to training and development, and other elements that attract potential employees and enhance their experiences once they are members of the organization. This definition is sweeping and inclusive, suggesting that the job of a manager of compensation may be broader and more diverse than building sound pay programs and providing adequate benefits. At its best, it includes an entire constellation of programs and practices designed to support the organization's strategic goals.

For the purposes of this chapter, space limitations require that we confine most of our discussion to the more basic forms of compensation: salary, incentives, and benefits. Incentive pay is still not pervasive in the nonprofit sector, particularly at nonexecutive levels, yet there is a trend to include them as part of the nonprofit pay package. Incentive pay is an avenue by which individual pay can be directly related to the "bottom line" results or mission of the organization, reducing fixed costs and encouraging top performance because it puts a percentage of an employee's pay "at risk." In times of tight budgets (as most are for nonprofits), pay programs that control fixed costs while increasing both individual and organizational performance are receiving more than passing attention from managers of nonprofit organizations.

Compensation Strategy and Organizational Mission

All organizations base their actions on goals that are either explicit or implicit. Strategic planning is done in well-managed organizations to ensure that current resources, financial, material and human, are used in the manner most effective to the organization's raison d'être. Organizations with effective performance management programs will require individual employees to set performance objectives that are based on unit goals, which in turn are driven by organizational goals. This "cascading" effect allows effective organizations to link broad, often ambitious goals and strategies with the activities of their individual workers. Thus, ultimately the individual employee is responsible for carrying out the fundamental mission of the organization. Because of this, it is imperative that the rewards system be integral to the nonprofit's mission and strategic plan and be consistent with the organization's goals, culture, and environmental pressures. Organizations need to decide where they want to go and how they will get there. Compensation is one of the many important gears in the total organizational performance machine that must be carefully tended, frequently lubricated and repaired, and upgraded or replaced if it no longer functions adequately in contributing to top performance.

For example, an organization that is changing its organizational structure must ensure that its pay strategy fits these changes. The most effective pay for self-directed work teams is probably not a traditional salary program; careful analysis of the goals of the work teams and their structures, the reasons why teams are being implemented, and the pay strategy of the organization all must be considered to determine the best approach.

It is imperative that workers are paid for what the organization wants to reward. This obvious yet critical fact is illustrated by Steven Kerr's well-known article, "On the Folly of Rewarding A, While Hoping for B," which cannot be quoted too often:

> Whether dealing with monkeys, rats, or human beings, it is hardly controversial to state that most organisms seek information concerning what activities are rewarded, and then seek to do (or at least pretend to do) those things, often to the virtual exclusion of activities not rewarded. The extent to which this occurs of course will depend on the perceived attractiveness of the rewards offered, but neither operant nor expectancy theorists would quarrel with the essence of this notion.
>
> Nevertheless, numerous examples exist of reward systems that are fouled up in that behaviors which are rewarded are those which the rewarder is trying to *discourage*, while the behavior he desires is not being rewarded at all. [Kerr, 1975, p. 769].

A familiar example of this mistake occurred frequently in the early 1980s when employees were given regular, annual cost-of-living increases. Although high inflation demanded some salary escalation to keep workers even with living costs, organizations were in effect paying their employees to merely show up at work, whether or not they were performing in the best interests of the organization. A better way to use pay to accomplish organizational goals is to direct the largest increases at those workers who contribute the most, not equally to all employees regardless of their performance. The opposite, a distasteful example, was a situation at Green Giant, in which employees who were rewarded for finding insects pieces in the vegetables began importing "home-grown" bug parts in order to increase their incentive rewards (as reported in Milkovich and Newman, 2008)!

The Need for a Rewards Policy

Environmental and market demands have significant impacts on rewards systems. Organizations that have jobs requiring extremely high levels of technical skill and expertise, such as medical doctors or engineers, must design systems that reward these key positions adequately. Management needs to ensure that qualified people are attracted and retained, while at the same time carefully balancing pay relationships across jobs within the company to avoid inequity.

Edward Lawler (1990, p. 11) recommends that managers should begin to develop an effective strategy "with an analysis of the outcomes or results they need from their pay system and then develop a core set of compensation principles and practices to support these directions." Aligning the reward system, including compensation, benefits, and work environment factors, to the organization's mission and strategic plan as well as its management style is critical. Thus, before a reward program is seriously considered, the executives and professionals responsible for designing it need to evaluate carefully the organization's goals, values, culture, and strategy to ensure that rewards play a key role in accomplishing organizational goals. The key point here is that the nonprofit's top management should carefully and strategically assess *what knowledge, skills, abilities, and outcomes the organization wants to reward*. This simple yet meaningful phrase should become the compensation manager's "motto," continually guiding him or her in making decisions about the content and process of the organization's total rewards strategy.

One way that many organizations define their total reward strategy is through the development, communication, and maintenance of a *reward policy*. This is generally a simple, relatively short statement that communicates how the organization plans to reward people, including pay, benefits, and work environment characteristics, how the system will be designed and maintained, and the philosophy of what rewards are supposed to accomplish. Also included should be a statement expressing the organization's intention to treat everyone fairly and equitably, regardless of race, sex, religion, age, disability, color, national origin and other protected classes relevant to local laws and organizational values or policies. Although the rewards policy should be brief, much concern and deliberation need to go into its development since the organization's top management must make a commitment to staunchly adhere to its precepts to maximize employee trust. The reward policy should then be communicated to employees along with other key organizational policies.

Using Consultants

Before embarking on any major new salary or benefits program, the nonprofit organization should consider the value and cost-effectiveness of contracting with a compensation consultant. Organizations on tight budgets, particularly nonprofits, often fall into the trap of trying to save money by developing major programs in-house. If current staff has the needed HR expertise, this may be the appropriate avenue to take. However, even if current staff members are equipped with necessary skills, the following points should be considered on the value of using consultants.

First, consultants generally have a wide range of experience across a number of organizations and therefore may know what will work best for any unique organization. Compensation programs, especially with regard to benefits, are sophisticated and complex systems and even HR professionals with basic compensation knowledge may not have the breadth and depth of experience to develop and install programs that are truly a "good fit."

Second, consultants usually have access to a vast amount of salary and benefits survey data or have easily accessible sources and will thus be able to assess external competitiveness better than can an organization alone.

Third, consultants are outsiders, and this gives them an extremely valuable commodity: objectivity. Since the consultant's salary will not be part of the new compensation program, unlike the in-house HR professional's, he or she will be in a better position to tell top managers or the board of directors about unpopular or expensive compensation issues (for example, critical positions that are dramatically underpaid relative to the market). Objectivity also is a great asset in explaining to employees why some jobs have been downgraded and that their topped-out employees (employees who are at the maximum of their pay grade and thus ineligible for salary increases) will not be receiving increases for the next year or so. In addition, if the consultant is to conduct a specially designed salary or benefits survey, other organizations may be more likely to participate and share their salary information since the consultant provides a greater guarantee of confidentiality than a rival organization.

The major disadvantage of using consultants is, of course, cost. But keep in mind the above-cited estimate of wage costs: often over 50 percent of total costs. Sometimes several thousand dollars in consulting fees is money extremely well spent if it is able to provide the organization with a compensation system that maximizes the value of the salary and benefit dollar.

To assist in-house compensation program development, HR professionals can gain useful technical knowledge through the certification program of WorldatWork (formerly the American Compensation Association). This program consists of nine seminars and exams in critical compensation areas (WorldatWork also offers benefits certification). Those serious about establishing, installing and maintaining a state-of-the-art rewards program should consider obtaining this certification.

What are the components of a sound salary and benefits program? We will begin with a discussion of base compensation, usually known simply as salary or wages. Executive pay and incentive programs in nonprofit organizations will be discussed before moving on to development of benefits packages.

Traditional Base Compensation Principles

Over the last fifteen years, there has been much discussion regarding the "end of the job" (Bridges, 1994). "Jobs" are tightly defined, predetermined, and controlled, and thus said to sometimes limit organizations in responding adequately to fast-changing competitive pressures. Rather, voices of reform recommend that work should be considered "roles" that are broader and more flexible. Given the competitive nature of labor markets as well as the need for organizations to maximize the value they receive from each individual, this makes some sense. Moving away from the attitude of "it's not in my job description" allows employers to use workers' KSAs (knowledge, skills, and abilities) to their utmost in accomplishing organizational and unit goals, while at the same time providing employment that may be more rewarding, challenging, and interesting than a traditional, narrowly-defined job.

"To Job or Not to Job": Job- or Person-Based Systems

However, jobs provide a number of practical advantages. They also do not seem to be disappearing into the mists of time, since most organizations continue to use them (Giancola, 2007). The "job" concept is superior to "nonjob" models because of its ease in recruiting, conducting market analyses of competitors' pay levels, and training design. But it is generally true that many jobs have increased in flexibility and, in order to achieve their missions, small organizations usually require workers who are willing to wear a number of hats. The point is that the way that management views how work will be accomplished, as either carefully prescribed "jobs," or as more loose and flexible "roles," will make a difference in the type of pay systems and procedures that should be developed. Thus, nonprofits should carefully analyze their organization's characteristics, the type of work that needs to get done and the type of people most likely to have these skills, and decide to what extent work should be conceived of as jobs or roles. One way to conceptualize this question is to ask whether the organization wants to pay for a *job* to be done, in which the work requires a defined set of tasks and duties that are relatively stable, and for which a reasonable number of candidates in the labor market could be found to fill them, or if the work requires a *person's* unique abilities and skills for a variety of changing organizational needs. Generally speaking, this needs to be determined organization-wide, not job-by-job or person-by-person, so that the entire pay structure is coherent and consistent.

Since evidence suggests that organizations, for-profit and nonprofit, have not abandoned the convenience of the job, but rather have merely broadened its content and flexibility, the emphasis of this chapter will be focused on more traditional job-centered compensation systems. For readers who believe a nonjob system would be more workable for their organizations, most compensation textbooks contain descriptions of specific nonjob techniques (examples include Bergman and Scarpello, 2000; Henderson, 2006; Milkovich and Newman, 2008).

Job or Work Analysis

As is true for many personnel practices (recruitment, staffing, performance management, training and development, and others), the foundation of salary systems is current, accurate, and thorough analysis of the work to be done. Traditionally called "job analysis," a variety of techniques can be used to observe, examine, record, and summarize the main components of jobs. However, given the interest in person-based ("nonjob") approaches, techniques are now being developed to analyze the work accomplished in organizations when it is done outside of a traditional job context. For example, work within an entire department, system, process, or skill set may be investigated as the unit of analysis, where multiple people may do many interchangeable tasks (Milkovich and Newman, 2008).

However, as noted above, since most organizations have retained the basic "job" concept for ease in recruitment, hiring, and compensation programs, job analysis is still a viable term. Through job analysis, data on the content of jobs are gathered, evaluated, quality-controlled, compiled, and summarized (usually in the form of job descriptions) so that jobs are thoroughly and accurately understood. This somewhat time-consuming process is absolutely necessary for at least two reasons. First, accurate job knowledge is critical in establishing *external competitiveness* in that jobs must be compared across organizations by the *content* of the job (what the people actually do), not merely by a job title that may or may not truly describe the job. Second, only by understanding jobs can the level of *internal equity* (discussed below) in the organization be assessed and, if necessary, adjusted. Since establishing internal equity involves comparing jobs, it naturally requires that accurate and current job information is available in a useable format.

Job analysis can be conducted with a number of techniques, depending on its final use (job analysis is also used in designing programs for training, recruitment, job design, as well as compensation). These techniques include interviews of incumbents and/or supervisors (either individually or in groups), observations of workers, highly structured questionnaires or checklists completed by the job incumbent (such as the well-known Position Analysis Questionnaire), or open-ended questionnaires completed by the incumbent and/or supervisor. The latter method is the one most frequently used by medium to small organizations, since it allows data to be gathered easily and relatively cheaply. Open-ended questionnaires are typically designed by the organization so that the data gathered fit the values and goals of the organization—in other words, they should collect data on *what the organization wants to pay for*. As will be discussed below, often the *compensable factors* that will be used in the job evaluation process are assessed through this questionnaire.

Organizations that do not have the resources to engage consultants or lack the expertise in-house to perform job analysis may find some relevant open-ended questionnaires on several public-domain Internet sites. However, it is critical to keep in mind two important points. First, job analysis, as mentioned above, should measure jobs (or work) in relation to what the organization wants to reward. Therefore, "off-the-shelf" techniques or questionnaires may turn into a mere waste of time that don't really measure the work in ways that are useful or meaningful to effective pay system development. Second, job (or work) analysis can become a highly-charged emotional and political activity in any organization, particularly if the results are to be used for pay determination. When employees know that job analysis results may make a difference in how their jobs are valued, they have a vested interest in consciously or unconsciously making their work sound as important and complex as possible. If they believe that the process was unfair, incomplete, or contaminated, serious intra-organizational problems could arise. Thus, it is strongly recommended that compensation experts be involved in this process as early as possible.

External Competitiveness

Over the last two decades, external competitiveness, or the need for organizations to identify their competitors for labor and set pay levels in response to them, has increased in importance. Several changes in the national (and global) economy have shifted the weight of pay system development from internal to external

considerations. A primary change is that American organizations now recognize that they exist in a highly competitive labor environment. Indeed, even in times of economic downturn, the "war" for talent continues for many technical and highly educated workers. Given projections that KSAs in the American workforce will not meet American business needs over the next few decades (Heneman and Judge, 2009), external competitiveness has moved to the front of the line in pay system design. Further, this increase in competition for highly skilled labor has discouraged workers from limiting themselves to one sector or another. Indeed, public sector and nonprofit organizations may find themselves in competition with for-profits for the same people who previously saw themselves as nonprofit workers. Thus, the ability to understand the entire labor market, both for- and nonprofit, enables the nonprofit compensation manager to make informed and intelligent decisions regarding total reward strategies. Finally, rapidly increasing technology requires hiring and retaining people with skills that are "market driven." As nonprofit organizations rely more heavily on automation of information, Internet fundraising, and other functions, the need for the salary system to respond quickly and effectively to market forces that dictate salaries for these positions is critical. Without adaptive systems to gauge and react to market changes, retention of highly skilled workers will be extremely difficult.

With Whom Do We Compete for Employees? After ensuring that job information is complete and up-to-date, the first question that must be answered is "What are the salary markets for the jobs in this organization?" In nearly every organization, several salary markets, or _"relevant labor markets,"_ will exist. The key to answering this question is to determine where in the labor market the needed KSAs exist. For example, clerical jobs are nearly always recruited locally, probably from both for-profit and nonprofit organizations, because that's where people with clerical KSAs can be found. Therefore, the relevant labor market for clerical jobs is usually a wide local market. While it is true that many nonprofits will be unable to meet the pay levels of large, private-sector companies, it is still critical to have information about the pay level in the entire relevant market. Some professional jobs that are technically or specialty oriented will most likely be recruited regionally, nationally, or even internationally, sometimes from other nonprofits with similar missions and goals, but sometimes from broader sources. Thus, the relevant labor market for specialty jobs may also include both for-profit and nonprofit firms. If key executive positions require skills specialized to particular nonprofit organizational needs, then their appropriate labor market will be national (or international) nonprofits in similar sectors. However, some executive roles may benefit from skills found outside the nonprofit arena. As in all positions, the appropriate relevant labor market for the nonprofit's executives

must also be carefully considered and chosen, based on the organization's goals and strategies.

What Data? After identifying the relevant markets, *benchmark jobs* should be identified. These are jobs upon which the salary system will be built, so they should be well-defined and clearly understood within the organization. Every organization has its own unique jobs that do not exist in the rest of the world and for which no market data are available. However, benchmark jobs should be those that (1) are easily found in other organizations within the relevant labor markets, (2) are relatively unchanging, (3) as a group, represent nearly all levels within the organization, (4) vary in levels of compensable factors (which will be discussed below), (5) have multiple incumbents, and (6) for which the organization is experiencing particular difficulty recruiting (Kovac, 2008; Wallace and Fay, 1988). Typically, it is desirable to choose a group of benchmarks representing a minimum 25 to 30 percent of all jobs in the organization, many more if the organization wishes its reward system to be market-driven.

A critical point in this process is to recognize that job *titles* are not determinants of benchmark jobs, job *content* is. Job descriptions created from the job analysis should be used to ensure valid market matches. Also, to avoid confusion, titles should accurately reflect the contents of the job and should not be manipulated to reward special employees or increase the prestige of the supervisor, as often happens in salary systems that are not adequately designed and maintained.

Salary data are generally collected from two broad sources: published salary surveys or surveys conducted by the organization or its consultants. Published surveys are undoubtedly the easiest to obtain but have drawbacks (Exhibit 25.1 lists a variety of published surveys; nonprofit organizations should be certain to use those relevant to the nonprofit sector). First, some are extremely expensive. Those published by national consulting firms can cost from a hundred to a few thousand dollars and more. Such cost issues may be counteracted by the payroll dollars saved in an effective salary administration program, and several organizations may form a consortium to purchase them jointly. These surveys are generally of very high quality, with the data "cut" in many useful ways (for example, by region, by type of industry, by budget size, and others). However, because many of these surveys are geared to the private sector, they may only have relevant data for a few jobs in a nonprofit organization. But for some high-level technical or specialized jobs, the data found in them may be essential. Luckily there are many cheaper published sources of salary data available, such as those published by other nonprofits, including professional associations and government entities.

EXHIBIT 25.1. SELECTED SALARY SURVEY SOURCES.

U.S. Department of Labor, Bureau of Labor Statistics

National Compensation Survey: http://www.bls.gov/ncs/ocs/home.htm
- Data for all fifty states and metropolitan areas are available at no charge; includes benefits data.

Professional Nonprofit Associations

American Society of Association Executives: http://www.asaenet.org
- Association Compensation & Benefits Study: includes many executive and nonexecutive positions

Nonprofit Industry Surveys

Abbott, Langer & Associates (http://www.abbott-langer.com/)
- All Nonprofits Salary Survey
- Benefits in Nonprofit Organizations Survey

Economic Research Institute (http://www.eri-nonprofit-salaries.com/)
- Multiple salary surveys for nonprofits, including executive compensation

Nonprofit Times (http://www.nptimes.com/)
- Comprehensive Nonprofit Compensation and Benefit Report

PAQ – SalaryExpert (http://www.salaryexpert.com)
- Nonprofit Comparables Data

Professionals for Nonprofits (http://www.nonprofitstaffing.com/Home.aspx)
- Offers free access to nonprofit salary surveys for New York City, New Jersey, and Washington D.C.

National Consulting Groups Publishing Surveys for Various Industries and Professions

Abbott, Langer & Associates (http://www.abbott-langer.com/)

Executive Alliance (http://www.executivealliance.com/)

The Hay Group: Hay PayNet® (http://www.haygrouppaynet.com/)

Hewitt Associates (http://www.hewittassociates.com)

Mercer Human Resources Consulting (http://www.mercer.com/home.htm)

Towers Perrin (http://www.towersperrin.com/tp/lobby.jsp?country=global)

Watson-Wyatt Data Services (http://www.watsonwyatt.com/)

Finding salary data for highly paid professional jobs that exist only in other, similar nonprofits may require a custom survey. An advantage of custom surveys is that the organization has control over the data that are retrieved. The main disadvantage is that, because surveying is another fairly sophisticated and technical activity, an organization must either have the internal staff with sufficient time and appropriate expertise or hire qualified consultants. Thus, custom surveys may turn out to be as or more expensive than purchased surveys.

Determining where relevant salary data can be found obviously should be driven by the relevant salary market(s). For local clerical markets, several sources are available. First, local human resources groups often publish salary surveys keyed to a general market. The Society for Human Resource Management has many local chapters across the country. Second, the Bureau of Labor Statistics has a rich variety of data available on its Web site (http://www.bls.gov/home.htm) at no charge. Third, municipalities (often through Chambers of Commerce) or states may conduct surveys of local markets which may be available for small fees. Nonprofit managers should be particularly aware of organizations such as Abbott, Langer and Associates and the American Society of Association Executives that publish data specifically for selected nonprofit markets (see Exhibit 25.1). Consultants are often helpful in identifying more obscure sources for published surveys unusual jobs, and associations representing specific occupations may produce surveys that are available at a reasonable cost. A word of caution, however: be sure that these surveys have been conducted using accepted and reputable survey methodologies. Sometimes such associations overvalue their constituents' worth to improve the profession's public image, so their data should be compared with other, more objective sources to ensure their validity.

Simple Internet search engines may be able to locate hard-to-find salary sources, but as any wise Web surfer knows, data from the Internet, particularly salary data, must be accepted with a degree of skepticism. Many managers who have had conversations about competitive salaries with their employees know that there is a seemingly infinite amount of Internet salary data available, and employees frequently use this information to argue for pay increases. It is therefore critical that the nonprofit compensation manager be able to understand the basics of good salary survey methodology, which are discussed below, and be able to communicate the importance of using only verifiably valid and reliable data in making pay decisions.

Using the Data. Good salary surveys report several statistics for each job, usually including the average salary, weighted average, minimum, maximum, median (50th percentile) and perhaps other percentiles. Generally, the most important

statistic in the salary survey is the weighted average, since it represents the average salary across all the job incumbents (not just across organizations), and thus better estimates labor market rates. Several points should be reviewed before using data from a salary source:

- How many organizations have participated? Make sure that data are representative of a sufficiently large sample.
- Are the organizations in the survey representative of the organization's relevant labor market(s)?
- How does the weighted average compare to the average salary? If they are dramatically different, it may mean that one very large organization's data are skewing the results, since weighted averages are weighted by the number of employees within each organization.
- How do the average and weighted average salaries compare with the 50th percentile (median)? Again, a large discrepancy could indicate a skewed distribution that may mean it is a nonrepresentative sample.

At least three different salary data sources should be collected for each benchmark job, more when possible. This helps to ensure that final market data averages are valid. Since survey data are collected at different points in time (high-quality surveys will cite the effective date of the data), data must be aged by a reasonable inflation factor so that all data are comparable. This factor should be based on the general increase in salaries and salary structures currently occurring in the market (sources for these statistics will be discussed later). Next, the individual data points need to be checked to see that they are within a reasonable range of each other; outliers, either much higher or lower than others, should be removed. Then, data for each job should be averaged, after which the jobs can be arrayed in order of market value.

A useful means of evaluating the organization's current standing in the market is through regression analyses. Using job evaluation points (to be discussed below) as the independent variable, one regression line should be calculated with market average salaries as the dependent. This regression line should be plotted and compared with the regression line for which current salaries is the dependent variable. By looking at the disparities between these two lines, the degree to which the organization conforms to the market can be ascertained. For example, such a comparison may show that the organization is paying competitively for lower level jobs, while upper levels jobs are being paid under their market rates (such as in Figure 25.1). Using these graphs to illustrate discrepancies helps explain compensation needs to decision makers, including boards of directors, who must consider economic impacts.

FIGURE 25.1. REGRESSION ANALYSIS ILLUSTRATING THE RELATIONSHIP OF CURRENT SALARIES TO MARKET DATA.

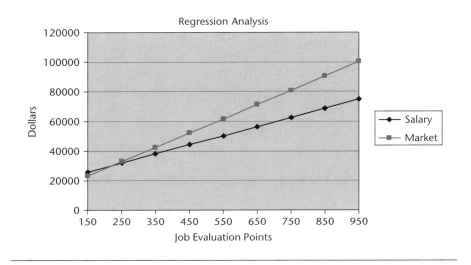

The convenience of adopting a job-based pay program is clearly seen when trying to gather market data for a nonjob-based pay program. Simply speaking, it is quite difficult to use market surveys to price "nonjobs," because such surveys are not designed for this purpose. Flexible, unique and highly adaptable "roles" defy collecting competitive salary data. Efforts have been made that involve extrapolating key skills from job-based salary data, but this strategy, while theoretically workable, is time-consuming and difficult; skill-based approaches to pay are workable only in limited circumstances and conditions and are beyond the scope of this chapter.

Internal Equity

Internal equity refers to the perception of fairness in pay for various jobs throughout the organization. In other words, in an internally equitable system, jobs that are of similar levels on key *compensable factors,* such as skill or knowledge required, supervisory responsibilities, accountability for budget and resources, complexity of the job, or working conditions, will be paid at the same general level. For example, a job of accounting clerk may require some post-high-school education or experience, knowledge of basic accounting principles, no supervisory responsibilities, and little accountability for financial resources. If this job is compared to a beginning employee benefits claim clerk, a job also requiring some post–high school education or experience, basic technical knowledge, no supervisory responsibilities and little accountability for financial resources, we would conclude that the jobs are essentially worth about the same to the organization. However, a custodian, as compared to those jobs, would probably not be valued as highly, since custodial work usually requires less technical knowledge and experience. In an equitable system, these differences in internal job value would be appropriately reflected in the pay structure; in a system that is not equitable, the custodian may be paid the same as or more than the accounting clerk or benefits claims clerk, or the benefits claims clerk may make significantly more or less than the accounting clerk. An important caveat here is that job evaluation addresses differences between job *content,* not employees' *performance* levels. We are interested in what the job requires, and not what any particular individual might be able to do or how well they do it.

Internal equity is established using some form of *job evaluation.* This broad term describes a number of methods by which jobs are valued within the organization. Two of the most prevalent in small to medium-sized organizations will be discussed here: slotting and point factor job evaluation.

Slotting. Slotting is appropriate for organizations that want to emphasize external competitiveness over internal equity, for those with a small number of jobs, for those which a great deal of market data are available or for those with flexible or quickly changing jobs. The slotting process begins with gathering as much market data as possible. After these data are tabulated and quality-controlled using the criteria presented above, the jobs are arrayed in order of their market value. Jobs for which no market data are available (usually jobs that are unique to the organization) are then *slotted* into this hierarchy. The slotting is done by comparing the job to those in the hierarchy and determining, based on the overall value of the job to the organization, where the job fits in the hierarchy. Slotting done in this manner is often referred to as a kind of "whole job" evaluation system, meaning that compensable factors (skill, education, working conditions, and others) are not systematically determined and compared, but that the job is looked at as a "whole." Of course, in practice, the cognitive decision processes that human beings naturally use tend to fall back on informally derived compensable factors. However, they are not formally defined or systematically applied.

In addition to allowing market responsiveness, the major advantage of the slotting method is savings of time, effort, and costs. Since a more elaborate system is time-intensive, slotting saves much staff time and effort. Also, the technical skill needed to develop and install other types of job evaluation systems is fairly high, and the cost of consultants in establishing internal equity can be avoided when slotting is used.

However, slotting has disadvantages. The most obvious is that some organizations have many jobs that are not found in the job market and thus market data may not be available for a large percentage of the organization's jobs. Second, because of the whole job technique, the system is generally lower in reliability (when two people independently slot jobs, they are likely to come up with different solutions) than is a point-factor system, and thus may be more likely to face challenges from employees.

Point-Factor Job Evaluation. Of the more complex job evaluation systems, the most common is point-factor evaluation. The well-known Hay system is a complex hybrid of the point-factor method. The basic steps in establishing and implementing a point-factor system involve

- Identifying and weighting a set of compensable factors that uniquely describe those job characteristics for which the organization wants to pay
- Establishing levels within each factor and assigning points to each level
- Carefully comparing each job to the factors and assigning points appropriate to each factor level which describes the job

The end result is a hierarchy that ranks the jobs from highest to lowest in their value to the organization.

Organizations have used a variety of compensable factors in their job evaluation systems, including the following:

- Accountability
- Complexity of job
- Consequence of errors
- Customer service responsibility
- Decision making
- Education and training
- Experience
- Independent judgment
- Interpersonal contacts
- Interpersonal skills
- Physical exertion
- Planning responsibility
- Problem solving
- Sales responsibility

- Scope of job
- Supervision
- Technical knowledge
- Working conditions

However, empirical research using factor analysis (a statistical procedure that defines basic underlying components) has found that these numerous factors generally reduce down to four basic concepts: skill, effort, responsibility, and working conditions.

Compensable factors appropriate for the organization are determined by a number of methods, ranging from sophisticated computer programs to hand-picking the factors that "sound right." However, top management must be involved in the choice of these factors. There are several reasons for this. First, top management is closest to the mission, goals, and strategy of the organization and can define what the organization wants to pay for and translate that information into the compensable factors. Second, top management has a broad view of the organization's functions and thus understands the scope and content of the jobs. Third, as in any management program, it is imperative that top management "buy-in" to the system. Nonprofit organizations should also consider the advisability of gaining board of directors' approval and may need to include its members in the actual factor determination process.

One of simplest and most straightforward methods used to guide top managers in factor choice is by using these steps:

1. The HR professional in charge of developing this program identifies a universe of appropriate compensable factors. This can be done by reviewing a set of factors such as those listed above and eliminating those not relevant to the organization. For example, sales responsibility or physical exertion might not be relevant to nonprofits and, if so, would be removed.
2. After identifying an appropriate universe, the HR professional should carefully explain the overall point-factor evaluation concept as well as the meaning of each factor to the top managers.
3. Top managers then should *individually* rank the factors.
4. The HR professional compiles those rankings and uses them to select a set of factors. While the number of factors needed to produce a workable job hierarchy can be as few as three or four, the key is to include enough to capture the major components for which the organization wants to pay. It is also advisable to consider those factors which may improve the system's acceptability to employees and management. Several years ago, it was not uncommon for job evaluation systems to include up to ten

compensable factors. Currently, given the increased emphasis on market data and consideration of the cost of complex systems, point-factor systems generally have between four and seven factors.

5. The HR professional presents this set to the top management group for discussion, asking them to ensure they completely yet concisely describe the job characteristics for which they are willing to pay.

After the final compensable factors are chosen, they should then be weighted according to the relative importance of the factors to each other, in light of the organization's mission and strategy. For example, an association of physicians is probably driven by jobs that are highly dependent on education and technical training, so that factor would be heavily weighted. "Consequence of errors" may be less important, so would be weighted accordingly. An easy method to accomplish this is to ask the top managers individually to divide 100 points among the set of factors. The HR professional can then compile their responses into one set of weightings, which top management as a group can again assess and approve.

After weighting the factors, they must be divided into *levels*. An easy example is education and training. Typical levels in this factor include

1. High school diploma or equivalent; basic reading skills required.
2. High school diploma or equivalent, plus ability to operate simple equipment such as word processors; basic office or technical skills.
3. Some advanced training, typically found in two-year college or certification program, or equivalent experience; ability to operate moderately complex equipment (such as for word processing); intermediate analytical skills.
4. Theoretical understanding of a body of knowledge similar to that acquired in an academic field of study. May include a bachelor's degree, extensive technical training, or equivalent experience.
5. Comprehensive understanding of one or several fields, normally gained through extensive study in an academic environment or business. May include a master's degree or equivalent experience.
6. Knowledge of a subject to a level that the incumbent is an authority in the field; may include doctoral degree or equivalent experience.

Parenthetically, note that "or equivalent" should be used for the education factor for two important reasons. First, it allows flexibility in staffing. Practically every organization will have individuals who may be formally "over-" or "underqualified" for their jobs but are performing adequately or better. Second, it provides some protection from legal liability. Because protected classes may be adversely impacted by educational requirements, these levels are not hard-and-fast requirements but are a general gauge of education that incumbents typically have.

If no outside consultant is assisting in the project, it would be helpful for the nonprofit executive to consult a compensation consultant or comprehensive textbook listing typical compensable factors. Defining appropriately sensitive factor levels requires a degree of expertise that generally comes only from previous experience. Points must also be assigned to each factor level within each factor, guided by the factor weightings. Table 25.1 illustrates a typical example of the assignment of these values.

The product of these efforts at this point is essentially a device by which all of the organization's jobs can be measured. The next major phase of the point-factor job evaluation process involves using this point-factor "yardstick" to measure jobs. Benchmark jobs are evaluated first. Building the salary system is easier if the benchmark jobs for which market data were collected are used as benchmarks in the job evaluation process.

Second, the individuals responsible for evaluating the jobs must be chosen. In the best of all possible worlds, a *job evaluation committee* made up of top managers is used. Under the guidance of an HR professional or compensation consultant, this group of five to eight executives spends several uninterrupted hours or even days carefully discussing each job, debating its rating on each factor and finally, reaching consensus on a final rating. Again, executives are ideal because they have a broad, organizational perspective and understand overall organizational functions, are closest to the strategic goals and values of the organization, and their participation makes them more likely to "buy-in" to the system. Also, this initial use of the new system on the benchmark jobs helps to more precisely define the meaning of the factors in the particular organizational context. Top managers then better understand and appreciate its relevance. However, the disadvantage is clear: the time and energy of executives is at a premium, particular in these days

TABLE 25.1. ASSIGNING POINTS TO FACTOR LEVELS

Factors	Weight	Points	1	2	3	4	5	6
Education and training	25%	250	50	75	100	150	200	250
Accountability	20%	200	35	75	100	135	175	200
Independent judgment	20%	150	25	50	75	100	125	150
Supervision	15%	100	15	30	45	60	80	100
Complexity of job	10%	100	15	30	45	60	80	100
Consequence of errors	10%	100	15	30	45	60	80	100
Total	100%	900						

of scaled-down management structures. Each nonprofit organization will need to carefully consider whether, or how much of, its executives' time should be used. A cheaper but less effective strategy is to use a middle-management committee to evaluate the benchmark jobs. (Committees made up of workers below middle-management are generally not recommended, since they become susceptible to political pressures from coworkers to over- or underrate certain jobs.)

After the job evaluation committee has evaluated the benchmark jobs, a subcommittee, often the HR professional and/or consultant and one top manager, evaluates the rest of the jobs. Even using time-saving tactics, the committee process can be extremely expensive in terms of executive time and productivity. An alternative but less effective process is for the HR professional, in conjunction with a consultant or other HR staff, to evaluate all jobs, and then gain top management approval for the job hierarchy.

Regardless of the evaluation process, the same principles should be followed in evaluating the jobs:

- Evaluators must understand all the factors and levels. Time should be allocated for discussion of the system and how it relates to the organization.
- Evaluators must thoroughly understand each job. This is where current and accurate job descriptions are essential. If necessary, the job's supervisor should be consulted during the discussion to ensure that essential job functions are understood.
- A critical point that evaluators should remember is that they are evaluating *jobs* and not people. It is essential that discussion center on the requirements of the job and not an unusually high (or low) performing job incumbent.
- Each job should be discussed in terms of how it rates on each factor and what specific job tasks or responsibilities relate to the factor.
- If possible, a consensus on the job's rating on each factor should be reached. Majority rule should be used only as a last option.

After all jobs have been evaluated, the point values should be entered into a spreadsheet (see an abbreviated example in Table 25.2). This enables the evaluators to "quality control" their results, ensuring that face-valid and sensible relationships between the jobs are maintained.

A final step in job evaluation is to review the hierarchy with each departmental manager. The array of jobs within the department, listed *without* point values should be presented to the manager (point values of jobs should be known only by the job evaluation committee and relevant HR staff in order to avoid misunderstandings among those who do not understand the scope or application of the evaluation system). He or she should check to see that this hierarchy

TABLE 25.2. JOB EVALUATION SPREADSHEET

Job	Education and Training	Accountability	Independent Judgment	Supervision	Complexity of Job	Consequence of Errors	Total
Receptionist	50	35	25	15	15	10	150
Accounting clerk	75	100	75	30	45	30	355
Administrative assistant	150	135	125	45	60	40	555
Development director	200	175	125	60	80	80	720
Program director	200	175	150	80	80	50	735

"makes sense" in the accepted understanding of the jobs' functions, values, and relationships. Some minimal fine-tuning may be needed. After all departments have reviewed these hierarchies, a spreadsheet illustrating all jobs within departments across the organization can be produced which may be reviewed by the top managers. This last step is to ensure that job relationships are equitable not only within departments, but across the organization.

Choosing and Maintaining the Right System. Regardless of the type of job evaluation method that is used, a system of regular review should be established so that jobs are analyzed and reevaluated about every three years, more often if they change frequently. Obviously, organizational needs, as well as jobs, change over time and a regular system is necessary so that internal equity is maintained. Often, HR departments will systematically review one-third of the jobs each year to eliminate having to face a major project every three years. In addition, supervisors should have a mechanism to appeal job evaluations to HR outside this regular cycle when they can substantiate a legitimate need to do so.

With innovative pay systems such as team-based pay, incentive systems, and skill-based pay increasing due to less traditional organizational structures, budget constraints, and the importance of market forces, the usefulness of extensive job evaluation programs has been questioned. All organizations, especially nonprofits, in which time and money are in extreme demand, need to decide the balance to strike between internal and external pressures and design an internal evaluation system that is the least administratively complex. In terms of administrative complexity, the point-factor system is definitely not for everyone.

Indeed, the hassles of creating an internally equitable salary structure are hard to exaggerate. They nearly always pay off in the long run, however. Although most managers believe that inequities with the external market will foster more pay dissatisfaction than inequitable internal relationships, experiences in the private sector with two-tiered pay systems provide a valuable lesson of the impact of internal inequity. These systems were designed to reduce costs in financially troubled employers by paying new hires dramatically less for the same jobs than previously hired incumbents, sometimes as little as one-half of the incumbents' pay.

Research and experience show not only that new employees show high levels of pay dissatisfaction, but longer-tenured, higher-paid employees are also extremely uncomfortable with the inherent inequities. Also, internal inequities will be experienced by the employee on a daily, even hourly basis, as he or she continually interacts with other workers. External market inequities, on the other hand, may only be directly experienced as one reads the classified advertisements, surfs the Internet, or has an occasional conversation comparing wages. Thus, every organization should be cognizant of the consequences of internal inequity and install, implement, and maintain a sound job evaluation program, no matter how simple or complex.

External Competitiveness and Internal Equity: What Roles Should They Play?

The competitive pressures of the external labor market, plus the importance of creating organizations in which employees believe they are paid equitably, require nonprofit managers to carefully weigh the relative importance of internal and external equity. It is possible that organizations that do not have to attract highly skilled, specialized, or in-demand workers may find their needs better served by ensuring first an equitable internal hierarchy of jobs, and then making sure that it generally matches the relevant market. Alternatively, organizations that are dependent on the attraction and retention of highly skilled workers will probably need to first focus on developing a system in which jobs are paid competitively, and then check to ensure that internal considerations are taken care of. As always, the mantra of "what is it that the organization wants to reward?" should inform and guide this strategic decision. It is upon this important decision that the amount of market data needed and the complexity of the job evaluation procedure should be chosen.

Building the Externally and Internally Equitable Salary Structure

A salary structure creates a means by which pay is set and administered. It serves to integrate the organization's policies relative to external competitiveness and internal equity in a manageable system that sets minimum and maximum pay levels for jobs, thereby serving to ensure that pay is within the range that supports the organization's rewards strategy.

Reconciling Contradictions Between the Data. It is likely that the job hierarchies generated from market analysis and job evaluation will not match exactly; in other words, the market will probably value jobs higher or lower than does the organization. This requires that the organization have a strategy regarding the relative importance of each. Some jobs, such as those with valuable and/or rare skill sets may need to be "market-driven," meaning that their values should be based primarily, if not solely, on current and accurate market data. An organization that has jobs that are particularly relevant to the organization's mission and strategy may choose to pay them above their market rates. An example from a for-profit organization may be helpful. In the banking industry, one of the most notoriously low-paid jobs is that of teller. However, a bank that has formulated a strategy of preeminent customer service might choose to pay its tellers above the market because it wants to attract, motivate, and retain the very best candidates. Thus, nonprofit HR managers must carefully consider what their strategy relative to internal and external equity should be, and whether it should differ for any particular jobs.

Pay Level Policy. As part of the rewards policy formulation, top managers must decide where they wish to stand relative to their job markets. This decision then translates directly into how the organization "prices" its jobs, a fundamental part of building the salary structure.

Most organizations in the private sector attempt to maintain their pay levels at the median of their relevant markets. This does not mean that every employee will be paid the going market rate, but that overall, the salary ranges and grades reflect the current market rates (more will be said about this later). Some organizations make policy decisions to pay at the 60th percentile or higher; they believe that paying premium salaries will ensure that they attract and retain the top performers in the job market. Some organizations may pay significantly under the market median; this strategy may be driven by the need for only low-skilled, easily hired employees performing easily acquired duties. Obviously, the pay level decision is critical to the organization's strategic planning, its long range goals and the current environmental challenges it faces.

Structuring the Structure. The HR professional or compensation consultant must make several decisions regarding the *salary structure*—the set of grades and their accompanying ranges. A salary grade involves several simple but key concepts: minimum, maximum, midpoint (or "control point"), and range spread.

The minimum is organization's policy of the minimum value that the job is worth. Generally, newly hired workers with little or no relevant job experience will be paid the minimum rate. The maximum reflects the most value the organization expects to receive from the job. Even if an incumbent performs the job superbly and has done so for the last fifty years, the job is simply worth no more than the maximum. In most cases, jobs of similar value will be grouped together in a single grade; systems that use only one job per grade are usually unwieldy and inefficient.

The midpoint, or control point, is a critical concept in base salary administration. It is the point in the salary range that is keyed to the organization's response to the market. For example, if the market rate for accountants is $4000 per month and the organization's policy is to pay at 110 percent of the market, the midpoint for the grade in which accountants are found will be $4400. New hires with little or no experience will be paid at the minimum of the range, and some longer-tenured accountants may be paid more, but generally the job of accountant, when performed by a fully-performing incumbent, is worth $4400 to that organization.

The term "control point" is preferable to "midpoint" for a couple of reasons, even though "midpoint" is more statistically descriptive. First, as we will see later, all employees should not expect to advance to the maximum of their job grade, unless their performance over time is exemplary. In an effective salary structure, an employee who meets expectations for the job should receive the value the job is worth on the market (or our reaction to the market as determined by our pay level policy). Using the term "midpoint" is often interpreted by employees to mean that they have another 50 percent of the salary structure in which to move. Only top performers, however, should be paid in the top half of the grade. Second, "control point" is descriptive of the midpoint's use in salary administration. It allows the organization to control costs around its policy toward the salary market.

Range Spread: Traditional or Broadbanding? The range spread is the difference between the maximum and the minimum, expressed as a percentage of the minimum. In older, more traditional salary systems, range spreads typically run from 35 to 50 percent, with the smaller ranges usually used for lower-level jobs. The idea here is that incumbents in lower-level jobs will stay in the range for less time than incumbents in higher-level jobs, since the lower jobs are less complex, easier to learn and incumbents will tend to be promoted quickly to higher levels. However, in the last decade or so, a useful concept called "broadbanding" has been adopted by organizations seeking to make their pay systems more flexible. Broadbanding collapses what would have been several grades into a broad

FIGURE 25.2. BROADBANDING SUPERIMPOSED ON A TRADITIONAL SALARY STRUCTURE.

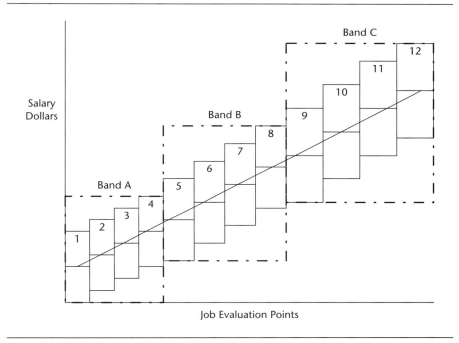

"band," creating a more flexible system in which the pay for jobs can be adjusted without reclassifying a position from one grade to another. Figure 25.2 illustrates this concept. It also allows more managerial discretion, in that a manager has a wider range within which to pay people. Since there are fewer bands than there are grades in a traditional salary structure, the broadbanded system is easier to administer and maintain. Although broadbanding may not formally assign a control point to the band, in practice there may be "zones" or "shadow ranges" within the band that are keyed to market rates (Klaas, 2002). In more traditional systems, salary grades group jobs together that are of the same value to the organization. In broadbanding, a certain amount of precision is lost, and jobs in the same band will differ more in their organizational values than they would in a traditional system.

Broadbanding systems are useful when flexibility and nontraditional career paths are the preferred strategy of the organization. However, because there are fewer guidelines (since there are fewer ranges there are thus fewer minimum and maximum pay rates in the system) there runs the risk of paying jobs over market rates, and the increased managerial discretion opens the door to wider potential for bias. As in all reward system decisions, the mission, organizational strategy and HR strategies need to be carefully considered in determining whether broad bands or more traditional ranges will be used.

Constructing Grades or Bands. Control point (or midpoint) progression, or the difference between the control points of two grades as expressed as a percentage of the lower grade's control point, should also be considered in constructing grades or bands. A key consideration here is the role of promotions to the organization (if the organization wants to encourage employees to higher levels of achievement via promotion, then making control points farther apart will provide substantial pay benefits to advancement). Also, if supervision is considered an important competency within the organization, larger progressions will more heavily reward those in supervisory positions. Sometimes organizations will split the structures into exempt (professional, supervisory, and managerial workers, including those exempt from the provisions of the Fair Labor Standards Act, who are not paid overtime) and nonexempt grades (those who are paid overtime) and use a larger control point progression for the exempt structure. The key issue is that job families have sufficient differentials between them to support the value of the jobs in the marketplace and within the organization.

Salary structures are built beginning with the control points that are determined after the reconciliation of job evaluation points and market data for benchmark jobs. Minimums and maximums of each band or grade are then calculated. The widths should depend again on strategic considerations: how long incumbents are expected to remain in their positions (longer time calls for wider grades or bands) and the degree to which promotional opportunities should be rewarded (greater emphasis on promotions calls for narrower grades or bands). It should be noted that creating a salary structure requires more art than science: the discrepancies in market and internal values must be managed while also creating a smooth progression up the grades that maintains appropriate relationships between them. Experience in building salary structures is recommended.

Maintaining the Structure. In order to maintain the salary structure, the market must be checked annually to ensure that the organization's grades or bands remain competitive. This is done through another kind of survey, a prototype of which is WorldatWork's annual *Salary Budget Survey* (available for a reasonable fee to nonmembers). This survey presents data regionally, by industry and by job level for present and anticipated structure increases. These data are presented as a percentage and represent the amount the surveyed companies increased their midpoints (minimums and maximums change accordingly) in the year and the amount by which they expect to increase them in the next year. Organizations will typically use this information to adjust their own structures to remain competitive, but usually do not correspondingly increase employees' wages unless an employee's salary is surpassed by the new minimum. Handling these "green circle employees" is discussed below.

Common Issues in Installing a New System. Upon installing a new salary system, it is likely that some employees' current salaries will be over the new maximums ("red circle" employees) or under the new minimums ("green circle" employees). Theoretically, red circle employees are being paid substantially over the market rate (or midpoint or control point) for the job. Therefore, it does not make sense to continue to increase their base pay and thus it is typically "frozen" until the structure's maximum catches up and exceeds it in the course of normal salary structure maintenance, as described above. To maintain their level of motivation, however, many organizations will provide these individuals with annual lump-sum bonuses based on performance. This strategy gives the employees additional income but does not add to the fixed costs of their base salaries. Green circle employees' salaries are substantially below the market rates for their jobs, and consequently should be moved at least to the new minimum as quickly as possible. For organizations with limited resources, that may mean giving small periodic increases to boost the salary gradually. In addition, some long-term employees may be faced with severe inequity if their salaries are at the minimum and new workers are hired in to work alongside them at the same pay level. In these cases, the person handling the HR process must recommend the best approach to balance equity with financial resources. Often a simple formula combining years of services and performance is created to move longer-term employees to a more equitable position in the grade or band.

Other Salary Administration Policies. Salary administration procedures must be written that coordinate with the goals, plans, and policies of the organization. There should be policies covering the salary impact of transfers, promotions, demotions, reclassifications (which happens when a job is reevaluated and placed in a different grade due to changes in its duties), and new hiring. It is essential that these be carefully thought out so that the intentions of the compensation plan are not subverted due to haphazard (and often nonmotivational) administrative procedures.

Pay satisfaction is popularly regarded as the worker's satisfaction with the level of salary and benefits he or she may receive. However, since research shows that pay satisfaction depends on the structure and administration of the program as well as salary and benefits levels and raises (for example, Heneman and Judge, 2000; Heneman and Schwab, 1985; Carraher, 1991), the wise HR professional will ensure that administrative processes are sound and equitable.

Increasing Individuals' Base Pay. In the past, many nonprofit and government organizations based salary increases on seniority rather than performance. In most cases, however, seniority-based pay is seen as strategically out of alignment with the leaner, more competitive operating environment and has thus been discontinued in favor of a merit system (merit pay generally refers to a salary increase based on the employee's performance appraisal; Deckop and Cirka, 2000). A 1997 survey found that two-thirds of nonprofit associations reported using merit increases for nonexecutives and only 2 percent relied on seniority-based pay (Casteuble, 1997). Although association practices may differ from those in other nonprofits, there is, in fact, a trend across the nonprofit sector to move into what has formerly been the domain of for-profit organizations: incentives, and sometimes even pay-at-risk plans.

These more innovative pay systems do not eliminate the need for sound base compensation programs, however. Individuals must still receive a base wage, which will continue to represent a substantial expense to the organization and must be managed carefully. Therefore, the executive in charge of compensation in the nonprofit must decide the best method with which to move employees through their grades or bands. In addition to merit and seniority-based systems, across-the-board or cost-of-living increases can also be used. However, like seniority-based pay, these alternatives increase the fixed costs of salaries in a manner that has no relationship to the employee's level of performance.

Communicating About Salary Plans

An effective compensation program should communicate about several basic areas to all employees (Rubino, 1997):

- The employee's job description and how it was developed (i.e., job analysis)
- The general methods by which jobs are evaluated
- How market data are collected and analyzed
- How performance relates to pay
- How performance is measured and appraised
- Administrative policies and procedures
- Benefit plans

However, explaining in depth the specific details about any of these elements can be counterproductive since reward plans are complex and difficult to understand for most employees. Introducing more information than is needed should be avoided, so employees are neither confused nor suspicious about how their rewards are determined.

Beyond these sensible recommendations, organizations will have to make strategic decisions regarding how much information about the plan should be available to employees. Some public organizations, like federal, state, and local governments, make data regarding all salary grades and ranges available to employees as well as taxpayers; even individual salaries can be easily discovered just by an Internet search. Other organizations are less open, some making discussion of individual salaries among employees a disciplinary offense. Generally speaking, most organizations make the minimum, midpoint, and maximum of a salary range available to the individuals whose jobs fall within it. In this way, employees are aware of the earning power of their present jobs.

A case can be made for making the entire salary structure (pay grades' minimum, midpoint, and maximum values) available to all employees because of the developmental (and thereby motivational) aspects. Theoretically, if individuals know the earning potentials of prospective jobs to which they may aspire, they may be motivated to acquire the necessary skills and experiences to get them there. Also, the career-tracking characteristics of this scheme should encourage employees to remain with the organization in order to achieve their personal career goals. However, if such career options do not exist for most employees in the organization and if the culture does not permit such disclosure, it should not be done. Newer, innovative management strategies like "open book management" argue in favor of increased openness about pay. However, like practically every human resource function, the method of communicating compensation plans must be carefully determined based on its impact on and coordination with the culture of the organization.

Incentive Pay in Nonprofits

As has already been discussed, over the last decade or so American business has had to become more competitive in many of its human resource practices. In many for-profit organizations, bonuses are now common at all levels of employees. Although some nonprofit organizations are so financially constrained that incentives may seem an impossible luxury, it is useful for the nonprofit executive or HR professional to be aware of them, since some of these systems may have direct applicability to nonprofits that have productivity or motivational issues.

The use of incentive plans is increasing rapidly in nonprofit organizations (Deckop and Cirka, 2000). Although cash incentives are common at the executive level, a large percentage of nonprofits provide some type of cash incentive to all employees (Klein, McMillan and Keating, 2002; Towers Perin, 1999). For the nonexecutive nonprofit employee, these are for the most part short-term incentives, designed to reward the employee for a performance window of year or less. Indeed, incentives can be effective in nonprofits if the following criteria are met (Wein, 1989).

- The top decision makers, including the board of directors, embrace a philosophy of pay-for-performance.
- Incentives are based on improvements to the organization's financial condition, either through generation of revenue or enhanced cost savings. A particularly apt candidate for incentives is the development officer, whose performance often has a direct and immediate impact on organizational revenue.
- The performance upon which the incentive is based is measurable and achievable, and includes nonfinancial measures that are critical to the organization's mission and strategy (such as quality of service delivery).
- Managers find financial rewards motivating.
- The amount of the incentive is large enough to "make a difference" in motivation.
- Incentives are awarded only to employees whose performance is above average, perhaps substantially above average.
- The incentive plan is communicated effectively and employees trust that their efforts will be appropriately rewarded.

These points underscore the case that has been made throughout this chapter: Any type of rewards strategy must be carefully considered and closely aligned with the organization's mission, strategy, and other HR policies and practices.

Types of Incentives

Simple short-term bonuses are probably the most widely understood type of incentive. These bonuses are based on a measure of performance over which the employee has some level of control, and can be awarded to individuals for individually-based performance, or to groups, departments, or units, depending on the appropriate level given the desired performance. "Spot awards," in which a supervisor allocates a pool of discretionary bonus money in relatively small amounts (usually $50 to $100) to employees for excellent performance in isolated events, can be powerful if carefully used.

Gain-sharing programs require significant up-front design time, but may be more acceptable to board and public stakeholders because, in the nonprofit context, they focus on cost-savings generated by employee performance. This type of program may be particularly appropriate for nonprofits that are experiencing unnecessarily high operating costs. Although these plans vary widely, they nearly always include some employee-participation mechanism whereby employees' ideas and initiatives not only encourage "buy-in" to the program but at least partially determine methods to save costs. Usually the organization will split the cost savings pool on an equal basis with the employees, and thus the plan benefits both the individual and the organization. The major downside to this type of program is that it involves defining a fairly complicated formula by which productivity gains are measured, which may necessitate hiring knowledgeable consultants to assist in the design and installation of the plan. Implementation of these complicated plans nearly always requires outside expertise.

Nonprofit organizations considering incentive plans should ensure that they remain in compliance with IRS regulations. Although detailed discussion of this is beyond the scope of this chapter, note that the IRS allows incentive plans as long as they do not violate rules that prohibit inappropriate private gain (see Chapter Two of this handbook for a legal discussion of appropriate personal benefit) (Klein, McMillan, and Keating, 2002).

Nonfinancial Incentives

Nonprofit organizations generally are not cash-rich. Board members or constituents may also be resistant to providing cash incentives to employees who "are just doing their jobs" and prefer those funds be directed at the organization's core mission. When such attitudes exist, it is encouraging to note that other types of incentives may be powerful, but less expensive motivators. For example, a popular nonfinancial incentive used by nonprofits is flextime. "Employee of the month" or awards of clothing with organizational insignia can often reap motivational returns whose value far exceeds the cost of the reward itself. Wise managers will carefully consider these options in their rewards strategies. Readers interested in a more complete discussion of these "nontraditional" incentives should refer to Mary Watson and Rikki Abzug's chapter on recruiting and retention (Chapter Twenty-four).

Executive Pay in Nonprofits

Although for-profit organizations are almost consistently under heavy fire by the media and labor groups for their top management compensation practices, such was not the case for top management of nonprofit organizations until the early 1990s when nonprofit salaries reported in the media were repudiated as out-of-hand, regardless of the market forces that probably made them necessary. It is imperative that top decision makers, including governing boards, understand that superior performance in top management positions is critical and that the best performers are often in very high demand in the marketplace. However, even reasonable levels of pay may seem unconscionable to the uneducated. Thus those involved in determining executive pay should be extremely thorough in their market analyses and decision making, and active in communicating about market pressures to the board and major contributors. Indeed, recent nonprofit excesses (such as Richard Grasso's executive pay package for leading the New York Stock Exchange), have resulted in increased nonprofit executive compensation IRS disclosure requirements (Cherry, 2009; Reilly and Cumpston, 2007).

The pay of the nonprofit executive group should be determined in a similar manner to that for other employees described earlier, using market data analyses, job evaluation, sound policies and procedures, and carefully designed incentive pay. External competitiveness issues are usually weighted much more heavily for top managers, for a couple of reasons. First, the location of these positions in the organization means that internal equity considerations are limited to those jobs below. Second, these are key jobs that are generally quite visible to organizations competing for talent. Thus, external factors are more salient for these positions. In addition, since the overall performance of the nonprofit in accomplishing its mission is more clearly dependent on top management than lower-level employees, an incentive program leveraged on achievement of mission and strategy should be seriously considered.

In response to the need for more market-based salaries, as well as external pressures for nonprofit executive pay to be related to organizational performance, nonprofits are increasingly turning to variable executive pay. In fact, about half of nonprofits report having executive bonus programs (Gaeta, 2003; Reilly and Cumpston, 2007). For-profits are often criticized not for their base salaries, which tend to be relatively modest ("relatively" is a key word here), but for their incentive pay, often in the form of annual bonuses or stock options. However, nonprofit organizations have less to worry about in this regard, since those nonprofit CEOs who are eligible for bonuses on average receive only about 15 percent of their base pay in incentives (Gaeta, 2003). In addition, nonprofits are often severely constrained by limited financial resources, making the magnitude of nonprofit executive pay, in comparison to their for-profit counterparts, seem quite modest. However, wise nonprofit decision makers will monitor the level and composition of executive compensation packages to ensure that they are not only appropriate given market forces and IRS constraints, but also acceptable to key stakeholders.

The most frequent method in nonprofit organizations for determining the basis for incentive pay is a relatively subjective board judgment. A better approach is to create executive performance measures that clearly delineate the criteria upon which a bonus will be paid. An obvious tactic is to link executive bonuses with operational cost savings, which also serves to fund the incentives. Another financial criterion is "program ratio," or the ratio of the amount spent on delivery of mission-related services to the total expenses. However, in addition to financial components, measures should also be considered that reflect accomplishment of the organization's mission and outcomes. Organizations that use tools such as the "balanced scorecard" often find it effective to link executive compensation to the results reported in such tools. (For a more thorough discussion of these measures and examples of how several nonprofits employ them, the reader should review "Nonprofits at the Crossroads: A New Look at Executive Incentives" by Gaeta [2003].)

It is often advisable, for obvious reasons, to contract with outside consultants to design the salary plan for top management. Not only do they have access to more data, they have the knowledge and objectivity needed to make recommendations to the board for paying these critical jobs.

Benefits

Careful design and implementation of benefits programs are essential in attracting and retaining a qualified workforce. Many job seekers are not willing to join an organization unless it offers a reasonable, if not generous, benefits package. The amount of money employers spend on benefits is staggering and continues to grow (costing the average U.S. employer around 40 percent of its total payroll (Milkovich and Newman, 2008)). Thus, it is more than a good idea to make sure that benefits are effective in helping to attract and retain good employees.

The breadth and depth of the topic of benefits could easily fill several volumes, so the scope of discussion presented here will be necessarily limited. The field has become highly technical and specialized, requiring the typical executive who is inexperienced in this area to solicit help from outside in order to ensure that the organization's benefits programs are competitive, appropriate for its employee base, and in full compliance with applicable law. Many consultants are available to assist the nonprofit in this quest, some who are also brokers selling the products and some who merely analyze organizational needs and make recommendations. Either type can be of great assistance to the nonprofit executive and board.

The same concepts of external competitiveness and internal equity applied to salary compensation are relevant in designing benefits programs. Organizations desiring to compete successfully for job candidates must design their benefits programs using current and reliable market data on the benefits offered by competitors. Benefits surveys are often included as adjuncts to salary surveys, and surveys specific to benefits are also available. Because of the divergence and variety of different packages, conducting a benefits survey from scratch can be extremely difficult, frustrating, and cumbersome. So if reliable and relevant data are available from a reputable published source, they are nearly always preferable to a survey conducted in-house.

Just as salary programs need to be developed with internal equity in mind, benefits programs should also consider factors internal to the organization. In other words, the program should meet key employee needs as well as satisfy the employer in terms of financial and other policy obligations.

In meeting employee needs, the executive should carefully consider the types and levels of benefits the employees want. Demographics of employee groups reflect differences in benefits attractiveness. For example, middle-aged or older employees may be more concerned with retirement and retiree health insurance than younger employees, whose interests may revolve around beginning families and whose desires may include health insurance (especially covering maternity expenses, family leave, and life insurance). However, it is a mistake to design benefits programs totally on demographics, since they are not always predictive of the benefits employees want. Employee surveys, focus groups, or other means of collecting data on the wants and needs of workers are essential.

One way that organizations can satisfy diverse employee groups is through flexible benefits, or "cafeteria plans." These plans can be structured in many ways and include many options. Using "125 plans," the IRS allows employees to deduct pretax earnings from their paychecks to set aside for particular benefits, such as child care or medical, vision, or dental costs. This option saves the employee taxes while allowing employees to choose benefits that are particularly attractive to them. The complexity and legal implications of these plans are such that external advice is often essential to executives contemplating the creation of such plans.

Benefits in the Rewards Policy

As discussed above, a rewards policy needs to be formulated that reflects and explains what it is the organization wants its rewards system to accomplish. Just as pay and work environment considerations are included, the role of benefits in the reward system needs to be clearly articulated. Information that should be considered for such a policy includes the following (McCaffery, 1983):

- The organization's desire to provide employees with meaningful welfare and security benefits.
- The organization's intention to design benefits to fit employee needs.
- The organization's desire to use benefits as a means to motivate and achieve desired levels of productivity.

- The philosophy and approach by which the program will be evaluated in relation to benefits costs, salary increases and external factors.
- How the organization plans to fund the benefits (most often, organizations require employees to pay at least part of the costs).
- The organization's intention to communicate effectively to explain benefits programs and changes to employees.
- The content of individualized annual statements regarding the value of benefits, company contributions, and employee costs.
- The market with which benefits will be compared.
- The requirement that trustees and carriers will submit detailed reports annually to management.
- The commitment that benefits plans will be assessed annually to ensure they meet the needs of changing demographics of the employee group.

Health Care

No one reading this book is ignorant of the crisis in health care that has confronted the U.S. for the past several decades. It continues to escalate and, as of this writing, the U.S. Congress has just recently passed and President Obama signed into law two major pieces of health reform legislation: the Patient Protection and Affordable Care Act and the Health Care and Education Reconciliation Act. The impact of this complex legislation remains to be seen, but it is intended to begin to resolve two of the most difficult challenges that the United States and many other nations face: controlling health care costs and ensuring access to all citizens. This legislation includes significant provisions and requirements related to workplace health insurance. The reader can find current information on this legislation and associated regulations and policies at www.healthcare.gov.

Nonprofit organizations must confront both problems of cost and access, directly in rising health insurance costs and indirectly by making the difficult decision of whether health benefits can be offered and to whom. As noted, emerging federal health care reform legislation may relieve organizations of some of these decisions. In the current system, however, many nonprofits, like many for-profits, simply cannot afford to offer even basic health benefits to all employees.

More than a decade ago, an initial response to health insurance cost issues was the implementation of managed care programs in nearly all organizations, profit and nonprofit. This is a broad term for a variety of programs from Health Maintenance Organizations (HMO), to Point of Service Plans (POS) Preferred Provider Organizations (PPO). These programs generally require significant monitoring and managing of individual health care occurrences, including ensuring that individual care selections are prudently chosen as well as confirming that the costs associated with them are reasonable. Although there are many variations, generally speaking HMOs require employees to choose physicians and other health-care providers who belong to a network; POSs and PPOs reward employees who choose within their networks but usually allow some coverage outside. In this way, employers can achieve reduced rates for medical services by either paying en masse for services or receiving discounts on certain procedures. However, most benefits professionals agree that managed care hasn't been the miracle cure for cost control that was hoped for (Employee Benefits Research Institute, 2009a).

Although traditional cost-containment strategies, such as raising copays and deductibles, encouraging preventative care, ensuring medical billing is accurate, and requiring second opinions, are still good ideas, new strategies to manage health care costs include (Cascio, 2009) the following:

- Form "purchasing coalitions" to negotiate for better rates with health care providers. Several jurisdictions have created "community health purchasing alliances" (CHPAs), organizations that are set up to create a group for which affordable health insurance is obtainable for small businesses. Florida, California, North Carolina, Connecticut, and Cleveland are among those jurisdictions that have such organizations (Volz, 1998).
- Treat hospitals, insurers and providers as any other type of vendor by making information about them easily accessible to employees (such as Internet resources) so they can make economical decisions.
- Offer flexible benefit plans that encourage employees to choose plans that meet their needs and also save costs.
- Create negotiation relationships directly with doctors to ensure the best prices.
- Ensure that patients have "preadmission certification" given by physicians before they enter the hospital.

Many organizations are now taking more innovative measures to control costs, through the use of "consumer driven" or "defined contribution" health care benefits. These attempt to push more decision-making responsibility about health care expenditures onto employees, through a variety of methods, from making multiple health care insurance choices available to employees, to giving employees extra cash and letting them purchase their insurance privately. Most common among these methods, however, are those that utilize some sort of health savings account (HSAs), or health reimbursement arrangements (HRAs). HSAs are funded through employee and employer contributions, and must be combined with high-deductible insurance plans. HRAs are funded solely by the employer, and may or may not be paired with high-deductible insurance, although in practice, they usually are (Employee Benefits Research Institute, 2009b).

The basic advantages in all these plans are that employers' costs become more fixed and administrative costs are reduced. For employees, particularly those with medical needs, the disadvantages may outweigh the advantages. Out-of-pocket costs may be higher, and they are required to better understand complex medical benefit plans and make more independent health care decisions. In the United States, all of these facets of employee health benefits will be affected by the requirements of the recently enacted health care reform legislation, although it is too early to know exactly what impact the new legislation will have on nonprofit employers and their employees.

Retirement Plans

In the past, retirement plans aimed to provide retirees with between 50 and 70 percent of their pre-retirement income. This was considered sufficient because, in retirement, work-related expenses are no longer accrued, employment deductions are no longer made, tax breaks give retirees a new advantage, and money is not put away for retirement any longer. However, since most retirees now have little desire to scale back their lifestyles and perhaps even look forward to doing things they didn't have time to do before, most financial consultants now recommend that future retirees plan for a larger income (for example, 80 to 100 percent of pre-retirement pay). In addition, Americans are living longer and more funds must be available for these longer retirements than previously planned.

Retirement income is usually achieved through the coordination of Social Security payments with income from retirement plans. Social Security is currently under Congressional reform, and proposals to make the program solvent in the future include decreasing scheduled benefit increases, changing the amount of contribution in relation to salary, and increasing the retirement age (Employee Benefit Research Institute, 2009c). Thus, Americans will need to be aware that these changes will undoubtedly decrease the percentage of retirement benefits they receive from Social Security.

Two broad types of retirement plans exist, defined benefit and defined contribution. Defined benefit plans traditionally have been the norm. Defined benefit plans define the income that the employee will receive upon retirement, usually based upon a percentage of the average compensation over all or a number of employment years. They require extensive actuarial support, making assumptions regarding future earning potential, number of years until retirement, and other pertinent factors. The contribution the employer makes is determined through actuarial assessments. Because of the expense of these programs and the requirement of a fairly large employee base, they are relatively rare in all but the largest nonprofit organizations, and their numbers are in decline in most sectors.

Defined contribution plans, on the other hand, define the amount that is put into some kind of investment vehicle. Therefore, the actual retirement income the employee will receive depends upon the success of the investment and is therefore unknown, but the amount contributed to the plan is defined. Often the investment is contributed by both the employer and employee. These are commonly found in nonprofit organizations in the form of tax-sheltered annuity programs (TSAs), or 403(b) plans.

Similar to for-profit 401(k) plans, TSAs allow employees to reduce taxable income by contributing a percentage of their salaries on a pretax basis to one or more qualifying annuities and mutual funds. Plans can include both an employer match along with the salary reduction or salary reduction alone. In 2010, individuals may contribute up to $16,500 a year. There are "catch-up" plans available for employees over 50 that allow greater annual contributions.

Retirement plans for nonprofits, like for-profit plans, are subject to massive IRS and other legislative regulations (especially the Employees' Retirement Income Security Act, or ERISA, and IRS codes); the substance of these is well beyond the scope of this chapter. Nonprofits and the HR professionals designing their retirement programs must take care to ensure compliance with these complicated regulations.

In general, defined contribution plans are the preferred choice of most nonprofit employers that are able to implement retirement plans. Thus it is important that employees are aware of the financial risks of such plans and their responsibility to participate. Over the years, the participation rate has risen to approximately 80 percent for those whose employers offer this option, partly because employers can now offer automatic enrollment in which employees must "opt out" rather than "opt in" (Businessweek.com, 2009). Many organizations offering defined contribution plans provide retirement or financial planning seminars to their employees many years before their normal retirement date. This type of training, which is generally free from providers or fairly inexpensive, can assist employees in feeling comfortable about their retirement prospects and can aid employers by increasing the commitment level of the employee to the organization.

Paid Time Off

Often nonprofit organizations can more easily offer paid time off than cash to reward performance. In today's business environment employees view vacations, holidays, and sick leave as an employment right and thus paid time off has become a standard part of the total compensation package. Determining the best mix of paid time off requires application of the same principles used to determine other reward components: internal equity and external competition considerations. The demographics of the employee base may affect the particular kind of paid time off employees prefer. Younger workers may prefer sick leave, personal time off, or family leave provisions in order to raise children. As employees age, there also may be more demand for family leave programs that allow middle-aged employees to care for elderly parents. However, as in all benefits matters, caution is advised about making unfounded assumptions based only on demographics. The best way to determine employee preferences is to ask them, via a survey or other methods. Questions regarding employee preferences in paid time off issues should be included in any surveys or focus groups the organization uses.

Competitive market pressures also must be taken into consideration. For example, one nonprofit organization gives its employees all working days between Christmas and New Years as paid holidays because a major for-profit employer a few blocks away has done so. Although this may be an unusual example, it shows the necessity for nonprofits to be aware of the time off policies of organizations with which they compete for labor. All organizations should carefully evaluate their options in light of their own particular labor market implications before setting their own policies.

Most American employees in medium and large organizations receive an average of eight paid holidays per year, nine days of vacation at one year of service, increasing to 19 days at 25 years of service (U.S. Department of Labor, 2006). Some organizations also offer floating holidays, or days that change depending on the calendar and the needs of the organization. For example, if Independence Day falls on a Thursday, Friday may be given as a floating holiday to create a four-day weekend.

Many organizations now offer what is frequently referred to as "paid time off" (PTO) or "personal days," often in lieu of sick leave, holidays, and vacation (Cyboran, 2008). Although policies vary dramatically, PTO offers a limited number of days that the employee may choose to take off for any personal reason, from sickness to birthdays to "mental health days." However, when PTO days are used up, additional time off for illness or any other reason must be taken without pay. The theory behind PTO is to encourage workers to take responsibility for their time off, and manage it in a way that fits their needs, whether it is to care for sick children, go to the doctor, or take care of other necessary personal business. Such programs can be effective in improving or maintaining trust in and commitment to the organization but must be carefully designed using employee preferences and historical absence data so the program is as effective as possible.

Other paid time off issues must be decided by the organization, including policies regarding jury duty, military leave, and death of a family member. Also, careful formulation of plans must be made to ensure that policies deal appropriately with overtime pay, shift differentials, incentive pay, status of paid time off provisions during probationary periods, accrual of time off not used, and other relevant issues. Of course, paid time off is usually coordinated with Family and Medical Leave Act (FMLA) requirements.

Tuition Reimbursement

About 80 percent of all U.S. companies provide tuition reimbursement (Ziehlke, 2004); a much smaller share of nonprofit employers provide this benefit. Many of these organizations provide tuition reimbursement only for their employees who are pursuing degrees. Most require the student employee to receive satisfactory grades as well as to be working on a degree that is somehow related to his or her current employment. Just as all compensation components need to be integrally linked to the organization's mission and strategic plan, tuition reimbursement programs should be carefully geared to an explicit career development philosophy that helps advance the organization's human resource strategy. In other words, nonprofits with limited resources need to understand what they are purchasing when they financially assist their student employees. It could be simply employee goodwill or a more strategic goal of training workers to address particular technological or professional needs as identified in the human resource planning process. As with any expenditure, management should direct its tuition funds deliberately.

Communication of Benefits to Employees

Although effective communication is essential in nearly all aspects of human resources, it may be that no other area is so critically dependent upon communication as is the benefit program. Although ERISA requires that employees receive an annual summary plan description covering retirement benefits, this is not sufficient. Not only do employees need to know what their benefits are in order to effectively utilize them, ensuring that they understand them is the only way for organizations to truly gain the "bang for their benefit bucks." After all, both profit and nonprofit organizations spend an enormous amount of money on benefits. To obtain the optimum level of motivation and commitment from employees requires communicating the value of what they are receiving. Indeed, implementing a good benefits communication program has been shown to increase employee satisfaction by 40 percent (Kislievitz, Debgupta, and Metz, 2006). McCaffery (1992) recommends several essential steps in effective communication:

- *Listen to employees.* Monitor the type of questions they ask, evaluate errors employees make in following procedures or filling out forms, listen to the employee "grapevine," and ensure upward communication channels are in place to monitor employee preferences.
- *Create and expand awareness.* Use "events-centered" communication that is structured around events such as time of hire, promotion, illness, or other relevant events that will make the information more salient, useable, and retainable to employees. Provide personalized reports that state clearly what

each individual receives and the monetary value of his or her benefits package. Incorporate regular reminders of the value of benefits in newsletters, paycheck inserts, posters, and other communications devices.

- *Build understanding.* Ensure literature is readable by evaluating the writing in benefits materials and use graphics and illustrations where appropriate. Communicate with employees face-to-face regularly to ensure employees understand their benefits.

- *Gain employee trust.* Train representatives to communicate effectively. Use nonsupervisory employees as benefits communicators so that knowledgeable and nonthreatening people are available to answer questions. Systematically audit benefits literature to ensure it reflects current programs. Install internal complaint procedures that go beyond the requirements of ERISA. Balance themes of benefits messages to counter any bad news with the proactive communication of positive plan features.

- *Ensure that the benefits communication budget is adequate.* A standard is to budget two to three percent of the total cost of benefits.

Justifying Rewards Costs to Directors

Some enhancements to total compensation programs may entail minimal cost increases but reap significant rewards in terms of increased employee satisfaction and retention or more successful recruitment. Often, however, improvements in salary and benefit programs result in potentially large financial outlays. In nonprofit organizations, as in many for-profit organizations, justifying such increases to boards of directors can be a formidable task. Faced with severe financial constraints and sometimes with constituent pressures, many directors are loath to approve policies that may have long-lasting and sizable financial impact. Therefore, the executive or HR officer who is in charge of formulating and proposing the program should follow some basic guidelines.

First, most of us realize that others will be more likely to accept a program if they are allowed some kind of input into it. Thus, no one should begin developing any part of the total compensation program without the knowledge and blessing of the CEO and board. He or she should carefully explain the need for the new program, and the means by which it will be developed and the method of installation. Graphs of turnover statistics, current salaries as compared to market data, and other preliminary information justifying the need for a new program should be presented concisely.

Second, directors should be informed throughout the process. Developing and installing a salary program can take anywhere from six weeks to one year, depending on the size of the employee base, the number of jobs, and the culture of the organization. As the project progresses, the board should be given regular updates.

Third, directors should be involved in critical aspects of the project. It is essential, for example, that they approve the final relevant labor market determination before salary data are gathered. Unless the directors feel comfortable with the specific data sources to which jobs are being compared, any market data, no matter now painstakingly collected, will be virtually useless. Also, if an executive job evaluation committee is used, make sure that at least some members of the board, preferably those of longer tenure and greater respect, be included on the committee. Ensure that the board knows that it will approve all final job hierarchies and salary structures. Include directors, where possible, on focus groups that assess employee needs and desires.

When nonprofit operational needs can be pressing, allocating money for salaries and benefits can be an imposing challenge. However, clear, concise and thorough justification and explanation of the needs, development process and final recommendations to boards of directors will allow them to make reasonable and sensible decisions regarding this critical financial issue.

Also critical is to ensure corporate and foundation funders, as well as other major donors, understand the necessity and process by which the compensation decisions are made. Although their communication and participation can be less involved, it is important that they believe the systems and processes by which these crucial decisions are made have been conducted knowledgeably, professionally, and conscientiously.

Summary

Organizations, nonprofit and for-profit, are being challenged to compete effectively. In order to do this, they must have qualified employees who are motivated to accomplish the strategic goals of the organization. Attraction, motivation, and retention of high-caliber employees require that total compensation systems be carefully and thoughtfully designed and implemented. Pay strategies must fit the organization's culture and goals; thorough consideration must be given to identifying the outcomes and behaviors the organization desires and designing reward strategies to ensure that they occur.

To do this, effective organizations must have up-to-date salary and benefits policies and communicate them to their employees. Second, organizations need to design and build effective base compensation programs, considering how external competitiveness and internal equity will be balanced. Although job evaluation programs can be effective in communicating management's intentions to pay equitably, it is important that these time-consuming and expensive systems not be overutilized. Third, management must decide how it plans to encourage the key behaviors needed to accomplish strategic goals. This may be done through group or individual incentive programs, merit pay programs, or other plans. Each system has advantages and disadvantages that need to be weighed and evaluated in light of each organization's unique culture and characteristics.

Fourth, it is critical that nonprofit organizations conscientiously evaluate necessary benefits levels. It is imperative that organizations understand both competitive pressures and employee desires. Finally, organizations need to design administrative policies and procedures that ensure that their salary and benefits programs are consistently, equitably, and effectively delivered to employees.

References

Bergman, T. J., and Scarpello, V. G. *Compensation Decision Making*. Chicago: Dryden Press, 2000.

Bridges, W. "The End of the Job." *Fortune*, 1994, Sept. 18, pp. 62–68.

Businessweek.com. "How does your 401k stack up?" http://images.businessweek.com/ss/09/03/0317_invest_retire/12.htm. Retrieved Dec. 14, 2009.

Carraher, S. M. "A Validity Study of the Pay Satisfaction Questionnaire." *Educational and Psychological Measurement*, 1991, *51*(2), 491–495.

Cascio, W. F. *Managing Human Resources: Productivity, Quality of Work Life, Profits* (8th ed.). New York: McGraw Hill, 2009.

Casteuble, T. "What Today's Association Executives Earn." *Association Management*, 1997, *49*(4), 53–61.

Cherry, B. "Disclosure rules to Build an Effective Executive Compensation Strategy." *The Free Library*. September 22, 2009. Retrieved May 22, 2010 from http://www.thefreelibrary.com/Disclosure rules to build an effective executive compensation . . . -a0210724248

Choate, P. "Today's Worker in Tomorrow's Workplace." *Journal of Business Strategy*, 1990, *11*(4), 4–7.

Christofferson, J., and King, B. "The 'It' Factor: A New Total Rewards Model Leads the Way." *workspan*, 2006, *4*(May), 2–8.

Cyboran, S. "Paid Time Off: Is It Right for Your Organization?" *workspan*, 4(May), 2008, 45–48.

Deckop, J. R., and Cirka, C. C. "The Risk and Reward of a Double-Edged Sword: Effects of a Merit Pay Program on Intrinsic Motivation." *Nonprofit and Voluntary Sector Quarterly*, 2000, *29*(3), 400–418.

Employee Benefits Research Institute. "Chapter 20: Health Benefits Overview." *Fundamentals of Employee Benefit Programs* (6th ed.), 2009a, http://www.ebri.org/pdf/publications/books/fundamentals/2009/20_Hlth-Bens-Ovrvu_HEALTH_Funds-2009_EBRI.pdf.

Employee Benefits Research Institute. "Chapter 29: Managing Health Care Costs." *Fundamentals of Employee Benefit Programs* (6th ed.), 2009b, http://www.ebri.org/pdf/publications/books/fundamentals/2009/29_Mng-Costs_HEALTH_Funds-2009_EBRI.pdf.

Gaeta, E. "Nonprofits at the Crossroads: A New Look at Executive Incentives." *WorldatWork Journal*, 2003, *12*(3), 64–71.

Giancola, F. "Dubious Rationale for a New Compensation Policy." *Employee Benefit Plan Review*, 2007, *61*(3), 11–13.

Henderson, R. I. *Compensation Management in a Knowledge-Based World* (10th ed.). Upper Saddle River, N. J.: Prentice Hall, 2006.

Heneman, H. G., and Judge, T. A. "Compensation Attitudes." In Sara L. Rynes and B. Gerhart (eds.), *Compensation in Organizations: Current Research and Practice*. San Francisco: Jossey-Bass, 2000, 61–103.

Heneman, H. G., and Judge, T. A. *Staffing Organizations* (6th ed.). New York: McGraw-Hill Irwin, 2009.

Heneman, H. G., and Schwab, D. P. "Pay Satisfaction: Its Multidimensional Nature and Measurement." *International Journal of Psychology*, 1985, *20*(2), 129–141.

Kerr, S. "On the Folly of Rewarding A, While Hoping for B." *Academy of Management Journal*, 1975, *18*(4), 769–783.

Kislievitz, M., Debjupta, S., and Metz, D. "Improving Employee Benefits Behavior Through Effective Communication." *WorldatWork Journal*, January 2006, 52–60.

Klaas, B. S. "Compensation in the Jobless Organization." *Human Resource Management Review*, 2002, *12*(1), 43–61.

Klein, A., McMillan, A., and Keating, K. M. "Long-Term Incentives in Not-for-Profits: An Emerging Trend." *WorldatWork Journal*, 2002, *11*(3), *63–71*.

Kovac, J. C. "Benchmark Jobs." *workspan, April 2008*, 50(4), 83.

Lawler, E. E. III. *Strategic Pay: Aligning Organizational Strategies and Pay Systems*. San Francisco: Jossey-Bass, 1990.

McCaffery, R. M. *Managing the Employee Benefits Program*. Boston, Mass.: PWS-Kent, 1983.

McCaffery, R. M. *Employee Programs: A Total Compensation Perspective*. Boston, Mass.: PWS-Kent, 1992.

Milkovich, G. T., and Newman, J. M. *Compensation* (9th ed.). New York: McGraw-Hill Irwin, 2008.

Reilly, M., and Cumpston, D. "Executive Compensation Issues for Nonprofit Boards." *workspan*, 2007, *5*, 41–46.

Rubino, J. A. *Communicating Compensation Programs*. Scottsdale, Az.: American Compensation Association, 1997.

Towers Perin. Management and Compensation Report for Nonprofit Organizations. New York: Towers Perin, 1999.

U.S. Department of Labor, Bureau of Labor Statistics. "National Compensation Survey: Employee Benefits in Private Industry in the United States, March 2006." Aug. 2006. http://www.bls.gov/ncs/ebs/sp/ebsm0004.pdf.

Volz, D. "If You Can't Beat 'Em." *Marketing Health Services*, Fall 1998, *18*(3), 10–14.

Wallace, M. J., and Fay, C. H. *Compensation Theory and Practice*. Boston, Mass.: PWS-Kent, 1988.

Wein, J. R. "Financial Incentives for Non-Profits." *Fund Raising Management*, 1989, *20*(7), 28–35.

Ziehlke, E. "Sharing the Costs." *Smart Business Columbus*, Jan. 2004. http://www.sbnonline.com/National/Article.aspx?CID=5600.

CHAPTER TWENTY-SIX

DESIGNING AND MANAGING VOLUNTEER PROGRAMS

Jeffrey L. Brudney

One of the most distinctive features of the nonprofit sector is its ability to harness the productive labor of literally millions of citizens in service to organizational goals without benefit of remuneration. Government organizations at the federal, state, and local levels also rely on substantial volunteer labor to pursue their public purposes. This remarkable achievement does not just happen spontaneously as a consequence of compelling agency missions, although, certainly, the desire to help people through donating time to a worthwhile cause is a powerful motivation for most volunteers. The credit belongs, instead, to the volunteer program, which allows citizens to realize the helping impulse as a well as a variety of other motives through work activities designed by the organization with the volunteer in mind to meet its needs and objectives. The volunteer program may be part of an organization that also has paid staff, or it may consist of a group or organization staffed entirely by volunteers.

An organized volunteer program provides a structure for meeting certain requisites: volunteers must be recruited; they must be screened and given orientation to the agency; they must be assigned to positions and afforded training as necessary; they must be supervised, motivated, and accorded appropriate recognition; they should be evaluated to assess the efficacy of their placement for themselves, as well as for the organization. This inventory focuses too narrowly on the volunteer, however, and overlooks the groundwork the organization must first lay for an effective program. The agency must determine its reasons for enlisting voluntary assistance and how it plans to involve and integrate citizen participants. Based on that philosophy, it must develop job descriptions for volunteer positions and arrange for orientation and training for employees expected to work with non-paid staff. The agency should make clear the importance of collaborating with volunteers and hold these employees accountable for doing so. Given the infrastructure that must be created to have an effective volunteer program, an agency must exhibit or reach a certain state of preparation or readiness (Brudney, 1995).

The volunteer program is a vehicle for facilitating and coordinating the work efforts of volunteers and paid staff toward the attainment of organizational goals. The core program functions that make this achievement possible can be grouped as follows:

- Establishing the rationale for volunteer involvement
- Involving paid staff in volunteer program design
- Integrating the volunteer program into the organization
- Creating positions of program leadership
- Preparing job descriptions for volunteer positions
- Meeting the needs of volunteers
- Recruiting and retaining volunteers
- Managing volunteers
- Evaluating and recognizing the volunteer effort

This chapter elaborates the essential components of the volunteer program and offers suggestions for increasing their effectiveness. Two caveats with respect to coverage are in order. First, one might reasonably add risk management for volunteers and volunteer programs to the listing above, since it has become a concern to host organizations (Herman and Jackson, 2001). This topic is the focus of Chapter Twenty-three in this handbook and will not be covered here.

Second, this chapter concentrates on "service" volunteers, individuals who donate their time to help other people directly, rather than on "policy" volunteers, citizens who assume the equally vital role of sitting on boards of directors or advisory boards of nonprofit organizations. The aspects of volunteer service that are unique to boards are discussed in Chapter Five of this volume. Although the demands of managing the performance and incorporating the benefits into the agency of these two types of volunteer activity are quite distinct, some overlap does exist. Service volunteers can bring a wealth of practical experience and knowledge that might prove a great asset to an advisory board; similarly, experience in direct service might usefully shape or sharpen the observations and insights of board members. Yet service volunteers may not always possess the breadth of perspective and background important to effective policymaking, or an interest in this pursuit, whereas board members may lack the immediate skills or motivation to perform well in a service capacity. As a result of such trade-offs, a great variety of practices governs the relationship between service and policy volunteering across the nonprofit sector. Some organizations encourage service volunteers to become board members, others permit the interchange, and still others prohibit it. The term "volunteer program" conventionally refers to the organization and management of service volunteers. This topic forms the core of this chapter.

Establishing the Rationale for Volunteer Involvement

No matter how overburdened an agency, constrained its human and financial resources, eager for fresh input and innovation, and enthusiastic about the potential contribution of citizens, organizational efforts to incorporate volunteers should not begin with recruitment. Unfortunately, well-intentioned but premature calls for (undifferentiated) "help" can breed apprehension among paid staff and frustration among volunteers, and exacerbate the very problems volunteerism was intended to solve. Because this scenario would reinforce negative stereotypes about volunteers and undermine their credibility as a vital service resource, it must be avoided. In fact, Susan J. Ellis (1994) begins *The Volunteer Recruitment Book* with the admonition (and chapter) "Recruitment Is the Third Step." The first step, treated in this section, is to determine why the organization wants volunteers; the second, discussed in a section below, is to design valuable work assignments for them (Ellis, 1994, pp. 5–6). The agency must resist the temptation to "call in the volunteers" until the groundwork for their sustained involvement has been put in place. "Throwing people at a problem" (rather than "money") is no way to solve it. The foundation for an effective volunteer program rests, instead, on a serious consideration by the agency of the rationale for citizen involvement and the development of a philosophy or policy to guide this effort. The initial step in planning the program should be to determine the purposes for introducing the new participants into the organization. For what reasons are volunteers sought?

Especially in times of fiscal exigency, top organizational officials will often express "cost-savings" as the primary reason for enlisting volunteers. Yet the claim is misleading (Brudney, 2003). In the first place, although the labor of volunteers may be "free" or donated, a volunteer program requires expenditures, for example, for orientation, training, reimbursement, promotion, materials, and so forth. In the second, for volunteers to finance cost-savings (rather than extend agency resources), cutbacks must be exacted somewhere in the agency budget. If cutbacks are to be visited on paid staff, officials risk the kind of resentments and antagonisms that have scuttled many a volunteer program.

A more accurate description of the economic benefits that volunteers can bring to an agency is "cost-effectiveness." When a volunteer program has been designed to supplement or complement the work of paid staff with that of citizens, volunteers can help an agency to hold costs down in achieving a given level of service or to increase services for a fixed level of expenditure (Brudney, 2003, 1990; Karn, 1982–1983, 1983; Moore, 1978). From the perspective of organizational efficiency, what volunteers offer is the capacity to make more productive application of existing funds and person-power. With a relatively small investment of resources, volunteers have the potential to increase the level and quality of services that an agency can deliver to the public. Although costs are not spared in this situation, to the degree that volunteers improve the return on expenditures, they extend the resources yet available to an agency to meet pressing needs for assistance and services.

Additional or different purposes may drive a volunteer program. The leadership of a nonprofit organization may decide to enlist volunteers to interject a more vibrant dimension of commitment and caring into its relationships with clients. Or the goal may be to learn more about the community, nurture closer ties to citizens, and strengthen public awareness and support. Volunteers may be needed to reach clients inaccessible through normal organizational channels, that is, to engage in "outreach" activities (for example, May, McLaughlin, and Penner, 1991; Dorwaldt, Solomon, and Worden, 1988; Young, Goughler, and Larson, 1986). They may be called upon to provide professional skills not readily available to an agency, such as computer programming, legal counsel, or accounting expertise. The purpose may be to staff an experimental or pilot program otherwise doomed to fiscal austerity. Enhancing responsiveness to client groups or establishing a community perspective internally offers still other rationales for volunteer involvement.

Volunteers also make excellent fundraisers. Because the public tends to perceive them as neutral participants who will not directly benefit from monetary donations to an agency, organizations very frequently enlist citizens for this task. In fact, in a 1989 national survey nearly half (48 percent) of the volunteers reported assignments in fundraising (Hodgkinson, Weitzman, Toppe, and Noga, 1992, p. 46). More recent survey research on volunteers shows that fundraising ranked first by frequency of mention as a volunteer assignment in surveys conducted in 1996 and 1994 (tied in 1994 with assisting the elderly, handicapped, social service recipients, or homeless not as part of an organization or group), although the percentages are much more modest (7.3 percent and 4.8 percent, respectively), probably due to differences in question wording (Hodgkinson and Weitzman, 1996, p. 34). That the list of possible purposes for establishing a volunteer program is lengthy attests to the vitality of the approach. Before seeking volunteers agency leaders should settle on the ends for their organization. An explicit statement of goals advances several important facets of program design and functioning. First, it begins to define the types of volunteer positions that will be needed and the number of individuals required to fill these roles. McCurley (2005) strongly cautions against overrecruitment. Such information is at the core of eventual recruitment and training of volunteers. Second, it aids in delineating concrete objectives against which the program might be evaluated once in operation. Just as in any organized effort, evaluation results are instrumental to strengthening and improving the program.

Finally, a statement of the philosophy underlying volunteer involvement and the specific ends sought through this form of participation can help alleviate possible apprehensions of paid staff that the new participants may intrude on professional prerogatives or threaten job security. Clarifying the goals for voluntary assistance can dampen idle, typically negative speculation and begin to build a sense of program ownership on the part of employees—especially if they are included in planning for the volunteer program (see below).

It should be acknowledged that simply stating the mission or goals for volunteer involvement (or for other organizational endeavors) is insufficient. Without follow-through or commitment, even the most laudable purposes can fall easy victim to failure and frustration. Worse, rhetorical support (alone) can breed cynicism and lack of trust that can be particularly difficult to overcome. In the wake of the tragic events of September 11, 2001, for example, President Bush seemed to have the moment and the oratory to galvanize the citizenry toward greater volunteerism, self-sacrifice, and responsibility for common purposes. Approximately one year later, editorialists began to question whether the social, moral, and political capital that grew out of that terrible day had already evaporated. "Mr. Bush continues to extol the virtues of voluntary service, and this is admirable. But it is hardly enough to resist the erosion in the level of public engagement as people return to everyday routines" (*New York Times*, 2002).

Involving Paid Staff in Volunteer Program Design

The support of top-level organizational officials is crucial to the establishment and vitality of a volunteer program (for example, Ellis, 1986; Valente, 1985; Farr, 1983; Scheier, 1981). Yet they are not the only ones who should be involved in defining the mission, philosophy, and procedures of the program. Paid staff, and if they are already known to the agency or can be identified, volunteers, should also be included in relevant meetings and discussions.

A precept in the field of organizational development is to include groups to be affected by a new policy or program in its design and implementation. Involvement adds to the knowledge base for crafting policy and inculcates a sense of ownership and commitment that can prove very beneficial in gaining acceptance for innovation. Because the incorporation of volunteers into an agency can impose dramatic changes in work life, the participation of paid staff is especially important (Graff, 1984, p. 17). The sharing of needs, perspectives, and information among agency leadership, employees, and prospective volunteers that ensues plays a pivotal role in determining how the volunteer program might be most effectively designed, organized, and managed to further attainment of agency goals. At the same time, the process helps to alleviate any concerns of paid staff regarding volunteer involvement and its implications for the workplace.

A primary purpose of the planning meetings and discussions is to develop policies and procedures governing volunteer involvement endorsed by all parties. Agency guidelines need not be lengthy, but they should address all major aspects of volunteer participation (see McCurley and Lynch, 1996, pp. 24, 195–202). Important aspects include

- Definition of volunteer
- Screening procedures
- Orientation and training
- Probationary period
- Assignment of volunteers
- Performance evaluation
- Benefits of service
- Length or term of service
- Grievance procedures
- Reimbursement policies
- Use of agency equipment and facilities
- Confidentiality requirements
- Disciplinary procedures
- Record-keeping requirements

In all areas these policies should be as comparable as possible to pertinent guidelines for paid staff.

Although some may lament the formality of conduct codes for volunteers as somehow inimical to the spirit of help freely given, this device is associated with positive results. Explicit policies for volunteers demonstrate that the agency takes their participation seriously and values their contribution to goal attainment. By setting standards as high for volunteers as for paid staff, an agency builds trust and credibility, increased respect and requests for volunteers from employees, a healthy work environment, and, perhaps most important, high-quality services (for example, McCurley and Lynch, 1996, 1989; Goetter, 1987; Deitch and Thompson, 1985; Wilson, 1984). A seasoned volunteer administrator advises, "One should not have different qualifications for staff than one has for volunteers doing the same work" (Thornburg, 1992, p. 18). These guidelines and expectations greatly facilitate organizing the volunteer program, handling problem situations, protecting rights, and managing for consistent results.

Some authorities go farther to argue that "Non-profits should treat volunteers as if they were paid employees" (Stoolmacher, 1991). They contend that the standard elements of volunteer administration in the United States, which have counterparts in paid employment—for example, interview, screening, placement, job description, orientation, supervision, ongoing training, performance review, maintenance of records, recognition, and fair and professional treatment—reduce the possibility for confusion and frustration on the part of volunteers that can result in an unsuccessful experience for both them and the organization. The "volunteers as unpaid staff" model is not without detractors (for example, Ilsley, 1990), and the approach should be amply leavened to take into account the needs, perspectives, and circumstances of volunteers so that volunteers are matched to missions and jobs for which they have interest, ability, skills, and input (Meijs and Brudney, 2007). Other scholars maintain that this "programme" (program) model of volunteer management may work well in certain circumstances (for example, in a larger volunteer program or in a program operated by a government agency or large nonprofit) but not in all, such as in a membership-based organization or a small cooperative (Meijs and Hoogstad, 2001).

Explicit policies for the volunteer program help solidify the "psychological contract" linking volunteers to the agency and, thus, may reduce withdrawal and turnover. In one study, Jone L. Pearce (1978, pp. 276–277) found that those organizations most successful in clarifying the volunteer-agency relationship suffered the lowest rates of turnover. These agencies distributed notebooks with all written policies, formal job descriptions, and training manuals to citizen participants. By contrast, the organization with the highest turnover in Pearce's sample provided none of this information to volunteers.

In more recent research, Steven M. Farmer and Donald B. Fedor (1999) investigated the effects of the psychological contract in a survey of 451 executive committee volunteers working in the chapters of a large, national, nonprofit fundraising health advocacy organization. Similar to the results of Pearce's (1978) study, Farmer and Fedor (1999) found that fulfillment (or violation) of the psychological contract affected the level of volunteer participation. Volunteers who reported that the organization had met their expectations participated more in the organization and perceived greater levels of organizational support for their involvement. In turn, perceived organizational support not only increased levels of participation but also reduced volunteers' turnover intentions. In another study, Matthew Liao-Troth (2001) found the attitudes of paid workers and volunteers holding similar jobs in a single hospital setting to be quite similar, including the psychological contract (with the exception of psychological contracts regarding benefits). Liao-Troth (2001, p. 437) concludes, "Volunteers may believe that they have made certain agreements with the organization as to what they will provide the organization and what the organization will provide them. If a manager is not aware of her or his volunteers' psychological contracts, then he or she may unintentionally violate the volunteers' psychological contracts, which can have negative consequences in terms of job performance."

Although volunteers may not be involved in initial discussions concerning volunteer program planning and design (at this stage they may not be known to the agency), once this effort is launched and in operation, they need to have input into major decisions affecting the program. Just as for paid employees, citizens are more likely to invest in and commit to organizational policies, and provide useful information for this purpose, if they enjoy ready access to the decision-making process. Participation in decision making is a key element of "empowerment" in volunteer administration, which is thought to result in increased ownership of the volunteer program by participants and, hence, greater commitment and effectiveness (for a full discussion, see Scheier, 1988a, 1988b, 1988–1989; Naylor, 1985). Formerly, this term seemed to center on citizen volunteers and expressed the idea that they should enjoy greater say in these programs, as well as greater recognition for the time, skills, and value they contributed. More recently, the term seems to have shifted to a focus on the administrators of these programs and expresses the conviction that they should have positions (and prerequisites), influence, authority, and status in host organizations commensurate with performing a very difficult but highly productive managerial task (for example, McCurley and Ellis, 2003b; Ellis, 1996).

Integrating the Volunteer Program into the Organization

As these comments suggest, the volunteer program must be organized to respond to the motivations and requirements of volunteers and employees. With respect to volunteers, the program should have mechanisms for determining the types of work opportunities sought and meeting those preferences, and for engendering an organizational climate in which volunteers can pursue their goals, with the acceptance, if not always the avid endorsement, of paid personnel. From the perspective of staff, the program must have structures and procedures in place to assume the task of volunteer administration and to generate a pool of capable citizens matched to the tasks of participating offices and departments.

To accomplish these goals, the volunteer program must be linked to the structure of the nonprofit or government host organization. A small nonprofit may accommodate volunteers with a minimum of structural adaptations, but larger agencies need to consider alternative structural configurations for integrating volunteers into their operations (Brudney, 1995; Valente and Manchester, 1984, pp. 56–57). In order of increasing comprehensiveness, these arrangements consist of ad hoc volunteer efforts, volunteer recruitment by an outside organization with the agency otherwise responsible for management, decentralization of the program to operating departments, and a centralized approach. Each option presents a distinctive menu of advantages and disadvantages.

Volunteer efforts may arise spontaneously in an ad hoc fashion to meet exigencies confronting an organization, especially on a short-term basis. Normally, citizens motivated to share their background, training, skills, and interests with organizations that could profit by them are the catalyst. Fiscal stress, leaving an agency few options, may quicken the helping impulse. The Service Corps of Retired Executives (SCORE), an association of primarily retired business persons who donate their time and skills to assist clients of the U.S. Small Business Administration, began in this way in the early 1960s; retired business executives approached the SBA to offer assistance with its huge constituency (Brudney, 1986, 1990). The responsiveness and alacrity with which an ad hoc effort can be launched and operating are inspiring: Within six months of its inception, SCORE supplied two thousand volunteers to the SBA. Crisis and emergency situations can provoke an even more spectacular response, mobilizing huge numbers of volunteers in a remarkably short time.

Spontaneous help from citizens can infuse vitality (and labor) into an agency and alert officials to the possibilities of volunteerism. Offsetting these benefits, however, is the fact that only selected parts or members of the organization may be aware of an ad hoc citizen effort and, thus, be able to take advantage of it. In addition, because energy levels and zeal wane as emergencies are tamed or fade from the limelight of publicity or attention, the ad hoc model of volunteer involvement is very vulnerable to the passage of time. A volunteer program requires not only a different type of ongoing, rather than sporadic, commitment from citizens, but also an organizational structure to sustain their contributions and make them accessible to all employees. Unless the agency takes steps to institutionalize participation, it risks squandering the long-term benefits of the approach. Almost from the start, the SBA and the SCORE volunteers worked to develop an appropriate structure. In 1989, they celebrated the twenty-fifth anniversary of a partnership that has brought a continuous stream of volunteers to the agency (13,000 volunteers in 1989 alone) and assistance to an estimated 2.5 million small businesspersons (National SCORE Office, 1989). By 2009, SCORE (2009) volunteers had assisted 8.5 million small businesses on behalf of the U.S. Small Business Administration.

A second option sometimes open to nonprofit agencies is to rely on the expertise and reputation of an established organization, such as the United Way and its affiliates, or a volunteer center or clearinghouse, to assist in the recruitment of volunteers but to retain all other managerial responsibilities internally. Since recruitment is the most fundamental program function and, arguably, the most problematic, regular, professional assistance with this task can be highly beneficial, particularly for an agency just starting a volunteer program. Some private business firms seeking to develop volunteer programs for their employees have extended this model: They find it advantageous to contract with local volunteer centers not only for help with recruitment but also other primary program functions, such as volunteer placement and evaluation (Haran, Kenney, and Vermilion, 1993). A large national network of volunteer centers and affiliates of the Points of Light Institute–HandsOn Network offers these services to nonprofit organizations and government agencies (Brudney, 2003).When this model is used, quality control presents a necessary caution, just as it does in the delegation of any organizational function. Recruiters must be familiar with the needs of the nonprofit agency for voluntary assistance, lest volunteers be referred who do not meet the desired profile of backgrounds, skills, and interests. A recruiter may also deal with multiple client organizations, so that the priority attached to the requests of any one of them is unclear. More important, trusting recruitment to outsiders is a deterrent to developing the necessary capacity in-house, which is an essential aspect of a successful volunteer program. By all means, organizations should nurture positive relationships with agencies in the community to attract volunteers and for other purposes. But they must avoid total dependence on external sources and endeavor to implement recruitment mechanisms of their own.

The volunteer program can also be decentralized in individual departments within a larger nonprofit organization. The primary advantage offered by this approach is the flexibility to tailor programs to the needs of specific organizational units and to introduce volunteers where support for them is greatest. Yet duplication of effort across several departments, difficulties in locating sufficient expertise in volunteer management to afford multiple programs, and problems in coordination—particularly, restrictions on the ability to shift volunteers to more suitable positions or to offer them opportunities for job enrichment across the organization—are significant liabilities.

In the public sector, the selective approach can unwittingly generate disincentives for managers to introduce volunteers (Brudney, 1989, p. 117). Top agency officials may mistakenly equate nonpaid work with "unimportant" activities to the detriment of a department's (and a manager's) standing in the organization, or they may seize upon the willingness to enlist volunteers as an excuse to deny a unit essential increases in budget and paid personnel. Such misunderstandings must be ameliorated prior to the introduction of volunteers.

Despite the limitations, the decentralized approach may serve an agency quite well in starting a pilot or experimental program, the results of which might guide the organization in moving toward more extensive volunteer involvement. Alternatively, a lack of tasks appropriate for volunteers in some parts of the agency or, perhaps, strong opposition from various quarters may confine voluntary assistance to selected departments. Among larger organizations that enlist volunteer assistance, the decentralized approach is likely most common.

The final structural arrangement is a centralized volunteer program serving the entire agency. With this approach a single office or department is responsible for management and coordination of the volunteer program. The volunteers may serve exclusively in this unit, or they may be deployed and supervised in line departments throughout the organization. The office provides guidelines, technical assistance, screening, training, and all other administration for volunteer activity throughout the agency. The advantages of centralization for averting duplication of effort, assigning volunteers so as to meet their needs as well as those of the organization, and producing efficient and effective voluntary services are considerable. However, the program demands broad support across the organization, especially at the top, to overcome issues that may be raised by departmental staff and any limitation in resources. When such backing is not forthcoming, the other structural arrangements may serve the nonprofit agency quite well. Although it may be tempting to conceive of the various structural arrangements as a progression from less to more "organized" volunteer involvement, they should instead be seen as corresponding to differences among agencies in acceptance and uses of volunteers.

Creating Positions of Program Leadership

Regardless of the structural arrangement by which the volunteer program is integrated into agency operations, this component requires a visible, recognized leader. All program functions, including those discussed above (developing a rationale for the volunteer effort, involving paid staff in program planning and design, housing the volunteer program), benefit from the establishment and staffing of a position bearing overall responsibility for management and representation of the volunteers. The position goes by a variety of names (for example, "Volunteer Coordinator"); here it is called the "Director of Volunteer Services" (DVS) to signify the importance of the role.

James C. Fisher and Kathleen M. Cole (1993, pp. 15–18) elaborate two approaches that organizations typically take in designing the volunteer management function: personnel management and program management. The personnel management approach is most common in organizations in which volunteers are deployed in several or many units or departments and have numerous responsibilities throughout the organization. In this configuration the volunteer program manager works with the line departments in all facets of volunteer administration and supports the line departments. However, the principal accountability of the volunteer is to the paid staff (or other) supervisor in the unit where the volunteer is housed. The volunteer administrator does not directly supervise the volunteer or provide training or evaluation. By contrast, in the program management approach the volunteer administrator normally supervises the volunteers, who are housed in a single unit under her or his leadership. As Fisher and Cole (1993, p. 18) explain, "In the program management approach, the volunteer administrator is a program developer as well as the leader of volunteer efforts integral to the organization's program delivery. In the personnel management approach, the volunteer administrator recruits, selects, and places volunteers and trains paid staff to work with them. In both approaches, the responsibilities of the volunteer administrator usually include job design, recruitment, interviewing, orientation, and recognition."

The manner by which the office of the director of volunteer services is staffed sends a forceful message to employees regarding the significance of the volunteer program to the agency and its leadership. Organizations have experimented with an assortment of staffing options for the post, including volunteers, personnel with existing duties, and employee committees. None so manifestly demonstrates a sense of organizational commitment and priorities as does a paid DVS position. Establishing the office as close to the apex of the agency's formal hierarchy as feasible conveys a similar message of resolve and purposefulness. Unfortunately, the evidence suggests that agencies do not always attend to supports for the position (for a review, see Brudney, 1992, pp. 272–273).

Based on a nationally representative sample of charities, the Urban Institute (2004) found that only about three out of five charities (62 percent) report that they have a paid staff person whose work responsibilities include management of volunteers. The presence of a paid staff coordinator does not mean that this official spends much time on volunteer administration, or that she or he has training in the field. Consistent with other research (Brudney, 2003, 1990), the paid staff coordinators of volunteers in the Urban Institute study devote about one-third of their time on the job to the volunteer function; the median paid staff volunteer coordinator in charities spends 30 percent of her or his time on this task. Full-time managers of volunteers are especially rare. In the sample of 1,753 charities, among those charities with a paid staff volunteer coordinator, only one in eight has a staff member who devotes 100 percent of her or his time to volunteer management. Across the sample of 541 religious congregations in the Urban Institute Study, only one congregation said that it has a full-time volunteer coordinator for its social service outreach activities.

Support for training of administrators of volunteers was somewhat better. About two-thirds of the paid staff coordinators in the charities (66 percent) reported a minimum level of training, defined as any formal training in volunteer administration, such as coursework, workshops, or attendance at conferences that focus on volunteer management. Support for the volunteer administrator increased with organizational size or resources. Based on these findings the Urban Institute (2004, p. 9) reported that the use of staff to manage volunteers by charities lags behind their parallel need and use of staff for fundraising, and concluded:

> Taken together, the findings regarding paid staff support for management of volunteers point to low professionalization and capitalization of volunteer administration in the United States. The fact that many coordinators are getting some training suggests that many are interested in learning about how to manage volunteers. However, the small amount of time spent on volunteer administration suggests that charities and congregations do not have the resources to allocate to volunteer management or that they devote their organizational resources primarily to other efforts.

These findings point to the ongoing need to press for greater organizational support for the director of volunteer services (DVS). For example, the DVS should enjoy prerogatives and responsibilities commensurate with positions at the same level in the agency hierarchy, including participation in relevant decision making and policymaking and access to superiors. In this manner the incumbent can represent the volunteers before the relevant department(s) or the organization as a whole, promote their interests, and help prevent officials from taking their contributions for granted. A part-time or full-time (as necessary) paid position lodges accountability for the program squarely with the DVS, presents a focal point for contact with the volunteer operation for those inside as well as outside the organization, implements a core structure for program administration, and rewards the office-holder in relation to the success of the volunteers.

In addition to these roles, the DVS has important duties that further substantiate the need for a dedicated position (Ellis, 1996, pp. 45–49). The DVS is responsible for volunteer recruitment and publicity, a critical function requiring active outreach in the community and highly flexible working hours. The incumbent must communicate with department and organizational officials to ascertain workloads and requirements for voluntary assistance. Assessing agency needs for volunteers, enlarging areas for their involvement, and educating staff to the approach (see above) should be seen not as a one-time exercise but as an ongoing responsibility of the DVS. The DVS interviews and screens all applicants for volunteer positions, maintains appropriate records, places volunteers in job assignments, provides liaison supervision, and monitors performance. The office must coordinate the bewildering variety of schedules and backgrounds brought by volunteers to the agency. The DVS also bears overall responsibility for orientation and training, as well as evaluation and recognition, of volunteers. Since employees may be unfamiliar with the approach, training may be appropriate for them as well; the DVS is the in-house source of expertise on all facets of volunteer involvement and management. Finally, as the chief advocate of the program, the DVS endeavors not only to express the volunteer perspective but also to allay any apprehensions of paid staff and facilitate collaboration.

Positions of leadership for the volunteer program require extensive interaction with new and continuing volunteers. Thus, as volunteer programs increase in size, the DVS will likely need to share leadership duties with designated volunteers and/or paid staff. Given the scope of the job tasks, clerical and other support for the leadership positions is highly advisable.

Preparing Job Descriptions for Volunteer Positions

The essential building block of a successful volunteer program is the job description. Paradoxically, no intrinsic basis exists to create (or classify) a position as "paid" or "volunteer." Even among agencies that have the same purpose or mission, or that work in the same substantive or policy domain, a given position can be classified differently (for example, business counselor, computer programmer, day-care provider, receptionist, ombudsperson). Within an agency, moreover, job definitions are dynamic, so that volunteers can give way to paid service professionals in some areas (for example, Ellis and Campbell, 2005; Park, 1983; Schwartz, 1977; Becker, 1964) and gain responsibility from them in others (for example, Brudney, 1986).

Without an intrinsic basis to designate a task or position as "volunteer" or "paid," the *process* by which work responsibilities are allocated assumes paramount importance. As elaborated above, the most enduring basis for an effective volunteer program is for top agency officials and employees (and if possible, volunteers) to work out in advance of program implementation explicit understandings regarding: the rationale for the involvement of volunteers, the nature of the jobs they are to perform, and the boundaries of their work (Ellis, 1986; Graff, 1984; Brown, 1981; Wilson, 1976). This agreement should designate (or provide the foundation for distinguishing) the jobs assigned to volunteers and those held by paid staff.

The second critical step in the job design process consists of a survey of employees, or perhaps personal interviews with them, to ascertain key factors about their jobs, and to make them aware of the potential contributions of volunteers. At a minimum, a survey should seek to identify those aspects of the job that employees most enjoy performing, those that they dislike, and those for which they lack sufficient time or expertise; the survey should also ascertain any activities or projects that employees would like to do but cannot find time to perform. Since employees may lack background information regarding the assistance that volunteers might lend to them and to the agency, the survey or interview, or alternatively in-service training, should provide resource materials regarding volunteers, such as a listing of the jobs or functions that unpaid staff are already performing in their agency or in similar organizations, new initiatives undertaken by volunteers beyond the time or expertise of paid staff, and skills and descriptions of available volunteers (compare McCurley and Lynch, 1996, pp. 25–26; McCurley and Lynch, 1989, pp. 27–28).

Popular stereotypes to the contrary, not all volunteer positions need be in supportive roles to employee endeavors. In some Maryland counties, for instance, paid staff have facilitated and supported the activities of volunteers in delivering recreation services, rather than the reverse (Marando, 1986). In the Court Appointed Special Advocates (CASA) and Big Brothers and Big Sisters programs, paid staff also facilitate and support the core work performed by volunteers. Many organizations rely on donated labor for highly technical, professional tasks, such as accounting, economic development, and computer applications, not provided by employees and which they otherwise could not afford or obtain. For example, organized into 364 chapters across the United States, the 12,400 volunteers of the Service Corps of Retired Executives (2009) provide business advice and counseling to the clients of the Small Business Administration well beyond the means and paid personnel of the SBA. Most important is that the delegation of tasks takes into account the unique capabilities that paid staff and volunteers might bring toward meeting organization needs.

To allocate work responsibilities among employees and volunteers, Susan J. Ellis (1996) suggests that an agency reassess the job descriptions of the entire staff, paid and unpaid. Prime candidates for delegation to volunteers are tasks with the following characteristics:

- Those that might be performed periodically, such as once a week, rather than on a daily or inflexible basis
- Those that do not require the specialized training or expertise of paid personnel
- Those that might be done more effectively by someone with specialized training in that skill
- Those for which the position occupant feels uncomfortable or unprepared
- Those for which the agency possesses no in-house expertise
- Those which might be performed "episodically," that is, on an occasional basis using very short time intervals
- Those which might be performed "virtually" or through computer technology such as e-mail or the Internet

The culmination of the task analysis should be a new set of job descriptions for employees and a second set for volunteers that are sensitive to prevailing organization conditions. Paid staff are primarily assigned to the most important, daily functions whereas volunteers handle work that can be done on a periodic basis or that makes use of the special talents for which the volunteers have been recruited (Ellis, 1996). The intent is to achieve the most effective deployment of both paid and nonpaid personnel. The respective tasks should be codified in formal job descriptions not only for paid but also nonpaid workers, with the stipulation that neither group will occupy the positions reserved for the other.

A pioneer in the field, Harriet H. Naylor (1973), insisted, "Most of the universally recognized principles of administration for employed personnel are even more valid for volunteer workers, who *give* their talents and time" (p. 173, emphasis in original). Her insight into the parallels between the administration of paid staff and volunteers is especially pertinent with respect to job specifications, placement, and orientation. Studies undertaken by the International City/County Management Association on volunteer programs in local governments indicate that "Volunteer job descriptions are really no different than job descriptions for paid personnel. A volunteer will need the same information a paid employee would need to determine whether the position is of interest" (Manchester and Bogart, 1988, p. 59). Specifications for volunteer positions should include (McCurley and Lynch, 1996, p. 30)

- Job title and purpose
- Benefits to the occupant
- Qualifications for the position
- Time requirement (for example, hours per week)

- Proposed starting date (and ending date, if applicable)
- Job responsibilities and activities
- Authority invested in the position
- Reporting relationships and supervision
- Evaluation
- Probationary period (if necessary)

The parallels to paid administration noted by Naylor (1973) and others continue beyond the job description to other key functions of the volunteer program. Applicants for volunteer positions should be *screened* for relevant competencies and interests, as well as pertinent background and qualifications. Especially for positions that call for contact with vulnerable populations such as youth and the infirm, reference or background checks should be conducted for volunteers (see Chapter Twenty-three for further discussion on this and related risk management matters). Volunteers should be *interviewed* by officials from the volunteer program, the agency, or both to ensure a suitable fit of citizen and organizational needs. These new members will require an *orientation* to the agency and its volunteer component. Among the topics that orientation activities should address are the overall mission and specific objectives of the organization, its traditions and philosophy, its operating rules and procedures, the rationale and policies of the volunteer program, and the roles and interface of paid and nonpaid staff members. Finally, as needed, *training* should be provided to volunteers to assume the organizational tasks assigned to them.

Emerging Jobs for Volunteers: Virtual Volunteering and Episodic Volunteering

As mentioned briefly above in the listing of organizational tasks that might be delegated to volunteers, virtual volunteering and episodic volunteering are emerging forms. Virtual volunteering refers to volunteering "at a distance" through electronic technology, including the Internet or e-mail (Murray and Harrison, 2002a, 2002b, 2005). In the 1999 edition of the Independent Sector survey of *Giving and Volunteering in the United States,* just 1 percent of respondents had learned about volunteering via the Internet, a finding that prompted the authors to conclude, "Few charities are maximizing the possibilities of the Internet to stimulate giving and volunteering" (Kirsch, Hume, and Jalandoni, 2000, p. 16). By the time of the 2001 *Giving and Volunteering* survey, however, 3.3 percent of a national sample of U.S. volunteers reported that they had learned about a volunteering opportunity via an Internet posting or responded to a solicitation over the Internet (Toppe, Kirsch, and Michel, 2002, p. 41). Also in the 2001 survey, among volunteers with Internet access, about 13 percent reported that they had used the Internet to search for or learn about volunteer opportunities. About 4 percent of volunteers with Internet access reported that they had volunteered over the Internet over the past year, performing such activities as mentoring, tutoring, or Web site development (Toppe, Kirsch, and Michel, 2002, p. 41). The USA Freedom Corps, an umbrella organization for coordination of volunteer programs in the U.S. federal government, relies on the nonprofit, online virtual volunteer service "VolunteerMatch" (www.volunteermatch.org) for much of its initial recruitment and information gathering. VolunteerMatch (2009) claims to have helped more than 70,500 participating nonprofit organizations and made 4.3 million volunteer referrals since 1998.

A study of virtual volunteering in Canada conducted by Vic Murray and Yvonne Harrison (2002a, 2002b) in 2001–02 yields similar findings. Murray and Harrison found that only about 4 percent of a sample of 1,747 potential volunteers who had used the online "Volunteer Opportunities Exchange" said that they had done any virtual volunteering in the past year. Of the 494 managers of volunteer resources surveyed across Canada as part of the study, only one-third reported having any openings for virtual volunteering, and over 70 percent of them reported making fewer than five such placements in the previous year. The study showed that the top three types of virtual volunteer assignments reported by mangers of volunteer resources were desktop publishing, Web site development and maintenance, and research. Despite the limited use of virtual volunteering found in their study, Murray and Harrison (2002a, p. 9) conclude, "Even though the demand for virtual volunteers may not be large at present, it is likely to grow in the future."

Murray and Harrison (2005, 2002a) attribute the relatively low incidence of virtual volunteering in Canada in 2001–2002 not to a lack of potential volunteers or "supply" but to a lack of organizational readiness or "demand." They speculate that the lack of demand could emanate from several sources, including a lack of organizational capacity (funds, skills) for developing virtual volunteering positions and recruitment and management systems, negative or uniformed attitudes toward electronic technology, a genuine shortage of volunteer work that lends itself to virtual volunteering, and even fear that the electronic technology may put charitable and nonprofit organizations at risk as consequence of anti-terrorism legislation (Murray and Harrison, 2005, p. 45). Murray and Harrison observe that this form of volunteering may require a review of all current volunteer (and possibly paid staff) positions to determine whether organizational work could be reengineered to become virtual rather than on-site (advice parallel to the discussion above regarding the possible reallocation of job tasks among paid staff and volunteers to achieve an efficient result). In addition, other major organizational changes to accommodate virtual volunteers are likely to prove necessary that could occasion reluctance, if not outright resistance. Once virtual volunteer jobs have been identified, defined, and posted, for example, training, supervision, recognition, and communication systems will probably need to be redesigned to support the new type of volunteer involvement.

Although the nature of virtual volunteering appears to be well understood, no universally accepted definition of episodic volunteering exists. Nancy Macduff (1995) characterizes episodic volunteers as those who give service that is short in duration (temporary) or at regular intervals for short periods of time (occasional). "A rule of thumb is that the episodic volunteer is never around longer than six months" (Macduff, 1995, p. 188). Michele A. Weber (2002, pp. 1–2) defines episodic volunteers as those who contribute their time sporadically, only during special times of the year, or consider it a one-time event. These volunteers give time without an ongoing commitment, often in the form of self-contained and time-specific projects. Weber (2002, p. 2) contrasts these volunteers with "periodic" volunteers, who give time at scheduled, recurring intervals, such as daily, weekly, or monthly. Macduff (1995, pp. 55–57) relates the growth in episodic engagement to the advent of "reflexive volunteering," in which citizens decide for themselves where, when, and how much to volunteer in creating their own "life biography." Formerly, "collective" forms of volunteering dominated, which were mediated much more strongly by organizational needs, demands, and mores.

The trend data made available by the Independent Sector Organization in its biennial national surveys illustrate the scope of episodic volunteering in the United States (Kirsch, Hume, and Jalandoni, 2000, p. 21). Over the period 1987 through 1998, reported rates of volunteering among the American public generally increased, with some perturbations. Yet the total number of hours contributed annually remained fairly constant (within the range of 19.5 to 20.5 billion) so that the average number of hours donated by volunteers on a weekly basis steadily diminished over the decade. The decline is substantial, a 25 percent decrease from an average of 4.7 hours contributed per week and 244.4 hours per year in 1987 to 3.5 hours weekly and 182.0 hours annually in 1998. Points of Light Institute CEO Michele Nunn (2000, p. 117) speculates, "This could be the result of broader participation levels of individuals who did not regularly volunteer," that is, episodic volunteers.

Given the vagaries of definition, estimates of the extent of episodic volunteering are not precise—although, as suggested by the comparative data, unquestionably substantial. According to the 1999 Independent Sector Organization survey, which assessed giving and volunteering behavior retrospectively for 1998, 39 percent of volunteers preferred to volunteer at a regularly scheduled time, weekly, biweekly, or monthly (Kirsch, Hume, and Jalandoni, 2000, p. 5).

By contrast, "For 41 percent of volunteers, serving is a sporadic, one-time activity;" another 9 percent reported volunteering only at special times of the year such as holidays or festivals. If Weber's (2002) distinction between periodic and episodic volunteering is accepted, 69 percent of volunteers could be classified as "periodic" in 2001, meaning that they volunteered at scheduled times recurring at regular intervals (for example, daily, weekly, monthly). The other 31 percent were "episodic volunteers" who contributed their time sporadically, during special times of the year, or regarded it as a one-time activity (Toppe, Kirsch, and Michel, 2002). With regard to the preference among potential volunteers for shorter-term, episodic engagements, Steve McCurley and Susan J. Ellis (2003b, p. 1) insist, "You can find similar data in Canada, Australia, the United Kingdom, and practically every other country that's done even a causal survey of volunteer attitudes."

McCurley and Ellis (2003b) argue that given the rising trend in short-term, episodic volunteering, the field is in danger of "using the wrong model" to design volunteer jobs, manage and supervise volunteer involvement, and integrate these vital human resources into host organizations. In light of changing volunteer attitudes, preferences, demographics, and availability, the traditional "volunteer as unpaid staff" model that conceived volunteers as holding long-term, continuous jobs albeit for many fewer hours than paid staff, may well be in need of refinement for large numbers of potential volunteers (Brudney and Meijs, 2009). Host organizations that wish to attract episodic volunteers must overcome several barriers, such as possibly antagonistic attitudes of long-term volunteers and paid staff regarding the value of episodic volunteering, agency preferences for continuous service, general resistance to change, and legal liabilities (Macduff, 1995, pp. 189–191).

To start or accommodate an episodic volunteer program, volunteer jobs will need to be shorter in duration; have a clearer, more limited focus; avoid those areas in which legal liability could be an issue (for example, direct contact with vulnerable populations); and have less intensive administrative procedures such as the extent of screening, interviewing, and training required for the job. An organization need not choose between having an episodic volunteer program and a more traditional one based on long-term volunteer involvement: the programs can exist side-by-side. In fact, Macduff (1995, p. 201) believes that "Supervision of short-term volunteers can be done quite effectively by long-term volunteers," a factor which would carry benefits for both parties as well as for the organization as a whole. I discuss the benefits of having such "career ladders" for volunteers for purposes of retention in the section that follows.

Virtual volunteering and episodic volunteering increase the demands on agencies and their directors of volunteer services to design positions strategically to integrate new forms of productive labor and to make attendant changes in the workplace—as well as to overcome the organizational and personal hurdles and obstacles likely to result. In a volunteer world in which traditional sources of recruitment are lagging, competition for recruits is keen, new forms of participation are gaining popularity, and agency workloads are expanding, organizational investment in these emerging forms of volunteering may well be worth the effort. In light of such trends, Brudney and Meijs (2009) conceive of volunteer energy as a natural resource that must be sustained through creative involvement by host organizations.

Meeting the Needs of Volunteers

To this point, the analysis has focused primarily on the demands of nonprofit and public organizations for attracting, structuring, and managing volunteer labor. Agency needs constitute only half of the equation for a successful volunteer program, however. The other half consists of meeting the needs of volunteers. An effective volunteer program marries organizational demands for productive labor with the disparate motivations that volunteers bring for contributing their time.

The theme of voluntary action gives to the study of nonprofit institutions much of its characteristic identity. Most nonprofit organizations are vitally dependent on volunteers to carry out missions and reach objectives. Accordingly, voluminous research has been concerned, directly or indirectly, with the motivations that spur volunteers. A basic conclusion emanating from this research is that these motivations are complex and multifaceted, and that they may serve a variety of functions for the individual volunteer, including values, understanding, career, social, esteem, and protective dimensions (Clary, Snyder, and Stukas, 1996; Clary, Snyder, and Ridge, 1992). As Clary and his colleagues point out, an understanding of volunteer motivations and the functions that they perform for individuals will assist nonprofit and government organizations in recruiting and retaining volunteers—as well as lead to more satisfying experiences for these citizen participants (Clary, Snyder, and Stukas, 1996, pp. 502–503).

Although the reasons for volunteering are rich and diverse, several large, national surveys extending for more than a quarter of a century reveal a markedly consistent (and interpretable) pattern of professed motivations. Table 26.1 displays the reasons for involvement in volunteer work expressed most often by representative samples of Americans over time in seven surveys, the earliest taken in 1965 and the latest in 1991. Other, more recent surveys of volunteers' professed motivations have been conducted, however, they are based on different items. The survey results summarized in Table 26.1 offer the most comprehensive and

TABLE 26.1. MOTIVATION FOR INVOLVEMENT IN VOLUNTEER WORK BY YEAR, 1965–1991 (IN PERCENTAGES)

Motivation	1965[a]	1974	1981	1985	1987	1989	1991
Help people	38	53	45	52	-	-	70
Do something useful	–	–	–	–	56	62	61
Enjoy doing volunteer work	31	36	29	32	35	34	39
Interest in activity or work	–	–	35	36	–	–	–
Sense of duty	33	32	–	–	–	–	–
Religious concerns	–	–	21	27	22	26	31
Could not refuse request	7	15	–	–	–	–	–
Friend or relative received service[b]	–	22	23	26	27	29	29
Volunteer received service	–	–	–	–	10	9	17
Learning experience[c]	–	3	11	10	9	8	16
Nothing else to do, free time	–	4	6	10	9	10	8
Thought work would keep taxes down	–	–	5	3	–	–	–

Note: The percentages do not sum to 100 because respondents were permitted multiple responses. A dash indicates that this option was not presented to respondents (not that 0.0 percent gave this response) In the 1965 and 1974 surveys, volunteers were asked about the reason for doing their first "nonreligious" volunteer work. In the 1981, 1985, 1987, 1989, and 1991 surveys, the motivations also pertain to "informal" volunteer work, that is, work that does not involve a private-sector association or formal organization.

[a]In the 1965 survey, the question of motivations for volunteering was presented to respondents as open-ended. The responses were coded into the categories shown in the table. In the other surveys, the respondents were presented with a listing of possible motivations for volunteering and were asked which were motivations for them (see Department of Labor, 1969, p. 9).

[b]In 1974, this category referred exclusively to respondents' children; in 1989, this category stated that a family member or friend would benefit.

[c]In the 1974 survey, this category referred to the idea that volunteer work can lead to a paid job.

Sources: The data are adapted from U.S. Department of Labor (1969); ACTION (1974); Gallup Organization (1981); and Hodgkinson and Weitzman (1986, 1988, 1990, 1992).

consistent set of items available regarding volunteer motivation. The length of the series reinforces the reliability of the responses.

According to the data presented in Table 26.1, the most common stimulus for volunteering is to "do something useful to help others" (or to "help people"), manifested by nearly a majority and often substantially more of the respondents in each survey. In addition, approximately one in four people mention "religious concerns." About 10 percent of volunteers, rising to 17 percent in 1991, state as a motivation that they had previously benefited from the activity; perhaps their volunteer work is motivated by a desire to "give something back" for the services or attention they had earlier received. Even allowing for the possibility of some socially desirable responses, the attention that such altruistic motivations seems to command is impressive. Although such professed altruistic motivations appear to drive a great amount of volunteering, more instrumental motivations are common as well. For example, in the survey findings summarized in Table 26.1, approximately 30 to 40 percent of the volunteers gave as reasons that they "enjoy doing volunteer work," or that they "had an interest in the activity or work." A substantial number of volunteers (22 percent to 29 percent), too, said that they have a friend or relative either involved in the activity in which they volunteer, or who would benefit from it.

In the surveys conducted in the 1980s, another 8 to 11 percent of respondents identified volunteering as a "learning experience" (16 percent in the 1991 survey). The educational or training benefits afforded by this opportunity are especially important to individuals who seek entry or reentry into the job market but lack requisite competencies or experience. According to one volunteer coordinator and consultant, "*Any* marketable skills can be strengthened and brought up to date in a well-structured volunteer setting" (O'Donald, 1989, p. 22; emphasis in original).

The data in Table 26.1 suggest that many people seem to hold both other-directed and self-directed motivations for volunteering simultaneously. In order to capture some of the richness of these motivations, the national surveys allowed multiple responses, and, indeed, in each survey the cumulative percentages surpass 100.0 percent. Volunteering, thus, appears to spring from a mixture of altruistic and instrumental motivations. Volunteers can—and most likely do—pursue both types of rewards simultaneously: one can certainly help others, derive strong interest and satisfaction in the work, learn and grow from the experience, and enjoy the company of friends and coworkers in the process. These rewards emanate from the quality and meaning of the volunteer experience. As Jon Van Til (1988, pp. 1–9) observes, volunteering is helping behavior deemed beneficial by participants, even though this action "may contribute to individual goals of career exploration and development, sociability, and other forms of personal enhancement." Thus, volunteering is "pro-social" rather than self-sacrificial, that is, activity intended to benefit others but not restricting possible benefits to the volunteers as well.

It is also worth noting in Table 26.1 what the volunteering impulse is not: very few citizens apparently engage in this activity with the motivation to spare organizational funds or the conviction that their "work would keep taxes down." Only 3 to 5 percent of volunteers profess these motivations. Although organizational pleas to "save money" with volunteers may be compelling to agency leaders, they apparently resonate with few volunteers.

How might these motivations evolve as individuals join organizations and engage in volunteer work? Strong altruistic or service motivations could reasonably lead individuals to seek productive outlets for donating their time.

As might be expected, however, once they have begun to assist an organization, the immediate rewards of the work experience—such as the social aspects of volunteering and the characteristics of the job they are asked to perform—tend to rise in salience.

For example, based on a study of diverse work settings, Pearce (1983) discovered that volunteers stated that they joined the organization for predominantly service reasons, but that friendships and social interaction became more influential in their decision to remain with it. Although the long-range rewards of helping others, supporting organizational goals, and making a contribution decreased in importance to them (albeit the scores remained at high levels), the rewards of meeting people and enjoying the company of friends and coworkers increased. Similarly, in a study of volunteers to local government, the importance attached by participants to doing something useful or benefiting a family member or friend diminished over time, but interest in or enjoyment of the work grew as a motivation (Sundeen, 1989).

Pearce concludes (1983, p. 148), "The rewards individuals expected from volunteering are often not the rewards most salient to them once they have become volunteers." If not anticipated and addressed, this shift in the expected rewards from the experience can result in rapid and ruinous turnover of volunteers. The volunteer program must be designed to counteract this possibility; fortunately, many options are open.

To reinforce volunteers' initial emphasis on service motivations, they might be placed in positions where they can contribute directly to organizational goals, for example, through contact with clients or participation in policy activities. Additionally, agencies should offer entry-level advisement and careful placement to assist volunteers in reaching their personal goals and attempt to foster a work environment conducive to their efforts. Training programs and orientation sessions should present an accurate picture of the rewards of volunteering, so that citizens—and the organizations they serve—do not fall prey to unrealistic expectations of the experience.

Agencies also need to respond to changes in the motivations of volunteers. While an organization may have a standard set of activities designed to recruit volunteers, retaining them is a dynamic process of reviewing performance, growth, and aspirations with the volunteer and modifying work assignments accordingly (McCurley and Lynch, 2005). In addition to the methods discussed above, to motivate the continued involvement of volunteers, organizations may offer a variety of inducements depending upon individual circumstances. These include a series of steps toward greater responsibilities (volunteer career ladders), participation in problem solving and decision making, opportunities for ongoing training, supportive feedback and evaluation, and letters of recommendation documenting work performed and competencies gained. I discuss volunteer recruitment and retention in more depth in the following section.

Recruiting and Retaining Volunteers

McCurley (2005, pp. 595–596) distinguishes three types of volunteer recruitment efforts for nonprofit and public organizations: concentric circles recruitment, warm-body recruitment, and targeted recruitment. Concentric circles recruitment is the most subtle and the most endemic, by some estimates practiced by as many as 94 percent of agencies (p. 596). It is intended to provide host organizations with a small but steady flow of volunteers; "turning up the heat" can yield more.

Underlying concentric circles recruitment is stakeholder interaction with the organization. An agency maintains daily contact with a variety of constituent populations or stakeholders, such as clients and their families, volunteers and their friends, staff members, people in the surrounding community, suppliers, vendors, and others. The stakeholders are aware of the existence of the agency, and many have experience with it either directly or indirectly (for example, through a relative or coworker). Their familiarity makes them more receptive to the agency than those who do not know the organization and its work, thus facilitating volunteer recruitment. In addition, this form of recruitment "makes use of the personal appeal factor by having individuals who already know the potential volunteer convey the recruitment message, thus piggybacking on their individual credibility" (p. 596). Volunteer recruitment proceeds in concentric circles, with the agency reaching out first to its stakeholders, who then carry the recruitment message to their networks, and so forth.

The other forms of volunteer recruitment identified by McCurley (2005) are more overt. "The warm-body recruitment campaign is used when the agency needs a relatively large supply of volunteers for tasks that can be easily taught to most people in a short period of time" (p. 595). Jobs of this nature might include staffing an event, such as a clean-up campaign, a fundraising gathering, or an awards luncheon or dinner; various "thons" (bike-a-thons, walk-a-thons, and so on) also use this technique to recruit volunteers. Although detailed job descriptions are not generally necessary for warm-body recruitment, screening, orientation, and training as necessary should be provided.

The final method of attracting volunteers is targeted recruitment, which "operates in exactly the opposite fashion as the warm-body campaign" (McCurley, 2005, p. 595). Whereas warm-body recruitment seeks large numbers of volunteers with undifferentiated talents and expertise, targeted recruitment is designed to attract fewer, select volunteers for jobs that require particular skills or interests or are appropriate for specific age or cultural groups (p. 596). According to McCurley (2005, p. 595), three questions guide the targeted recruitment campaign:

1. What skills or aptitudes are needed to perform the job? This aspect considers the characteristics of the persons sought for the job.
2. Where and how can the organization find people with the requisite skills and interests? This aspect considers connections to these people, including work settings, educational attainment, leisure organizations and activities, relevant publications, and areas of the community.
3. What motivations might appeal to the persons sought? This aspect considers the psychological and other needs to be met through the job.

The intent of shaping and limiting the recruitment message and information dissemination process is to generate a small but sufficient number of suitable volunteer applicants.

Brudney (2003, p. 290) has elaborated the various strategies organizations can use to attract volunteers. The first set pertains to the volunteer motivations of volunteers. Job design strategies concentrate on meeting the needs and motivations of volunteers for interesting and meaningful work, including opportunities for advancement. Closely related, human capital strategies enable participants to raise their market value for paid employment through acquiring contacts, training, and references in the volunteer environment. Ceremonial strategies allow volunteers to join groups and organizations that are important to them, work with like-minded individuals, meet policymakers and other dignitaries, and receive public recognition for service. Similarly, policy strategies, such as service on boards of directors, organizational commissions, task forces, and panels, afford volunteers the opportunity to participate actively in organizational governance.

The second set of strategies focus on making the volunteer job and setting more attractive to volunteers. Organizational change and development strategies center on building an agency culture receptive to volunteers. This relationship begins at the outset of volunteer contact with the agency; research suggests that host organizations do not routinely attend to welcoming, or even informing, volunteers very well (Hobson and Malec, 1999). Facilitation strategies aim to make volunteer opportunities more readily available through such means as extending hours to volunteer beyond traditional (agency) work hours, reimbursing volunteers' out-of-pocket expenses, and providing child care as needed. Similarly, flexibility strategies broaden the nature of volunteer work to make it more convenient, and often enjoyable, to the volunteer. Examples include jobs that can be performed outside the agency (for example, at home or in the automobile), or by groups of people the volunteer knows and values (for example, the family, religious congregation, work unit, or organization), or by electronic means, such as the Internet. Finally, outreach strategies encompass publicizing the agency volunteer program both more widely and strategically to stakeholders (see above), to other groups and organizations (workplace, school, religious institutions, neighborhood groups, civic and other associations, and so on), and to electronic media.

The strategies to attract volunteers are, fortunately, rich and varied. However, the competition among nonprofit, government, and even for-profit organizations for them is intense (Brudney, 2003), and the rate of volunteering in the United States has not increased but remained relatively stable between 26 and 28 percent over the period 2002–2008 (Bureau of Labor Statistics, 2009). Paradoxically, some evidence suggests that organizations are succeeding in the "recruitment wars." The Corporation for National and Community Service (2007) (CNCS) reports that between 2005 and 2006 fully one-third of U.S. volunteers did not continue volunteering. Since the volunteer rate has been steady, organizations seem to be replenishing the stock of lost volunteers.

Retention, though, is another matter. Confronted with the attrition in volunteering in the U.S. study, former CNCS Chief Executive Officer David Eisner warned, "This report is a wakeup call for any group that uses volunteers: If you want to keep them, you need to give them serious and meaningful work that affects change in your community; and you have to remember to train, manage, and thank them the way you would any valued colleague" (CNCS, 2007, p. 1). Far less is known—and published—about retaining volunteers than recruiting them (Brudney and Meijs, 2009).

Based on a nationally representative sample of charities, Hager and Brudney (2008) found that retaining volunteers is associated with organizations adopting recommended practices for managing volunteers, especially offering recognition activities for volunteers, training and professional development opportunities for them, and screening procedures to identify suitable volunteers and to match them with appropriate jobs or tasks in the agency. "These volunteer management practices all center on making the experience worthwhile for the volunteer" (Hager and Brudney, 2008, p. 20). Adoption of the volunteer management practices was not widespread among the charities, however: less than half of them reported that they had eight of nine recommended volunteer management practices in place "to a large degree" (see, for example, Urban Institute, 2004). Hager and Brudney (2008) report other steps that charities can take to increase volunteer retention and their "volunteer management capacity," including creating a culture that is welcoming to volunteers, allocating sufficient resources to support them, providing a worthwhile and productive volunteer experience that citizens will want to repeat and share, and enlisting volunteers in recruiting other volunteers.

In *Keeping Volunteers,* Steve McCurley and Rick Lynch (2005) corroborate these findings. They also provide many more guidelines for retaining volunteers. They recommend, for example, seeing to the motivational needs of volunteers (see above), letting volunteers do the work they want to do consistent with organizational needs, thanking volunteers, making sure that volunteers feel connected to the organization and are invested in its mission, setting high standards for volunteers, listening carefully to volunteers and providing feedback especially concerning accomplishments and goal achievement, instilling organizational values, detecting and ameliorating volunteer burnout, encouraging incremental commitment for short-term volunteers, and developing career ladders for volunteers to offer them new and expanded opportunities.

Organizations tend to use a common set of methods and approaches for attracting new volunteers focusing on concentric circles recruitment, warm-body recruitment, and targeted recruitment (McCurley, 2005). They rely on recruitment strategies that appeal to the motivations of volunteers or that make the job or organizational setting more attractive to them (Brudney, 2003). Recruitment focuses on the pool of prospective volunteers as a whole, rather than particular volunteers. Many of the techniques for retaining volunteers are geared or oriented to the individual volunteer, with the goal of attending to her or his specific needs for ongoing stimulation, fulfillment, and engagement which will likely change over time with the volunteer experience. It is little wonder then that host organizations encounter difficulties in retaining volunteers.

Managing Volunteers

Managing volunteers is different than managing employees. Volunteers are much less dependent on the organization to which they donate their time than are paid staff members, who must earn their livelihood from it. Volunteers can usually leave the organization and find comparable opportunities for their labor with far less effort and inconvenience than can employees. As a result, nonprofit managers and supervisors do not have as much control over volunteer workers.

These differences in control help explain some oft-noted characteristics of volunteers in the workplace. Volunteers can afford to be more selective in accepting job assignments. They may insist on substantial flexibility in work hours. They may not be as faithful in observance of agency rules and regulations, particularly those they regard as burdensome or "red tape." Part of the reason may stem from the fact that nearly all who volunteer do so on a part-time basis and, thus, can be expected to have less information about organizational policy and procedures. Too, many consider these aspects of the job and agency as inimical to the spirit and practice of help freely given, and choose to evade or even ignore them. Social interaction is part of the fun and spark of volunteering, and participants may place high value on this feature of the experience (see above).

Given the relative autonomy of volunteers, a heavy-handed approach to supervision can be expected to elicit antagonism and turnover rather than productivity and compliance. Standard organizational inducements for paid employees, such as pay, promotion, and perquisites, are not operative for volunteers. Conventional organizational sanctions are likely to prove unavailing. For example, referring a problem to hierarchical superiors for resolution or disciplinary action (or threatening to do so) is far less apt to sway volunteers than employees.

These considerations may leave the impression that volunteers cannot be "managed," but that conclusion is unfounded. In reviewing certain "myths" (as he calls them) that people sometimes have about volunteers, Brudney (2003, pp. 291–292) debunks this notion, as well as the equally popular view that volunteers cannot be terminated or "fired." He prescribes a reasonable course for the manager to take should a serious problem arise and persist with a volunteer: ascertain the facts of the situation, be firm in explaining both the problem and the consequences of further violation, and follow through according to agency policy if the problem continues. Eminent management authority Peter F. Drucker (1990, p. 183) agrees that in cases of egregious misconduct, volunteers "must be asked to leave." Countenancing the transgression sends the wrong message to employees, other volunteers, and agency clients that staff (nonpaid or paid) are free from organizational direction and oversight.

The message for management is decidedly more positive: the foundation for effective management of volunteers rests on applying different techniques and incentives than commonly used for paid employees to motivate and direct work behaviors toward agency goals. Managerial investment in building trust, cooperation, teamwork, challenge, growth, achievement, values, excitement, and commitment are much more effectual strategies for this purpose than are the conventional methods. In their highly influential study *In Search of Excellence*, Thomas J. Peters and Richard H. Waterman (1982) maintain that "America's best-run companies" use the same approach for paid employees—with enviable results. Although a common admonition in this literature is to manage volunteers as if they were employees (for example, Stoolmacher, 1991), this research suggests that it is equally persuasive to recommend "managing employees as if they were volunteers" (Smith and Green, 1993).

Based on a careful examination of a volunteer program servicing a large, urban public library system, Virginia Walter (1987, p. 31) found that administrators who embraced this style of "management-by-partnership" enjoyed greater success in dealing with volunteers and meeting objectives than did those officials intent on control. In a major study of the volunteer SCORE program (Service Corps of Retired Executives) sponsored by the U.S. Small Business Administration (SBA), Brudney (1990, pp. 112–114) arrives at a similar conclusion. The volunteer business counselors who assisted the SBA sometimes fit the stereotypes attributed to volunteer workers. For example, they displayed low tolerance for necessary government paperwork and "bureaucracy," uneven knowledge of SBA rules and procedures, and keen interest in deciding what cases they would accept (or reject) for counseling. Yet SBA staff rated the performance of the volunteers as comparable to their own on signal dimensions, including quality and timeliness of services to clients, and dependability in work commitments. Like Walter (1987), Brudney (1990) attributes these beneficial results to the partnership approach to managing the volunteer program practiced by the SBA and SCORE.

A successful volunteer program must do more than advance changes in managerial style. It must also institute a framework or infrastructure to facilitate successful volunteer integration and involvement in the organization. To channel volunteer talents and energies productively, agencies must elucidate the behaviors expected from unpaid staff. Probably no factor aids more in supervising volunteers (and paid staff) than placing them in positions where they can put their strongest motivations and best skills to work. The procedures discussed earlier in this chapter offer a viable means to elaborate and promote mutual understanding of the volunteer-agency relationship. Developing a coherent philosophy for volunteer involvement, preparing guidelines for the volunteer program, creating formal positions for volunteers, preparing the relevant job descriptions, interviewing and screening applicants and placing them in mutually satisfactory work assignments, and presenting orientation and training are potent means to define what volunteer service means to the agency and to citizens, and to coordinate the needs and motives of both parties. Jean Baldwin Grossman and Kathryn Furano (2002, p. 15) similarly identify three elements as "vitally important to the success of any volunteer program": screening potential volunteers to ensure appropriate entry and placement in the organization; orientation and training to provide volunteers with the skills and outlook needed; and management and ongoing support of volunteers by paid staff to ensure that volunteer time is not wasted but used as productively as possible.

Effective management of volunteers, thus, calls for more than changes in managerial style, although these adjustments are certainly important. The volunteer program must also provide an infrastructure to impart a shared conception of volunteer service. Absent such a framework, managerial adaptations in themselves are likely to prove insufficient. As Grossman and Furano (2002, p. 15) aptly summarize, "No matter how well intentioned volunteers are, unless there is an infrastructure in place to support and direct their efforts, they will remain ineffective at best or, worse, become disenchanted and withdraw, potentially damaging recipients of services in the process."

Evaluating and Recognizing the Volunteer Effort

Researchers contend that the evaluation function is carried out less often and less well than the other central elements of a volunteer program (for example, Allen, 1987; Utterback and Heyman, 1984). Survey research undertaken on volunteer programs in government bears out this contention. In a study of 534 cities over 4,500 population that enlisted volunteers in the delivery of services, Sydney Duncombe (1985, p. 363) found that just a handful (62 or 11.6 percent) had made an evaluation study; a study of 189 state agencies reported a comparable rate (13.6 percent) (Brudney and Kellough, 2000, p. 123). Understandably, organizations that rely on the assistance of volunteers may be reluctant to appear to question through evaluation the worth or impact of well-intentioned helping efforts. In addition, officials may be apprehensive about the effects of an evaluation policy on volunteer recruitment and retention, and on public relations. Nevertheless, for individual volunteers and the paid staff who work with them, as well as for the volunteer operation as a whole, evaluation and recognition activities are essential program functions.

Evaluation of Volunteers and Employees

The fears of organizational leadership notwithstanding, volunteers have cogent reasons to view personnel assessment in a favorable light. A powerful motivation for volunteering is to achieve worthwhile and visible results; evaluation of performance can guide volunteers toward improvement on this dimension. No citizen contributes his or her time to have the labor wasted in misdirected activity, or to repeat easily remedied mistakes and misjudgments. That an organization might take one's work so lightly as to allow such inappropriate behavior to continue is an insult to the volunteer and an affront to standards of professional conduct underlying effectiveness on the job. Clients and host organizations suffer the brunt of these lapses. Evaluation of performance, moreover, is actually a form of compliment to the volunteer (Ellis, 1986, pp. 81–82). A sincere effort at appraisal indicates that the work merits review, and that the individual has the capability and will to do a better job. For many who contribute their time, volunteering offers an opportunity to acquire or hone desirable job skills, build an attractive résumé for purposes of paid employment (see above), or both. To deny constructive feedback to those who give their time for organizational purposes, and who could benefit from this knowledge and hope to do so, is a disservice to the volunteer.

Open to nonprofit organizations are an assortment of procedures for carrying out evaluation of volunteer performance. Often the employee to whom the volunteer reports will prepare the appraisal. Or the responsibility may rest with the director of volunteer services or with the personnel department in larger organizations. A combination of these officials might also handle the task. To complement this agency-based perspective, volunteers might evaluate their own accomplishment and experience in the agency, as suggested by some authorities (for example, Manchester and Bogart, 1988; McHenry, 1988). The assessment should tap volunteer satisfaction with important facets of the work assignment, including job duties, schedule, support, training, opportunities for personal growth, and so on. The self-assessment is also a valuable tool to obtain feedback on the management and supervision of volunteers; employees should learn from the process as well. Regardless of the type of evaluation, the goal ought to be to ascertain the degree to which the needs and expectations of the volunteer and the agency are met, so that job assignments can be continued, amended, or redefined as necessary.

Agency officials might recognize and show their appreciation to volunteers through a great variety of activities: award or social events (luncheons, banquets, ceremonies), media attention (newsletters, newspapers), certificates (for tenure or special achievement), expansion of opportunities (for learning, training, management), and, especially, personal expressions of gratitude from employees or clients. A heart-felt ''thank you'' may be all the acknowledgment many volunteers want or need. Others require more formal recognition. The director of volunteer services should make letters of recommendation available to all volunteers who request them. Recognition is a highly variable activity that, optimally, should be tailored to the wants and needs of individual volunteers.

Some agencies choose to recognize volunteers who evince especially strong potential, and who seek paid employment with the agency, by considering them for such positions when available (for example, police auxiliaries). One volunteer administrator refers to this process as a ''try before you buy'' opportunity for paid staff (Thornburg, 1992, p. 20). The advantages offered by this procedure notwithstanding, volunteering should not be seen as a necessary credential or requirement for paid employment with a nonprofit or government organization.

In general, volunteer-based services require the participation of not only volunteers but also paid staff. If organizational officials are committed to having employees and volunteers work as partners, program functions of evaluation and recognition should apply to both members of the team. Though frequently neglected in job analysis, employees expected to work with volunteers should have pertinent responsibilities written into their formal job descriptions. Equally important, performance appraisal for the designated positions must assess requisite skills in volunteer management. Just as demonstrated talent in this domain should be encouraged and rewarded, an employee's resistance to volunteers, or poor work record with them, should not go overlooked and, implicitly, condoned in the review. As necessary, the organization should support training activities for paid staff to develop competencies in volunteer administration.

Similarly, recognition activities for volunteer programs normally focus on citizen participants, rather than on both members of the team. Employees value recognition as well, especially when awards ceremonies, social events, media coverage, agency publications, and the like bring their efforts and accomplishments with volunteers to the attention of organizational leadership. In addition, feedback on employee achievement from volunteers and the director of volunteer services belongs in agency personnel files. By taking seriously the evaluation and recognition of paid staff with regard to their collaboration with volunteers, nonprofit and government officials provide incentives for an effective partnership.

Evaluation of the Volunteer Program

The overriding goal of a volunteer program ought to be to exert a positive effect on the external environment, better the life circumstances of agency clients, or both. Periodically, agencies that mobilize volunteers for such purposes should undergo evaluation of the impact or progress they have registered in ameliorating the conditions or problems identified in their mission statements. Too often, what passes for "evaluation" of the volunteer program is a compilation of the number of volunteers who have assisted the organization, the hours they have contributed, and the amount of client contacts or visits they have made.

A highly recommended but more complicated evaluation procedure is for agencies to calculate the total "equivalent dollar value" of all the jobs or services performed by volunteers, based on the market price for the labor the organization would otherwise have to pay to employed personnel to accomplish the same tasks (for example, Ellis, 1996; Karn, 1982–1983, 1983). Anderson and Zimmerer (2003) demonstrate that estimating the dollar value of volunteer work is open to a variety of options: At least five methods are available, based on the average wage, the average nonagricultural wage rate (as released annually by the U.S. Bureau of Labor Statistics and used by the Independent Sector organization), a "living wage" (based on dollars required to subsist or cost of living aligned with the federal poverty level), comparable worth (equivalent dollar valuation), and minimum wage. Fringe benefits ranging from 10 to 12 percent may also be included in the calculation.

Impressive and significant though these data may be—normally documenting tremendous levels of contributed effort and monetary value across nonprofit and public institutions—they tap the inputs or resources to a volunteer program, rather than its results or accomplishments. Some researchers complain, too, that this approach slights the monetary costs associated with the volunteer program, for example, for paid staff supervision, reimbursement for expenses, training of volunteers, and use of organizational resources and facilities (Quarter, Mook, and Richmond, 2003, p. 46; Utterback and Heyman, 1984, p. 229). To correct for this problem, in his analysis of the Service Corps of Retired Executives (SCORE) volunteer program sponsored by the U.S. Small Business Administration (SBA), Brudney (1990, pp. 40–51) applied a cost-effectiveness model in which both the equivalent dollar value of volunteer services as well as the costs or expenses associated with the volunteer program are taken into account, thus resulting in a cost-effectiveness ratio. Brudney's (1990, p. 48) study documented that for every dollar the SBA invested in support of the SCORE program, the agency garnered volunteer services worth from $1.11 to $1.86. Katharine Gaskin (2003, 1999a, 1999b) similarly proposed a "Volunteer Investment and Value Audit" (VIVA) in which a cost-benefit analysis is performed based on the ratio of the comparative market value of the functions performed by volunteers to the organization's expenditures on volunteers. In an evaluation of volunteer programs cross-nationally, Gaskin (2003, p. 46) reports very high cost-benefit ratios or returns on the investment in volunteers ranging from 1:1.3 to 1:13.5, a finding that indicates that for every British pound invested in volunteers the "return" varied from 1.3 to 13.5 pounds. Nonprofit organizations should consider additional forms of evaluation of the volunteer program. Much as they might be expected to do for any other operational unit, at regular intervals agency officials should assess the outcomes of the volunteer program against its stated goals or mission. Volunteer activity is other-directed; it should do more than gratify citizen participants and accommodate employees. Officials need to review the aggregate performance of the volunteers in assisting clients, addressing community problems, expediting agency operations, and meeting further objectives. Not only does the assessment yield information that can improve functioning of the program, but also it reinforces for all concerned—citizens, paid staff, and agency clients alike—the importance attached by the organization to the volunteer component. Smith and Ellis (2003) propose, conceptually, an ambitious evaluation of volunteer programs to incorporate their contribution to economic capital, physical capital, human capital, social capital, and cultural capital. Although such a methodology has not yet been developed, Smith and Ellis (2003, p. 52) point out that a concentration on the economic impacts of volunteering to the exclusion of impacts in these other areas not only gives "a very partial picture of the total value of volunteering" but also is potentially damaging in that it serves to "reinforce the notion that volunteering is all about saving money." Similarly, economist Eleanor Brown (1999) recommends that we consider the value of the time and service donated to the volunteer as well as to the organization. She points out that standard accounting of volunteer time also overlooks the less tangible benefits of volunteering (for example, training, career development, and so on) and the benefits that may accrue to third parties such as fellow citizens from the time devoted to people and valued causes.

A second type of evaluation, also recommended, pertains to assessing the processes of a volunteer program. Officials should determine that procedures to meet essential program functions discussed in this chapter (such as volunteer screening and placement) are in place, and that they are operating effectively. Additionally, the evaluation should attempt to gauge the satisfaction of volunteers and paid staff members with the program, as well as their perceptions concerning its impact on clients and the external environment. Continuing struggles with, for example, recruiting suitable volunteers, arresting high rates of volunteer burnout and turnover, relieving staff antagonisms, reaching mutually agreeable placements, and so forth, point to flaws in program design that must be addressed. By diagnosing such difficulties, a process evaluation can enhance progress toward achievement of program objectives.

Jack Quarter, Laurie Mook, and Betty Jane Richmond (2003) have extended the evaluation of volunteer programs—as well as the evaluation of the activities of nonprofit organizations and cooperatives—by placing them in the broader context of "social accounting." Quarter, Mook, and Richmond (2003) focus on valuing the contributions of volunteers to the organization and its clients, and the larger social impacts of these organizations, for example, their effects on clients, the community, the environment, and on the volunteers themselves. As these authors note, conventional accounting practices overlook these aspects, even though they are among the most important effects of nonprofit organizations: "Even though volunteers in the United States and Canada contribute the equivalent full-time work of almost 10 million people per year . . . the value of this work, estimated to be over $250 billion, is not recognized in conventional accounting" (Quarter, Mook, and Richmond, 2003, p. 131). Quarter, Mook, and Richmond introduce new types of accounting statements intended to assess the social impacts of nonprofit organizations and volunteers, including the Socioeconomic Impact Statement, the Socioeconomic Resource Statement, the Expanded Value Added Statement, and the Community Social Return on Investment Model.

Summary and Conclusion

According to the *2001 Survey of Giving and Volunteering in the United States* conducted for Independent Sector (Toppe, Kirsch, and Michel, 2002), 44 percent of adults over the age of 21 volunteered with a formal organization in 2000. On average, they volunteered 15 hours in the preceding month. Of these formal volunteers, 69 percent reported they volunteered on a regular basis, monthly or more often. In the month prior to the survey, 27 percent had volunteered, averaging 24 hours of time donated in that month. In all, an estimated 83.9 million adults formally volunteered in 2000, giving approximately 15.5 billion hours. The formal volunteer workforce represented the equivalent of over nine million full-time employees, with an estimated dollar value of $239 billion. Based on a different sample design and methodology, surveys of volunteering conducted annually by the Bureau of Labor Statistics/Current Population Survey beginning in 2002 put the volunteer rate of Americans at 26–28 percent, lower than in the 2001 Independent Sector Survey but still substantial (Bureau of Labor Statistics, 2009).

The key to integrating this staggering volume of talent and energy into nonprofit and government organizations is the volunteer program. Using the information presented in this chapter, a nonprofit leader will be able to implement the central elements that will be essential to a successful organizationally-based volunteer program. The key elements are as follows:

- The program should begin with the establishment of a rationale or policy to guide volunteer involvement.
- Paid staff must have a central role in designing the volunteer program and creating guidelines governing its operation.
- The volunteer program must be integrated structurally into the nonprofit organization.
- The program must have designated leadership positions to provide direction and accountability.
- The agency must prepare job descriptions for the positions to be held by volunteers, as well as see to the related functions of screening, orientation, placement, and training.
- The volunteer program must attend to the motivations that inspire volunteers and attempt to respond to them, with the goal of meeting both these needs and the needs of the organization.
- Volunteers must be attracted and recruited to the organization and retained for service.

- Managing volunteers for best results typically requires adaptations of more traditional hierarchical approaches toward teamwork and collaboration.
- All components of the volunteer effort—citizens, employees, and the program itself—benefit from evaluation and recognition activities.

This list is ambitious, yet well within the reach of most nonprofit and government organizations. So, too, are the advantages to be derived from delivering an effective volunteer program.

References

ACTION. *Americans Volunteer, 1974.* Washington, D.C.: ACTION, 1974.

Allen, N. J. "The Role of Social and Organizational Factors in the Evaluation of Volunteer Programs." *Evaluation and Program Planning*, 1987, *10*(3), 257–262.

Anderson, P. M., and Zimmerer, M. E. "Dollar Value of VolunteeTime: A Review of Five Estimation Methods." *Journal of Volunteer Administration*, 2003, *21* (2), 39–44.

Bureau of Labor Statistics. "Volunteering in the United States, 2008." Available at http://www.bls.gov/news.release/volun.nr0.htm. Retrieved November 2, 2009.

Becker, D. G. "Exit Lady Bountiful: The Volunteer and the Professional Social Worker." *Social Service Review*, 1964, *38* (1), 57–72.

Brown, E. "Assessing the Value of Volunteer Activity." *Nonprofit and Voluntary Sector Quarterly*, 1999, *28*(1), 3–17.

Brown, K. "What Goes Wrong and What Can We Do About It?" *Voluntary Action Leadership*, 1981 (Spring), 22–23.

Brudney, J. L. "The SBA and SCORE: Coproducing Management Assistance Services." *Public Productivity Review*, 1986, no. 40 (Winter), 57–67.

Brudney, J. L. "The Use of Volunteers by Local Governments as an Approach to Fiscal Stress." In T. N. Clark, W. Lyons, and M. R. Fitzgerald (eds.), *Research in Urban Policy, Volume 3*. Greenwich, Conn.: JAI Press, 1989.

Brudney, J. L. *Fostering Volunteer Programs in the Public Sector: Planning, Initiating, and Managing Voluntary Activities*. San Francisco: Jossey-Bass, 1990.

Brudney, J. L. "Administrators of Volunteer Services: Their Needs for Training and Research." *Nonprofit Management and Leadership*, 1992, *2* (Spring), 271–282.

Brudney, J. L. "Preparing the Organization for Volunteers." In T. D. Connors (ed.), *The Volunteer Management Handbook*. New York: Wiley, 1995, 36–60.

Brudney, J. L. "Supplanting Common Myths with Uncommon Management: The Effective Involvement of Volunteers in Delivering Public Services." In S. W. Hays and R. C. Kearney (eds.), *Public Personnel Administration: Problems and Prospects* (4th ed.). Upper Saddle River, N. J.: Prentice Hall, 2002, 287–300.

Brudney, J. L., and Kellough, J. E. "Volunteers in State Government: Involvement, Management, and Benefits." *Nonprofit and Voluntary Sector Quarterly*, 2000, *29*(March), 111–130.

Brudney, J. L., and Meijs, L.C.P.M. "It Ain't Natural: Toward a New (Natural) Resource Conceptualization for Volunteer Management." *Nonprofit and Voluntary Sector Quarterly*, 2009, *38* (August), 564–581.

Brudney, J. L., with Kim, D. *The 2001 Volunteer Center Survey: A Report On Findings And Implications*. Washington, D.C.: Points of Light Foundation, 2003.

Clary, E. G., Snyder, M., and Ridge, R. "Volunteers' Motivations: A Functional Strategy for the Recruitment, Placement, and Retention of Volunteers." *Nonprofit Management and Leadership*, 1992, *2*(4), 333–350.

Clary, E. G., Snyder, M., and Stukas, A. A. "Volunteers' Motivations: Findings from a National Survey." *Nonprofit and Voluntary Sector Quarterly*, 1996, *25*(4), 485–505.

Corporation for National and Community Service. "New Federal Report Shows Volunteering Strong in America, but 1 in 3 Volunteers Dropped Out in 2006." Available at http://www.nationalservice.org/about/newsroom/releases_detail.asp?tbl_pr_id=682. Retrieved Nov. 1, 2007.

Deitch, L. I., and Thompson, L. N. "The Reserve Police Officer: One Alternative to the Need for Manpower." *Police Chief*, 1985, *52*(5), 59–61.

Dorwaldt, A. L., Solomon, L. J., and Worden, J. K. "Why Volunteers Helped to Promote a Community Breast Self-Exam Program." *Journal of Volunteer Administration*, 1988, *6*(4), 23–30.

Drucker, P. F. *Managing the Non-Profit Organization: Practices and Principles*. New York: Harper-Collins, 1990.

Duncombe, S. "Volunteers in City Government: Advantages, Disadvantages and Uses." *National Civic Review*, 1985, *74*(9), 356–364.

Ellis, S. J. *The Volunteer Recruitment Book*. Philadelphia: Energize, 1994.

Ellis, S. J. *From the Top Down: The Executive Role in Volunteer Program Success* (revised ed.). Philadelphia: Energize, 1996.

Ellis, S. J., and Campbell, K. H. *By the People: A History of Americans as Volunteers*. New Century Edition. Philadelphia: Energize, 2005.

Farr, C. A. *Volunteers: Managing Volunteer Personnel in Local Government*. Washington, D.C.: International City Management Association, 1983.

Farmer, S. M., and Fedor, D. B. "Volunteer Participation and Withdrawal: A Psychological Contract Perspective on the Role of Expectations and Organizational Support." *Nonprofit Management and Leadership*, 1999, *9*(4), 349–367.

Fisher, J. C., and Cole, K. M. *Leadership and Management of Volunteer Programs: A Guide for Volunteer Administrators*. San Francisco: Jossey-Bass, 1993.

Gallup, Inc. *Americans Volunteer, 1981*. Princeton, N.J.: Gallup Organization, 1981.

Gaskin, K. "Valuing Volunteers in Europe: A Comparative Study of the Volunteer Investment and Value Audit." *Voluntary Action*, 1999a, *2*(1), 35–49.

Gaskin, K. *VIVA in Europe: A Comparative Study of the Volunteer Investment and Value Audit*. London, UK: Institute for Volunteering Research, 1999b.

Gaskin, K. "VIVA in Europe: A Comparative Study of the Volunteer Investment and Value Audit." *Journal of Volunteer Administration*, 2003, *21*(2), 45–48.

Goetter, W. G. J. "When You Create Ideal Conditions, Your Fledgling Volunteer Program Will Fly." *American School Board Journal*, 1987, *194*(6), 34–37.

Graff, L. L. "Considering the Many Facets of Volunteer/Union Relations." *Voluntary Action Leadership*, 1984 (Summer), 16–20.

Grossman, J. B., and Furano, K. "Making the Most of Volunteers." 2002. Available at Public/Private Ventures, www.ppv.org.

Hager, M. A. and Brudney, J. L. "Management Capacity and Retention of Volunteers." In Matthew Liao-Troth (ed.), *Challenges in Volunteer Management*. Charlotte, N.C.: Information Age Publishing, 2008, 9–28.

Haran, L., Kenney, S., and Vermilion, M. "Contract Volunteer Services: A Model for Successful Partnership." *Leadership*, 1993 (January-March), 28–30.

Herman, M. L., and Jackson, P. M. *No Surprises: Harmonizing Risk and Reward in Volunteer Management*. Washington, D.C.: Nonprofit Risk Management Center, 2001.

Hobson, C., and Malec, K. "Initial Telephone Contact of Prospective Volunteers and Nonprofits: An Operational Definition of Quality and Norms for 500 Agencies." *Journal of Volunteer Administration*, 1999, *17*(4), 21–27.

Hodgkinson, V. A., and Weitzman, M. S. *The Charitable Behavior of Americans: A National Survey*. Washington, D.C.: Independent Sector, 1986.

Hodgkinson, V. A., and Weitzman, M. S. *Giving and Volunteering in the United States: Findings from a National Survey*. Washington, D.C.: Independent Sector, 1988.

Hodgkinson, V. A., and Weitzman, M. S. *Giving and Volunteering in the United States: Findings from a National Survey*. Washington, D.C.: Independent Sector, 1990.

Hodgkinson, V. A., and Weitzman, M. S. *Giving and Volunteering in the United States: Findings from a National Survey*. Washington, D.C.: Independent Sector, 1992.

Hodgkinson, V. A., and Weitzman, M. S. *Giving and Volunteering in the United States: Findings from a National Survey*. Washington, D.C.: Independent Sector, 1996.

Hodgkinson, V. A., Weitzman, M. S., Toppe, C. M., Noga, S. M. *Nonprofit Almanac, 1992–1993: Dimensions of the Independent Sector*. San Francisco: Jossey-Bass, 1992.

Ilsley, P. *Enhancing the Volunteer Experience*. San Francisco: Jossey-Bass, 1990.

Karn, G. N. "Money Talks: A Guide to Establishing the True Dollar Value of Volunteer Time, Part I." *Journal of Volunteer Administration*, 1982–83, *1* (Winter), 1–17.

Karn, G. N. "Money Talks: A Guide to Establishing the True Dollar Value of Volunteer Time, Part II." *Journal of Volunteer Administration*, 1983, *1* (Spring), 1–19.

Kirsch, A. D., Hume, K. M., and Jalandoni, N. T. *Giving and Volunteering in the United States: Findings from a National Survey 1999 Edition*. Washington, D.C.: Independent Sector, 2000.

Liao-Troth, M. A. "Attitude Differences Between Paid Workers and Volunteers." *Nonprofit Management and Leadership*, 2001, *11*(4), 423–442.

Macduff, N. "Episodic Volunteering." In T. D. Connors (ed.), *The Volunteer Management Handbook*. New York: Wiley, 1995, 9–28.

Macduff, N. "Principles of Training for Volunteers and Employees." In R. D. Herman (ed.), *The Jossey-Bass Handbook of Nonprofit Leadership and Management* (2nd ed.). San Francisco: Jossey-Bass, 2005, 703–730.

Manchester, L. D., and Bogart, G. S. *Contracting and Volunteerism in Local Government: A Self-Help Guide*. Washington, D.C.: International City Management Association, 1988.

Marando, V. L. "Local Service Delivery: Volunteers and Recreation Councils." *Journal of Volunteer Administration*, 1986, *4*(4), 16–24.

May, K. M., McLaughlin, R., and Penner, M. "Preventing Low Birth Weight: Marketing and Volunteer Outreach." *Public Health Nursing*, 1991, *8*(2), 97–104.

McHenry, C. A. "Library Volunteers: Recruiting, Motivating, Keeping Them." *School Library Journal*, 1988, *35*(8), 44–47.

McCurley, S. "Keeping the Community Involved: Recruiting and Retaining Volunteers." In R. D. Herman (ed.), *The Jossey-Bass Handbook of Nonprofit Leadership and Management* (2nd ed.). San Francisco: Jossey-Bass, 2005, 587–622.

McCurley, S., and Ellis, S. J. "Is Volunteer Management Superior to Employee Management?" 2003a, *3*(2). Available at http://e-volunteerism.com/.

McCurley, S., and Ellis, S. J. "Thinking the Unthinkable: Are We Using the Wrong Model for Volunteer Work?" 2003b, *3*(1). Available at http://e-volunteerism.com/.

McCurley, S., and Lynch, R. *Essential Volunteer Management*. Downers Grove, Ill.: VMSystems and Heritage Arts Publishing, 1989.

McCurley, S., and Lynch, R. *Keeping Volunteers*. Olympia, Wash.: Fat Cat Publications, 2005.

McCurley, S., and Lynch, R. *Volunteer Management: Mobilizing All the Resources in the Community*. Downers Grove, Ill.: Heritage Arts Publishing, 1996.

Meijs, L. C. P. M., and Brudney, J. L. "Winning Volunteer Scenarios: The Soul of a New Machine." *International Journal of Volunteer Administration*, 2007, *24* (Oct.), 68–79.

Meijs, L. C. P. M., and Hoogstad, E. "New Ways Of Managing Volunteers: Combining Membership Management And Programme Management." *Voluntary Action*, 2001, *3*(3), 41–61.

Moore, N. A. "The Application of Cost-Benefit Analysis to Volunteer Programs." *Volunteer Administration*, 1978, *11*(1), 13–22.

Murray, V., and Harrison, Y. "Virtual Volunteering: Current Status and Future Prospects." 2002a. Available at the Canadian Centre for Philanthropy, www.nonprofitscan.ca.

Murray, V., and Harrison, Y. "Virtual Volunteering in Canada." 2002b. Available at www.nonprofitscan.ca.

Murray, V., and Harrison, Y. "Virtual Volunteering." In J. Brudney (ed.), *Emerging Areas of Volunteering* (2nd ed.). Indianapolis, Ind.: Association for Research on Nonprofit Organizations and Voluntary Action, 2005, 33–50.

National SCORE Office. *This Is SCORE*. Washington, D.C.: National SCORE Office, 1989 (NSO-86002 [4/89]).

Naylor, H. H. *Volunteers Today— Finding, Training and Working with Them*. Dryden, New York: Dryden Associates, 1973.

Naylor, H. H. "Beyond Managing Volunteers." *Journal of Voluntary Action Research*, 1985, *14*(2, 3), 25–30.

New York Times. "An Uncertain Trumpet." Editorial. Sept. 8, 2002.

Nunn, M. "Building the Bridge from Episodic Volunteerism to Social Capital." *Fletcher Forum of World Affairs*, 2000, *24*(2), 115–127

O'Donald, E. "Re-Entry Through Volunteering: The Best Jobs that Money Can't Buy." *Voluntary Action Leadership*, 1989 (Fall), 22–27.

Park, J. M. *Meaning Well Is not Enough: Perspectives on Volunteering*. South Plainfield, N.J.: Groupwork Today, 1983.

Pearce, J. L. "Something for Nothing: An Empirical Examination of the Structures and Norms of Volunteer Organizations." Doctoral dissertation, Yale University, 1978.

Pearce, J. L. "Participation in Voluntary Associations: How Membership in a Formal Organization Changes the Rewards of Participation." In D. H. Smith and J. Van Til (eds.), *International Perspectives on Voluntary Action Research*. Washington, D.C.: University Press of America, 1983.

Peters, T. J., and Waterman, R. H. Jr. *In Search of Excellence: Lessons from America's Best-Run Companies*. New York: Warner Books, 1982.

Quarter, J., Mook, L., and Richmond, B. J. *What Counts: Social Accounting for Nonprofits and Cooperatives*. Upper Saddle River, N.J.: Prentice Hall, 2003.

Scheier, I. H. "Positive Staff Attitude Can Ease Volunteer Recruiting Pinch." *Hospitals*, 1981, *55*(3), 61–63.

Scheier, I. H. "Empowering a Profession: What's in Our Name?" *Journal of Volunteer Administration*, 1988a, *6*(4), 31–36.

Scheier, I. H. "Empowering a Profession: Seeing Ourselves as More than Subsidiary." *Journal of Volunteer Administration*, 1988b, *7*(1), 29–34.

Scheier, I. H. "Empowering a Profession: Leverage Points and Process." *Journal of Volunteer Administration*, 1988–89, *7*(2), 50–57.

Schwartz, F. S. "The Professional Staff and the Direct Service Volunteer: Issues and Problems." *Journal of Jewish Communal Service*, 1977 (2), 147–154.

Service Corps of Retired Executives (SCORE). "About SCORE." Available at http://www.score.org/explore_score.html. Retrieved Nov. 2, 2009.

Smith, A. C., and Green F. B. "Managing Employees as if They Were Volunteers." *SAM Advanced Management Journal*, 1993, *58*(3), 42–46.

Smith, J. D., and Ellis, A. "Valuing Volunteering." *Journal of Volunteer Administration*, 2003, *21*(2), 49–52.

Stoolmacher, I. S. "Non-Profits Should Treat Volunteers as if They Were Paid Employees." *Chronicle of Philanthropy*, July 16, 1991, *3*(19), 34–35.

Sundeen, R. A. "Citizens Serving Government: Volunteer Participation in Local Public Agencies." In *Working Papers for the Spring Research Forum*. Washington, D.C.: Independent Sector, 1989.

Thornburg, L. "What Makes an Effective Volunteer Administrator? Viewpoints from Several Practitioners." *Voluntary Action Leadership*, 1992 (Summer), 18–21.

Toppe, C. M., Kirsch, A. D., and Michel, J. *Giving and Volunteering in the United States 2001: Findings from a National Survey*. Washington, D.C.: Independent Sector, 2002.

Urban Institute. 2004. *Volunteer Management Capacity in America's Charities and Congregations: A Briefing Report*. Washington, D.C. Available at http://www.urban.org/UploadedPDF/410963_VolunteerManagment.pdf. Accessed Nov. 11, 2009.

U.S. Department of Labor. *Americans Volunteer*. Washington, D.C.: Department of Labor, Manpower Administration, 1969.

Utterback, J., and Heyman, S. R. "An Examination of Methods in the Evaluation of Volunteer Programs." *Evaluation and Program Planning*, 1984, *7*(3), 229–235.

Valente, M. G. "Volunteers Help Stretch Local Budgets." *Rural Development Perspectives*, 1985, *2*(1), 30–34.

Valente, C. F., and Manchester, L. D. "Rethinking Local Services: Examining Alternative Delivery Approaches." Washington, D.C.: International City Management Association *Information Service Special Report* (12), 1984.

Van Til, J. *Mapping the Third Sector: Voluntarism in a Changing Social Economy*. New York: Foundation Center, 1988.

VolunteerMatch. "At-A-Glance VolunteerMatch." Available at http://www.volunteermatch.org/about/volunteermatch_fact_sheet.pdf. Retrieved Nov. 2, 2009.

Walter, V. "Volunteers and Bureaucrats: Clarifying Roles and Creating Meaning." *Journal of Voluntary Action Research*, 1987, *16*(3), 22–32.

Weber, M. A. "What Can Be Learned about Episodic Volunteers from a National Survey of Giving and Volunteering?" Paper presented at the Annual Meeting of the Association for Research on Nonprofit Organizations and Voluntary Action. Montreal, Quebec, Canada, November 14–16, 2002.

Wilson, M. *The Effective Management of Volunteer Programs*. Boulder, Colo.: Johnson, 1976.

Wilson, M. "The New Frontier: Volunteer Management Training." *Training and Development Journal*, 1984, *38*(7), 50–52.

Young, C. L., Goughler, D. H., and Larson, P. J. "Organizational Volunteers for the Rural Frail Elderly: Outreach, Casefinding, and Service Delivery." *Gerontologist*, 1986, *26*(4), 342–344.

CONCLUSION

The Future of Nonprofit Leadership and Management

David O. Renz

This third edition of the *Jossey-Bass Handbook of Nonprofit Leadership and Management*, which is being issued fifteen years after the first edition, describes a nonprofit sector that is very different from that of the inaugural edition. The field has grown and developed in important and amazing ways, some very positive and some less so, and the content of the work of the typical nonprofit leader and manager is quite different from those earlier days. True, the purpose and functional content of nonprofit management remains substantially the same: it is the process of planning, organizing, and leading the work of the organization, including establishing goals, developing organizational strategies, securing and allocating resources, organizing the work, recruiting and mobilizing the work force to do it, supervising the implementation of the work, evaluating the degree to which the organization is accomplishing its goals, and then refining plans to sustain and enhance the organization's performance.

And yet, as Lester Salamon explains well in Chapter Three of this volume, the context of nonprofit leadership and management has changed so much that it is not at all the same work. Some things have become easier, yet much has become dramatically more complex and challenging. In his chronicle of the changes that have led to today's demanding environment, Salamon identifies four key types of challenges:

- The challenges of *finance*, from federal retrenchment to the changing nature of public support to a decline in the share of private giving relative to nonprofit need

- The challenges of more and different kinds of *competition*, ranging from intrasector competition among nonprofits for time, talent, and treasure to intersector competition as nonprofits and for-profits compete for attention, credibility, and business as they jockey for the opportunity to provide services in an increasingly sector ambivalent marketplace
- The challenges of *effectiveness* that derives from the increased demands for nonprofits to demonstrate and prove performance, results, and accountability
- The challenges of *technology,* as new and increasingly sophisticated digital technologies and social media become available to both the sector and to a good share of its constituents, leading to heightened expectations for new levels of communication, engagement, and responsiveness—and to new definitions of effectiveness

Today is indeed a new day for the typical nonprofit leader and manager!

And, Salamon suggests, tomorrow promises more—more of the same, plus more that will be different. Among the emerging opportunities he describes are the following:

- Major social and demographic shifts, fueling exceptional changes in the composition and character of every society on the planet, including exceptional growth in the size of an aged population, more women in the workforce, exceptional growth in the number of children living in single-parent households, and major changes in the balance among the many racial and ethnic groups that comprise civil societies across the globe
- New forms of philanthropy, some employing new strategies and vehicles and enabled or energized by new technologies, some fueled by the increasingly large intergenerational transfer of wealth
- Greater visibility and policy salience as the value and potential for impact of nonprofit organizations are recognized and embraced by political and institutional leaders
- Resumption of governmental spending on social welfare and other civil society programming

Gowdy and associates at LaPiana Consulting, in a similar assessment prepared recently for the Irvine Foundation (2009), assert that the nonprofit sector today is at a unique point in time, "an inflection point" that will fundamentally reshape the sector. They argue that successful nonprofit leaders and managers must build their capacity to be attuned to rapid and continual shifts to manage strategically in the fundamentally new operating environment that is emerging as the result of the *convergence* of five central trends (and it is the aggregate result of these five trends *as they interact* that is most important, they explain). These trends are

- Demographic shifts redefine participation, including the emergence of increasingly intergenerational and multicultural workplaces that effectively address issues of engagement, inclusion, and equity.
- Technological advances abound, including the rise of social media and "new ways of communicating, demanding greater openness and transparency" (p. 10) that both enable and require nonprofits to strategically leverage and facilitate collaborative engagement.
- Networks (technological *and* social) enable dialogue, work, and even decision making to be organized in multiple new and relatively more fluid ways.
- Interest in civic engagement and volunteerism is rising, reflecting both growing expectations for new levels and multiple forms of engagement and heightened expectations of nonprofits that they will create opportunities better tailored to the times and ways that these participants wish to become involved.
- Sectoral boundaries are blurring as nonprofits, for-profits, and even governmental agencies compete and collaborate in increasingly diverse ways, ways that both enhance and sometimes confuse opportunities for the creation of both private wealth and social capital.

Salamon characterizes the nonprofit sector as a "resilient sector," capable of successfully addressing and leveraging these trends as it strives to adapt and develop. Nonetheless, he also warns,

> The context of nonprofit management has changed massively in recent years. Up to now, nonprofit managers have had to fend for themselves in deciding what risks it was acceptable to take in order to respond to this changing context. Given the stake that American society has in the preservation of these institutions and in the protection of their ability to perform their distinctive roles, this may now need to change. Americans need to rethink in a more explicit way whether the balance between survival and distinctiveness that nonprofit institutions have had to strike in recent years is the right one for the future, and, if not, what steps might now be needed to allow nonprofit managers to shift this balance for the years ahead. (p. 97)

The Successful Nonprofit Leader and Manager of the Future

What does all of this mean for the future of nonprofit leadership and management? It certainly suggests that the work of leaders and managers will become even more complex and demanding. It also suggests that, while passion and commitment are essential to success, effective leaders and managers need more to succeed. The knowledge, skills, and abilities explained in this handbook are central to the future success of the typical nonprofit leader and manager.

Some worry, as we continue to professionalize the management of the sector, that the distinctive character of nonprofits in civil society will be lost. But there is no reason to believe that this must be the case. Indeed, drawing on a key marketing concept, we can and must remember to regularly and clearly articulate the key differentiators that distinguish nonprofit organizations from all others. If professionalization and education are implemented appropriately, the sector will not lose its way because at core effective management must be grounded and defined in mission accomplishment. So the challenge, in difficult times, is to never forget why we do what we do. This is the essence of effective nonprofit leadership. I am optimistic that we are very unlikely to forget our mission—our volunteers and donors and community leaders will not let this happen. Although the sector's public trust ratings are less than I'd like, it remains true that the average citizen values the nonprofit sector and considers it an essential part of a viable society. We know this, in part, because year after year we continue to see citizens across the world taking the time to create thousands of new nonprofits (and a good share of them are all-volunteer organizations) to address their community's needs and interests.

From the perspective of nonprofit management and leadership, how do we ensure the sector does not lose its distinctiveness and viability? My answer is that we lead and manage effectively! Every one of the chapters of this handbook explains a unique facet of how we ensure that our sector and its organizations remain vital, viable, and distinctive. At core, this has four dimensions:

Govern, Lead, and Manage with Strategic Focus

Fundamentally, strategic leadership and management constitute the process of making choices about the best and most effective ways to achieve the intended purpose of the organization (that is, the mission). As Robert Herman argues in the second edition of this volume (2005), it is imperative that every nonprofit is "managing toward the morality of the mission." It is when a nonprofit's leaders and managers forget to or fail to keep the mission, vision, and values of the organization as the foundation for the decisions they make that we have the greatest potential for losing our way. Many of the trust and accountability problems of the sector derive from our key stakeholders' fears that we are not in fact doing this and doing it well—they are warning us to take the fundamentals seriously.

Do Not Fall Prey to the "Run It Like a Business" Clichés

The oft-uttered admonition to "run it like a business" is valid advice—until it's not! Many of the most spectacular failures of nonprofit leadership and management exemplify the cultural contradictions of our sector, when nonprofit leaders think they can operate as a conventional business would operate—only to find that they had violated important conventions and rules (some written and some not) about what is acceptable for a nonprofit to do. All organizations today operate in an environment of increasingly complex competing and conflicting values and expectations. But businesses ultimately have the option of ignoring or shortchanging some values and expectations in favor of others. Nonprofit leaders and managers, however, must recognize *and accommodate* a much larger array of stakeholders' competing values and perspectives as they determine what their organizations should do, how they should do it, and how to judge effectiveness and success.

Among the key distinctions: at its core, a business serves a market niche as long as it is profitable; when it's no longer profitable the well-managed business will leave the niche to pursue something that has greater promise for profit. A business is obligated, as a matter of responsible use of the owners' assets, to leave a niche or market when it cannot achieve an appropriate return on those assets (at whatever level of return is deemed acceptable by those owners). Alternatively, by definition and mandate associated with charity status, the typical nonprofit operates in a market where profitability is less viable (that is, the economist's concept of market failure). Indeed, in recent years, some nonprofits have been threatened with or even lost their exempt status because there was no clear distinction between their enterprise and a for-profit business. The nonprofit is mission-bound to stay in its specific (tax-exempt) business if at all possible, so key decisions turn on whether it is feasible to remain in the market (with some form of subsidization, including but not limited to tax exemption) to continue to serve its clients.

Market and Communicate Effectively

Nonprofit leaders must become more effective at explaining the true characteristics of the nonprofit world. We have failed to help many of our key constituents—including many who govern, manage, staff, and volunteer for our own organizations—understand the nature of the sector and its organizations. Earlier in this volume, Lester Salamon observes,

> Thanks to the pressures they are under, and the agility they have shown in
> response to them, American nonprofit organizations have moved well beyond

the quaint Norman Rockwell stereotype of selfless volunteers ministering to the needy and supported largely by charitable gifts. Yet popular and press images remain wedded to this older image and far too little attention has been given to bringing popular perceptions into better alignment with the realities that now exist, and to justifying these realities to a skeptical citizenry and press. (p. 96)

Three chapters of this handbook are dedicated to the processes by which we engage, inform, and educate our key constituencies through marketing, through strategic communications, and through advocacy. We must be effective in using the guidance and insights of these fields as we lead and manage.

Perform Well and Deliver Social Value

Ultimately, people value nonprofits for the social value they add. If nonprofits do not deliver on their missions, communities legitimately ask why they should allow them and subsidize them. The ultimate judgment in the test of whether we are effectively "managing toward the morality of the mission" comes directly from our performance and from our ability to demonstrate that progress is being made. Our constituents and stakeholders want us to succeed, and the reason they will maintain or even increase their support is because they see the value in what we seek to accomplish. There is no question that the nature of the problems and needs addressed by the nonprofit sector is such that progress can be slow, difficult, and hard to demonstrate. For that reason, the work of marketing and communication is integral to this element. But, as Greg Dees explains in Chapter Ten, there is only one bottom line in the nonprofit world—it is the creation of social value. Without social value that derives from the effective practice of nonprofit leadership and management, the legitimacy of the field disappears and we run the danger of becoming "just another business out to make a buck."

Does Nonprofit Management Differ from For-Profit Management?

Some question whether there is any substantive difference between "nonprofit management" and management in other types of organizations. After all, every one of the nonprofit management functions that has been explained in this handbook is important to the effective management of every organization. And the tasks of management described herein are essential to the management of profit-making organizations too. So is there a difference? At core, whether in nonprofit or for-profit organizations, the central purpose of management is the same. However, there are particular dimensions to *nonprofit* management that are important to recognize because they have a distinct impact on the success of those who do this work.

The Unique Legal Context. To state the obvious, the nonprofit sector in the United States and most other nations of the world is legally distinct from the other sectors. It is neither for-profit business nor government, even as it carries certain characteristics of each, and this difference in legal context is significant to the practice of management (most notably, it limits the range of strategic options available to the leadership team). As explained in Chapter Two, in most nations the organizations that are qualified as "nonprofit" organizations receive this distinction because they have agreed to limit the nature and scope of their work. They have secured special privileges, such as tax-exempt status, but the price of these privileges is that these nonprofit (and nongovernmental) organizations must constrain their activities to those that address broader social or charitable purposes. Such distinctiveness applies to much of the nonprofit sector across the globe, although it is essential to recognize that there is great variation in the laws of different nations with regard to permissible and impermissible nonprofit activity. Thus, it is essential that a nonprofit manager manage with respect to the legal context of each nation in which his or her organization operates.

The Unique Ownership Structure. One of the legal differences that becomes significant to management is that of organizational ownership. In the United States and many other nations, it is generally not possible to own (that is, to have an equity stake such as stock) a nonprofit charitable organization. In practical terms, the typical U.S. charity is "owned" by the community or segment of the community that it exists to serve. Thus, its governing board and management must act as stewards of the assets of the organization on behalf of the community, even as there is no singular and clear external source of accountability or control over the affairs of the organization. Such diffusion of control and accountability creates both unique opportunities and complications for nonprofit management (for more on this, see Chapter Four, "The Many Faces of Nonprofit Accountability").

The Unique Political and Cultural Context. The aforementioned legal and ownership differences couple with the unique political context of the nonprofit sector to further complicate the work of nonprofit management. One result of the nonprofit's diffuse and unclear accountability is that the typical organization has multiple significant stakeholders, and many think they are "in charge." These stakeholders bring diverse and conflicting performance expectations to bear on the organization and, therefore, on its management team. In today's environment of heightened concern for accountability and performance, the management team cannot afford to overtly ignore most such expectations, even when they are inconsistent. Thus, one of the most challenging tasks of *nonprofit* management is to select a course of action that strikes a reasonable balance among the divergent expectations and demands of the organization's multiple stakeholders. This requires that management be especially politically sophisticated and sensitive to the external environment.

Further, efficiency in the social sector cannot be assessed as it is in business. A sector that serves to address the expressive and artistic needs of a community cannot legitimately be judged by the same criteria as those that serve instrumental functions. Indeed, this is where part of the paradox of the sector arises—for many seek to turn the sector into a purely instrumental form (and in its own way, government has done more to create this dynamic than any other part of society). However, for some nonprofits, their mere existence *is* the outcome their stakeholders seek, and we should never forget this in our press to enhance effectiveness and accountability. I am reminded of the truth of this every year as thousands (really, tens of thousands) of citizens, all over the world, invest an incredible amount of time in the founding and nurturing of nonprofits that generate only goodwill, fellowship, camaraderie, and enhanced sense of community. In a broader sense, this too is a market phenomenon, yet it is not the rational-logical resource-maximizing dynamic of some economic theories—and it cannot and should not be reduced to such.

The Unique Financial and Capital Structure. Further complicating the unique work of nonprofit management is a financial context that is much more complex than that of similarly sized for-profit businesses. The typical nonprofit's complicated mix of clients and markets, which correlates directly to complicated business models grounded in diverse and inconsistent funding and financing models, makes the work of nonprofit management distinctive. The typical for-profit business gets its financial support from a relatively uncomplicated set of sources; nonprofits increasingly must fund and finance their operations with a mix of philanthropic resources and earned income derived from a relatively diverse set of sources. Each source imposes its own expectations for operations, management performance, and organizational accountability. Among the most demanding are the governmental sources, since acceptance of funds from government typically intensifies the demands for procedural as well as performance accountability.

Many of these distinctions are subtle yet very real, demanding, and potentially disabling to the unprepared leader or manager. Successful business entrepreneur turned nonprofit leader and consultant, Mario Morino, described from personal experience the nature of these differences in a 2007 speech. Among the differences he articulated for his business colleagues:

- Context has an extremely significant function. . . . The issue itself may be crystal clear to you, but understanding the context within which the issue is framed is key (and the difference between success and failure).
- All organizations deal with external factors, but social sector organizations confront and work through more outside conditions beyond their control and that are more social and people-based in nature.
- Not all business entrepreneur traits transfer well. Some of the characteristics that were effective in the private sector may not work now. . . . The highly driven nature, the adrenaline kick-in, the brashness that is valued in business settings, the "take it on at all costs" mentality, all have their consequences in a world where relationship, context, and social complexity play such important roles in being effective.
- Many of the factors vital to success are outside of your immediate control—the multiplicity of stakeholders, the interdependency of "supply chains," and the expectations society places on nonprofits.
- Don't assume market forces. . . . Do not make the assumption that the market forces at work in the private sector—or the systems and discipline they introduce—carry over to the social sector.
- Government funding and programs are important. There is a romantic, idealistic view that we can scale solutions without government funding. In some areas this may be true and, when possible, we should do all we can to make this a reality. But in areas where public funding approximates from 85 to 95 percent of the available funding (for example, human services), this is simply not realistic (Morino, 2007, pp. 4–5).

Conclusion

Nonprofit organizations play increasingly significant and diverse roles in the development and maintenance of civil society throughout the world. Thus, the demand for sophistication and skill in leading and managing these organizations is growing. Leaders from across the globe are asking more and more of nonprofit organizations—more with regard to creativity, more with regard to responsiveness, more with regard to impact and results.

A new generation of nonprofit managers is preparing to lead these important organizations—a generation that understands the increasingly complex nature of the work of nonprofit management. This new generation of nonprofit managers understands that although passion and dedication are essential to the future of the nonprofit sector and continued development of global civil society, passion and dedication alone are inadequate. It is through the effective practice of leadership and management that the organizations of the third sector will continue to grow and develop in their capacity to successfully address the needs of a diverse and complicated world.

The practice of nonprofit leadership and management is riddled with paradox and contradiction. Indeed, it always has been. Central to public service and community leadership roles is the need to find ways to address and reconcile (to the greatest degree possible) a host of competing values and tensions. But I'd suggest that we're heading into a new era—new for the sector and new for those who aspire to lead and manage it. Nonprofits will play even more roles of pivotal significance in the shared-power global environment of tomorrow, and their leaders and managers must become adept at understanding and addressing the needs and challenges of an environment characterized by greater variation and complexity, coupled with cycles of change that are deeper and faster than we traditionally have known. The pace of change and the extent of that change will demand a greater level of knowledge, sophistication, and skill from those who aspire to lead and manage these organizations.

These are exciting and challenging times for those who lead and manage nonprofit organizations, and the sector's capacity to deliver on its promises to serve our communities and citizens well hinges directly on the effectiveness of its leaders and managers. Similar to the editions that precede, this third edition of *The Jossey-Bass Handbook of Nonprofit Leadership and Management* presents the latest and most relevant leadership and management information available for this extensive topic. The authors and I have taken care to integrate the best of what we know about current practice with the guidance and insight that derives from the latest in research and theory. Our goal is that this edition, similar to its predecessors, will become a valued and widely used reference and resource, providing current and emerging leaders and managers with the knowledge and insight that will enable them to make the difference they aspire to make for years to come.

References

Gowdy, H., Hildebrand, A., LaPiana, D., and Campos, M. M. "Convergence: How Five Trends Will Reshape the Social Sector." San Francisco: The James Irvine Foundation, 2009.

Herman, R. "Conclusion: The Future of Nonprofit Management." In R. Herman (ed.), *The Jossey-Bass Handbook of Nonprofit Leadership and Management.* San Francisco: Jossey-Bass, 2005, pp. 731–735.

Morino, M. "Business Entrepreneurs & Philanthropy: Potential and Pitfalls." A Keynote Speech to Legacy 2007, The National Philanthropic Trust, Washington D.C., September 28, 2007.

NAME INDEX

SUBJECT INDEX

A

Abbott, Langer & Associates, 719, 720

ABC, *See* Activity-based costing (ABC)

Absorption process, 592

Accident insurance, 665

Account structure, 631–632; articulation needs, 632; information needs, 631–632; resource providers, 631; senior managers and governing bodies, 631

Accountability, 101–121, 193–195; adaptive learning, 113–114; answerability/justification, 102; board of directors, 105, 133, 152–153; compliance-driven, 102, 116; core components of, 102; defined, 102; disclosure statements and reports, 108, 117; downward, 103; enforcement/sanctions, 102; establishing, 346; evaluation and performance assessment, 109, 117; for finances, 105; and

governance, 104–105; improving, 116; legal, 675–685; mechanisms, 107–114; membership organizations, 103; moral, 675–685; movement, 433–435; organizational mission, 106–107; participation, 111–113, 114; and performance, 105; performance-based, 105–106; policy advocacy networks, 104; as relational concept, 104; relationships, 103; self-regulation, 110, 117; service organizations, 103–104; strategy-driven, 116–117; transparency, 61, 102; and trust, 101; upward, 103

Accountability, Learning, and Planning System (ALPS), 114

Accounting: differential-cost, 580, 602–623; full-cost, 580–581; practices, 476; responsibility, 580, 622, 623, 636–638; software, 476–477; systems, 476–477

Accounts, chart of, 476

Accreditation movement, 572–573

ACTION, 774

ActionAid International, 114

Activism and the law, 355–356

Activity-based costing (ABC), 592–600; in the economics department, 596–599; indirect cost pools, 592; system development, 592–596

Adaptive learning, 113–114

Administrative Cost to Expenditures (ACE) ratios, 443

Adoption: and diffusion, 315–316; of a strategic marketing mindset, 302–303

Advanced Institute of Management Research Web site, 390

Advertising: art of investing in, 344; forms of, 343–344

Advocacy, 347–374, *See also* Lobbying; Social change movements; activities constituting, 351–352; advancing as a field, 372–373; Advocacy and Organizing Cycle, 369; advocacy capacity, building, 358–360; Advocacy